EAT
BETTER
LIVE
BETTER

EAT BETTER LIVE BETTER was edited and designed by
The Reader's Digest Association Limited, London

First Edition Copyright © 1991
The Reader's Digest Association Limited
Berkeley Square House, Berkeley Square, London w1x 6AB
Copyright © 1991 Reader's Digest Association Far East Limited
Philippines Copyright © 1991 Reader's Digest Association Far East Limited
Reprinted with amendments 1993

Printed in Great Britain
ISBN 0 276 420 37 3

READER'S DIGEST

EAT BETTER LIVE BETTER

Published by The Reader's Digest Association Limited

LONDON · NEW YORK · SYDNEY · CAPE TOWN · MONTREAL

CONTENTS

CONTRIBUTORS	6
INTRODUCTION	7~8
Buying and Cooking for Health	**9~28**
Buying Food	9
Understanding Food Labels	10~11
Cooking Food	12~18
Vegetables	12~13
Fruit	13~14
Fish	14~15
Poultry	15~16
Meat	16~18
Reheating Food	18
Storing for the Unexpected	18
The Store Cupboard	19
The Healthy Kitchen	20~21
Microwave Cooking	20
Kitchen Utensils	20~21
Refrigerators	21
Freezers	21
Freezing and Thawing Food	22~26
Making Stocks	27~28

∽
THE RECIPES
29~340

SOUPS AND STARTERS
31~74

SALADS AND RAW FOOD DISHES
75~116

PASTA AND RICE DISHES
117~142

FISH AND SHELLFISH
143~170

BEEF, LAMB AND PORK DISHES
171~210

POULTRY AND GAME
211~236

ONE-POT DISHES
237~258

VEGETABLE DISHES
259~294

DESSERTS
295~320

SNACKS, DRINKS AND SANDWICHES
321~340

∽

Food and Your Body 341~368

The Nutrients in Our Food 341

Proteins 341~342

Fats 342~343

Carbohydrates 343~344

Salt 344~345

Fibre 345

Vitamins and Minerals 345

Major Sources and Functions 346~348

How Our Bodies use Food 349~351

Digestion 349

Fuel for the Body 349

Metabolism 349~350

Glucose for Energy 350

Storing Food for Energy 350~351

Focus on Everyday Food and Drink 351~355

Organic Foods 355

Food Irradiation 355

Food Directory 356~368

Eating and Exercise for a Healthy Life 369~386

The Great British Diet 369

Planning for Health 369

The Balanced Diet 370~371

Daily Menu Planning Guide 370

Exercise 371~379

Warming Up and Cooling Down 372~373

Which Sport is Best for You? 375

The Live Better Workout 376~377

Eating to Look Better 378~381

Fitting Health into your Lifestyle 381~382

Alcohol 382~384

How to Monitor your Drinking 383

Coping with Stress 384

Sleep 384~385

Food Poisoning and other Food Scares 385~386

Common Food Myths 386

Special Diets for Special Needs 387~401

Food and Growth 387~388

Slimming for the Overweight 388~393

Who is Overweight? 389

Crash Dieting 389~390

Monitoring Your Weight 390~391

Seeing an Improvement 390~391

Which Diets Work? 391~393

Slimming Advice 393

Vegetarianism 393~395

Digestive Problems 395~396

The Heart 396~398

Heart Disease 397~398

Diabetes 398~399

Food Allergies and Sensitivities 399~400

Diet and Cancer 400~401

Arthritis 401

Convalescing 401

Index 402~415

Acknowledgments 416

EDITOR
Alasdair McWhirter

ART EDITOR
Iain Stuart

CONTRIBUTORS

THE PUBLISHERS WISH TO THANK THE FOLLOWING
CONSULTANTS, EXPERTS AND ARTISTS FOR THEIR VALUABLE
CONTRIBUTIONS TO CREATING *EAT BETTER LIVE BETTER*

Cookery Consultant
Pat Alburey

Recipes Created by
Pat Alburey · Jane Foster · Carol Pastor · Jennie Reekie
Dr Mary Skinner · Jane Suthering · Jeni Wright

Recipes photographed, prepared and styled by

PHOTOGRAPHERS	Martin Brigdale	Laurie Evans	Clive Streeter	Simon Wheeler
HOME ECONOMISTS	Berit Vinegrad	Maxine Clarke	Lyn Rutherford	Stephen Wheeler
STYLISTS	Andrea Lambton	Lesley Richardson	Maria Kelly	Rebecca Gillies

Artists
Malcolm McGregor · Precision Illustration

Nutritional Consultant Editor
Moya de Wet, BSc, SRD

Nutritional Consultants
Adriana Cuff, BSc, SRD
Caroline Elson, BSc, SRD
Patricia Heavens, BSc, SRD
Michael Turner, PhD, FIFST, FRSH, FIBiol
Nutritional and Dietetic Consultants

Exercise Consultant
Ru-tee Block

Cover Photograph
Photograph by Vernon Morgan, food prepared by
Alyson Birch and styled by Maria Jacques

INTRODUCTION

Most people tend to think of healthy eating as a minefield of do's and don'ts, but *Eat Better Live Better* shows how food should be seen as something to be enjoyed as well as being good for you. Good health depends on what people eat and how much exercise they take. Using this book, you can get the balance right for you and your family.

The British Diet

There are many good things about the typical diet people eat in Britain, malnutrition for example is extremely rare, but unfortunately the British diet also has its problems. Because we eat so many fatty foods, this country has one of the highest rates of heart disease in the world – ten times the rate in Japan. In Britain, more people die from heart disease than from cancer, strokes and all accidents put together.

There has recently been a massive amount of research into diet and food safety. *Eat Better Live Better* gives a clear, up-to-date view on the real dangers – based on fact, not on alarmist claims and quirky theories. A clear message has emerged from all the confusion of what is, and is not, good for you – the best diet is a varied and well-balanced one. Very few foods are bad for you if they are eaten in moderation. It is perfectly all right to eat a bar of chocolate or have an extra roast potato, as long as your diet is balanced from day to day.

Recipes for Health

Most of this book is made up of over 300 delicious recipes specially created for *Eat Better Live Better*. All of them are written in easy-to-follow stages and are photographed in full colour. They cater for every occasion. Some can be made in five minutes, while more sophisticated dishes will impress your family and friends. There are many exciting new recipes to encourage a varied diet, and also traditional favourites made with all the flavour but with much less fat, cholesterol and sugar.

Apart from the recipes, there are four other sections in the book. The first section, Buying and Cooking for Health, gives advice on what to look for in shops and what to avoid. Confusing terms on food labels are explained and useful tips are given on how valuable nutrients can be kept in food when cooking or storing it.

Food and How to Enjoy It

After the recipes, Food and Your Body describes in simple language what the basic building blocks of food are and then goes on to tell the fascinating story of how food is converted to energy or to living tissue like skin, bone and muscle. There is also a large reference section giving basic nutritional information and handy tips on a wide range of food and drink. Eating and Exercise for a Healthy Life provides practical advice on living and eating sensibly. Food scares are put firmly into perspective, and you can check to see if you and your family have a balanced diet. You can read about how our diet affects the way we look and how well we sleep. Exercise is an important part of feeling healthy. There are simple exercises, designed specially for this book, which need no special equipment and are suitable for all ages.

Diets for Special Needs

The final section, Special Diets for Special Needs, is written for those with particular dietary requirements. These might include people who want to lose weight, vegetarians, diabetics and people who suffer from allergies or heart disease. There are dozens of delicious recipes for people with any of these special needs.

There is no magic diet to make excess weight fall off and there is no secret formula to prevent illness. But by eating sensibly and taking regular exercise, you will feel better, have more energy, be less prone to illness and be ready to enjoy life to the full. With this book you can choose to eat better, live better and maybe live longer too.

∞

Buying and Cooking for Health

Our quality of life, how we look and how we feel, is directly affected by the nutrients contained in the food we eat. Proteins help build and repair muscle, blood and skin, and keep our bodies working efficiently. Carbohydrates provide vital energy for heat and movement. Fats keep body tissues in good repair and are important for skin and hair. Vitamins help prevent disease and regulate many of our body's inner functions. Minerals are vital for the formation of bones and teeth, blood-clotting and the operation of the nervous system. These nutrients often need to work together, so it helps to eat a well-balanced diet.

Techniques for Healthy Cooking The following chapter explains simply how various methods of preparation and cooking affect the taste, appearance and nutritional value of individual foods. There are guidelines on choosing the best equipment and utensils for the kitchen, how to store food, and how to cook healthily and still produce delicious meals.

Buying Food

We now have an almost overwhelming choice of food and places to buy it; from the local butcher and baker to the new 'megastore' on the outskirts of town. Exotic foods are brought to our supermarkets from all over the world, and fresh fruit and many vegetables are available throughout the year.

Price and convenience are important factors for the consumer, but so is the quality of food. Thanks to refrigeration and better transport we are now eating more and more fresh produce, which naturally has a much higher vitamin and mineral content than food that has been preserved, refined or processed. Even in the last five or ten years it has become easier to buy high-quality fresh foods – the raw ingredients for a good diet and a healthy life.

Where to Buy? In the large supermarket chain stores, fruit and vegetables are as fresh as those bought from a greengrocer or market, but they may cost more. Similarly, prepackaged meat bought at the supermarket is usually of the same quality as meat bought from the butcher, but it may be difficult to find exactly the type, cut and quantity of meat you require. There is little or no difference between an in-store bakery and most bakers' shops. Most large supermarket chains now offer an excellent selection of wines which are hand-picked by experts and sold at prices that compare well with most off-licences.

Large supermarket chains have strict regulations regarding the shelf life of their products, and you can be almost certain that the food in these stores is fresh. Any food that passes its sell-by date is removed and usually destroyed. To limit this waste, foods that are nearing their sell-by dates are reduced in price for immediate sale. By shopping just before closing time, especially on Saturdays, you may pick up some bargains, but be sure to check the sell-by date to see how quickly the food should be eaten.

Food and Safety

Food poisoning can be a widespread and serious problem, but one which you can guard against by using common sense and by taking basic precautions. Bacteria can contaminate food at any stage between production and the dinner table. Although there are now stringent standards for food hygiene, food safety is ultimately left to the consumer.

Cleanliness is a vital consideration when buying food. If shop assistants have dirty hands or nails, or even if they are smoking, they could be breaking the law and be posing a risk to hygiene. Always check the sell-by dates on packaged foods. Avoid packages

---

'In one week a family of four will typically consume 16 pints (9 litres) of milk, 9lb (4kg) of meat, 10 eggs, 29½lb (13kg) of fruit and vegetables and 8lb (3.6kg) of bread.'

---

that are damaged, such as badly dented tins, and look out for frozen-food cabinets that are unclean or overfilled – which can often stop food being frozen properly. Ensure that fresh meat is well wrapped and never buy cracked or dirty eggs.

Convenience Foods

Ready-to-cook and ready-to-eat foods are now universally available; but these are not the only convenience foods. In general, any foods which have been processed, such as tinned, frozen or packaged foods, can be termed convenience foods. These processing methods have overcome seasonal fluctuations in food supplies and save time for the consumer, but they often result in foods containing considerably more fat, refined sugar and salt than fresh food alternatives.

Food Processing Ready-made dishes are made in the conventional way from raw ingredients, then they are cooled very rapidly and either frozen or stored in their chilled form. Although ready-made meals are popular and convenient, they are often expensive and contain additives and preservatives to ensure that they reach you in a palatable condition. It is important to follow the storage and cooking instructions on the packet.

Canning food is a good way of storing it for long periods of time, although most tinned vegetables and fruit have lower vitamin contents compared with fresh or frozen varieties.

Freezing does little harm to most vegetables and because they are usually frozen immediately after

picking their vitamin and mineral content is often higher than fresh produce bought from your local greengrocer or supermarket.

Understanding Food Labels

By law, manufacturers must supply a list of ingredients on the wrapping of processed foods. Other information on calories, protein, carbohydrate and fat content is not required by law, but many manufacturers are now supplying this. Until labelling is standardised in 1992 (in line with the European Community's regulations), a lot of this information can be confusing and even misleading; making it difficult for the consumer to make true comparisons between brands.

Ingredients are given in descending order of volume – the first ingredient listed makes up the largest part of the product. Water and sugar are often near the top of the list. Check for different kinds of sugars which can be listed separately. Nutritional values are given per 3½oz (90g), or per 3½fl oz (100ml) for fluids, or per average serving.

Additives used as ingredients must be listed, and are grouped in the following categories according to their chief function: antioxidant, colour, emulsifier, flavouring, preservative, and stabiliser. The general medical view is that additives are safe and do no harm to the majority of people, but if you want to avoid them, it is important to understand the labels.

Here is an alphabetical list that will help you to understand the terms used on food labels:

Additives These usually appear at the end of the ingredients, grouped under their category headings (flavouring, preservative, antioxidant, emulsifier, stabiliser or colour) and itemised by their code number, full chemical name, or both. Flavourings, however, do not have to be itemised. Code numbers that are preceded by the letter E show that the additive has been approved for use in all European Community countries. Additives whose code has no E have been approved only in the UK.

Antioxidant An additive that delays or prevents food from turning rancid or changing in taste, smell and appearance. Code numbers run from 300 to 322.

Calorie A measure of the energy value of food, correctly called kilocalorie (kcal). The metric equivalent, the kilojoule (kJ) is equal to about 4.2 calories.

Carbohydrate The primary source of our energy, consisting of sugars and starches found in plant matter, especially root vegetables such as potatoes and turnips, and grains such as wheat and rice.

Colour Additives that impart a characteristic or appetising colour to foods, or intensify the colour. About half the permitted colours are extracts from natural sources, but the rest are man-made.

Dextrose A form of sugar found in animal and plant tissue and derived artificially from starch.

Emulsifier An additive that helps distribute particles evenly in liquids and prevents mixtures such as oil and water from separating into layers; used in salad creams, ice creams and margarines. Code numbers run from 400 to 495.

Energy See calorie.

Enriched Some of the nutrients that were lost during the processing have been put back into the food.

Fat A nutrient that provides a concentrated source of energy. Labels may list them as saturated fats (mainly from animals) and monounsaturated and polyunsaturated fats (usually from vegetables).

Flavouring There are over 2000 flavourings; many are herbs and spices, but some are man-made. A manufacturer can currently use the word 'flavouring' without specifying what it contains.

Fortified Extra nutrients that were never present in a certain food have been added to it during processing. For example, breakfast cereals are often fortified with vitamins and minerals.

Fructose A form of sugar found in fruit and honey which is often used as a food preservative and as an intravenous nutrient.

Glucose A form of sugar found in fruit and starches.

Kcal, Kcalorie, kJ, Kjoule and Kilojoule See calorie.

Lactose A form of sugar found in milk.

Maltose A form of sugar found in malt and cereals.

Meat Products Foods described as consisting of 'meat products' often contain a large amount of fat. For example, beef sausages only need to have 50 per cent meat content – half of which can be fat.

Preservative An additive that helps prevent deterioration until its 'sell-by' or 'best-before' date. Preservatives slow the development of bacteria and other microorganisms that would make food go off and cause food poisoning. The most widely used preservative is sulphur dioxide, used in wine, beer and soft drinks. Code numbers run from 200 to 283.

Protein A nutrient needed for repair and growth of body tissue. Found in fresh foods, dairy products, nuts, grains, pulses and some vegetables.

RDA The Recommended Daily Amount an adult should consume to prevent any type of deficiency developing, as specified by the government. Labels show the percentage of vitamins and minerals found in a serving, compared to the RDA.

Stabiliser An additive that prevents oil and water from separating, and affects the texture and body of foods. Most stabilisers derive from natural sources. Code numbers run from 400 to 495.

Starch See carbohydrate.

Sucrose A form of sugar.

Sugar free The product does not contain sucrose, but may contain other sweeteners such as concentrated fruit juice or honey. 'No added sugar' simply means the product is already sweet enough.

Sweeteners Artificial sweeteners have a sweet taste but few, if any, calories. They have to be tested for safety and comply with government regulations.

Some additives do not have to be declared on labels, namely substances that help to keep food in good condition such as enzymes used to tenderise meat, and additives used solely as processing aids such as the enzyme rennet in dairy products. Certain products do not have to list their ingredients at all, such as bread, most alcoholic drinks and anything with only one ingredient, like milk and honey.

Cooking

Many nutrients are inevitably lost and destroyed before food reaches the table – through natural chemical changes that take place when foods are exposed to air, immersed in water and subjected to heat. But it is quite easy to keep the loss of nutrients to a minimum. Well-cooked food can have as much as three times the nutritional value of food that has been cooked badly – it looks and tastes better too.

Vegetables

Vegetables provide us with a vital source of vitamins and minerals, but these nutrients are often lost during storage, preparation and cooking, when they are kept in unsuitable conditions for long periods, for example, or soaked in water before cooking. However, most of these losses can easily be avoided.

Storing Vegetables

To obtain the maximum goodness from vegetables, they should be eaten as quickly as possible after harvesting. It is best to buy fresh vegetables daily and to prepare and cook them on the same day, but this is not always practical.

Preventing Deterioration Before storing vegetables, check them over and discard any that have been eaten by insects, bruised or damaged. There is no need to wash earth off garden vegetables before storing them as the soil will help retain nutrients.

Vegetables deteriorate quickly after harvesting. Deterioration is caused by the chemical reactions of enzymes (proteins that break down food) naturally present within vegetables that remain active long after harvesting. These chemical reactions can be slowed down for as long as one week by storing vegetables carefully. Leafy greens and salads store well under cool, dark and slightly humid conditions. The bottom drawer in a refrigerator is a good place for these vegetables to be stored in polythene bags or containers. Less fragile vegetables such as potatoes,

marrows, turnips, carrots and swedes should be kept in a cool, dark, airy place such as a larder, a well-ventilated cupboard or a cellar.

Preparation Before Cooking

All vegetables should ideally be prepared just before cooking, but if you have to prepare them in advance, keep them refrigerated. Keeping any cutting you do to a minimum also prevents nutrients being lost.

Washing Vegetables Wash vegetables just before they are peeled or cut. After washing, shake off most of the water – if absorbed, it can lengthen the cooking time. Never leave vegetables standing in water – it allows the vitamins to leach out.

Peeling and Chopping

Take care not to remove too many of the outside leaves or stalks from cabbages, sprouts, broccoli, cauliflowers or curly kale unless they are very tough. Generally speaking, the darker the leaves are, the more nutrients and flavour they contain. However, the thicker stalks from spinach leaves and the hard core of cabbages should be removed.

Peeling Vegetables It makes best nutritional sense to cook and eat vegetables with their skins on. Most of their fibre content is contained within the skin and a lot of the vitamins are just below it. The skin also helps to prevent vitamins and minerals from escaping into the water. But most root vegetables, such as swedes, parsnips and older carrots, have tough, thick skins and are better peeled.

Chopping Vegetables When it is appropriate, cook vegetables whole to preserve nutrients. Choose those of a similar size or, when necessary, cut them into equal size pieces to ensure even cooking. Chopping often bruises tender, leafy greens, so tear spinach, lettuces and fresh herbs.

Cooking Vegetables

The best way to get every available vitamin and mineral from vegetables is to eat them raw, but cooking is usually necessary for taste and variety.

Most vegetables should only be cooked until they are just tender, retaining a slight crispness. They are ready when the tip of a knife goes easily into the vegetable but meets with slight resistance.

Loss of Nutrients There are three major factors that contribute to the loss and destruction of vitamins and minerals:
1. The leaching of water-soluble vitamins and minerals into the cooking water.
2. The prolonged heating of vegetables.
3. The action of plant enzymes which are activated by heat before the temperature is high enough to destroy them, which is why most vegetables should be cooked in water that is already boiling.

It is impossible to prevent entirely any one of these factors from taking place during cooking, but with care and accurate timing most nutrients can be retained in bright and tasty vegetables.

Boiling Vegetables There are two main methods of boiling vegetables that will produce colourful, flavoursome vegetables that are still full of goodness:
1. Cook even-sized vegetables with a little water in a pan with a well-fitting lid, so that any vegetables not immersed in the water will be steamed. This allows only a small amount of nutrients to leach out into the water, but it can also prevent flavour-spoiling sulphur gases from escaping. If green vegetables are overcooked in a covered pan, they may discolour.
2. Cook vegetables in a large amount of boiling water, immersing all the vegetables. Potatoes will have a better texture if they are started off in cold water and brought to a gentle boil. Although a few more nutrients are lost, these can be saved if the cooking water is used for stocks, soups or stews.

'Refreshing' vegetables, after they have been cooked, by quickly running them under cold water, ensures vegetables keep their colour and flavour.

Steaming Vegetables Steaming is an excellent way of retaining maximum flavour, colour and nutrients. Steaming is particularly suited to root vegetables, cauliflower and broccoli. Leafy vegetables are not suitable as they take longer to cook by this method and so lose more nutrients.

Vegetables can be cooked in a special tiered steaming saucepan, or in a wire or expanding metal basket which will hold them above the water. The water should already be boiling before the vegetables are put into the steamer.

Pressure Cooking Pressure-cooked vegetables are cooked very quickly at a high temperature, in a minimum amount of water. It is probably the best method of all for retaining nutrients, but timing is critical and can be difficult to control.

Baking Vegetables Although baking takes a long time, vegetables retain a lot of their nutrients. Potatoes, squashes and onions can be baked in their skins, preferably wrapped in foil to retain moisture and speed up cooking.

Stir-frying The Chinese method of stir-frying has long been recognised as one of the healthiest ways to cook most vegetables. Finely sliced vegetables are cooked very quickly in a very small amount of oil. They keep their colour and almost all their nutrients.

Cooking with Pulses Pulses, such as dried peas, beans and lentils, are virtually fat free, high in fibre and contain protein, vitamins and minerals. Pulses are also cheap to buy and very filling.

Some kidney-shaped beans contain a toxin which must be destroyed before they can be eaten.

Destroying Toxins in Beans Place the dried beans in a saucepan, cover them with cold water and bring to the boil. Boil rapidly for 10 minutes, drain them in a colander and rinse well. Simmer in fresh water until tender. Only add salt after cooking to prevent toughness. Always drain and rinse tinned beans.

Fruit

One of the simplest and most enjoyable ways to improve your health is to eat plenty of raw fruit, which retains all of its vitamins and minerals.

Storing Fruit

Fruits begin to deteriorate quickly once they have ripened and should usually be eaten as soon as possible after picking or buying. More often than not, fruits such as pears, peaches, avocados, mangoes, pawpaws and pineapples are harvested in an unripe condition so that they are just ripe for eating by the time they reach the shops. Some fruits may be sold in a very unripe state and these should be avoided because, even if they ripen later, their flavour will never be very good.

Most ripe fruit will keep for a few days in a cool, airy place. Highly perishable soft fruits, like raspberries and strawberries, are better stored in the refrigerator, preferably spread out on plates or trays. Remove them from the refrigerator at least an hour before eating, as this will allow them to return to room temperature and restore their flavour.

Storing oranges and lemons in the vegetable compartment of the refrigerator helps slow down dehydration and keeps them fresh for longer.

Preparing Fruit

Maximum nutritional value and fibre will be obtained from fruits that are eaten whole and, where appropriate, with their skins on. The smaller fruit is cut up, the more vitamins and minerals will be lost.

Cut juicy fruit over a bowl to catch the vitamin-rich juice, and serve it with the fruit.

With the possible exception of strawberries, raspberries and loganberries, all fruit should be washed to remove traces of fertilisers, pesticides and the wax coating sprayed onto apples and citrus fruits. Wash the fruit under cold water (never leave it to soak) and pat dry with paper towels. Wash soft fruit gently, or simply brush any dirt away.

Apples, pears, bananas and peaches contain tannin, which causes their peeled flesh to turn brown when exposed to air. This has little effect nutritionally but looks unattractive. To prevent this, brush fruit with a little lemon juice.

When sieving fruit for purées, use a nylon or non-reactive stainless-steel sieve. Although sieved fruit makes excellent purées, it contains less fibre.

Cooking Fruit

The vitamins in fruit are not as vulnerable as those in vegetables, because fruits are more acidic, and the acidity protects vitamin C during cooking. All fruits should be cooked in a stainless-steel or enamel pan.

Most fruits cook in their own juices and require only 2-3 tablespoons of water in the saucepan to prevent scorching. Firm fruits, like pears and peaches, require longer cooking and must be covered with water or sugar syrup. Some vitamins and minerals will leach out into the cooking liquid, but nothing is lost when the juices are served with the fruit. Any leftover juice can be kept and used to make healthy drinks, diluted with water, soda water or milk.

Very acidic fruits such as blackcurrants, rhubarb and some varieties of gooseberries must be cooked

'Bananas, apples, oranges and most other fruits can help people lose weight. They release their energy slowly and their high fibre content makes you feel full for longer.'

to make them more palatable and digestible. They may also need to have some sugar added to sweeten them. On average, only 4-6oz (115-175g) of sugar is needed for every pound (450g) of fruit, depending on tartness. This can be reduced to 2-3oz (50-75g) per pound, or even less if the fruit is sweet. A lower amount of sugar results in a fresher, fruitier flavour.

Fish

Because fish and shellfish are highly perishable, they are best eaten on the day they are caught or bought. Select fresh fish with bright eyes, red gills, shiny scales and firm flesh, take it home immediately and refrigerate until needed. Fish can be stored for a day if it is rinsed and dried with paper towels, put on a clean plate, covered and refrigerated.

Preparing Fish for Cooking

You can either prepare fish yourself or ask your fishmonger to do it for you. Before cooking, all fish must be gutted, washed and dried with paper towels. It may also be filleted or boned.

Cooking Fish

When fish is cooked to perfection, the result is delicious white or pink opaque flaky flesh that separates easily. Due to its high moisture content, fish may be cooked without any liquid added to it. You can wrap it in foil, parchment or even a clean newspaper and allow it to cook in its own juices. Never use lemon juice or wine if cooking fish in foil because the acid in these dressings combines with the fish oils and will react with the aluminium, allowing some of it to get into the food.

White Fish

White fish is particularly suited to very gentle poaching in fish stock or milk. The cooking liquids from these methods are full of nutrients and can be used to make a sauce or a fish soup.

White fish is also good baked in foil or parchment. You can try cooking it with moist vegetables like tomatoes, leeks and onions. When baking fish, add just enough liquid to prevent sticking.

*'In 1989 the medical journal **Lancet** reported that eating oily fish twice a week could cut the risk of a heart attack by almost a third. Steaming, grilling, poaching and microwaving are all good cooking methods which protect valuable fish oils.'*

Steaming is an excellent method of cooking fish, as the hot vapour cooks it quickly while retaining the goodness and flavour.

Whole fish like sole or thick cutlets of fish may be lightly brushed with oil or butter to prevent drying out, then cooked under a grill or over a barbecue. Oily fish, such as mackerel, are even better suited to being grilled or barbecued. Their oil makes them virtually self-basting and keeps them moist.

Shellfish

Shellfish cook very quickly and timing is crucial, as they become tough and rubbery when overcooked. Most shellfish, such as mussels, need only a few minutes in boiling water or stock – as soon as they open, they are ready to eat.

Raw Fish

Raw fish is exceptionally nutritious, but it should never be eaten unless it is absolutely fresh and from clean waters. Prepare raw fish by slicing it very thinly, and serve with pickles or a fresh dill and mustard sauce. Halibut, tuna, sole, salmon and squid all taste delicious when prepared in this way.

Raw fish can also be cured or marinated in lemon or lime juice; the citric acid turns the translucent flesh opaque, giving it a cooked appearance. All fish should be refrigerated whilst marinating.

Poultry

Poultry is a good source of protein and is relatively inexpensive compared with beef, lamb and pork. It is also much lower in fat if the skin is removed.

Storing Poultry

Once bought, poultry should be kept in the refrigerator for no longer than 2 days, unless the 'eat-by' date on the packet states otherwise. Poultry bought from the supermarket should be unwrapped before refrigeration and any pink juices, that may contain bacteria, in the bottom of the plastic bags or polystyrene trays should be wiped away with kitchen paper. Fresh poultry, bought from a butcher, is usually quite dry. Place the poultry on a rack standing on a plate or tray, and cover with foil to prevent it drying out. Always remove the bird's giblets and store them separately – they may be used for making stock.

Preparing Poultry

Before cooking poultry, rinse the cavity with cold water, then dry the bird with paper towels.

If frozen poultry has not been completely thawed before cooking it will not cook right through or kill off any bacteria. The bacteria will then multiply and contaminate the meat, especially if it is left to stand for any length of time after cooking.

Stuffing Poultry Birds are often stuffed to add flavour and moisture to the meat. Any stuffing should be cold before use. A warm stuffing creates ideal conditions for bacteria to thrive. Once a bird has been stuffed it should be put straight in the oven. An alternative to conventional stuffing is to place fresh or dried herbs, a clove-studded onion, some celery or a cut orange in the bird's cavity. Birds with white meat are best for stuffing, as the fat from birds like ducks or geese usually seeps into the stuffing.

Cooking Poultry

With the exception of duck breasts, which may be eaten slightly pink, poultry should never be served in an underdone state. When roasting poultry the fat under the skin keeps the meat moist and supplies most of the flavour. When the skin is removed, the flesh can dry out while cooking. The ways of keeping meat moist, outlined below and opposite, usually apply to poultry too. You can remove poultry skin when cooking in stews or casseroles as the cooking liquid stops the flesh from drying out.

Ducks and geese are much fattier than chicken or turkey. Pricking their skin before roasting on a rack will allow much of the excess fat to run out.

Test whole birds for readiness by sticking a skewer into the thickest part of the thigh, allowing the juices to escape. If the juices run pink, continue cooking for 10 minutes and test again. The juices will be a clear, yellowy colour when the bird is ready.

Roasting Times As a very general rule, allow about 15 minutes for every 1lb (450g) of chicken or turkey. Poultry should be roasted initially at a high temperature – about 230°C (450°F, gas mark 8) – for 15-30 minutes to seal in the flavour and moisture, and to colour the skin. Cooking should then be completed at about 180°C (350°F, gas mark 4). This method also helps to draw off excess fat. Turn large birds over halfway through cooking. Cover a bird with foil if it becomes too brown or dry.

Meat

Meat is a good source of protein, vitamins, fats and minerals. Very little happens to the protein during cooking, unless it is overcooked, and most of the vitamins and minerals in meat are saved during cooking because any rich-tasting juices that seep out are usually served as sauces or gravy.

Meat is left to age or mature for several days before reaching the shops, to enable the flavour to develop and allow enzymes to break down tough tissues,

leaving the meat tender. It is traditionally hung in a moist, airy atmosphere. Beef and pork are hung for up to ten days and lamb is hung for up to a week.

Buying leaner cuts of meat is an effective way of reducing the amount of fat in your diet. However, even when all the visible fat is removed from meat,

In Britain, meat accounts for 22 per cent of fat in our diet. Lamb is the fattiest meat, followed by beef, pork and then game.

as much as 30 per cent of the total weight can still be invisible fat contained within the flesh. There are cooking methods, however, that help reduce the invisible fat as well as the visible.

Keeping Meat Fresh

Beef and pork can be kept in the refrigerator for up to 4 days, lamb should only be kept for 3 days. If you have to keep the meat for more than a day, unwrap it when you get home and pat it dry with paper towels to remove the moisture. Place the meat on a rack over a plate or tray and cover it.

Preparation Before Cooking

When removing fat from pork or lamb chops, trim it down rather than removing it completely so that the chops will retain their shape. Large joints of meat can have the fat completely removed. Fat trimming is particularly recommended for lamb. Meats that have no fat need care to prevent drying. Use the following methods to keep meat moist and flavoursome:
1. Before roasting or grilling, lightly smear the meat with cholesterol-free olive oil. This protects the surface yet seals in the meat juices. A sprinkling of fresh or dried herbs and crushed garlic rubbed over the surface of meat adds extra flavour.
2. Salt draws off moisture from raw meat and makes it dry, so season meat just before serving.
3. Marinating meat in wine, herbs and spices before cooking tenderises the meat and adds flavour. The marinade can also be used as a sauce.
4. A moist stuffing stops small cuts drying out.
5. Meat should be removed from the refrigerator about 45 minutes before cooking so that it reaches room temperature. If it is too cold, the outside of the

Roasting Meat

The best method for roasting beef, lamb and pork is to place it in a very hot oven for 10-15 minutes to sear the outside. Then reduce the temperature to cook the meat more slowly. After the initial searing, the meat may be covered with foil to keep its moisture. You can use chart below to check cooking times.

Meat		Roasting Times	Cooking Instructions
Lamb	Medium rare	12 minutes per 1lb (450g) plus 12 minutes	Roast at 230°C (450°F, gas mark 8) for 15
	Medium	15-20 minutes per 1lb (450g) plus 15 minutes	minutes, then reduce to 180°C (350°F, gas
	Well done	20-25 minutes per 1lb (450g)	mark 4) and continue cooking until done.
Beef	Rare	15 minutes per 1lb (450g) plus 15 minutes	Roast at 230°C (450°F, gas mark 8) for 15
	Medium	20 minutes per 1lb (450g) plus 20 minutes	minutes, then reduce to 180°C (350°F, gas
	Well done	25 minutes per 1lb (450g) plus 25 minutes	mark 4) and continue cooking until done.
Pork	Well done	25-30 minutes per 1lb (450g) For crispy crackling, the temperature can be turned up again for the last 5-10 minutes.	Roast at 200°C (400°F, gas mark 6) for 15 minutes, then reduce to 160°C (325°F, gas mark 3) and continue cooking until done.

meat will cook before the rest, especially if the meat is being grilled or fried and the cooking time is short.
6. Before roasting meat, place it on a rack to allow fat to drip below during cooking.
7. Tenderise tough steaks by pounding muscle fibres in the meat with a wooden mallet or rolling pin.

Cooking Meat

More fat and juices are lost from meat when the temperature is high. Therefore, meat that is cooked slowly over a gentle heat will be more tender. Slow cooking is always better for cheaper cuts of meat.

Fat-trimmed beef or lamb is more likely to be tender if it is cooked fairly rare. Beef and lamb cooked to give pink, juicy flesh is perfectly safe from contamination by bacteria. Rolled joints, stuffed or unstuffed, should always be cooked thoroughly. Pork must be cooked thoroughly to prevent the risk of a parasitical disease called trichinosis.

Meat Thermometers To be really certain that meat is cooked properly, you can test it with a meat thermometer. This is done by inserting the thermometer into the flesh at its thickest part, away from any bone, about 15-30 minutes before the end of the calculated cooking time.

The thermometer should read as follows:

Beef, rare 60°C (140°F); medium 70°C (158°F); well done 75°C (167°F).
Lamb, medium rare 60°C (140°F); medium to well done 63-80°C (145-176°F).
Pork, well cooked 75°C (167°F).

After cooking the meat, leave it standing in a warm place for 10 minutes – if necessary, cover it with foil to keep it hot. During this time the meat's internal temperature will increase slightly and will equalise throughout the meat. The flesh will also reabsorb its juices and become firm, making it easier to carve.

Removing Fat from Roasting Juices Most of the fat can be carefully skimmed off the juices in the pan. A better way of removing fat is to pour the juices into a tall jug and stand it in a bowl of cold water. The fat will then rise and solidify – it can then easily be spooned off. Reheat the sauce in the pan, scraping any crusty brown pieces left into the sauce.

Grilling Meat

Grilled and barbecued meat retains all its nutrients and requires little or no fat for cooking. The grill or barbecue fire should be very hot to seal the meat

17

straight away, after which the heat can be lowered. Always brush the grill rack with oil first – preferably olive oil – to prevent sticking.

Braising and Stewing

These methods involve slow cooking in water, stock or wine, either on the stove or in the oven. Dishes or saucepans with well-fitting lids are essential, to stop too much steam escaping.

Braising or stewing methods are excellent for cooking leaner cuts of meat that must be kept moist, and for tougher cuts that need slow, gentle cooking. All the nutrients from the meat and any vegetables are saved in the cooking liquids.

Braising Meat Large pieces of meat are placed in a covered pan on a bed of herbs and vegetables which keeps the meat just above the water.

Stewing Meat Chunks or cubes of meat should be cooked in just enough liquid to cover them.

Removing Fat from Casseroles Fat can be skimmed off the top of casseroles at intervals. If the stew is made a day early, then cooled and refrigerated overnight, the fat will solidify on the surface and can be lifted off. Reheat thoroughly before serving.

Frying Meat

Frying meat in a lot of fat is not recommended. When frying is essential to seal meat, use a nonstick frying pan and brush it with olive oil. Meat can also be sealed in a heated dry pan – a few pieces at a time. Cook mince slowly so that it releases as much of its fat as possible, which can then be poured away.

Reheating Food

One of the most common causes of food poisoning is the growth of bacteria in reheated food. To kill the bacteria before consumption, food must be thoroughly heated at high temperatures. No foods should be reheated more than once – meat stocks and other foods which are repeatedly heated and cooled encourage bacteria to grow. The standing times given for microwave foods are vital for ensuring that they have been cooked right through.

Eating Leftovers Cold It is generally safer and healthier to eat leftover foods cold, especially roast meats and cooked fish. Cold cooked vegetables are better tossed into salads, as more of their vitamins are lost through reheating.

Storing for the Unexpected

A well-stocked store cupboard is often a godsend. When unexpected guests drop in, or when work commitments or illness prevent you from shopping, you can still conjure up nutritious and tasty meals.

Tinned Foods Although they are not quite as high in nutrients as their fresh or frozen counterparts, tinned foods are convenient and have a long shelf life. Tinned tomatoes are useful for making sauces to go with pasta and rice, and exotic tinned foods such as superior soups and stews, artichoke hearts and lychees are useful for unexpected entertaining.

If you live in an area where extreme winter weather is a hazard, which may cut off the power and heating in your home, make sure you have a good stock of foods rich in fats and high in calories to provide your body with energy and warmth.

Buying for Storing Choose foods that are in good condition and avoid anything nearing its 'sell-by' date. Check the date-stamping on all vacuum-packed and dried foods. Do not buy any cartons that look swollen; any tins that are dented, rusty, swollen or showing signs of leakage; or torn packets of dried food. Avoid any frozen food with broken packaging or signs of freezer burn – white spots on the surface.

Ensuring it Keeps Well Dried and tinned goods should be kept in a cool, dry store cupboard. Use up older tins and packets first to avoid any wastage.

The Store Cupboard

Basic Ingredients It is generally useful to keep a refrigerator well stocked with eggs, butter, cheese and other everyday foods. Vacuum-packed meats and fish have quite a long refrigerator life, but once opened, must be treated as fresh. Keep your store cupboard stocked with flour, sugar, salt, coffee, tea, breakfast cereals, stock cubes, gravy powders, reduced-sugar jams and spreads, oil and vinegar, herbs, spices and sauces. In addition to these, the following foods are recommended:

Item	Information	Storage Time
Dried Food		
Pasta and rice	These form the basis for many meals. They are filling, easy to cook and nutritious. Store in a sealed packet or airtight jar.	2 years
Dried beans and pulses	These provide plenty of protein and fibre. Dried peas and beans often need long soaking and cooking but are useful for long periods of emergency. Store in a sealed packet or airtight jar.	Pulses – 18 months Lentils – 2 years
Dried milk powder	Whole and skimmed varieties are a good substitute for fresh. Store in an airtight jar or tin.	6 months
Dried fruits	Apricots, prunes, currants and raisins may be added to desserts or cereals. Store them in an airtight container in a cool place.	6 months
High-fibre biscuits	These are a good source of energy in emergencies. Keep in a sealed packet or airtight jar.	6 months
Nuts	Nuts and nut products, like peanut butter, are rich in fat and protein and provide a concentrated source of energy. See packet for 'best-before' date.	Vacuum-packed nuts – 1 year
Tinned Foods		
Vegetables	Common varieties such as carrots, mushrooms, peas and sweetcorn kernels can be kept, and unusual ones such as asparagus spears, artichoke hearts, ratatouille, bamboo shoots and water chestnuts for variety.	2 years
	Tomatoes are an essential part of any emergency store. Use them in soups, casseroles and sauces, and for adding flavour to many dishes.	2 years
	Baked beans, butter beans and red kidney beans are some of the precooked beans available in tins. They are all extremely nutritious and do not need to be soaked.	2 years
Fruits	They provide energy and vitamins.	18 months
Fish and meats	These are invaluable sources of protein and provide the foundation for many dishes.	Meat – 1½ -2 years Fish – 1 year
Soups	These are quick and nourishing. Condensed varieties can also be used as sauces.	2 years
Drinks	Long-life drinks, such as carton fruit juices, UHT milk and additive-free cordials, are ideal.	Cordials and fruit juices – 8-12 months, UHT milk – 3 months

The Healthy Kitchen

A well-planned kitchen with plenty of work space and good lighting is easy to keep clean and much more enjoyable to cook in. Kitchens should also be well ventilated and have a fairly constant temperature – not too hot, or bacteria will breed quickly.

Microwave Cooking

Most foods, especially vegetables and fish, will cook faster in a microwave and in very little liquid – just the right conditions for preserving nutrients.

Know Your Microwave

Before using a microwave, it is essential to read the manufacturer's manual so that you understand exactly how your oven works. You should also find out what the wattage output of your oven is – they range from 400 to 750 watts. Microwaves with a lower wattage output will take longer to cook food. Recommended cooking times for foods will be given in the manual and they should be followed closely.

Cold Spots Microwaves cause molecules in the food to vibrate. This vibrational energy can heat food to 100°C (212°F) – easily hot enough to kill bacteria. However, as the microwaves bounce off the metal oven walls inside the cooker in a set pattern there may be a few small areas or 'cold spots' that are missed. It is possible for bacteria to survive in 'cold spots', which could then lead to food poisoning. To avoid this problem, food must be regularly turned to ensure even cooking and the destruction of bacteria. It also helps to choose foods that are of equal size.

Standing Time Microwaves may not always penetrate right through to the centre of large pieces of food, such as joints of meat or poultry. In such cases, the standing time allows the cooking to be completed by residual heat gradually spreading right through to the centre of the food. If food is still not cooked after a standing period, it may be given a second burst in the microwave, followed by another standing period. Recommended standing times appear in all instruction manuals.

Kitchen Utensils

The following list of utensils gives advice on how to equip your kitchen with safe, effective and durable equipment that will help to ensure the food you cook is nutritious, hygienic and flavoursome.

Knives Sharp stainless-steel knives do not taint or discolour food. Blunt knives can bruise food and so destroy nutrients.

Chopping Boards A traditional hardwood chopping board ensures a good contact between the knife and the food, and prevents slipping. Strong odours from onions, garlic and fish can be removed by sprinkling bicarbonate of soda onto a wet board before scrubbing with hot soapy water, rinsing and drying. Always scrub the board well after cutting raw meat. Laminated and hard resin boards are usually more hygienic than wooden ones but not so easy to cut on.

Tea-towels One of the biggest health hazards in a kitchen are dirty tea-towels – bacteria thrive on them.

Bowls and Jugs The most hygienic bowls and jugs are made from heat-resistant glass or stainless steel; neither of which retain odours or react with acidic foods. Germs can breed in cracks in glazed earthenware bowls, and plastic bowls can absorb strong flavours that may taint other foods.

Spoons Wooden spoons will not scratch a saucepan's lining and expose the base metal, which may react with acidic foods. Stainless-steel spoons (as well as peelers, graters and whisks) are good for other uses.

Sieves and Colanders All sieves and colanders need careful cleaning as food often gets trapped in them. Nylon or plastic sieves and colanders may eventually buckle if repeatedly used with boiling liquids.

Saucepans Good heavy-based saucepans allow even conduction of heat and have tightly fitting lids.
   Stainless-steel pans do not react with food in any way but are not always the best conductor of heat, and some foods stick to them. A heavy-gauge stainless-steel pan with an aluminium or copper base

(to help spread the heat evenly) should last well and is suitable for cooking almost any food.

Copper pans are the best conductors of heat – perfect for both rapid sautéing and slow cooking, but they react with acidic foods (particularly fruits).

Heavy cast-iron pans with vitreous-enamel linings are good for long, slow cooking. If their enamel becomes chipped, they may react with acidic foods.

Nonstick saucepans and frying pans allow food to be cooked with little or no fat.

Lightweight aluminium pans react badly with acidic food and can sometimes buckle over intense heat. They are also difficult to keep clean.

Food Processors and Blenders If the cutting blades become blunt they will bruise food, so either replace them or send them away to get them sharpened.

Roasting and Baking Tins Heavy-gauge enamel, cast-iron, and stainless-steel roasting tins will not buckle or react with acidic foods. They conduct heat evenly, and are therefore less likely to burn food. Dry tins thoroughly after use to avoid rusting.

Glazed Earthenware Oven-proof earthenware does not conduct heat well and so is good for slow cooking.

Woks Very little fat is needed to cook food in woks, because they conduct heat quickly and evenly.

Steamers Traditional steamer saucepans have a normal saucepan base and a perforated steamer pan that fits inside. You can also buy a fold-out stainless-steel steamer which fits any saucepan, and is perfect for cooking small quantities of food. If you have a wok, use a Chinese bamboo steamer.

Foil Aluminium foil should not be used with acidic foods such as lemons and vinegar, which corrode it.

Plastic Film Recent research suggests that plastic film may react slightly with foods that have a high fat content, if it is in direct contact with them. Use non-toxic plastic film for microwave cooking.

Refrigerators

A refrigerator helps to keep food fresh because the cold slows down the growth of bacteria. Keep the temperature between 0°C (32°F) and 5°C (41°F) –

temperature dials are not always accurate, so it may be worth checking the temperature with a thermometer. Make sure that the refrigerator is cold enough in the summer, when warm air gets in every time the door is opened. Never leave the refrigerator open for long periods. Hot foods should be cooled before they are placed in the refrigerator or freezer.

Defrosting and Cleaning A refrigerator that needs defrosting will not work efficiently. Even a refrigerator that defrosts automatically has to be emptied for cleaning. Remove the food and cover it with blankets or newspapers to keep it cool. Clean the refrigerator with warm water and bicarbonate of soda.

Keeping Foods Separate To prevent the spread of bacteria, different foods should be kept separately. Never allow raw meats or poultry to come into contact with cooked foods or any food that is to be eaten raw. Each time cooked meats are removed from the refrigerator they collect bacteria, so only remove them when necessary.

Covering foods helps to prevent them drying out and stops strong smells developing. Keep cheeses in non-airtight containers, and eggs in the egg rack or an open bowl, so that air can circulate around them.

Freezers

As long as the temperature is kept at −18°C (0°F) or below, most perishable foods can safely be kept for months in a freezer. Every food has a different chemical make-up, and some frozen foods keep their flavour, colour and texture better than others.

Defrosting and Cleaning To function properly, freezers must be defrosted from time to time: chest models once a year, and upright models two or three times a year. Try to run food stocks down before defrosting. If you cannot borrow space in a neighbour's freezer, pack food in insulated bags, picnic boxes or newspaper.

Defrosting can take several hours, but putting bowls of hot water in the freezer will speed the process. Freezers that defrost automatically still need to be emptied for cleaning. The temperature must reach −18°C (0°F) again before restocking.

Freezing and Thawing Food

This chart gives the length of time that foods can safely be kept frozen without their flavour or texture being badly impaired. It also gives tips on wrapping food for the freezer, spells out any special preparation that is necessary and lists thawing times.

Before vegetables are frozen they should be blanched (cooked in fast boiling water for about 1 minute), then 'refreshed' by draining them in a colander and immediately run under cold water and dried. This process helps frozen vegetables keep their flavour and colour. Most fruit and vegetables benefit from being cooked straight from the freezer.

Because food expands as it freezes, it is often important to leave 'head space' at the top of freezer

Food	Preparation	Packaging	Tips	Storage (mths)	Thawing (hrs/lb) in the refrigerator	Thawing (hrs/lb) at room temperature
Meat						
Beef, lamb and pork joints	Cut joints to required size. Cover protruding bones with foil. Bone joints if desired, roll and tie into shape.	Wrap tightly in polythene or foil. Overwrap large joints with extra layers for protection.	Boning joints before freezing saves valuable space. Pork joints will only store for 9 months.	9-12	5	2
Beef steaks	Trim off fat. Separate pieces with freezer paper or foil.	Wrap tightly in strong foil, polythene bags or freezer paper.	Divide into portions required for one family meal.	9-12	5	2
Pork and lamb chops	Stack with double sheets of freezer paper for easy separation.	Wrap tightly and secure with freezer tape. Polythene bags or plastic containers.	Pork chops must be thawed in the refrigerator.	3-4	5	2
Minced meat	Divide into portions. Omit seasoning.	Sealed freezer bags.	Only freeze very fresh mince.	1-2	6	1-1½
Sausages (shop bought)	No preparation necessary.	Sheet polythene or freezer bags. Wrap tightly and seal well.	Homemade sausages can be stored for up to 6 months.	3	6	1½ -2
Fish						
Whole white and oily fish	Scale and remove head, backbone, fins, tail and gut. Wrap tightly.	Sheet polythene, freezer paper or foil.	Oily fish will only store for 3 months.	3-6	6-10	3-5
Fish steaks and fillets	Keep portions separate with double sheets of freezer paper.	Wrap tightly as for whole fish and secure with freezer tape.	Dry fish with kitchen paper before freezing.	3-6	6-10	3-5
Crab	Cook meat for 15 minutes per 1lb (450g). Remove meat from body and claws.	Polythene bags or containers. Pack leaving ½in (15mm) head space.	Pack white and brown meat separately.	1	10-12	3

bags or containers. All foods should be sealed and labelled with the contents and date.

The faster food is frozen the less it is damaged by the freezing process and the better it will keep. If possible, chill food in the refrigerator before it is frozen and lower the temperature of the freezer. Your freezer manual will give advice on how much food can safely be frozen all at one go.

Since large amounts of food take longer to thaw than smaller quantities, thawing times are expressed as the number of hours needed to thaw 1lb (450g) of a particular food. To maintain texture and stop bacteria multiplying, it is best to thaw food slowly in a refrigerator. However, times are given for thawing food at room temperature as well in a refrigerator. While food is thawing, loosen its wrapping.

The chart also lists foods that should never be frozen and others that do not freeze well. Unwashed food, especially poultry, should never be frozen – it dramatically increases the risk of food poisoning.

Food	Preparation	Packaging	Tips	Storage (mths)	Thawing (hrs/lb) in the refrigerator	Thawing (hrs/lb) at room temperature
Fish *continued*						
Prawns and shrimps	May be frozen in single layers on trays for easy removal.	Polythene containers or freezer bags. Chill and pack leaving 1½in (40mm) head space.	Prawns can be frozen raw or cooked. To cook, boil for 5 minutes, cool and shell.	1	6-8	1½ -2
Mussels	Cook and remove from shells.	Pack in plastic boxes, leaving ½in (15mm) head space.	Strain cooking liquid and pour over mussels.	1	6-8	1½ -2
Poultry and Game						
Whole birds	Clean outside and in with kitchen paper. Protect protruding bones with foil.	Seal in freezer bag, squeezing out as much air as possible.	Giblets may be wrapped and placed in the body cavity if used within 3 months. Otherwise, store separately.	3-6	12-36	–
Portions	Joint the bird if necessary, and wipe with kitchen paper.	Plastic containers. Wrap portions individually.	Any trimmings may be frozen separately and used for making stock.	As for whole birds	8-10	–
Soups						
	Strain, cool and remove surplus fat.	Rigid polythene containers. Leave 1-2in (25-50mm) of head space in containers.	Mixing frozen vegetable purées and vegetable stock makes delicious soups.	2-3	–	1-2
Sauces						
	Cool, strain if desired and remove surplus fat.	Pour into rigid containers. Leave 1-2in (25-50mm) head space.	Add cream after thawing.	2-3	–	1-2
DO NOT FREEZE	Sauces made with a lot of cream, cheese or milk may separate when frozen.					

continued on next page

				Storage (mths)	Thawing (hrs/lb) in the refrigerator	Thawing (hrs/lb) at room temperature
continued from previous page						
Food	**Preparation**	**Packaging**	**Tips**			
Vegetables						
Beans (French and runner)	Wash, top and tail, blanch, refresh and drain.	Polythene bags, containers or cartons. Pack leaving head space.	Cut the beans, slice them or leave whole.	12	–	–
Peas	Shell, blanch, refresh and drain.	Pack with ½in (15mm) head space in polythene bags or containers.	Squeeze out as much air as possible if using bags.	12	–	–
Broccoli	Wash and split into florets. Blanch, using 1 teaspoon salt to 2 pints (1.1 litres) water. Refresh and drain.	Polythene bags. No head space needed.	Choose tight, compact, dark green heads.	12	–	–
Brussels sprouts	Trim discoloured leaves and wash. Grade into sizes, blanch, refresh and drain.	Polythene bags. No head space needed.	Freeze even-sized sprouts together.	12	–	–
Carrots	Trim, wash and peel. Blanch, refresh and drain.	Polythene bags. Pack with ½in (15mm) head space.	Slice or dice if desired.	12	–	–
Cauliflower	Trim and separate into small florets. Blanch, refresh and drain.	Polythene bags. No head space needed.	Check for dirt and insects in florets.	6	–	–
Corn on the cob	Remove outer green leaves and silk. Blanch cobs of similar size together, cool and drain.	Freezer wrap.	If desired, remove kernels after blanching, slicing closely to the cob with a sharp knife.	12	–	–
Potatoes	Boil new potatoes until almost ready, drain and cool.	Polythene bags. Squeeze air out from bags before freezing. Pack with no head space.	Old potatoes should be cooked, mashed with milk and beaten egg to freeze.	12	6	1½
Spinach	Wash carefully, blanch, refresh and drain.	Polythene bags or containers. Pack leaving ½in (15mm) head space.	Blanch a small amount of spinach at a time.	12	–	–
DO NOT FREEZE	Whole tomatoes, marrow, cucumber, salad leaves and most herbs retain their flavour, but their high water content leaves them mushy when thawed.					
Dairy						
Cream	Freeze double cream (over 40% butterfat) and clotted cream only.	Polythene containers. Allow 1in (25mm) head space.	Add 1 tablespoon sugar to 1 pint (570ml) cream to prolong storage time.	4	8	1-2

Food	Preparation	Packaging	Tips	Storage (mths)	Thawing (hrs/lb) in the refrigerator	Thawing (hrs/lb) at room temperature
Dairy *continued*						
Butter	Freeze butter in its original packaging.	If it has become soft, overwrap it.	Salted butter will store for longer than unsalted.	6-12	12	1-2
Cheese	Hard cheeses only – divide into 8oz (225g) portions. Grate if desired.	Freezer wrap.	Soft cream cheese may be blended with other foods for a dip and stored for 2 months.	2-6	12	–
DO NOT FREEZE	Milk, single cream, whipping cream, sour cream and most yoghurts tend to separate when frozen. Soft cheese loses its texture and much of its flavour. Whole eggs should never be frozen – they will burst. Eggs in cooked dishes, such as custard, may be grainy after freezing. Egg yolks should be frozen with 1 teaspoon salt or 1 tablespoon sugar for every 6 yolks to stop them becoming gelatinous. Freeze egg yolks and unwhipped egg whites separately. Never freeze whipped egg whites.					
Fruit						
Apples	Wash, peel, core and slice. Place in salted water and blanch, or steam, until pliable but not pulpy. Or cook until completely softened with 3oz (75g) sugar to each 1lb (450g) of prepared apples. Cool before freezing.	Pack in polythene containers, freezer bags or waxed cartons, leaving head space.	To pack, either sprinkle sugar between layers; 2-3oz (50-75g) per 1lb (450g) of fruit, or sub-merge in a cold sugar syrup: dissolve 8oz (225g) sugar in 1 pint (570ml) of water, bring to the boil and boil for 1 minute. Allow to cool.	9	7-8	3½ -4
Blackberries	Remove hulls and wash if necessary. Drain. Pack with sugar or syrup as for apples.	Polythene containers or waxed cartons, leaving head space.	Add crumpled waxed or greaseproof paper to hold berries under syrup.	12	6-7	2-3
Cherries	Stalk, stone, wash and dry. Pack with sugar or syrup as above.	Freezer bags, polythene containers or waxed cartons.	Turn fruit over in the sugar until it is dissolved.	6	7-8	3-4
Gooseberries	Top and tail, wash, drain thoroughly and pack with sugar or syrup.	Freezer bags.	Layer the gooseberries with sugar. Use up to 1lb (450g) of sugar to 5lb (2.3kg) of gooseberries.	12	7-8	3-4
Peaches	Wash, stone and peel. Pack with sugar or syrup.	Polythene containers or waxed cartons.	Add 1 tablespoon of lemon juice to each pint (570ml) of syrup to preserve colour.	9	7-8	3-4

continued on next page

continued from previous page					Thawing (hrs/lb) at room temperature	
					Thawing (hrs/lb) in the refrigerator	
Food	Preparation	Packaging	Tips	Storage (mths)		
Fruit *continued*						
Plums	Halve and stone. Dry or syrup pack.	Polythene containers or waxed cartons.	Add a piece of crumpled waxed or greaseproof paper to hold the fruit under the syrup.	9	7-8	3-4
Raspberries	Remove hulls. Do not wash. Pack with sugar or syrup.	Polythene containers or waxed cartons. Leave head space.	May be frozen without sugar in single layers on trays before packaging.	12	6-7	2-3
Rhubarb	Wash, trim and cut into pieces. Drop in boiling water for 1 minute, cool and pack dry or in sugar.	Freezer bags if dry, polythene containers for syrup. Leave head space.	Stew before freezing if desired.	12	7-8	3-4
Strawberries	Remove hulls. Pack with sugar or syrup, or open freeze without sugar as for raspberries.	Polythene containers or waxed cartons.	Freeze strawberries crushed or puréed if desired.	12	6-7	2-3
DO NOT FREEZE	Bananas turn black when frozen.					
Baking						
Bread (unbaked)	Complete the kneading of the dough.	Large, lightly greased polythene bag.	Tie the bag but leave space for rising.	5-8 weeks	12	3-6
Bread (baked)	Freeze freshly baked bread only.	Ungreased polythene bag with tight seal.	Crisp crusts on bread will start to fall away after one week.	4 weeks	12	3-6
Cakes	Freeze whole or sliced and wrapped.	Freezer wrap or foil within rigid container.	Ensure icing is set before freezing. Cakes made without fat store for half the time given.	8-10	12	4
Pastry	Freeze pies or tarts with unbaked pastry. Store unbaked pie tops or tart shells separated with paper or foil.	Freezer or cling wrap. Extra foil or polythene will hold shapes.	Uncooked pastry will cook from the freezer.	4-6	–	2-4
DO NOT FREEZE	Uncooked pastry or batter made with yeast may not rise properly after freezing. Frosting and fillings for cakes can be frozen but may require special attention. Glacé icings may crack, fillings made with whipped cream may separate and frostings with a high egg content, such as royal icing, may dry out. To freeze a frosted pastry or cake without spoiling the decoration, freeze it unwrapped for a short time until very firm, then wrap and freeze it again.					
	Jelly and aspic lose their texture when frozen and need to be melted and reset before serving. Foods with a high salt content do not freeze well.					

Stocks

A good stock can make all the difference to soups, sauces and casseroles. The long, slow cooking of meat, bones and vegetables with herbs and spices allows flavours to mingle and concentrate.

Most good supermarkets now sell fresh stock. Commercial stock cubes may be convenient but they are no substitute for the real thing – they contain a lot of monosodium glutamate and other synthetic flavourings and have virtually no nutritional value.

If you have a freezer it is worth making stocks in large quantities, since they can be frozen for up to 6 months. Make sure frozen stock is well labelled.

Making stock is an ideal way of using up almost any leftovers. The following stock recipes have no added salt and very little fat.

Vegetable Stock

The aim is to make a well-flavoured liquid rather than a soup when cooking vegetable stock. This stock will keep up to a week in the refrigerator or up to 6 months in a freezer.

MAKES : *4-5 pints (2.3 - 2.8 litres)*
PREPARATION TIME : *20 minutes*
COOKING TIME : *3 hours*

INGREDIENTS
1lb (450g) leeks
4 large sticks celery
8oz (225g) onions
1½ lb (700g) carrots, swedes and turnips
1 clove garlic
2-3 sprigs parsley
2-3 sprigs thyme
2 bay leaves
20 black peppercorns

Wash the leeks and celery, keeping only the white parts of the leeks. Peel the onions, carrots, swedes and turnips. Roughly chop all the vegetables and put them into a large saucepan. Add the unpeeled garlic,

herbs, peppercorns and 6 pints (3.4 litres) of cold water and bring to the boil. Reduce the heat, partially cover with a lid, and simmer for 3 hours. Allow to cool, then sieve into a bowl. Refrigerate or freeze.

Chicken or Veal Stock

To make veal stock use 6lb (2.7kg) of uncooked veal bones instead of the chicken pieces in this recipe. Turkey can also be substituted. All giblets except the liver can be used to make chicken stock. For a clear stock, do not let the stock boil. The stock can be refrigerated for 3 days or frozen for 5 months.

MAKES : *7 pints (4 litres)*
PREPARATION TIME : *20 minutes*
COOKING TIME : *4 hours*

INGREDIENTS
6lb (2.7kg) boiling fowl and giblets or
6lb (2.7kg) legs, trimmings or uncooked bones
8oz (225g) carrots
8oz (225g) onions
3 sticks celery
1 large leek
3 cloves
1 clove garlic
3-4 sprigs thyme
3-4 sprigs parsley
2 bay leaves
24 peppercorns

If using a boiling fowl, cut it into large pieces. Wash the pieces and giblets and put them into a very large saucepan. Add 8 pints (4.5 litres) of cold water and bring slowly to the boil. Peel the carrots and onions. Wash the celery and the leek. Roughly chop all the vegetables and press the cloves into a slice of onion.

As soon as the stock boils, reduce the heat and add all the remaining ingredients to the pan. Partially cover the pan with a lid, and simmer gently for 3½ -4 hours, regularly skimming off any surface scum.

Sieve into a large bowl and cover with a clean cloth. Discard the chicken and vegetables. Allow the stock to cool, then refrigerate overnight.

Next day, remove all the solidified fat from the surface of the stock. Freeze or refrigerate.

Beef Stock

Beef stock needs long, slow cooking. If you keep the skin on the clove of garlic, the stock will have a subtle garlic flavour. You can refrigerate the stock for 3 days or freeze it for up to 5 months.

MAKES: 6½ pints (3.5 litres)
PREPARATION TIME: 20 minutes
COOKING TIME: 6 hours
CHILLING TIME: Overnight
OVEN: Preheat to 220°C (425°F, gas mark 7)

INGREDIENTS
4½ lb (2kg) chopped marrow bones
1 chopped oxtail
4 large onions
4½ lb (2kg) shin of beef
8oz (225g) carrots
4 sticks celery
1 large leek
4 cloves
1 clove garlic
3-4 sprigs thyme
3-4 sprigs parsley
2 bay leaves
24 black peppercorns

Place the marrow bones and oxtail in a roasting tin. Peel three of the onions and add them to the tin. Cook in the oven for 1 hour, until the bones and onions are well browned.

Cut the shin of beef into cubes. Peel the remaining onion, the carrots, and wash the celery and leek. Press the cloves into the whole onion and cut all the other vegetables into thick slices.

Remove the tin from the oven, and put the bones and onions into a very large saucepan. Add the cubed beef and 8 pints (4.5 litres) of cold water. Bring to the boil slowly.

Pour off the fat in the roasting tin. Add ½ pint (285 ml) of cold water and place over a moderate heat. Bring to the boil, while scraping the brown residue from the bottom. Add the liquid to the pan.

When the stock starts to boil, reduce the heat immediately and add all the remaining ingredients. Partially cover with a lid, and simmer gently for 5 hours, regularly skimming scum from the surface. Sieve into a large bowl and cover with a clean cloth. Discard the bones, meat and vegetables.

Let the stock cool, then refrigerate overnight. Next day, remove the solidified fat from the surface and then freeze or refrigerate.

Fish Stock

A good fish stock will add depth of flavour to any fish dish. It is particularly useful for making delicious fish soups. Fish stock is also perfect for poaching fish. Almost any trimmings of white fish can be used to make stock, except the gills, as long as they are clean. Take care not to cook fish stock for too long, otherwise it will start to smell strongly and take on a bitter taste. Fish stock can be refrigerated for 2 days or frozen for 2 months.

MAKES: 4 pints (2.3 litres)
PREPARATION TIME: 20 minutes
COOKING TIME: 40 minutes

INGREDIENTS
3lb (1.4kg) white fish trimmings (head and bones)
1 leek
1 stick celery
1 large onion, or 5 shallots
1 carrot
Juice of 1 lemon
1 sprig parsley
1 sprig thyme
8 white peppercorns
1 pint (570ml) dry white wine
Freshly ground black pepper

Wash the fish trimmings and place them in a large saucepan. Wash the leek and celery, keeping only the white parts of the leek. Peel the onion, or the shallots, and the carrot, then thinly slice all the vegetables. Add all the ingredients to the pan. Pour in 3 pints (1.7 litres) of cold water and slowly bring to a boil, then reduce the heat immediately. Skim any scum off the surface at regular intervals. Simmer gently for 30 minutes. Season lightly with freshly ground black pepper, if desired, and sieve into a large bowl. Allow to cool. Freeze or refrigerate.

THE RECIPES

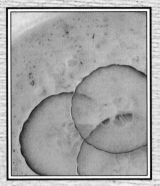

**SOUPS &
STARTERS**
31-74

**SALADS &
RAW FOOD DISHES**
75-116

**PASTA & RICE
DISHES**
117-142

**FISH &
SHELLFISH**
143-170

**BEEF, LAMB & PORK
DISHES**
171-210

POULTRY & GAME
211-236

ONE-POT DISHES
237-258

**VEGETABLE
DISHES**
259-294

DESSERTS
295-320

**SNACKS, DRINKS &
SANDWICHES**
321-340

ABOUT THE RECIPES

This book is about enjoying food and feeling good about it. All 306 recipes have been specially created and photographed for *Eat Better Live Better*. Not only will they provide you with scores of new ideas for healthy eating, but they will also show you how to prepare and cook old favourites in a healthier way.

Most of the recipes are designed to give 4 servings, but many have tips on adapting a meal for more or less people and provide imaginative ways of using up leftovers. The ingredients are listed in a logical order and the preparation and cooking times are always stated. The recipes encourage the use of fresh ingredients, but if any may be tricky to find, substitutes are given.

The recipe instructions are written in easy-to-follow stages, explaining all the culinary terms as they crop up. They include serving suggestions and give advice on which vegetables or wine go particularly well with a dish. Beautiful colour photographs of every recipe whet the appetite and give you hundreds of ideas on presenting food.

Calories per serving and basic nutritional information are given for each recipe, enabling you to plan a well-balanced diet. Although many of the dishes are low in calories, there are also plenty of recipes for those with healthy appetites. People with special needs, such as vegetarians or those with heart disease, diabetes or common food allergies, will find dozens of delicious recipes that are suitable for them. But, above all, the recipes are for people who want to be healthy and still enjoy their food.

SOUPS & STARTERS

A tremendous range of colours and textures can be used when preparing light and healthy appetisers. Choose from simple or exotic starters, and hearty or refreshing soups. Spices, herbs and garnishes add the final touch.

∽

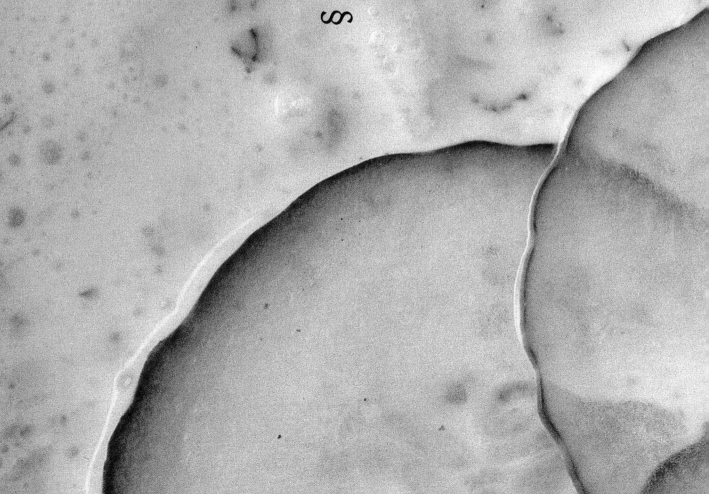

Bouillabaisse

This nutritious thick fish soup is based on a famous recipe from Marseilles, where it is traditionally made with a spiny scorpion fish called rascasse. Sea bass, sole, flounder or snapper are substituted here, or you can use a mixture of all four. Bouillabaisse is a meal in itself and goes well with garlic bread.

SERVES 4
PREPARATION TIME : *20 minutes*
COOKING TIME : *15 minutes*

INGREDIENTS
4 small fillets of sea bass, sole, flounder or
snapper, weighing 1½lb (700g)
4oz (115g) squid (optional)
1 medium onion
2 cloves garlic
1 leek
1 red or yellow pepper
1 tablespoon virgin olive oil
2 tomatoes
1 pint (570ml) fish stock or
equivalent fish stock cubes
3fl oz (90ml) dry white wine
1 bay leaf
½ teaspoon fennel seeds
2 sprigs fresh thyme or ½ teaspoon dried
2 splashes tabasco sauce
Salt and freshly ground black pepper
4 sea or bay scallops
2 tablespoons chopped parsley

Calories per serving : 315 · High in vitamin C and calcium from tomatoes and vegetables · High in iron and protein from fish

Finely chop the onion, garlic, leek and de-seeded pepper. Heat the oil in a large saucepan and cook the vegetables for 3-4 minutes. Add 1 fish fillet, the tomatoes, fish stock, wine, bay leaf, fennel seeds, thyme, tabasco, salt and pepper and cook for 5 minutes. Break up the cooked fish fillet with a fork.

Add the other fillets, and the optional squid, in one layer and top with the scallops. Cover and simmer for another 5 minutes. Sprinkle with parsley.

A chunky French soup of fish, herbs and wine.

Gazpacho

Gazpacho originated in southern Spain, as a peasant soup of bread, garlic, olive oil and water. This recipe, which requires no cooking, is one of the most popular variations, using summer salad ingredients for a colourful and sweeter-tasting soup.

SERVES 4
PREPARATION TIME : *20 minutes*
CHILLING TIME : *1-2 hours*

INGREDIENTS
1oz (25g) fresh white breadcrumbs
2 tablespoons olive oil
¼ teaspoon paprika
8oz (225g) tomatoes
3 spring onions
1 small clove garlic
½ small cucumber
½ red pepper
½ yellow pepper
Juice of 1 lime or 1 teaspoon red wine vinegar
16fl oz (475ml) tomato juice
Salt and freshly ground black pepper

Calories per serving : 145 · Low in calories and sodium · Cholesterol free · High in vitamin C from tomatoes and tomato juice

Bring ¼ pint (150ml) of water to the boil, then mix it in a bowl with the breadcrumbs, oil and paprika. Put the mixture to one side.

Dip the tomatoes into hot water for 30 seconds, then cold water for 1 minute, until the skins can be easily removed. Cut the tomatoes in half, remove all the seeds and finely dice the flesh. Trim the spring onions and peel the garlic. Peel the cucumber, and finely dice it with the peppers and spring onions.

Blend the breadcrumb mixture, cucumber, peppers, spring onions and garlic in a liquidiser until fairly smooth. Stir in the lime juice.

Add this mixture to the tomato juice and diced tomatoes, season to taste, and chill. Serve cold.

A modern variation of traditional Spanish gazpacho makes a refreshing starter or light summer snack.

Hard-Boiled Eggs with Pesto

Pesto is a thick basil sauce from Genoa in Italy. Although it is easy to make, you can use 4 table-spoons of ready-made pesto sauce instead. Home-made sauce can be sealed and refrigerated for a week. You will need a liquidiser for this recipe.

Fresh tomato complements rich, pesto-filled eggs.

SERVES 4
PREPARATION TIME : *10 minutes*
COOKING TIME : *10 minutes*

INGREDIENTS
4 eggs
1 small clove garlic
2 large sprigs basil
1oz (25g) pine nuts
1oz (25g) grated Parmesan cheese
1 tablespoon virgin olive oil
Freshly ground black pepper
2 beef or large tomatoes for garnish

Calories per serving : 180 · Low in sodium · High in protein from eggs

Hard-boil the eggs for 10 minutes. Cool them under running water and shell, then cut in half lengthways and remove the yolks.

To make the pesto, crush the garlic and place it in the liquidiser along with the basil sprigs and pine nuts, reserving some basil leaves for garnish. Blend until smooth. Add the egg yolks and cheese and blend again, then add the olive oil and quickly blend once more. Season to taste, using plenty of pepper.

Pile the pesto mixture into the hollows of the egg whites and serve garnished with slices of tomato and the reserved basil leaves.

Spinach Triangles with Tomato and Basil Sauce

These light triangles, filled with nutritious spinach, are made from filo pastry. This pastry is made from very pliable dough that can be pulled and rolled until wafer thin – making remarkably light pastry casings.

SERVES 4
PREPARATION TIME : *30 minutes*
COOKING TIME : *35 minutes*
OVEN : *Preheat to 190°C (375°F, gas mark 5)*

INGREDIENTS
2lb (900g) fresh spinach
1 tablespoon virgin olive oil
½ tablespoon freshly squeezed lemon juice
¼ teaspoon nutmeg
Salt and freshly ground black pepper
2oz (50g) butter
8oz (225g) packet filo pastry
TOMATO SAUCE
2lb (900g) fresh tomatoes
1 red or Spanish onion
1 bunch fresh basil
1½ tablespoons virgin olive oil

Calories per serving : 420 · High in fibre, protein, calcium and iron from spinach · High in vitamin C from tomatoes

Crispy filo-pastry cases filled with spinach on a bed of fresh tomatoes mixed with onion and fresh basil.

Wash the spinach thoroughly and place it in a large pan of salted water. Bring to the boil and cook over a moderate heat for 2 minutes, until just tender.

Drain the spinach well, transfer to a mixing bowl and mix in 1 tablespoon of olive oil, the lemon juice, nutmeg and season to taste.

Melt the butter in a pan. Lightly butter 8 sheets of pastry, laying each new sheet on top of the last one. Cut into rectangles, 8 × 4in (200 × 100mm), and spoon a tablespoon of spinach onto one end of each piece – about 1in (25mm) from the edge. Fold one corner of pastry over the spinach, fold the pointed edge back over the strip, and fold over the remaining flap to form a triangle. Seal any open edges. Place the triangles on a greased baking tray and bake in a preheated oven for about 20 minutes, or until the pastry is crispy and golden.

Meanwhile, plunge the tomatoes in boiling water for 30 seconds, then cold water for 1 minute, so that the skins can be easily peeled away. Finely chop the tomatoes, onion and basil.

Heat 1½ tablespoons of oil in a frying pan. Gently cook the onion for 5 minutes, until golden and transparent. Add the tomatoes and basil and season with salt and plenty of black pepper. Simmer for 10 minutes until the oil separates from the tomatoes. Divide the tomato sauce between 4 large plates and serve the triangles on top.

Fresh Vegetable Timbale

This vegetable dish has a lovely soft consistency. Its asparagus flavour is complemented by the subtle aftertastes of the herbs and vegetables. Peak season for asparagus is spring. The individual timbales may be turned out onto plates for serving, or left in their baking dishes for a more rustic effect. You will need a liquidiser for this recipe.

SERVES 4
PREPARATION TIME : *45 minutes*
COOKING TIME : *1 hour 10 minutes*
OVEN : *Preheat to 160°C (325°F, gas mark 3)*

INGREDIENTS
8oz (225g) fresh asparagus
1 leek or ½ medium onion
3oz (75g) mushrooms
1 bay leaf
¼ teaspoon dried thyme
½ teaspoon salt
3 spring onions
1oz (25g) fresh spinach
6 parsley sprigs
1½ oz (40g) butter
6 eggs
1 tablespoon grated Parmesan cheese
¼ teaspoon white pepper
Generous pinch of ground nutmeg
1 slice brown toast

Calories per serving : 255 · High in protein and iron from eggs

Wash the asparagus, cut off the tough ends of the stalks and put them in a saucepan. Roughly chop the leek or onion, and the stalks of the mushrooms. Add these to the saucepan along with the bay leaf, thyme and salt. Cover with ¾ pint (450ml) of water, bring to the boil, simmer for 25 minutes and drain, reserving the vegetable stock.

While the stock is cooking, cut the tips off the asparagus and reserve. Chop the remaining stalks, the spring onions, the spinach, the parsley and the mushroom caps, and put all the ingredients into a frying pan with 1oz (25g) of the butter over a medium heat for 3 minutes, stirring occasionally.

Add the vegetable stock and simmer for 10 minutes, until the asparagus stalks are tender. Reserving the liquid, drain the vegetables and liquidise them. Add ⅓ pint (190ml) of the stock to the purée, and salt to taste. Beat the eggs thoroughly with a fork or a whisk, stir them into the purée and

Fresh asparagus tips decorate small soufflé pots of pureéd vegetables mixed with eggs and Parmesan. The soufflés have an intense flavour of asparagus and are delicious eaten with freshly baked bread.

add the Parmesan, white pepper and ground nutmeg.

Crumble the toast into breadcrumbs, butter 4 small soufflé dishes and coat with the breadcrumbs. Fill each just over half full with the vegetable mixture. Place the dishes in a baking pan and fill the pan with enough hot water to come halfway up the sides of the dishes. Bake for 40 minutes, or until set.

Whilst they are cooking, put the asparagus tips and the remaining vegetable stock in a pan, gently bring to the boil and simmer for 5 minutes until the tips are tender. Drain the tips and refresh them by running them quickly under a cold tap – this helps to keep them looking fresh and green.

When the timbales are cooked, slice the asparagus tips down the middle and use to garnish each soufflé dish. Serve immediately.

Carrot, Tomato and Cardamom Soup

Cardamom is a rich, aromatic spice that belongs to the ginger family – the most prized spice in the world after saffron. Choose fresh green or white pods for this soup, as the small, dark seeds retain essential oils that are missing in ready-ground supplies. You will need a liquidiser for this recipe. You may like to try serving this soup with Indian breads, such as nan or paratha.

SERVES 4
PREPARATION TIME : *15 minutes*
COOKING TIME : *40 minutes*

INGREDIENTS
9 cardamom pods
10oz (275g) fresh tomatoes
10oz (275g) carrots
1½ tablespoons sunflower oil
1 onion
1¾ pints (975ml) vegetable or chicken stock
Salt and and freshly ground black pepper
Fresh coriander or parsley for garnish

Calories per serving : 90 · Low in calories
High in fibre from vegetables

Carrots and tomatoes are blended to make a vivid red-orange soup which is rich and smooth. The addition of cardamom creates an Eastern flavour.

Roughly crush the cardamom pods using a pestle and mortar or the end of a rolling pin. Place all the pods and seeds in a piece of muslin and tie securely with string.

Skin the tomatoes by plunging them into a bowl of hot water for 30 seconds, then cold for 1 minute, until the skins can be easily removed using your fingers. De-seed the tomatoes, trim the carrots, and roughly chop them both.

Heat the oil in a large saucepan and finely chop the onion. Cook the onion over a medium heat until transparent. Add the carrots and tomatoes and stir for 2-3 minutes.

Add the stock and wrapped cardamom pods, then bring to the boil. Reduce the heat and simmer for about 30 minutes until the carrots are tender. Remove the cardamom from the saucepan and leave to cool, then squeeze the muslin out over the saucepan, extracting all the juices.

Purée the vegetables and their liquid in a liquidiser, then return to the saucepan and reheat gently. The soup may be kept warm over a low heat until ready to serve, but you may need a little extra stock or water to thin it.

Season with salt and freshly ground black pepper to taste, garnish with a sprinkling of chopped coriander or parsley, and serve immediately.

Crab Chowder

Chowders are thick and substantial American soups, although the name comes from the French word *chaudière*, meaning 'stew pot'. Ingredients vary but usually contain fish or shellfish. Plump sweetcorn, either fresh or frozen, is used for this chowder.

SERVES 4
PREPARATION TIME : *20 minutes*
COOKING TIME : *45 minutes*

INGREDIENTS
6oz (175g) white crabmeat
2 cobs sweetcorn or 4oz (115g) sweetcorn kernels
1 small onion
1 stick celery
½ small green pepper
1 medium potato
4 rashers lean bacon
1 tablespoon virgin olive oil
1 bay leaf
½ teaspoon paprika
1½ pints (850ml) vegetable or chicken stock
½ pint (285ml) semi-skimmed milk
1 tablespoon cornflour
2 tablespoons freshly chopped parsley
Salt and freshly ground black pepper

Calories per serving : 230 · High in zinc and vitamin C · High in protein from bacon and crab

Bacon gives this crab soup a smoky flavour.

If using fresh sweetcorn, remove the husks and silky threads, then cook the cobs in boiling water with a pinch of sugar for about 15 minutes until tender. Drain and cool, then cut away the kernels. If using tinned or frozen kernels, cook according to packet instructions, then drain and cool.

Finely chop the onion, celery, pepper and potato. Remove the rinds from the bacon and cut into small pieces. Heat the oil in a large saucepan, add the bacon and cook gently until lightly browned.

Add the onion, celery and pepper to the saucepan and cook for 5 minutes, stirring occasionally. Next add the potato to the saucepan with the bay leaf, paprika and stock and bring to the boil. Reduce the heat, cover and simmer for 20 minutes.

Mix the milk with the flour and stir into the soup with the sweetcorn and crab. Simmer for 10 minutes. Discard the bay leaf, add the parsley and season.

Spicy Garlic Prawns

Garlic has a natural affinity with prawns; enhancing their subtle flavour without being overpowering. You can use other vegetables such as aubergine, broccoli or cauliflower instead of the courgettes.

SERVES 4
PREPARATION TIME : *5 minutes*
COOKING TIME : *15 minutes*

INGREDIENTS
8oz (225g) peeled prawns
1lb (450g) courgettes
4 garlic cloves
1 green chilli
1 tablespoon sunflower oil
1 level teaspoon grated fresh ginger
2 large tomatoes
3 tablespoons chopped coriander
¼ teaspoon ground turmeric
½ teaspoon cumin seeds
1 tablespoon lemon juice
Salt and white pepper

Calories per serving : 160 · High in protein, calcium and iron from prawns

A variety of textures, tastes and colours make this spicy prawn and courgette dish a popular light starter.

Cut the courgettes into sticks about 3in (80mm) long and ¼in (5mm) thick. Peel and crush the garlic, de-seed and finely chop the chilli. Heat the oil in a pan and gently fry the garlic, grated ginger and chilli for about 3 minutes. De-seed and roughly chop the tomatoes and add them to the pan. Increase the heat and cook for a further 4 minutes, stirring frequently.

Add all the remaining ingredients to the pan and cook for 2 minutes, stirring occasionally. Season to taste and serve as a hot starter or light snack. Serve the dish piping hot straight from the pan, if you wish. Take care not to overcook the ingredients.

Butternut Squash and White Bean Soup

In North America, farmers grow a great range of squashes, including the succulent butternut variety. It tastes similar to pumpkin, which could be substituted in this recipe. You will need a liquidiser.

SERVES 6-8
PREPARATION TIME : *20 minutes*
SOAKING TIME : *Overnight*
COOKING TIME : *1½ hours*

INGREDIENTS
1 butternut squash or 1 small pumpkin
8oz (225g) dried white beans
1 onion
2 cloves garlic
3 pints (1.7 litres) vegetable or chicken stock
1½ teaspoons dried thyme
1 bay leaf
¾ pint (450ml) semi-skimmed or whole milk
Salt and freshly ground black pepper
½ teaspoon paprika
Celery leaves for garnish

Calories per serving : 145 · Low in calories, fat and cholesterol · High in iron, protein and fibre from the beans and onion

Soak the beans overnight in cold water. Drain them and place in a large saucepan. Roughly chop the onion and garlic and add them to the pan with 2 pints (1.1 litres) of the stock, 1 teaspoon of the dried thyme and the bay leaf. Bring to the boil then reduce the heat. Cover and simmer for about 1½ hours until the beans are tender.

Peel the butternut and discard the seeds and membrane. Finely dice the flesh and simmer in the reserved stock and thyme for 15 minutes until tender.

Allow to cool, then remove the bay leaf from the beans, add the butternut squash, milk and stock mixture and purée in a liquidiser until smooth.

Return to the pan and reheat gently. Season to taste, sprinkle paprika in the centre of each serving and garnish with the chopped celery leaves.

Butternut blended with white beans and herbs.

Three Bean Pâté

This creamy-smooth pâté is very easy to prepare – perfect if you have visitors at short notice. If you do not have fresh herbs to hand, tabasco or chilli powder can be used for flavouring instead. Tahini paste, made from sesame seeds, separates easily, so always stir well before measuring it out. You will need a food processor for this recipe.

SERVES 10
PREPARATION TIME : *15 minutes*

INGREDIENTS
14oz (400g) tin flageolet beans
15oz (425g) tin borlotti beans
15oz (425g) tin cannellini beans
4-6 cloves garlic
¼ pint (150ml) tahini paste
Juice of 2 lemons
1 small bunch fresh parsley
1 teaspoon fresh thyme
Salt and freshly ground black pepper
Parsley sprigs for garnish

Calories per serving : 180 · Low in sodium and cholesterol · High in protein and fibre from beans

Put all the beans in a colander and rinse them thoroughly under cold running water. Peel and crush or finely chop the garlic cloves and place them in a food processor with the beans, tahini paste, lemon juice, parsley and thyme.

When the mixture has been puréed, season to taste with salt and freshly ground black pepper. Process the pâté again until creamy, adding 2 or 3 tablespoons of hot water. Turn it into a bowl and swirl the surface with a palette knife. Garnish with parsley sprigs and serve with raw vegetables, such as radishes, celery, carrots and cauliflower florets, and fingers of warm pitta bread or Melba toast.

The pâté can be made a day in advance if it is stored in an airtight container and refrigerated. It can also be frozen for up to a month. Defrost in the container, then blend in the food processor until smooth, adding a little hot water if necessary.

This creamy-smooth vegetarian pâté is lifted with herbs and lemon juice, and served with crudités and toast.

Eggs with Blue Cheese and Ricotta

Although egg yolks contain some cholesterol, there is no need to cut them out from a healthy diet altogether. This is because egg yolks (along with seeds and soya beans) also contain lecithin; a fatty substance which helps to break down cholesterol and keep fats moving through the blood stream. This dish can be served with a tomato salad.

SERVES 4
PREPARATION TIME : *5 minutes*
COOKING TIME : *25 minutes*
OVEN : *Preheat to 190°C (375°F, gas mark 5)*

INGREDIENTS
2oz (50g) blue Brie
4 tablespoons milk
2 tablespoons chopped chives
8oz (225g) Ricotta
Salt and freshly ground black pepper
4 eggs

Calories per serving : 205 · High in protein and calcium from eggs and cheese

Remove the rind from the Brie. Chop the cheese, then mash it in a basin using a fork. Gradually beat in half the milk, the chives, the Ricotta and finally the last of the milk. Season with freshly ground black pepper. Alternatively, blend the Brie and milk together in a liquidiser, then add the chives, Ricotta and pepper.

Lightly oil 4 small ramekins and divide the cheese mixture between them. Mould the mixture in each dish to provide hollows for the eggs. Break an egg into each dish and season with a little salt and plenty of freshly ground black pepper.

Cover each ramekin with a piece of foil and stand in a roasting tin containing 1in (25mm) of hot water.

Bake for about 20 minutes or until the whites have set but the yolks are still soft. Serve straight from the oven with buttered toast fingers.

Watercress Soup

The peppery flavour of watercress lends itself well to soups, and this dish can be served hot or cold as a refreshing summer soup. As watercress is highly perishable, buy it no more than one day before you intend to use it. Choose fresh, bright green watercress with crisp leaves. Pick off any roots and damaged leaves. The potatoes need not be peeled if their skins are good. You will need a liquidiser.

SERVES 4
PREPARATION TIME : *20 minutes*
COOKING TIME : *25 minutes*

INGREDIENTS
2-3 bunches watercress
1 small onion
1lb (450g) potatoes
1 pint (570ml) vegetable or chicken stock
½ pint (285ml) semi-skimmed or whole milk
¼ teaspoon ground nutmeg
1 tablespoon lemon juice
Salt and freshly ground black pepper
1 tablespoon natural yoghurt

Calories per serving : 140 · Low in calories, fat, cholesterol and sodium

Serve with lightly buttered toast fingers on the side.

Clear glassware and plenty of ice make a refreshing presentation idea for cold watercress soup.

Chop the onion and dice the potatoes, then place them in a large saucepan with the stock, milk and nutmeg. Bring to the boil, then reduce the heat, cover and simmer for 15-20 minutes until the potatoes are tender.

Meanwhile, pick over and wash the watercress, reserving a few sprigs for garnish. Add the cress and the lemon juice to the saucepan, remove from the heat immediately and allow to cool a little.

Purée the mixture in a liquidiser until smooth. Return to the saucepan, reheat gently and season. Carefully swirl a little yoghurt into the centre of each bowl and garnish with the watercress leaves.

Bresaola with Pears

Air-dried beef fillets are produced in mountainous regions throughout Europe – examples are *bresaola* in Italy, *bundnerfleisch* in Germany, and *viande sechée* in Switzerland. Tender, lean cuts of meat are matured for two months until they turn a dark red colour. Balsamic vinegar is a sweet and sour Italian red wine vinegar, aged in barrels for up to 50 years. If balsamic vinegar is difficult to find, you can use the same amount of cider vinegar with two generous pinches of caster sugar.

SERVES 4
PREPARATION TIME : *10 minutes*

INGREDIENTS
4oz (115g) bresaola – about 12 slices
2 small ripe dessert pears
1 tablespoon balsamic vinegar
4oz (115g) medium-fat curd cheese
Freshly ground black pepper to taste
Red oak-leaf lettuce for garnish

Calories per serving : 135 · Low in calories and sodium

Peel, halve and core the pears. Cut each half into slices and brush them with a little vinegar. Beat the curd cheese, then mix in the remaining vinegar. Arrange the bresaola, pears and cheese. Add pepper to taste and garnish with lettuce.

Finely sliced dried beef fillets with fresh pears.

Asparagus with Orange Dressing

The highly desirable, succulent asparagus came from northern Italy. It was grown in the 16th century in the heart of Venice to replace original crops of corn and flax. It has now become so popular that the British import it from many different countries and grow a small amount on home soil. Asparagus is at its best and is slightly cheaper in May and June, when in season, but it is available from shops throughout the year. The orange dressing originates from a Maltese recipe which makes a refreshingly light accompaniment for this simple starter.

Succulent asparagus spears make a luxurious starter served with a tangy citrus fruit and parsley dressing.

SERVES 4

PREPARATION TIME : *20 minutes*

COOKING TIME : *11 minutes*

INGREDIENTS

1lb (450g) fresh asparagus

DRESSING

Grated peel of ½ orange

3 tablespoons orange juice

1 tablespoon lemon juice

Salt and freshly ground black pepper

¼ teaspoon mustard powder

3 tablespoons virgin olive oil

Pinch of caster sugar

1 spring onion

1 small bunch parsley

1 orange for garnish

Calories per serving : 195 · Low in cholesterol · High in vitamin C from asparagus and citrus juice

Rinse the asparagus and remove the base of any tough stems. If possible, cook the asparagus upright with the tips above the level of the cooking water. Boil gently for 8 minutes or until just tender. Drain and rinse quickly under cold water, then pat dry.

Bring ¼ pint (150ml) of water to the boil in a small pan. Add the grated orange peel and boil for 3 minutes. Remove the peel and stir in the orange and lemon juice, salt, pepper, mustard powder, oil and sugar until well mixed. Finely chop the spring onion and 1 tablespoon of parsley. Mix well.

Peel the orange, cutting away all the pith, and slice out individual segments by cutting against each side of the segment's skin.

Put the asparagus on individual plates and pour the dressing over evenly. Garnish with sprigs of parsley, orange segments and very thin strips of orange peel, if desired.

Spiced Lentil Soup

Lentils are a cheap and excellent source of protein, and often take the place of meat in a vegetarian diet. As well as being a staple food of India, this popular pulse is widely used throughout Europe. This recipe

This hearty lentil soup is a version of Indian dahl.

is a thinned version of an Indian dish called dahl, and tastes delicious served with fresh bread, especially Indian breads such as nan or roti.

SERVES 4

PREPARATION TIME : *15 minutes*

COOKING TIME : *1 hour*

INGREDIENTS

4oz (115g) red lentils

2oz (50g) carrots

4oz (115g) potatoes

1 small onion

1 tablespoon virgin olive oil

1 teaspoon cumin powder

2 teaspoons coriander powder

1 teaspoon turmeric

1 dried red chilli

2 pints (1.1 litres) vegetable or chicken stock

Salt and freshly ground black pepper

2 tablespoons natural yoghurt (optional)

Parsley or coriander leaves for garnish

Calories per serving : 205 · Low in cholesterol · High in fibre, iron and protein from the lentils

Wash the lentils thoroughly in cold water, drain and reserve. Finely dice the carrots, potatoes and onion. Heat the oil in a large saucepan and cook the onion until transparent. Add the spices and cook for 2-3 minutes, stirring continuously.

Put the carrots and potatoes in the saucepan with the lentils and stock. Bring to the boil, reduce the heat and simmer for 1 hour until tender.

Season to taste and, if desired, serve topped with a spoonful of natural yoghurt and a sprinkling of freshly chopped parsley or coriander leaves.

Watercress Mousse with Red Pepper Sauce

The Persians and Romans considered watercress to be extremely healthy, and the Greeks thought it was a brain food and a cure for deranged minds. Sweet peppers are the fruit of an American shrub, long cultivated by the natives in tropical and southern America. You will need a liquidiser for this recipe.

SERVES 4
PREPARATION TIME : *30 minutes*
SETTING TIME : *2 hours*
COOKING TIME : *15 minutes*

INGREDIENTS
MOUSSE
3oz (75g) watercress
1 tablespoon lemon juice
2 teaspoons powdered gelatine or agar agar
3 spring onions
8oz (225g) medium-fat curd cheese
4 tablespoons semi-skimmed milk
Salt and freshly ground black pepper
SAUCE
2 red peppers
½ clove garlic
A pinch of caster sugar
4 tablespoons olive oil
1 tablespoon lemon juice
Salt and freshly ground black pepper
4 sprigs watercress

Calories per serving : 265 · Low in cholesterol and sodium · High in vitamin C from watercress and peppers · High in protein from cheese and milk

Lightly oil 4 ramekins (yoghurt tubs would also make suitable mould dishes for this recipe) of approximately 3fl oz (90ml) capacity.

Pour 1 tablespoon of cold water and the lemon juice into a cup, sprinkle over the gelatine, or agar agar, and leave to soften for 5 minutes. Stand the cup in a pan of hot water until the gelatine dissolves.

Finely chop the watercress and spring onions. Tip the cheese into a basin and beat in the milk, then stir

An elegant cheese mousse, speckled with watercress and surrounded by a colourful roasted pepper purée.

in the watercress, spring onions, and seasoning. Add the gelatine to the cheese mixture, beat well, and divide between 4 moulds. Put into the refrigerator and leave for 2 hours, until set.

Place the red peppers under a hot grill for 15-20 minutes, turning occasionally to cook on all sides, until the skin blackens and chars. Remove and allow to cool, then peel off the skin and discard the core and seeds. Reserve ¼ of one pepper for garnish. Crush the garlic, place it in a liquidiser with the caster sugar and the rest of the pepper flesh, and process. When smooth, gradually add the oil, lemon juice, and seasoning.

To serve, dip the moulds into very hot water for 10 seconds and invert onto small plates. Pour sauce round each mousse. Garnish with strips of roasted red pepper and sprigs of watercress.

Parsnip and Apple Soup

Parsnips were more widely used in earlier times; often in ways that would now seem unusual. The Elizabethans, for example, used parsnips with apples to make bread. Parsnips are an autumn vegetable, and their flavour improves after a sharp frost. You will need a liquidiser for this recipe.

SERVES 6
PREPARATION TIME : *20 minutes*
COOKING TIME : *25 minutes*

INGREDIENTS
1lb (450g) parsnips
1 medium onion
3 tablespoons virgin olive oil
9oz (250g) Cox's apples
½ teaspoon ground nutmeg
1½ pints (850ml) vegetable or chicken stock
½ pint (285ml) whole or
semi-skimmed milk
Salt and freshly ground black pepper (optional)
A few sprigs parsley for garnish

Calories per serving : 120 · Low in calories and
cholesterol · High in fibre from vegetables

Finely chop the onion. Heat 2½ tablespoons of the oil in a large saucepan, and cook the onion over a medium heat until transparent. While the onion is cooking, peel, trim and roughly chop the parsnips. Reserving 1 small apple for garnish, peel, core and roughly chop the others.

Stir the nutmeg into the onion, and add the parsnips, chopped apple and stock. Bring to the boil, then reduce the heat and simmer for about 20 minutes until the parsnips are tender. Remove from the heat and allow to cool slightly.

Meanwhile, wash, core and cut the reserved apple into thin slices, leaving on the reddish skin. Fry the slices quickly for 1 minute in the remaining oil, then put to one side.

Blend the apples, vegetables and their liquid in a liquidiser until smooth. Stir in the milk and reheat gently, seasoning to taste. Pour the soup into individual bowls and serve garnished with the apple slices and parsley.

Apple slices make an attractive garnish when gently fried, as the red of the skin spreads throughout the fruit.

Tomato, Avocado and Mozzarella Antipasto

This traditional Italian dish is known as 'Tricolore' – the red tomatoes, the white Mozzarella cheese and the green of the avocado or basil leaves representing the three colours of the Italian flag. The subtle flavour and rich texture of the avocado adds a sense of luxury to the dish. It is high in vitamins and, unusually for a fruit, 20 per cent of its weight is made up of essential polyunsaturated oils. Replacing unsaturated oils in a diet, with polyunsaturated oils, can significantly lower a person's cholesterol level. Typically, this dish is made with either avocado or basil, but this version uses both to make a simple, nutritious and eye-catching starter.

A favourite Italian antipasto of different tastes and textures represents the three colours of the Italian flag.

INGREDIENTS

4 large ripe tomatoes
1 large ripe avocado
8oz (225g) Mozzarella
2 teaspoons red wine vinegar
½ teaspoon caster sugar
8 fresh basil leaves for garnish

DRESSING

2 tablespoons virgin olive oil
Freshly milled black pepper
a pinch of salt
1 teaspoon dried oregano

Calories per serving : 380 · High in protein from Mozzarella, and calcium and zinc from avocados

Wash, core and slice the tomatoes and sprinkle them with the vinegar and sugar.

Slice the Mozzarella thinly. To halve the avocado, make a deep encircling cut from the neck down to the base and back up to the neck. Sharply twist the avocado to separate the two halves. Holding the half containing the stone, lightly chop at the stone with a sharp knife until the blade becomes lodged. Give the knife a sharp twist to dislodge the stone and cut the flesh into lengthwise slices.

Arrange the various slices on individual plates, alternating red, white and green colours. Mix the olive oil, black pepper, salt and oregano in a small bowl and sprinkle the dressing evenly over each plate. Garnish with the basil leaves.

French Onion Soup

The French have long regarded this warming soup as an antidote to fatigue, chills, head colds and even hangovers. From ancient times onions have been regarded as a medicine for many ills, and they still play a part in contemporary folk medicine. This soup is quite delicious and the melted cheese and French toast with mustard adds extra punch to the flavour. Use large Spanish onions which are much sweeter than British ones.

Onion soup topped with toasts and melting cheese.

INGREDIENTS

1lb (450g) large Spanish onions
1oz (25g) butter
1 tablespoon virgin olive oil
¼ teaspoon sugar
2½ pints (1.4 litres) beef or vegetable stock
Salt and freshly ground black pepper
4 slices French bread
1½ teaspoons French mustard
2oz (50g) grated Gruyère cheese
2 tablespoons brandy (optional)

Calories per serving : 195 · High in calcium

Peel and slice the onions into rings. Heat the butter and oil in a large saucepan, add the onions and sprinkle over the sugar. Cook over a low heat for about 15 minutes, stirring occasionally, until the onions are soft. Gradually stir in the stock and season to taste. Bring the mixture to the boil and simmer, uncovered, for 45 minutes.

Toast the bread slices and dip each slice into the soup. Spread the mustard on the soaked toasts and pile on the grated cheese. Grill the toasts again until the cheese melts and turns golden-brown.

Add the optional brandy to the soup and float a slice of cheese toast in each serving.

Mushroom Soup

This recipe provides a refreshing starter for any time of the year. Choose flat, or field mushrooms, to give the soup a really good flavour. You will need a liquidiser for this recipe.

A light mushroom soup with an intense flavour.

SERVES 4
PREPARATION TIME : *30 minutes*
COOKING TIME : *35 minutes*

INGREDIENTS
14oz (400g) flat or field mushrooms
1 leek or ½ medium onion
1 carrot
1 clove garlic
1 medium potato
2 tablespoons virgin olive oil
1 bay leaf
½ teaspoon mixed dried herbs (thyme,
savory, tarragon)
1 teaspoon chopped fresh tarragon
or ½ teaspoon dried tarragon
2 pinches nutmeg
Juice of ½ lemon
Salt and white pepper

Calories per serving : 145 · Low in calories and cholesterol · High in fibre from vegetables

Chop the leek or onion, the carrot and garlic and dice the potato. Heat the oil in a large frying pan. Reserve a few small mushrooms for the garnish, take the stalks off the rest, then add both the caps and stalks to the pan with the leek or onion, potato, carrot, garlic, bay leaf and mixed herbs. Cook for 10 minutes over a fairly high heat, stirring constantly.

Add 2 pints (1.1 litres) of water. Simmer for 25 minutes and add the tarragon, nutmeg and lemon juice. Blend the vegetable broth in a liquidiser, season to taste and reheat gently.

Clean and cut the reserved raw mushrooms into thin slices. Add the mushroom slices and serve.

Lebanese Cucumber Soup

This simple, cold soup is popular throughout the Middle East because it is so refreshing in warm weather. The addition of fresh mint adds to the cooling effect. Choose a live, natural yoghurt as it is particularly beneficial to the digestive system.

SERVES 4
PREPARATION TIME : *20 minutes*

INGREDIENTS
1 medium cucumber
2 spring onions
1 clove garlic
8fl oz (225ml) carton natural low-fat yoghurt
2½fl oz (75ml) sour cream
1 tablespoon chopped fresh mint
Mint sprigs for garnish
1 pinch ground cumin
1 teaspoon lemon juice
Salt and freshly ground black pepper

Calories per serving : 90 · High in calcium from yoghurt · Low in sodium, fat and cholesterol

Reserving a small amount of cucumber for garnish, peel the rest and finely grate or chop it over a bowl to catch any liquid. Trim the spring onions and finely chop the bulbs and about 3in (80mm) of the green stalk. Crush and finely chop the garlic.

Mix the grated or chopped cucumber and its liquid with all the other ingredients and stir well until smooth. Season to taste with salt and black pepper.

Chill the soup mixture in the refrigerator until required, then divide into 4 soup bowls, garnish with sprigs of fresh mint and thin slices of cucumber.

Cooling cucumber is mixed with natural yoghurt, sour cream, herbs and spices for a refreshing summer soup.

Mussels in White Wine

Mussels are now farmed in Britain to provide cheap and nutritious shellfish all year round. This recipe is an excellent example of traditional French and Belgian cuisine. The mussels can be steamed in their own juices, retaining plentiful amounts of protein and trace elements. Serve with crusty bread.

SERVES 4
PREPARATION TIME : *40 minutes*
COOKING TIME : *15 minutes*

INGREDIENTS
4lb (1.8kg) bag of mussels
2 cloves garlic
2 sticks celery
2 shallots
2 tablespoons virgin olive oil
¼ pint (150ml) dry white wine
2 tablespoons fresh chopped parsley
2 tablespoons chopped celery leaves or lovage
Freshly ground black pepper

Calories per serving : 150 · Low in cholesterol · High in protein, calcium, iron and zinc from mussels

Discard any mussels that have open shells. Scrub and wash the remainder thoroughly to remove any barnacles, grit or weed. Gently pull out the hairy beard on each mussel and discard. Place the mussels in a large saucepan. Add at least ½ pint (285ml) of water with a dash of white wine if desired, cover tightly and cook over a high heat for 3-5 minutes until the shells open, shaking the pan from time to time. You may need to cook the mussels in batches.

When all the shells are open, remove them from the saucepan. Discard any closed shells. Strain the cooking liquid through fine muslin and reserve.

Finely chop the garlic, celery and shallots. Heat the oil in a saucepan and sauté the chopped ingredients for 5 minutes. Add the liquid from the mussels and the white wine and bring to the boil. Add the mussels, cover and simmer for 3-4 minutes.

Serve the mussels and sauce in soup plates. Sprinkle with freshly chopped herbs and a generous helping of black pepper.

Sea-fresh mussels cooked with white wine and herbs.

Parsnip and Cumin Soup

The naturally sweet and nutty flavour of parsnips combines well with spicy cumin seeds to make a thick, warming soup. Parsnips are available most of the year, but avoid large, tough ones with woody cores. You will need a liquidiser for this recipe.

SERVES 4
PREPARATION TIME : *10 minutes*
COOKING TIME : *30 minutes*

INGREDIENTS
1lb (450g) parsnips
2 onions
1 tablespoon virgin olive oil
2 teaspoons ground cumin seeds
1½ pints (850ml) chicken stock
Salt and freshly ground black pepper
Paprika for garnish

Calories per serving : 145 · Cholesterol free · Low in calories · High in fibre from vegetables

Peel and chop the parsnips and onions, then heat the oil in a saucepan and fry them for 5 minutes over a medium heat. Sprinkle in the cumin and cook for a further 3-4 minutes.

Add the stock, cover and simmer gently for 20 minutes or until the parsnips are tender.

Remove from the heat and blend in a liquidiser. Reheat gently and season to taste.

Pour into individual bowls, sprinkle with a little paprika and serve.

The delicious nutty-sweet taste of parsnips with onions is lifted by the addition of spicy ground cumin seeds and a sprinkling of paprika. Serve with hot bread for a warming starter or filling snack.

Baked Scallops with Garlic and Herbs

The season for scallops is autumn to spring, and a sweet sea-salt smell indicates their freshness. The fishmonger will open and clean them for you, but they are usually already presented on the flat half of their shells. Alternatively, frozen scallops are available from many large supermarkets. Larger scallops, such as the Great scallop or King scallop, are best for this dish.

SERVES 4
PREPARATION TIME : *15-20 minutes*
COOKING TIME : *12-15 minutes*
OVEN : *Preheat to 200°C (400°F, gas mark 6)*

INGREDIENTS
12 large scallops
2 cloves garlic
2 tablespoons chopped parsley
2 tablespoons virgin olive oil
Salt and freshly ground black pepper
Lemon wedges for garnish

Calories per serving : 215 · Low in sodium and cholesterol · High in protein from scallops

Wash fresh scallops thoroughly under cold running water, discarding any fringe-like membrane and dark organs to leave the clean, white muscle and orange roe. If you have any hollow undershells, reserve 4 of them as serving dishes – scrub them thoroughly and boil for 5 minutes. Thaw frozen scallops and wipe them dry.

Crush the garlic and mix with the parsley and oil in a bowl. Add the scallops, stir gently and season.

Place 3 scallops in each shell and cook in the oven for 10 minutes. Garnish with lemon wedges.

A traditional French recipe for baked scallops.

Figs with Prosciutto Ham and Goat Cheese

Although this Italian dish is very simple to make, it has an elaborate combination of textures and flavours. Fresh, ripe figs are best for this recipe and the peak season is early to late summer. If you cannot find any prosciutto, use some other sort of Italian parma ham.

SERVES 4
PREPARATION TIME : *10 minutes*

INGREDIENTS
4 slices prosciutto
4 fresh, ripe figs
4oz (115g) soft goat cheese
2oz (50g) fromage frais
12 fresh basil leaves

Calories per serving : 95 · Low in calories and cholesterol · High in protein from ham, and calcium from cheese

Carefully slice the figs into fan shapes with a sharp serrated knife, and arrange on the plates with the slices of ham.

Italian-inspired ripe figs, goat cheese and prosciutto.

Combine the goat cheese and fromage frais by mashing with a fork until smooth. Tear 4 basil leaves into small strips and stir into the cheese. Divide the mixture into round portions and arrange them on the plates. Garnish with the remaining basil leaves and serve immediately.

Vegetable Platter

Fresh, uncooked vegetables are one of the best sources of vitamins, minerals and fibre, and the raw energy that they provide is known to help combat tiredness, stress and disease. Select only the smallest and choicest young vegetables for this colourful platter. The two spicy sauces can either be spooned onto the plate, or served separately as dips. You will need a liquidiser or sieve for this recipe.

SERVES 4
PREPARATION TIME : *1½ hours*
COOKING TIME : *15 minutes*

INGREDIENTS
8 radishes
8 spring onions
8 baby carrots
10 baby sweetcorn
16 mangetout
4 cherry tomatoes
12 small button mushrooms
½ cucumber
2 Little Gem lettuces
Sprigs of watercress for garnish
PEPPER SAUCE
2 large red peppers
½ teaspoon caster sugar
Salt and freshly ground black pepper
A few drops of tabasco sauce
MUSTARD SAUCE
2 teaspoons Dijon mustard
¼ pint (150ml) Greek yoghurt
Salt and freshly ground black pepper

Calories per serving : 140 · Low in calories, fat and cholesterol · High in fibre and iron from vegetables High in protein

A summer platter of fresh and colourful raw vegetables ready to dip in mustard and red pepper sauces.

Grill the peppers for about 15 minutes, turning occasionally, until the skin wrinkles but does not burn. Remove and allow to cool. Meanwhile, make the mustard sauce by blending the mustard and Greek yoghurt together, and seasoning with a little salt and pepper. Refrigerate until needed.

Remove the skin and seeds from the cooled peppers and liquidise the flesh, or pass it through a sieve to make a purée. Stir in the sugar, a little salt and pepper, and a few drops of tabasco sauce to taste. Refrigerate until needed.

Wash the vegetables. Clean the mushrooms, slicing the larger ones in half. Slice the cucumber, and divide the lettuce into individual leaves.

Arrange on a large platter, spoon the dressings into small bowls, garnish with cress and serve.

Spinach and Salmon Terrine

Pale pink salmon and deep green spinach are used in this terrine to create a beautiful starter that is quite simple to make. Although the redcurrant sauce is not an essential part of the dish, it makes an impressive accompaniment if you are serving the terrine at a dinner party. Choose fresh, young spinach with tender leaves – peak season is late spring. The recipe can be made a day in advance if desired, and you will need a liquidiser and a medium-sized loaf tin.

SERVES 6-8
PREPARATION TIME : *40 minutes*
CHILLING TIME : *Overnight*
COOKING TIME : *1 hour*
OVEN : *Preheat to 180°C (350°F, gas mark 4)*

INGREDIENTS
1lb (450g) fresh young spinach
1lb (450g) salmon, skinned and boned
3 large eggs
1 teaspoon salt
Freshly ground black pepper
1 level teaspoon ground nutmeg
¼ pint (150ml) single cream
REDCURRANT SAUCE
8oz (225g) redcurrant jelly
Juice of 1 orange
Peel of ½ orange
1 teaspoon white wine vinegar
Pinch of salt
Fresh redcurrants for garnish (optional)

Calories per serving : 295 · High in calcium, iron and vitamin C from spinach · High in protein from salmon

Butter the loaf tin and line its base with buttered greaseproof paper. Wash the spinach, removing any large stalks or veins, and pat the leaves dry. Cut two-thirds of the salmon into ¾in (20mm) cubes, and roughly cut up the remaining third. Break the eggs into the liquidiser, and then add the roughly cut salmon, salt, pepper and nutmeg. Gradually feed in

A wonderful ensemble in pink and green. Chunky, juicy salmon set in spinach and a redcurrant and orange sauce provide luxurious flavours, while fresh redcurrants add a colourful garnish.

all the spinach while puréeing the salmon mixture.

Once everything has been finely puréed, stir in the cream and cubes of salmon. Pour the mixture into the prepared loaf tin and cover with foil.

Place two folded sheets of newspaper in the bottom of a large ovenproof dish or deep baking tray, stand the loaf tin on the paper, and fill with boiling water to within ½in (15mm) of the rim of the loaf tin. The paper prevents the bottom of the terrine from cooking too fast, and from turning brown. Cook for 1 hour, until the spinach mixture has set, then cool and refrigerate.

Cut the orange peel into large pieces. Place all the ingredients for the sauce in a pan and heat gently. Stir until all the redcurrant jelly has melted. Remove the pieces of orange peel before serving.

When the terrine is quite cold, turn it out of the tin and carefully remove the greaseproof paper. With a sharp knife cut into ½in (15mm) slices with a gentle sawing action, and put them on individual dessert plates. Just before serving, pour a little of the warm redcurrant sauce around each slice and garnish with a small bunch of redcurrants.

Courgette Soup

Courgettes are dwarf members of the squash family that includes marrows, cucumbers and melons, and although courgettes are always thought of as vegetables they are in fact fruits. Their delicate flavour makes a deliciously light soup that is heightened by the flavour of the fresh herbs, the nutmeg and the tangy cheese. The lemon juice is just enough to give the soup a refreshing twist without making it at all sour. You will need a liquidiser.

SERVES 4
PREPARATION TIME : *30 minutes*
COOKING TIME : *15 minutes*

INGREDIENTS
1½lb (700g) small courgettes
1 medium onion
1 clove garlic
2 tablespoons olive oil
2 tablespoons plain flour
2 pints (1.1 litres) unsalted chicken or vegetable stock
3oz (75g) blue cheese, or Parmesan, grated
Juice of ½ small lemon
½ teaspoon ground nutmeg
Salt and freshly ground black pepper
2 tablespoons low-fat natural yoghurt
2 tablespoons chopped parsley
1 tablespoon chopped chives

Calories per serving : 260 · Low in cholesterol · High in protein from cheese and yoghurt, calcium from yoghurt and iron from courgettes

---

Wash and trim the courgettes. Grate the courgettes by hand, or if you have a food processor with a grating attachment you can use that. Roughly chop the onion and finely chop or crush the garlic. Heat the olive oil in a large pan, add the onion and garlic, and cook over a moderate heat for 5 minutes or until translucent, stirring occasionally.

Add the courgettes and continue cooking and stirring for another 3 minutes. Sprinkle the flour over the courgettes and stir it in thoroughly for 1 minute. Add the stock and gently bring to the boil, reduce the heat and simmer for 5 minutes. Allow to cool a little, then liquidise the soup and stir in all the grated cheese. Then add the lemon juice and stir in the nutmeg, salt and pepper. If necessary, return the soup to the pan to reheat. Garnish with a swirl of yoghurt and the chopped parsley and chives. Serve immediately.

A taste of summer is contained in this pale green blend of courgettes, Parmesan, herbs and spices. Lemon juice adds a tangy freshness and the low-fat yoghurt and chives make a healthy garnish.

Prawn and Mango Cocktail

The prawn cocktail takes on a new life using fresh fruits and spicy seasonings. If you prefer, you can substitute a fresh tomato for the mango, adding 2 tablespoons of natural yoghurt to the dressing, and a dash of tabasco instead of the chilli.

Spicy fruits and seafood make a refreshing starter.

SERVES 4
PREPARATION TIME : *10 minutes*
MARINATING TIME : *2 hours*

INGREDIENTS
8oz (225g) peeled prawns
1 large ripe mango
1 lime
½ sweet red pepper
½ sweet yellow pepper
1 teaspoon finely chopped green or red chilli
2 tablespoons chopped coriander or parsley leaves
2 tablespoons virgin olive oil
1 Little Gem lettuce

Calories per serving : 145 · High in protein from prawns · High in vitamin C from mango

Peel the mango, remove the stone and chop finely. Juice the lime and core and dice the peppers.

Put the mango, lime juice, peppers, chopped chilli and coriander, or parsley, in a bowl, then add the prawns and marinate in the refrigerator for 2 hours.

Drain the liquid and mix it with the olive oil to make a dressing. Wash, dry and shred the lettuce and spoon on the prawns, mango and peppers.

Vegetable Terrine

This delicate, creamy mousse is studded with colourful vegetables and served in a pool of tomato sauce. Both terrine and sauce can be prepared 48 hours in advance. You will need a liquidiser and a 2 pint (1.1 litre) loaf tin for this recipe.

SERVES 8-12
PREPARATION TIME : *1-1½ hours*
CHILLING TIME : *Overnight*

INGREDIENTS
TERRINE
30 large spinach leaves
5oz (150g) fine green Kenyan beans
6oz (175g) carrots
6 tinned artichoke hearts
1 envelope powdered gelatine
or 1 level teaspoon agar agar
3 × 7oz (3 × 200g) packets medium-fat soft cheese
½ lemon
Salt and freshly ground white pepper
2 egg whites
Chervil for garnish
TOMATO SAUCE
4 large ripe tomatoes
2 tablespoons tomato purée
2½fl oz (75ml) dry white wine
1 tablespoon red or white wine vinegar
½ -1 teaspoon caster sugar
Tabasco sauce or cayenne
Salt and freshly ground black pepper

Calories per serving : 105 · High in protein and vitamin C from vegetables · Low in cholesterol

Brush the inside of a 2 pint (1.1 litre) loaf dish or tin lightly with oil and set aside.

Wash the spinach leaves thoroughly, removing any large stalks. Blanch the leaves in boiling salted water for 20 seconds. Reserving the water, lift out the

Spinach covers a terrine of delicately layered vegetables in a light cheese mousse, lying in a fresh tomato sauce.

spinach with a slotted spoon, rinse quickly under cold running water, then pat dry. Line the bottom and sides of the loaf dish or tin with the leaves, letting them hang over the sides.

Top and tail the beans and cook them in the spinach water for 5 minutes. Lift out, rinse and pat dry. Peel the carrots and cut into thin sticks. Cook for 5 minutes in the same water, lift out, rinse and dry. Reserve 3fl oz (90ml) of the cooking water. Rinse the artichokes, pat dry, and cut into thin rings.

Sprinkle the gelatine over the water in a heatproof bowl and leave to soak until spongy. Stand the bowl in a saucepan with enough hot water to come halfway up the sides. Heat gently until the gelatine dissolves. Remove from the water and allow to cool.

Finely grate the lemon rind and squeeze the juice. Put the cheese in a bowl with the lemon rind, juice, salt and white pepper. Gradually beat in the dissolved gelatine or agar agar. In a separate bowl, whisk the egg whites until stiff, fold them gently into

the cheese mixture and season with salt and pepper.

Spoon a quarter of the cheese mixture into the loaf tin, level the surface, and arrange the beans lengthways on top to form a single layer. Press down gently. Cover with a second quarter of the cheese and a layer of the carrots. Repeat with another quarter of the cheese and a layer of artichokes placed cut side down. Top with remaining cheese and cover with the overlaying spinach leaves. Cover and chill in the refrigerator overnight.

Make the sauce by roughly chopping the tomatoes, placing them in a liquidiser with the remaining sauce ingredients and reserved vegetable cooking water. Liquidise until very smooth, then work through a sieve into a bowl. Season to taste.

To serve, run a palette knife between the spinach leaves and the tin. Invert the terrine onto a serving plate or board and cut into 12 slices using a sharp knife and a sawing action. Garnish with the chervil and serve with the sauce ladled around the terrine.

Split Pea Soup with Ham and Celeriac

Pea and ham soup is a famous English farmhouse dish that dates back to the Middle Ages. Water is the only liquid added, as the ham makes its own stock while cooking. The meat may be soaked overnight in cold water and a little milk to help draw out the salt. Substitute celery for the celeriac if you wish.

SERVES 8
PREPARATION TIME : *20 minutes*
COOKING TIME : *2-2½ hours*

INGREDIENTS
1 smoked ham knuckle
1lb (450g) yellow or green split peas
1 medium onion
1 large carrot
8oz (225g) celeriac
Few sprigs fresh thyme
1 bay leaf
Freshly ground black pepper

Calories per serving : 225 · High in iron, fibre and zinc from vegetables · High in protein from ham

Wash the split peas thoroughly in a sieve or colander to remove any dust and grit. Finely chop the onion, and finely dice the carrot and celeriac.

Drain the ham, if soaked, and place in a large saucepan with 3 pints (1.7 litres) of water and all the ingredients except the pepper. Bring to the boil, reduce the heat, then cover and simmer for about 2 hours. Stir frequently and add extra water if necessary. Alternatively, cook the ham for 1 hour in a pressure cooker.

Stick a skewer into the ham to check if it is tender. Cook for a further 30 minutes if required. Remove the ham from the saucepan. Allow the soup to cool and the fat to rise to the surface. Discard the fat.

If you are adding the ham back to the soup, discard all the fat and bones and chop the meat finely, or shred by sticking a fork in the ham and tearing it with another fork. Season with pepper to taste, reheat gently and serve.

Colourful split peas brighten this farmhouse soup.

Tomato and Basil Soup

Fresh tomato soup is highly superior to tinned varieties. Sun-ripened tomatoes give the sweetest flavour, so this soup is ideally made in the summer with almost overripe tomatoes. The pasta may be omitted or replaced by the same amount of rice.

SERVES 4
PREPARATION TIME : *15 minutes*
COOKING TIME : *30 minutes*

INGREDIENTS
2lb (900g) ripe tomatoes
2 tablespoons olive oil
2 cloves garlic
2 tablespoons tomato purée
1¼ pints (725ml) vegetable stock
1 teaspoon caster sugar
1½ oz (40g) small pasta shapes
1 bunch fresh basil or lovage
Salt and freshly ground black pepper

Calories per serving : 160 · Low in calories and cholesterol · High in fibre from vegetables, and vitamin C from tomatoes

Chop the tomatoes. Heat the oil in a saucepan and gently sauté the garlic for 2-3 minutes. Add the tomatoes, tomato purée, stock and sugar. Bring to the boil, reduce the heat and simmer for 20 minutes.

Summer-ripe, puréed tomatoes enhanced by basil.

While the soup is simmering, cook the pasta shapes in boiling, salted water until tender. Drain and keep to one side in cold water.

Pass the tomatoes and liquid through a sieve, or purée in a liquidiser and pass through a fine sieve.

Drain the pasta and add to the soup. Reheat gently. Reserving 6 whole leaves, finely chop the basil and stir into the soup. Season to taste, garnish with the basil leaves and serve.

Goat Cheese Toasts

The sun-dried tomatoes and roasted peppers used in this recipe can be bought from delicatessens or some large supermarkets, or you can roast fresh peppers yourself. If possible, use Italian bread or rolls as their texture is particularly suitable for this dish. Chèvre is a popular French goat cheese.

Red or white wine goes well with tangy cheese toasts.

SERVES 6
PREPARATION TIME : *20 minutes*
COOKING TIME : *3 or 28 minutes with fresh peppers*
OVEN : *Preheat to 220°C (425°F, gas mark 7)*

INGREDIENTS
5oz (150g) goat cheese
2 roasted sliced red peppers in oil
or 2 fresh red peppers
1 thin Italian loaf or baguette
2 tablespoons virgin olive oil
2 tablespoons fromage frais
½ tablespoon fresh basil or ½ teaspoon dried
½ tablespoon fresh thyme or ½ teaspoon dried
½ tablespoon fresh marjoram or ½ teaspoon dried
2 sliced sun-dried tomatoes in oil
Freshly ground black pepper
GARNISH
1 head radicchio
1 head Little Gem lettuce
3 tablespoons virgin olive oil
2 teaspoons balsamic or white wine vinegar

Calories per serving : 170 · Low in cholesterol
High in protein from goat cheese

To roast fresh peppers, cook them in the oven for 25 minutes, turning once, until blackened and blistered. Cool under cold, running water and peel the skins. Remove the seeds and cut the flesh into thin strips, then put to one side.

Slice the bread into 12 pieces of ¼in (5mm) thickness. Brush one side of each slice with olive oil and toast in the oven to lightly colour both sides.

Mix the cheese and fromage frais together with a fork until smooth. Chop the herbs and then mix half the basil, thyme and marjoram in with the cheese.

When you are ready to serve, spread the cheese mixture onto the toasted bread and lay thin strips of either sun-dried tomatoes or red peppers diagonally over the cheese. Place the toasts on a baking tray and bake in the preheated oven for about 3 minutes.

Sprinkle with the remaining herbs and freshly ground black pepper to taste. If using the garnish, wash, dry and roughly chop the salad greens, sprinkle over with the oil and vinegar, and arrange with the toasts on individual plates and serve.

Broccoli, Almond and Nutmeg Soup

Broccoli originates from Mediterranean countries and is especially popular in Italy. It is best bought in this country between mid-winter and late spring. You will need a liquidiser for this recipe.

Smooth green soup decorated with toasted almonds.

SERVES 6
PREPARATION TIME : *20 minutes*
COOKING TIME : *25 minutes*

INGREDIENTS
1lb (450g) broccoli
1 medium onion
1 medium potato
2½ tablespoons virgin olive oil
1½ pints (850ml) vegetable or chicken stock
3oz (75g) flaked almonds
½ pint (285ml) semi-skimmed or whole milk
1 generous pinch nutmeg
Salt and freshly ground black pepper

Calories per serving : 195 · Low in cholesterol and sodium · High in fibre and vitamin C from broccoli

Trim and divide the broccoli into florets. Reserve 2oz (50g) and roughly chop the rest. Chop the onion and dice the potato into cubes. Heat 2 tablespoons of oil in a saucepan and cook the onion over a medium heat until transparent. Add the potato and chopped broccoli with the stock. Bring to the boil, then simmer for 20 minutes until the potato is tender.

Heat the rest of the oil in a frying pan and add the flaked almonds, stirring gently. Remove as soon as they go brown.

Reserve some almonds and put the rest in a liquidiser with the vegetables and their liquid. Blend until smooth. Return to the saucepan, add the milk and reheat. Add the nutmeg and season with salt and freshly ground black pepper.

Break the remaining broccoli into small florets, cook in ¼ pint (150ml) of boiling water for 2-3 minutes and drain the water into the soup. Garnish with the small florets and remaining almonds.

Thai Chicken and Coconut Soup

A hint of chilli adds piquancy to this creamy Thai soup. This traditional recipe will introduce those unfamiliar with Thai food to one of the healthiest and most flavoursome of all cuisines.

SERVES 4
PREPARATION TIME : *20 minutes*
COOKING TIME : *15 minutes*

INGREDIENTS
2 boned and skinned chicken breasts
2 × 15oz (425g) tins coconut milk
½ pint (285ml) chicken stock
4 spring onions
4 stalks lemon grass, or grated rind of ½ lemon
Juice of 2 limes
1 teaspoon grated fresh ginger
3 teaspoons anchovy essence
1 teaspoon soy sauce
12 small red chillis
4 lime leaves (optional)
6 sprigs fresh coriander

Calories per serving : 460 · High in vitamin C from citrus fruits · High in protein from chicken

Oriental flavours in an unusual blend of spices, chicken and coconut scented with lemon grass and coriander.

Pour the stock and coconut milk into a large pan. If using creamed coconut, place in a pan with the stock and heat gently until the blocks have melted.

Slice the spring onions. If you are using lemon grass, cut off the base of each stalk, peel away the tough outer layers and discard. Finely chop the bottom 4in (100mm) of each stalk and discard the rest. Add the lemon grass or grated lemon peel to the pan with the lime juice, grated ginger, anchovy essence, soy sauce, whole chillis, spring onions and optional lime leaves.

Heat the soup to just below boiling point. Cut the chicken breasts into 1in (25mm) strips, add to the pan and simmer for 10 minutes. Reserve 4 small sprigs of coriander, chop the remainder and the bottom 1in (25mm) of the stalks. Add to the pan. Pour the soup into bowls, garnish with coriander sprigs and serve. Do not eat the chillis or lime leaves.

Chicken Satay

In Indonesian and Malay cooking, roasted peanuts are pounded into a paste to provide the basis for satay sauce. This low-fat version of satay has all the flavour of an authentic Malaysian recipe and complements the chicken perfectly. Look for organic peanut butter in your supermarket or food store – it is made purely from peanuts, with nothing added. Wooden skewers are available from oriental food shops and some department stores.

SERVES 6
PREPARATION TIME : *30 minutes*
MARINATING TIME : *1 hour*
COOKING TIME : *15 minutes*

INGREDIENTS
1¾lb (800g) boned chicken breasts
½ medium onion
2 cloves garlic
2 tablespoons soy sauce
¼ teaspoon chilli powder
12 spring onions (optional)
1 cucumber
1 lime or lemon
SATAY SAUCE
4oz (115g) crunchy peanut butter
2 tablespoons soy sauce
2 tablespoons clear honey
2 tablespoons lime or lemon juice
¼ teaspoon chilli powder

Calories per serving : 95 · Low in calories and fat
High in protein from chicken

Peel and roughly grate the onion and peel and crush the garlic cloves. Remove the skin from the chicken, cut the meat into small pieces and place in a bowl with the onion and garlic. Add the soy sauce and chilli powder and mix well. Cover and leave to marinate in a cool place for at least 1 hour, turning the chicken occasionally.

Soak 12 small wooden or bamboo skewers in cold water and preheat the grill.

To make the spring onion tassels, wash and trim the spring onions, leaving 2-3in (50-80mm) of stalk.

Rich Indonesian peanut sauce spices up chicken.

With a sharp knife make parallel vertical cuts in the stalks to form delicate tassels. Put the spring onions in iced water in the refrigerator for 1 hour to make the tassels fan out.

Thread all the chicken cubes onto the soaked skewers and cook under a hot grill for 8-10 minutes, turning occasionally.

Pour any leftover marinade into a saucepan, add the sauce ingredients and bring to the boil. Simmer, while stirring, for 3-5 minutes until thickened.

Arrange 2 skewers of chicken on each of 6 plates. Slice the cucumber and cut the lime or lemon into wedges, and use, together with the spring onion tassels, to garnish each serving. Divide the sauce between 6 small bowls and serve hot.

Roquefort Pears

The tangy flavour of the blue Roquefort cheese makes a delicious contrast to the sweetness of dessert pears. But if you wish, you can substitute Gorgonzola or Stilton cheese, which are not so expensive. For a richer flavour you can use a few tablespoons of whipping or double cream instead of the yoghurt. The stuffing and sauce can be made up to 4 hours in advance if kept covered in a cool place, but if possible the pears should not be peeled and stuffed until just before you are ready to eat.

SERVES 4
PREPARATION TIME : *25 minutes*

INGREDIENTS
4 ripe dessert pears
3oz (75g) Roquefort cheese
3oz (75g) skimmed milk soft cheese
¼ pint (150ml) natural low-fat yoghurt
Cayenne pepper
2oz (50g) shelled walnuts
1 tablespoon chopped fresh tarragon
or ½ teaspoon dried
A little lemon juice
1 teaspoon tarragon wine vinegar
or white wine vinegar
Lamb's lettuce, or 8 small lettuce
leaves for garnish
Tarragon sprigs for garnish

Calories per serving : 245 · High in fibre · High in protein and calcium from milk, cheese and yoghurt

Put the Roquefort cheese in a bowl and mash well with a fork. Beat in the soft cheese, 1 tablespoon of the yoghurt, and the cayenne pepper. Transfer half of this stuffing mixture to a second bowl. Reserving 8 walnut halves for garnishing, chop the rest and stir them into one of the bowls, along with the chopped tarragon.

Peel and halve the pears. Remove the cores from the pears with a teaspoon and hollow out the cavities from 4 halves to make them slightly larger. Slice 4 halves lengthways and brush all over with a little lemon juice to prevent them from discolouring. Pat the pears dry, then fill the hollowed-out cavities with the nutty stuffing.

To make the dish look more attractive, fan the sliced pears out on individual plates and place a stuffed pear on each plate. Gradually whisk the remaining yoghurt into the cheese mixture in the second bowl, and then add the wine vinegar to make a smooth dressing. Spoon the dressing carefully over the pears. Roughly chop the remaining walnuts and scatter over the pears. Garnish with the lettuce and tarragon sprigs and serve immediately.

Visually appealing, these sweet dessert pears are filled with tangy blue cheese and yoghurt with walnuts.

65

Avocado and Orange Salad

Avocado pears are an excellent source of vitamins, minerals and essential oils. They are available all year round, and their rich creamy flesh goes well with citrus fruits. To test for ripeness, the fruit should give when touched, especially at the neck.

SERVES 4
PREPARATION TIME : *30 minutes*

INGREDIENTS
1 large or 2 small avocados
3 large oranges
½ cucumber
Fresh dill for garnish
DRESSING
3 tablespoons fresh orange juice
1 tablespoon red wine vinegar
1 teaspoon grain mustard
1 tablespoon virgin olive oil
2 teaspoons finely snipped chives
Salt and freshly ground black pepper

Calories per serving : 230 · Low in cholesterol · High in fibre from the vegetables · High in vitamins A, B and C from the avocados and oranges

Oranges and cucumber complement rich avocados.

Peel the oranges and cut away all the pith. Then carefully cut between the skin of each segment, working over a bowl to catch and reserve the juice.

Peel and thinly slice the cucumber, then halve and de-seed the slices to make crescent shapes. Cut the avocado in half lengthways and remove the stone, then peel and dice the flesh.

Put all the dressing ingredients into a bowl, add the orange juice and whisk well together. Add the avocado and mix gently to coat it in the dressing.

Serve alternating slices of orange and cucumber with avocado in the middle. Spoon over the dressing and garnish with dill before serving.

Country Baked Mushrooms

The stuffing in this recipe absorbs the cooking juices from the mushrooms, making it juicy and full of flavour. The mushrooms can be stuffed ready for baking 24 hours in advance, if covered and stored in an ovenproof dish in the refrigerator. This dish makes a delicious vegetarian starter or main course if it is served with warm bread and a salad.

SERVES 4
PREPARATION TIME : *25 minutes*
COOKING TIME : *15 minutes*
OVEN : *Preheat to 190°C (375°F, gas mark 5)*

INGREDIENTS
10oz (275g) large open cup mushrooms
or flat field mushrooms
2 garlic cloves
Finely grated rind of 1 lemon
1½oz (40g) wholemeal breadcrumbs
1 tablespoon fresh chopped marjoram
1 tablespoon fresh chopped parsley
3 tablespoons virgin olive oil
Salt and freshly ground black pepper
Fresh parsley sprigs for garnish
Lemon wedges for garnish

Calories per serving : 135 · Low in calories and cholesterol

Stuffed crispy mushrooms can be served with dry French cider or a red wine, such as a full-bodied Beaujolais.

Prepare mushrooms by wiping clean with a damp cloth, or washing quickly and drying thoroughly. Carefully remove the stalks and chop them finely. Crush the garlic and grate the lemon rind, then place them both in a bowl with the mushroom stalks, breadcrumbs, herbs, and 1½ tablespoons of the olive oil. Add salt and freshly ground black pepper to taste and then stir well to mix all the ingredients.

Brush the bottom of a shallow ovenproof dish with 2 teaspoons of oil. Arrange the mushrooms in a single layer in the dish. Divide the stuffing equally amongst the mushrooms and sprinkle over the remaining oil. Bake in the oven for 15 minutes. Serve hot, garnished with fresh herbs and lemon wedges.

Cabbage and potato soup spiked with hot red chilli.

Potato, Cabbage and Chilli Soup

This satisfying, slightly spicy soup is ideal for a cold night. Cabbage used to help farm workers survive long winters, but today it is valued for being nutritious. Kale, which is even higher in vitamin C, may be substituted for cabbage – eaten regularly it is believed to ease high blood pressure and reduce the risk of getting certain cancers.

SERVES 4
PREPARATION TIME : *20 minutes*
COOKING TIME : *40 minutes*

INGREDIENTS
½ small cabbage or 8oz (225g) kale
10oz (275g) potatoes
1 fresh red chilli, or ¼ teaspoon red chilli powder
1 large onion
2 cloves garlic
2 tablespoons virgin olive oil
2 pints (1.1 litres) of vegetable or chicken stock
Salt and freshly ground black pepper

Calories per serving : 260 · Low in cholesterol · High in fibre and vitamin C from cabbage and onion High in iron from cabbage

Peel and finely chop the onion and peel, crush or finely chop the garlic. Finely slice the chilli. Heat the olive oil in a large saucepan and add the onion, garlic and chilli or chilli powder. Cook on a high heat for 3 minutes, stirring occasionally. Dice the potatoes into ½in (15mm) cubes and add them with ½ pint (285ml) of the stock to the pan. Cover and simmer for 5 minutes.

Wash the cabbage and cut it into 1in (25mm) squares. Add the cabbage to the pan, so that it lies on top of the other ingredients, cover and steam for 5 minutes.

Add the rest of the stock, bring to the boil and simmer for 30 minutes. Use a wooden spoon pressed against the side of the pan, or a potato masher, to break down the potatoes. Add salt and plenty of freshly ground black pepper to taste, and serve.

Game and Brandy Soup

Wood pigeon is available all year round from butchers and some supermarkets and is surprisingly inexpensive. It can be bought in both fresh and frozen forms and, as with all wildfowl and game, the meat is exceptionally lean. Other game, such as quail, may be substituted – 4 quail to replace 2 pigeons. Serve with fresh bread.

SERVES 4
PREPARATION TIME : *30 minutes*
COOKING TIME : *1½ hours*

INGREDIENTS
4 wood pigeons
1 tablespoon vegetable oil
1 onion
2 sticks celery
1 carrot
½ tablespoon plain flour
3 tablespoons brandy
3 pints (1.7 litres) chicken stock
1 bouquet garni
Salt and freshly ground black pepper

Calories per serving : 235 · Low in cholesterol · High in iron and protein from game birds

Remove the breasts from the wood pigeons and keep to one side. Chop the remains of the carcasses and trimmings into small pieces.

Heat the oil in a large saucepan, add the chopped carcasses and cook over high heat for 5-10 minutes, stirring occasionally until well browned. While the carcasses are browning, finely dice the onion, celery and carrot and add to the saucepan. Cook for 5 minutes, stirring occasionally.

Stir in the flour and cook for 1-2 minutes until well browned. Standing well clear, pour in the brandy and set it alight. Wait for the flame to die, add the stock and bouquet garni and bring to the boil.

Add 4 tablespoons of water to the boiling stock, reduce the heat, cover and simmer for 1 hour, stirring from time to time. Pass the soup through a fine sieve or muslin cloth, pressing out all the juices into a clean saucepan.

Thinly slice the reserved wood-pigeon breasts and add them to the pan. Simmer for 7 minutes then season to taste. This soup will keep in the refrigerator for 2-3 days and freezes well.

Wood pigeons, root vegetables and herbs, laced with brandy, make a warming soup for a winter's night.

Artichoke Cups with Cottage Cheese

The modern globe artichoke originated in Italy, where it was first recorded in Naples in 1400. The peak season is in spring and autumn. Choose compact green heads with no dark patches or dry streaks. Fresh artichokes are available in green-grocers and some supermarkets or, alternatively, you can buy them tinned. Artichokes are best cut up with stainless-steel knives and cooked in stainless-steel saucepans, as some people claim contact with other metals darkens their colour and gives them a harsher flavour.

SERVES 4
PREPARATION TIME : *25 minutes*
MARINATING TIME : *1 hour*
COOKING TIME : *25 minutes*

INGREDIENTS
4 large or 12 baby globe artichokes
2 lemons
Rind of 1 lemon
DRESSING
1 small clove garlic
1 tablespoon white wine vinegar
1 tablespoon chopped chervil
1 tablespoon chopped parsley
1 teaspoon Dijon mustard
1 tablespoon virgin olive oil
Salt
FILLING
8oz (225g) low-fat cottage cheese
2 tablespoons finely snipped chives
Freshly ground black pepper
1 oak-leaf lettuce
Chervil or parsley sprigs for garnish

Calories per serving : 110 · Low in calories
and cholesterol

Squeeze and strain the juice from the lemons into a large bowl. Put the lemon rind into a saucepan and fill with water. Bring to the boil.

Prepare each artichoke by cutting the stalk off

Artichoke hearts with cottage cheese and herbs.

level with the base. Working from the base, bend back and pull off the first four rows of the outer, darker leaves until you reach the inner, lighter leaves. Chop off the pointed top, leaving the base part of the artichoke, and then trim off any tough green parts around the outside. Put the prepared pieces into the lemon juice to prevent discoloration.

Lightly salt the boiling water, add the artichokes, reduce the heat, and partially cover with a lid. Cook for 25 minutes until tender. Meanwhile, crush the garlic and blend well in a bowl with the other dressing ingredients. In another bowl, mix the cottage cheese with the chives and some black pepper. Cover and refrigerate until needed.

Pour the artichokes into a colander and rinse well under cold running water. Drain upside down on kitchen paper. Carefully scoop out and discard the hairy chokes with a teaspoon. Put the artichoke hearts into the dressing and turn them gently until well coated. Cover and refrigerate for 1 hour.

Fill the cups with the cottage cheese and serve with oak-leaf lettuce on individual plates. Garnish with the chervil or parsley and sprinkle a little of the dressing on the lettuce.

Crudités with Tofu Mayonnaise

Tofu is a low-fat, high protein bean curd made from soya beans, and a popular ingredient in Japanese cooking. It makes an excellent vegetarian starter or light lunch. The mayonnaise can be made up to 24 hours in advance if stored in an airtight container in the refrigerator. The vegetables can be tossed in their dressing up to 2 hours in advance if stored in the same way and drained before serving. You will need a liquidiser for this recipe, and a food processor with a grating disc would be an advantage.

Healthy tofu and vegetables make a crunchy starter.

SERVES 6
PREPARATION TIME : *30 minutes*
COOKING TIME : *2 minutes*

INGREDIENTS

TOFU MAYONNAISE
10½ oz (300g) carton firm silken tofu
2 tablespoons virgin olive oil
2 tablespoons lemon juice
2 cloves garlic
Salt and freshly ground black or white pepper

CRUDITÉS
½ lemon
½ lime
½ orange
6oz (175g) celeriac
4 tablespoons virgin olive oil
6oz (175g) small courgettes
1 tablespoon cardamom pods
6oz (175g) carrots
6oz (175g) raw or cooked beetroot
2 teaspoons cider vinegar
1 tablespoon finely chopped fresh dill
or 1 heaped teaspoon dried dill
Salt
Freshly ground white pepper
Freshly ground black pepper

Calories per serving : 205 · Low in cholesterol · High in calcium from the tofu · High in fibre from the vegetables

Make the tofu mayonnaise by liquidising all the ingredients until smooth. Add salt and pepper to taste, then turn into a serving bowl. Cover and chill in the refrigerator while preparing the vegetables.

Squeeze the juice and finely grate the rind of the lemon, lime and orange, and put to one side. Peel and grate the celeriac and place it in a bowl. Toss in a dressing made with 1 tablespoon of the olive oil, the grated lemon rind and juice, and salt and white pepper to taste.

Top and tail the courgettes and cut them into sticks if desired. Place in a bowl and toss in a dressing made of 1 tablespoon of the olive oil, the grated lime rind and juice, and seasoning.

Dry fry the cardamom seeds in a nonstick frying pan for about 2 minutes until toasted, then crush in a mortar and pestle, or use a rolling pin and remove the husks. Peel and grate the carrots. Place in a bowl and toss in a dressing made of 1 tablespoon of the olive oil, the grated orange rind and juice, the toasted cardamom seeds, and salt and freshly ground black pepper to taste.

Peel and grate the beetroot. Place in a bowl and toss in a dressing made of 1 tablespoon of the olive oil, the cider vinegar, dill and salt and freshly ground white pepper to taste.

Arrange neat mounds of all 4 vegetables separately on individual plates, draining them with a slotted spoon if watery, and serve the tofu mayonnaise separately as a dip.

71

Crab with Marinated Sweet Peppers and Filo Pastry

Fresh crab is a good source of protein, and can be bought prepared from a fishmonger. Always eat the crabmeat within 24 hours of purchase. The tartlet cases can be made in advance and kept in an airtight container in the freezer. They only take 5 minutes to defrost. You will need 8 patty tins measuring 4in (100mm) diameter at the top and 2½in (65mm) at the base, and a round, 3½in (90mm) biscuit cutter.

SERVES 4
PREPARATION TIME : *30 minutes*
MARINATING TIME : *1 hour*
COOKING TIME : *35 minutes*
OVEN : *Preheat to 190°C (375°F, gas mark 5)*

INGREDIENTS
8oz (225g) fresh white prepared crabmeat
MARINADE
2 large red peppers
2 cloves garlic
2 tablespoons virgin olive oil
2 tablespoons lemon juice
½ teaspoon sugar or clear honey
Salt and freshly ground black pepper
FILO TARTLET CASES
Three 14 × 7½in (355 × 190mm) sheets
filo pastry
1oz (25g) butter
Few sprigs fresh dill or watercress

Calories per serving : 235 · Low in cholesterol · High in protein, zinc and iron from crabmeat · High in vitamin C from peppers and lemon juice

Lay the peppers on a baking tray and bake in a preheated oven for about 30 minutes until they are blackened and blistered. When cool, peel away the skin and discard the seeds. Cut into sticks and place in a small bowl.

Peel and crush the garlic. Whisk together all the ingredients for the marinade and stir in the peppers.

Delicate cases made from filo pastry contain fresh crab and strips of marinated sweet peppers.

Leave covered in the refrigerator to marinate for approximately 1 hour.

Meanwhile, prepare the filo cases. Spread melted butter finely over one sheet of filo pastry. Lay over a second sheet and butter again, finally lay a third sheet on top. Stamp out 8 circles from the three-layered piece of filo with a round biscuit cutter, and use them to line the 8 individual patty tins. Prick the bottom of each, then bake for 6-8 minutes until golden. Allow to cool before filling.

Lightly break up the crabmeat and mix it in with the peppers and marinade. Divide this mixture between the filo cases and garnish with the dill or watercress. Serve cold or slightly warm.

Spicy Spinach Soup with Coconut

This particular combination of coconut and spices is popular in India. The addition of spinach may seem unusual, but it adds flavour and substance. It is important to use fresh root ginger which is available in most greengrocers and supermarkets. You will need a liquidiser for this recipe.

SERVES 4
PREPARATION TIME : *30 minutes*
COOKING TIME : *25 minutes*

INGREDIENTS
1lb (450g) fresh spinach
6oz (175g) potatoes
2 tablespoons virgin olive oil
1 clove garlic
2 teaspoons cumin powder
1 teaspoon turmeric
2oz (50g) desiccated coconut
2½ pints (1.4 litres) vegetable or chicken stock
1in (25mm) piece fresh ginger
Salt and freshly ground black pepper
Natural yoghurt or single cream for garnish

Calories per serving : 240 · Low in cholesterol · High in fibre and iron from spinach

Wash the spinach well under cold running water. Chop it finely and discard any old leaves or tough stalks. Cut the potatoes into cubes. Heat the oil in a large saucepan and add the garlic and spices. Cook over a medium heat for 2-3 minutes, stirring occasionally, to release the aromas.

Add the spinach, potatoes and coconut to the saucepan and stir until the spinach has wilted. Take care not to overcook the spinach.

Pour in the stock and bring to the boil, then reduce the heat and simmer for about 15 minutes until the potato is tender. Meanwhile, peel and finely grate the fresh ginger.

Blend the contents of the saucepan together in a liquidiser until smooth. Return to the saucepan and reheat gently. You may choose to thin the soup by adding a little extra stock or water if necessary.

Stir in the ginger and season to taste. Garnish each portion with a spoonful of natural yoghurt or single cream. Serve this soup in individual portions or in a large soup tureen.

Eastern spices blend with coconut, potatoes and spinach to give this attractive green soup an exotic flavour.

Smoked Salmon Rolls with Light Cheese Mousse

Smoked salmon with a tangy herb and cheese filling makes a luxurious starter. The addition of a little mayonnaise gives the filling a creamy texture but it is not essential and reduced calorie mayonnaise can be used as an alternative. You can also find 'very low-fat' cottage cheese in the shops which contains practically no fat. Dill is a herb that has a special affinity with fish, and it makes an excellent foil for this creamy-rich starter.

SERVES 4
PREPARATION TIME : *30 minutes*
CHILLING TIME : *2 hours*

INGREDIENTS
4oz (115g) packet smoked salmon (4 large slices)
1½ teaspoons powdered gelatine
4oz (115g) very low-fat natural cottage cheese
Grated rind of ½ lime or lemon
1 tablespoon lime or lemon juice
1 heaped tablespoon mayonnaise
2 tablespoons freshly snipped chives
1 tablespoon freshly chopped dill
Freshly ground black pepper
Dill sprigs or whole chives for garnish
Lime or lemon wedges for serving

Calories per serving : 135 · Low in calories · High in protein from salmon

Sprinkle the gelatine over 2 tablespoons of water in a small, heatproof bowl. Leave to soak for about 5 minutes, until spongy. Drain off any liquid from the cottage cheese and press through a fine sieve into a bowl. Leave to one side.

Stand the bowl of gelatine in a saucepan containing enough hot water to reach halfway up the side of the bowl. Heat gently until all the grains of gelatine have completely dissolved. Remove the bowl from the water and leave to cool briefly.

Stir the dissolved gelatine into the sieved cottage cheese until evenly mixed. Finely grate the lime or lemon rind and add, along with the juice, mayonnaise, chopped herbs and black pepper. Beat well to mix and cover the bowl. Chill the mousse in the refrigerator for 1 hour, or until the mousse is just set.

Cut each salmon slice in half lengthways and grind black pepper over each piece. Place equal amounts of the cheese mousse in neat mounds at the end of each piece of salmon. Carefully roll the salmon around the mousse and arrange seam side down on a board. Cover and chill in the refrigerator for at least 1 hour.

Serve the salmon rolls on individual plates with a garnish of dill sprigs or whole chives and lime or lemon wedges. Granary, rye or pumpernickel bread also go well with this dish.

Smoked salmon rolled around a creamy mousse of cottage cheese and herbs makes a luxurious starter.

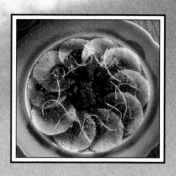

SALADS &
RAW FOOD DISHES

*Fresh, uncooked foods are the healthiest of all.
Boost your intake of raw vegetables by mixing them with
fruits, cheeses, grains, pulses and meat, in
a variety of irresistible salads.*

cs

Beetroot and Orange Salad

When buying beetroot, look for those with loose but undamaged skins. Choose small or medium varieties as large ones may be tough. You can buy them raw and then cook them yourself. Wash the beetroot thoroughly, then plunge them into boiling, unsalted water, cover and cook for between 15 minutes and 1 hour, depending on their size. Drain and cool the beetroot quickly under cold, running water before peeling. The unusual flavour of this salad complements cold meats such as pork, duck, goose and game particularly well.

Sweet and sour flavours mingle in this colourful salad. It can be served on its own or with cold meats.

INGREDIENTS
1lb (450g) beetroot
2 large oranges
SALAD DRESSING
2 teaspoons celery seeds
3 tablespoons white wine vinegar
2 teaspoons caster sugar
2 tablespoons sunflower or groundnut oil
Salt and freshly ground black pepper

Calories per serving : 150 · Low in fat and cholesterol · High in dietary fibre from beetroot

To make the dressing, lightly crush the celery seeds in a mortar using a pestle, or with the end of a rolling pin, and place them in a small saucepan. Add the wine vinegar, sugar and ¼ pint (150ml) water. Boil for 8-10 minutes until the liquid has reduced to about 2 tablespoons. Strain into a bowl and put to one side to cool.

Using a sharp knife, peel the oranges, cutting away the pith and the skin. Slice the oranges into rings, catching any juice in a bowl to add to the dressing.

Peel and thinly slice the beetroot, cubing a small amount to place in the centre of the dish. Arrange the beetroot and orange slices alternately. Mix the oil with the vinegar mixture, add salt and black pepper to taste and beat well with a fork. Pour the dressing over the salad and serve. For extra garnish, arrange thinly pared strips of orange peel over the salad.

Crab, Orange and Avocado Salad

The flavours, colours and textures of this simple salad complement each other perfectly. Sprinkling the avocado with lemon juice prevents the flesh from discolouring, and enables you to prepare the salad up to 1 hour in advance. Fresh, prepared crab meat is readily available from supermarkets and fishmongers. Serve as a starter with fresh bread, or as an accompaniment to other salads.

Fresh crab with lightly dressed avocado and oranges.

INGREDIENTS
8oz (225g) fresh, prepared or tinned crab
2 large oranges
2 avocados
2 teaspoons lemon juice
Parsley or dill sprigs for garnish
DRESSING
Juice of ½ orange
1 teaspoon whole grain mustard
1 tablespoon virgin olive oil
Salt and freshly ground pepper

Calories per serving : 320 · High in dietary fibre from avocado · High in protein and iron from crab

Peel the oranges with a sharp knife – cutting a little into the flesh so that you remove the skin and all the pith from the segments. Catch any juice that falls in a bowl, and reserve for the dressing. Slice the oranges thinly into rounds across the core.

Cut the avocados in half lengthways, remove the stone, peel the skin, and sprinkle the flesh with the lemon juice. Drain any water from the crab. Arrange the avocado, orange and crab on individual plates.

Mix the dressing ingredients together, season to taste and sprinkle over the salad. Garnish with parsley or dill sprigs and serve.

Californian Strawberry and Spinach Salad

Many chefs in California delight in creating imaginative dishes by combining unusual ingredients. This eye-catching salad is easy to prepare, and can be served as a light starter or side salad.

SERVES 4
PREPARATION TIME : *20 minutes*
COOKING TIME : *5 minutes*
OVEN : *Preheat to 200°C*
(400°F, gas mark 6)

INGREDIENTS
2oz (50g) shelled whole fresh almonds
8oz (225g) fresh young spinach
1lb (450g) ripe strawberries
1 bulb fennel
DRESSING
Juice of ½ orange
1 teaspoon smooth French mustard
2 tablespoons virgin olive oil
1 tablespoon fruit vinegar or white wine vinegar
Salt and freshly ground black pepper

Calories per serving : 215 · High in iron and fibre
from spinach · High in vitamin C from strawberries

Spinach and fruit combine to create an exotic salad.

Roast the almonds on a baking tray in the oven for about 7 minutes, shaking the tray and checking frequently to avoid burning. When they are well roasted, tip them into a heat-proof bowl.

Wash the spinach thoroughly and pat dry. Discard any coarse leaves, or stems. Wash, hull and halve the strawberries. Wash the fennel. Remove the feathery tops and hard base, and cut into thin strips.

To make the dressing, put all the ingredients in a screw-top jar and shake vigorously, then taste and adjust the seasoning.

Put the salad into a large bowl, pour over the dressing and toss thoroughly. Try to leave plenty of strawberries on top of the salad when serving.

Chickpea Salad

Chickpeas are a nutritious legume, and are high in fibre, protein, vitamins and minerals. They are popular all over the Mediterranean and have always been an important ingredient in Arab cuisine. Chickpeas come in large and small varieties which can be used in numerous dishes. Their rich nutty flavour lends itself to salads, soups and stews, and they are used to make creamy dips such as the Middle-Eastern purée called 'hummus' – which is the Arab word for chickpea. Tinned varieties have already been cooked and retain their original flavour. They are readily available from supermarkets and grocers. This salad is easy to prepare and goes well with cold ratatouille.

SERVES 4
PREPARATION TIME : *5 minutes*

INGREDIENTS
1¼ lb (575g) tinned chickpeas
6 spring onions
2 tablespoons virgin olive oil
Juice of ½ lemon
4 tablespoons chopped parsley
Salt and freshly ground black pepper
1 lemon for garnish

Calories per serving : 290 · Low in cholesterol
High in fibre and iron from chickpeas

Chickpeas are grown all around the world and are known by many different names; garbanzo in Spain, cece in Italy and channa in India. This Mediterranean salad of chickpeas, spring onions and parsley is lightly dressed in lemon juice and olive oil, and garnished with lemon wedges.

Drain and rinse the tinned chickpeas, drain again, and then put them to one side.

Trim and wash the spring onions, then finely slice the bulb and about 3in (80mm) of the green stalk into thin rings, and put to one side.

In a large serving bowl, blend the oil and lemon juice together by whisking thoroughly. Add the drained chickpeas, spring onions and chopped parsley. Season to taste with salt and freshly ground black pepper and then thoroughly toss the salad.

Cut the lemon into wedges for garnish, and arrange them over the top of the salad.

Pasta Salad with Fresh Vegetables

Italian cooks are very particular when it comes to cooking pasta. Overcooked pasta can be watery and unappetising. The Italians cook it 'al dente', which means firm to the bite. When the pasta is cooked in this way it not only tastes better, but sauces adhere to it and it is well suited for salads. Choose rigatoni, penne or shell-shaped pasta for this recipe. The onion is pickled to add a piquancy to the salad, but the pickling is not essential if you are in a hurry. Choose vegetables that are very fresh and firm. The pasta and raw cooked vegetables add interesting textures, and the addition of goat's cheese gives the dish a tangy flavour.

SERVES 4
PREPARATION TIME : *30 minutes*
MARINATING TIME : *3 hours*
COOKING TIME : *15 minutes*

INGREDIENTS
12oz (350g) pasta
1 red onion
1 teaspoon cider vinegar
3oz (75g) small broccoli
8oz (225g) small courgettes
2 stalks celery
½ cucumber
2 small carrots
1 large beef tomato or 8 cherry tomatoes
3 tablespoons fresh basil leaves
3 tablespoons virgin olive oil
Salt and freshly ground black pepper
2oz (50g) goat's cheese (optional)

Calories per serving : 440 · High in dietary fibre from pasta and vegetables · High in iron from broccoli High in vitamin A from carrots and courgettes High in vitamin C from tomatoes

To pickle the onion, peel, then slice it thinly and place in a bowl. Cover with boiling water and allow to stand for 30 seconds. Drain and return to the bowl with just enough cider vinegar to cover the slices. Store in the refrigerator to marinate for 3 hours.

Cook the pasta in boiling salted water, according to the instructions on the packet, leaving it slightly firm. Meanwhile, break the broccoli into very small florets and add to a pan with just enough boiling water to cover them. Add a pinch of salt and blanch for 2 minutes. Drain and put to one side.

Trim and dice the courgettes and celery into ½in (15mm) cubes. Peel and dice the cucumber and carrots, and dice the tomato into cubes of the same

Fragrant basil and crunchy vegetables served with rigatoni pasta in a simple olive-oil dressing. This tasty pasta salad makes a colourful main course, especially if goat's cheese is crumbled over it.

size. If using cherry tomatoes, simply halve them. Combine the vegetables together in a serving bowl. Drain the onion and add to the bowl, along with the broccoli and basil. Mix thoroughly.

Drain and rinse the pasta in cold water, then drain again thoroughly and add to the bowl with the olive oil. Toss well and season to taste. Sprinkle with crumbled goat's cheese, if desired, and serve cold.

Cracked Wheat Salad with Lime

This dish, also known as tabbouleh, is popular throughout the Middle East, but probably originated in The Lebanon. It is made from cracked wheat, or bulgur, which is wheat that has been parboiled, then dried and broken or cracked into small pieces. The fresh lime juice makes this a particularly light and refreshing salad, and in the summer it is the ideal accompaniment to grilled or barbecued fish or meat. Tabbouleh will keep for a day or two if covered and stored in the refrigerator, but ideally the lime juice should not be added until the salad is required.

SERVES 4
PREPARATION TIME : *25 minutes*
SOAKING TIME: *20 minutes*

INGREDIENTS
4oz (115g) bulgur wheat
4oz (115g) mangetout
2 spring onions
2 ripe tomatoes
4oz (115g) cucumber
3 tablespoons fresh chopped parsley
3 tablespoons fresh chopped mint
3 tablespoons virgin olive oil
Juice of 1 large or 2 small limes
Salt and freshly ground black pepper
A few sprigs of mint or flat-leaf parsley
Cucumber or tomato for garnish (optional)

Calories per serving : 210 · Low in cholesterol · High in dietary fibre from cracked wheat · High in vitamin C from tomatoes and cucumber

Place the bulgur wheat in a bowl and cover with boiling water. Leave to soak for 20 minutes.

Meanwhile, bring a saucepan of water to the boil and add the mangetout. Bring the water back to the boil, then immediately drain the mangetout. Place the mangetout in cold, or preferably iced, water to refresh them. This will help them to keep their bright green colour.

Drain the mangetout thoroughly, then cut them into thin strips crossways. Trim the spring onions and finely chop the bulbs and 3in (80mm) of the green stalks. Finely chop the tomatoes and dice the cucumber. Put all the vegetables together in a bowl.

Drain the bulgur wheat thoroughly. Preferably, drain it in a colander or sieve and shake well to remove all the water, before mixing it with the vegetables. Chop the fresh herbs and add them to the bowl. Add the olive oil and lime juice and season generously to taste. Mix well.

Spoon the mixture onto a serving dish and garnish with fresh herbs. To decorate, edge the salad with thinly sliced cucumber or diced tomato.

Lime juice, fresh mint and parsley flavour this exotic Middle-Eastern assortment of cracked wheat and vegetables to make an unusual and filling dish to serve as part of a summer lunch.

Slices of sweet dessert apples and nutty celeriac dressed with mayonnaise and served on a bed of crispy lettuce.

Celeriac and Apple Salad

Celeriac is a variety of celery that is grown for its nutty, edible root. It has a rough, brownish skin and white flesh, and can be eaten cooked as a hot vegetable or grated raw in salads. The peak season is from March to October, and you should choose vegetables with small heads and firm, clean roots. This light, crisp salad goes well with cold pork or ham. Use a low-calorie mayonnaise, if you prefer. A food processor with a grating disc is helpful when preparing this dish.

SERVES 4-6
PREPARATION TIME : *10 minutes*

INGREDIENTS
1lb (450g) celeriac
Juice of 1 lime
2 crisp dessert apples
3 tablespoons low-calorie mayonnaise
Freshly ground black pepper
1 Little Gem or other lettuce for garnish

Calories per serving : 40 · Low in fat and cholesterol
High in dietary fibre from celeriac

82

Trim and peel the celeriac and slice or grate it finely into a bowl, using a sharp knife or food processor. Pour over the lime juice and mix thoroughly.

Peel the apples and remove the cores. Grate the apples, then add them to the celeriac along with the mayonnaise and season with black pepper.

Toss the apples and celeriac well together so that the mayonnaise coats each piece. Arrange the crisp lettuce leaves in an attractive pattern on a serving plate. Add an extra grating of black pepper at the last moment and serve this crunchy salad with hot, crusty French bread.

Wholewheat Pasta Salad

Britain surprisingly exports wholewheat pasta to Italy. It is made with high-quality flour that retains all the goodness and fibre of whole wheat. Use long strands of pasta, such as tagliatelle, and a low-calorie mayonnaise if preferred. The dressing in this recipe is light and slightly piquant, and the salad makes a refreshing change from potatoes when served with cold meats, fish or poultry.

SERVES 4
PREPARATION TIME : *25 minutes*
COOKING TIME : *10 minutes*

INGREDIENTS
6oz (175g) wholewheat pasta
2 sticks celery
12 small radishes
3oz (75g) button mushrooms
3 tablespoons low-calorie mayonnaise
4 tablespoons fromage frais
1 tablespoon tarragon or white wine vinegar
¼ teaspoon mustard powder
Salt and freshly ground black pepper
1oz (25g) raw cashew nuts (optional)
1 tablespoon chopped chives

Calories per serving : 245 · Low in cholesterol · High in dietary fibre from pasta · High in protein from nuts and fromage frais

Place the pasta in a large pan of boiling, salted water. Cook according to the instructions on the packet, leaving the pasta cooked but slightly firm. Drain, rinse in cold water and drain again thoroughly.

Meanwhile, prepare the vegetables. Wash, trim and chop the celery into matchsticks, trim the radishes and clean and quarter the mushrooms.

In a mixing bowl, blend the mayonnaise, fromage frais, tarragon or white wine vinegar, mustard powder and pepper to taste. Stir in the drained pasta, mushrooms, celery, radishes and optional nuts, and mix well. Taste and adjust the seasoning.

Spoon the salad into a shallow salad bowl and arrange so that the pasta is piled up with radishes, celery, mushrooms and cashew nuts, if used. Then sprinkle the salad with the chives and serve.

Wholewheat pasta mixed with crunchy vegetables sprinkled with fresh chives and served with a light red wine from the Loire region. Fromage frais and low-calorie mayonnaise make a low-fat dressing.

Three Bean Salad

This simple side salad would go well with spicy Indian-style meals, and can be made quickly from canned beans that do not require overnight soaking and cooking. The red pepper and Spanish onion provide a crisp contrast to the soft texture of the pulses. This salad, without the lettuce, can be made up to 24 hours in advance if it is kept covered in the refrigerator, but it should be left to stand at room temperature for 20 minutes before serving.

A colourful array of beans and peppers served on a bed of crisp lettuce with a lime and coriander dressing.

Kippers and mushrooms covered in a spicy dressing.

SERVES 6-8
PREPARATION TIME : *20 minutes*
STANDING TIME : *30 minutes*

INGREDIENTS

1 × 15oz (425g) tin red kidney beans
1 × 15oz (425g) tin borlotti beans
1 × 14oz (400g) tin flageolet beans
1 large red pepper
½ large Spanish onion
1 garlic clove
1 tablespoon coriander seeds
4 tablespoons fresh chopped coriander
3 tablespoons virgin olive oil
Juice of 1 lime
Salt and freshly ground black pepper
1 lollo biondo or other curly leaved lettuce

Calories per serving : 390 · High in fibre, protein and iron from beans

Drain the tinned beans and rinse under cold running water, then shake in a sieve to drain and combine in a large salad bowl.

Halve, de-seed and thinly slice the pepper. Thinly slice the onion and crush the garlic. Combine the pepper, onion and garlic with the beans.

Dry-fry the coriander seeds for a few minutes, stirring constantly until their aroma is released, then remove and crush in a mortar with a pestle. Add to the salad with the chopped coriander and mix well.

Whisk the oil and lime juice together, pour over the bean mixture, season and mix well. Cover the bowl and leave to stand at room temperature for at least 30 minutes, stirring occasionally.

Arrange the lettuce leaves in a large serving bowl, spoon the salad into the centre and serve.

Kipper and Mushroom Salad

Once considered a poor man's food, kippers are now widely popular – especially since it has been proved that oily fish is good for the heart. Serve with boiled new potatoes for a light main course.

SERVES 4
PREPARATION TIME : *15 minutes*
MARINATING TIME : *4-12 hours*

INGREDIENTS

4 large kipper fillets
8oz (225g) mushrooms
1 small red pepper
2 tablespoons chopped parsley

DRESSING

Juice of 1 lemon
2 teaspoons chilli sauce or ½ teaspoon tabasco
4 tablespoons single cream
3 tablespoons olive oil
Freshly ground black pepper

Calories per serving : 550 · High in protein and iron from fish · High in vitamin C from pepper

Skin the kipper fillets, then cut them across the grain into ¼in (5mm) strips and put them into a bowl. Slice the mushrooms. Halve and de-seed the red pepper, and slice into 2in (50mm) strips. Add the mushrooms and pepper to the kipper.

Whisk the lemon juice and chilli sauce or tabasco together in a bowl. Keep whisking and add the cream slowly, then stir in the oil and season to taste. Pour the dressing over the kipper salad, cover and leave to marinate in the refrigerator for at least 4 hours.

When chilled, remove from the bowl using a slotted spoon and arrange in a serving dish. Whisk the sauce well, pour over the salad, sprinkle with the chopped parsley and serve.

Mangetout and Bacon Salad

The mangetout, also known as the sugar pea and snow pea, is an important vegetable in French and Chinese cooking. The pea, which should remain crisp when cooked, is eaten in its entirety, and this accounts for its French name meaning 'eat all'. The pods should have both tips trimmed and their string removed before washing and drying. To keep the salad low in fat, the croutons are browned in the oven rather than fried. You can serve this dish as a lunchtime snack, a side salad or even as a starter.

SERVES 4
PREPARATION TIME : *10 minutes*
COOKING TIME : *12 minutes*
OVEN : *Preheat to 190°C (375°F, gas mark 5)*

INGREDIENTS
1lb (450g) mangetout
6-8 rashers lean back bacon
2 slices bread
DRESSING
1½ tablespoons virgin olive oil or hazelnut oil
½ tablespoon white wine vinegar
Salt and freshly ground black pepper

Calories per serving : 230 · High in dietary fibre from bread and mangetout · High in protein from bacon

Remove the crust from the bread, cut it into tiny cubes and spread out on a baking sheet. Brown lightly in the oven for about 12 minutes.

Meanwhile, remove the rind and excess fat from the bacon and cut the flesh into ½in (15mm) wide strips. Cook in a dry frying pan over a moderate heat, until crisp and lightly golden. Keep the bacon warm.

Whisk the dressing ingredients together in a small bowl and bring a saucepan of water to the boil.

Add the mangetout to the boiling water and cook for 3-4 minutes until the pods are tender yet still crunchy. Meanwhile, preheat a serving bowl.

Plunge the mangetout into ice-cold water to keep them crisp, and then pat them dry. Either leave the mangetout whole or cut them in half.

Pour the dressing into the warmed bowl, add the mangetout, bacon and croutons, season to taste and toss well together. This salad is particularly delicious served slightly warm, with fresh crusty wholemeal bread and a crisp dry white wine.

A feast of bacon, mangetout and crunchy croutons.

Indonesian Pineapple Salad

This exotic but simple recipe is based on an Indonesian dish called Rojak, traditionally served with a spicy peanut dressing. The dressing can be prepared in advance and refrigerated.

An Indonesian salad to complement cold meats; full of contrasting tastes and served with a rich peanut sauce.

SERVES 4
PREPARATION TIME : *25 minutes*

INGREDIENTS

8oz (225g) fresh or tinned pineapple
7oz (200g) bean sprouts
2 medium carrots
½ large cucumber
4 spring onions
3oz (75g) roasted peanuts

DRESSING

2 tablespoons crunchy peanut butter
2 tablespoons sunflower oil
4 teaspoons soy sauce
A good pinch of chilli powder or cayenne pepper
Freshly ground black pepper

Calories per serving : 330 · Low in cholesterol · High in dietary fibre from pineapple and peanuts · High in vitamin C from fruit and vegetables

If using fresh pineapple, cut away the plume and base of the pineapple, then remove the peel and cut the flesh into bite-size chunks. Catch any juice that falls in a bowl and reserve for the dressing. If using tinned pineapple, reserve 4 tablespoons of the drained juice, and cut the fruit into chunks.

Rinse and drain the bean sprouts. Discard any discoloured parts and pat dry. Peel and coarsely grate the carrots. Cut the cucumber into sticks about the same length as the bean sprouts, discarding the seeds if desired. Trim the spring onions and slice diagonally into the same length again. Reserving a third of the peanuts for garnish, roughly chop the rest. Put all the prepared ingredients in a large bowl and toss thoroughly to mix.

To make the dressing, put the peanut butter in a jug and gradually whisk in the reserved pineapple juice, oil and soy sauce. Add the chilli powder or cayenne, and season to taste with pepper.

Add the dressing to the salad ingredients and toss thoroughly. Garnish with the reserved peanuts and serve at room temperature.

87

A colourful plate of red-skinned apple, refreshing rocket leaves and freshly cut slivers of tangy Parmesan.

Parmesan, Rocket and Apple Salad

Rocket looks rather like dandelion leaves but it has the texture of crisp lettuce. It is commonly grown in the Mediterranean region and is very popular in Italy, where it is usually known as ruchetta. Its spear-shaped leaves have a delicious, spicy bitterness which is excellent combined with other salad greens and mixed pieces of hot, crispy bacon. In this recipe, its unique mustardy, lemon flavour complements the tangy Parmesan and the sweetness of the apple. You can buy small packets of rocket in large supermarkets, or bunches in Italian delicatessens or good greengrocers. Young spinach or sorrel leaves make a good substitute if rocket is not available. Try serving this salad with French bread.

SERVES 4
PREPARATION TIME : *15 minutes*

INGREDIENTS
6oz (175g) rocket, spinach or sorrel leaves
4oz (115g) block fresh Parmesan
2 Cox's apples or 1 large red-skinned apple
DRESSING
2 tablespoons virgin olive oil
Juice of ½ orange
2 teaspoons white wine vinegar
1 teaspoon smooth French mustard
½ teaspoon horseradish sauce
Salt and freshly ground black pepper

Calories per serving : 240 · Low in cholesterol · High in dietary fibre from rocket and apples

Wash the rocket, or spinach or sorrel, removing any large stems or damaged leaves. Dry the leaves in a salad spinner or with kitchen paper. Cut any rind off the Parmesan, and using a mandolin, cheese parer, or just a sharp knife, cut large slivers of Parmesan as thinly as possible. Do not worry if the slices crumble or break – they will still look attractive.

Mix all the ingredients for the dressing together in a bowl and season to taste with salt and black pepper. Wash, but do not peel, the apple. Quarter the apple, remove and discard the core and dice it into ½in (15mm) cubes. Mix the apple with the rocket, spinach or sorrel, and dressing in a salad bowl. Scatter over the Parmesan shavings and serve.

Apricot and Rice Salad

Apricots were cultivated in China as long ago as 2000 BC, and are a popular ingredient in Middle-Eastern cookery. Their tart, tangy taste combines well with brown rice to make a simple salad, and the sherry vinegar brings out the nutty flavour of the rice. Buy dried, ready-to-cook apricots that do not need soaking, and easy-cook rice.

SERVES 4-6
PREPARATION TIME : *10 minutes*
STANDING TIME : *1 hour*
COOKING TIME : *30 minutes*

INGREDIENTS
8oz (225g) long grain brown rice
1 yellow or red pepper
8oz (225g) dried apricots
4in (100mm) piece of cucumber
3oz (75g) pumpkin seeds
2 fresh apricots
Sprigs of parsley for garnish
DRESSING
3 tablespoons grapeseed or sunflower oil
1½ tablespoons sherry vinegar
1 teaspoon grainy mustard
Freshly ground black pepper

Calories per serving : 490 · High in dietary fibre from apricots · High in iron from apricots and rice

Cook the rice according to the packet instructions and mix the dressing ingredients together.

Drain the rice and turn into a bowl. Add the dressing, mix well and leave to cool for 1 hour.

Halve and de-seed the pepper and cut into 2in (50mm) strips. Roughly chop the apricots and dice the cucumber into ½in (15mm) cubes. Mix the peppers, apricots, cucumber and pumpkin seeds with the rice. Season to taste and garnish.

Rice salad with fresh apricots and pumpkin seeds.

89

Thai Fish Salad

The bright exotic colours of mangoes, papayas and tomatoes make this dish look as spectacular as it tastes. The salad is beautifully light, with just a hint of spice from the chilli. If the monkfish is left out, it makes an excellent dish for vegetarians. Make sure the mangoes and papayas are really ripe – they should give a little when squeezed gently.

SERVES 4
PREPARATION TIME : *35 minutes*
COOKING TIME : *3 minutes*

INGREDIENTS
12oz (350g) monkfish tail
Juice of 2 large or 3 small limes
1 level teaspoon caster sugar
1 teaspoon anchovy essence
2 ripe mangoes
2 ripe papayas
1 bunch spring onions
1 red or green chilli
1 large beef tomato
½ cucumber
4 sprigs coriander
8 basil leaves
2 Little Gem lettuce
A pinch of salt

Calories per serving : 300 · High in fibre and vitamin A from fruit · High in protein and iron from fish High in vitamin C from fruit and lettuce

Squeeze the limes and pour the juice into a large bowl. Mix in the sugar and anchovy essence.

Peel the mangoes, cut them in half and discard the stones. Peel the papayas, cut them in half and scoop out the seeds. Cut the fruits into 2in (50mm) strips and place in the bowl with the lime juice.

Trim and slice the spring onions, de-seed and chop the chilli, dice the tomato and cucumber into 1in (25mm) cubes and add them to the bowl.

Keeping a few coriander leaves for garnish, shred the rest of the coriander and basil leaves and add them to the bowl. Wash the lettuce, pat dry and arrange on individual plates. Chop the remaining

Monkfish mixed with ripe fruit and a hint of spice.

lettuce heart, add it to the salad and toss thoroughly.

Remove the tough thin membrane of the fish with a sharp knife and cut down each side of the central bone to remove the fillets. Dice the flesh into 1½in (40mm) cubes and put in a pan with ½ pint (285ml) water and the salt. Bring slowly to the boil, then cover and simmer gently for 3 minutes.

While the fish is cooking, divide the salad among the plates. Drain the monkfish and add to the salads while the pieces are still warm. Garnish with the reserved coriander leaves and serve immediately.

Oriental Salad with Fruit

The persimmon is the national fruit of Japan and resembles a tomato with a papery blossom at one end. Persimmons are now stocked in some large supermarkets, and you should choose soft ripe fruits that are bright orange, with thin skins and the stalks attached. Peak season is autumn to winter. If hard to find – papayas or mangoes can be used as substitutes. You will need a liquidiser for this recipe.

SERVES 4-6
PREPARATION TIME : *10 minutes*

INGREDIENTS
8oz (225g) mixed salad greens, such as frisée,
mâche or lollo rosso
2 oranges
4 tinned water chestnuts
2 teaspoons sesame seeds
1 pear
2 ripe persimmons
DRESSING
1 ripe persimmon
1 tablespoon rice or fruit vinegar
1 teaspoon sesame oil
½ teaspoon lemon juice
¼ teaspoon Worcestershire or soy sauce
Salt and freshly ground black pepper

Calories per serving : 220 · Low in fat and
cholesterol · High in fibre from fruit and salad

Wash and dry the salad greens and chill them in the refrigerator. Peel the oranges and separate them into segments, discarding the pips and any tough skin or pith. Cover the segments and chill.

Slice the water chestnuts, cover with water and put in the refrigerator. Toast the sesame seeds over a medium heat in a small frying pan, without oil, and leave to one side.

To make the dressing, peel the persimmon and place it in the liquidiser, together with ½ cup of water, the vinegar, sesame oil, lemon juice, Worcestershire or soy sauce and ½ teaspoon of salt. Blend until smooth, then add black pepper to taste and chill in the refrigerator.

When ready to serve, peel and slice the pear and the remaining persimmons. Remove the dressing, oranges and chestnuts from the refrigerator. If the dressing has separated, whisk it together with a fork. Mix the salad greens with the dressing and arrange the mixture on large plates. Garnish with the oranges, water chestnuts and persimmon and pear slices. Sprinkle with the toasted sesame seeds and serve immediately.

Exotic fruits served with a spicy dressing and sprinkled with toasted sesame seeds create a taste of the East.

Waldorf Salad

The Waldorf salad owes its name to the Waldorf Astoria Hotel in New York, where the recipe was first created. In this version, soft cheese made from skimmed milk keeps the dressing low in fat.

SERVES 4
PREPARATION TIME : *15 minutes*

INGREDIENTS
12oz (350g) celery
3oz (75g) shelled walnut halves
3 red apples
Juice of ½ lemon
2oz (50g) sultanas
1 large lettuce heart
DRESSING
4 tablespoons fromage frais
1 tablespoon lemon juice
1 tablespoon mayonnaise
1 tablespoon walnut oil
Salt and white pepper

Calories per serving : 250 · Low in cholesterol ·
High in protein and dietary fibre

Waldorf salad served with a light Chardonnay wine.

Mix all the dressing ingredients together and season to taste. Beat vigorously with a fork until the mixture is thick and smooth. Leave to one side.

Wash and trim the celery stalks and roughly chop them, reserving a few celery leaves for garnishing the salad. Roughly chop 2oz (50g) of the walnut halves. Wash, quarter, core and roughly chop the apples, leaving the peel on.

Place the apples in a large bowl, pour over the lemon juice and mix thoroughly. Add the celery, walnuts and sultanas to the bowl. Taste and adjust the seasoning, if necessary.

Line a shallow bowl with the lettuce leaves. Spoon the salad into the bowl, and carefully pour over the dressing. Garnish with the remaining walnut halves and celery leaves and serve immediately.

Winter Salad with Goat's Cheese

Most soft goat's cheese is full fat, but its strong flavour means that only a small quantity is required. French goat's cheese, known as chèvre, is one of the most popular types of goat's cheese and is widely available in supermarkets. A light French red wine, such as Brouilly, goes well with this dish.

SERVES 4
PREPARATION TIME : *15 minutes*

INGREDIENTS
½ frisée lettuce
or 1 Little Gem lettuce
1 small radicchio
1 head chicory
2 sticks celery
2oz (50g) walnuts
4oz (115g) goat's cheese
DRESSING
2 teaspoons mild whole grain French mustard
1 teaspoon clear honey
1 tablespoon red wine vinegar
3 tablespoons walnut or olive oil

Calories per serving : 240

Served with French bread and red wine, this winter salad provides a tasty, light meal or a satisfying starter.

Roughly chop the walnuts, place them in a bowl and crumble over the goat's cheese.

Thoroughly wash and dry the lettuce, radicchio, chicory and celery. Tear the lettuce, radicchio and chicory into pieces and slice the celery. Line the base of a salad bowl, or a serving platter, with the greens.

Thoroughly mix up all the ingredients for the dressing. Pour the dressing in with the celery, walnuts and cheese and toss well. Spoon the mixture over the greens and serve.

Salmon Tartare

Salmon has a particularly high content of fish oils which helps people to maintain soft skin and glossy hair. In this dish the combination of raw and smoked salmon served with a dill sauce creates both a luxurious and a nutritious dish. Salmon is hung in dense smoke, usually produced from smouldering wood chips, for several hours. This gives it the delicate smoked-salmon flavour. Serve this dish with a large green salad and chunks of brown bread.

SERVES 4
PREPARATION TIME : *15 minutes*

INGREDIENTS
1lb (450g) fresh salmon
6oz (175g) smoked salmon
2 tablespoons tarragon vinegar
Salt and freshly ground black pepper
Sprigs of fresh dill for garnish
DILL SAUCE
4 tablespoons mayonnaise
or reduced-calorie mayonnaise
4 tablespoons sour cream
2 tablespoons fresh chopped dill
1 tablespoon chopped chives
or ½ teaspoon dried chives
Salt and freshly ground black pepper

Calories per serving : 310 · High in protein and
vitamin D from salmon

Carefully skin and bone the salmon (or ask your fishmonger to do this for you). Cut the fresh salmon into cubes using a sharp knife and place the cubes in a bowl. Cut the smoked salmon into very fine slivers and put to one side.

Add the vinegar to the bowl and season with a little salt, some dill and plenty of black pepper. Arrange the salmon on a serving platter with the fresh fish on one side and the smoked fish on the other. Garnish with the dill.

Blend the mayonnaise, sour cream, dill, chives, salt and freshly ground black pepper together in a bowl to make the dill sauce. Serve the sauce in a separate serving dish or bowl along with the salmon.

Raw and smoked salmon with a creamy dill sauce.

Marinated Mushroom and Artichoke Salad

This Middle-Eastern inspired side salad also makes a light, refreshing starter. It is perfect for serving with barbeçued meat, poultry or fish. The mushrooms are blanched to prevent them from discolouring.

SERVES 4-6
PREPARATION TIME : *25 minutes*
MARINATING TIME : *4-24 hours*

INGREDIENTS
1lb (450g) small white button mushrooms
8oz (225g) tin artichoke hearts
3 tablespoons lemon juice
2 teaspoons coriander seeds
½ teaspoon cumin seeds
1 clove garlic
2 tablespoons virgin olive oil
2 tablespoons cider vinegar
2 tablespoons clear honey
2 tablespoons chopped fresh coriander
Salt and freshly ground black pepper
Raw red and white onion rings for garnish
Fresh coriander leaves for garnish

Calories per serving : 140 · Low in fat · High in iron
from artichokes and mushrooms

Trim the base of the mushroom stalks and wipe them clean. Drain the tinned artichoke hearts and put them in a large bowl.

Bring a saucepan of water to the boil, add 1 tablespoon of lemon juice and the mushrooms. Cook in boiling water for 1 minute. Drain the mushrooms and rinse them in cold water. Drain again, pat dry, and add them to the artichokes.

Crush the coriander, the cumin seeds and the peeled garlic in a mortar with a pestle, or on a board with a rolling pin. Heat 1 tablespoon of the oil in a pan, add the crushed mixture and stir-fry for 1 minute. Then add the remaining lemon juice, the vinegar and honey. Stir-fry for a further 2 minutes. Pour the mixture over the mushrooms and artichokes, add the remaining oil and stir until the mushrooms are coated. Add the chopped coriander, season to taste, and stir again. Cover and chill in the refrigerator for 4 hours, stirring occasionally.

Peel and slice a mixture of red and white onions into rings and arrange around the edge of a serving platter or dish. Toss the mushrooms and artichokes well and spoon them into the centre. Garnish the onion rings with coriander leaves and serve chilled.

The salad can be left covered to marinate for up to 24 hours. Serve with warm pitta bread.

Middle-Eastern flavours of cumin and coriander make this dish of artichokes and mushrooms highly aromatic.

Swedish Dill and Cucumber Salad

Cucumber salads are popular in Sweden where they are traditionally served with fish. This dish would go well with cold poached salmon in summer or hot smoked fish in winter. Choose a firm cucumber and either peel away the skin completely or peel away strips down the length of the cucumber with a vegetable peeler to give a striped effect. This salad can be made up to 5 hours in advance if kept covered in the refrigerator.

SERVES 4
PREPARATION TIME : *30 minutes*
MARINATING TIME : *2 hours*

INGREDIENTS
1 large cucumber
Salt
Dill sprigs for garnish
DRESSING
3 tablespoons white wine vinegar
2 tablespoons caster sugar
2 tablespoons chopped fresh dill

*Calories per serving : 50 · Low in calories,
fat and cholesterol*

Wash the cucumber and peel if desired. Cut in half crossways and slice as thinly as possible. Place the slices in a colander and sprinkle each layer with a little salt. Cover with a plate, place a heavy weight on top, and leave to stand for 30 minutes to draw out excess water from the cucumber.

Meanwhile, put the wine vinegar and sugar in a small saucepan with 4 tablespoons of water. Bring to the boil for 1 minute, then remove and leave to cool.

Rinse the salted cucumber slices under cold running water, pat dry and place in a large bowl.

Stir the dill into the dressing. Pour the dressing over the cucumber and mix well. Cover the bowl and leave the cucumber to marinate in the refrigerator for about 2 hours, stirring occasionally.

When ready, transfer the salad to a serving platter, garnish with dill sprigs and serve immediately.

Thinly sliced marinated cucumber with fresh dill.

Warm Duck Salad

This warm salad, made with marinated duck breast, can be served alone as a light meal or as a starter. The salad is enhanced by mushrooms coated in herb dressing and served with mixed salad greens.

SERVES 4-6
PREPARATION TIME : *35 minutes*
MARINATING TIME : *At least 1 hour*

INGREDIENTS
2 duck breasts
12 medium mushrooms
2 tablespoons virgin olive oil
½oz (15g) unsalted butter
1 clove garlic
½ teaspoon balsamic or cider vinegar
1 tablespoon lemon juice
1 small radicchio lettuce
1 bunch watercress
1 head of curly endive or escarole
1 tablespoon chopped parsley
1 tablespoon chopped fresh basil
MARINADE
2 shallots or 1 small onion
1 tablespoon lemon juice
1 tablespoon virgin olive oil
1 tablespoon fresh mixed herbs
Salt and freshly ground black pepper

*Calories per serving : 205 · High in protein from
duck · High in iron from duck and watercress*

Skin the duck breasts and cut them into long, thin slices. Finely chop the shallots or onion and mix all the marinade ingredients together in a large bowl, seasoning generously. Place the duck strips in the marinade, cover and leave in the refrigerator overnight, or for at least 1 hour.

Wipe the mushrooms clean and slice them thinly. Reserving the marinade, drain the duck strips. Heat 2 tablespoons of oil and the unsalted butter in a pan, add the duck strips and sauté for 2-3 minutes.

Quickly transfer the duck to a separate dish and add the mushrooms to the pan, with a little more butter, if necessary. Sauté for 2-3 minutes over a high heat, stirring occasionally.

Peel and slice the garlic. Add the marinade to the mushrooms with the garlic, vinegar and lemon juice. Reduce the mixture in the pan by boiling for 2 minutes. Return the duck to the pan, coating each strip with the mixture, and take off the heat.

While the dressing is cooling, wash and dry the mixed salad leaves, divide them between plates and top with the duck strips. Remove the garlic from the dressing and pour it over the salads. Garnish with parsley and basil and serve.

Marinated strips of duck breast, mushrooms and dressing warm the salad without wilting the salad greens.

Tomato, Orange and Fennel Salad

Use only firm, ripe and flavourful tomatoes for this recipe. Locally grown tomatoes that have ripened naturally are best. This salad can be made up to 2 hours before serving if kept cool and covered. Serve with crusty garlic bread as a starter, or as a side salad with barbecued poultry or fish.

SERVES 4-6
PREPARATION TIME : *25 minutes*
STANDING TIME : *30 minutes*

INGREDIENTS
6 medium ripe tomatoes
4 small oranges
1 bulb fennel
2 tablespoons orange juice
2 tablespoons lemon juice
3 tablespoons virgin olive oil
2 tablespoons fresh basil
½ teaspoon French mustard
½ teaspoon caster sugar
Salt and freshly ground black pepper
Basil leaves for garnish

Calories per serving : 210 · Low in cholesterol · High in dietary fibre from oranges and tomatoes

Remove the tomato skins by plunging each tomato into hot water for 30 seconds, then cold water for 1 minute, until the skins are cool enough to be peeled away with your fingers. Core and slice the tomatoes into thin rings.

Using a sharp knife, peel the oranges, cutting away all the white pith and skin. Slice into rings, catching any juice in a bowl and reserving it for the dressing. Trim the feathery leaves from the fennel bulb and reserve for garnish, then slice the bulb into rings. Arrange the tomato, orange and fennel alternately on individual plates.

Add the measured orange juice to that collected in the bowl, together with the lemon juice, olive oil, basil, mustard and sugar. Season to taste and beat well with a fork, then drizzle the mixture over the salad and allow it to stand in a cool place for 30 minutes, so the salad absorbs the flavours of the dressing. Just before serving the salad, garnish it with the reserved fennel fronds or basil leaves.

Slices of raw fennel, similar in taste to anise, are served with oranges, tomatoes and garlic toasts.

Old English Vegetable Salad

This recipe is a variation of 'salmagundi', a special salad that was served at lavish banquets during the 17th and 18th centuries. Today it makes an excellent buffet centrepiece, or main-course lunch served with wholemeal bread. You can vary the ingredients according to personal taste and seasonal availability. For example, vegetarians can substitute cheese wedges and grapes for the meat.

SERVES 6
PREPARATION TIME : *45 minutes*

INGREDIENTS
*12oz (350g) boneless cooked chicken
or turkey breasts
12oz (350g) young carrots
4oz (115g) whole baby sweetcorn
Salt
12oz (350g) waxy new potatoes
4oz (115g) frozen petits pois
2 eggs or 6-8 quail's eggs
3 medium ripe Mediterranean tomatoes
½ large cucumber
6oz (175g) ham
Parsley or chervil sprigs for garnish*
DRESSING
*1 small bunch spring onions
1 clove garlic
4 tablespoons virgin olive oil
1 tablespoon white wine vinegar or lemon juice
1 teaspoon French mustard
Salt and freshly ground black pepper*

*Calories per serving : 300 · High in dietary fibre from
corn and potatoes · High in vitamin A from
carrots and peas and vitamin C from tomatoes*

Cut the chicken or turkey breasts into thin strips. Scrape the carrots and cut into 3in (80mm) strips.

Add the baby sweetcorn to a saucepan of boiling water with a good pinch of salt and boil for about 5 minutes until tender yet crisp. Reserving the water, rinse the sweetcorn under cold running water, cut in half lengthways and put to one side.

Scrub the potatoes but do not peel them. Boil in the reserved water for 15-20 minutes until tender, then drain and leave to cool.

Meanwhile, cook the frozen peas according to the instructions on the packet, and hard-boil the eggs.

To remove the tomato skins, plunge them into a bowl of hot water for 30 seconds, then cold for 1 minute, until cool enough to peel the skins with your fingers. Core and slice into thin rings. Shell and thinly slice the hard-boiled eggs or shell and halve the quail's eggs, reserving a few unshelled for garnish. Thinly slice the cucumber. Cut the ham into

strips and slice the cooled potatoes into thin rings.

To make the dressing, trim the spring onions and thinly slice the bulb and about 3in (80mm) of the green stalk. Crush the garlic. Mix the spring onions and garlic with the remaining dressing ingredients and season to taste.

Arrange the potatoes in circles on a large platter with the peas and quail's eggs on top. Add the rest of the meat and vegetables in a fan extending outwards with slices of egg and onion piled in the centre. Drizzle over the dressing, and garnish with fresh sprigs of parsley or chervil and the unshelled quail's eggs. Serve immediately.

Slices of new potatoes, peas and quail's eggs circle a fan of chicken, ham and fresh vegetables to provide a decorative centrepiece for a dining table or buffet.

Caesar Salad

This salad originated in Italy, but is now popular throughout America. The final addition of the egg and lemon juice used in the recipe, binds the salad together into a delicious whole.

SERVES 4
PREPARATION TIME : *20 minutes*
MARINATING TIME : *30 minutes*
COOKING TIME : *5 minutes*

INGREDIENTS
2 slices bread
2 cloves garlic
4 tablespoons virgin olive oil
5 anchovy fillets
¼ teaspoon Worcestershire sauce
¼ teaspoon dry mustard
1 cos or romaine lettuce
Salt and freshly ground black pepper
1 tablespoon wine vinegar
1 egg
Juice of ½ lemon
2oz (50g) grated Parmesan cheese

Calories per serving : 280 · High in protein from eggs, anchovies and cheese

Crispy croutons and Parmesan cover a simple salad.

Peel and chop the garlic and cut the bread into cubes. Add the garlic to the oil and leave for 30 minutes to marinate. Sauté the bread cubes in 2 tablespoons of the garlic oil in a frying pan until just lightly toasted. Remove and drain on kitchen paper.

Mash the anchovy fillets in a small bowl, add the Worcestershire sauce and mustard and put aside.

Wash and dry the lettuce, then tear the leaves into pieces. Place these in a salad bowl, season to taste and combine them with the mustard and anchovy mixture. Mix the vinegar with the remaining garlic oil and pour over the lettuce.

Beat the egg in a bowl and pour it over the salad along with the lemon juice. Add the croutons and grated Parmesan cheese, toss vigorously and serve.

Warm Salad of Scallops

Scallops can be bought frozen or fresh, still in their fan-shaped shells. It is not necessary to buy large, expensive scallops, the smaller queen variety are just as good. This salad makes a perfect starter – very tasty but not too filling.

SERVES 6
PREPARATION TIME : *20 minutes*
COOKING TIME : *5 minutes*

INGREDIENTS
12oz (350g) fresh or frozen scallops
Salt
6oz (175g) mangetout
1 small lollo rosso or oak-leaf lettuce
2oz (50g) corn salad or small, raw spinach leaves
2in (50mm) piece fresh ginger
2 tablespoons virgin olive oil
1 tablespoon light soy sauce
3 tablespoons dry sherry

Calories per serving : 165 · High in protein from scallops · High in iron from scallops and spinach

Trim the mangetout and blanch in salted, boiling water for 2 minutes. Drain and refresh in cold water.

Wash and dry the lollo rosso and the corn salad or spinach leaves. Divide between 6 small plates, with the mangetout. Cover and chill until required.

Oak-leaf lettuce makes a beautiful background for pan-fried scallops and mangetout scented with fresh ginger.

Peel the ginger and slice it into very thin strips. Blanch the strips by plunging into boiling water for 30 seconds. Then put into ice-cold water, drain and pat dry. Mix the olive oil with the soy sauce. Cut large scallops into three but leave small ones whole.

Pour the sherry into a small saucepan and bring to the boil. Add the scallops, cover with a lid and cook for 2 minutes or until the scallops are just cooked, shaking the pan continually.

Remove the scallops from the pan and divide between the 6 plates. Scatter the strips of ginger over the scallops. Add 3 tablespoons of the liquid left in the pan to the soy sauce mixture. Shake well, pour the dressing over the 6 servings and serve at once.

Tomato, Pepper and Olive Pasta Salad

The tomatoes, peppers and garlic used to make the tomato sauce for this salad are baked in their skins, rather than fried in oil. The skins are then easily peeled away, leaving soft, sweet-tasting vegetables that complement the saltiness of the olives. This salad goes well with Italian salami, Italian breads such as ciabatta, and Chianti wine. Garnish with sprigs of rosemary and marjoram for an attractive finish. You will need a liquidiser for this recipe.

Cooked penne pasta is dressed with fresh tomato sauce and spooned into an attractive serving bowl. The dish is complemented with juicy black olives and fresh sprigs of rosemary and marjoram.

SERVES 4
PREPARATION TIME : *10 minutes*
COOKING TIME : *30 minutes*
OVEN : *Preheat to 200°C (400°F, gas mark 6)*

INGREDIENTS
6 large, ripe tomatoes
2 medium red peppers
4 cloves garlic
4 fresh rosemary sprigs
8oz (225g) penne or shell pasta
½ teaspoon caster sugar
Salt and freshly ground black pepper
16 black olives
1 sprig fresh basil leaves
1 teaspoon fresh marjoram
1 teaspoon fresh chopped chives
2oz (50g) Parmesan cheese

Calories per serving : 360 · High in dietary fibre from pasta and vegetables · High in protein from cheese and vitamin C from tomatoes and peppers

Wash and dry the tomatoes and peppers. Cut the peppers in half and remove the seeds, then place them in a roasting tray with the tomatoes and garlic cloves. Cover with two of the rosemary sprigs, reserving the other two for garnish, and bake in the oven until soft – about 15 minutes for the tomatoes and garlic and 25 minutes for the peppers.

In the meantime, add the pasta to a pan of salted, boiling water. Cook according to the instructions on the packet, leaving the pasta cooked but slightly firm. Drain, rinse in cold running water and drain again. Put to one side.

When cool enough to handle, peel away the pepper and tomato skins. Snip an end off each garlic clove and squeeze the inner clove out from the skin. Place the tomatoes, peppers, sugar and garlic in a liquidiser and blend to a thick sauce.

Season the sauce to taste and stir in the olives. Mix the pasta with the tomato sauce. Tear the basil leaves and add them to the pasta with most of the marjoram and chives. Garnish with the remaining rosemary sprigs and herbs. Serve the salad cold in a large bowl or serving platter with freshly grated Parmesan cheese served separately in a bowl.

Squid and Tomato Salad

Whole squid can be bought fresh or frozen. It is best to use fresh, tender baby squid for this salad – small squid tend to have a fresher taste. If larger squid are used, cook them for a little longer until just soft. Squid is not very difficult to prepare, but most fishmongers will prepare them for you.

SERVES 4
PREPARATION TIME : *45 minutes*
CHILLING TIME : *1 hour*
COOKING TIME : *6 minutes*

INGREDIENTS
1lb (450g) squid
1 small onion
¼ pint (150ml) dry white wine
1 tablespoon virgin olive oil
1 tablespoon white wine vinegar
Salt and freshly ground black pepper
1 tablespoon fresh chopped dill
12oz (350g) tomatoes
4 spring onions
Dill sprigs for garnish
Lemon wedges for garnish

Calories per serving : 190 · Low in cholesterol
High in protein and iron from squid

To prepare the squid, pull the head and all its attachments out of the body sac, in a gentle but firm motion. Cut the tentacles away from the head and then remove the hard beak from the centre of the tentacles. Remove the transparent pen that emerges from the body and separate the fins. Pull off the purplish skin covering the body and fins. Rinse the body, tentacles and fins thoroughly. Slice each body into rings, cut the wings into ¼in (5mm) thick slices, and leave the tentacles whole.

Put the onion into a saucepan with the wine and bring to the boil. Add all the squid, cover and cook very gently for 5 minutes, or until tender. Pour through a sieve into a bowl and discard the onion. Reserve about 2 tablespoons of the cooking liquid in the bowl and allow to cool, then whisk in the oil, vinegar, salt and pepper. Add the squid and dill and mix together thoroughly. Then cover and chill in the refrigerator for approximately 1 hour.

Just before serving, plunge the tomatoes into a bowl of hot water for 30 seconds, then cold for 1 minute, until cool enough to peel off the skins with your fingers. De-seed and dice the tomatoes. Trim the spring onions, and finely slice the bulb and about 1in (25mm) of the stalk.

Mix the diced tomatoes with the thinly sliced spring onions and slices of squid. For an attractive effect, you can arrange slices of beef tomato around the side of the serving dish, or individual plates. Spoon the squid mixture onto the dish, or plates, and garnish with delicate sprigs of dill and some thinly cut lemon wedges. Serve immediately with fresh wholemeal or cracked wheat bread.

Slices of tender squid are served with tomatoes, spring onions and dill mixed with a vinaigrette.

Fresh Pear Salad

Pears and nuts make a crisp and slightly sweet salad. Use any dessert pears, such as Doyenné du Comice (usually known as Comice), Williams, Packham or Conference. Try to choose ones that are ripe but firm. Another variation of this salad, with an Italian influence, can be made by adding 2 tablespoons of crumbled blue cheese. You can use any combination of the lettuces that are listed in the recipe. Serve as a starter, side salad or light main course.

Fresh pear slices with pecan nuts, blue cheese and crisp salad greens make a crunchy, slightly sweet salad.

Prawns, cauliflower and pasta with light rosé wine.

INGREDIENTS
2 ripe dessert pears
1 Webb's Wonderful, oak-leaf or lollo rosso lettuce
1 spring onion
2 tender stalks celery
2 tablespoons walnuts or pecans
2 tablespoons blue cheese (optional)
DRESSING
1 small clove garlic
1 tablespoon fruit vinegar
2 tablespoons virgin olive oil
½ tablespoon salt
Freshly ground black pepper

Calories per serving : 195 · Low in cholesterol · High in dietary fibre from lettuce and pears

Wash and dry the lettuce leaves and cut them into thin strips. Trim the base of the spring onion and finely chop the bulb and about 3in (80mm) of the green stalk. Trim and chop the celery into thin slices.

Lightly toast the walnuts or pecans in a dry pan for 2 minutes, without burning, and put to one side.

Peel and crush the garlic and mix the dressing ingredients in a bowl. Peel and slice the pears and cover with dressing to prevent discolouring.

Combine all the ingredients together with the dressing, crumble in the optional blue cheese, toss well and serve immediately.

Prawn, Cauliflower and Pasta Salad

The anchovy essence used in this salad dressing greatly enhances the flavour of the prawns. It is available in bottles from large supermarkets. You can use either fresh or frozen cooked prawns. This dish can be made several hours in advance if kept covered in the refrigerator, and allowed to stand at room temperature for 20 minutes before serving. Serve as a light main course with French bread, chilled dry white or rosé wine, or dry French cider.

SERVES 4
PREPARATION TIME : *30 minutes*

INGREDIENTS
8oz (225g) cooked peeled prawns
8oz (225g) cauliflower florets
Salt
8oz (225g) small green pasta shapes
Sprigs of coriander or parsley for garnish
DRESSING
2 tablespoons low-calorie mayonnaise
1 tablespoon virgin olive oil
2 teaspoons anchovy essence
Freshly ground white pepper

Calories per serving : 305 · High in dietary fibre from cauliflower and pasta · High in protein from prawns

If using frozen prawns, defrost them and pat dry thoroughly. Divide the cauliflower florets into small sprigs, discarding the stalk ends, and add to a saucepan of salted, boiling water. Bring back to the boil and blanch for 2 minutes until tender yet crisp. Lift the florets from the pan with a slotted spoon and rinse under cold running water. Drain and pat dry.

Add the pasta shapes to the boiling water and cook according to packet instructions. When cooked, the pasta should still be slightly firm. Drain, rinse under cold running water and drain well.

Whisk the dressing ingredients in a salad bowl, add the cauliflower, pasta and prawns, and toss. Season to taste with pepper, garnish with coriander or parsley and serve.

Radicchio adds a splash of colour to this salad.

Tuna and Bean Salad

Originating from southern Italy, where the local people eat a healthy diet of fresh vegetables, herbs, fruit and olive oil, this dish uses tinned flageolet beans which look most attractive with the tuna. If wished, you can substitute cannellini or borlotti beans. Serve with warm wholemeal bread or rolls.

SERVES 4
PREPARATION TIME : *15 minutes*

INGREDIENTS
7oz (200g) tin tuna in brine
2 × 14oz (400g) tins flageolet beans
1 small red onion
2 tablespoons fresh chopped parsley
Radicchio or lettuce leaves for garnish
DRESSING
1 lemon
3 tablespoons virgin olive oil
Salt and freshly ground black pepper

Calories per serving : 320 · High in fibre and iron from beans · High in protein from fish and beans

Rinse the beans well, drain thoroughly and put them into a large serving bowl and set aside.

To make the dressing, squeeze the juice of half a lemon and mix it with the olive oil, then add salt and freshly ground black pepper to taste. Pour over the beans and toss well. Peel and thinly slice the onion and drain the tinned tuna. Flake the tuna and then fold it gently into the beans together with the onion.

Add the chopped parsley and season to taste. Add a little more lemon juice if wished. Wash and pat dry the radicchio or lettuce leaves, then tear them and arrange on individual plates. Spoon on the tuna and beans and serve.

Spinach, Smoked Chicken, Avocado and Mushroom Salad

This salad is easy to make and its creamy piquant dressing really brings it alive. Fresh, raw spinach is extremely healthy as none of its minerals or vitamins have been destroyed by cooking. If you cannot find any smoked chicken breasts or you are worried about sodium in your diet, maize-fed or normal chicken breasts are a good alternative. Hot garlic bread goes especially well with this salad.

This delicious salad makes a healthy main course.

SERVES 4
PREPARATION TIME : *30 minutes*
COOKING TIME : *20 minutes*
OVEN : *Preheat oven to 190°C (375°F, gas mark 5)*

INGREDIENTS

2 smoked, skinned and boneless chicken breasts
1 tablespoon virgin olive oil
12oz (350g) fresh young spinach
6oz (175g) button mushrooms
4 spring onions
1 large ripe avocado
Squeeze of lemon

DRESSING

1 clove garlic
4 tablespoons Greek or natural yoghurt
Juice of 1 orange
1½ teaspoons white wine vinegar
1 teaspoon French mustard
½ teaspoon tabasco
Freshly ground black pepper
2 tablespoons fresh chopped parsley for garnish

Calories per serving : 230 · High in protein from chicken · High in iron and carotene from spinach

Put the chicken breasts on an oiled baking tray and cook for 10 minutes on each side.

Meanwhile, wash all the spinach, discarding any large or discoloured leaves and coarse stalks. Tear any large leaves into smaller pieces and dry them in a salad-spinner or with kitchen paper.

To make the dressing, chop or crush the garlic and thoroughly mix all the ingredients, apart from the parsley, and season with plenty of black pepper.

Wash and slice the mushrooms. Wash, trim and slice the spring onions – only use the white bulb and bottom 3in (80mm) of the stems. Cut the avocado in half, discard the stone and peel, then dice the flesh into ¾in (20mm) cubes and sprinkle with the lemon juice to stop the avocado discolouring.

When the chicken is cooked, cut it into bite-size chunks and stir any juices into the dressing. While the chicken is still warm, mix all the ingredients for the salad in a large salad bowl. Serve the dressing separately in a small jug, or bowl, with the chopped parsley sprinkled over it.

Raw root vegetables make a light and crunchy salad.

Mixed Root Salad

Grated raw root vegetables are a rich, natural source of vitamins, minerals and fibre. Look for young vegetables that are small and firm. A food processor with a grating disc is helpful when making this salad.

SERVES 4
PREPARATION TIME : *10 minutes*

INGREDIENTS

8oz (225g) celeriac
8oz (225g) carrots
8oz (225g) kohlrabi
1 head chicory
1 teaspoon caraway seeds
1 tablespoon chopped chives

DRESSING

2 tablespoons virgin olive oil
½ teaspoon French mustard
1 tablespoon orange juice
2 teaspoons white wine or tarragon vinegar
Salt and freshly ground black pepper

Calories per serving : 130 · Low in fat and cholesterol · High in fibre from root vegetables

Peel and grate the celeriac, carrots and kohlrabi, and place in a bowl. Combine the dressing ingredients and pour over the vegetables. Spoon the salad into a serving dish, arrange the chicory leaves around it, sprinkle over the seeds and garnish with chives.

Turkish Salad

Rocket (or roquette) is a member of the mustard family, and its leaves have a slight sharpness that combines well with other greens. Rocket grows in Turkey almost like a weed. It is served there as a simple salad; in generous quantities with lemon wedges, or in a mixed salad with Feta cheese and mint. In this recipe the ratio of rocket to lettuce can be varied according to taste and availability. Choose fresh-smelling rocket with long, crisp leaves. This salad could be served as a starter, with warm fresh Greek or Turkish bread, or as a light side salad.

A mixed Turkish salad served in traditional style with Feta cheese and black olives garnished with mint.

INGREDIENTS

4oz (115g) crisp lettuce, such as Webb's or Iceberg
2oz (50g) rocket
3 tomatoes
4oz (115g) cucumber
1oz (25g) onion or spring onion
8 black olives
4oz (115g) Feta cheese
8 small sprigs mint

DRESSING

2 tablespoons olive oil
2 teaspoons lemon juice
1 teaspoon brown sugar
Pinch of mustard powder
Salt and freshly ground black pepper

Calories per serving : 150 · High in vitamin C from
tomatoes, cucumber and lemon

Wash the salad leaves and pat dry, then tear them into bite-size pieces. Wash all the remaining salad vegetables. Cut the tomatoes, cucumber and onion into varying shapes, by dicing some and slicing others, to add interest.

Arrange the salad leaves in a bowl or shallow dish and sprinkle the chopped ingredients on top. Stone and slice the olives and crumble the Feta cheese. Chop half the mint and sprinkle it over the salad, along with the olives and Feta.

Combine all the ingredients for the salad dressing and pour over the salad. Garnish with the remaining mint sprigs and serve immediately.

Sweet Pepper and Basil Salad with Feta

Feta cheese is a soft, white Greek cheese made from goat's or ewe's milk. Its tangy flavour combines with the pepper and basil to give a distinctive and refreshing taste. The peppers are cooked so that the skins burn and can be easily removed. Add the torn basil leaves just before serving.

Red and yellow peppers brighten up a simple salad.

INGREDIENTS

2 large red peppers
2 large yellow peppers
½ head frisée lettuce
6oz (175g) Feta cheese
Large sprig fresh basil leaves

DRESSING

4 spring onions
3 tablespoons virgin olive oil
1 tablespoon white wine vinegar
1 teaspoon fennel seeds (optional)
Salt and freshly ground black pepper

Calories per serving : 145 · Low in cholesterol · High
in vitamin C from peppers and lettuce

Bake the peppers in the oven for about 20 minutes, turning them two or three times, until their skins are blackened and blistered.

Trim the spring onions and thinly slice the bulb and green stalk. Mix with the remaining dressing ingredients and season to taste. Wash and dry the lettuce and put to one side.

Remove the peppers. When cool, peel off the skins, then halve, de-seed and cut into thin strips.

Shred the lettuce and arrange on individual plates with the peppers. Pour over the dressing, crumble the cheese over, and season with pepper. Garnish with torn basil leaves, and serve.

Gazpacho Salad

This crunchy and colourful salad gets its name from a famous chilled Spanish soup called Gazpacho, which originally came from the mountainous region of Andalusia in the south. There it is made from a mixture of tomatoes, cucumbers, peppers, garlic, olive oil and wine vinegar, all of which are included in this recipe. Another southern Spanish touch is added with the inclusion of toasted almonds for the garnish. This salad is perfect for summer, when vegetables are sweet, ripe and full of flavour.

A refreshing Spanish salad combines the traditional ingredients for Gazpacho. The cucumber adds its crunchy texture and cool flavour, while the spicy dressing and toasted almond garnish make this an unusual summer salad.

SERVES 6
PREPARATION TIME : *40 minutes*
CHILLING TIME : *30 minutes*

INGREDIENTS
1lb (450g) ripe tomatoes
1 large green pepper
1 large yellow pepper
½ small cucumber
A few black olives (optional)
2oz (50g) toasted almond flakes
DRESSING
3 or 4 cloves garlic
2oz (50g) ground almonds
3 tablespoons virgin olive oil
6 tablespoons tomato juice
2 tablespoons red or white wine vinegar
¼ teaspoon cayenne pepper or chilli powder (optional)
Salt and freshly ground black pepper

Calories per serving : 215 · Low in cholesterol · High in fibre from almonds, peppers and tomatoes
High in vitamin C from peppers

To remove the tomato skins, plunge the tomatoes into a bowl of hot water for 30 seconds, then into a bowl of cold water for 1 minute, until cool enough to peel off the skins with your fingers. Core and dice the peeled tomatoes into ½in (15mm) cubes.

Remove the stalks from the green and yellow peppers, then halve and de-seed them and cut them into thin strips. Cut the cucumber into strips about the same size as the peppers.

To make the dressing, finely chop or crush the garlic, and put it in a small bowl with the ground almonds. Whisk in the oil, tomato juice and wine vinegar – mixing thoroughly. Season to taste with cayenne or chilli, and salt and pepper.

Arrange the vegetables on a large serving dish or platter, or simply toss them together in a deep salad bowl. Pour over a small amount of the dressing, then cover and chill for 30 minutes.

Remove the chilled salad from the refrigerator and pour over the remaining dressing – or serve the dressing separately on the side. Garnish with the optional black olives and toasted almond flakes.

Mixed Sprout Salad with Tahina Dressing

Tahina is an oily paste made from sesame seeds that are roasted and ground. It is a staple food in most countries around the eastern end of the Mediterranean, and is used in Middle-Eastern cookery to give a strong nutty flavour to salads and sauces. It is available from large supermarkets, Greek shops and delicatessens. Bean sprouts are an extremely economical and nutritious food; the vitamin content of the seeds actually increases once the seeds have germinated. Some health shops even sell seeds which you can sprout yourself at home in jars. As they grow so quickly, it is possible to have a constant supply of fresh, organic vegetables. If you have any difficulty obtaining alfalfa sprouts or seeds, use double the amount of bean sprouts, or 6oz (175g) of bean sprouts with 2oz (50g) of cress.

SERVES 4
PREPARATION TIME : *10 minutes*

INGREDIENTS
4oz (115g) bean sprouts
4oz (115g) alfalfa sprouts
1 small red pepper
4oz (115g) white radish or mooli
Salt and freshly ground black pepper
1 lemon
Parsley sprigs for garnish
DRESSING
Juice of ½ lemon
1 clove garlic
2½ tablespoons tahina
2 teaspoons virgin olive oil
2 tablespoons chopped parsley

Calories per serving : 105 · Low in cholesterol · High in vitamin C from bean sprouts

---

Wash the bean and alfalfa sprouts in cold water, and then pat them dry thoroughly. Halve, de-seed and finely slice the pepper. Cut away the leaves and rootlets from the radish, and peel and slice it thinly. Combine the sprouts, pepper and radish in a bowl.

Season with salt and ground black pepper to taste.

To make the dressing, squeeze the lemon and peel and crush the garlic. Spoon the tahina paste into a separate bowl and beat in 3 tablespoons of warm water. Stir in 1 tablespoon of lemon juice and the oil, then add the garlic and parsley and mix thoroughly.

Cut the lemon into wedges. Turn the salad into a serving dish, and garnish with the lemon wedges and parsley. Serve the tahina dressing separately.

Finely sliced red pepper gives a splash of colour to this crunchy salad. Bean and alfalfa sprouts are tossed over the vegetables before the dish is garnished with lemon wedges and parsley. The rich nutty flavour of the tahina makes the salad taste quite substantial.

Salade Niçoise

Arguments are still raging in Nice about the true ingredients of their famous Salade Niçoise. You can vary the ingredients in this nutritious, low-calorie version according to season.

SERVES 4
PREPARATION TIME : *25 minutes*
COOKING TIME : *15-20 minutes*

INGREDIENTS
8oz (225g) tuna fish in brine
8oz (225g) small new potatoes
3oz (75g) french beans
4 eggs
1lb (450g) tomatoes
8 anchovy fillets
12 black olives
DRESSING
1 clove garlic
3 tablespoons virgin olive oil
1 tablespoon wine vinegar
Salt and freshly ground black pepper
Parsley for garnish

*Calories per serving : 355 · High in protein
from tuna fish and beans*

Scrub the new potatoes and cook them in boiling, lightly salted water for 15-20 minutes. Top and tail the beans and cook in boiling water for 3 minutes.

A light tuna salad from the south coast of France.

Hard-boil the eggs for 8 minutes and put to one side.

Cut the tomatoes and boiled eggs into quarters. Put them into a salad bowl with the anchovy fillets, olives and cooked new potatoes, which you can halve or quarter, depending on size.

To make the dressing, peel and crush the garlic, mix it with the oil and vinegar and season to taste. Flake the tuna, toss the salad with the dressing and garnish with finely chopped parsley before serving.

Wild Rice, Orange and Hazelnut Salad

Traditionally harvested by the American Indians, wild rice contains more protein than ordinary rice. Here the nutty flavours of wild rice and hazelnuts combine with a citrus dressing to make a refreshing salad. Brown rice can be used as a substitute.

SERVES 4-6
PREPARATION TIME : *25 minutes*
COOKING TIME : *30-40 minutes*
OVEN : *Preheat to 180°C (350°F, gas mark 4)*

INGREDIENTS
8oz (225g) wild rice
1 teaspoon salt
1 orange
3oz (75g) hazelnuts
4 tablespoons currants
1 fennel bulb
1 apple
Salt and freshly ground black pepper
DRESSING
3 spring onions
4 tablespoons lemon juice
1 teaspoon balsamic or cider vinegar
1 tablespoon fresh chopped parsley
1 tablespoon fresh chopped fennel leaves
¼ teaspoon crushed fennel seeds
3 tablespoons virgin olive oil
1 tablespoon hazelnut oil

*Calories per serving : 350 · Low in cholesterol · High
in dietary fibre from wild rice*

A tempting combination of roast hazelnuts and the dark kernels of wild rice lifted by a sharp citrus dressing.

Rinse the wild rice, soak for 45 minutes and drain. Bring 2½ pints (1.4 litres) of water to the boil with ½ teaspoon of salt, add the rice, cover and simmer for 30 minutes, until tender. Drain and set aside.

Grate the orange finely then squeeze the juice and put to one side with the peel.

Roast the hazelnuts on a baking tray in the oven for 6-8 minutes. Place the currants in a bowl, cover with hot water and soak for 5 minutes. Drain and cover with orange juice. Cool the roasted nuts, rub away the skins with your fingers and chop roughly.

Finely chop the spring onion bulbs and roughly chop 1 tablespoon of the green stalks. Mix with the grated orange peel, lemon juice, parsley, vinegar, remaining salt, fennel leaves and seeds, and oils. Drain the orange juice from the currants.

Slice the fennel, core and dice the apple and stir into the rice with the currants. Mix thoroughly with 1 tablespoon of the dressing. Before serving, add the remaining dressing and nuts, season and toss well.

San Francisco Salad

This colourful orange and walnut salad is traditionally decorated with edible nasturtium flowers. Some larger supermarkets sell nasturtium flowers and bags of ready-prepared mixed salad greens. You can buy rocket separately from good supermarkets and greengrocers. The rocket gives this salad a distinctive lemon and mustard taste.

SERVES 4-6
PREPARATION TIME : *15-20 minutes*

INGREDIENTS
8oz (225g) mixed green salad leaves (curly endive, rocket, nasturtium, lamb's lettuce)
2oz (50g) radicchio
2 large oranges
3oz (75g) shelled walnuts
2 tablespoons walnut oil
2 teaspoons clear honey
Large pinch of mustard powder
Salt and freshly ground black pepper
Nasturtium flowers for garnish

Calories per serving : 195 · Low in cholesterol · High in dietary fibre from salad greens

---

Mixed salad greens with oranges and walnuts.

Wash the green salad leaves and radicchio very thoroughly and pat dry. If necessary, tear the leaves into small pieces with your fingers.

Using a sharp knife, peel the oranges, cutting away all the pith and skin. Catch any juice in a salad bowl. Cut the oranges into segments between the membranes and put to one side.

Finely chop half the walnuts and put them into the bowl with the walnut oil. Then add the honey and mustard, season to taste with salt and freshly ground black pepper and beat well with a fork.

Add the salad leaves to the bowl with the orange segments and the remaining walnuts. Toss all the ingredients gently, then garnish with nasturtium flowers and serve immediately.

Potato Salad with Walnut and Lemon Dressing

Many varieties of waxy new potatoes are well suited for salads – the pink fir apple is especially good. Serve this delicious summer salad as a starter, or as a main course with cold ham or chicken.

SERVES 4
PREPARATION TIME : *20 minutes*
COOKING TIME : *12-18 minutes*

INGREDIENTS
8oz (225g) waxy new potatoes
1 small crisp green lettuce
1 small radicchio
A few leaves of frisée or oak-leaf lettuce
1 medium Cox's pippin apple
2oz (50g) walnut halves
DRESSING
½ pint (285ml) crème fraîche
1¼ tablespoons white wine vinegar
1¼ tablespoons lemon juice
Salt and freshly ground black pepper

Calories per serving : 160 · Low in cholesterol · High in dietary fibre from potatoes

---

The slightly bitter taste of radicchio complements a lemony crème fraîche dressing to make a refreshing salad.

Wash and drain the potatoes, removing any eyes or dark patches. Steam or boil whole for 14-18 minutes with the skins on. Meanwhile, trim, wash, dry and shred the salad leaves. Finely chop the apple and place in a bowl with the salad leaves and walnuts. When the potatoes are cooled, add them to the bowl.

Whisk together the dressing ingredients, pour over the salad, toss lightly and serve.

Marinated Fish in Lime Juice

A marinade is a liquid in which ingredients are soaked, so that they become tender and aromatic. This South American dish, known as Ceviche, was first introduced in Peru. It is still eaten there today, in the traditional style, with strips of hot red chilli. Marinated fish has become very popular in recent years and, as long as the fish is absolutely fresh, it tastes delicious. This recipe uses oregano and coriander to complement the fish. A dash of tabasco gives extra bite, and the thinly sliced onion adds a lovely sharpness. The fish is marinated for several hours in orange and lime juice which gives it a cooked appearance, while still retaining all the delicacy and flavour of the fresh fish. Any white fish fillets can be used in this recipe, such as haddock, cod, sole or plaice.

SERVES 4
PREPARATION TIME : *30 minutes*
MARINATING TIME : *5-12 hours*
COOLING TIME : *1 hour*

INGREDIENTS
1½lb (700g) white fish fillets
1 medium onion
1 orange
4 limes
2 teaspoons fresh chopped oregano
or 1 teaspoon dried oregano
2 tablespoons fresh chopped coriander
4 tablespoons virgin olive oil
1 teaspoon caster sugar
1 teaspoon tabasco
Salt and freshly ground black pepper
1 large lettuce heart
1 lime for garnish

Calories per serving : 280 · High in protein from fish · Low in fat

Originally from Peru, this raw-fish dish is healthy, appetising and simple to make. The fish is marinated for several hours in a combination of citrus juices, coriander leaves, pungent oregano and a dash of tabasco. Serve on a bed of crisp lettuce.

Skin the fish and cut into bite-size pieces. Chop the onion and place in a bowl with the fish. Squeeze the orange and 4 limes, then pour the juice over the fish and onion. Cover and place in the refrigerator for at least 5 hours, until the fish is opaque.

Add the chopped herbs to the fish, along with the olive oil, caster sugar and tabasco. Season to taste and mix thoroughly. Leave for 1 hour in a cool place, allowing the flavours to infuse.

Shred the lettuce and divide between 4 plates. Pile the marinated fish into the centre of the lettuce. Slice the remaining lime into wedges and use for garnish.

PASTA & RICE DISHES

Pasta, rice and grains form the basis for the healthy Mediterranean diet. Dozens of delicious sauces can be added to make nutritious starters or simple but exciting main courses.

Italian Pea and Ham Risotto

In northern Italy, where rice dishes are as popular as pasta dishes are in the south, this recipe is called 'Risi Bisi'. It is important to use an Italian short-grain rice to make this simple but tasty risotto.

SERVES 4
PREPARATION TIME : *10 minutes*
COOKING TIME : *30-35 minutes*

INGREDIENTS
12oz (350g) Italian short-grain risotto rice
4 thin slices lean cooked ham
½ large onion
2 tablespoons virgin olive oil
½ oz (15g) butter
2 pints (1.1 litres) chicken or vegetable stock
¼ pint (150ml) dry white wine
3oz (75g) frozen peas
Salt and freshly ground black pepper
2oz (50g) freshly grated Parmesan cheese

Calories per serving : 500 · High in fibre from rice
High in protein from ham, cheese and peas

Remove any fat from the ham. Cut the ham into thin slices and leave to one side. Finely chop the onion. Heat the oil and butter in a large saucepan over a gentle heat and cook the onion for 5 minutes, until soft and golden. Mix the rice with the onion and continue cooking it over a moderate heat for 5-7 minutes, until the grains of rice begin to burst. Meanwhile, heat the stock.

Stir the wine into the rice until it has been absorbed. Add ¼ pint (150ml) of the hot stock. Mix well and cook over a moderate heat until the stock has been absorbed, stirring continuously.

Continue cooking for 20 minutes, adding the remaining stock in ¼ pint quantities, until the rice is tender yet firm and the texture is creamy. Add the peas with the last measure of stock and season to taste. Fold in the ham and 1oz (25g) of the Parmesan. Divide the mixture between serving bowls, sprinkle with the remaining Parmesan and serve.

Spaghetti with Mussels

In southern Italy, this traditional dish is called 'Spaghetti con Cozze'. If wished you can use a wholemeal spaghetti for extra fibre, and substitute baby clams for the mussels. Serve in soup bowls.

SERVES 4
PREPARATION TIME : *30 minutes*
SOAKING TIME : *2-4 hours*
COOKING TIME : *15 minutes*

INGREDIENTS
2½ lb (1.1kg) mussels
¼ pint (150ml) dry white wine or fish stock
4 shallots
1 clove garlic
1 stick celery
1 teaspoon caster sugar
4 tablespoons chopped parsley
1 tablespoon olive oil
14oz (400g) spaghetti
Salt and freshly ground black pepper

Calories per serving : 490 · High in fibre from spaghetti · High in protein and iron from mussels

A favourite creamy risotto of northern Italy.

Succulent mussels cooked gently in white wine, or stock, go beautifully with spaghetti to make an elegant dish.

Wash the mussels thoroughly in two or three changes of cold water. Remove the beards from the mussels and discard any shells that are broken. Then sharply tap the mussels one by one, and throw them away if they do not close. Leave all the remaining mussels to soak in cold water for 2-4 hours to get rid of any sand or grit.

Pour the wine or fish stock into a large pan. Finely chop the shallots, crush the garlic, chop the celery and add to the pan, together with the sugar and half the chopped parsley. Simmer gently for 5 minutes. Increase the heat, add the mussels, cover the pan and cook for another 5 minutes, shaking the pan continuously until all the shells are open. Remove and discard any shells that remain closed.

Bring a large pan of water to the boil – without adding salt. Add the olive oil and spaghetti and cook, according to the instructions on the packet, leaving the pasta cooked but firm to the bite.

Meanwhile, tip all the cooked mussels into a muslin-lined colander, reserving the juices. Boil the juice for a few minutes until it has been reduced by half. Remove the mussels from their shells, keeping a few unshelled ones aside for garnish.

Drain the spaghetti and tip it back into the pan along with the reduced mussel stock, and cook gently together for 2 minutes. Then add the mussels and the other half of the parsley, and mix well and season to taste. Divide between the warmed soup bowls, garnish with the reserved mussels and serve.

Spanish Rice

This recipe is based on the famous Spanish dish 'paella', which is usually made with rounded, short-grain rice. It was originally cooked by Spanish peasants in a large, shallow pan called a 'paellera', over a charcoal fire in the open air. This low-fat version retains all the goodness and variety of the traditional dish, but uses long-grain brown rice for added fibre and a pleasant texture. Serve with a red wine punch such as Spanish sangria, or a Spanish red wine such as Rioja.

SERVES 4

PREPARATION TIME : *20-25 minutes*

COOKING TIME : *50 minutes*

INGREDIENTS

4 skinned chicken thighs
2 tablespoons olive oil
2 medium onions
1 clove garlic
1 large, ripe tomato
1 red pepper
8oz (225g) easy-cook, long-grain brown rice
¼ teaspoon ground turmeric
1 pint (570ml) chicken stock or water
3oz (75g) low-fat garlic sausage
1 teaspoon paprika
4oz (115g) frozen peas
6oz (175g) unshelled prawns
Salt and freshly ground black pepper

Calories per serving : 420 · High in fibre from rice
High in protein from chicken, prawns and sausage
High in vitamin C from peppers and tomatoes

Large prawns, chicken, garlic sausage and spices combine to create a festive rice dish that the Spanish traditionally cook for special family occasions.

Heat the oil in a large frying pan. Add the chicken thighs and fry them briefly over a moderate heat until golden-brown on both sides. Remove from the heat and put to one side.

Chop the onions and crush the garlic. Dice the tomato into ½in (15mm) cubes. Halve, de-seed and dice the pepper. Reduce the heat of the pan, add the onions and garlic and cook gently for 5 minutes. Add the tomato and pepper and cook for 2 minutes, before adding the rice and turmeric and cooking for a further 2 minutes, while stirring.

Pour the stock or water into the pan and bring to the boil. Replace the chicken, cover and cook over a moderate heat for 20 minutes.

Chop the garlic sausage and stir it into the pan with the paprika and peas. Cook for about 10 minutes, without stirring, until all the liquid has been absorbed and the rice is cooked.

Reserve 4 prawns in their shells for garnish and peel the rest. Add the peeled prawns to the pan and cook for 2 minutes. Taste and adjust the seasoning. Turn the mixture into a serving dish, garnish with the reserved prawns and serve.

A tarragon and wine sauce sets off the combination of chicken and artichokes. Crisp green vegetables add freshness and colour to this delicious pasta dish.

Chicken, Artichoke and Tarragon Pasta

Many of Europe's most interesting country recipes come from Provence, where Italian and French cuisines have been combined over the years. This dish has a fresh lemony tang which is complemented by the tarragon – one of the most popular herbs in southern France. The green vegetables make this pasta dish a complete meal in itself. Serve with one of the wines of Provence, such as Côtes du Luberon, Côtes du Ventoux or Coteaux d'Aix en Provence.

SERVES 4
PREPARATION TIME : *25 minutes*
COOKING TIME : *45 minutes*

INGREDIENTS
12oz (350g) green tagliatelle
2 uncooked chicken breasts or half a chicken
1 large onion
3 tablespoons virgin olive oil
2 tablespoons sherry vinegar or white wine vinegar
2 glasses vermouth or white wine
Juice of 1 lemon
14oz (400g) tinned artichoke hearts
3oz (75g) small mangetout
4oz (115g) broccoli
1 tablespoon fresh tarragon or 1 teaspoon dried
1 teaspoon caster sugar
4 tablespoons strained Greek yoghurt
Salt and freshly ground black pepper

Calories per serving : 300 · High in iron from chicken · High in vitamin C from lemon and broccoli

Cut the chicken breasts into 2in (50mm) strips. Peel and chop the onion finely. Heat 2 tablespoons of the olive oil in a frying pan, then add the vinegar and onion, and cook for 3 minutes over a medium heat. Add the chicken and cook for a further 3 minutes, stirring occasionally. Add the vermouth or wine, and the lemon juice, and reduce the heat so that the sauce is just simmering.

Meanwhile, drain the tin of artichokes and cut them into bite-size pieces. Trim the mangetout and break up the broccoli into tiny florets. Roughly chop the tarragon leaves, discarding the stalks, and add them to the chicken in the frying pan, along with the sugar and artichokes. Stir in the yoghurt, adjust the seasoning and continue to simmer over a low heat.

Add the pasta and remaining oil to a large pan of boiling salted water, and cook according to the instructions on the packet. Add the mangetout and broccoli florets to a smaller pan of boiling salted water and cook for 2-3 minutes.

Drain the pasta and vegetables as soon as they are cooked. Spoon the chicken, artichokes and sauce over the pasta, and arrange the green vegetables around the plate. Serve immediately.

A feast of oyster, chestnut and open cup mushrooms served with linguine makes a warming vegetarian dish. The thin strips of pasta are dressed with yoghurt and white wine and sprinkled with fresh parsley.

Linguine with Mushroom Sauce

Mushrooms are the fruits of certain fungi. There are an estimated 40,000 species growing wild around the world, and attempts to cultivate them have been made from the earliest times, by the ancient Greeks and Romans. The combination of mushrooms used in this recipe is only a guide, and you should choose according to personal taste and availability. Buy fresh, firm, blemish-free mushrooms. Cut the large mushrooms into thin slices, and leave the small varieties whole. This dish can be served as a starter, or as a simple main course with a salad.

SERVES 4
PREPARATION TIME : *20 minutes*
COOKING TIME : *25 minutes*

INGREDIENTS
10oz (275g) linguine pasta
1 medium onion
1 clove garlic
2 tablespoons virgin olive oil
8oz (225g) open cup mushrooms
3 tablespoons chopped parsley
2 small glasses dry white wine
5oz (150g) oyster mushrooms
5oz (150g) chestnut mushrooms
Salt and freshly ground black pepper
8fl oz (225ml) Greek yoghurt

Calories per serving : 300 · Low in cholesterol · High in fibre from pasta and mushrooms · High in protein from pasta and yoghurt

Chop the onion finely and crush the garlic. Heat the olive oil in a saucepan, add the onion and garlic and cook for 5 minutes over a gentle heat, until softened but not browned. Bring a pan of lightly salted water to the boil, ready for the pasta.

Meanwhile, wipe all the mushrooms clean on kitchen paper. If it is necessary to wash them, quickly rinse them in a colander under a cold tap. Finely chop the open cup mushrooms, and add them to the pan with the onion and garlic. Continue cooking gently until the mushrooms soften. Add 2 tablespoons of the chopped parsley and the wine, then bring to the boil and cook for 2-3 minutes until the wine has almost evaporated. Reduce the heat.

Add the linguine to the pan of boiling water and cook according to the packet instructions, leaving the pasta cooked but slightly firm.

Meanwhile, slice the remaining mushrooms. Add them to the reduced mushroom mixture and season with salt and pepper. Cover and cook gently for 5 minutes, until the mushrooms are just tender.

Drain the linguine, then return it to the saucepan and stir in the yoghurt. Pour the mushroom mixture onto the linguine, toss lightly together, then spoon onto serving plates. Sprinkle with the remaining parsley and serve immediately.

Baked Polenta with Tomato and Cheese

Polenta is made from cornmeal and is a staple food of northern Italy. It can be served as a soft, thick purée, or, as in this recipe, it can be left to set in a baking dish and then sliced. All manner of toppings can be added to baked polenta, so you can vary the ingredients according to availability. Fontina is a mild Italian cheese that is soft, yet firm enough to slice. If wished, you can substitute another soft cheese, such as Italian Ricotta Mozzarella. You will need a liquidiser for this recipe.

SERVES 4
PREPARATION TIME : *30 minutes*
COOKING TIME : *1 hour 30 minutes*
OVEN : *Preheat to 200°C (400°F, gas mark 6)*

INGREDIENTS
10oz (275g) polenta
8 thin slices ham or prosciutto
1 large onion
2 cloves garlic
1 tablespoon virgin olive oil
1 bay leaf
2 tablespoons fresh parsley
1 tablespoon chopped fresh basil
1¾ lb (800g) tinned whole tomatoes
½ teaspoon sugar
Salt and freshly ground black pepper
½ oz (15g) butter
6oz (175g) Fontina or other mild soft cheese
4oz (115g) goat or blue cheese
2 tablespoons fresh mixed herbs

Calories per serving : 620 · High in fibre from polenta · High in protein from ham and cheese High in vitamins A and C from tomatoes

Stir the polenta into a large pan of salted boiling water. Cook over a moderate heat, stirring continually for 5 minutes, then frequently for a further 35 minutes, until the polenta becomes very thick.

Meanwhile, cut the ham slices into strips, and finely chop the onion and garlic. Heat the olive oil in a frying pan and cook the onion, garlic, bay leaf, chopped parsley and basil over a gentle heat for 5 minutes. Add the tomatoes, breaking them up with a spoon. Increase the heat and cook for 15 minutes, until the mixture is soft.

Remove the bay leaf and blend the mixture in a liquidiser until smooth. Add the sugar and season to taste. Return to the pan and simmer for 10 minutes, until quite thick. Taste and adjust the seasoning.

Turn the cooked polenta into a buttered baking tray and leave to cool for 30 minutes, until firm, then turn out and cut into slices. Butter a gratin or baking dish, and spread a thin layer of tomato sauce over the bottom. Place the polenta slices in the dish in a single layer. Mix the ham strips with a small amount of the tomato sauce and spread over the polenta. Slice the Fontina and place the slices over the meat, then spread over the remaining sauce.

Break the goat or blue cheese into small pieces and sprinkle over the top, adding a little more black pepper. Bake, uncovered, for 30 minutes, then remove and sprinkle with the fresh mixed herbs. Serve immediately.

Two cheeses blend with polenta in a tomato sauce.

Simple Mediterranean flavours of olive oil, garlic, pine nuts and spinach turn spaghetti into an enticing dish.

Spaghettata

Spaghettata, or spaghetti with olive oil and garlic, is a very simple and quick dish which requires only a handful of basic ingredients. This is a good dish to make when provisions are running low. It makes a nourishing and filling meal which is excellent for lunch or supper, or when guests turn up unexpectedly. This recipe also uses spinach and pine nuts, but you can vary the ingredients and add grated cheese, tinned anchovies or shellfish for extra substance and flavour. Freshly chopped herbs also add their own distinctive taste.

SERVES 4
PREPARATION TIME : *2-3 minutes*
COOKING TIME : *12 minutes*

INGREDIENTS
12oz (350g) spaghetti or wholemeal spaghetti
1½ lb (700g) fresh spinach
5 tablespoons virgin olive oil
4 cloves garlic
2oz (50g) pine nuts
Salt and freshly ground black pepper

Calories per serving : 530 · High in fibre and protein from pasta · High in iron, vitamins A and C from spinach · Low in cholesterol

Wash the spinach, discarding any discoloured leaves and tough stalks. Add it to a pan of salted boiling water and cook for 1 minute. Drain in a colander, refresh under cold running water, and drain again. Squeeze the spinach to get rid of as much water as possible, chop it roughly and set aside.

Put the spaghetti in a pan of salted boiling water, with 1 tablespoon of the oil to prevent sticking. Cook according to the instructions on the packet, leaving the pasta cooked but slightly firm.

Meanwhile, preheat the grill to a moderate heat. Crush the garlic. Heat the remaining oil in a large saucepan, and cook the garlic over a gentle heat until soft and golden. Roast the pine nuts under the grill until lightly browned, taking care not to burn them, and add them to the pan.

Drain the spaghetti well. Add it to the garlic and pine nuts. Mix in the spinach thoroughly, season to taste, and serve immediately.

Polenta with Chicken Livers and Sage

Made from cornmeal, polenta is a kind of Italian semolina. There are two types of polenta; finely ground or coarse. Although the cooking method is the same for both, finely ground polenta is easier to work with. You might like to try an Italian smoked ham in this dish, such as pancetta.

Polenta is eaten with many dishes in northern Italy.

SERVES 6
PREPARATION TIME : *15 minutes*
COOKING TIME : *1 hour*

INGREDIENTS
10oz (275g) polenta
2 slices bacon or Italian smoked ham
1 small onion
2 sprigs parsley
8oz (225g) fresh mushrooms
1½ oz (40g) butter
1lb (450g) chicken livers
3 tablespoons white wine
1 tablespoon shredded fresh sage
Salt and freshly ground black pepper
Fresh sage leaves for garnish

Calories per serving : 400 · High in protein and iron from liver and bacon · High in vitamin A from liver

Bring 2½ pints (1.4 litres) of water to the boil, add 1 tablespoon of salt and reduce to a simmer. Slowly add the polenta, stirring constantly for 5 minutes, then frequently for 25 minutes.

Meanwhile, remove the rinds and excess fat from the bacon. Chop the bacon or ham and onion into small pieces. Finely chop the parsley and slice the mushrooms. Melt 1oz (25g) of butter in a pan and sauté the bacon or ham and onion for 8 minutes over a medium heat. Stir in the parsley, chicken livers and mushrooms and cook for 4-5 minutes. Stir in the wine and sage, season, and cook for 2 minutes. As soon as the polenta is cooked, stir in the remaining butter. Spoon into serving bowls, pour over the chicken-liver sauce, garnish with sage and serve.

Fresh springtime vegetables mixed with fettucine.

Fettucine Primavera

'Primavera' is Italian for 'springtime' and this recipe uses fresh spring vegetables, which can be varied according to availability. A healthy pasta sauce is made with olive oil, yoghurt and low-fat cheese.

SERVES 4
PREPARATION TIME : *15 minutes*
COOKING TIME : *30 minutes*

INGREDIENTS
10oz (275g) fettucine
4oz (115g) broccoli florets
4oz (115g) cauliflower florets
2 small young carrots
2oz (50g) small white button mushrooms
1 small red pepper
1 small green pepper
1 medium onion
3oz (75g) low-fat Cheddar cheese
2 tablespoons virgin olive oil
4 tablespoons low-fat yoghurt
2 tablespoons whipping cream
Generous pinch of cayenne pepper
Salt and freshly ground black pepper

Calories per serving : 420 · High in fibre from vegetables · High in protein from cheese · High in vitamins A and C from vegetables

Bring a large saucepan of salted water to the boil. Meanwhile, trim and divide the broccoli and cauliflower into small florets. Peel the carrots and cut into small sticks about 2in (50mm) long. Slice the mushrooms thinly with the stalks still attached. Halve, core and de-seed the peppers, then cut them lengthways into thin strips. Thinly slice the onion and grate the cheese.

Blanch the broccoli, cauliflower and carrots in the boiling water for 2 minutes. Reserving the water, lift the vegetables from the water with a slotted spoon and put them in a colander, then drain again.

Bring the pan of water to the boil again, ready to cook the pasta, adding more water if necessary.

Meanwhile, heat the oil in a saucepan or casserole dish. Add the sliced onion and cook over a gentle heat for 7-8 minutes, stirring frequently. Add the peppers and mushrooms and cook for a further 5 minutes, stirring frequently. Remove the pan from the heat and stir in the yoghurt, cream, 2oz (50g) of the cheese, and the cayenne. Season to taste with salt and pepper, and set aside.

Cook the pasta according to the packet instructions, leaving the pasta cooked but slightly firm to the bite. Towards the end of the cooking time, return the sauce to a very gentle heat and add the blanched vegetables. Stir the sauce and vegetables until heated through, taking care not to let the mixture boil, then taste and adjust the seasoning.

Drain the pasta well and put into a serving bowl. Pour over the sauce and sprinkle with the remaining cheese. Serve immediately.

Crab Cannelloni with Tomato Sauce

Cannelloni is a large pipe-shaped pasta and, unlike most other pastas, it does not need to be pre-boiled. Use a fresh Parmesan cheese and grate it yourself; the best kind is called Parmigiano-Reggiano, and it is available from large supermarkets and Italian delicatessens. This recipe uses a crab and spinach stuffing instead of the traditional meat filling, which makes for a much lighter dish, and the fresh tomato sauce is low in calories but high in vitamin C. You will need a liquidiser for this recipe.

SERVES 6
PREPARATION TIME : *50 minutes*
COOKING TIME : *40 minutes*
OVEN : *Preheat to 190°C*
(375°F, gas mark 5)

INGREDIENTS
18 dried cannelloni tubes
1lb (450g) fresh white crabmeat
or 2 × 7oz (200g) tins crabmeat
8oz (225g) frozen spinach
3 tablespoons chopped fresh basil
or 1 teaspoon dried
Salt and freshly ground black pepper
3oz (75g) fresh Parmesan
Sprigs of thyme, parsley or basil for garnish
TOMATO SAUCE
1 medium onion
1 large carrot
1 medium stick celery
4 cloves garlic
1 tablespoon virgin olive oil
3 × 14oz (400g) tins plum tomatoes
6 tablespoons dry white wine
4 teaspoons sugar
2 bay leaves
1 teaspoon each chopped fresh thyme, parsley and
basil, or ½ teaspoon each dried
2 level teaspoons salt
Freshly ground black pepper

Calories per serving : 620 · High in protein from crab
and cheese · High in iron and carotene from spinach

To make the tomato sauce, peel and finely chop the onion and carrot. Trim and finely chop the celery and crush the garlic. Put the oil into a medium saucepan, add the chopped vegetables and garlic, and sauté gently until soft.

Add the remaining tomato sauce ingredients and bring to the boil. Turn the heat down and leave to simmer for 15 minutes, stirring occasionally to break up the tomatoes. Allow to cool for 5 minutes, then pour into a liquidiser and purée, thinning the sauce by adding a little water if necessary. Put the tomato sauce to one side. Drain the crab, if using tinned. Place in a bowl and flake the flesh with a fork.

Heat the spinach in a saucepan with a tablespoon of water, or as instructed on the packet, for about 4 minutes. Drain thoroughly and add to the crab. Mix the basil with the crab and spinach, and season with salt and pepper.

Divide the filling equally between the cannelloni tubes and spoon in. Pour half the tomato sauce into a large ovenproof dish, and place the filled tubes on top, then pour the remaining sauce over them.

Bake for 30 minutes. Meanwhile, grate half the Parmesan cheese and slice the rest into shavings for garnish. Remove the cannelloni from the oven and sprinkle the grated Parmesan over the baked sauce, then bake for a further 10 minutes. Garnish with sprigs of herbs and the Parmesan shavings, and serve immediately.

Along Italy's west coast, nutritious crabmeat is often substituted for beef, as in this delicious pasta bake.

Couscous with Seven Vegetables

Couscous is the name given to both the national dish of Morocco, and the durum wheat pasta granules from which it is made. The granules are placed in a colander or steamer that is lined with cheesecloth or a clean tea towel and steamed over a saucepan containing a broth. As the broth is heated, steam starts to rise and cooks the couscous. Slowly the couscous absorbs the delicious flavours of the vegetables, meat and spices. The couscous is dried and separated several times to give a light, moist texture. This is not as complicated as it sounds, but it is possible to buy precooked couscous.

SERVES 4-6
PREPARATION TIME : *1 hour*
COOKING TIME : *1¼ hours*

INGREDIENTS
1lb (450g) couscous
1½ -2lb (700-900g) lamb shoulder or neck
2 cloves garlic
2 medium onions
2 tablespoons virgin olive oil
2 tablespoons butter
2 cinnamon sticks
2 teaspoons coarse salt
2 teaspoons freshly ground black pepper
1 chilli pepper
½ teaspoon saffron
½ teaspoon turmeric or paprika
10 sprigs parsley
10 sprigs coriander
4 carrots
3 small turnips
3 courgettes
1 aubergine
3 tomatoes
1¼ lb (575g) can chickpeas

Calories per serving : 685 · High in fibre from chickpeas and couscous · High in protein and iron from meat and vitamins A and C from vegetables

Place the couscous in a bowl and cover with cold water. Drain immediately through a fine sieve and return to the bowl. Work the couscous with your fingers to separate the granules. Leave to stand.

Meanwhile, dice the lamb into 2in (50mm) cubes, finely chop the garlic and slice the onions into rings. Prepare the broth by putting the lamb, garlic, onions, oil, butter, cinnamon sticks, salt, pepper, chilli pepper, saffron, turmeric or paprika, 6 sprigs of parsley, 6 sprigs of coriander, and 3 pints (1.7 litres) of water into a large pan. Bring to the boil.

Work the couscous between your fingers again and place 8 tablespoons of it into the lined colander,

over the gently simmering broth. When steam rises through, add the rest and steam for 30 minutes.

To prepare the vegetables, peel and quarter the carrots and turnips. Trim and quarter the courgettes and slice the aubergine. Quarter and seed the tomatoes. Drain and rinse the chickpeas.

Remove the colander and empty the steamed couscous into a large flat pan. Sprinkle with a small glass of salted water. Separate the grains with your fingers, spread the couscous out and leave to dry.

Meanwhile, add the carrots and turnips to the broth and steam for 10 minutes. Then stir in the aubergines, courgettes and tomatoes, and just enough water to cover all the vegetables, if there is insufficient. Return the couscous to the colander and steam for 20 minutes. Add the chickpeas to the broth and steam for a final 10 minutes.

Reserving the broth liquid, drain the vegetables and meat. Heap the couscous onto a large, warmed serving plate and moisten with ¼ pint (150ml) of the broth and make a hollow in the middle. Spoon the meat and vegetables into the hollow. Chop the remaining herbs for garnish and serve.

Moroccan couscous, made from durum wheat, piled with fresh vegetables and scented with herbs.

Mixed Fish Lasagne

You can vary the fish used in this dish according to personal taste and availability, although it is best to include one smoked variety. The fillets will need to be skinned and boned, or you can ask the fishmonger to do this for you. If using 'easy-cook' lasagne, save the liquid from the can of sweetcorn to add to the sauce. The lasagne will not cook evenly if it overlaps in the oven, so use a square or rectangular oven dish if possible.

SERVES 4-6
PREPARATION TIME : *20 minutes*
COOKING TIME : *1 hour*
OVEN : *Preheat to 200°C
(400°F, gas mark 6)*

INGREDIENTS
12oz (350g) fresh cod fillet
12oz (350g) smoked cod fillet
1 medium onion
1½ oz (40g) butter
1½ oz (40g) plain flour
1 pint (570ml) semi-skimmed or whole milk
1 bay leaf
1 tablespoon olive oil
6oz (175g) lasagne or spinach lasagne
2 tablespoons chopped parsley
*1 × 7oz (200g) tin sweetcorn (no salt or
sugar added)*
Salt and freshly ground black pepper
1½ oz (40g) Parmesan cheese
Parsley for garnish

*Calories per serving : 460 · High in fibre from pasta ·
High in protein from fish, cheese and milk*

Skin and bone the fillets of fish and cut into 1in (25mm) squares. Peel and finely chop the onion. Melt the butter in a frying pan, add the chopped onion and cook gently for 5 minutes. Stir in the flour, cook for a further minute, then gradually stir in the milk and bring to the boil.

Remove from the heat and add the bay leaf and the fish. Mix well, cover and leave aside for 20 minutes, and the sauce will start to cook the fish.

A textured lasagne, rich with fish, cheese and herbs.

Add the oil and lasagne to a very large saucepan of salted boiling water, and cook according to the instructions on the packet. Drain thoroughly.

Stir the fish and remove the bay leaf, then stir in the chopped parsley. Drain and reserve the sweetcorn liquid if you are adding this to the sauce. Stir in the sweetcorn and season to taste. Line a square or rectangular ovenproof dish with a quarter of the sauce, cover with a third of the lasagne, add another quarter of the sauce and layer with more lasagne and continue, finishing with a layer of sauce.

Grate the Parmesan cheese and sprinkle evenly over the top, then place in the oven and bake for 45 minutes, until the top is golden-brown and the lasagne is bubbling. Garnish with parsley and serve.

Pasta Quills with Salmon, Broccoli and Tarragon

The Italians call the hollow quill-shaped pasta used in this recipe 'penne'. As with all pasta, the healthiest kind is the hard, high-protein variety made with durum wheat, which preserves the wheatgerm. If desired, you can substitute canned salmon or chopped smoked salmon for the fresh salmon.

SERVES 4
PREPARATION TIME : *20 minutes*
COOKING TIME : *20 minutes*
OVEN : *Preheat to 110°C (225°F, gas mark ¼)*

INGREDIENTS
10oz (275g) pasta quills
8oz (225g) broccoli
½ tablespoon virgin olive oil
8oz (225g) fresh salmon
1 glass white wine or vermouth
8 sprigs fresh tarragon
6oz (175g) low-fat fromage frais
6 tablespoons single cream
2 teaspoons lemon juice
Salt and freshly ground black pepper
8 lemon wedges for garnish

Calories per serving : 460 · High in protein from salmon, cheese and cream · High in iron from salmon · High in fibre from broccoli · High in vitamin C from lemon juice and broccoli

Break up the broccoli into bite-size florets and finely dice any stalks. Cook the pasta quills in boiling salted water with a dash of oil for 10 minutes, then add the broccoli and cook for a further 2 minutes.

Meanwhile, cut away any skin from the salmon, dice the flesh into 1in (25mm) cubes and remove any bones. Put the fish into a large pan with a pinch of salt, the wine or vermouth, and enough water to cover the fish. Gently bring to the boil and simmer for 3 minutes. Transfer into a bowl with a slotted spoon, cover and keep warm in the oven.

Remove the leaves from 4 of the tarragon stalks, chop them finely and combine with the fromage frais and single cream. Stir into the fish juices remaining in the pan and heat very gently until just warmed. Drain the pasta and broccoli in a colander. Reserve a few of the broccoli florets for garnish and add the rest of the broccoli and pasta to the tarragon sauce. Stir in the lemon juice, season to taste, and reheat gently for 2 or 3 minutes.

Remove the salmon from the oven. Spoon the pasta onto plates, arranging the salmon cubes over the top. Garnish with the broccoli florets, sprigs of tarragon and lemon wedges. Serve immediately.

Juicy chunks of fresh salmon with tender green broccoli tossed in a tangy tarragon, wine and lemon sauce.

A dry white wine goes well with this hearty dish of fettucine noodles, basil and sweet red and yellow peppers. A hot red chilli makes the dish slightly spicy.

Fettucine with Two Pepper Sauce

Fettucine is a fresh, noodle-shaped pasta made with eggs and plain wheat flour – which results in a lighter dough than pasta made with durum wheat. Available from Italian delicatessens and most large supermarkets, it only takes a few minutes to cook. The bright red and yellow of sweet peppers adds colour to this dish, which can be served as a starter or, with additional pasta, as a main course. You will need a liquidiser for this recipe.

SERVES 4
PREPARATION TIME : *15 minutes*
COOKING TIME : *40 minutes*
OVEN : *Preheat to 240°C
(475°F, gas mark 9)*

INGREDIENTS
*1lb (450g) fettucine
3 red peppers
3 yellow peppers
2 large onions
4 cloves garlic
1 red chilli pepper
1½ tablespoons virgin olive oil
Salt and freshly ground black pepper
2 sprigs rosemary
1 bay leaf
Fresh basil leaves for garnish*

Calories per serving : 460 · Low in cholesterol · High in fibre, protein and iron from fettucine · High in vitamin C from peppers

Place the whole peppers on a baking tray and bake in the oven for 20-25 minutes, until the skins are charred and blistered. Put to one side to cool.

Meanwhile, chop the onions into small cubes, finely chop the garlic, and de-seed and finely slice the chilli pepper.

Pour the oil into a frying pan and sauté the onions and garlic over a moderate heat for 10 minutes, until soft and lightly coloured. Remove half the onions from the pan and keep to one side.

With your fingers, peel away the charred skins from the cooled peppers, then halve and de-seed them. Keeping the yellow peppers to one side, add the red peppers to the onions in the pan, along with the chilli pepper, and stir-fry for 3-4 minutes.

Pour the contents of the pan into a liquidiser with 3 tablespoons of water and blend until smooth, then season to taste with salt and pepper.

Stir-fry the yellow peppers with the rosemary, bay leaf and reserved onions in the pan for 3-4 minutes. Remove the herbs and blend until smooth in the liquidiser, then adjust the seasoning.

Cook the fettucine in salted boiling water for a few minutes, or according to the instructions on the packet, leaving the pasta cooked but slightly firm. Meanwhile, gently reheat the red and yellow pepper sauces separately.

Drain the pasta and transfer to serving plates. Pour over the sauces separately, allowing them to merge if wished, garnish with the basil leaves and serve.

Nutty Fruit Risotto

This combination of fruit, nuts and spices has a distinctive Middle-Eastern flavour. Ready-to-eat, mixed dried fruit is easy to obtain at supermarkets and adds a naturally sweet taste to the risotto. This recipe uses sunflower seeds, which are an excellent source of nutrients, including iron, and vitamins B and E. Choose unsalted nuts for this dish, such as peanuts, cashews and pine nuts. This nutritious main course is especially suitable for vegetarians, but it also goes well with lean ham, chicken and turkey. Any leftovers are excellent served cold and tossed in a little French dressing.

SERVES 4
PREPARATION TIME : *10 minutes*
COOKING TIME : *35 minutes*

INGREDIENTS
10oz (275g) Italian easy-cook brown rice
9oz (250g) packet ready-to-eat dried fruit salad
5 celery sticks
1 large onion
2 tablespoons groundnut or sunflower oil
½ oz (15g) butter
1 teaspoon ground cinnamon
1 teaspoon ground ginger
Salt and freshly ground black pepper
2 tablespoons fresh coriander
5oz (140g) mixture of sunflower seeds and nuts

Calories per serving : 500 · Low in cholesterol · High in fibre from brown rice, dried fruit and nuts High in iron from brown rice and dried fruit

---

Roughly chop the fruit salad. Trim and roughly chop the celery sticks. Peel and finely chop the onion. Heat the oil and butter in a large pan until the butter melts. Add the onion and celery and cook over a

gentle heat, stirring frequently, for 8 minutes, until the vegetables are soft and golden, but not brown.

Add the chopped fruit, and 1½ pints (850ml) of water. Bring to the boil, then cover the pan and simmer for 10 minutes.

Add the rice, ground cinnamon and ginger. Season to taste with salt and freshly ground black pepper, and stir to mix thoroughly. Cover and cook over a low to moderate heat, according to the time on the rice packet instructions, until the rice is cooked and all of the liquid has been absorbed.

Chop the fresh coriander. Fold in the sunflower seeds and nuts, and half the coriander. Taste and adjust the seasoning, then transfer the risotto to a serving bowl and sprinkle with the remaining coriander. Serve immediately.

A dish of rice scented with cinnamon and ginger and textured with dried fruits, sunflower seeds and nuts, conjures up the distinctive taste of the Middle East.

Creamy Mushroom and Walnut Pasta

Yoghurt replaces the rich cream and butter sauce traditionally used in this recipe – yet it still has a rich and creamy taste. The farfalle pasta used in this recipe is one of the prettier shapes; resembling bow ties or butterflies. Serve as a starter or main course with a light red wine, such as a Brouilly or Chinon.

SERVES 4
PREPARATION TIME : *10 minutes*
COOKING TIME : *15-20 minutes*

INGREDIENTS
12oz (350g) farfalle pasta
4oz (115g) shelled walnuts
½ medium onion
10oz (275g) field mushrooms
1 clove garlic
½ oz (15g) butter
2 tablespoons virgin olive or walnut oil
8fl oz (225ml) Greek strained yoghurt
2 tablespoons fresh chopped parsley
Salt and freshly ground black pepper

Calories per serving : 315 · High in protein and fibre from nuts and pasta

Butterfly pasta with field mushrooms and walnuts.

Bring a saucepan of lightly salted water to the boil, ready for the pasta. Wrap the walnuts in a clean tea towel and roughly crush them with a rolling pin.

Add the pasta to the pan of boiling water and cook according to the instructions on the packet, leaving the pasta cooked but slightly firm.

Meanwhile, peel and finely chop the onion. Wipe the mushrooms clean on kitchen paper, or quickly rinse them in a colander under a cold tap, and thinly slice them. Finely chop the garlic, or crush it in a mortar with a pestle. Gently melt the butter in a large pan and add the walnuts. Cook them over a gentle heat for 2-3 minutes, stirring frequently, until they turn a deeper colour – taking care not to burn them.

Remove the walnuts and put them to one side. Wipe the pan clean and add the olive or walnut oil and onion to the pan. Cook over a moderate heat for 7-8 minutes, stirring occasionally, until the onion is soft and golden. Add the mushrooms and garlic, then turn to a high heat and cook for 5 minutes, stirring continuously, until the juices run and the mushrooms are tender.

Remove the pan from the heat. Add the walnuts and yoghurt, 1 tablespoon at a time, mixing well after each addition. Return the pan to a very low heat and continue stirring until the yoghurt is heated through – taking care not to let the yoghurt boil and separate. Add half the parsley and season to taste with salt and freshly ground black pepper.

Drain the pasta quickly and immediately mix it with the sauce. Taste and adjust the seasoning. Transfer the pasta and its sauce to serving plates. Sprinkle over the remaining parsley and serve.

Spaghetti Bolognaise

Over 200 pasta shapes have been invented to date, but the long-established favourite is spaghetti; and even this can be bought in a large assortment of thicknesses and lengths. 'Spaghettini' are thin strands of spaghetti and 'spaghettoni' are thick. This recipe is a healthy version of a traditional Italian dish. The use of lean meat reduces the fat content, and by cooking it slowly you will need less oil. If wished, you can use wholewheat spaghetti for extra fibre, and replace some of the minced beef with extra mushrooms. Serve with a green salad.

Spaghetti with a rich beef, wine and tomato sauce, cooked with fresh herbs, makes a delicious pasta favourite.

SERVES 4
PREPARATION TIME : *10 minutes*
COOKING TIME : *1 hour*

INGREDIENTS
1lb (450g) spaghetti
1 large onion
2 cloves garlic
6oz (175g) mushrooms
1 tablespoon virgin olive oil
1lb (450g) minced beef
14oz (400g) tin tomatoes
2 tablespoons chopped fresh thyme, marjoram and
parsley, or 2 teaspoons dried mixed herbs
1 tablespoon tomato purée
1 teaspoon English mustard
1-2 glasses red wine
1 bay leaf
Salt and freshly ground black pepper
4oz (115g) Parmesan cheese

Calories per serving : 685 · High in fibre from pasta
High in protein and iron from beef

Finely chop the onion. Crush the garlic and thinly slice the mushrooms. Heat the olive oil in a pan and sauté the onion and garlic over a low heat for 15 minutes, until soft and lightly coloured. Add the mushrooms and stir-fry over a moderate heat for a further 3 minutes. Spoon the mixture into a bowl and leave to one side.

Reduce the heat and add the minced beef. Cook slowly over a low heat for 5 minutes until the meat juices appear, breaking up the meat with a spoon. Raise to a moderate heat and cook for another 5 minutes, until browned. Bring a large pan of water to the boil, ready to cook the spaghetti.

Drain the tin of tomatoes, then add them to the pan with the minced beef, along with the onion and mushroom mixture, the mixed herbs, tomato purée, mustard, wine and bay leaf. Bring to the boil, then reduce the heat and leave to simmer slowly for 30 minutes, adding more wine if necessary to keep the sauce moist. Remove the bay leaf and season.

Cook the spaghetti in the pan of boiling water, according to the instructions on the packet, leaving the pasta cooked but slightly firm. Drain and serve with the bolognaise sauce, and a bowl of Parmesan to pass around.

Chicken and Mushroom Risotto

A true Italian risotto should have a thick and creamy consistency, which can only be obtained by using the right kind of short-grain rice. Many supermarkets sell 'Italian risotto rice', but it is worth a visit to an Italian delicatessen to buy Arborio rice, which is better still and will provide the thickest, creamiest rice. This recipe provides a practical means of using up small amounts of leftover poultry or meat. After a roast chicken dinner, the chicken carcass can be boiled up with onions, carrots and herbs to make the stock for this recipe.

A creamy mushroom risotto, with tender chicken pieces and pine nuts flavoured with white wine and parsley.

SERVES 4
PREPARATION TIME : *15 minutes*
COOKING TIME : *40 minutes*

INGREDIENTS
8oz (225g) cooked chicken
2 medium onions
1 clove garlic
6oz (175g) mushrooms
2 tablespoons virgin olive oil
8oz (225g) Italian risotto or Arborio rice
¼ pint (150ml) dry white wine
¾ pint (450ml) chicken stock
Salt and freshly ground black pepper
1oz (25g) pine nuts
2 tablespoons chopped parsley

Calories per serving : 400 · High in fibre from rice
High in protein from chicken

Chop the onions, crush the garlic and slice the mushrooms. Dice the chicken. Heat the oil in a saucepan and gently fry the onions and garlic for 5 minutes. Add the mushrooms and fry for 2 minutes, then stir in the rice for a further 2 minutes. Add the wine and stir until absorbed by the rice.

Add half the stock and bring to the boil, then lower the heat and simmer gently, stirring frequently, until the stock has been absorbed. Add the remaining stock and simmer very gently, stirring frequently, until absorbed. After about 15 minutes, mix in the diced chicken and cook for 5 minutes, until the rice is creamy and tender but firm to the bite.

Season to taste and turn into a serving dish. Sprinkle with the nuts and parsley before serving.

Pasta with Courgette and Carrot Ribbons

Green and white tagliatelle – also known as Paglia e fieno – looks especially attractive mixed with carrot and courgette ribbons. The green pasta is made with spinach. You can substitute spaghetti if necessary. Choose firm courgettes with glossy, unblemished skins for this vegetarian main course or starter.

Fresh courgette and carrot strips add crunch to pasta.

SERVES 6
PREPARATION TIME : *10-15 minutes*
COOKING TIME : *10-15 minutes*

INGREDIENTS
1lb (450g) green and white tagliatelle
1lb (450g) carrots
1lb (450g) courgettes
2 cloves garlic
2 tablespoons fresh basil
5 tablespoons virgin olive oil
2 tablespoons pine nuts
Salt and freshly ground black pepper

Calories per serving : 470 · High in fibre and protein from pasta and nuts · High in iron from pasta and courgettes and vitamin A from carrots

Peel the carrots and top and tail the carrots and courgettes. Using a vegetable peeler, shred them into ribbons. Cut wide ribbons into thinner strips with a knife. Finely chop the garlic and basil.

Blanch the courgettes and carrot ribbons in boiling salted water for 1 minute. Drain, rinse under cold running water, and drain again.

Cook the pasta according to the packet instructions, leaving the pasta cooked but slightly firm. Meanwhile, heat the oil in a large saucepan or casserole dish. Add the courgette, carrot, pine nuts, garlic and basil, and toss over a moderate heat until the vegetables are heated through and coated in oil.

Drain the pasta and add it to the saucepan or casserole. Toss well, season to taste and serve.

Turmeric gives this rice dish its slightly golden colour, and combines with cardamom to add a distinctive Middle-Eastern aroma. Rice, pine nuts and raisins provide the pilaf with an interesting texture.

Persian Pilaf

In the Middle East and India, pilafs are served as a side dish instead of plain boiled rice. But they can also form a vegetarian main course, topped with plain yoghurt and accompanied with Indian bread, such as nan or chappati. Pilafs are traditionally made with clarified butter (ghee), but this recipe uses groundnut oil, which is healthier. In India and the Middle East, the rice is gently simmered until all the cooking liquid has evaporated or been absorbed. Use basmati rice for this dish – its fine texture and sweet

aroma are especially suitable for Middle-Eastern cooking. The crust that forms at the bottom of the rice is considered a great delicacy in Persian cookery. Called 'tahdiq' it is reserved for special guests. Serve the pilaf as a starter or main dish with a green salad and freshly chopped mint, if desired.

SERVES 4-8
PREPARATION TIME : *10 minutes*
STANDING TIME : *15 minutes*
COOKING TIME : *25 minutes*

INGREDIENTS
12oz (350g) basmati rice
1 medium onion
8 cardamom pods
4 medium, ripe tomatoes
3 tablespoons groundnut oil
½ teaspoon ground turmeric
Salt and freshly ground black pepper
3oz (75g) pine nuts
2oz (50g) raisins or currants
Fresh coriander for garnish (optional)

Calories per serving : 460 · Low in cholesterol · High in fibre from rice, nuts and currants

Put the rice in a sieve and rinse under cold running water until the water runs clear, then put to one side. Chop the onion finely. Crush the cardamom pods into a fine powder in a mortar with a pestle, or with a rolling pin on a flat surface.

Plunge the tomatoes into a bowl of hot water for 30 seconds, then cold for 1 minute, until cool enough to peel off the skins with your fingers. Roughly chop the peeled tomatoes.

Heat the oil in a heavy saucepan or flameproof casserole dish. Then add the onion, cardamom and turmeric, and cook over a gentle heat, stirring frequently, for about 7-8 minutes, until the onion is soft, but not brown. Add the chopped tomatoes and the rice. Mix well with the onion, then pour in 1 pint (570ml) of boiling water. Stir well and season to taste, then cover the pan tightly with a well-fitting lid and cook over a very low heat for 15 minutes, without lifting the lid.

Uncover the pan, add the pine nuts and raisins or currants and fork through gently. Cover with the lid again, turn off the heat and leave the pan to stand for a further 15 minutes without lifting the lid. Taste and adjust the seasoning. Transfer to a warm serving dish, or you can leave it in the cooking dish so that the 'tahdiq', or rice crust, is preserved in the bottom of the bowl. Garnish with fresh sprigs of coriander and serve immediately.

Pasta Provençale

The most common vegetables in Provençale cooking – aubergines, courgettes, peppers, tomatoes and onions – make a colourful and delicious sauce for pasta. The fusilli pasta used in this recipe comes in the shape of small twists. If you have a bottle of red wine open, add a glass to give the sauce a lift. Freshly grated Parmesan or Cheddar can be served separately for sprinkling over the pasta. Serve with a mixed or green salad for a healthy vegetarian main course, or it can be eaten on its own as a snack.

SERVES 4
PREPARATION TIME : *10-15 minutes*
COOKING TIME : *45 minutes*

INGREDIENTS
10oz (275g) fusilli pasta
2 medium-sized courgettes
1 small aubergine
1 red pepper
1 yellow pepper
1 medium onion
1-2 cloves garlic
1lb (450g) tinned chopped tomatoes or
fresh ripe tomatoes
2 tablespoons virgin olive oil
1 tablespoon tomato purée
2 teaspoons chopped fresh basil
1 teaspoon dried herbes de Provence
Salt and freshly ground black pepper
1 glass red wine (optional)
3oz (75g) Parmesan or Cheddar cheese (optional)

Calories per serving : 180 · Low in cholesterol · High in fibre from pasta · High in vitamin C from peppers and tomatoes

Trim the courgettes, peel the aubergine, and halve and de-seed the peppers, then cut the vegetables into thin strips, about ½in (15mm) thick. Thinly slice the onion and crush the garlic. If using fresh tomatoes, plunge them into a bowl of hot water for 30 seconds, then cold for 1 minute, until cool enough to peel off the skins with your fingers.

Heat the oil in a heavy saucepan or casserole dish. Add the chopped onion and cook over a gentle heat for about 7-8 minutes, stirring frequently, until the onion is soft. Add the peppers and cook for a further 5 minutes, stirring often. Then mix in the courgette and aubergine strips, and the garlic. Cook for 5 minutes, stirring, then add the tomatoes, tomato purée and herbs. Season to taste.

Bring to the boil, stirring often. Then lower the heat, half cover the pan and simmer for 20 minutes. Stir occasionally and add a little water, or wine, if the sauce seems dry. Warm a large serving bowl.

Meanwhile, cook the pasta according to the packet instructions, leaving it cooked but slightly firm. Grate the cheese if using it.

Drain the pasta and turn into the warmed bowl. Pour the sauce over the pasta and toss well. Garnish with slivers of Parmesan and serve.

A light but warming dish of fusilli pasta coated in a basil and tomato sauce, served with peppers, aubergines, courgettes, garlic and herbes de Provence.

Fresh Tagliatelle with Tomatoes and Olives

Popular Italian black olives include the slightly acid Liguria, the salty Lugano, the mild Ponentine, and the slightly wrinkled Gaeta. Olives complement a typical, slightly sweet, tomato sauce and pasta. Be careful not to overcook the fresh tagliatelle.

SERVES 4

PREPARATION TIME : *10 minutes*

COOKING TIME : *40 minutes*

INGREDIENTS

1lb (450g) fresh tagliatelle
1 medium onion
2 cloves garlic
3 tablespoons olive oil
1½ lb (700g) tomatoes
1 tablespoon fresh chopped oregano
2 tablespoons white wine (optional)
2oz (50g) black olives
Salt and freshly ground black pepper
3oz (75g) grated Parmesan cheese
Oregano leaves for garnish

Calories per serving : 580 · High in fibre from pasta · High in protein from cheese and pasta

A simple, tasty dish that uses the flavours of Italy.

Finely chop the onion and crush the garlic. Heat the oil in a pan and gently fry the onion and garlic for 5 minutes, stirring occasionally.

Immerse the tomatoes in a bowl of boiling water for 30 seconds, then cold for 1 minute, until cool enough to peel off the skins with your fingers. Chop the peeled tomatoes roughly.

Add the tomatoes, oregano and optional wine to the pan, then cover and cook gently for 20-25 minutes, until the tomatoes are quite soft.

Meanwhile, add the pasta to a pan of boiling salted water and cook according to the packet instructions – 3-4 minutes is usually enough.

Stone and chop the olives and stir them in with the tomatoes. Heat gently for 5 minutes and adjust the seasoning. Drain the pasta and turn it into a serving dish. Pour over the tomato sauce, sprinkle over the Parmesan cheese, garnish with oregano and serve.

Quick Spaghetti Carbonara

'Spaghetti alla Carbonara' is the Italian version of bacon and eggs; it is very easy to make. Beaten eggs, added to the spaghetti before the rest of the sauce, are cooked immediately by the heat of the pasta.

SERVES 4

PREPARATION TIME : *10 minutes*

COOKING TIME : *20 minutes*

INGREDIENTS

1lb (450g) spaghetti or wholewheat spaghetti
2 tablespoons virgin olive oil
1 medium onion
8 rashers smoked bacon
4oz (115g) mature Cheddar or fresh Parmesan cheese
3 eggs
3 tablespoons milk or 4 tablespoons double cream
Salt and freshly ground black pepper
3 tablespoons fresh chopped parsley

Calories per serving : 680 · High in fibre from pasta High in protein and iron from bacon and eggs

The strong flavour of smoked bacon in 'Spaghetti alla Carbonara' is softened by the creamy mixture of the cheese, milk and eggs. Season the dish with plenty of freshly ground black pepper.

Preheat 4 serving plates. Bring a large saucepan of salted water to the boil and add 1 tablespoon of the olive oil and the spaghetti. Cook the pasta according to the instructions on the packet – it should be tender but still firm to the bite.

Peel and chop the onion. Heat the rest of the oil in a frying pan and briefly fry the bacon until just cooked on both sides. Remove the bacon from the pan, leaving the cooking juices behind. Add the onion to the pan and cook for 4 minutes over a medium heat, stirring occasionally, until it softens and begins to turn golden.

While the onion is cooking, chop the bacon into large squares and discard the rinds. Grate the cheese onto a plate, then beat the eggs thoroughly with a fork in a small bowl.

When the onions are cooked, add the bacon squares and milk or cream to the pan and season to taste. Reduce the heat.

Drain the cooked spaghetti and return it to the pan. Quickly stir in the beaten eggs and the grated cheese. Stir in the remaining ingredients and divide between the heated plates. Garnish with the parsley and extra twists of black pepper, and serve.

141

Cannelloni Stuffed with Spinach and Cheese

'Cannelle' means pipes in Italian, and 'cannelloni' means large pipes. This pasta dish is baked in a herby tomato sauce made with tinned, chopped tomatoes – which are useful for making quick and tasty sauces – especially if you add some extra fresh ingredients to give more flavour and body. If wished you can substitute basil or parsley for the oregano. Serve as a starter or main course, with a fresh, crispy salad and an Italian red wine such as a Chianti Classico. You will need a 12 × 9in (300 × 230mm) baking dish for this recipe.

Tubes of pasta filled with a delicious mixture of spinach and creamy cheese baked in a rich tomato sauce flavoured with oregano, garlic and red wine.

SERVES 4-6
PREPARATION TIME : *45 minutes*
COOKING TIME : *20-25 minutes*
OVEN : *Preheat to 180°C (350°F, gas mark 4)*

INGREDIENTS
12 dried cannelloni tubes
1lb (450g) frozen or 2lb (900g) fresh spinach
8oz (225g) curd cheese
Freshly grated nutmeg
Salt and freshly ground black pepper
2 × 14oz (400g) tins chopped tomatoes
1-2 cloves garlic
2 tablespoons fresh oregano or 2 teaspoons dried
4 tablespoons red wine (optional)
1oz (25g) Parmesan cheese

Calories per serving : 460 · High in protein from cheese and pasta · High in iron and carotene from spinach · High in vitamins A and C from tomatoes

If you are using frozen spinach, thaw and boil in a saucepan over a high heat for 2 minutes, stirring all the time. Turn the spinach into a fine sieve and press it with the back of a spoon to extract any remaining liquid. If you are using fresh spinach, wash it thoroughly, discarding any discoloured leaves or tough stalks, and then chop roughly. Put the wet spinach in a pan and cover. Cook for 2-3 minutes until the leaves wilt, and drain well.

Transfer the spinach to a bowl, add the curd cheese and nutmeg, and season to taste. Beat well to mix. Divide the spinach and cheese mixture equally between the cannelloni tubes and spoon it in.

Put the chopped tomatoes into the saucepan. Finely chop the garlic and herbs and add to the tomatoes with the optional wine, and season to taste. Bring to the boil, stirring to break up the tomatoes as much as possible.

Pour enough of the tomatoes into a 12 × 9in (300 × 230mm) baking dish to cover the bottom. Lay the cannelloni tubes in the dish, side by side in a single layer, so that they form two rows of tubes that fit snugly together. Pour over the remaining tomato mixture. Grate the Parmesan and sprinkle evenly over the cannelloni. Bake for 20-25 minutes, until bubbling. Serve straight from the dish.

FISH & SHELLFISH

An abundance of fresh fish and seafood
is available all year round for creative meals
that are high in protein and low in calories. Fish is
easily digested, and fish oils help to fight
heart disease when eaten regularly.

Crisp mangetout, mango and succulent prawns cooked in soy sauce flavoured with sherry and ginger.

Prawn, Mangetout and Mango Stir-fry

An ancient form of Chinese cooking; stir-frying was developed in poor farming areas where there was a lack of fuel. The intense heat, built up from a small fire, cooks the thinly sliced food very quickly. The heat seals in the food's nutrients, making it one of the healthiest ways to cook. Stir-frying has another advantage – only a small amount of oil is needed. Although it is possible to use an ordinary frying pan, a Chinese wok is best for stir-fry dishes, as its shape ensures that the heat is evenly distributed all over the pan. The subtle flavours of ginger and soy sauce in this recipe enhance the sea-fresh prawns. Serve with freshly cooked rice or noodles.

SERVES 4
PREPARATION TIME : *15 minutes*
COOKING TIME : *5 minutes*

INGREDIENTS
8oz (225g) peeled prawns
1 medium onion
6oz (175g) mangetout
1 large ripe mango
1 tablespoon vegetable or sesame oil
2 teaspoons grated fresh ginger
1 tablespoon dry sherry
1 tablespoon soy sauce
1 level teaspoon cornflour

Calories per serving : 245 · High in fibre and vitamin C from mangetout and mango · High in protein

Halve and thinly slice the onion. Top and tail the mangetout. Peel and slice the mango.

Heat the oil in a wok or large frying pan and stir-fry the onion and coarsely grated ginger for 2-3 minutes until just tender. Add the mangetout and prawns and stir-fry for 1 minute.

Add the mango, sherry and soy sauce, and fry for 1 minute while mixing the cornflour with 1 tablespoon of water. Add the cornflour to the pan, cooking and stirring for another 1-2 minutes, until the sauce thickens. Serve immediately.

An elegant dish of fresh sole and salmon roulades.

Sole and Salmon Roulades

Rouler means 'to roll' in French, hence the name roulade. In this elegant dish for special occasions, fillets of sole are rolled around delicate slivers of smoked salmon. The peas in the roulade sauce add bright colour and a slightly sweet flavour. Serve with new potatoes and a selection of fresh vegetables. You will need a liquidiser for this recipe.

SERVES 4
PREPARATION TIME : *20 minutes*
COOKING TIME : *25 minutes*
OVEN : *Preheat to 190°C (375°F, gas mark 5)*

INGREDIENTS
8 small fillets Dover or lemon sole
4oz (115g) smoked salmon
½ oz (15g) butter
Salt and freshly ground black pepper
¼ pint (150ml) white wine
4 spring onions
4oz (115g) frozen peas
4 sprigs of chervil or parsley

Calories per serving : 425 · High in protein from fish · High in iron from salmon

Skin the fillets of sole and divide the salmon into 8 pieces. Lay a piece of salmon over the skin-side of each sole fillet and roll up from head to tail. Place the rolls in a buttered ovenproof dish, season with pepper and pour over the wine. Cover the dish with a lid or foil and bake for 15 minutes. Switch off the oven and remove the fish. Reserving the cooking juices, lift the fish onto a serving dish, cover, and put to one side in the warmed oven.

Trim and finely chop the spring onions. Strain the cooking juices through a sieve into a saucepan. Add the peas, spring onions and chervil or parsley. Bring to the boil and simmer gently for 4 minutes.

Strain the sauce through a sieve into a liquidiser and blend, then pass the sauce through a sieve into a saucepan. Season and reheat. Pour the sauce around the fish roulades and serve.

Spicy Prawns with Chinese Noodles

Both Italy and China lay claim to having been the first country to invent pasta; the Italians with their spaghetti, and the Chinese with their delicious egg noodles. Noodles are still a staple food in northern China, where it is too cold to grow rice. There they are made from wheat flour and water, while in southern China eggs are added. Egg noodles can be bought dried or fresh from large supermarkets, delicatessens and Chinese grocers. If wished, you can substitute Italian egg noodles. The spicy, hot oriental prawns in this recipe are stir-fried in a wok or nonstick frying pan. Some red chillies are much hotter than others, so use them with caution if you are unfamiliar with a particular variety. It is always safest to remove the hot seeds.

SERVES 5
PREPARATION TIME : *15 minutes*
COOKING TIME : *12 minutes*

INGREDIENTS
12oz (350g) Chinese egg noodles
6 medium tomatoes
1-2 fresh red chillies
6 spring onions
2-3 cloves garlic
2in (50mm) piece fresh root ginger
2½ tablespoons groundnut or sunflower oil
8oz (225g) large peeled prawns
1 tablespoon tomato purée
Salt and freshly ground black pepper

Calories per serving : 440 · High in vitamin C from tomatoes · High in protein from prawns

A fiery mixture of chillies, spring onions, garlic and fresh ginger served with egg noodles and stir-fried prawns.

146

To remove the skins, plunge each tomato into a bowl of hot water for 30 seconds, then cold for 1 minute, until cool enough to peel off the skins with your fingers. Cut the flesh of each tomato into 8 segments.

Trim both ends of each chilli and slit them in half lengthways. Hold the chillies under running water and rub away some, or all, of the seeds. Trim the spring onions, and slice the bulb and about 3in (75mm) of the green stalk. Peel and finely chop the garlic and peel and grate the ginger.

In a wok or heavy nonstick frying pan, heat 2 tablespoons of the oil over a moderate heat for 1-2 minutes, until hot. Add the spring onions and ginger and stir-fry for 2-3 minutes, until just softened. Remove and drain on kitchen paper.

Add the prawns and chillies to the wok or pan and stir over a moderate heat for 1-2 minutes. Remove and drain on kitchen paper. Cook the egg noodles in boiling, salted water according to the instructions on the packet. Preheat a large serving bowl.

Meanwhile, add the remaining oil and the garlic to the wok or pan and stir-fry over a moderate heat for 2-3 minutes, until the garlic is just golden. Add the tomatoes, increase to a high heat and cook for 2 minutes, stirring continually. Add the tomato purée, season with salt and pepper to taste and mix thoroughly. Return the prawns and other drained ingredients to the wok or pan and mix again. Heat through for 1 minute then remove from the heat.

Drain the noodles and transfer them to the heated serving bowl. Pour the prawn mixture over the top and serve immediately.

Monkfish with Leeks

Monkfish tail has a mild, sweet flavour with a firm texture that holds its shape well during cooking. In this recipe the fish is simply steamed on top of the heated vegetables. Because of the way leeks grow, dirt is found between the layers of the leaves and you should take care to wash the leeks thoroughly. Trim off the rootlets and remove any tough outer leaves, then split the leeks lengthwise and hold under cold running water. Chinese cabbage has a crunchy texture and a faint flavour of mustard that lends itself well to this dish. Serve with mashed or new potatoes sprinkled with ground nutmeg.

Monkfish on a bed of tender steamed vegetables.

SERVES 4
PREPARATION TIME : *15 minutes*
COOKING TIME : *20 minutes*

INGREDIENTS
1lb (450g) monkfish tail
½ tablespoon lemon juice
Salt and freshly ground black pepper
3 leeks
6oz (175g) mushrooms
6oz (175g) Chinese cabbage
1oz (25g) butter

Calories per serving : 165 · Low in fat · High in fibre from vegetables · High in protein from fish

Trim any pieces of tough membrane, skin and gristle from the fish. Cut into 4 pieces, discarding the backbone, sprinkle over the lemon juice and season.

Finely chop the leeks, mushrooms and cabbage. Melt the butter in a pan, add 4 tablespoons of water and the leeks, cover and cook over a gentle heat for 10 minutes, stirring occasionally. Add the mushrooms and cabbage, cover again and cook gently for 5 minutes. Season to taste.

Place the fish on top of the vegetables in the pan, add another 4 tablespoons of water, cover and cook for 5 minutes, until the fish is cooked through. Lift out the fish pieces, arrange them on a serving dish surrounded by the vegetables and serve.

Baked Cod with Devilled Topping

Devilled dishes first appeared on English menus early in the 18th century, when hot spicy devilled sauces were a popular means of disguising poor quality meat. They were also a tasty way to use up leftovers. This recipe goes particularly well with mashed potatoes, baked tomatoes and courgettes.

SERVES 4
PREPARATION TIME : *10 minutes*
COOKING TIME : *20 minutes*
OVEN : *Preheat to 200°C (400°F, gas mark 6)*

INGREDIENTS
4 × 6oz (175g) pieces cod fillet
1 medium onion
1oz (25g) unsalted butter
1 teaspoon Worcestershire sauce
1 teaspoon English mustard
1 teaspoon curry paste
1oz (25g) fresh breadcrumbs

Calories per serving : 175 · Low in fat · High in protein · Good source of vitamin B12 from cod

Spicy devilled topping adds zest to baked cod fillets.

Skin, wash and dry the fish fillets, and arrange them in a lightly oiled baking dish.

Peel and finely chop the onion. Melt the butter in a pan, then add the onion and remaining ingredients. Mix well and spread evenly over the 4 fish fillets.

Bake the fillets in the oven for 20 minutes, and serve immediately.

Salmon, Halibut and Vegetable Pasta

Fish is one of the healthiest of all high-protein foods. It is low in fat and contains valuable oils in its flesh that some scientists believe can lower the levels of cholesterol in the body. This nutritious fish pasta is brought alive by its sweet and sour orange and dill sauce. Serve as a main course, or by reducing the quantities you can serve it as a colourful starter. Use either white or green fresh tagliatelle.

SERVES 4
PREPARATION TIME : *40 minutes*
COOKING TIME : *30 minutes*

INGREDIENTS
1lb (450g) fresh tagliatelle
1 medium onion
2 tablespoons olive oil
1 tablespoon white wine or dill vinegar
1 large glass dry white wine
Juice of 2 oranges
2 tablespoons granulated sugar
1½ tablespoons chopped fresh dill
8oz (225g) fresh salmon
8oz (225g) fresh halibut
4oz (115g) small French beans
4oz (115g) broccoli
3 tablespoons strained Greek yoghurt
Salt and freshly ground black pepper

Calories per serving : 520 · High in fibre from beans and broccoli · High in protein and iron from fish

Finely chop the onion. Heat 1½ tablespoons of oil in a large frying pan over a medium heat. Add the onion and vinegar and cook for 5 minutes, stirring

Pasta with tempting chunks of salmon and halibut, fresh green vegetables and an orange and dill sauce.

occasionally, until the onion starts to brown. Add the wine, orange juice, sugar and most of the dill – reserving a few sprigs for garnish – then reduce the heat and stir occasionally, until the sauce simmers.

Use a sharp knife to skin the fish. Removing any bones, cut the flesh into 1in (25mm) cubes.

Bring a large and a small pan of water to the boil. Top and tail the beans and break the broccoli into small florets. Add the beans to the small pan and cook for 1 minute, then add the broccoli florets and cook for a further 2 minutes. Drain the vegetables in a colander and refresh them by running them under cold water for just a few seconds. This stops the vegetables from cooking any more and helps them to retain their bright green colour and crispness. Drain them once more, and keep them warm in a low oven.

Add the pasta to the large pan with the remaining olive oil and cook according to the packet instructions. Bring a small pan of water to the boil, reduce to a moderate heat and add the diced fish. Poach gently for 2-3 minutes, then drain. Meanwhile, stir the yoghurt into the sauce in the frying pan, season to taste, and continue to simmer.

Drain the cooked pasta and divide between plates. Spoon over the sauce and add the diced fish. Then carefully arrange the vegetables by pressing them into the pasta so that they look bright and fresh. Garnish with the reserved dill sprigs and serve.

Mackerel with Rhubarb and Apple Sauce

In Britain, fresh mackerel are in season all year round, but they are at their best between April and June. This recipe has a fruity rhubarb sauce and goes well with potatoes and peas or green beans.

SERVES 4
PREPARATION TIME : *30 minutes*
COOKING TIME : *25 minutes*

INGREDIENTS
4 fresh mackerel
1 teaspoon virgin olive oil
Freshly ground black pepper
1 red-skinned apple
Parsley or watercress sprigs for garnish
SAUCE
6oz (175g) young pink rhubarb
6 tablespoons apple juice
½ oz (15g) butter

Calories per serving : 425 · High in protein and vitamin D from mackerel

A sharp, fruity sauce complements grilled mackerel.

Preheat the grill to a medium setting. Remove the heads from the fish, cut each fish open along the stomach, remove the entrails and wash thoroughly. Press hard along the length of the fish to loosen and remove the backbone, cutting it at the tail end.

To make the sauce, cut the rhubarb into 1½in (40mm) chunks and place in a saucepan with the apple juice. Simmer for 10 minutes until the mixture is soft, then beat in the butter and keep warm.

Meanwhile, place the fish on a lightly oiled baking tray and grill them for 5-7 minutes on either side, sprinkling with a little freshly ground black pepper before turning.

Pour the sauce over the mackerel and garnish with the apple slices, parsley or watercress sprigs.

Salmon Kedgeree

Usually made with smoked haddock and served at breakfast, this fish and rice dish is turned into a very special lunch or supper meal when it is made with fresh salmon. If wished, you can poach the fish in white wine rather than milk.

SERVES 4-6
PREPARATION TIME : *15 minutes*
COOKING TIME : *30 minutes*

INGREDIENTS
12oz (350g) fresh salmon fillets
2 eggs
12oz (350g) basmati rice
1 green pepper
3 celery sticks
1 small onion
2 tablespoons groundnut oil
1½ pints (850ml) fish or chicken stock
2 teaspoons curry powder
¼ teaspoon cayenne pepper
Salt and freshly ground black pepper
½ pint (285ml) skimmed or semi-skimmed milk
2 tablespoons fresh parsley

Calories per serving : 455 · High in protein from eggs, salmon and milk · High in iron from curry powder and eggs · High in vitamin C from pepper

In India, during the last days of the Raj, the British adopted a rice and lentil dish called 'khichri' and turned it into 'kedgeree' by replacing the lentils with fish and eggs. This dish goes well with bread and a green salad.

Hard-boil the eggs and put to one side in their shells. Put the rice in a sieve, rinse under cold running water until it runs clear. Set aside to drain.

Halve, core and de-seed the green pepper, then dice finely. Trim and chop the celery sticks into small pieces. Peel and chop the onion finely.

Heat the oil in a large pan. Add the chopped vegetables and cook over a moderate heat for 10-15 minutes, stirring frequently, until softened. Meanwhile, heat the stock in a separate pan.

Add the curry powder and cayenne pepper to the vegetables and stir constantly for 2 minutes. Stir in the rice, then slowly stir in the hot stock. Bring to the boil, stirring constantly, then lower the heat and season with salt and black pepper. Cover and simmer for 15 minutes, until the rice is tender but still firm to the bite, and almost all the stock has been absorbed.

Meanwhile, shell the hard-boiled eggs and put to one side. Put the fish fillets skin-side down in a single layer in a frying pan. Pour over the milk and add enough water to just cover the fish. Season with pepper to taste and bring to the boil. Lower the heat, cover and simmer very gently for 8 minutes, basting occasionally, until cooked through. Remove the fish from the liquid and flake into large pieces over a plate, discarding the skin and bones.

When the rice is cooked, remove the pan from the heat and gently fold in the flaked fish and freshly chopped parsley. Adjust the seasoning and transfer to a serving dish. Cut the hard-boiled eggs into quarters or eighths and use to garnish the kedgeree. Serve immediately.

Succulent baby squid are spiced with a piquant tomato and pepper sauce, and garnished with herbs.

Grilled Squid with Tomato and Pepper Sauce

Just after they have been caught, squid are amongst the most beautiful of all sea creatures (firm with shimmering iridescent colours), but within minutes they take on the familiar white appearance seen on the fishmonger's slab. In this recipe the squid are served with a piquant tomato sauce, a traditional Catalan recipe. Squid freeze well – they can even be tenderised by the process. Squid are easy to prepare but fishmongers will do it for you.

SERVES 4-6
PREPARATION TIME : *45 minutes*
COOKING TIME : *40 minutes*

INGREDIENTS
1½ lb (700g) baby squid
2 tablespoons olive oil
4 tablespoons white wine
SAUCE
1 red chilli
3 sweet red peppers
2oz (50g) blanched almonds
8oz (225g) ripe tomatoes
3 cloves garlic
3 tablespoons virgin olive oil
2 tablespoons wine vinegar
Salt and freshly ground black pepper
Sprigs of fresh basil or thyme for garnish

Calories per serving : 340 · Cholesterol free · High in protein from squid and almonds · High in vitamin C from peppers and tomatoes

To make the sauce, preheat the grill on a medium-high setting. Slice open and de-seed the red chilli. Put it on a baking tray with the 3 sweet peppers, almonds and unpeeled tomatoes and garlic. Sprinkle all the vegetables with 1 tablespoon of oil and put under the grill. Watch them carefully, removing the almonds after 5 minutes, or as soon as they start to turn brown. The garlic and tomatoes should be grilled for 10-15 minutes until they have softened. Turn the peppers occasionally and grill for about 25 minutes until their skins are black and blistered.

Meanwhile, prepare the squid. Pull the head and the innards attached to it away from the body in a gentle but firm motion. Cut away the tentacles from the head and then remove the hard beak from the centre of the tentacles. Remove the transparent pen that emerges from the body and separate the fins. Pull off the purplish skin covering the body and the fins. Rinse the body, fins and tentacles.

Grind the almonds in a pestle and mortar or in a food processor. Then peel the peppers, tomatoes and garlic. De-seed the peppers and chop the chilli, tomatoes and the peppers finely. Preheat the grill.

Slice the squid on one side so you can spread them

out flat over a baking tray and sprinkle them with 2 tablespoons of oil and the white wine. Place them about 3in (75mm) under the grill and heat for 10 minutes, until they have turned golden and opened.

Meanwhile, combine the sauce ingredients in a pan, stirring in the remaining 2 tablespoons of oil and the vinegar. Season to taste. Warm the sauce over a gentle heat. As soon as the squid are ready, garnish with the herbs and serve.

Crab Cakes

This recipe uses both the white crab meat, found in the crab's claws, and the brown meat from the main shell. When buying prepared crab meat from your fishmonger or supermarket, make sure that the meat is fresh and firm. Serve these cakes with a fresh tomato or tartare sauce, and a green salad.

SERVES 4
PREPARATION TIME : *20 minutes*
CHILLING TIME : *1 hour*
COOKING TIME : *30 minutes*
OVEN : *Preheat to 220°C (425°F, gas mark 7)*

INGREDIENTS
4oz (115g) prepared fresh or tinned crab meat
1¼ lb (575g) potatoes
*2 tablespoons fresh or 2 teaspoons dried
chopped chives*
Juice of ½ lemon
1 teaspoon Worcestershire sauce
3-4 drops tabasco sauce
2 egg yolks
Salt
1 tablespoon olive oil
Lemon wedges for garnish
COATING
2 tablespoons wholemeal flour
Salt and freshly ground black pepper
4oz (115g) fresh wholemeal breadcrumbs
2 egg whites

Calories per serving : 345 · High in fibre from wholemeal flour and potatoes · High in protein from crab and egg · High in zinc from crab

---

Peel and roughly chop the potatoes, then cook them in salted, boiling water for 10-15 minutes, until just tender. Drain and return to the pan and cook over a low heat for 1-2 minutes to evaporate as much water from the potatoes as possible.

Mash the potatoes thoroughly and put them into a bowl. Add the chopped chives to the potatoes, along with the crab meat, lemon juice, Worcestershire sauce and tabasco. Bind the mixture together with the egg yolks and season to taste with salt.

Place the bowl in the refrigerator and leave to chill for 1 hour, then roughly mould the mixture into 4 cakes, each about ½in (15mm) thick.

To make the coating, put the flour onto a flat plate and season to taste. Put the breadcrumbs onto a second flat plate. Pour the egg whites into a shallow bowl, whisk them lightly with a fork and mix in ¼ teaspoon of salt and a generous amount of pepper. Dip the cakes in the flour, then in the egg white and finally in the breadcrumbs.

Place the cakes on a nonstick baking tray and pour over the oil. Bake in the oven for about 15 minutes, until crisp and golden-brown.

Remove from the oven, lift the cakes from the tray and arrange them on a serving dish. Garnish with the lemon wedges and serve immediately.

Crab cakes coated in a little wholemeal flour and breadcrumbs make an appetising meal seasoned with spicy tabasco and Worcestershire sauce.

Plaice with Watercress Sauce

Watercress is one of Britain's oldest culinary plants; still prized for its highly nutritious content (a good source of minerals, and vitamins A and C) and for the freshness it brings to any sauce. You will need a liquidiser for this recipe.

SERVES 4
PREPARATION TIME : *10 minutes*
COOKING TIME : *15 minutes*

INGREDIENTS
4 large or 8 small fillets of plaice
2 tablespoons vegetable oil
Salt and freshly ground black pepper
Watercress sprigs for garnish
SAUCE
1 small onion
½ oz (15g) butter
1 bunch watercress
5 tablespoons half or single cream
1oz (25g) soft low-fat cheese
Salt and freshly ground black pepper

Calories per serving : 290 · High in protein from fish · Good source of vitamin B12 from fish

A light cheese and watercress sauce with plaice.

To make the sauce, peel and finely chop the onion. Melt the butter in a pan and gently fry the onion for 5 minutes. Add the watercress, reserving a few sprigs for garnish, and cook for a further 2-3 minutes, stirring continually, until the watercress is wilted but no colour is lost.

Tip the watercress and onion into a liquidiser and blend until smooth. While the liquidiser is running, add the cream and low-fat cheese until the mixture is well blended.

Line a grill pan with lightly oiled foil and lay the plaice fillets on the grill rack inside it. Brush the fillets lightly with oil and season to taste.

Cook the fillets under a hot grill for 5-8 minutes, until just cooked through and lightly golden.

Meanwhile, pour the sauce back into the pan, reheat gently for 2 minutes, and turn into a small serving bowl. Transfer the cooked fish to the heated plates, garnish with watercress sprigs and serve with the watercress sauce.

Spanish Marinated Cod

Cod fillets can make a healthy treat when cooked at home. Here, they are marinated Spanish-style in a mixture of lemon juice, garlic and herbs. This dish goes particularly well with a tomato salad and can be served with either potatoes or rice.

SERVES 4
PREPARATION TIME : *5 minutes*
MARINATING TIME : *1½ -2½ hours*
COOKING TIME : *10 minutes*

INGREDIENTS
1½ -2lb (700-900g) cod fillet
1 bay leaf
2 tablespoons virgin olive oil
Juice of 1 lemon
1-2 cloves garlic
2 teaspoons ground coriander
Salt and freshly ground black pepper
4 lime wedges and fresh parsley sprigs for garnish

Calories per serving : 250 · High in protein from fish · Good source of vitamin B12 from fish

A fresh mixed salad goes beautifully with Spanish-style cod fillets that have been marinated with coriander.

To make the marinade, tear the bay leaf into 3 pieces. Place the bay leaf, oil, lemon juice, peeled garlic, coriander and seasoning in a shallow dish and whisk together with a fork.

Cut the fish into 4 pieces and immerse, skin sides up, in the marinade. Leave to marinate for at least 1½ hours, turning and basting two or three times.

Preheat the grill. Place the pieces of fish in an ovenproof dish, skin side down, and spoon over the remaining marinade. Cook for 10 minutes under a moderately hot grill, basting occasionally with the marinade, until the fish is golden-brown.

Lift the pieces of fish from the dish and arrange on serving plates. Spoon over the remaining marinade and garnish each piece of fish with a slice of lemon and a sprig of parsley. Serve immediately.

Trawlerman's Stew

Because of its abundance and succulent thick white fillets, cod has been popular in many countries since medieval times. This recipe is based on a stew that has been popular for centuries in the remote fishing villages of the French Basque. If you have the time, it is worth making your own fresh fish stock for a fuller flavour. Serve in soup bowls with crusty French bread on the side.

SERVES 4
PREPARATION TIME : *20 minutes*
COOKING TIME : *35 minutes*

INGREDIENTS
1½ lb (700g) cod fillet
Salt and freshly ground black pepper
1 large onion
2 cloves garlic
1 green pepper
2 tablespoons virgin olive oil
1lb (450g) potatoes
6 medium tomatoes
½ pint (285ml) fish stock
1 teaspoon dried oregano
Fresh parsley for garnish

Calories per serving : 355 · High in fibre from vegetables · High in protein from cod · High in vitamin C from potato, tomato and pepper

Skin the cod fillet, then wash and pat dry. Cut into 8 pieces and season generously.

Peel and finely chop the onion and garlic. Halve and de-seed the green pepper, then slice it into strips. Heat the oil in a flameproof casserole and add the onion, garlic and pepper, then cook for 5 minutes, until the onion is transparent. Meanwhile, scrub the potatoes and dice them into large pieces, and quarter the tomatoes.

Add the potatoes, stock and oregano to the casserole. Cover and simmer for 20 minutes, then add the tomatoes and arrange the fish pieces on top. Cover and simmer for a further 10 minutes.

Chop the parsley, sprinkle it over the casserole and serve immediately.

Steaming bowls of fish stew make a hearty meal.

Mexican-style Trout

Trout belong to the same family as salmon and are now farmed in Britain as well as many other parts of the world. Deliciously fresh wild trout are also available from most fishmongers. Although they are more expensive than the farmed varieties, they are a good source of fish oils, which are believed to help prevent heart disease when eaten on a regular basis.

SERVES 4
PREPARATION TIME : *15 minutes*
COOKING TIME : *40 minutes*
OVEN : *Preheat to 180°C (350°F, gas mark 4)*

INGREDIENTS
2 large 1½ lb (700g) or 4 small gutted trout
1 large onion
1 red pepper
2 tablespoons olive oil
1 dessertspoon sherry or white wine vinegar
Juice of 2 limes
3 tablespoons fresh chopped parsley
2 dashes tabasco sauce
Salt and freshly ground black pepper
AVOCADO DIP
1 ripe avocado
1 tablespoon natural yoghurt

Calories per serving : 425 · High in protein from trout · High in vitamin C from limes and pepper

Peel and thinly slice the onion. Halve, de-seed and dice the pepper. Heat the oil in a frying pan, add the onion and vinegar and cook over a moderate heat for 5 minutes. Add the pepper and cook for a further 2 minutes. Then add the juice of one of the limes, 2 tablespoons of the parsley, and the tabasco. Mix thoroughly and remove from the heat.

Brush an ovenproof dish with a little oil, place the trout in the dish and season lightly. Spoon over the onion and pepper mixture. Tighty cover the dish with foil and bake in the oven for about 30 minutes.

Meanwhile, halve the avocado and remove the stone, then peel away the skin. Blend the avocado, the juice of the second lime, and the yoghurt together in a liquidiser – or mash them together with a fork. The dip can be gently heated before serving but should not be kept warm for too long.

Garnish the baked trout and the dip with the remaining parsley. Serve the dip with the fish or in a separate bowl.

Mexican-style trout cooked with onion and peppers in lime juice and tabasco, and served with an avocado dip.

Juicy chunks of monkfish are spiced with coarsely crushed black peppercorns, and poached in fish stock with a little cream and brandy. Served with carrot and courgette ribbons, it makes a light and beautiful dish.

Peppered Monkfish Fillets

Monkfish is traditionally known as the 'poor man's lobster', because it used to be substituted for the real thing. It has recently become a popular dish in its own right, however, featuring regularly on restaurant menus. Despite its ugly appearance – with its huge head and gaping mouth – its firm flesh is succulent with a mild, sweet flavour, making it an excellent and versatile fish to cook and eat. Monkfish is also easy to prepare, as it has no fine bones. It tastes particularly good when spiced, as in this recipe, which uses black peppercorns. Fish stock is now available in large supermarkets, or you can make your own using the backbone, skin, and any other trimmings from the monkfish.

SERVES 4
PREPARATION TIME : *30 minutes*
COOKING TIME : *25 minutes*

INGREDIENTS
2 × 1lb (450g) monkfish tails
Salt
1 teaspoon coarsely crushed black peppercorns
1 tablespoon virgin olive oil
½ oz (15g) unsalted butter
¼ pint (150ml) fish stock
1 teaspoon arrowroot
4 tablespoons half cream
2 tablespoons brandy (optional)

Calories per serving : 160 · High in protein and good source of vitamin B12 from monkfish

Remove the skin from the fish, and as much of the pink membrane as possible. Remove the fillets by cutting along either side of the central bone, then wash and pat them dry.

Gently rub a little salt, and the coarsely crushed black peppercorns, evenly into the fish.

Heat the oil and butter in a frying pan and cook the fish for 10 minutes over a medium heat, turning occasionally until the fillets are well sealed. Add the fish stock, then cover and simmer for 10 minutes.

Mix the arrowroot with 1 tablespoon of cold water and stir the mixture into the pan, along with the cream and brandy. Cook for a few minutes, stirring until thickened, then remove and serve.

Ash Wednesday Fish Pie

According to a religious tradition, the consumption of all meats, eggs and dairy produce is forbidden during the 40 days of Lent – hence the use of milk, fat and eggs for pancakes on Shrove Tuesday. This filling pie upholds the Ash Wednesday tradition, and is a perfectly suitable meal for anyone who is allergic to dairy produce.

Hot fish pie with a potato and parsnip topping.

SERVES 4
PREPARATION TIME : *20 minutes*
COOKING TIME : *45 minutes*
STANDING TIME : *40 minutes*
OVEN : *Preheat to 200°C (400°F, gas mark 6)*

INGREDIENTS
1lb (450g) haddock fillets
1 medium onion
4oz (115g) oyster or button mushrooms
2oz (50g) sunflower margarine
1½ oz (40g) flour
½ pint (285ml) fish or vegetable stock
Salt and freshly ground black pepper
PIE TOPPING
12oz (350g) potatoes
12oz (350g) parsnips
1oz (25g) sunflower margarine
½ teaspoon freshly grated nutmeg
Salt and freshly ground black pepper

Calories per serving : 390 · High in fibre from vegetables · High in protein from haddock

Skin the haddock fillets and cut them into 1in (25mm) pieces. Peel and finely chop the onion. Clean and chop the mushrooms. Heat the margarine in a large pan, add the onion and mushrooms and gently fry them for 8 minutes.

Stir in the flour and cook over a moderate heat for 2-3 minutes. Gradually stir in the fish or vegetable stock and bring to the boil, stirring continually.

Turn off the heat, stir in the fish and season with salt and black pepper. Cover the pan and leave it for 30 minutes, during which time the heat from the sauce and pan will start to cook the fish.

To make the topping, peel and roughly chop the potatoes and parsnips and cook them in salted, boiling water for 15 minutes, until tender. Drain and mash the vegetables together, then beat in the margarine, the nutmeg and plenty of black pepper and a little salt.

Turn the fish mixture out of the pan into an ovenproof dish. Spread the parsnip and potato topping over the top and rough up lightly with a fork.

Place the dish in the oven and bake for 25 minutes until the top is golden-brown. Serve immediately.

Tender salmon steak flavoured with balsamic vinegar and fresh dill makes an easy but luxurious main course.

Salmon with Dill

Balsamic vinegar, which lends its unique sweet and sour flavour to this delicate fish dish, comes from the town of Modena in northern Italy, where it has been produced for centuries. There they claim that the vinegar is only usable after ten years, and at its very best after 100 years. Balsamic vinegar is available from delicatessens and large supermarkets, or you can substitute white wine or dill vinegar. Salmon, with its firm, sweet-tasting flesh, lends itself well to the different flavours of balsamic vinegar and fresh dill, but you should take special care not to overcook it. Serve with baby new potatoes, steamed in their skins, fresh broccoli, mangetout or French beans, and carrots cut into matchsticks.

SERVES 4
PREPARATION TIME : *10 minutes*
COOKING TIME : *8-10 minutes*
OVEN : *Preheat to 220°C (425°F, gas mark 7)*

INGREDIENTS
4 salmon steaks, each weighing 6oz (175g)
5 teaspoons virgin olive oil
4 tablespoons balsamic vinegar or white wine
or dill vinegar
Salt and freshly ground black pepper
8 fresh dill sprigs

Calories per serving : 535 · High in protein from salmon · Good source of vitamin B12 from salmon

Cut 4 squares of greaseproof paper and 4 of foil, each one large enough to enclose 1 salmon steak. Brush 1 teaspoon of olive oil onto the paper squares and then place a salmon steak on each square. Drizzle 1 teaspoon of olive oil and 1 tablespoon of vinegar over each steak, season with salt and pepper to taste, and top with 2 dill sprigs.

Wrap the salmon steaks carefully in the paper squares and then wrap these in the foil squares. Place the wrapped steaks on a baking sheet and cook in the oven for 8-10 minutes, until the salmon is just opaque in the centre.

Unwrap the foil, and then the paper, and carefully place the salmon steaks with their dill sprigs on serving plates. Serve immediately.

Trout Parcels with Cucumber and Lemon

Hundreds of recipes have been created for this popular and delicious fish. Many Victorian recipes used a traditional English method of baking trout which involved wrapping the fish in a double thickness of newspaper and then soaking it under running water. As soon as the paper dried out in the oven, the fish was perfectly cooked. Nowadays, most people prefer to use greaseproof paper, which also keeps the moisture in. Serve with boiled or new potatoes and a green vegetable or a crisp salad.

Juicy pink trout with a creamy cucumber sauce.

SERVES 4
PREPARATION TIME : *20 minutes*
COOKING TIME : *15 minutes*
OVEN : *Preheat to 180°C (350°F, gas mark 4)*

INGREDIENTS
4 small gutted fresh trout
1 lemon
4 sprigs parsley
SAUCE
½ medium cucumber
2 spring onions
Rind and juice of 1 lemon
1oz (25g) unsalted butter
1 tablespoon plain flour
4 tablespoons half cream
1 tablespoon fresh chopped parsley
Salt and freshly ground black pepper

Calories per serving : 310 · High in protein from fresh trout

Wash the trout thoroughly and remove any black skin inside the fish by rubbing it with a little salt. Dry the fish with kitchen paper. Cut the lemon into slices and place a few slices and a parsley sprig in each belly cavity. Wrap the fish, individually, in a double thickness of newspaper or greaseproof paper. Wet the parcels under cold running water and place on a baking tray. Bake for 15 minutes.

Meanwhile, peel and dice the cucumber. Trim the spring onions and slice the bulb and bottom 3in (80mm) of the green stalk. Juice the lemon and finely grate the rind. Melt the butter in a saucepan and sauté the cucumber for 1-2 minutes until just tender. Remove with a slotted spoon and put aside.

Gradually stir the flour into the saucepan, mixing well, then add the cream a little at a time, stirring continuously. Return the cucumber to the pan, along with the spring onion, lemon juice and rind, and chopped parsley. Add a little water if necessary to maintain a creamy consistency, and season to taste with salt and freshly ground black pepper. Continue stirring and cooking for 3 minutes, until thickened, then pour the sauce into a jug or sauceboat.

Unwrap the trout and arrange on a serving plate. Serve the sauce separately.

Skate with Tarragon Dressing

Skate are related to sharks and sting rays. They have a kite-shaped body with a long tail, and are usually very large. Fishmongers rarely display skate whole, preferring to skin and joint them. It is always best to get the fishmonger to skin the fish for you, as it is easier to cook. Skate is never cooked when it is absolutely fresh, as a glutinous coating sticks to the skin for a few hours after it has been caught. Once poached in a little water with wine or vinegar, however, this coating is removed. Sometimes small nuggets of tail flesh called 'skate nobs' are available from fishmongers, which can be floured and fried in butter, but it is the ribbed wings that are considered

to be the best part. The French consider skate wings to be a great delicacy, and they have a famous recipe called 'Raie au Beurre Noir', in which the fish is lightly seasoned and simply cooked in golden-brown butter. The tarragon and lemon dressing in this recipe provides an exciting alternative.

Delicate skate wings poached in wine and served with a light, slightly piquant lemon dressing.

SERVES 4
PREPARATION TIME : *15 minutes*
COOKING TIME : *15-20 minutes*

INGREDIENTS
1 large skinned skate wing weighing
approximately 2lb (900g)
4fl oz (115ml) dry white wine or vermouth
½ lemon
1 small onion
3 tarragon stalks
6 peppercorns
½ teaspoon salt
4 sprigs tarragon for garnish
DRESSING
1 tablespoon chopped tarragon
1 lemon
4 tablespoons virgin olive oil
Salt and freshly ground black pepper
2 dashes tabasco
1 generous pinch caster sugar

Calories per serving : 415 · High in protein from skate · Good source of vitamin B12 from skate

Rinse the skate under cold water and pat dry. Cut into 4 evenly sized portions.

Pour 6fl oz (175ml) of water and the wine, or vermouth, into a pan large enough to hold the skate. Cut off the rind from half a lemon in large strips, avoiding as much pith as possible, and squeeze the juice into a bowl. Peel, chop and quarter the onion. Add the lemon rind and juice, onion, tarragon stalks, peppercorns and salt to the pan, and bring slowly to the boil.

Add the pieces of skate, cover the pan and simmer gently for about 15 minutes or until the skate is cooked through.

Meanwhile, to make the dressing, finely chop the tarragon and squeeze all the juice out of the lemon. Then combine all the remaining ingredients for the dressing in a small pan and heat gently for 2-3 minutes and whisk thoroughly.

Lift the skate out of the pan with a slotted spoon, leaving all the strips of lemon peel behind. Arrange the skate on a serving plate, spoon over the dressing, garnish with tarragon sprigs and serve immediately.

Cajun-Creole Cod

This quick and simple recipe is a medley of two delicious cuisines. Cajun and Creole cookery reflect the French and Spanish influences that the settlers had on local produce in New Orleans and the West Indies. This dish goes well with nutty brown rice and a crisp green salad, or a seasonal green vegetable.

SERVES 4
PREPARATION TIME : *10 minutes*
MARINATING TIME : *½ -2 hours*
COOKING TIME : *10 minutes*

INGREDIENTS
4 thick cod steaks, each weighing about 6oz (175g)
20 whole black peppercorns
10 allspice berries
1 teaspoon coriander seeds
2 dried red chillies
2 cloves garlic
2 tablespoons virgin olive oil
1oz (25g) unsalted butter
Juice of 1 lime
Lime wedges for garnish
Coriander sprigs for garnish

Calories per serving : 285 · Low in cholesterol
High in protein from cod

Crush the peppercorns, allspice, coriander, chillies and garlic in a mortar with a pestle. Rub both sides of each fish steak with this mixture, then cover the steaks and leave them to marinate in the refrigerator for at least 30 minutes.

Preheat a low oven and warm a serving platter. Heat the oil and butter in a pan until the mixture foams. Add the cod steaks and cook over a moderate heat for 5 minutes on each side, pressing down firmly with a fish slice occasionally, until the centre of each steak is opaque. Reserving the rest of the ingredients in the pan, transfer the fish to the warmed serving platter, then cover and keep hot.

Return the pan to a high heat. Add the lime juice and stir until bubbling. Pour this mixture over the cod steaks. Garnish with the lime wedges and coriander sprigs and serve immediately.

Cod steaks marinated with spices and then pan fried.

Plaice with Orange and Lemon Sauce

Fish fillets are rolled around a healthy citrus, herb and nut stuffing in this recipe. Good herbs to use are parsley, chervil, dill, chives, marjoram and oregano. If desired, you can substitute fish or chicken stock, or water for the white wine.

SERVES 4
PREPARATION TIME : *30 minutes*
COOKING TIME : *20 minutes*
OVEN : *Preheat to 180°C (350°F, gas mark 4)*

INGREDIENTS
4 large or 8 small plaice fillets
2oz (50g) flaked almonds
1 orange
1 lemon
1 medium egg
3oz (75g) granary or wholemeal breadcrumbs
4 tablespoons chopped fresh herbs
Salt and freshly ground black pepper
1 large glass dry white wine
½ oz (15g) butter

Calories per serving : 280 · High in fibre from bread and almonds · High in protein from fish and egg
High in vitamin C from orange and lemon

Skin the fish fillets. If using 4 large fillets, cut each one in half lengthways to make 8 fillets. Wash, pat dry, and set aside.

Spread the almonds out on a baking sheet and cook them in the oven for 6-8 minutes – checking them regularly as they burn easily – until they are a pale biscuit colour. Remove and chop the almonds, then set them aside.

To make the stuffing, finely grate the rinds and squeeze the juice of the orange and lemon. Beat the egg in a bowl. Reserving a little orange rind for garnish, add the remaining rinds to the bowl, along with 1 tablespoon of the orange juice, the almonds, breadcrumbs, and half of the chopped herbs. Season and stir well until evenly mixed, adding a little more orange juice if the stuffing is dry.

Spread out 8 fish fillets, skin side up, on a work surface. Place an equal amount of stuffing along the centre of each fillet, then roll up each fillet around its stuffing and secure with wooden cocktail sticks.

Place the rolled fillets upright in a baking dish. Pour the lemon juice, any remaining orange juice and the wine over the fillets, and season. Cover and bake for 15 minutes, or until the fish is just opaque.

Remove the cooked plaice rolls, and drain the cooking liquid into a saucepan. Carefully remove the cocktail sticks, keeping the fish in the baking dish.Cover again and return to the warm oven.

Boil the cooking liquid for 5 minutes, or until reduced by a third. Remove from the heat, stir in the butter and remaining chopped herbs, and season.

Arrange the fillets on dinner plates, and spoon over the sauce. Garnish with the orange rind and serve immediately.

Orange and lemon sauce gives a tangy taste to a light dish of herb-stuffed plaice that is served with spinach.

Marinated Mackerel with Tarragon

Dill is the herb most commonly used for marinating fish, but there is no reason why other herbs such as tarragon or parsley cannot be used. Mackerel is one of the most nutritious fish, as it is rich in the special oils that are now thought to help prevent heart disease. Ask the fishmonger to gut and fillet the fish for you. Serve with a salad and new potatoes.

SERVES 4
PREPARATION TIME : *10 minutes*
MARINATING TIME : *36-48 hours*

INGREDIENTS
2 gutted and filleted mackerel, each weighing about 1lb (450g)
4 tablespoons fine sea salt
3 tablespoons caster sugar
3 tablespoons chopped tarragon
Sprigs of fresh tarragon for garnish
SAUCE
2 tablespoons smooth French mustard
2 teaspoons clear honey
1 tablespoon lemon juice
3 tablespoons olive oil
1 tablespoon chopped chives

Calories per serving : 490 · High in protein from fish · High in vitamin D from fish

Wash the fillets and trim away the inside of the belly cavity. To make the marinade, mix together the salt, sugar and tarragon, and sprinkle a third of the mixture over the bottom of a large dish. Lay two fillets in the dish, skin-side down, and sprinkle over another third of the mixture. Lay the remaining fillets on top, skin-side up, and sprinkle over the remaining mixture. Place in the refrigerator for at least 36 hours, turning the fish several times.

Lift the fillets out of the marinade and cut the flesh away from the skin into neat strips – as if slicing smoked salmon. Arrange on a large serving platter and garnish with sprigs of fresh tarragon.

To make the sauce, spoon the mustard into a bowl. Gradually stir in the honey, lemon juice, oil and chopped chives. Pour into a jug or sauceboat, and serve separately with the fish.

Tarragon cuts through the rich flavour of mackerel.

Roast Monkfish Tail

Monkfish are also known as angel sharks. They have a strange, flattened appearance and it is their tail section that is the most popular part for cooking; one tail section providing two large fillets. Serve the dish with boiled potatoes and a selection of vegetables.

SERVES 4
PREPARATION TIME : *20 minutes*
COOKING TIME : *40 minutes*
OVEN : *Preheat to 200°C (400°F, gas mark 6)*

INGREDIENTS
2½ lb (1.1kg) monkfish tail
1 small onion
2 tablespoons virgin olive oil
½ teaspoon fennel seeds
⅓ teaspoon ground anise or star anise
4 tablespoons dry vermouth
Salt and freshly ground black pepper
12 cherry tomatoes
Coriander sprigs for garnish (optional)

Calories per serving : 340 · High in protein and vitamin B12 from monkfish

Remove the tough grey skin and pink membrane from the monkfish tail. Wash and dry the fish and secure it evenly with fine string, so that its shape is held during cooking.

Finely chop the onion, and heat the oil in a large frying pan over a medium heat. Sauté the onion, fennel seeds, ground anise or star anise in the pan for 2-3 minutes, until the onion is transparent.

Add the monkfish to the frying pan and cook for about 5 minutes, until the fish is sealed on all sides. Remove from the heat, pour over the vermouth and season to taste with salt and freshly ground black pepper. Transfer the contents to a roasting tin or gratin dish, placing the monkfish on the top, and roast in the oven for 30 minutes.

Add the tomatoes to the roasting tin or gratin dish, and cook for a further 5 minutes, then remove from the oven and garnish the fish with coriander sprigs, if desired. Serve immediately from the gratin dish, or on individual plates.

A festive dish of roast monkfish tail is cooked with aromatic fennel seeds, dry vermouth and cherry tomatoes.

Haddock Fillets with Coriander and Orange

Coriander seeds are one of the world's most popular flavourings. They have a faint orange flavour which complements the orange sauce in this recipe and goes particularly well with fish. If you have the time to make one, a fresh fish stock is best for this recipe.

SERVES 4

PREPARATION TIME : *20 minutes*

COOKING TIME : *30 minutes*

OVEN : *Preheat to 200°C (400°F, gas mark 6)*

INGREDIENTS

4 × 6oz (175g) pieces skinned haddock fillet
Salt and freshly ground black pepper
1 tablespoon plain flour
1 tablespoon sesame seeds
2 tablespoons ground coriander seeds
Finely grated rind and juice of 1 large orange
½ oz (15g) unsalted butter
1 tablespoon virgin olive oil
SAUCE
½ pint (285ml) fish stock
1 teaspoon cornflour
4 tablespoons half cream

Calories per serving : 170 · High in protein and iron from fish · High in vitamin C from orange

An aromatic orange sauce transforms fresh haddock.

Wash, pat dry and season the fish pieces. Mix the flour, sesame seeds, coriander and half the orange rind together and coat the fish with the mixture.

Heat the butter and oil together and brush half the mixture lightly onto a nonstick baking tray. Arrange the fish on the tray and pour the remaining butter and oil over the top. Bake in the oven for 15 minutes.

Pour the stock, orange juice and remaining rind into a wide, shallow pan. Fast boil the mixture to reduce by half. Mix the cornflour and 2 tablespoons of water into a smooth paste, stir in the cream, then slowly add to the stock, stirring until thickened. Serve the fish and the sauce separately.

Spicy Fish with Mangoes

Grey mullet is a particularly suitable firm-fleshed fish for this dish, as it grills easily and is relatively inexpensive. You can, however, use any firm white fish, such as cod, swordfish or monkfish. Choose ripe mangoes with a sweet smell and taut skin. This dish goes well with Basmati rice, cooked with 2 tablespoons of desiccated coconut. The marinade can be prepared up to 12 hours in advance.

SERVES 4

PREPARATION TIME : *45 minutes*

MARINATING TIME : *4-12 hours*

INGREDIENTS

1 large grey mullet, filleted
3 tablespoons chopped fresh coriander
1 mango or 3 medium tomatoes
Sprigs of coriander for garnish
MARINADE
3 cloves garlic
2in (50mm) piece fresh ginger
16fl oz (475ml) low-fat yoghurt
1 teaspoon chilli powder
Juice of 1 lemon
Salt

Calories per serving : 200 · High in protein from fish · High in calcium from yoghurt

Grey mullet is marinated in a spicy mixture of garlic, ginger and yoghurt, then grilled and garnished with exotic mango slices for a fruity, scented flavour. This recipe also makes an excellent barbecue dish.

To make the marinade, crush the garlic and cut the ginger into matchsticks. Empty the yoghurt into a dish large enough to hold the fish fillets and add the garlic, ginger, chilli powder, lemon juice, chopped coriander and salt. Place the fish in this mixture and turn to make sure it is well coated. Cover and leave for at least 4 hours in the refrigerator.

When the fish is ready, preheat the grill and remove the fish from the marinade. Reserve half this marinade and discard the rest. Place the fish in an ovenproof dish under the grill at a medium heat for 15 minutes, then turn the fish over carefully and grill for 15 minutes more until it has just cooked through.

Meanwhile, preheat a low oven. Chop the fresh coriander finely and add it to the marinade, then pour the mixture into a saucepan and heat gently for 4-5 minutes. Remove from the heat, pour the marinade into a jug or sauceboat and keep warm in the oven. Peel and slice the mango or, if using tomatoes, cut them into quarters.

Remove the fish from the grill. Cut each fillet in two and arrange on a serving platter. Garnish with mango or tomato slices, and coriander sprigs. Pour over the marinade and serve.

Prawn Skewers with Lime and Tamarind

The tamarind, or Indian date tree, has been grown in India for centuries. It is the sweet and sour-tasting pulp around the tamarind seeds that is used in cooking; one of the most popular ingredients in Asian cuisine. Small jars of the concentrated fruit used in this recipe are sold in good Asian shops, delicatessens and some large supermarkets. The spicy, marinated prawns go well with plain boiled rice and a lightly dressed mixed salad.

SERVES 4
PREPARATION TIME : *45 minutes*
MARINATING TIME : *1 hour or overnight*
COOKING TIME : *10 minutes*

INGREDIENTS
2lb (900g) whole uncooked prawns
2 teaspoons tamarind concentrate
3 tablespoons brandy
1-2 dried red chillies
1 small onion
2 cloves garlic
2 tablespoons olive oil
Pinch of saffron threads
Rind and juice of 1 lime
2 tablespoons clear honey
2oz (50g) creamed coconut
Fresh coriander leaves for garnish

Calories per serving : 500 · High in protein, calcium, iron and zinc from prawns

If necessary, cut the heads off the uncooked prawns. Peel the prawns carefully, leaving the bodies intact, then cut along the length of their backs and discard the dark threads of intestine. Wash and pat dry.

Mix the tamarind concentrate and the brandy together until smooth. Finely chop the chillies. Peel and finely chop the onion and garlic cloves. Heat the oil in a small saucepan and cook the chillies, onion, garlic and saffron for 5 minutes until soft, then remove from the heat. Finely grate the rind of the lime and squeeze the juice, then add the rind and juice to the saucepan, along with the honey and the tamarind mixture.

Marinate the prawns in this mixture for at least 1 hour in a cool place, turning occasionally. Preheat the grill on a medium-high setting.

Reserving the marinade, thread the prawns onto 4 wooden skewers and place them under the grill for 3 minutes, until the prawns are firm and pink.

Meanwhile, gently heat the marinade in a small pan. Stir in the creamed coconut until it melts. If the sauce is too thick, add a little water and simmer gently for 2 minutes.

Garnish with the coriander leaves and serve the sauce separately.

Skewered prawns are marinated in a mixture of tamarind, chillies, garlic and brandy to make a rich and spicy Asian dish that is served with rice.

BEEF, LAMB & PORK DISHES

Red meat can play an important part in a balanced diet. Healthy barbecues and filling stews are contrasted by tender ethnic dishes accompanied by vegetables, fruits and nuts from the Orient and the Middle East.

Spicy Lamb Kebabs with Yoghurt and Cucumber Sauce

In this recipe the oriental method of marinating meat and fish with soy sauce and ginger is combined with the cooling effect of yoghurt and cucumber that is favoured in Indian and Middle-Eastern cuisines.

The Chinese have used both ginger and soy sauce for centuries. Soy sauce was first used in sauces more than 400 years ago, and ginger reached southern Europe before Roman times. The lamb can be marinated up to 48 hours in advance, and the sauce can also be prepared ahead and refrigerated. The kebabs can then be assembled and cooked or barbecued when required. They go well with rice and a tomato salad. The yoghurt and cucumber sauce should be served separately. Bay leaves can also be used as a garnish.

Lamb kebabs are marinated in ginger and two different soy sauces before being grilled. A refreshing sauce made of creamy yoghurt, fresh mint and cucumber balances the oriental spices beautifully.

Tender lamb's liver baked with sage and rosemary.

SERVES 4
PREPARATION TIME : *20 minutes*
MARINATING TIME : *12-48 hours*
COOKING TIME : *15-20 minutes*

INGREDIENTS
1½ lb (700g) lamb neck fillets
3 teaspoons fresh root ginger
3 tablespoons light soy sauce
3 tablespoons dark soy sauce
SAUCE
12 baby onions or shallots
½ cucumber
1 clove garlic
2 teaspoons chopped fresh mint or
1 teaspoon dried mint
¼ pint (150ml) natural yoghurt
Salt and freshly ground black pepper

Calories per serving : 350 · High in protein, iron and zinc from lamb · High in protein from yoghurt

Cut the lamb into bite-size pieces and place in a large bowl. Peel and grate the ginger. Combine the ginger and the two soy sauces and add to the lamb. Mix well until the meat is completely covered with the sauce. Cover and leave to marinate in the refrigerator for at least 12 hours, stirring once or twice.

To make the sauce, cook the onions in boiling water for 5 minutes then drain and remove the skins. Grate the cucumber coarsely and crush the garlic. Combine with the chopped mint and yoghurt, and season to taste. Cover and store in the refrigerator until required.

Preheat the grill. Thread lamb pieces and onions alternately onto 4 kebab sticks and grill, turning and basting frequently, for 15-20 minutes.

Lamb's Liver Parcels with Herbs

Baking liver in greaseproof paper keeps it moist and tender without using any fat. Most herbs can be used with liver, including chives, dried mixed herbs and parsley, or the stronger rosemary and thyme.

SERVES 4
PREPARATION TIME : *5 minutes*
COOKING TIME : *4 minutes*
OVEN : *Preheat to 220°C (425°F, gas mark 7)*

INGREDIENTS
1lb (450g) lamb's liver
Salt and freshly ground black pepper
2 sprigs fresh sage or rosemary

Calories per serving : 205 · High in protein, iron, zinc, and vitamin A from liver

Put a baking tray in a hot oven for at least 5 minutes.

Slice the liver thinly. Take a sheet of greaseproof paper about 12in (300mm) long. Fold it in half and cut out the shape of a semicircle. Then open it out.

Lay the slices of liver on one half of the paper, about 1in (25mm) from the edge. Season with salt and pepper, and add herbs as desired.

Fold the paper over the liver. Working along the rounded edge, turn over the edges of paper making little pleats to completely enclose the meat, but stop about ½in (15mm) from the straight edge. Blow as much air as possible into the bag through the gap, then seal it with a final pleat.

Remove the baking tray from the oven and lay the parcel on it. Replace the tray in the oven and bake for 4 minutes only.

Take the tray out of the oven, split open the bag, and arrange the liver and its juices on a plate.

A sweet and juicy mango is delicious with lamb.

Grilled Lamb Cutlets with Spiced Mangoes

Known as the 'Apple of the Tropics', mangoes have been grown in India for 4000 years, but they have only recently been used in Western cuisine. At first their use was restricted to desserts, but now they appear in salads, starters and main dishes. The taste is acid-sweet, the aroma of spring pine wood. When buying, choose fruits with a sweet smell and taut skin, no soft spots. They will keep for up to two weeks in the refrigerator. Mango slices are delicious with lamb, pork, duck and goose. Serve with rice, preferably Basmati, and crisp green vegetables such as mangetout or broccoli.

SERVES 4
PREPARATION TIME : *15 minutes*
COOKING TIME : *15 minutes*

INGREDIENTS
8 lamb cutlets
1 large clove garlic
Salt and freshly ground black pepper
1 large ripe mango
2 tablespoons white wine vinegar
2 tablespoons soft brown sugar
½ teaspoon ground cinnamon
½ teaspoon ground ginger
Coriander sprigs for garnish

Calories per serving : 450 · High in protein from lamb · High in carotene from mangoes

Turn on the grill to a moderately high heat. Peel and cut the garlic in half, then rub the cut surface over the cutlets and season them with salt and pepper. Grill the cutlets for about 7 minutes on each side. Preheat a serving dish.

Working over a bowl to catch any juice – peel the mango and cut it into slices. Scrape all the flesh off the skin and put it into a small saucepan, together with any mango juice caught in the bowl. Add the vinegar, sugar and spices, and heat gently until the sugar has dissolved. Increase the heat slightly, and add the mango slices. Cover and cook for about 5 minutes.

Arrange the cutlets on the heated serving dish, together with the mango slices. Garnish with the coriander and serve immediately.

Calf's Liver with Lime and Sage Leaves

Calf's liver is one of the most tender meats. When it has been pan-fried for just a minute or two on each side, its velvety texture almost melts in the mouth. Calf's liver is sometimes sold with a layer of fat left around it, which can be easily removed with a knife. Lamb's liver can provide a cheaper alternative, but the meat is not quite so tender.

SERVES 4
PREPARATION TIME : *10 minutes*
COOKING TIME : *10 minutes*

INGREDIENTS
8 thin slices calf's liver,
each weighing 1½ -2oz (40-50g)
1 tablespoon plain flour
Salt and freshly ground black pepper
2 tablespoons virgin olive oil
12 fresh sage leaves
Juice of 1 lime

Calories per serving : 225 · High in protein,
vitamin A and iron from liver

If you have a whole liver, cut off any exposed ducts or connective tissue, peel off the outer membrane and slice the liver diagonally, removing any internal ducts. If desired, you can soak the liver in milk to tone down its strong flavour, but it should not be blanched as this will toughen it. Season the flour generously with salt and pepper, then sprinkle the slices of liver with the flour on both sides.

Heat the oil in a large saucepan and quickly fry the sage leaves, until they begin to give off their aroma. Remove from the pan and reserve. Make sure the pan is really hot before frying the liver slices for 1-2 minutes on each side. If necessary, keep the first batch warm whilst cooking the rest of the meat.

Return the sage leaves to the pan, sprinkle the lime juice over the liver and warm gently for 1 minute. Serve immediately.

Sage was one of the first herbs to be used in British cooking. It complements tender calf's liver beautifully.

Pan-fried Steak with Green Peppercorn Sauce

As a variation on pepper steak, the peppercorns in this recipe are used to flavour the sauce rather than the steak itself. These steaks should be served as quickly as possible after being cooked.

SERVES 4
PREPARATION TIME : *5 minutes*
COOKING TIME : *7-12 minutes*

INGREDIENTS
4 × 6oz (175g) sirloin steaks
2 shallots
1 teaspoon green peppercorns
2 teaspoons coarse grain mustard
2 tablespoons brandy
8fl oz (225ml) strained Greek yoghurt
or ¼ pint (150ml) single cream
Juice of ½ lemon
Salt and freshly ground black pepper

Calories per serving : 260 · High in protein from beef

Trim excess fat from the steaks. Place some of the fat into a nonstick frying pan and cook over a medium heat to render it. Discard any solid fat.

Raise the heat to high and fry the steaks in the pan for 2 minutes each side. Reduce the heat and cook for up to 2-3 more minutes each side. Eight minutes'

Steak served with a mustard and peppercorn sauce.

time will give a well-done steak; reduce the cooking time by half for rare meat. Remove the steak from the pan and keep warm in the oven.

Chop the shallots finely and add to the pan juices. Cook over a low heat, stirring until lightly coloured. Add the crushed peppercorns, mustard and brandy. Stir in the yoghurt or cream and lemon juice; heat gently and then serve with new potatoes and a salad or crisp vegetables.

Mixed Bean Chilli Con Carne

This heart-warming dish is particularly appropriate for cold winter nights. Minced meat is usually used, but chopped meat makes it more substantial. Add more chilli powder for a spicier dish.

SERVES 6
PREPARATION TIME : *50 minutes*
COOKING TIME : *1 hour*

INGREDIENTS
1½ lb (700g) lean skirt of beef
14oz (400g) tin flageolet beans
14oz (400g) tin black-eye beans
14oz (400g) tin red kidney beans
2 medium onions
2 fresh green chillies
1 large green pepper
1 tablespoon virgin olive oil
3 cloves garlic
2 teaspoons chilli powder
1 teaspoon ground cumin
1 teaspoon cumin seeds
1 teaspoon dried oregano
2 × 14oz (400g) tinned tomatoes
1 tablespoon tomato purée
¼ pint (150ml) beef stock
Salt and freshly ground black pepper
2 tablespoons fresh chopped coriander
6 sprigs of coriander for garnish

Calories per serving : 400 · High in protein from beef
and beans · High in vitamin C from tomatoes

A spicy Mexican chilli con carne made with chopped beef, tomatoes, a variety of beans and fresh coriander.

Trim any excess fat from the beef and chop the meat finely. Pour the tinned beans into a colander or sieve, rinse well under cold water and leave to drain. Peel and chop the onions, and de-seed and chop the chillies. Halve, de-seed and slice the green pepper.

Heat the oil in a large saucepan and add the onions, chillies and the green pepper. Cook over a moderate heat for about 5 minutes until the onion has softened and gone transparent, then remove the vegetables from the pan with a slotted spoon and set aside. Increase the heat under the pan, add the chopped beef and cook for 5 minutes until it is well browned. Meanwhile, crush the garlic.

Return the onion, chillies and pepper to the pan, and then stir in the crushed garlic, chilli powder, ground cumin, cumin seeds and oregano. Cook for 1-2 minutes over a medium heat.

Sieve the tinned tomatoes and add them to the pan along with the tomato purée and beef stock. Season lightly with salt. Stir in the beans and slowly bring to the boil, stirring continuously. Reduce the heat to a low setting, cover with a tightly fitting lid or foil and cook for about 30 minutes.

Add the fresh chopped coriander to the pan and, keeping the pan uncovered, cook for a further 15 minutes to reduce the liquid. Season with black pepper to taste. Garnish with the sprigs of coriander and serve piping hot in deep bowls.

177

Yorkshire Puddings with Minced Beef and Horseradish

Yorkshire pudding was traditionally served with lettuce sauce or gravy as a preamble to roast beef in Yorkshire homes. The individual puddings in this recipe make wonderful crisp containers for savoury minced beef. The batter and minced beef may be prepared several hours in advance if kept in the refrigerator. You can use six 4in (100mm) tins or patty pans.

SERVES 4-6
PREPARATION TIME : *20 minutes*
COOKING TIME : *50 minutes*
OVEN : *Preheat to 220°C (425°F, gas mark 7)*

INGREDIENTS
BATTER
4oz (115g) plain flour
Salt
1 egg
¼ pint (150ml) semi-skimmed milk
2 tablespoons virgin olive oil
FILLING
2 large onions
1 tablespoon olive oil
1lb (450g) lean minced beef
¾ pint (450ml) beef stock
1 large carrot
4 tablespoons horseradish relish
1 tablespoon Worcestershire sauce
A few drops gravy browning (optional)
Salt and freshly ground black pepper
Parsley sprigs for garnish

Calories per serving : 290 · High in protein from beef, milk and eggs · High in zinc from beef

Sift the flour and a pinch of salt into a bowl. Beat in the egg, milk and ¼ pint (150ml) of cold water, to give a smooth batter.

Place a teaspoon of oil in each of the Yorkshire pudding tins, or ½ teaspoon if using patty pans, and

Golden Yorkshire puddings with horseradish mince.

place in the oven for 2-3 minutes, until very hot. Divide the batter between the tins and bake for 40 minutes (30 minutes for smaller ones) until risen.

Meanwhile, chop the onions and sauté them in 1 tablespoon of olive oil until transparent. Add the minced beef and cook until well browned on all sides. Stir in the stock and simmer for about 10 minutes. Grate the carrot ready for the garnish.

Stir in the horseradish relish, Worcestershire sauce, and a few drops of gravy browning if wished. The mixture should be moist with the stock, but not sloppy. Season to taste.

Fill the Yorkshire puddings with the minced beef and top each one with a little grated carrot. Garnish each pudding with a sprig of parsley and serve.

Roast Leg of Lamb with Barley, Apricot and Mint

Barley is the most digestible of cereals and goes particularly well with lamb. You can use the barley cooking water to make the gravy. It can also be used as the base for a nutritious lemon barley water drink. Serve hot with potatoes and a selection of colourful vegetables, or cold with a salad.

SERVES 8
PREPARATION TIME : *1 hour*
COOKING TIME : *2 hours*
OVEN : *Preheat to 180°C (350°F, gas mark 4)*

INGREDIENTS

4lb (1.8kg) boned leg of lamb
2oz (50g) pot barley
2 teaspoons arrowroot powder
½ pint (285ml) lamb stock or barley water
Fresh mint sprigs for garnish

STUFFING

1 large onion
3oz (75g) mushrooms
3oz (75g) dried apricots
4 tablespoons fresh mint
1 tablespoon olive oil
Salt and freshly ground black pepper

Calories per serving : 600 · High in protein, iron, zinc and vitamin B12 from lamb · High in fibre from apricots, barley and vegetables

Wipe boned lamb inside and out and leave to one side. Wash the barley thoroughly in a sieve under running water, then cook in boiling water for about 45 minutes, until just tender.

To make the stuffing, roughly chop the onion, mushrooms, dried apricots and mint. Heat the oil over a moderate heat and sauté the onion and the mushrooms for 5 minutes until soft. Take off heat, stir in apricots and mint, and season to taste.

Reserving the barley cooking water, if you are using this instead of lamb stock, drain barley and stir into stuffing mixture.

Fill leg of lamb with stuffing and close with skewers or string, either by hand or with a trussing or darning needle. Weigh the lamb to calculate cooking time, allowing 30 minutes per 1lb (450g) for well done, 20-25 minutes for pink to medium.

Place the meat in a roasting tin – and cover with foil if cooking a well-done joint, basting occasionally. Remove from the tin and leave to stand in a warm place for 10 minutes before carving.

For gravy, mix arrowroot with 1 tablespoon cold water, add to pan juices with barley water or stock. Cook until thick, strain into sauceboat and serve.

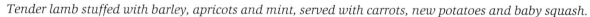

Tender lamb stuffed with barley, apricots and mint, served with carrots, new potatoes and baby squash.

Succulent pork stuffed with prunes served with a sloe gin sauce, broad beans, squash and baby cauliflowers.

Roast Loin of Pork with Prunes and Sloe Gin

Sloe gin is English in origin, and was very popular in Victorian times. It is made by marinating small black 'sloe' berries, harvested in late autumn, in corked bottles of gin with added sugar for several months. The berries are either pricked or crushed to release their flavour and colour. The result is a delicious purple liqueur used in many recipes at the turn of the century. It balances the richness of the pork in this particular dish. Ordinary gin may be substituted if you have trouble finding sloe gin.

The pork may be stuffed with the prunes up to a day in advance of cooking, and kept covered in the refrigerator until required. Serve the pork in thin slices on warmed plates with a selection of colourful vegetables. The sauce should be served separately.

SERVES 6-8
PREPARATION TIME : *15 minutes*
COOKING TIME : *1¼ -1½ hours*
OVEN : *Preheat to 190°C (375°F, gas mark 5)*

INGREDIENTS
3lb (1.4kg) loin of pork
12 ready-to-eat prunes
½ pint (285ml) white grape juice
½ pint (285ml) chicken stock
2 shallots
12 crushed juniper berries
3 tablespoons sloe gin
1 teaspoon arrowroot powder or cornflour
Salt and freshly ground black pepper

Calories per serving : 340 · High in protein, zinc and vitamin B12 from pork

Bone the pork, and remove the rind and excess fat from the surface. Using a sharp knife, make a large hole through the centre of the eye of the loin and press the prunes into it.

Place the pork and prunes in an ovenproof dish just big enough to hold the meat, and pour over the grape juice and stock. Peel and chop the shallots, and add to the dish with the crushed juniper berries. Roast in the oven for 1¼ -1½ hours until tender. Remove the pork from the dish and allow to rest in a warm place for 5 minutes before carving.

Transfer the cooking juices in the dish to a small pan and add the sloe gin. Then mix the arrowroot or cornflour with 1 tablespoon of cold water until smooth, and add to the pan. Cook over a medium heat, stirring until thickened. Add the meat juices to the sauce and strain into a sauceboat.

Pork Chops with Orange and Ginger

Both oranges and root ginger are thought to have originated in China. This dish is an adaptation of a traditional dish still served in the fertile but hilly province of Hunan in central China.

SERVES 4
PREPARATION TIME : *15 minutes*
COOKING TIME : *1-1¼ hours*
OVEN : *Preheat to 180°C (350°F, gas mark 4)*

INGREDIENTS
4 pork chops
1 large onion
2 teaspoons fresh root ginger
1 tablespoon vegetable oil
1 teaspoon arrowroot powder or cornflour
¼ pint (150ml) orange juice
¼ pint (150ml) chicken stock
1oz (25g) raisins
Salt and freshly ground black pepper
1 tablespoon chopped parsley for garnish

Calories per serving : 555 · High in protein and vitamin B12 from pork

Preheat the grill. Trim the rind and excess fat from the pork; which can be either spare rib or loin chops. Grill the chops for about 4 minutes, browning well on both sides. Place the chops in an ovenproof dish in a single layer.

Chop the onion finely, and peel and grate the fresh root ginger. Heat the oil in a small saucepan and sauté the onion over a medium heat for 8 minutes until transparent. Add the ginger and cook for a further 30 seconds, stirring continually.

Mix the arrowroot powder or cornflour with 2 or 3 teaspoons of the orange juice until smooth, then add to the saucepan. Add the remaining orange juice and all of the stock. Stir in the raisins and gently bring to the boil, stirring continually. This sauce may be made a day ahead if kept covered in the refrigerator.

Pour the sauce over the chops, cover and bake for about 45 minutes until thoroughly cooked and tender. If wished, you can remove the lid about 20 minutes before the end of cooking to brown the chops a little more. Season the dish with salt and freshly ground black pepper. Garnish with chopped parsley and serve immediately.

Pork chops baked with a delicious orange, raisin and ginger sauce, served with beans, broccoli florets and slivers of courgette. Jacket or new potatoes go well with the dish.

This spicy Mexican dish topped with avocado sauce is fun to prepare and makes a really tasty meal.

Beef Tacos

This recipe has been adapted from traditional Mexican cuisine. A taco is a tortilla, or Mexican-style flatbread, that has been wrapped around some sort of filling – in this case beef. Ready-made corn tacos are available from supermarkets and are simply heated to contain the filling of your choice. Serve these tacos as a light lunch or supper dish. You will need a liquidiser for this recipe.

SERVES 4
PREPARATION TIME : *30 minutes*
COOKING TIME : *35 minutes*
OVEN : *Preheat to 180°C (350°F, gas mark 4)*

INGREDIENTS
1½ lb (700g) lean minced beef
2 tablespoons virgin olive oil
2 medium onions
2 cloves garlic
1 green chilli
4 tomatoes
14oz (400g) tin pinto or borlotti beans
1 teaspoon ground cumin
Salt and freshly ground pepper
½ small Iceberg lettuce
AVOCADO SAUCE
1 ripe avocado
1 green chilli
½ small onion
1 clove garlic
1 squeeze lemon juice
3 tablespoons virgin olive oil
Salt and freshly ground pepper
1 tomato
12 taco shells

Calories per serving : 625 · High in protein and zinc from meat · High in fibre from beans

Heat 2 tablespoons of oil in a nonstick frying pan and quickly fry the beef over a moderate heat until it browns. Peel and chop all the onions for the beef mixture and avocado sauce, crush all 3 garlic cloves, and de-seed and finely chop the 2 green chillies – keeping the sauce ingredients to one side. Add the 2 medium onions, 2 garlic cloves and 1 green chilli to the pan. Lower the heat slightly and cook for 5 minutes, stirring frequently.

Immerse all of the tomatoes in boiling water for 30 seconds, then cold water for 1 minute, until cool enough to peel away the skins with your fingers. De-seed and chop the tomatoes and drain the tin of beans. Add 4 of the tomatoes, the beans and the cumin to the pan, cover and simmer gently for 30 minutes. Season to taste.

Meanwhile, to make the avocado sauce, peel the

avocado and remove the stone. Blend the avocado in a liquidiser with the chopped chilli, onion, crushed garlic and lemon juice until smooth. Gradually pour in the oil while the motor is still running. Taste and adjust the seasoning, transfer into a basin and stir in the last chopped tomato.

Lay the tacos on a baking sheet and heat in the oven for 5 minutes, then shred the lettuce for garnish. Hold the heated tacos carefully in a clean tea towel and pile 2 heaped tablespoons of the beef mixture into each shell. Scatter the shredded lettuce over the shells, top with the avocado sauce and arrange on a serving platter. Serve immediately.

Veal with Balsamic Vinegar and Sultanas

Balsamic vinegar is a red wine vinegar from Modena in northern Italy. Its distinctive sweet and sour taste is achieved after it has been left to mature in wooden cases for between 3 and 12 years, or preferably even longer for a richer taste. If it is unavailable, sherry vinegar makes a perfectly good substitute. This dish should be served with a colourful selection of fresh vegetables, such as carrots and mangetout.

SERVES 4
PREPARATION TIME : *10 minutes*
SOAKING TIME : *20 minutes*
COOKING TIME : *15 minutes*

INGREDIENTS
4 large veal cutlets or escalopes
1 glass red wine
3oz (75g) sultanas
1oz (25g) butter
1 tablespoon virgin olive oil
1 teaspoon sugar
Pinch of cinnamon
2 tablespoons balsamic or sherry vinegar
Salt and freshly ground black pepper
2oz (50g) pine nuts

Calories per serving : ·380 · High in protein from veal
Low in cholesterol

Pour the red wine into a small saucepan and bring to the boil. Remove from the heat, add the sultanas, and leave them to soak for at least 20 minutes.

Meanwhile, heat the butter and oil in a frying pan, add the veal and sauté for 5 minutes until brown on both sides. Remove the veal from the pan and place it in an oven on a low setting to keep it warm.

To make the sauce, add the soaked sultanas and wine to the pan, along with the sugar, cinnamon and vinegar. Boil the mixture for 2 minutes, until the liquid is slightly reduced, stirring continuously.

Remove the veal from the oven and place it on a serving dish, season to taste and pour over the sauce. Sprinkle with pine nuts and serve immediately.

Pan-fried veal with balsamic vinegar and sultanas.

Braised Pork with Leeks

A hallmark of Normandy cooking is the use of cider. This dish is a variation on one of the region's most ancient recipes – loin of pork gently braised in cider. Braising is an excellent method of ensuring that the lean pork stays moist and succulent.

SERVES 4
PREPARATION TIME : *10 minutes*
COOKING TIME : *1¾ hours*
OVEN : *Preheat to 160°C (325°F, gas mark 3)*

INGREDIENTS
*2lb (900g) joint boned and rolled lean
loin of pork
6 leeks
8fl oz (225ml) dry cider
2 tablespoons chopped fresh sage
or 2 teaspoons dried sage
Salt and freshly ground black pepper*

*Calories per serving : 430 · High in protein from
pork · High in vitamin C from leeks*

Leeks served with pork cooked with sage in cider.

Trim off the roots and the top 2in (50mm) of the leeks, then wash thoroughly to remove any sandy grit between the leaves. Chop all the leeks into 1in (25mm) rounds and place in a flameproof casserole.

Heat a nonstick frying pan and cook the joint, fat side down, at medium to high heat, browning and sealing on all sides.

Place the joint in the casserole. Pour the cider over, sprinkle with the sage, and season to taste. Bring the liquid to the boil on top of the cooker. Then cover, and place in the oven for 1¾ hours. Towards the end of the cooking time, warm a serving dish.

When cooked, lift the joint out of the casserole and place it on the heated dish. Remove the leeks with a slotted spoon and place around the joint. Skim off any fat from the liquid in the pan, and serve separately in a jug. Complement with baked or boiled potatoes and carrots.

Sussex Lamb Chops

The sweetness of the English Bramley apple in the sauce for these lamb chops is perfectly balanced by the sharpness of the cider vinegar. You can mash the apple to make a purée or you can blend the cooked apple in a liquidiser for an even smoother sauce.

SERVES 4
PREPARATION TIME : *10-15 minutes*
COOKING TIME : *30-35 minutes*

INGREDIENTS
*4 × 6oz (175g) loin lamb chops
1 tablespoon plain flour
½ teaspoon ground allspice
Salt and freshly ground black pepper
1 medium onion
3 celery sticks
1 large Bramley apple
2 tablespoons groundnut oil
2 tablespoons cider vinegar
4 fresh rosemary sprigs
Apple slices for garnish (optional)*

*Calories per serving : 370 · High in protein, iron,
zinc and vitamin B12 from lamb*

Apple, rosemary and a little allspice turn lamb chops into a special meal, washed down with some cider.

Trim all excess fat from the lamb chops. Mix the flour with the allspice and a little seasoning. Coat the chops with this mixture and set aside.

Finely chop the onion and celery and then wash, quarter, core and roughly chop the Bramley apple.

Heat the oil in a nonstick frying pan, add the chops and cook over a moderate heat until lightly coloured on all sides. Remove the chops from the pan and drain on absorbent kitchen paper.

Add onion and celery to the pan. Mix well, adding a few tablespoons of water if the mixture becomes dry. Cook over a gentle heat for 5 minutes, stirring constantly, then add the chopped apple and ½ pint (285ml) water. Mix well and slowly bring to the boil, then add the cider vinegar and season to taste.

Return the chops to the pan and top with rosemary sprigs. Cover and cook gently for 25-30 minutes until tender. Baste and turn frequently. Place the chops on top of the sauce on a serving dish or on individual plates and garnish with the apple slices if desired.

Steak with Oranges and Walnuts

You can use any type of steak for this dish, including fillet steak, sirloin, rump or minute steaks. Ready-shelled walnuts are easiest to use for this recipe, but if you choose to buy fresh walnuts in their shells, check to see that the seal between the two halves of the shell is intact. The oranges add a tangy flavour as well as a vivid colour to this simple steak recipe. Heat a large dish, ready for serving.

SERVES 4
PREPARATION TIME : *10 minutes*
COOKING TIME : *10 minutes*

INGREDIENTS
4 steaks
2 oranges
1 lettuce heart
1½ oz (40g) walnuts
1½ tablespoons fresh chives
1½ tablespoons virgin olive oil
Salt and freshly ground black pepper

Calories per serving : 305 · High in protein and zinc from beef · High in vitamin C from oranges

Bring a small pan of water to the boil. Pare a thin slice of orange peel from one of the oranges and cut it into matchsticks. Blanch the matchsticks in boiling water for 1 minute, drain and leave to one side.

Peel both the oranges with a sharp knife, cutting away all the white pith. Remove the segments over a basin by cutting them along either side of their membranes. Squeeze any remaining juice from the orange into the basin.

Wash and shred the lettuce and finely chop the walnuts and chives. Heat the oil in a large frying pan over a moderate heat, add the orange segments and juice, chopped walnuts and chives and bring to the boil. Cook for about 2 minutes, until the juice is syrupy, then transfer to a warm bowl.

Season the steaks with salt and black pepper and add them to the pan. Fry the steaks over a high heat on both sides until cooked according to the thickness of the meat and your personal taste – about 3 minutes on each side for a rare steak and 4-5 for a well-done steak. When the steaks are nearly cooked, pour the sauce over them and cook for another minute. Arrange the steaks and sauce on the heated serving dish and keep warm.

Keeping to a high heat, add the remaining oil to the pan and cook the shredded lettuce for just 1 minute. Add the orange matchsticks and stir well. Scatter the lettuce and orange rind over the steaks and serve immediately.

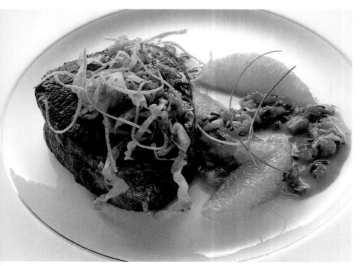

The sweet taste of orange and the nutty texture of walnuts complement a tender steak beautifully.

Baked Ham with Apricots and Candied Sweet Potatoes

Labels on many bacon and gammon joints often advise against soaking before cooking. However, when baking rather than boiling a joint, the meat loses some of its juices making it more salty, so it is advisable to soak the meat to remove as much of the salt as possible. The sweet potato, often wrongly identified as the yam, is 'candied' by adding natural sweeteners such as sugar and honey. Apricots add their own sweetness, alternatively nectarines or peaches can be used instead. This dish makes a colourful and festive main course.

INGREDIENTS

*2lb (900g) smoked joint lean shoulder
bacon or gammon
1 medium onion
6 peppercorns
6 coriander seeds
2lb (900g) sweet potatoes
2 tablespoons sunflower oil
8oz (225g) fresh apricots
Grated rind and juice of 1 orange
1oz (25g) muscovado sugar
1 tablespoon grain mustard
1 tablespoon clear honey
30 cloves*

*Calories per serving : 480 · High in protein and zinc
from pork · High in carotene and vitamin C from
orange, apricots and sweet potatoes*

Honey-glazed ham with apricots and sweet potatoes.

Cover the meat with cold water and leave in a cool place to soak for 4 hours, then drain. Place the joint on a piece of foil large enough to wrap and seal it. Chop the onion finely and sprinkle over the joint, along with the cloves, peppercorns and coriander seeds. Wrap the meat and seal the edges, then cook in the oven for 1 hour and 20 minutes.

Bring a pan of salted water to the boil. Peel the sweet potatoes and cut them into 2in (50mm) cubes. Add them to the pan of water and return to the boil. Simmer for 7 minutes.

Meanwhile, heat the oil in a small roasting tin in the oven. Drain the potatoes. Remove the tin from the oven and add the potatoes to it, coating them evenly with the oil. Replace in the oven and cook for 30 minutes. Halve the apricots. Grate the orange rind into a bowl and squeeze in the juice.

Add the apricots to the tin and the sugar to the orange juice and rind. Pour the orange mixture over the apricots and potatoes and return the tin to the oven for a further 30 minutes, basting two or three times, until most of the sugar and orange mixture has caramelised around the potatoes. Meanwhile, warm a dish with a lid.

Reserving the sugar mixture, remove the potatoes and apricots from the tin with a slotted spoon and place them in the warmed dish.

Remove the meat from the oven and take it out of the foil. Reserve the cooking juices. Increase the oven temperature to 220°C (425°F, gas mark 7). Peel off the skin from the meat and score the fat with crisscrossed cuts. Mix the mustard with the honey and spread it over the fat and press the cloves in to make a pattern. Place in a roasting tin or dish and cook in the oven for 10 minutes, basting two or three times, until the fat is golden-brown.

Meanwhile, make the sauce by mixing the sugar mixture and reserved meat juices in a pan and bring to the boil on top of the stove.

Cut the meat into slices and arrange on a serving platter, or if you prefer, carve the ham at the table. Lay the potatoes and apricots around the meat and serve the sauce separately in a small jug.

Lamb with Yoghurt and Indian Spices

This recipe is based upon an Indian festival dish called 'Raan', in which the lamb is marinated in a rich mixture of yoghurt and spices and then cooked gently in the oven. Spices like cumin, ginger, chillies and colourful turmeric make this a spectacular and delicious dish.

After the lamb has been left marinating in the yoghurt for two days it is so tender that it almost falls off the bone, and can be served with a spoon rather than a carving knife. Although you must plan ahead to make this recipe, it is actually very simple to prepare and it always looks impressive. For an Indian-style buffet – serve with curried vegetables, rice, hot pepper relishes and chutneys.

SERVES 6

PREPARATION TIME : *15-20 minutes*

MARINATING TIME : *2 days*

COOKING TIME : *2½ hours*

OVEN : *Preheat to 220°C (425°F, gas mark 7), reduce to 160°C (325°F, gas mark 3)*

INGREDIENTS

4lb (1.8kg) leg of lamb

2 teaspoons cumin seeds

2 teaspoons coriander seeds

Seeds of 6 cardamom pods

2in (50mm) piece fresh root ginger

4 cloves garlic

4 cloves

2 dried red chillies

2 teaspoons ground turmeric

2 teaspoons salt

¾ pint (450ml) natural low-fat yoghurt

3 tablespoons lemon juice

Toasted almonds to garnish

2 tablespoons soft brown sugar

Fresh coriander sprigs for garnish

Calories per serving : 585 · High in protein from the lamb and yoghurt. High in iron, vitamin B12 and zinc from the lamb

Trim the fat from the lamb. Score the meat deeply in a crisscross pattern with a knife. Dry-fry the cumin, coriander and cardamom in a pan for 2-3 minutes until their aroma is released. Set aside.

Grind the peeled ginger and garlic to a paste in a mortar and pestle with the dry-fried seeds, the cloves and chopped chillies. Transfer to a bowl, add the turmeric, salt, yoghurt and lemon juice, and mix well. Spread the yoghurt mixture over the lamb and

right into the scored meat. Cover loosely with foil. Marinate in the refrigerator for two days.

When ready to cook, preheat the oven and leave the lamb at room temperature for 1 hour. Taking care not to burn them, toast the almonds on a flat roasting tin in the oven for 8 minutes and set aside.

Place the lamb on a rack in a roasting tin and sprinkle with the sugar. Roast in the oven for 20 minutes. Reduce the oven temperature and remove the lamb, baste well, then cover with foil and return to the oven. Basting frequently, continue roasting for 2-2¼ hours, until the meat is very tender.

Let the lamb stand, still covered, for 20 minutes. Garnish with the toasted almonds and coriander.

Cardamom, coriander and cumin add spice to this aromatic Indian dish which is served with hot pepper relishes and chutneys.

Roast Fillet of Beef with Bacon and Mushrooms

Fillet of beef is excellent when simply roasted and is enormously popular. Wrapping the beef in bacon helps to keep it moist during cooking. To make the sauce, use a well-flavoured stock – fresh stocks are available in cartons at most large supermarkets. Serve the roast fillet with a selection of crisp vegetables, such as mangetout, baby carrots and tiny brussels sprouts.

SERVES 6
PREPARATION TIME : *30 minutes*
COOKING TIME : *35-55 minutes*
OVEN : *Preheat to 200°C (400°F, gas mark 6)*

INGREDIENTS
1½ lb (700g) fillet of beef
8 rashers streaky bacon
1 small onion
½ oz (15g) unsalted butter
12oz (350g) mushrooms
2 teaspoons fresh chopped thyme
or 1 teaspoon dried thyme
1 teaspoon arrowroot powder or cornflour
2 tablespoons whole or semi-skimmed milk
Salt and freshly ground black pepper
1 tablespoon plain flour
1 tablespoon English mustard
¾ pint (450ml) beef stock

Calories per serving : 320 · High in protein, iron and zinc from beef and bacon

Trim any fat or sinew from beef. Remove the rinds from the bacon and set the rashers aside. Place rinds in a large frying pan and cook over medium heat until some of the fat is rendered. Discard rinds.

Peel and finely chop the onion. Melt the butter in the pan, and sauté the onion until transparent. Chop the mushrooms finely and add to the pan with the thyme. Cook over a high heat, stirring frequently, until the mixture is dry.

Mix the arrowroot or cornflour into the milk until smooth and add to the mushrooms. Stir well and

Bacon and chopped mushrooms surround tender beef.

cook over a medium heat until the mixture thickens and becomes firm. Season to taste and leave to cool.

Lay bacon rashers on a piece of greaseproof paper so they overlap slightly, making a 'sheet' of bacon.

Spread the mushroom mixture evenly over the bacon, then place the beef fillet on top. Carefully wrap the bacon around the beef, securing it at intervals with cocktail sticks, skewers or string.

Place the beef on a rack in a roasting tin and cook in the oven for 45 minutes for medium-cooked beef, 35 minutes for rare and 55 minutes for well-done.

Turn off oven. Remove beef from the tin and keep warm on a serving plate in the oven. Mix a little of the cooking juices into the flour until smooth. Add to roasting-tin juices and cook over medium heat, stirring continually until bubbling. Add mustard and stock, a bit at a time, for the sauce. Simmer for 5 minutes until slightly thickened, season to taste, and strain into sauceboat. Serve beef in thick slices.

Lincolnshire Sausages with Lentils

A hearty and nutritious dish, this is really a meal in itself and does not need any other vegetables to be served with it. Lincolnshire sausages are available from butchers and some supermarkets.

SERVES 4
PREPARATION TIME : *15 minutes*
SOAKING TIME : *3-12 hours*
COOKING TIME : *1½ hours*
OVEN : *Preheat to 180°C (350°F, gas mark 4)*

INGREDIENTS
1lb (450g) Lincolnshire sausages
12oz (350g) green lentils
4 rashers smoked streaky bacon
4 medium onions
1 large clove garlic
1 tablespoon virgin olive oil
2 bay leaves
2 pints (1.1 litres) light vegetable stock
Salt and freshly ground black pepper

Calories per serving : 680 · High in protein from sausage and bacon · High in fibre from lentils

Put the lentils in a large bowl, cover with cold water and leave to soak for at least 3 hours.

Cut the rinds off the bacon and put them in a flameproof casserole over a high heat until some of the fat has melted. Keeping this fat in the casserole, discard the rinds. Chop up the bacon and quickly fry it in the fat for 5 minutes.

Peel and quarter the onions and crush the garlic. Reduce the heat, add the oil, onions and garlic, and cook gently for a further 5 minutes. Stir in the lentils and bay leaves and toss them lightly in the oil. Then pour over the stock and bring to the boil. Cover the casserole with a lid and put into the oven for 1 hour.

Lightly brown the sausages in a nonstick frying pan (this is not to cook them, but just to make them look more appetising). Stir the casserole contents well, then bury the sausages in the dish. Cover the dish again and replace in the oven for a further 30 minutes. Check after 15 minutes and, if the dish is becoming too dry, add an additional ¼ pint (150ml) of stock or water. Taste, and season before serving.

Lincolnshire sausages are flavoured with black pepper and sage, but any spicy sausage can be used for this dish.

A tasty casserole of minced lamb, fennel and artichoke hearts cooked with rosemary, coriander and tomatoes.

Lamb, Fennel and Artichoke Hotchpotch

If ready-minced lamb is unavailable, buy a boned half shoulder of lamb and mince it at home. Fennel has been used in European cooking since ancient times. It has a lovely anise flavour, and is used to make a Spanish after-dinner liqueur called hierbas. When buying fennel, choose firm, crisp bulbs that are a pale greenish-white with fresh-looking tops. The coriander adds its musky, orange aroma to complement the fennel, artichoke and lamb. This aromatic dish may be prepared 1-2 days in advance if stored in the refrigerator. It will then need reheating in the oven, or simmering with a little added stock to moisten it. Garnish with the parsley and the retained fennel fronds, and serve immediately. The dish goes well with potatoes or freshly cooked brown rice and a simple green salad with a light French dressing.

SERVES 4
PREPARATION TIME : *15 minutes*
COOKING TIME : *45 minutes*

INGREDIENTS
1lb (450g) lean minced lamb
2 fennel bulbs, each weighing 8oz (225g)
1 medium onion
2 cloves garlic
1 tablespoon virgin olive oil
2 teaspoons ground coriander
Salt and freshly ground black pepper
14oz (400g) tin chopped tomatoes
3 sprigs fresh rosemary or 1 teaspoon dried
14oz (400g) tin artichoke hearts
Chopped parsley and fennel fronds for garnish

Calories per serving : 260 · High in protein from lamb · High in vitamin C from tomatoes

192

Peel the outside of each fennel bulb to remove any coarse strings. Trim root and stalk ends, then cut each bulb in 8 wedges. Retain any fluffy green fronds for garnish. Cook the fennel wedges in boiling salted water for 5 minutes, then drain and put to one side.

Chop the onion and garlic finely. Heat the oil in a large frying pan and sauté the onion with the garlic and ground coriander over a medium heat for 8 minutes, until the onion is transparent. Add the lamb and cook, stirring occasionally, for about 10 minutes, until the meat is well browned on all sides.

Add the seasoning, chopped tomatoes, rosemary and fennel, then cover and simmer for 25 minutes.

Drain and halve the artichokes and stir into the pan. Simmer for 5 minutes, garnish and serve.

Navarin of Lamb

The traditional British lamb hotpot is cooked French style in this recipe, with the addition of tomatoes and garlic. A bouquet garni, a herb mixture that includes sprigs of thyme and parsley and a bay leaf, is also added to flavour the dish while cooking.

SERVES 4
PREPARATION TIME : *25 minutes*
COOKING TIME : *2¼ -2½ hours*
OVEN : *Preheat to 160°C (325°F, gas mark 3)*

INGREDIENTS
1-1½ lb (450-700g) neck fillet of lamb
4 medium onions
4 medium carrots
4 small turnips
8 small potatoes
2 cloves garlic
1 pint (570ml) lamb stock
2 tablespoons tomato purée
Bouquet garni
2 sprigs fresh rosemary
2 teaspoons cornflour
Salt and freshly ground black pepper
Parsley for garnish

Calories per serving : 495 · High in protein from lamb · High in carotene from carrots

Cut the lamb into 1½ -2in (40-50mm) chunks. Peel and quarter the onions. Peel the carrots and halve them crossways. Peel and halve the turnips, peel the potatoes and crush the garlic. Place the lamb chunks in the oven in a flameproof casserole dish with all of the vegetables.

Add the lamb stock, crushed garlic, tomato purée, bouquet garni and rosemary sprigs to the casserole dish and bring slowly to a simmer. Cover with a lid, or foil, and cook in the oven for about 2¼ hours until the meat is really tender.

Mix the cornflour and 1 tablespoon of cold water until smooth and stir into the casserole. Cook, stirring over a medium heat until the gravy starts to thicken slightly. Remove the bouquet garni and the rosemary sprigs. Season to taste with salt and freshly ground black pepper, garnish with freshly chopped parsley. Serve straight from the casserole or on individual plates when desired.

Savoury navarin of lamb flavoured with an aromatic bouquet garni, and garnished with fresh chopped parsley. The French serve this dish with chunks of fresh bread to help mop up the delicious juices.

Pork Chops with Barbecue Sauce

'Barbecue' originated from the Mexican-Spanish word *barbacoa*, describing meat grilled over a green wood fire. Although primitive, barbecuing is one of the healthiest ways of cooking, for it allows any fat to drip from the food. It also seals in all the flavours of the food. This recipe uses a delicious homemade version of American barbecue sauce, which was probably adapted from the devilled sauces made with strong mustard that have been used in British cooking for centuries. This dish may be prepared a day in advance if refrigerated and then reheated in the oven or simmered gently. Serve with natural yoghurt, filled jacket potatoes and a green salad.

Pork chops, a cool green salad and jacket potatoes are set off by a traditional spicy American barbecue sauce.

SERVES 4
PREPARATION TIME : *20 minutes*
COOKING TIME : *45 minutes*
OVEN : *Preheat to 180°C (350°F, gas mark 4)*

INGREDIENTS
4 spare rib chops
1 medium onion
1 tablespoon virgin olive oil
3 teaspoons horseradish sauce
1 teaspoon mustard powder
1 teaspoon celery seeds
14oz (400g) can chopped tomatoes
2 tablespoons honey
1 tablespoon malt vinegar
1 tablespoon Worcestershire sauce
Chopped parsley for garnish

Calories per serving : 610 · High in protein, vitamin B12 and iron from pork

Chop the onion roughly. Heat the oil in a saucepan and sauté the onion over a medium heat for 8 minutes until transparent. Add all the other sauce ingredients. Cover and simmer for 10 minutes.

Meanwhile, trim any rind and fat from the spare rib chops and place them in an ovenproof dish large enough to hold them in a single layer.

When ready, spoon the barbecue sauce over the chops, cover and bake in the preheated oven for 45 minutes until thoroughly cooked and tender. Garnish with parsley and serve immediately.

Chinese Spare Ribs with Five-Spice Marinade

Pork ribs are more commonly known as Chinese or American spare ribs, reflecting their popularity in both countries. In this dish they are marinated in five-spice powder, which is often used in Chinese cooking. It is a brown powder made up of ground star anise, fennel, cinnamon, cloves and szechuan pepper, and is available from oriental shops and supermarkets. The ribs are best left to marinate for up to 24 hours to absorb the flavours.

An exotic five-spice powder enhances these pork ribs.

SERVES 4
PREPARATION TIME : *15 minutes*
MARINATING TIME : *1-24 hours*
COOKING TIME : *50 minutes to 1 hour*
OVEN : *Preheat to 180°C (350°F, gas mark 4)*

INGREDIENTS
2½ lb (1.1kg) pork spare ribs
2 cloves garlic
1in (25mm) fresh root ginger
2 teaspoons curry powder
2 teaspoons five-spice powder
2 tablespoons light soy sauce
2 tablespoons dry sherry or dry white wine
2 tablespoons clear honey

Calories per serving : 450 · High in protein from pork · High in iron from pork and curry powder

Cut the sheets of ribs into individual pieces by slicing between the bones with a sharp knife.

Crush the garlic or chop it finely, and peel and finely grate the ginger. Combine with the remaining ingredients in a bowl.

Lay the ribs in a large dish, pour the marinade over them and toss well until evenly coated. Cover and leave in a cool place for at least 1 hour.

Toss the ribs once more, then place them in a large roasting tin, in a single layer.

Cook in the preheated oven for 50 minutes to 1 hour, turning and brushing with the marinade from time to time, until the ribs are well browned. Serve immediately.

Irish Stew

Traditionally, Irish stew is made with the rather fatty middle neck chops or 'scrag end' of lamb. This recipe uses lean neck fillet instead. The dish is made of layers of meat and vegetables, creating a truly hearty meal. The herbs thyme and rosemary complement the lamb, and potatoes add a fresh touch to the dish. Serve with crunchy carrots and a seasonal green vegetable, adding bright colour.

SERVES 4
PREPARATION TIME : *30 minutes*
COOKING TIME : *2½ -3 hours*
OVEN : *Preheat to 180°C (350°F, gas mark 4)*

INGREDIENTS
1lb (450g) lean neck of lamb fillet
2lb (900g) potatoes
2 large onions
2 teaspoons fresh chopped rosemary
or 1 teaspoon dried
2 teaspoons fresh chopped thyme
or 1 teaspoon dried
Salt and freshly ground black pepper
Rosemary and thyme sprigs for garnish

Calories per serving : 390 · High in protein from lamb and potatoes · High in iron and zinc from lamb · High in fibre from potatoes

Trim away any fat from the lamb and cut the meat into thin slices. Scrub the potatoes and slice into very thin rounds. Slice the onions into rings.

Line the bottom of a casserole dish with a layer of potatoes, then a layer of onion rings and a layer of lamb. Sprinkle with a little rosemary and thyme and season. Continue layering in this way, finishing with a layer of potatoes on top.

Pour in enough water to half fill the casserole dish and slowly bring to the boil. Cover with foil and the casserole lid and cook in the oven for 2½ -3 hours, until the potatoes and lamb are tender. Uncover the casserole for the last 20-30 minutes of cooking to brown the potatoes.

Garnish with rosemary and thyme sprigs and serve straight from the casserole dish.

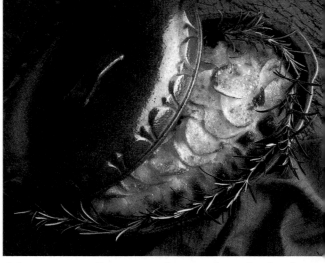

Crispy potato slices cover layers of tender lamb sprinkled with thyme and rosemary. The dish is also garnished with a ring of rosemary sprigs.

Pork, Potato and Apple Cakes

Potato cakes have long been a favourite in the north of England and in Scotland, where they are usually served with bacon for breakfast. Serve these cakes with apple sauce or gravy for a light lunch or supper. They may be made and shaped and kept covered in the refrigerator for up to 12 hours. Once cooked they should be eaten immediately.

SERVES 4
PREPARATION TIME : *35 minutes*
COOKING TIME : *25-30 minutes*

INGREDIENTS
8oz (225g) minced raw pork
1lb (450g) potatoes
4oz (115g) cooking apple
2oz (50g) onion
1 tablespoon fresh sage
Salt and freshly ground black pepper
2 tablespoons vegetable oil
2 dessert apples
8 sage leaves for garnish

Calories per serving : 340 · High in dietary fibre from potatoes and cooking apples · High in protein from pork

Peel the potatoes and cut into even-sized pieces. Steam or cook in boiling salted water for about 20 minutes until tender. Drain thoroughly and mash well. Add the minced pork.

Finely chop or grate the cooking apple and onion and add to the potato. Chop the sage, add to the mixture and season generously. Work the mixture together until evenly combined. With lightly floured hands, shape the mixture into 8 cakes.

Heat the oil in a nonstick frying pan on a medium heat, and cook the cakes for 12-15 minutes, turning them occasionally until golden-brown on both sides. To check that the mixture is cooked, insert a skewer into the centre of one cake and leave it there for 10 seconds. Draw the skewer out and touch it. If it feels hot then the mixture is cooked.

While the cakes are cooking, core and cut the dessert apples into quarters. Fry the apple and sage leaves in a small amount of hot oil until the apples are cooked through and the sage leaves are crisp. Serve the cakes with an apple quarter and a sage leaf on top of each one.

Pork, potato and apple cakes garnished with crisp fried apple and sage leaves. They are still served with bacon for breakfast in some parts of northern England and Scotland, but they are just as good for lunch or supper.

Szechuan Pepper Lamb

Szechuan pepper, also known as 'fagara' or anise pepper, is used in a wide range of dishes from eastern China. These aromatic peppercorns are the dried berries of an oriental shrub, and they can be bought from large supermarkets as well as Chinese stores. In China, the peppercorns are roasted until crisp, ground, and mixed with a little salt for a table condiment. In this dish, Szechuan pepper adds a sharp, tangy flavour to the lamb, while the dried red chillies make it quite hot and spicy. The lamb is first chilled in a freezer, making it easier to slice.

SERVES 4

PREPARATION TIME : *15-20 minutes*
FREEZING TIME : *½ -1 hour*
COOKING TIME : *25 minutes*

INGREDIENTS

12oz (350g) lean lamb leg steak
1 tablespoon Szechuan peppercorns
1 or 2 dried red chillies
2 medium red peppers
6 spring onions
2 teaspoons cornflour
2 tablespoons shoyu or low-sodium soy sauce
2 tablespoons dry sherry
2 tablespoons dark soft brown sugar
2 tablespoons groundnut oil
Salt and freshly ground black pepper

Calories per serving : 280 · High in protein and zinc from lamb · High in vitamin C from pepper · Low in cholesterol (less than one egg)

Wrap the lamb in foil and place it in the freezer for at least 30 minutes. Unwrap the lamb and slice it by cutting across the grain into very thin slivers.

Dry-fry the peppercorns for 2-3 minutes until their fragrance is released, then crush in a mortar and pestle with the dried red chillies. Put the lamb, peppercorns and chillies in a bowl and stir well to mix. Cover and set aside.

Halve and de-seed the peppers, then slice them lengthways into thin strips. Trim the spring onions and slice them on the diagonal into 1½in (40mm)

Tangy Szechuan pepper, spicy red chillies and a little sherry flavour the lamb in this oriental dish.

lengths. Put the cornflour in a measuring jug and add the shoyu or soy sauce, sherry and sugar, and stir well to mix into a smooth paste.

Heat half the oil in a wok or frying pan. Add the red peppers and spring onions and stir-fry over a gentle heat for 3-4 minutes until softened. Remove with a slotted spoon and set aside on kitchen paper.

Heat the remaining oil in the pan, add the lamb in batches and stir-fry over a moderate to high heat for 3-4 minutes until crispy and tender. Remove the lamb with a slotted spoon and set aside with the red peppers and spring onions.

Stirring all the time, pour boiling water gradually into the cornflour mixture up to the ½ pint (285ml) mark. Mix thoroughly to ensure that the cornflour is evenly distributed, then pour the liquid into the pan and stir to scrape up all the sediment. Bring gently to the boil, stirring constantly, then simmer until thickened and return the lamb and vegetables to the pan. Stir to coat in the sauce, season to taste and serve immediately.

Baked Spare-rib Chops with Sweet Potato and Pumpkin

This recipe is one of the favourite ways of preparing pork chops in the West Indies. Pumpkins and sweet potatoes are amongst the most common vegetables used on the islands. In England, pumpkin is widely available in the autumn, but Indian and West Indian shops have a supply throughout the year.

SERVES 4
PREPARATION TIME : *25 minutes*
COOKING TIME : *2 hours*
OVEN : *Preheat to 190°C (375°F, gas mark 5)*

INGREDIENTS
4 pork spare-rib chops
1lb (450g) pumpkin
1lb (450g) sweet potatoes
1 red pepper
1 onion
Few sprigs fresh thyme
1 pint (570ml) chicken stock
Salt and freshly ground black pepper
2 teaspoons West Indian hot chilli sauce (optional)

Calories per serving : 645 · High in protein and zinc from pork · High in carotene, vitamin C and vitamin A from pumpkin and sweet potato.

Wipe the chops and cut away any rind. Discard the seeds from the pumpkin, cut away the skin, and dice into ¾in (20mm) cubes.

Peel and dice the sweet potatoes into similar-sized cubes and then put them in water to stop them discolouring. Halve and de-seed the pepper and cut it into small squares. Peel and finely chop the onion.

Mix all the vegetables in an ovenproof dish, add the sprigs of thyme, cover with stock and season to taste. If desired, add the West Indian hot chilli sauce.

Place the chops on top of the vegetables and season lightly. Cover with foil and bake in the oven for about 2 hours until the vegetables and meat are tender – removing the foil about 30 minutes before the end of the cooking time to brown the chops. Serve immediately.

The sweet flavour of the tender vegetables and the spicy chilli sauce used in this simple pork recipe are typical of West Indian cooking.

Wiltshire Ham Cooked in Cider

Cider-making spread to the West Country after the Norman Conquest in 1066, and by the 13th century, cooking in cider had become a speciality of the region. A strong dry cider with a hint of apple subtly flavours the ham. This traditional dish can be served hot with potatoes, green vegetables and Cumberland sauce, which is a savoury fruit sauce sharpened by red currants and sometimes cranberries. It can also be served cold with salad, pickles and crusty bread.

From the Old English word 'hamm' (a thigh), ham is the salted back leg of the pig. Wiltshire ham is mild, since it is not matured as long as some other hams.

SERVES 6-8
PREPARATION TIME : *20 minutes*
COOKING TIME : *1¼ hours*
SOAKING TIME : *Overnight*

INGREDIENTS
3lb (1.4kg) gammon joint
1 teaspoon ground mace
1 teaspoon ground allspice
12 cloves
1 pint (570ml) dry cider
1 tablespoon chopped sage, thyme or parsley
SAUCE
Grated rind and juice of ½ orange and ½ lemon
8oz (225g) redcurrant jelly
1 large glass port or red wine
Pinch of cayenne pepper
1 tablespoon Worcestershire sauce

Calories per serving : 440 · High in protein, iron, zinc and thiamin from pork

Soak the ham overnight in cold water. Place the ham with its cooking ingredients in a large pan with a tightly fitting lid. Pour in enough hot water to cover the ham, and bring to the boil. Reduce the heat, cover and simmer for 1¼ hours.

Meanwhile, grate the orange and lemon rinds and strain the juices into a bowl. Heat the redcurrant jelly in a small saucepan. Add the port and bring gently to the boil, stirring frequently. Reduce the heat and simmer until the liquid has thickened and reduced by about one-third.

Stir in the orange and lemon rinds and juice, add the cayenne pepper and the Worcestershire sauce and mix well. The sauce can be served warm or cold. Drain the ham and place on a carving dish.

Chinese Rolled Beef with Vegetables

These beef rolls, filled with a colourful vegetable stuffing, are cooked very quickly in the Chinese tradition, which retains their colour and flavour. White turnip or celeriac are alternatives for kohlrabi.

Thin slices of entrecote steak wrapped around brightly coloured vegetables and served in an oriental sauce.

SERVES 4
PREPARATION TIME : *45 minutes*
COOKING TIME : *15 minutes*

INGREDIENTS
8 × 2oz (50g) slices entrecote steak
2oz (50g) leeks
2oz (50g) carrots
2oz (50g) green beans
2oz (50g) kohlrabi
4 teaspoons vegetable oil
8 small shallots
1 tablespoon red wine vinegar
½ pint (285ml) red wine
¼ pint (150ml) beef stock
1 tablespoon oyster sauce
1 tablespoon soy sauce
1½ teaspoons arrowroot powder or cornflour

Calories per serving : 310 · High in protein from beef
High in carotene from carrots and kohlrabi

Trim the strip of fat from the edge of each slice of beef and discard.

Cut all the vegetables, except the shallots, into thin fingers, plunge them into boiling water for 30 seconds to blanch and drain.

Cover each piece of beef with an equal amount of vegetables and roll the beef around them. Secure each roll with a cocktail stick, then trim the sticks with scissors so that they do not protrude and the rolls can be evenly browned.

Heat 1 tablespoon of the oil in a large frying pan over a medium heat and brown the beef rolls on all sides for about 5 minutes. Remove from the pan.

Cut the shallots into thin rings. Add the remaining oil and the red wine vinegar to the pan and sauté the shallots for about 5 minutes until they are transparent and the vinegar is reduced. Add the wine, stock, oyster sauce and soy sauce, then heat to a simmer. Mix the arrowroot or cornflour with 1 tablespoon of water, stirring into the sauce until thickened.

Return the beef rolls to the pan and simmer for 5 minutes. Remove the cocktail sticks and serve with plain rice and vegetables or a side salad.

Tender chunks of beef cooked in red Burgundy and beef stock. As the casserole cooks, all the flavours from the vegetables mingle with the taste of beef, wine and smoky bacon – making a delicious, rich gravy.

Beef Bourguignonne

This recipe is based on the traditional French boeuf bourguignonne, or beef braised in Burgundy wine. The braising technique stops evaporation and keeps in all the aromas as it is slowly cooked. Like many stews and casseroles, this dish benefits from being made a day or two in advance and stored in the refrigerator, allowing the meats and vegetables to marinate in the red wine stock. Extra marinating heightens the flavour of the meat. The dish can then be reheated in the oven or simmered. A little extra stock may be required to moisten it when reheating. Serve hot, garnished with chopped parsley and potatoes or bread and crisp green beans or broccoli.

SERVES 4

PREPARATION TIME : *25 minutes*

COOKING TIME : *2½ -3 hours*

OVEN : *Preheat to 160°C (325°F, gas mark 3)*

INGREDIENTS

1-1½ lb (450-700g) braising steak
4oz (115g) lean smoked bacon
1 clove garlic
6oz (175g) large button mushrooms
1lb (450g) small onions or shallots
1 bouquet garni
¾ pint (450ml) beef stock
½ pint (285ml) red Burgundy wine
Salt and freshly ground black pepper
2 teaspoons cornflour
Parsley for garnish

---

*Calories per serving : 310 · High in protein, zinc
and iron from beef and bacon*

Cut off the bacon rinds and fry them gently in a flameproof casserole dish in the oven until some of the fat starts to melt. Discard rinds, add the rashers and fry for 2 minutes each side. Drain bacon on kitchen paper and cut into small pieces.

Cut the beef into 1½in (40mm) cubes, crush the garlic and add them to the casserole along with the cleaned mushrooms, peeled onions, bouquet garni, stock and wine. Season to taste.

Bring the casserole to simmering point then cover and bake in the oven for 2½-3 hours until the meat is tender. Remove and stir occasionally.

Mix the cornflour and water together to make a smooth paste and stir into the casserole. Cook over a medium heat, stirring until thickened. Adjust the seasoning and serve.

Pork Chops with Juniper Berries

There are 40-50 species of juniper berries, each taking a full three years to develop. They are used in brines for pickling meat, and marinades and stuffings for game and birds. Their slightly astrin-

Marinating pork chops with oil and juniper berries is an easy way to turn them into something special.

gent flavour enhances many dishes and is particularly good with fatty meats such as pork. Serve with apple sauce or jelly and a selection of vegetables.

SERVES 4

PREPARATION TIME : *5 minutes*

MARINATING TIME : *1 hour*

COOKING TIME : *15 minutes*

INGREDIENTS

4 pork chops
12 juniper berries
2 tablespoons sunflower oil
Salt and freshly ground black pepper

---

*Calories per serving : 640 · High in protein, iron and
vitamin B12 from pork*

Crush the juniper berries with a pestle and mortar, or with a rolling pin on a board, and put into a bowl. Stir in the oil and mix thoroughly.

Brush the chops on both sides with the crushed berries and oil, and season with salt and pepper. Lay the chops in a dish and leave at room temperature to marinate for 1 hour.

Turn the grill onto a medium heat for about 3 minutes before using. Grill the chops on each side for about 7 minutes. Serve immediately.

Pork Chops with Savoy Cabbage

This simple version of a traditional French country casserole dish makes a robust and tasty winter meal. Savoy cabbage has a delicate flavour and a crunchy texture, making it perfect for baking.

SERVES 4

PREPARATION TIME : *20 minutes*

MARINATING TIME : *4-24 hours*

COOKING TIME : *1½ hours*

OVEN : *Preheat to 180°C (350°F, gas mark 4)*

INGREDIENTS

4 pork chops

2lb (900g) savoy cabbage

Salt and freshly ground black pepper

MARINADE

1 medium onion

2 cloves garlic

½ pint (285ml) red wine

6 parsley stalks

1 sprig rosemary

6 peppercorns

6 coriander seeds

1 bay leaf

2 tablespoons virgin olive oil

Calories per serving : 590 · High in protein from pork · High in fibre from cabbage

Peel and roughly chop the onion. Crush the garlic. Put onion and garlic into a saucepan with the rest of the marinade ingredients, and slowly bring to the boil. Remove from heat and allow to cool.

Place chops in a shallow dish. Pour over marinade and refrigerate overnight, or at least 4 hours.

Set a pan with a little salted water on the hob to boil. Shred the cabbage. Cook in the boiling water for 5 minutes, then drain. Tip half the cabbage into a casserole and place the chops on top. Cover the chops with the remaining cabbage, then strain the marinade over the cabbage.

Place a lid over the casserole and cook in the oven for 1½ hours. Adjust the seasoning and serve.

The savoy cabbage comes from Savoie, France, where this dish has been served since the Middle Ages.

Braised Beef with Guinness

Guinness lends this casserole its rich brown colour and flavour. Use a casserole with a tightly fitting lid to keep in all the aromas and goodness. This dish benefits from being prepared 1-2 days ahead and refrigerated, letting the flavours mellow and mature.

SERVES 4

PREPARATION TIME : *20 minutes*

COOKING TIME : *3¼ hours*

OVEN : *Preheat to 160°C (325°F, gas mark 3)*

INGREDIENTS

1½ lb (700g) braising steak

2 large onions

4oz (115g) small mushroom caps

4 large carrots

4 sticks celery

½ teaspoon dried mixed herbs

1 bay leaf

1 tablespoon tomato purée

1 teaspoon brown sugar

1 pint (570ml) beef stock

½ pint (285ml) Guinness

1 tablespoon cornflour

Salt and freshly ground black pepper

Parsley for garnish

Calories per serving : 305 · High in protein from beef High in vitamin A and carotene from carrots

Cut the steak into 1½in (40mm) cubes. Quarter the onions and halve the mushroom caps. Quarter the carrots and celery crossways. Place the meat and vegetables in an ovenproof casserole, along with the mixed herbs, bay leaf, tomato purée, sugar, beef stock and Guinness. Stir to mix thoroughly.

Gently bring the stew to the boil, then cover and transfer to the preheated oven. Cook very gently for 3 hours until the meat is really tender.

Mix the cornflour with 1 tablespoon of water until smooth, then stir into the casserole. Bring to the boil, stirring until thickened. Adjust seasoning to taste.

Transfer to a serving dish, garnish with freshly chopped parsley and serve immediately.

Guinness adds a rich Irish flavour to this heart-warming dish of braised beef served with mashed potato and peas.

Beef Strips with Almonds and Sherry Vinegar

Sherry vinegar was first produced by accident in Andalusia, in southern Spain, when an old sherry barrel 'turned' and became vinegary. A pleasant and slightly nutty taste was produced which became popular with the locals, and sherry vinegar has been sold commercially ever since. Warm a large dish or individual plates ready for serving.

The nutty taste of sherry vinegar combines with the delicate flavour of almonds to enhance the beef.

SERVES 4
PREPARATION TIME : *10 minutes*
COOKING TIME : *12 minutes*

INGREDIENTS
1lb (450g) rump steak
Salt and freshly ground black pepper
3 tablespoons virgin olive oil
2oz (50g) blanched almonds
1 bunch spring onions
1½ tablespoons sherry vinegar

Calories per serving : 300 · High in protein and zinc from beef · High in fibre from almonds

Cut the steak into 2in (50mm) by ¼in (5mm) strips and season with salt and black pepper.

Heat 2 tablespoons of olive oil in a frying pan and gently fry the almonds for 1-2 minutes, until golden. Remove from the pan with a draining spoon and place in a ceramic bowl.

Trim and slice the onions, add them to the pan with ½ tablespoon of vinegar and cook over a high heat for 5 minutes, until the onions turn golden. Remove from the pan using a draining spoon and mix with the almonds.

Increase the heat and add the remaining oil. Quickly fry the steak until it is lightly browned on all sides. Pour over the remaining sherry vinegar and then add the almonds and onions to the pan. Heat together for 2-3 minutes, adjust the seasoning, and serve as quickly as possible.

Curried Lamb with Aubergine and Chickpeas

This mild curry is delicately flavoured with sweet spices, typical of Middle-Eastern cooking. The long, slow cooking of the lamb shoulder makes the meat tender and flavoursome, and the finished dish can be kept warm over a gentle heat until required. Serve with freshly cooked rice or warm Indian bread, natural yoghurt and a selection of chutneys.

Chickpeas are very nutritious as well as tasty and, until recently, they were the staple food for the Arab armies.

SERVES 4-6
PREPARATION TIME : *30 minutes*
SOAKING TIME : *Overnight*
COOKING TIME : *1½ hours*

INGREDIENTS
½ shoulder boned lamb
2 medium onions
2 cloves garlic
1 tablespoon ground coriander
2 teaspoons ground cumin
1 teaspoon ground cinnamon
10oz (275g) dried chickpeas
1 pint (570ml) lamb stock
1lb (450g) young aubergines
1 teaspoon salt
2oz (50g) creamed coconut
1 teaspoon lemon juice
Fresh coriander for garnish

Calories per serving : 190 · High in protein from lamb and chickpeas · High in fibre from chickpeas

There are three cycles of lamb; baby, spring and yearling. The older the lamb, the stronger the taste, so a younger lamb might be better for this delicate dish. Cut the lamb into 1in (25mm) cubes, discarding the excess fat, and finely chop the onions and garlic. Place the lamb in a large frying pan over a medium heat and quickly brown on all sides.

Add the onions, garlic and spices, stirring until the onion is transparent. Add the soaked, dried chickpeas and the stock. Bring to the boil, then reduce the heat and simmer for 45 minutes.

Meanwhile, to extract any bitter juices from the aubergines, cut into small cubes, sprinkle with the salt and leave to one side for about 30 minutes. Be sure not to buy mature aubergines, as they are much more likely to be bitter. Look for aubergines which are shiny and do not have any brown or soft spots, they should also be weighty and firm. After about 30 minutes, rinse the aubergines thoroughly, then add to the lamb and simmer for a further 45 minutes until the meat is tender. Crumble the creamed coconut into the pan and add the lemon juice.

Transfer to a serving dish, sprinkle with freshly chopped coriander and serve.

Pork Tenderloin in Filo Pastry with Orange Sauce

Pork tenderloin is very lean and can be slightly dry when cooked, but by stuffing the meat and wrapping it in pastry, you can retain the moisture and the flavour. For the orange sauce, use a well-flavoured stock rather than stock cubes. Fresh stock is now available in cartons from supermarkets if you have no time to make your own. You will also need some fine cotton string to bind the stuffed pork.

SERVES 4
PREPARATION TIME : *45 minutes*
COOLING TIME : *1 hour*
COOKING TIME : *30 minutes*
OVEN : *Preheat to 200°C (400°F, gas mark 6)*

INGREDIENTS
1lb (450g) pork tenderloin
5 teaspoons vegetable oil
3 sheets filo pastry
Flat-leaf parsley for garnish
STUFFING
2oz (50g) dried peaches
2oz (50g) bacon
1 small onion
1 tablespoon vegetable oil
1 tablespoon fresh chopped parsley
½ oz (15g) pistachio nuts
2oz (50g) fresh breadcrumbs
SAUCE
1 orange
¾ pint (450ml) chicken stock
2 teaspoons arrowroot powder or cornflour
2 spring onions
1 tablespoon Grand Marnier or Cointreau (optional)
1 teaspoon lemon juice
Salt and freshly ground black pepper

Calories per serving : 600 · High in protein and iron from pork and bacon · High in fibre from peaches

---

Trim any excess fat and sinew from the pork. Make a deep cut along the length of the meat and open it out. Place the meat on a sheet of plastic film and lay another sheet over it. Using the end of a rolling pin, or a wooden mallet, beat the meat from the centre out to the sides, until it is quite thin, then set it aside.

To make the stuffing, first cover the dried peaches with boiling water. Chop the bacon and onion finely. Heat the oil in a small frying pan and sauté the onion over a moderate heat for 4 minutes, then add the bacon and cook for a further 4 minutes, stirring occasionally. Chop the parsley and pistachio nuts finely, chop the peaches and add to the pan with the breadcrumbs. Season with salt and pepper.

Uncover the pork and lay the stuffing along its length. Fold the ends in and then the sides, and tie securely, at intervals, with string.

Heat 3 teaspoons of the oil in a frying pan, and cook the pork over a high heat to seal in the juices, turning the pork to make sure that all sides are sealed. Leave to cool at room temperature for about 1 hour, then carefully remove the string.

Lay the sheets of filo pastry on top of each other and place the pork on top, in the centre. Fold over the ends and then roll the pork in the pastry. Place on a lightly oiled baking tray. Brush with the remaining oil and sprinkle with water. Bake in the preheated oven for 30 minutes until crisp and golden.

While the pork is cooking, pare the rind of the orange thinly, cut it into fine matchstick strips and set aside. Cut the orange in half, squeeze the juice and pour it into a small saucepan with the stock. Bring to the boil and continue to boil uncovered until the juice has been reduced to ½ pint (285ml).

Mix the arrowroot powder or the cornflour with 1 tablespoon of water until smooth, and stir into the orange juice. Simmer until thickened. Slice the spring onions finely and add them to the sauce with the remaining ingredients and the orange strips. Simmer for 2-3 minutes, then season to taste. Pour into a warmed sauceboat.

Make sure you have a very sharp knife to cut the pork into slices. Serve garnished with small sprigs of flat-leaf parsley.

Succulent pork tenderloin in light filo pastry with a refreshing orange sauce. The pastry keeps the meat moist and full of flavour while cooking.

Beef, Raisin and Walnut Burgers

An unusual variation on the traditional hamburger, this version is moistened with bulgar wheat and raisins. Bulgar is one of the main staple foods of the Middle East. It is used in 'kibbeh', mixed with lamb and onions and served with lemon juice, olive oil and parsley. The wheat has a pleasant nutty flavour,

A tasty variation of the traditional hamburger using bulgar wheat, raisins and walnuts.

when soaked in water it expands and becomes quite tender. Serve these burgers with a salad or cooked vegetables, or in a burger bun with a low-calorie mayonnaise. They should be served as soon as they are cooked, but the raw mixture may be made up, shaped, and refrigerated up to 12 hours in advance.

SERVES 8
PREPARATION TIME : *25 minutes*
COOKING TIME : *15 minutes*

INGREDIENTS
1lb (450g) lean minced beef
2oz (50g) bulgar wheat
2oz (50g) raisins
4oz (115g) onion
1 clove garlic
1oz (25g) walnut pieces
1 tablespoon olive oil
1 egg
4 tablespoons fresh parsley
2 tablespoons Worcestershire sauce
½ tablespoon vegetable oil
1 teaspoon salt
Freshly ground black pepper

Calories per serving : 230 · High in protein and zinc from beef and egg · High in dietary fibre from raisins and bulgar wheat

Soak the bulgar wheat and the raisins in boiling water for 15 minutes. Drain thoroughly and squeeze out any excess moisture by wrapping the mixture in a clean kitchen cloth and wringing out the liquid. Place the mixture in a bowl.

Finely chop the onion and garlic and chop the walnuts. Warm the oil over a medium heat in a frying pan and sauté the onion, garlic and walnuts for about 5 minutes until the onion is transparent.

Add the onion mixture and the minced beef to the bulgar and raisins. Beat the egg and add it, along with the remaining ingredients, to the mixture. Mix well, then shape into 8 burgers.

Add the vegetable oil to a nonstick frying pan and cook the burgers over a medium heat for about 15 minutes, turning occasionally until thoroughly cooked. If desired, a higher heat will give a crispy brown crust. Season to taste and serve.

POULTRY & GAME

Chicken is extremely versatile, and is an excellent source of protein. Richly flavoured game is usually much less fatty than other meats and is delicious combined with fruit.

Chicken Strips in Yellow Bean Sauce

The secret to stir-frying poultry is to cut the boneless meat neatly, making sure that the pieces are the same size, so that they cook evenly and remain juicy. Yellow bean paste is made from soya beans, the most nutritious of all legumes, being very high in protein.

SERVES 4
PREPARATION TIME : *15 minutes*
COOKING TIME : *10 minutes*

INGREDIENTS
1lb (450g) skinless and boneless chicken breasts
1 fresh green chilli
3 tablespoons yellow bean paste
1½ tablespoons soy sauce
2 tablespoons honey
1½ tablespoons dry sherry
2 teaspoons cornflour
2 tablespoons virgin olive oil
2oz (50g) cashew nuts

Calories per serving : 315 · Low in cholesterol · High in protein from chicken and soya beans

Cut the chicken into thin, even strips. De-seed and slice the chilli into fine rings. Combine the yellow bean paste, soy sauce, honey and sherry together in a bowl. Then mix the cornflour with 3 tablespoons of

Honey adds sweetness to this spicy Chinese dish.

water until smooth, then add to the paste mixture.

Heat half the oil in a wok or frying pan over low heat and brown cashews evenly. Remove from pan.

Add the remaining oil to the pan and increase to a high heat. Add the chicken and chilli and stir-fry for 2-3 minutes until sealed on all sides.

Add the sauce to the pan and stir over a medium heat until the chicken is evenly glazed and the sauce is thickened. Add the cashew nuts and serve at once.

Roast Stuffed Venison

Venison is the leanest of all the red meats and is comparatively low in cholesterol. Most venison eaten in Europe is farmed in New Zealand, and is surprisingly inexpensive to buy. Ask your butcher to bone the joint of venison for you. Calvados is a delicious French brandy made from apples and is available from off-licences and large supermarkets. Serve this dish with a selection of root vegetables.

SERVES 4
PREPARATION TIME : *40 minutes*
COOKING TIME : *2 hours*
OVEN : *Preheat to 200°C (400°F, gas mark 6)*

INGREDIENTS
4lb (1.8kg) leg
or 3lb (1.4kg) shoulder boned venison
1 venison sausage or 4 slices streaky bacon
1 teaspoon butter or vegetable oil
1 clove garlic
1 apple
1 onion
½ teaspoon marjoram
Salt and freshly ground black pepper
2 tablespoons vegetable oil
½ pint (285ml) dry or medium-dry cider
1 bay leaf
½ teaspoon ground allspice
4fl oz (115ml) beef or venison stock
½ glass Calvados
½ lemon

Calories per serving : 735 · High in iron from venison · High in protein from venison and bacon

Calvados brandy and a tasty stuffing add a delicious potency to the self-basting sauce in this venison dish.

If using venison sausage, remove the meat from the casing. Add the butter or vegetable oil to a frying pan and sauté the meat over a moderately high heat for 5 minutes until it is partially cooked. If using bacon, cut the rashers into ¼in (5mm) pieces, blanch in boiling water for 3 minutes, then drain, pat dry and add them to an oiled frying pan.

Crush the garlic and peel and chop the apple and onion into ¼in (5mm) pieces. Add the garlic, apple and onion to the pan and cook for 5 minutes, while stirring, until the vegetables are tender. Add the marjoram, ½ teaspoon of salt and ¼ teaspoon of black pepper and cook for a further minute. Remove the pan from the heat and allow to cool.

Lay the venison leg or shoulder flat and sprinkle with salt and pepper. Spread the sausage or bacon mixture over the flat surface of the venison, then roll up and tie the meat in three places with string.

Heat 2 tablespoons of vegetable oil in a casserole dish just large enough to hold the venison. Brown the venison over a high heat for 1-2 minutes on each side. Add the cider, bay leaf and allspice and bring to a simmer. Lay a piece of greaseproof paper over the venison and cover it with a lid. Turn the oven temperature down to 190°C (375°F, gas mark 5) and cook for 1½ hours. Add more cider if it evaporates too quickly. Preheat a serving plate.

Remove the casserole from the oven, place the venison on the serving plate and keep warm.

Place casserole over moderately high heat and add the beef stock (or venison stock made from the bones), and the Calvados. Boil uncovered until it has reduced down to ½ pint (285ml). Add the lemon juice, adjust seasoning and stir.

Slice the venison into ½in (15mm) thick slices and serve with the sauce separately.

213

Mango not only makes this dish appealing to the eye, its exotic flavour also complements the duck.

Roast Duck with Mango Sauce

Ducks have been eaten in Europe and China for thousands of years. When the Greeks and Romans ate them, they reserved the brains and breasts for gourmets. The British traditionally eat roast duck, and this is the healthiest way to cook it, as most of the fat drains from the duck. The skin may also be removed after cooking to further reduce the calories. Peak season for mangoes is autumn to late winter. Choose a ripe mango with a sweet smell and taut skin, which gives slightly to the touch. Serve the duck portions with the sauce spooned over the top. Small new potatoes, mangetout and crisp broccoli florets go particularly well with this dish.

SERVES 4
PREPARATION TIME : *30 minutes*
COOKING TIME : *1¼ hours*
OVEN : *Preheat to 200°C (400°F, gas mark 6)*

INGREDIENTS
1 oven-ready duck weighing about 5lb (2.3kg)
1 medium onion
1 lime or lemon
1 bay leaf
1 large ripe mango
1 tablespoon cornflour
Salt and freshly ground black pepper

Calories per serving : 625 · High in iron, zinc and protein from duck

Reserve the duck giblets. Cut the duck in half by cutting either side of the backbone and through the breastbone. Then cut each half between the leg and breast to make four portions. Remove and reserve the wing tips for the stock, along with the backbone.

Prick the skin of the portions several times with a metal skewer and then place them on a roasting rack in a roasting tin. Roast the duck portions for 1 hour.

Roughly chop the onion. Using a vegetable peeler, cut strips of zest from the lime or lemon.

To make a good stock, place the onion, giblets, backbone, wing tips, bay leaf and half the zest in a saucepan with about 1½ pints (850ml) of water. Cover the pan and simmer for 1 hour.

Cut rest of zest into thin strips. Place in a bowl, cover with boiling water for a few minutes; drain.

Peel the mango and cut away the flesh. Cut the large pieces into small cubes and then scrape any remaining fruit from the stone. Put to one side.

Reserving ½ pint (285ml) of stock, strain the pan. Mix the cornflour with a little water; stir into the stock. Stir over a medium heat until thickened. Add the mango and zest, then season to taste.

Pigeons with Chicory

Pigeons are among the cheapest game fowl available, and their rich, lean meat lends itself well to braising with vegetables; a combined roasting and stewing technique used in this Belgian recipe.

Pigeon with leeks, bacon, chicory and redcurrant jelly.

SERVES 4
PREPARATION TIME : *20 minutes*
COOKING TIME : *2¼ hours*
OVEN : *Preheat to 150°C (300°F, gas mark 2)*

INGREDIENTS
4 pigeons
1 tablespoon virgin olive oil
4 rashers lean bacon
2 leeks
2 chicory heads
4fl oz (115ml) chicken stock
1 bouquet garni
3 tablespoons redcurrant jelly
Salt and freshly ground black pepper

Calories per serving : 620 · High in protein and iron from pigeon · High in fibre from vegetables

---

Gently heat the oil in a large flameproof casserole and fry the pigeons until well browned on all sides. Remove from the pan and put to one side.

Remove the rinds from the bacon and cut the rashers into pieces. Lower the heat, add the bacon to the dish and cook for 5 minutes. Meanwhile, wash and trim the leeks and then cut them in half, once widthways and again lengthways, to provide 8 pieces. Add the leek to the dish and cook gently for 2-3 minutes, stirring frequently.

Wash the chicory heads, discarding any wilted outer leaves, and halve them lengthways. Add the chicory heads to the dish. Stir the mixture well, and then cover the dish tightly and cook gently for 8 minutes, stirring occasionally.

Pour over the chicken stock and add the bouquet garni. Place the pigeons on top of the chicory and leeks, cover again and cook in the oven for 2 hours. Preheat a large serving dish.

Remove the casserole from the oven and lift the pigeons onto the heated serving dish. Remove the leeks and chicory with a draining spoon and arrange around the birds. Cover and keep warm.

Boil the liquid remaining in the dish rapidly over a high heat until it has reduced by half. Turn the heat down and add the redcurrant jelly. Stir until the jelly has melted. Taste and adjust the seasoning. Serve the sauce separately.

Chicken with Cheese and Courgette Stuffing

A light cheese and courgette stuffing helps to keep this simple roast chicken moist during cooking and adds to its flavour. For the best-tasting chicken, use one that has been free-range or corn-fed. Serve it with potatoes, carrots and leeks, or cold with a salad.

SERVES 4
PREPARATION TIME : *30 minutes*
COOKING TIME : *1¼ hours*
OVEN : *Preheat to 190°C (375°F, gas mark 5)*

INGREDIENTS
1 oven-ready chicken weighing about 3½ lb (1.6kg)
12oz (350g) courgettes
3oz (75g) fresh breadcrumbs
7oz (200g) low-fat soft cheese
½ oz (15g) fresh chives
Salt and freshly ground black pepper
1 tablespoon virgin olive oil
1 tablespoon plain flour
¼ pint (150ml) chicken stock

Calories per serving : 480 · High in protein from cheese and chicken · High in iron from breadcrumbs

The stuffing turns roast chicken into a special meal.

Wipe the chicken inside and out with a piece of kitchen towel, and trim and discard any excess fat.

Thickly slice the courgettes and steam them for 5 minutes. Leave to cool, then chop finely.

Combine the courgettes, breadcrumbs, cheese and chives in a bowl, and season and spoon the stuffing into the body cavity. Pin the flap of neck skin under the bird with a skewer. Brush the bird with oil and place in a roasting tin in the oven.

After 30 minutes, cover the chicken skin with foil if it is getting too brown. Roast for 1¼ hours or until the juices are clear when a skewer is run through the thick part of the thigh. When cooked, leave the chicken to rest for 5 minutes.

Put the flour into a cup. Add 2 tablespoons of chicken juices and mix to a smooth paste. Stir the mixture into any juices left in the roasting tin. Slowly add the stock, stirring until the sauce thickens, and simmer for 2-3 minutes. Season the sauce. Remove the stuffing and serve it separately in a small bowl.

Orange Chicken

This simple recipe is based on a popular Malaysian dish with a fruity sauce. Oriental chefs sometimes slice their meat half-frozen, helping them to cut it very finely. Serve with brown rice or egg noodles.

SERVES 4
PREPARATION TIME : *10-15 minutes*
COOKING TIME : *15-20 minutes*

INGREDIENTS
4 boneless chicken breasts, each weighing about 5oz (150g)
2 tablespoons shoyu or soy sauce
1 bunch spring onions
3 oranges (juice from 2, segments from 1)
2 tablespoons groundnut oil
4oz (115g) frozen peas
2 teaspoons soft brown sugar
Salt and freshly ground black pepper
Fresh coriander for garnish (optional)

Calories per serving : 290 · High in protein from chicken and peas · High in vitamin C from oranges

Skin the chicken breasts. If using frozen chicken, wait until it is partially thawed before cutting it into thin strips. If using fresh chicken breasts, pound with a mallet or rolling pin to flatten them before cutting crossways into ½in (15mm) thick slices. Place the slices in a shallow dish, then add shoyu or soy sauce and stir well to mix. Cover and set aside.

Trim the spring onions and slice them crossways into 1½in (40mm) lengths. Cut away the rind, pith and skin of one orange and slice out the segments with a knife. Squeeze the juice from the oranges.

Heat the oil in a wok or large frying pan. Add the chicken slices in batches and stir-fry over moderate to high heat for 3-4 minutes, until the meat turns white, then remove and set aside. Stir-fry the spring onions for 2 minutes. Remove and set aside.

Add the orange juice to the pan along with the frozen peas and sugar. Bring to the boil, stirring all the time, then simmer for 3 minutes. Remove the peas with a slotted spoon and set aside.

Bring the orange juice to the boil again, stirring constantly and boiling rapidly until reduced by half. Turn the heat down and return the chicken to the pan, with the onions, peas and orange segments. Heat through gently, then season to taste. Sprinkle with coriander if desired, and serve immediately.

Fresh oranges add sweetness and bright colour to this Malaysian chicken dish. The shoyu or soy sauce gives an authentic oriental flavour. Served with brown rice or egg noodles, this dish makes an easy but delicious supper.

Olives, lemon, bacon and herbs enhance this dish.

Mediterranean Drumsticks

Olives, lemon and garlic give this chicken dish its Mediterranean flavour. The drumsticks are browned to give the dish an attractive finish without adding extra fat – the skins may be removed to reduce the fat content even more. Serve with a green salad or green vegetables and fresh, crusty bread.

SERVES 4
PREPARATION TIME : *15 minutes*
COOKING TIME : *1½ hours*
OVEN : *Preheat to 180°C (350°F, gas mark 4)*

INGREDIENTS
8 large chicken drumsticks
4 rashers streaky bacon
2 medium onions
1 clove garlic
12oz (350g) potatoes
2oz (50g) pitted green olives
Juice of 1 lemon
½ pint (285ml) chicken stock
Freshly ground black pepper
1 teaspoon dried herbes de Provence
2 teaspoons cornflour
Chopped parsley for garnish

Calories per serving : 340 · High in protein from chicken and bacon

Remove the skins from the drumsticks if preferred, using short strokes of a knife while gently peeling it away. Remove the rinds from the bacon and place them in a large frying pan over a medium heat. Cut the bacon into pieces and add them to the pan. Cook for about 5 minutes until crisp, then remove the bacon pieces from the pan.

Brown the drumsticks in the bacon fat for about 10 minutes, turning for even colour. If you have skinned the chicken, you may have to add some of the skin to the pan for browning. Discard any skin or bacon rinds once the chicken is browned.

Meanwhile, peel and roughly chop the onions, peel and crush the garlic, scrub the potatoes and cut them into ½in (15mm) cubes. Place the onions, garlic and potatoes in a flameproof casserole.

Add the drumsticks to the casserole with the olives, lemon juice, chicken stock and bacon pieces. Season with pepper, add the herbes de Provence and cover and cook in the oven for 1½ hours, removing the lid after 1 hour. Preheat a serving dish.

Spoon the cooked drumsticks and the vegetables into the warmed serving dish to keep them hot while the sauce is being prepared.

For the sauce, mix the cornflour and 2 tablespoons of water to create a smooth paste. Add this paste to the liquid in the casserole dish. Bring the sauce to the boil, stirring it until it has thickened slightly. Spoon the sauce over the drumsticks and sprinkle with the fresh chopped parsley. Serve immediately with fresh bread and green vegetables or a salad.

Rabbit Stew with Pears

Rabbit should be meltingly tender and its gamey flavour goes beautifully with the sweet pears in this recipe. Be wary of the difference between hare and rabbit – hare has red meat whereas rabbit is much paler, it can be almost white. If buying rabbit from a butcher, ask to have it skinned and cut into pieces. Alternatively, rabbit pieces can be bought from a supermarket. All the bones can easily be removed after cooking. When choosing pears, look for firm fruit with the stalk attached and which yields slightly to the touch at the stalk end.

SERVES 4-6
PREPARATION TIME : *1 hour*
COOKING TIME : *2 hours*
OVEN : *Preheat to 150°C (300°F, gas mark 2)*

INGREDIENTS

1 or 2 rabbits or rabbit pieces
weighing 3lb (1.4kg)
4oz (115g) streaky bacon
2 tablespoons vegetable oil
3 tablespoons unsalted butter
Salt and freshly ground black pepper
½ teaspoon dried herbes de Provence
2 medium-sized onions
4 shallots
2 cloves garlic
5 tablespoons smooth Dijon mustard
½ pint (285ml) dry white wine
1 tablespoon fresh ginger
2-3 ripe pears
1 teaspoon sugar
2 tablespoons single cream
Juice of ½ lemon
3 tablespoons fresh chives

Calories per serving : 615 · High in dietary fibre from vegetables · High in protein from rabbit and bacon High in vitamin B12 from rabbit

Cut the bacon into 1in (25mm) squares. Fry them in a frying pan until the fat melts, then remove them from the pan and drain them on kitchen paper. In the same frying pan, add the vegetable oil and 2 tablespoons of the butter. Add the rabbit pieces and cook until brown, and then lay them with the bacon in a casserole dish and sprinkle with ground black pepper, herbs and a little salt. Then set aside.

Chop the onions and shallots finely, and crush the garlic cloves. Drain all but 2 tablespoons of the vegetable oil from the frying pan. Sauté the onions, garlic and shallots until they are soft (about 6-8 minutes), and then drain.

Pour the juices that have accumulated in the bottom of the casserole into a small bowl. Add the Dijon mustard and the onion mixture to the bowl. Mix the sauce well and pour it over the rabbit and bacon layer in the casserole.

Add the white wine to the frying pan and bring it to the boil. Skim off any scum that may rise to the surface and pour the white wine into the casserole. Cover with a sheet of buttered greaseproof paper, butter-side down, and a tight-fitting lid. Cook for 2 hours in the oven until tender.

Meanwhile, peel and grate the fresh ginger. Peel and slice the pears, and sauté them with the ginger in the remaining butter. Sprinkle them with the sugar and set the mixture aside.

When the rabbit is cooked, remove it from the casserole and put on a large serving dish, and keep it warm in the oven. Boil the casserole liquid until it reduces to about ¾ pint (450ml). Add the single cream to bind it, and then the squeezed juice from the lemon. Season to taste. Chop the fresh chives and stir them in together with the pear and ginger mixture. Heat the sauce through thoroughly, stirring occasionally. Spoon the sauce and the pears over the rabbit and serve immediately.

Tender rabbit with sweet pears and ginger. Once regarded as a poor man's food, it is now imported from China and served in the smartest restaurants.

Pigeon and Apricot Stir-fry

Pigeon was once such a popular food in Europe that many homes had their own pigeon lofts. Country boys used to keep young pigeons for eating by tying a string to each pigeon's leg. The string was threaded down through the nest, where a stick was tied to the other end. The birds could move, but not fly away, ensuring a fat bird for the table.

Today, pigeons are a favourite ingredient in Cantonese and Middle-Eastern cookery. This recipe uses the Middle-Eastern method of cooking the bird with spices and dried fruit. Pigeons are supposedly at their best from midsummer until the end of September, when many of the birds are young.

Apricots have been cultivated in China since 2000 BC. When they are dried they become quite tart, making this dish slightly tangy. The texture and flavour of the pine or cashew nuts also adds to the dish. Serve with rice or potatoes, and a green salad.

The rich dark meat of the pigeon is a delicacy across many parts of Europe and Asia. This Middle-Eastern recipe enhances it with a hint of cinnamon.

SERVES 4
PREPARATION TIME : *30 minutes*
COOKING TIME : *10 minutes*

INGREDIENTS
3 pigeons
2 tablespoons virgin olive oil
2oz (50g) pine nuts or cashews
2 cloves garlic
3 sticks celery
3 shallots
4oz (115g) dried apricots
1 teaspoon ground cinnamon
1 teaspoon cornflour
1 tablespoon brown or Worcestershire sauce
1 tablespoon chopped parsley
Salt and freshly ground black pepper
2 fresh apricots for garnish (optional)

Calories per serving : 600 · High in protein and iron from pigeon · High in carotene from apricots

Cut away the breasts from the pigeons by slitting closely along the breastbone to loosen the meat. Cut any excess bone from the breasts. Chop the meat finely and put it to one side.

Heat half of the olive oil in a frying pan and cook the pine nuts or cashews over a low heat until they are an even golden-brown colour. Remove the nuts and put them to one side.

Crush the garlic cloves. Trim the celery of its leaves and chop it and the shallots very finely. Chop the dried apricots very finely. Add the remaining olive oil to the frying pan and cook the garlic, celery and shallots, stirring constantly for about 30 seconds. Add the chopped pigeon and the cinnamon and cook the mixture for about 2 minutes, stirring continually until the pigeon meat is browned and sealed on all sides.

When the meat is sealed and browned, stir in the dried apricots. Mix the cornflour with 4 tablespoons of water until it is smooth. Then add it to the pan, stirring frequently until it has thickened. Stir in the brown or Worcestershire sauce, nuts and chopped parsley. Season to taste with salt and ground black pepper. Garnish with celery leaves or fresh apricot slices if desired, and serve immediately.

Grilled Baby Chickens with Chilli

In this recipe the baby chickens, or poussins, are 'spatchcocked' – split and flattened before grilling. The birds are then cooked Cajun-style, using chilli powder and peppers to make a spicy stuffing.

SERVES 4
PREPARATION TIME : *20 minutes*
MARINATING TIME : *4-24 hours*
COOKING TIME : *30 minutes*

INGREDIENTS
4 baby chickens or poussins
Lemon wedges for garnish
STUFFING
2 red peppers
2 small onions
3 cloves garlic
2 teaspoons chilli powder or to taste
3 tablespoons virgin olive oil
Salt

Calories per serving : 615 · High in protein from chicken · Low in cholesterol (without chicken skin)

Spicy stuffing is pushed under the skin of each bird.

Cut down each side of the bird's backbone to remove it. Lay the birds breast down on a board and press on the breastbone to flatten them. Using your fingers, carefully loosen the skin from the flesh right across the breast, and a little way down the thighs, taking care not to tear it, ready for the stuffing.

Halve, de-seed and roughly chop the peppers. Peel and roughly chop the onions, and crush the garlic. Put all stuffing ingredients except oil into a liquidiser and purée. Keeping the liquidiser running, gradually pour in oil until blended. Season with salt.

Spoon a quarter of stuffing between the flesh and skin of each bird, smoothing evenly. Refrigerate for between 4 and 24 hours. Grill the birds under low heat for 30 minutes. Garnish and serve.

Casserole of Duck with Peaches

Peaches make an excellent addition to the slightly gamey flavour of duck, and here they are complemented by a hint of sage. Barbary, Muscovy or the Nantois breeds of duck are less fatty than others.

SERVES 4
PREPARATION TIME : *35 minutes*
COOKING TIME : *1½ hours*
OVEN : *Preheat to 180°C (350°F, gas mark 4)*

INGREDIENTS
4lb (1.8kg) duck
Salt and freshly ground black pepper
½ lemon
6 shallots
1 clove garlic
2½ oz (65g) butter
1 tablespoon virgin olive oil
1 tablespoon chopped fresh parsley
1 bay leaf
4 fresh sage leaves
1 glass dry white wine
8fl oz (225ml) veal or chicken stock
3 large peaches
1½ tablespoons balsamic vinegar
2 teaspoons sugar

Calories per serving : 790 · High in iron, zinc and protein from duck

The sweet flavour of ripe peaches mingles with fresh sage and dry white wine to complement rich gamey duck.

Rinse inside the duck and pat it dry. Rub the inside with a little salt, pepper and half a lemon.

Peel and finely chop the shallots and garlic. Melt 1oz (25g) of the butter with the virgin olive oil in a casserole. Sauté the shallots, garlic, chopped parsley, bay leaf and 2 sage leaves for 4 minutes.

Place the duck on top and add ¼ pint (150ml) water and ½oz (15g) butter. Cover and cook in the oven for 50 minutes, basting frequently with water and butter, and turning to make sure it cooks evenly.

Turn the oven down low. Remove the duck from the casserole and keep it warm in the oven. Pour away the fat from the casserole, then add half the wine and boil for 2 minutes. Reduce the heat and add the stock, cooking gently for 5-8 minutes. Strain into a bowl, and discard the onion and garlic. Return the liquid to the casserole and simmer for 5 minutes. Adjust seasoning.

Dice the peaches into ½in (15mm) cubes. Sauté over a medium-high heat in 1oz (25g) butter and balsamic vinegar for 1 minute, then add the sugar and remaining wine and sage. Cook for 1 minute. Remove the peaches and keep warm. Skim any fat off the stock before adding it to the casserole. Bring the sauce to the boil and simmer for 3-4 minutes. Spoon the sauce and peaches over the duck. Serve.

223

Quail with Apples and Raisins

When roasting small birds like quail, it is important to stop the meat from drying out. This can be done by placing a rasher of fat bacon around the bird, but surrounding the bird with liquid – in this case stock and apple juice – works just as well.

SERVES 4
PREPARATION TIME : *15 minutes*
SOAKING TIME : *1-2 hours*
COOKING TIME : *30 minutes*
OVEN : *Preheat to 220°C (425°F, gas mark 7)*

INGREDIENTS
8 quails
2oz (50g) raisins
2 tablespoons brandy
2 small apples (Cox's or similar dessert apples)
1 teaspoon fresh thyme
¼ pint (150ml) unsweetened apple juice
½ pint (285ml) chicken stock
Freshly ground black pepper

Calories per serving : 690 · High in both protein and iron from quail

Quail is the smallest European game bird, kept moist in this recipe with chicken stock and apple juice.

Place the raisins in a basin, pour over the brandy and leave to soak for 1-2 hours, until the raisins have absorbed the brandy and become plump.

Remove any giblets from the quails and core and chop the apples, leaving the skins intact. Add the apples to the raisins with the thyme and mix well. Use this mixture to stuff the quails and place the stuffed birds in an ovenproof dish.

Pour over the apple juice and stock and season with black pepper. Roast the birds in the oven for 30 minutes, basting them two or three times with the liquid. Preheat a serving dish.

Lift the birds out of the dish, place them on the serving dish, then cover and keep warm. Strain the cooking liquid into a pan and boil rapidly to reduce by half. Pour it around the quails and serve.

Pheasant with Grapes and Kiwi Fruit

Pheasants are usually sold by the brace – a cock and a hen. The cock pheasant is leaner and more suitable for casseroling than the plumper hen which roasts well, so try to buy two cock pheasants for this dish. Kiwi fruit contains an enzyme which helps the digestion of some meats.

SERVES 4
PREPARATION TIME : *20 minutes*
COOKING TIME : *2 hours*
OVEN : *Preheat to 150°C (300°F, gas mark 2)*

INGREDIENTS
2 pheasants
2 tablespoons virgin olive oil
2 sticks celery
2 medium onions
½ pint (285ml) red wine
1 sprig rosemary
Salt and freshly ground black pepper
2 kiwi fruit
8oz (225g) black grapes

Calories per serving : 700 · High in protein from pheasant · High in fibre from vegetables

A lovely blend of gamey pheasant and sweet fruit.

Skin the pheasants and cut them into wing and leg joints. Heat the oil in a flameproof casserole and fry the joints over a high heat for a few minutes until thoroughly browned. Then remove them from the casserole and put to one side.

Chop the celery sticks and peel and chop the onions. Add them to the casserole and cook over low heat for 5 minutes. Pour in the wine and bring to the boil, then add the rosemary and replace the pheasant joints. Season with salt and pepper.

Cover the casserole dish and cook in the oven for 2 hours, until the pheasant is quite tender.

Peel the kiwi fruit, and cut it into ½in (15mm) cubes. Halve and de-seed the grapes.

Remove the casserole from the oven, lift out the pheasant joints onto the heated serving dish and keep warm. Remove the rosemary sprig.

Tip the celery, onions and grapes into a liquidiser, blending until smooth. Sieve the mixture into a saucepan. Bring to the boil and add the fruit. Cook for 1-2 minutes. Spoon the sauce over the pheasant joints and serve immediately.

Chicken in Mustard Sauce with Leeks

This delicious and filling dish uses the most basic of British foods, and takes very little time to make. The leeks, which are the sweetest of the onion family, offer a tasty contrast to the flavours of the bacon and mustard sauce. Look for fresh, young leeks which are mainly white, not green.

SERVES 4
PREPARATION TIME : *15 minutes*
COOKING TIME : *30 minutes*

INGREDIENTS
4 boneless and skinless chicken breasts
8oz (225g) leeks
pepper
8 rashers streaky bacon
1 tablespoon olive oil
1 tablespoon mustard powder
1 tablespoon plain flour
¾ pint (450ml) chicken stock
Freshly chopped parsley to garnish

Calories per serving : 195 · Low in cholesterol and fat · High in protein from chicken

Wash and cut the leeks into rings and reserve. Cut the pieces of chicken in half crossways and season with pepper. Then remove the rind from the bacon and lightly cook the rashers in the oil in a large nonstick frying pan over a low heat.

Stretch out each rasher of bacon, using the back of a knife, and then wrap one around each piece of chicken. Secure each rasher with a cocktail stick.

Place the chicken in the frying pan and stir in the mustard powder and the plain flour. Cook for 1-2 minutes, then stir in stock and bring to the boil. Reduce the heat and add the leeks. Cover and simmer for about 15 minutes until the leeks are tender. Garnish with parsley and serve.

Chicken breasts wrapped in bacon with tender leeks.

Chicken Goulash

Goulash originated in Hungary, and one of its most important ingredients is paprika which, together with tomatoes, produces a rich, deep red sauce. The best paprika still comes from Hungary, where it is produced in varieties that range from mild to very hot. Caraway seeds are added for texture and to help give the sauce its characteristic flavour. Traditionally, goulash is made with veal or pork, but it is adaptable to most meats, particularly chicken. Serve with jacket or mashed potatoes and steamed green vegetables, such as cabbage and green beans.

Mouth-watering Hungarian goulash brimming over with chicken, onions and mushrooms. Paprika gives colour and adds a spicy bite to the dish.

SERVES 4
PREPARATION TIME : *10 minutes*
COOKING TIME : *1 hour*

INGREDIENTS
8 boneless chicken thighs
2 medium onions
1 tablespoon paprika
1 teaspoon caraway seeds
4oz (115g) button mushrooms
14oz (400g) tin tomatoes
½ pint (285ml) chicken stock
Freshly chopped parsley for garnish

*Calories per serving : 185 · Low in fat
and cholesterol · High in protein from chicken
High in vitamin C from tomatoes*

Remove the skins from the chicken thighs. Heat a little of the skin in a nonstick frying pan and add the chicken. Cook over a medium heat for about 15 minutes, until well browned on all sides.

Meanwhile, peel and roughly chop the onions. Remove the chicken from the frying pan, discard the skin, and pour away all but 1 tablespoon of fat. Cook the onions in the pan with the paprika and caraway seeds for about 3 minutes, then add the mushrooms and cook for about 2 minutes.

Add the tomatoes and the stock and bring to the boil. Reduce the heat to a simmer, then add the chicken. Cover the pan and simmer for about 30-35 minutes, until the chicken is tender.

Remove the lid and reduce the liquid to a sauce consistency by fast boiling for 5-10 minutes, stirring frequently. Then sprinkle with the freshly chopped parsley and serve immediately.

Turkey Stir-fry

The Chinese, who originated the stir-fry method of cooking, consider it unlucky to cut food straight across, which is why the ingredients in their dishes are always cut on a slant. Served with a little boiled or fried rice, this dish makes a complete meal for four. You can vary the ingredients to include green pepper, carrot, cucumber and Chinese leaves.

A delicious mixture of bright, crunchy vegetables and turkey, quickly stir-fried and flavoured with sesame seeds.

SERVES 4
PREPARATION TIME : *20 minutes*
COOKING TIME : *12 minutes*

INGREDIENTS

1lb (450g) turkey breast fillets
Salt and freshly ground black pepper
1 red pepper
1 courgette
2oz (50g) dwarf corn spears
2oz (50g) button mushrooms
5 spring onions
2oz (50g) mangetout
3 tablespoons sunflower or olive oil
1 clove garlic
2oz (50g) broccoli florets
3 tablespoons light soy sauce
4oz (115g) bean sprouts
1 teaspoon sesame oil
1 tablespoon toasted sesame seeds

Calories per serving : 280 · High in vitamin C from broccoli and courgette · High in protein from turkey

Cut the turkey fillets into strips about 2in (50mm) long and ¼in (5mm) thick. Season with salt and black pepper. De-seed the pepper, top and tail the courgette and cut both into thin strips. Cut the corn spears in half, slice the mushrooms and cut the spring onions into 1in (25mm) lengths. Top and tail the mangetout. Preheat a large serving dish.

Heat 1½ tablespoons of the oil in a wok or large frying pan. Add the turkey fillets and cook for 3-4 minutes, stirring continually, until they are golden-brown. Remove the turkey from the wok or pan with a draining spoon and put it to one side.

Add the remaining oil to the pan and peel and crush the garlic. Place the garlic, pepper, broccoli florets, courgette and corn spears in the pan and cook for 2-3 minutes, stirring all the time.

Then add the mangetout, mushrooms and spring onions, cook for 2 minutes and reduce the heat. Replace the turkey fillets and pour over the soy sauce. Stir in the bean sprouts and cook for a further 2-3 minutes, until the meat is piping hot.

As soon as it is done, carefully turn the mixture into the preheated serving dish. Sprinkle with the sesame oil and the toasted sesame seeds. Serve the dish immediately.

Duck, Bean and Vegetable Stew

A selection of beans, such as white haricot, pinto, barlotti and kidney, may be used for this recipe. They can either be dried or tinned. Look for dried pulses which have a plump appearance and a bright colour. Be wary of older pulses as they take longer to cook, and may fall apart during cooking. Dust is a clear sign of age. Pulses should also be of the same size so they will cook evenly. Some supermarkets sell mixtures of dried beans which are ideal for stews, but these need soaking overnight. If you need to soak them, use a large bowl as they tend to double in volume. Soak in cold water for 6-8 hours or overnight, and discard any that float to the top.

INGREDIENTS
4 boned duck breast portions
4 small turnips
4 carrots
8oz (225g) dried beans
8oz (225g) small onions or shallots
14oz (400g) fresh or canned tomatoes
1 pint (570ml) chicken stock
1 large glass of red wine (optional)
2 bay leaves
3 sprigs of fresh thyme
2 sprigs of fresh rosemary
Salt and freshly ground black pepper

Calories per serving : 400 · High in calcium from beans and duck · High in vitamin A from carrots High in vitamin C from tomatoes

Nutritious beans, colourful vegetables and the rich flavour of duck create a wonderful stew that warms the heart on the coldest winter evening.

Duck meat varies according to the breed. Barbary duck is good to use because it is less fatty and has generous amounts of firm breast meat. Boned duck breasts are available from all good butchers and supermarkets. This dish can be complemented with fresh, crusty bread.

If there is a need to bone the duck breasts, remove the skin from the portions. Skinning the duck is easy when short, sharp strokes are made with a knife while peeling the skin back.

Once the skin has been removed, turn the pieces bone-side up and cut and scrape out the bones. Remove the tendon from the centre of each breast, stroking with a knife to strip it. Trim the meat. Replace the inner fillet if it detaches from the meat.

After boning them, cut each breast portion in half, crossways. Peel and halve the turnips. Quarter the carrots crossways and drain the beans if they were soaked. Soaking can involve cold water or speeding the process with hot water. If you do soak, be sure to use a large pot as the beans will probably double in size. Place them in a large flameproof casserole dish with all of the remaining ingredients, except for the salt and black pepper.

Bring the ingredients to the boil, then reduce the heat and simmer for 1½ -2 hours, until the beans are tender. Remove the lid from the casserole for the last 20 minutes of cooking to allow the sauce to reduce. Season to taste with the salt and freshly ground black pepper, and remove the herb sprigs if desired. Serve piping hot with the crusty bread.

Chicken Breasts with Raspberry Vinegar

This tasty dish uses pink peppercorns, which are sold in many specialist delicatessens and some large supermarkets. They are the berries of a small South American shrub, and are very decorative. If pink peppercorns are difficult to find, white or green peppercorns can be used instead. Aromatic raspberry vinegar adds an unusual twist to the dish. Serve with scrubbed new potatoes tossed with some chopped fresh herbs, and a fresh green vegetable.

Luscious raspberries and bright pink peppercorns add flavour and colour to pan-fried chicken breasts.

SERVES 4
PREPARATION TIME : *10-15 minutes*
COOKING TIME : *25-30 minutes*

INGREDIENTS
*4 skinned boneless chicken breasts
each weighing about 5oz (150g)
1 tablespoon pink peppercorns
½ large Spanish onion
2 tablespoons groundnut oil
Salt and freshly ground black pepper
3 tablespoons raspberry vinegar
2 teaspoons redcurrant jelly
Fresh or frozen whole raspberries to garnish
Sprigs of parsley or mint to garnish*

Calories per serving : 245 · High in protein from chicken · Low in cholesterol

Place the chicken breasts on a board and cover with greaseproof paper. Pound the chicken with a meat mallet or a rolling pin to flatten it slightly. Crush the pink peppercorns and rub them over the chicken. Finely chop the onion.

Heat the groundnut oil in a nonstick frying pan, then add the chicken breasts and cook over a moderate heat for about 5 minutes on each side or until the flesh is tender and white through to the centre. When it is cooked, remove the chicken from the pan with a slotted spoon, cover and keep hot.

Add the onion to the frying pan and cook over a low heat for about 10-15 minutes, until it is soft and transparent. Stir the onion frequently, taking care not to let it brown. Warm 4 dinner plates.

Meanwhile, cut each chicken breast on the diagonal into ½in (15mm) slices. Sprinkle the slices with salt and freshly ground black pepper to taste. Cover chicken again and keep hot.

Add the raspberry vinegar and the redcurrant jelly to the onion and mix well. Bring to the boil over a high heat, stirring all the time. Lower the heat to moderate and cook for a few more minutes, stirring constantly, until the mixture is reduced to a glaze.

Put the chicken slices on the previously warmed dinner plates and spoon the onion mixture over the top. Serve hot, garnished with the fresh or frozen raspberries and the sprigs of parsley or mint.

Venison Stew with Fruit

The fruit sauce and scented spices in this recipe complement the sweet, succulent gamey flavour of the venison beautifully, while the beer adds to its richness. Venison is best bought in the autumn or winter, when the meat is likely to be young and fresh. Ask the butcher to bone the meat if it has not already been done. Serve with rice or potatoes.

SERVES 4-6
PREPARATION TIME : *1 hour*
COOKING TIME : *2 hours*

INGREDIENTS

3lb (1.4kg) shoulder or leg of venison, boned
2 medium-sized onions
4 cloves garlic
1 small green chilli pepper
4 tablespoons olive oil
1 heaped teaspoon ground cumin
2 teaspoons ground oregano
14oz (400g) tin chopped tomatoes
1¾ pints (1 litre) beef stock
1 pint (570ml) dark beer
2 Granny Smith or other dessert apples
6oz (175g) pineapple (preferably fresh)
1 teaspoon cinnamon
1 tablespoon cider vinegar
¼ teaspoon ground allspice
2 teaspoons salt
2 teaspoons sugar
½ tablespoon chilli powder (or cayenne)
⅓ pint (190ml) water
3 tablespoons peanut or groundnut oil
or any vegetable oil

Calories per serving : 675 · High in protein from venison · High in vitamin C from tomatoes · High in fibre from onions, tomatoes and apples

Chop the onions coarsely, crush the garlic and chop the chilli pepper very finely. Heat the olive oil in a large casserole over medium heat and sauté the onion, garlic and chilli for 10 minutes or until soft, stirring occasionally. Drain, remove and set aside.

Put the cumin and oregano into a small pan and

The sweetness of pineapple is delicious with venison.

heat gently until they release their scent. Put aside.

Cut the venison into 2in (50mm) cubes and brown them in the remaining oil. Add the onion mixture and spices. Cook, stirring constantly, for 5 minutes.

Add the chopped tomatoes, beef stock and dark beer to the meat. Bring to the boil, then lower the heat and simmer for 1½ -2 hours until it is tender.

While the meat is cooking, peel the apples and pineapple (if using fresh). Dice coarsely and purée in a blender with the cinnamon, vinegar, allspice, salt, sugar and chilli powder with ⅓ pint (190ml) water. Heat peanut or other oil and sauté the mixture for 3 or 4 minutes until most of the liquid evaporates.

When the meat is cooked, take it out of the liquid and lay it on a warm dish. Add the fruit mixture to the casserole, mix with the liquid. If a thicker sauce is preferred, mix 1 teaspoon of cornflour with a little water and stir it into the cooking liquid. Simmer the sauce gently for 5 minutes, stirring it continuously. Pour the sauce over the meat, and serve.

Turkey and Spinach Rolls

Thin escalopes of turkey are best for this recipe, but you can also use turkey breast slices. To flatten the breast slices, you can place them between two pieces of plastic film or greaseproof paper and hit them with a wooden meat mallet or a rolling pin.

SERVES 4
PREPARATION TIME : *15 minutes*
COOKING TIME : *30 minutes*
OVEN : *Preheat to 190°C (375°F, gas mark 5)*

INGREDIENTS
4 × 3oz (75g) turkey escalopes
Salt and freshly ground black pepper
1lb (450g) spinach
½ small green pepper
1 clove garlic
1oz (25g) pine nuts
½ oz (15g) butter

Calories per serving : 155 · High in iron from spinach · High in protein from turkey

A nut and spinach spiral fills the tender turkey rolls.

Season the turkey escalopes. Wash all the spinach thoroughly and remove the stalks. Cook in a small amount of salted boiling water for 3 minutes, until just tender. Turn into a sieve and drain well, pressing to remove all liquid. Chop finely and place in a bowl.

De-seed the pepper, blanch in boiling salted water for 1 minute, then drain and finely dice. Add to the spinach, together with the crushed garlic and pine nuts. Season to taste.

Divide the spinach mixture into 4 servings and spread over the turkey escalopes, to within ¼in (5mm) of their edges. Roll each piece up and place in an ovenproof dish. Dot each one with a little butter and bake in the oven, basting two or three times, for 30 minutes. Remove and serve immediately.

Chicken Tikka

Chicken tikka is one of the healthier, lower-fat dishes served in Indian restaurants and is very easy to prepare. Recipes for this dish vary considerably, and in this recipe the quantities of spices can be adjusted to suit your personal taste. Serve chicken tikka with rice and a small mixed salad.

SERVES 4
PREPARATION TIME : *20 minutes*
MARINATING TIME : *2 hours*
COOKING TIME : *20 minutes*
OVEN : *Preheat to 220°C (425°F, gas mark 7)*

INGREDIENTS
4 boned and skinned chicken breasts
1 clove garlic
8 tablespoons natural yoghurt
1 tablespoon tomato purée
1½ teaspoons ground cumin
1 teaspoon coriander
1 teaspoon ground turmeric
½ -1 teaspoon chilli powder
½ teaspoon ground ginger
1 tablespoon fresh chopped coriander
Salt and freshly ground black pepper

Calories per serving : 170 · High in protein from chicken and yoghurt · Low in cholesterol

Succulent chicken tikka flavoured with a selection of aromatic spices which can be varied according to taste. Using skinned chicken breasts helps to make this dish low in fat and calories.

If you need to bone and skin the chicken breasts, strip off the skin by peeling it back with one hand while detaching it with short, sharp strokes of a knife. When the skin is removed, turn the pieces bone side up and scrape and cut out the bones. Strip the tendon from the middle of each breast cleanly, and trim the meat.

Lay the chicken breasts in a shallow dish. Crush the garlic and mix it with all the other ingredients thoroughly. Pour the mixture all over the chicken breasts, then cover the dish and leave it to marinate for at least 2 hours.

Place the marinated chicken on a rack in the oven and position a baking tin underneath to catch any juices. Cook for 25 minutes, or until the chicken is cooked through, and serve immediately.

Casserole of Pheasant with Chestnuts and Orange

In Britain, pheasants are in season from October to February, during which time birds should be readily available from butchers at very reasonable prices. The natural sweetness of the chestnuts, heightened by the orange juice, combines perfectly with game. When buying chestnuts, look for smooth, shiny shells and nuts that feel firm and solid.

SERVES 6
PREPARATION TIME : *20 minutes*
COOKING TIME : *1 hour*
OVEN : *Preheat to 160°C (325°F, gas mark 3)*

INGREDIENTS
1 brace oven-ready pheasants
500g can whole chestnuts in water
or 1lb (450g) fresh chestnuts
1 medium onion
3oz (75g) butter
2 tablespoons plain flour
1 pint (570ml) chicken or game stock
1 tablespoon redcurrant jelly
Juice and finely grated rind of 1 orange
1 teaspoon wine vinegar
Salt and freshly ground black pepper
1 bay leaf
Orange slices for garnish

Calories per serving : 680 · High in protein from pheasant · High in vitamin C from oranges

Cut each pheasant into 4 pieces with a sharp knife or kitchen scissors. If using fresh chestnuts, score a cross on the side of each nut with a sharp, pointed knife. Drop the scored chestnuts into boiling water and leave for 2 minutes. Drain and peel away the shells and skin. Finely chop the onion.

Melt the butter in a frying pan over a moderate heat. Add the pheasant pieces and cook for about 3 minutes on each side until browned. Transfer the pheasant to a lidded casserole dish.

The pheasant stays moist in this delicious casserole.

Add the onion to the hot butter and cook until it is lightly golden. Stir-fry the chestnuts with the onion for 2 minutes and then transfer to the casserole dish using a draining spoon.

Mix the flour with the residue in the saucepan and leave to bubble and lightly brown for 3-4 minutes, stirring occasionally. Add the stock and bring to the boil. Stir in the redcurrant jelly, orange juice, grated orange rind and wine vinegar.

Pour all the contents of the saucepan over the pheasant, season and add the bay leaf. Cover and cook in the oven for 1 hour, stirring occasionally. Transfer the pheasant pieces, onion and chestnuts to a hot serving dish. Strain the cooking juices over the finished dish, garnish with orange slices, and serve.

Chicken Yakitori

This is one of Japan's favourite dishes. The chicken can either be grilled or barbecued – the cooking time remains the same. For an authentic touch, use sake, the Japanese rice wine, instead of the dry sherry suggested here, and shoyu, Japanese soy sauce, which is both lighter and healthier than its Chinese equivalent. Both are essential in Japanese cooking. Serve with plain boiled rice and an oriental stir-fry of colourful vegetables such as baby sweetcorn, red peppers, mangetouts and bean sprouts.

INGREDIENTS

2 skinned boneless chicken breasts
6 skinned boneless chicken thighs, total 12oz (350g)
8oz (225g) chicken livers, fresh or frozen
2 cloves garlic
1in (25mm) piece fresh root ginger
6 black peppercorns
4 tablespoons dry sherry or sake
4 tablespoons shoyu or soy sauce
2 teaspoons soft brown sugar
4 spring onions for garnish

Calories per serving : 305 · High in protein from chicken and liver · High in iron and zinc from liver

If you are using frozen chicken livers, defrost them thoroughly. If you need to bone the chicken breasts, strip the skin and turn the pieces bone side up. Cut away the bones and remove the tendons by stroking them with a knife. Then trim the meat and cut the breasts, thighs and livers into large cubes of the same size, and set them aside.

Crush the garlic and ginger with the peppercorns in a mortar and pestle. Place them in a shallow dish and add the sake or sherry, shoyu or soy sauce and sugar. Stir well to mix, then add the cubes of chicken and liver. Cover the dish and leave it to marinate for at least 30 minutes, stirring occasionally to ensure the chicken is evenly coated.

Preheat the grill to a high temperature. Reserving the marinade, thread the chicken and chicken liver pieces alternately onto skewers. Place them on a lightly oiled grill rack and grill them for 10 minutes, turning frequently and basting with the reserved marinade. Garnish with spring onion tassels if desired and serve freshly cooked.

Shoyu, sake and ginger give chicken a truly oriental flavour, while a bright, crunchy stir-fry adds freshness.

Farmhouse Chicken Casserole

The distinctive flavour of dry cider complements the flavour of this casserole. However, you could use dry white wine to make a lighter dish for variety, or if you prefer not to use alcohol at all, chicken stock is a perfectly good alternative. This simple casserole can be made a day in advance if desired. Simply reduce the cooking time by 10-15 minutes and keep the casserole covered in the refrigerator until required. Then add the button mushrooms and gently reheat for 15 minutes until piping hot. This dish is a meal in itself, and does not need any side dishes.

Tender chicken quarters flavoured with thyme and rosemary, and cooked with colourful vegetables. Dry cider adds sweetness and a hint of apple to the sauce.

SERVES 4
PREPARATION TIME : *20 minutes*
COOKING TIME : *1½ hours*
OVEN : *Preheat to 180°C (350°F, gas mark 4)*

INGREDIENTS
4 chicken quarters
8oz (225g) baby onions
8oz (225g) new potatoes
12 baby carrots
8oz (225g) large button mushrooms
2 tablespoons plain flour
Salt and freshly ground black pepper
3 tablespoons groundnut oil
¾ pint (450ml) dry cider
2 teaspoons chopped fresh rosemary
2 teaspoons chopped fresh thyme
1 bay leaf
Fresh herbs for garnish

Calories per serving : 520 · High in protein from chicken · High in carotene from carrots

Skin the chicken quarters and peel the onions. Scrub the potatoes, cutting them in half if they are large. Scrape the carrots and wipe the mushrooms clean.

Season the flour with salt and black pepper and coat the chicken. Heat 2 tablespoons of groundnut oil in a large casserole dish. Add the chicken quarters and cook over a moderate heat for 10-15 minutes, until lightly browned on all sides.

When browned, remove the chicken and drain it on kitchen paper. Heat the remaining groundnut oil in the casserole dish. Add the onions and cook over a gentle heat for about 5 minutes until they have just turned golden. Stir in any remaining flour, then gradually pour in the dry cider, stirring continually.

Bring the mixture to the boil, then lower the heat and return the chicken to the casserole dish. Add the potatoes, carrots and herbs, and season to taste. Cover the casserole, transfer to the oven and cook for 45 minutes, stirring occasionally.

Add the button mushrooms and cook for a further 15 minutes, or until the chicken quarters are very tender. Taste and adjust the seasoning if necessary. Garnish the casserole with fresh herbs and serve it straight from the dish.

ONE-POT DISHES

Wholesome casseroles shut out the cold of winter. Cooked in rich sauces made with vegetables, fruits, herbs and spices, they need little accompaniment and are simple to make.

∽

Paella Catalana

Among the many variations of paella – Spain's most famous dish – this recipe is particularly colourful. It comes from the north-east coast of Spain, and reflects the abundance and variety of the region's seafood. To cut down on preparation time, you can buy cleaned squid from a fishmonger or a large supermarket. Serve with crusty French bread, a crisp green salad, and a full-bodied wine like Rioja.

SERVES 6
PREPARATION TIME : *1 hour*
COOKING TIME : *1 hour*
OVEN : *Preheat to 180°C (350°F, gas mark 4)*

INGREDIENTS
1lb (450g) cleaned squid
4 cloves garlic
½ pint (285ml) red wine
24-30 mussels
1 medium onion
4 tablespoons fresh parsley
1 medium yellow pepper
4 medium ripe tomatoes
1lb (450g) monkfish fillet
12 large raw prawns
2 tablespoons virgin olive oil
2½ pints (1.4 litres) fish or chicken stock
1lb (450g) Italian easy-cook brown rice
4oz (115g) frozen peas or petits pois
Salt and freshly ground black pepper

Calories per serving : 595 · High in protein from fish and seafood · High in fibre from brown rice and vegetables · High in vitamin C from tomatoes

Halve 2 of the cloves of garlic and put them in the bottom of an ovenproof dish. Slice the body of the cleaned squid into thin rings, and then cut its tentacles into small evenly sized pieces. Put the squid on top of the garlic and pour over half the red wine. Cover and cook for 1 hour in the oven, stirring occasionally, until the squid is tender.

Meanwhile, scrub the mussels under cold running water and scrape off all the beards and barnacles.

Halve another clove of garlic, then finely chop the onion and parsley. Place the garlic halves, half of the chopped onion, the parsley, mussels and the rest of the red wine in a wide shallow pan, or casserole, with a tightly fitting lid. Cover the pan and bring to the boil, shaking frequently until all of the mussels are open. Reserving the cooking liquid, lift the mussels out of the pan with a slotted spoon and set them aside. Discard any of the mussels that have not opened.

Halve, de-seed and roughly chop the pepper. Plunge the tomatoes into a bowl of hot water for 30 seconds, then into cold water for 1 minute, until cool enough to peel off the skins with your fingers. Chop the tomatoes roughly. Crush the remaining garlic with ½ teaspoon of salt.

When the squid is cooked, reserve the cooking liquid and drain. Remove the garlic halves and put the squid and the cooking liquid to one side.

Skin the monkfish fillet, cutting off as much of the tough grey membrane as possible, with a filleting or other sharp knife. Cut the fish into bite-sized chunks. If desired, reserve some whole prawns for garnishing, or leave their tail flanges on. Shell the rest of the prawns with your fingers. Then making a shallow cut along the back of the prawn, remove the dark intestinal vein that runs along the back.

Heat all the olive oil in a large pan and add the monkfish and prawns. Cook over a moderate heat for 5 minutes, stirring gently. Remove with a slotted spoon and set aside. Add the pepper, tomatoes and the remaining onion and garlic. Cook for about 15 minutes, stirring frequently, until thickened.

Heat the stock in a separate pan until it is just simmering. Meanwhile, stir the brown rice into the pan, then pour in the reserved liquid from the mussels and squid. Gently bring to the boil and simmer uncovered until almost all of the liquid has been absorbed by the rice. Stir occasionally.

As the amount of hot stock needed will vary according to the absorbency of the rice you are using, add it gradually in measures of about ½ pint (285ml) at a time. Cook over a moderate heat and stir frequently until each measure has been absorbed by the rice. After 30 minutes all the stock should be absorbed, and the rice should be just tender.

Add the frozen peas, then after 1-2 minutes the monkfish, prawns and squid, and stir gently until heated right through. Season to taste and serve.

In Spain, paella is usually made for special social or family celebrations. In Catalonia this colourful dish is traditionally cooked outdoors, over a charcoal fire in a large double-handled pan called a 'paellera'.

The couscous in this Moroccan national dish absorbs all the flavour of the chicken, vegetables, herbs and aromatic spices but still remains beautifully light.

Moroccan Chicken Couscous

Although couscous looks like a grain, it is actually a form of Moroccan pasta made from durum wheat. It is cooked by steaming it over a stew or broth. It can be bought from most health food shops and large supermarkets. Buy the precooked variety for this recipe to save time. Moroccan cooks often serve the cooking liquid from their couscous dishes separately – usually in two jugs with one containing spicy flavourings, such as harissa. If harissa sauce is difficult to find, you can add some extra ground cumin and coriander to one jug for variety.

SERVES 4-6
PREPARATION TIME : *30 minutes*
COOKING TIME : *2¼ hours*

INGREDIENTS
4-6 chicken quarters
4oz (115g) tin chickpeas
1 large Spanish onion
4 medium carrots
4 small turnips
or 2 medium swedes
2 potatoes
2 courgettes
4 tablespoons virgin olive oil
1lb (450g) precooked couscous
½ teaspoon ground cinnamon
3-4 drops orange-flower water (optional)
2 tablespoons seedless raisins
Salt and freshly ground black pepper
Fresh coriander leaves for garnish
SPICY PASTE
2 tablespoons tomato purée
2 cloves garlic
1 teaspoon paprika
1 teaspoon ground cumin
1 teaspoon ground coriander
1 teaspoon ground turmeric
¾ teaspoon cayenne

Calories per serving : 435 · Low in cholesterol
High in fibre and vitamin C from vegetables

Drain and rinse the chickpeas, place them in a large casserole and cover with cold water. Bring to the boil, then drain and rinse under cold water.

Skin the chicken quarters and cut them into large, bite-sized pieces. Peel and thinly slice the onion, scrape the carrots and cut them into thick rounds. Peel the turnips or swedes and the potatoes and cut them into large chunks. Top and tail the courgettes and slice thinly. Mix the ingredients for the spicy paste together in a small bowl.

Heat 2 tablespoons of the oil in a large flameproof casserole. Add the onion and cook gently for 10 minutes, stirring frequently, until softened. Add the spicy paste and mix well, then the chickpeas, and cover and simmer for 1 hour. Place the chicken into the casserole and cover with more cold water. Bring to the boil, lower the heat, cover the pan and simmer for 30 minutes, stirring occasionally.

Meanwhile, place the couscous in a bowl, add a pinch of salt and cover with boiling water. Leave to stand, stirring occasionally, until all the water has been absorbed. Stir in the remaining oil, cinnamon and optional orange-flower water.

Add all the vegetables except the courgettes to the stew and stir well. To steam the couscous, put it in a large colander, place on top of the stew and cover tightly with a lid or with foil. Cook over a moderate heat for about 30 minutes, until the steam starts to rise through the couscous. Add the courgettes and the raisins to the stew 15 minutes before the end of the cooking time and season to taste.

To serve, pile the couscous on a wide, flat, serving dish. Remove the chicken, chickpeas and vegetables from the cooking liquid with a slotted spoon and arrange over the couscous and moisten with a few spoonfuls of cooking liquid. Garnish with coriander. Serve the remaining liquid separately.

Smoked Pork and Haricot Beans

This is a low-fat version of Boston Baked Beans, using a lean, smoked, pork-loin joint rather than the traditional fatty belly of pork. You can soak the joint in water overnight to make it less salty.

Home-cooked pork and beans is a filling family dish.

SERVES 6
PREPARATION TIME : *20 minutes*
SOAKING TIME : *Overnight (optional)*
COOKING TIME : *3¼ hours*
OVEN : *Preheat to 180°C (350°F, gas mark 4)*

INGREDIENTS
1½ lb (700g) smoked pork joint
12oz (350g) dried haricot beans
1 medium onion
2 celery sticks
2 carrots
3 tablespoons black treacle
2 tablespoons tomato purée
2 teaspoons English mustard powder
½ teaspoon ground allspice
Salt and freshly ground black pepper

Calories per serving : 340 · Low in cholesterol and fat · High in protein and fibre from pork and beans High in vitamin B12, iron and zinc from pork

---

Blanch the pork before cooking to ensure that the finished dish will not be salty. Put the pork loin in a flameproof casserole and cover with water. Bring to the boil, then drain off the water and set aside.

Rinse and drain the beans. Place in the casserole and cover with fresh cold water. Do not add salt to beans during cooking as this will toughen them. Bring to the boil, then drain and rinse under cold running water and set aside. Chop the onion. Trim the celery and scrape the carrots, then chop them roughly. Place vegetables and beans in casserole.

Mix the black treacle, tomato purée, mustard and allspice in a jug with ¼ pint (150ml) of cold water and freshly ground black pepper to taste. Add the mixture to the casserole and stir well to mix, then cover with plenty of cold water and bring to the boil. Remove any scum from the surface with a slotted spoon, cover with a lid, then transfer the casserole to the oven and cook for 2½ hours, stirring occasionally, and adding more water if it becomes dry.

Add the pork to the beans, pushing it well down into the casserole. Cover and continue cooking for 45 minutes, until the beans are tender, then season to taste. Lift the pork out of the casserole, carve into meat slices and arrange on plates with the beans.

Ham and Sweetcorn Chowder

Chowder is an American name given to particularly thick and filling soups. This recipe, which uses ham, potatoes and sweetcorn, comes from New England and is substantial enough to serve as a nourishing and tasty main dish. As long as you use lean ham, it is low in fat. The cheese topping can be omitted for an even lower fat version. Serve piping hot with chunks of wholemeal bread and a salad.

A thick broth full of sweetcorn, potatoes, herbs and large chunks of ham is topped with grilled cheese to make a homely and satisfying family meal.

SERVES 4
PREPARATION TIME : *10 minutes*
COOKING TIME : *35 minutes*

INGREDIENTS
1½ lb (700g) old potatoes
6oz (175g) lean cooked ham
½ large Spanish onion
1 pint (570ml) skimmed or semi-skimmed milk
1¼ pints (725ml) chicken stock or water
1 teaspoon dried mixed herbs
½ teaspoon paprika
Freshly ground black pepper
12oz (350g) tinned or frozen sweetcorn
2 tablespoons freshly chopped parsley
2oz (50g) Parmesan cheese
2oz (50g) low-fat Cheddar cheese

Calories per serving : 495 · High in fibre from vegetables · High in protein from ham

Peel the potatoes. Discarding any fat, dice the ham and potatoes into ½in (15mm) cubes. Finely chop the onion and add it to a casserole with the potatoes.

Pour in the milk and stock, or water, and bring to a boil. Lower the heat, add the mixed herbs, ¼ teaspoon paprika and season with pepper. Half cover the pan and simmer for 20 minutes.

Preheat the grill on a high temperature. Add the ham and sweetcorn to the pan and simmer for 5 minutes, while stirring. Remove the pan from the heat, mix in the parsley and adjust the seasoning. Pour the chowder into 4 heat-proof serving bowls.

Grate and mix the cheeses together and sprinkle over the top of the chowders. Place the bowls under the grill for 3-4 minutes until the cheese is brown. Sprinkle with the remaining paprika and serve.

Braised Beef with Field Mushrooms

Brisket is an inexpensive cut of meat which becomes tender and absorbs the flavours of the herbs and vegetables when cooked slowly. Field mushrooms make a rich dark gravy to serve with the meat.

Large field mushrooms add their intense flavour to tender beef and create a rich dark sauce with the meat juices.

SERVES 4

PREPARATION TIME : *20 minutes*

COOKING TIME : *2¼ hours*

OVEN : *Preheat to 160°C (325°F, gas mark 3)*

INGREDIENTS

2 tablespoons sunflower or virgin olive oil
1½ -2lb (700-900g) boned and rolled
lean brisket of beef
2 large onions
2 cloves garlic
1lb (450g) large flat or field mushrooms
1 tablespoon freshly chopped thyme or
1 teaspoon dried
Salt and freshly ground black pepper
1 tablespoon freshly chopped parsley

Calories per serving : 295 · High in protein, iron and
zinc from beef · High in fibre from vegetables

Heat 1 tablespoon of the cooking oil in a flameproof casserole. Then, over a high heat, quickly brown the meat on all sides. Remove the browned beef from the casserole and set aside. Turn the heat down low.

Chop the onions. Add the remaining tablespoon of olive oil. Next add the onions and cook gently for about 5 minutes. Crush the garlic and roughly chop all the flat or field mushrooms. Stir in the garlic, mushrooms and thyme to the cooked onions. Mix well, then cover the casserole with a lid or piece of foil and cook gently for about 10 minutes.

Season the mushroom mixture to taste with salt and freshly ground black pepper and lay the meat on top. Cover the casserole again and cook in the oven for 1¾ hours. Preheat a large serving dish.

As soon as the beef is cooked, remove it from the oven and place it in the centre of the heated serving dish. Remove the mushrooms from the casserole with a slotted spoon and arrange them around the meat. Sprinkle over the freshly chopped parsley. Serve the cooking juices separately in a small jug.

Turkey Hotpot

Traditional English hotpots made with crispy potato toppings have long been a winter family favourite. Lean turkey ensures the dish is healthy as well as satisfying. Spinach or cabbage go well with this dish.

SERVES 6
PREPARATION TIME : *45 minutes*
COOKING TIME : *2½ hours*
OVEN : *Preheat to 180°C (350°F, gas mark 4)*

INGREDIENTS

1½ lb (700g) boneless turkey breasts
1 tablespoon virgin olive oil
1 large onion
8oz (225g) carrots
8oz (225g) swede
8oz (225g) turnips
3 sticks celery
1 large leek
1oz (25g) plain flour
14oz (400g) can chopped tomatoes
¾ pint (450ml) chicken stock
2 teaspoons fresh thyme or 1 teaspoon dry
2 tablespoons chopped parsley
Salt and freshly ground black pepper
2lb (900g) large potatoes
1oz (25g) butter

Calories per serving : 405 · High in protein and iron from turkey · High in fibre from vegetables

Cut the turkey breasts into 1in (25mm) cubes. Heat the olive oil in a large casserole dish. Add the turkey pieces and cook over a moderate heat for 5 minutes, stirring continually, until lightly browned. Remove the turkey with a slotted spoon, leaving the oil in the dish, and put to one side.

Thinly slice the onion, carrots, swede, turnips, celery and leek. Add them to the oil remaining in the dish and cook for 2-3 minutes, turning continually.

Return the turkey to the dish and stir in the flour. Add the canned tomatoes, stock and herbs. Season lightly to taste and bring to the boil.

Scrub and peel the potatoes, then thinly slice them. Remove the dish from the heat and arrange

A mixture of turkey and vegetables hidden under a blanket of crispy potatoes makes a tasty winter meal.

the potato slices to cover the top of the turkey and vegetables, starting from the outside and working inwards, overlapping in concentric circles. Dot the potatoes with little bits of butter.

Cover the dish with a lid, or with foil wrapped tightly over it, and cook in the preheated oven for about 1¾ hours, then uncover and cook for a further 45 minutes until the potatoes are really crisp and golden. Serve immediately.

Italian Meatball Casserole

This is a quick and simple top-of-the-stove casserole. It is important to use really lean mince to make the meat balls. As shop-bought mince tends to be quite fatty, buy a piece of beef and have a butcher mince it, or mince it yourself at home. It is best to buy the minced meat on the day that you are going to use it – never refrigerate it for more than two days. This Italian-style dish goes well with either fresh bread, pasta, potatoes or rice, and a simple green salad.

SERVES 4
PREPARATION TIME : *30 minutes*
COOKING TIME : *20 minutes*

INGREDIENTS
1lb (450g) lean minced beef
1 medium onion
Salt and freshly ground black pepper
1 tablespoon Worcestershire sauce
SAUCE
12oz (350g) large courgettes
1 large red pepper
4oz (115g) large button mushrooms
2 tablespoons virgin olive oil
14oz (400g) can tomatoes
1 teaspoon dried oregano
2 teaspoons arrowroot powder

Calories per serving : 295 · High in protein and iron from mince · High in vitamin C from vegetables

Peel and finely chop the onion, then combine all the ingredients for the meatballs in a large mixing bowl, adding 1 teaspoon of salt and ½ teaspoon of freshly ground black pepper. Shape the meat mixture into 24 balls, pressing each one firmly to hold its shape, then put them to one side.

Slice the courgettes. Halve and de-seed the red pepper and cut it into 1in (25mm) squares. Clean and slice the button mushrooms.

Heat the olive oil in a large frying pan or in a flameproof casserole with a tightly fitting lid, and brown the meatballs evenly over a medium heat for about 5 minutes.

Remove the meatballs from the pan and add the mushrooms to it, frying them quickly for 2 minutes. Return the meatballs to the pan and add the other vegetables, tomatoes and oregano. Gently bring to the boil, cover and simmer for 15 minutes.

Mix the arrowroot with 1 tablespoon of cold water until smooth, then stir it into the casserole and continue cooking over a moderate heat until the sauce has thickened. Serve immediately.

Savoury meatballs, mushrooms, red pepper and courgettes covered in a rich Italian tomato and oregano sauce.

A bright orange squash with a succulent turkey-and-mint filling makes an appealing and well-balanced meal.

Baked Squash with Turkey

Squashes are members of the gourd family and are native to the Americas. A variety of different types are available throughout the year, but it is the larger summer squashes that are most suitable for stuffing, such as the acorn squash, or kabocha, which has a dark green skin and yellow flesh, the pale-skinned scalloped squash, or the common vegetable marrow – available from late spring to early autumn. This recipe uses a turkey mince, which can be found in many of the larger supermarkets and butchers – or you can mince your own. It makes an excellent low-fat stuffing and has more flavour than chicken. Serve with rice or potatoes and a green salad.

SERVES 4
PREPARATION TIME : *20 minutes*
COOKING TIME : *1½ hours*
OVEN : *Preheat to 180°C (350°F, gas mark 4)*

INGREDIENTS
1 × 2lb (900g) squash
2 tomatoes
1 medium onion
1 tablespoon fresh mint
12oz (350g) minced turkey
3oz (75g) wholemeal breadcrumbs
Salt and freshly ground black pepper

Calories per serving : 215 · Low in fat · High in fibre from breadcrumbs · High in protein from turkey

Wash and trim the stem of the squash, then cut a slice off the top of the squash and scoop out the seeds with a teaspoon and discard. Put to one side.

To prepare the stuffing, plunge the tomatoes into a bowl of boiling water for 30 seconds, and then a bowl of cold water for about 1 minute, until the skins are cool enough to peel off with your fingers. De-seed and chop the tomatoes. Peel and finely chop the onion, and chop the mint. Then mix the minced turkey, breadcrumbs, onion, tomatoes, mint and seasoning in a bowl. Push as much of the mixture into the squash as possible.

Put the squash into a small roasting tin and bake in the oven for 1½ hours.

When the squash is cooked, place it on a heated serving dish, carefully slice it and serve immediately.

Chicken Simmered with Spicy Dried Fruit

In Morocco this dish is called 'Tagine', named after the earthenware pot in which it is traditionally cooked. Dried fruits are one of the most popular ingredients in Middle-Eastern cooking, and in this recipe the spicy fruit keeps the chicken really juicy and tender. Most good supermarkets sell ready-to-eat dried fruit salad, which does not need soaking.

SERVES 4
PREPARATION TIME : *10 minutes*
COOKING TIME : *45 minutes*

INGREDIENTS
4 × 10oz (275g) chicken quarters
½ pint (285ml) chicken stock
¼ pint (150ml) orange juice
2 teaspoons paprika
2 teaspoons ground ginger
½ teaspoon ground cinnamon
¼ teaspoon ground allspice
9oz (250g) packet ready-to-eat dried fruit salad
Salt and freshly ground black pepper

*Calories per serving : 180 · Low in fat
and cholesterol · High in protein from chicken*

To prepare the chicken, remove all of the skin and any fat from the quarters.

Pour the chicken stock and the orange juice into a flameproof casserole, then add the spices and stir it well. Add the dried fruit and bring slowly to the boil, stirring continuously. Then add the chicken quarters and season to taste. Baste the chicken pieces well with the liquid.

Lower the heat and cover the pan with a tightly fitting lid, then simmer very gently for about 30-35 minutes, until the chicken is tender. Lift the lid occasionally during the cooking, and stir the chicken and dried fruit to ensure that they cook evenly.

Taste and adjust the seasoning with salt and ground black pepper, then serve immediately.

Tender chicken with sweet dried fruit and spices.

247

Steamed Chicken with Coriander Stuffing

The humble chicken has not always been regarded as a commonplace food. In the middle of the 18th century the English valued some breeds so highly, such as the enormous Cochin China fowl, that they paid the price of three cows or a small flock of sheep for just a single bird. This recipe requires only an inexpensive roasting chicken. Steaming a chicken keeps it very moist and full of flavour, but you will need a large saucepan or casserole for this dish.

SERVES 4
PREPARATION TIME : *50 minutes*
COOKING TIME : *1½-2 hours*

INGREDIENTS
3lb (1.4kg) roasting chicken
2 medium onions
4 small turnips
6 medium carrots
1 tablespoon virgin olive oil
Peeled zest of 1 lemon
½ pint (285ml) chicken stock
STUFFING
4oz (115g) tomatoes
2oz (50g) mushrooms
3oz (75g) wholemeal breadcrumbs
3 tablespoons chopped coriander
Freshly ground black pepper
1 tablespoon lemon juice
3 tablespoons chicken stock

Calories per serving : 465 · High in fibre from wholemeal breadcrumbs and vegetables

Skin the tomatoes by plunging them into boiling water for 30 seconds and then into cold water for 1 minute. The skins should peel away very easily. De-seed the tomatoes and roughly chop them. Finely chop the mushrooms.

To make the stuffing, place the breadcrumbs in a basin with the tomatoes, mushrooms and coriander. Season with black pepper, and then bind with the lemon juice and the chicken stock. Remove any

A tasty coriander, tomato and mushroom stuffing helps to keep the chicken moist while it is cooking.

excess fat from inside the bird, then stuff the bird with the breadcrumb mixture.

Peel and quarter the onions and turnips and peel and roughly chop the carrots. Heat the olive oil in a large saucepan and fry the onions, turnips and carrots gently for about 5 minutes. Add the lemon zest and the chicken stock.

Place the chicken on a rack or stand so that it sits inside the saucepan without touching the stock or vegetables. A 6in (150mm) loose-bottomed cake tin (without the base) would be ideal.

Add the chicken to the saucepan. Cover it tightly, bring to the boil and cook gently for about 1½ -2 hours, or until the juices from the chicken thigh are quite clear when it is skewered.

Lift the chicken onto a serving dish. Remove the vegetables from the saucepan with a draining spoon and arrange them around the chicken. Serve the juices separately in a jug.

Lamb Stew with Lentils and Spinach

The lentils in this recipe gradually absorb the meat juices and spices to take on a rich, mellow flavour. Always pick over the lentils before cooking, to remove any small stones. Use fresh spinach when possible, choosing greens with small tender leaves that are springy to the touch; the peak season is late spring. This dish goes well with a side serving of fresh yoghurt and sliced cucumber.

SERVES 4-5
PREPARATION TIME : *35 minutes*
SOAKING TIME : *overnight*
COOKING TIME : *1½ hours*

INGREDIENTS

1½ lb (675g) shoulder of lamb
½ lb (225g) green or brown lentils
1lb (450g) fresh spinach
or 8oz (225g) frozen chopped spinach
1 onion
2 cloves garlic
2 carrots
1½ oz (40g) butter
1 tablespoon virgin olive oil
14oz (400g) tin peeled tomatoes
Salt and freshly ground black pepper
2 dried chilli peppers (optional)
½ teaspoon cumin
½ teaspoon ground coriander
2 tablespoons parsley or fresh coriander

Calories per serving : 590 · Low in cholesterol · High in protein, fibre and iron from lamb and spinach

Wash the lentils in cold water. If necessary, soak them overnight, and then drain. Soaking shortens cooking time and prevents splitting. However, most lentils are tender enough to need little or no soaking.

Trim the fat from the lamb and dice the meat into 1in (25mm) cubes. If you are using fresh spinach, wash it thoroughly. Finely slice the onion and garlic, and peel and slice the carrots into rounds.

Place ½oz (15g) of the butter and the olive oil into a large flameproof casserole. Heat until the butter melts and sizzles, and then add the lamb cubes, stirring until they are sealed and browned. Leaving the fat in the casserole, remove the lamb with a slotted spoon and keep it to one side.

Add the onion, garlic and carrots to the casserole and cook over a moderate heat until softened. Next add the tomatoes, lamb pieces, 1 teaspoon of salt, ½ teaspoon of pepper, optional chillies, lentils and enough water to just cover the mixture. Stir in the cumin and simmer for 1¼ hours, until the lentils are cooked. Add a little more water if the mixture begins to dry. Set the mixture aside when cooked.

Cook the spinach in 1oz (25g) of the butter with a little salt and the ground coriander. Reheat the lentil mixture and stir in the cooked spinach. Sprinkle with chopped parsley or fresh coriander and serve.

A yoghurt and cucumber sauce can be served with the spicy lentils and tender lamb in this colourful stew.

Mushroom Bake

This unusual German dish can be made using open cup, button, oyster or chestnut mushrooms, or with any combination of these varieties. The gammon can be left out of the recipe to make a vegetarian dish.

SERVES 4
PREPARATION TIME : *15 minutes*
COOKING TIME : *40-45 minutes*
OVEN : *Preheat to 200°C (400°F, gas mark 6)*

INGREDIENTS
1½ lb (700g) mushrooms
3oz (75g) sweet-cured gammon rashers
1 medium onion
½ tablespoon virgin olive oil
2 tablespoons brandy
1 tablespoon plain flour
¼ pint (150ml) sour cream
Salt and freshly ground black pepper
2oz (50g) low-fat Cheddar cheese
½ oz (15g) fresh wholemeal breadcrumbs
12 green stuffed olives
Sprigs of parsley for garnish

Calories per serving : 390 · Low in cholesterol · High in protein from gammon, cheese and breadcrumbs

Wash the mushrooms and pat dry. Cut the gammon rashers into thin strips and roughly chop the onion.

Heat the oil in a flameproof casserole dish with a tightly fitting lid. Add the gammon and onion and cook gently for 5 minutes until lightly browned. Pour in the brandy, heat for a few seconds, then, standing well clear, ignite with a match.

When the brandy flames have subsided, stir in the flour and sour cream. Heat the sauce gently for 5 minutes, stirring constantly. Do not allow it to boil. Add the mushrooms and remove the casserole from the heat. Season to taste, then cover tightly with a lid. Bake in the oven for 25-30 minutes, until the mushrooms are tender but not overcooked. Remove from the oven and uncover. Preheat the grill.

Grate the cheese, mix with the breadcrumbs and sprinkle over the mushrooms. Brown under a hot grill. Slice olives and chop parsley for the garnish.

The gammon gives the mushrooms a smoky flavour.

Pot-roasted Chicken with Cranberries

The slightly sharp taste of cranberries complements poultry beautifully. During winter you can buy fresh cranberries imported from North America. You can buy frozen or tinned varieties all year round.

SERVES 4
PREPARATION TIME : *10 minutes*
COOKING TIME : *1 hour 20 minutes*
OVEN : *Preheat to 190°C (375°F, gas mark 5)*

INGREDIENTS
3lb (1.4kg) roasting chicken
8oz (225g) cranberries
1 tablespoon raw brown sugar
Grated rind of 1 orange
Juice of 2 oranges
Salt and freshly ground black pepper
4 sprigs rosemary
1 tablespoon honey

Calories per serving : 595 · High in protein and zinc from chicken

Choose a casserole or covered roasting tin to fit the chicken snugly. Put the cranberries, sugar, orange rind and juice into the casserole and mix together.

Remove any giblets from the chicken and season the bird lightly inside and out with salt and black pepper. Place it on top of the cranberries with the rosemary, cover and cook in the oven for 1 hour. Warm a dish ready for serving.

Remove the cover and smear the honey over the chicken. Continue cooking for a further 20 minutes, basting frequently with the cooking juices, until the chicken is golden-brown.

Lift the chicken from the casserole and place it on the serving dish. Discard the rosemary sprigs. Remove the cranberries with a draining spoon and arrange them around the chicken. Carefully skim off and discard any fat from the cooking juices. Serve the cooking juices separately in a sauceboat.

Cranberries have a refreshing sharpness which balances the sweetness of the honey and orange in the sauce. Together with the side vegetables, the cranberries' deep-red colour gives this dish a really festive appearance.

Traditional Pot Roast Beef

This recipe uses an old-fashioned way of preparing a large piece of meat that requires long, slow cooking. The stock from the vegetables combines with the meat juices to create a delicious sauce, flavoured with a bay leaf and a little thyme.

SERVES 6-8
PREPARATION TIME : *25 minutes*
COOKING TIME : *3 hours*
OVEN : *Preheat to 160°C (325°F, gas mark 3)*

INGREDIENTS
*2½ lb (1.1kg) piece of rolled brisket,
forerib or topside of beef
2 medium onions
2 carrots
2 sticks celery
1 tablespoon vegetable oil
2 parsley sprigs
½ teaspoon dried thyme
1 bay leaf
½ pint (285ml) beef stock
2 teaspoons arrowroot powder
Salt and freshly ground black pepper*

*Calories per serving : 460 · High in protein,
iron and zinc from beef*

Tender roast beef cooked in a rich warming sauce.

Roughly chop the onions, carrots and celery sticks. Heat the oil in a casserole or large frying pan and brown the meat well on all sides.

Add the vegetables to the casserole with the herbs and stock. Cover and cook for about 3 hours in the oven until the meat is really tender.

Remove the meat from the dish and leave it to rest in a warm place. Strain the cooking juices into a saucepan through a sieve. Keep the vegetables warm until required.

Mix the arrowroot powder and 1 tablespoon of cold water until smooth, then add to the saucepan and cook over a medium heat, stirring all the time until thickened. Season to taste.

Cut the beef into thick slices, spoon the sauce over and serve with the vegetables immediately.

Sausages with Grapes and Cider

Umbria is a beautiful part of Italy that is famous for its salami and sausages, and this wholesome dish is based upon a traditional peasant recipe from the region. You can either use crisp seedless grapes, or larger grapes that need to be halved and seeded before they can be used. This dish goes well with potatoes or fresh bread, and a very simple side salad of radicchio or frisée lettuce.

SERVES 4
PREPARATION TIME : *10 minutes*
COOKING TIME : *25 minutes*

INGREDIENTS
*8 country-style pork sausages with herbs
2 tablespoons virgin olive oil
16 sage leaves
2 medium onions
8oz (225g) seedless green grapes
¼ pint (150ml) dry cider
1 teaspoon arrowroot powder or cornflour
Salt and freshly ground black pepper*

*Calories per serving : 345 · High in protein from
sausages · High in potassium from grapes*

Spicy sausages, cider, sage and crisp sweet grapes combine to make a simple but delicious main course.

Heat the oil in a frying pan and gently fry the sage leaves for a few minutes until they give off their aroma. Remove from the pan and keep to one side.

Cut the onions into rings, add them to the pan and cook over a medium heat for 8 minutes, or until softened. Remove and put to one side.

Cook the sausages in the same pan over a medium heat for about 10 minutes, turning occasionally until they are well browned on all sides. Return the onions and sage leaves to the pan, add the grapes, and then stir in all the dry cider.

Mix the arrowroot powder or cornflour with 1 tablespoon of cold water and add to the pan, stirring until the sauce has thickened. Cover and simmer for 5 minutes. Season, using plenty of black pepper, and serve straight from the pan.

Chicken, Potato and Butter-bean Stew

This heart-warming chicken stew is given a decorative touch with a patterned potato topping. Sweet potatoes are very easy to mash, and their delicious flavour makes an interesting addition to poultry and game. Serve the stew with crunchy vegetables, such as lightly cooked mangetout or French beans.

SERVES 4
PREPARATION TIME : *20 minutes*
COOKING TIME : *1 hour 20 minutes*
OVEN : *Preheat to 180°C (350°F, gas mark 4)*

INGREDIENTS
4 chicken breasts, skinned and boned
4oz (115g) tinned butter beans
1 medium onion
¾ pint (450ml) chicken stock
1 pinch of saffron
8oz (225g) carrots
6oz (175g) leeks
2 teaspoons fresh thyme and parsley
or 1 teaspoon dried thyme and parsley
Salt and freshly ground black pepper
2 teaspoons snipped chives
TOPPING
12oz (350g) sweet potatoes
12oz (350g) English potatoes
¼ pint(150ml) whole or semi-skimmed milk
1 pinch powdered cinnamon

Calories per serving : 445 · High in protein from chicken and milk · High in fibre from vegetables

Peel and slice the onion. Pour the chicken stock into a pan and add the onion and the saffron. Bring to the boil, reduce the heat and leave to simmer briskly, uncovered, for 15 minutes.

Meanwhile, slice both the carrots and the leeks into regular-sized rounds. In a 2 pint (1.1 litre) flat, ovenproof dish, layer the chicken breasts with the thyme, parsley, carrots and leeks. Pour over the saffron and onion stock. Season to taste with salt and freshly ground black pepper, cover and cook in the

Chicken and butter beans topped with crisp potato.

oven for 40 minutes, stirring well halfway through.

While the casserole is cooking, peel and cut the sweet potatoes into rounds 1in (25mm) thick. Cook the rounds in boiling water for about 15 minutes until soft, then drain and mash them thoroughly, adding half the milk and the cinnamon.

Peel and cut the English potatoes into similar-sized round pieces and cook them in boiling water for 15-20 minutes. Drain, add the remaining milk, and mash thoroughly.

When the casserole is cooked, remove the lid and stir in the butter beans. Cover with the mashed sweet potatoes and English potatoes, arranging them by hand, or using a piping bag in a striped manner if desired. Return the casserole to the oven and bake for a further 40 minutes until the topping is lightly crisp and golden. Garnish with the snipped chives and serve immediately.

Guinea Fowl with Red Cabbage

Guinea fowl has a very distinctive flavour – it is not quite as 'gamey' as pheasant, but is much richer than chicken. The sweetness of cooked red cabbage blends perfectly with guinea fowl, and stops it from becoming too dry during cooking.

SERVES 4
PREPARATION TIME : *15 minutes*
COOKING TIME : *1¾ hours*
OVEN : *Preheat to 180°C (350°F, gas mark 4)*

INGREDIENTS
2 guinea fowl
2 tablespoons virgin olive oil
2 medium onions
2 shallots
1 small red cabbage
3oz (75g) raisins
6 juniper berries
2 large sprigs thyme or 1 teaspoon dried
2 large pieces orange peel
¼ pint (150ml) chicken stock
Salt and freshly ground black pepper
1 tablespoon white wine vinegar

Calories per serving : 585 · Low in cholesterol · High in protein and iron from guinea fowl

Heat the olive oil in a flameproof casserole dish and add the guinea fowl. Quickly fry the birds over a moderate to high heat, turning them over so that they are lightly and evenly browned on all sides. Remove the guinea fowl from the casserole dish and put them to one side.

Peel and chop the onions and the shallots and add them to the dish. Lower the heat and gently cook for about 5 minutes. Wash the red cabbage thoroughly and shred it. Add it to the casserole dish along with the raisins. Mix well and cook gently for a further 5 minutes, stirring the mixture frequently.

Crush the juniper berries and add them, with the thyme and orange peel, to the dish. Pour the stock over the dish and season with salt and freshly ground black pepper. Place both guinea fowl on top of the cabbage mixture, cover and cook in the oven for 1½ hours. Warm a dish ready for serving.

Remove the casserole dish from the oven. Lift the guinea fowl onto the serving dish and remove all the orange peel. Mix the wine vinegar in with the cabbage, and adjust the seasoning. Carefully spoon the cabbage around the birds and serve.

Red cabbage adds its sweet flavour and deep colour to this tasty and warming dish of braised guinea fowl.

Spicy Arrabbiata Pasta

The spicy tomato sauce used in this recipe is called 'Arrabbiata' in Italy and is made with chillies and vodka. It is traditionally served with pasta quills, but any other pasta shapes can be used. Serve this dish with a green salad tossed in a garlic vinaigrette, and an Italian red wine such as a Chianti or Barolo.

SERVES 4
PREPARATION TIME : *10 minutes*
COOKING TIME : *35 minutes*

INGREDIENTS
10oz (275g) plain or wholemeal pasta shapes
2 red chillies
½ Spanish onion
1 clove garlic
3oz (75g) low-fat Cheddar cheese
3 tablespoons virgin olive oil
2 teaspoons white wine vinegar
1 tablespoon chopped fresh oregano
or 1 teaspoon dried
14oz (400g) tinned tomatoes
2 tablespoons tomato purée
1 teaspoon sugar
Salt and freshly ground black pepper
1 large glass red wine
1 tablespoon shredded fresh basil
4 tablespoons vodka (optional)

Calories per serving : 445 · Low in cholesterol · High in iron and fibre from wholemeal pasta

Half fill a flameproof casserole with water and bring it to the boil. De-seed the hot, red chillies and finely chop them along with the onion and garlic. Grate the cheese onto a plate and set aside.

Pour 1 tablespoon of the oil into the casserole of boiling water and cook the pasta according to the packet instructions, leaving it cooked but slightly firm. Leave the pasta to drain in a colander.

Add the remaining 2 tablespoons of olive oil and the white wine vinegar to the casserole and cook the onion for 5 minutes over a moderate heat, stirring

Vodka adds an unusual twist to this tomato sauce.

occasionally. Preheat the grill to a high temperature.

Stir the garlic, chillies, oregano, tomatoes and tomato purée into the onion, breaking up the tomatoes with a wooden spoon. Lower the heat and add the sugar, then season to taste and add the wine. Simmer gently for 10 minutes, stirring occasionally, then add the shredded basil and optional vodka.

Stir the pasta into the sauce, level the surface of the mixture, and sprinkle the grated cheese over the top. Place the casserole under the grill and cook for about 5 minutes, until the cheese is golden-brown and bubbling. Serve straight from the casserole.

Chop Suey

This well-known dish gets its name from the Chinese word *zasui*, meaning 'bits and pieces'. It provides a quick and efficient means of using up leftover pork, chicken and vegetables, by combining them with fresh ingredients in a sweet and sour sauce. If you have any cooked meat left over from a meal, you could use it to replace the chicken and pork in this recipe. Serve with rice or noodles.

SERVES 4
PREPARATION TIME : *30 minutes*
COOKING TIME : *20 minutes*

INGREDIENTS
1 large boneless chicken breast
6oz (175g) pork fillet (tenderloin)
8 spring onions
1 medium red pepper
3 carrots
3 celery sticks
1 × 8oz (225g) tin sliced bamboo shoots
3 tablespoons sunflower oil
4oz (115g) bean sprouts
Salt and freshly ground black pepper
SAUCE
2 teaspoons cornflour
2 tablespoons shoyu or light soy sauce
2 tablespoons dry sherry
1 tablespoon clear honey
1 teaspoon white wine vinegar

Calories per serving : 250 · Low in cholesterol

Skin the chicken breast and place it on a chopping board along with the pork. Cover the meat with greaseproof paper and flatten with a meat mallet or the end of a rolling pin. Then cut diagonally into thin slices, about ¼in (5mm) thick.

Trim and slice the spring onions. De-seed and halve the red pepper and slice it into thin strips. Scrape the carrots, trim the celery and cut both into thin strips to equal the pepper. Drain the bamboo shoots and cut them into thin strips. Mix all the ingredients for the sauce together in a jug and stir in 6 tablespoons of cold water.

Heat 2 tablespoons of the oil in a wok or frying pan. Add the chicken and pork in batches and stir-fry over a moderate to high heat for about 3-4 minutes until the meat has changed colour. Remove the meat with a slotted spoon and drain on kitchen paper.

Heat the remaining oil in the pan, add the spring onions, red pepper, carrots and celery and stir-fry for 5 minutes. Rinse and dry the bean sprouts then add them with the bamboo shoots and stir in the sauce. Increase to a high heat and stir-fry until the sauce boils and thickens. Return the chicken and pork to the pan and stir-fry until heated and evenly mixed. Season to taste before serving.

This oriental dish is brimming with tender meat and crunchy vegetables coated in a sweet and sour sauce.

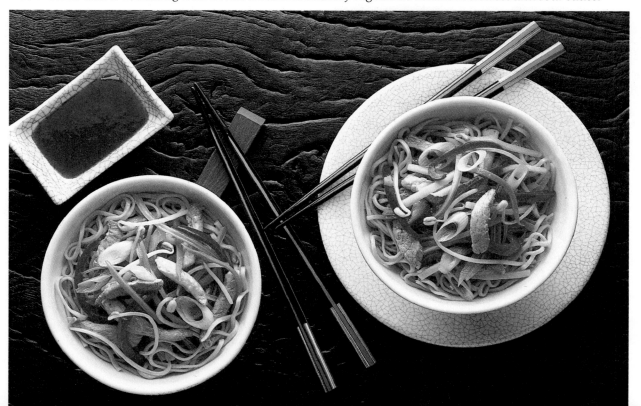

Hungarian Pork Goulash

Goulash is a traditional, spicy Hungarian dish, and although there are several variations of it, a true goulash should always contain onions and sweet paprika. A truly authentic goulash recipe requires pork fat, but this healthier yet equally flavoursome version substitutes a small amount of virgin olive oil instead. The dill-pickled cucumbers make this recipe slightly tangy. Serve this dish with a simple salad or a mixture of vegetables. Hungarians often eat bread with their goulash to help mop up the delicious sauce.

Sour cream tops a traditional Hungarian goulash of pork and potatoes cooked in a rich wine sauce.

SERVES 4
PREPARATION TIME : *30 minutes*
COOKING TIME : *2 hours 20 minutes*
OVEN : *Preheat to 180°C (350°F, gas mark 4)*

INGREDIENTS
1¾ lb (800g) lean leg of pork
1 tablespoon virgin olive oil
2 large onions
1 clove garlic
1-2 tablespoons sweet paprika
½ oz (15g) plain flour
¼ pint (150ml) dry white wine
½ pint (285ml) chicken stock
1 tablespoon tomato purée
Salt and freshly ground black pepper
1lb (450g) small new potatoes
3 large dill-pickled cucumbers
2 tablespoons sour cream
1 tablespoon chopped parsley

Calories per serving : 520 · High in protein from pork and potatoes · High in vitamin B12, zinc and iron from pork · High in fibre from potatoes

Remove all the excess fat from the pork and cut the meat into 1in (25mm) cubes. Heat the olive oil in a flameproof casserole and cook the pork cubes, a few at a time, over a high heat, until lightly browned all over. Remove from the dish and set aside.

Peel and chop the onions and peel and crush the garlic. Turn down to a moderate heat and add them to the casserole. Cook gently for about 5 minutes until soft and lightly browned, then stir in the garlic, paprika and flour. Cook for a further minute, and then add the wine, stock and tomato purée. Bring to the boil while stirring continually.

Return the pork to the casserole dish and season lightly with salt. Scrub the new potatoes and add them to the dish. Bring to the boil once more, remove from the heat and cover with a tightly fitting lid or foil. Place in the oven and cook for 2 hours. Slice the dill-pickled cucumbers and add them to the dish during the last 10 minutes of cooking.

Just before serving, season with pepper, spoon the sour cream on top of the meat, dust with paprika, if required, and sprinkle with chopped parsley.

VEGETABLE DISHES

New ideas for tasty main courses help vegetarians get all the vitamins, minerals and protein they need. The exciting range of fresh vegetables now available can also be used to make delicious side dishes which are so important in a meal.

∽

Leeks with Red and Yellow Peppers

Leeks were considered to be a delicacy in Greek and Roman times, and they have been popular in Europe ever since. A mixture of parsley, basil and thyme goes well with this dish of tender vegetables.

SERVES 4
PREPARATION TIME : *15 minutes*
COOKING TIME : *15 minutes*

INGREDIENTS
5 leeks
2 large yellow peppers
1 large red pepper
1½ oz (40g) butter
Salt and white pepper
1 tablespoon virgin olive oil
1½ tablespoons fresh mixed herbs

Calories per serving : 180 · High in dietary fibre and vitamin C from peppers and leeks

Top and tail the leeks and remove any tough outer leaves. Wash the leeks carefully to remove any grit, then slice them into thin rounds. Halve and de-seed

This bright vegetable dish makes its own sweet sauce.

the peppers and then slice them thinly into strips.

Melt the butter in a pan with 3 tablespoons of water, then add the leeks and a little salt. Cover the pan and cook the leeks over a medium heat for 8-10 minutes until tender.

Uncover the pan, add the oil and raise the heat. Sauté the peppers for 2 minutes. Add a little more water, lower the heat and cook for 2 minutes more until the peppers are soft and there is a sweet sauce in the pan. Add the herbs, season and serve.

Spicy Mexican Pizza

An important ingredient in Mexican cooking is chorizo, a spicy smoked sausage, which is an optional extra in this vegetable pizza. There are over 100 regional varieties from Mexico and Spain.

SERVES 4-6
PREPARATION TIME : *30 minutes*
COOKING TIME : *35-40 minutes*
OVEN : *Preheat to 200°C (400°F, gas mark 6)*

INGREDIENTS
PIZZA BASE
12oz (350g) wholemeal flour
3 teaspoons baking powder
¼ teaspoon salt
1oz (25g) butter
1 medium egg
6fl oz (175ml) skimmed milk
TOPPING
2 small fresh red or green chillies
1 small sweet green pepper
1 red onion
1 clove garlic
2oz (50g) Fontina or Mozzarella cheese
2oz (50g) mature Cheddar cheese
1oz (25g) smoked Gouda cheese
10 red or yellow cherry tomatoes
3 tablespoons virgin olive oil
6oz (175g) chorizo or spicy salami
2 tablespoons shredded fresh coriander

Calories per serving : 460 · High in vitamin C from chillies · High in protein from egg and milk

Spicy chorizo and aromatic coriander add their distinctive flavours to this colourful Mexican pizza.

For the base, sift the flour, baking powder and salt into a mixing bowl, and tip in the bran remaining in the sieve. Rub in the butter and make a well in the centre of the flour. In a separate bowl, beat the egg and mix it with the skimmed milk. Pour into the flour and mix to form a soft dough. Knead it on a lightly floured surface until smooth. Roll out into a round measuring 12in (300mm) in diameter. Lightly oil a large baking sheet and place the dough in the centre.

De-seed the chillies and sweet pepper. Slice the pepper, onion and garlic. Slice the cheeses thinly and cut the tomatoes in half. Arrange the chillies, onion, garlic and pepper on the pizza and sprinkle over 1 tablespoon of oil. Bake for 15 minutes.

Remove from the oven and sprinkle all but a small handful of the cheese over the pizza and add the cherry tomatoes. Sprinkle with another tablespoon of the oil and bake for a further 15 minutes.

Slice the chorizo into rounds. Remove the pizza and add the rest of the cheese and the chorizo. Sprinkle with the remaining oil. Bake for 5 minutes more. Garnish with coriander and serve.

Cabbage with Walnuts and Sesame Seeds

A few walnuts, sesame seeds and half a glass of white wine can turn a cabbage into an extremely tasty and elegant vegetable dish. The wine and sugar in this recipe help to keep the cabbage tasting sweet, and as long as the cabbage is not overcooked it will smell fresh and appetising. Cabbage should be tender but still slightly crisp after it has been cooked. Fish goes especially well with this dish but it is also excellent with most chicken and pork dishes.

SERVES 4
PREPARATION TIME : *15 minutes*
COOKING TIME : *6 minutes*

INGREDIENTS
1½ lb (700g) savoy or white cabbage
1 tablespoon walnut or olive oil
4oz (115g) shelled half walnuts
2oz (50g) sesame seeds
1oz (25g) butter
½ glass white wine or vermouth
½ teaspoon ground nutmeg
1 teaspoon sugar
Salt and freshly ground black pepper

Calories per serving : 285 · Low cholesterol · High in fibre from cabbage and walnuts · High in vitamin C from cabbage

Put the oil in a large frying pan and add the walnuts. Cook over a moderate heat for 2-3 minutes, taking care not to burn them, then add the sesame seeds and cook for another 2 minutes, until lightly toasted. Remove from the pan and set aside.

Wash the cabbage thoroughly, discarding any damaged or coarse leaves. Cut out the tough heart of the cabbage with a sharp knife and chop the cabbage into very thin shreds.

Add the butter and wine, or vermouth, to a large pan and add the cabbage and cook for 4-5 minutes, stirring frequently. Then mix in the nutmeg, sugar, sesame seeds and walnuts. Season to taste, transfer to a serving dish and serve.

Crunchy strips of savoy cabbage are sautéed in a little butter and wine. With the added flavour and texture of toasted walnuts and sesame seeds, an ordinary vegetable is transformed into a sophisticated dish.

Red Cabbage Ragout with Chestnuts

Apples, onions and spices, together with wine and vinegar, are traditional ingredients to cook with red cabbage. The red wine helps the cabbage keep both its colour and flavour and the long, slow cooking method used in this recipe allows it to absorb all the flavours, giving it a sweet and sour taste. This dish is normally served hot with game and meat dishes, but it is also delicious cold, with a salad.

SERVES 6-8
PREPARATION TIME : *25 minutes*
COOKING TIME : *2½ hours*
OVEN : *Preheat to 150°C (300°F, gas mark 2)*

INGREDIENTS

2lb (900g) red cabbage
2 Granny Smith apples
1 medium onion
1oz (25g) butter
1 tablespoon virgin olive oil
2 tablespoons redcurrant jelly
1-2 teaspoons crushed juniper berries
2 bay leaves
1 sprig fresh rosemary
2 tablespoons red wine vinegar
Large glass of red wine or port
½ teaspoon cinnamon
½ teaspoon mace
10oz (275g) tin whole peeled chestnuts
Salt and freshly ground black pepper
1 tablespoon chopped parsley

Calories per serving : 165 · Low in fat and
cholesterol · High in protein from nuts

The rich flavour of red cabbage, apples and chestnuts is heightened by subtle spices and juniper berries to make a colourful and heart-warming vegetable dish.

Finely shred the cabbage. Peel, core and slice the apples and finely chop the onion. Reserve a small knob of butter and add the rest to a large frying pan with the oil, then add the onion and cook over a moderate heat for 5 minutes until soft. Reduce the heat and spoon the redcurrant jelly into the pan with the onion. Stir for 1-2 minutes until the jelly has melted. Pour the mixture into a large, deep casserole.

Fill the casserole with layers of the shredded cabbage, sliced apple and juniper berries, then press the bay leaves and rosemary into the centre.

Mix the red wine vinegar with the red wine or port, add the cinnamon and mace. Pour this mixture over the casserole and cover with a piece of buttered greaseproof paper and a tightly fitting lid.

Cook in the oven for 2 hours and 10 minutes – check occasionally to see that all the liquid has not evaporated – and adding a little vegetable stock, wine or water if necessary. Drain the chestnuts and mix them into the casserole. Season, return to the oven and cook for a further 20 minutes. The dish can be kept warm for a while, but do not sprinkle over the fresh parsley until you are ready to serve.

Sweet Peppers in Honey and Soy Dressing

Sweet peppers are members of the capsicum family, being milder relatives of the spicy hot chilli pepper. This brightly coloured oriental vegetable dish goes particularly well served hot with chicken, fish or shellfish. It can also be served cold as a starter.

Crunchy peppers in a slightly sweet oriental sauce will brighten up any meal with a splash of colour.

SERVES 4
PREPARATION TIME : *30 minutes*
COOKING TIME : *2½ minutes*

INGREDIENTS
2 red peppers
2 yellow peppers
4oz (115g) mangetout
8 spring onions
1-2 cloves garlic
1 tablespoon clear honey
2 tablespoons light soy sauce
1 tablespoon sesame oil
2 tablespoons sunflower oil
1oz (25g) pine nuts or unsalted cashews

Calories per serving : 170 · High in vitamin C from peppers · High in protein from nuts

Halve and de-seed the peppers, and then chop them into matchstick-size strips. Trim the ends and the strings of the mangetout. Trim the roots and stalks of the spring onion, leaving about 3in (80mm) of stalk above the bulb, and chop them roughly. Finely chop the cloves of garlic.

Mix the honey and soy sauce together in a small bowl and leave to one side. Heat the two oils together in a wok or frying pan over a high heat until sizzling hot, then add the peppers, mangetout and garlic, and stir-fry for 1 minute. Add the spring onions and nuts and continue to stir-fry for another minute. Add the honey and soy mixture and stir well to coat the ingredients for a further 30 seconds.

Transfer the mixture with the juices to a heated serving bowl and serve immediately.

Braised Vegetable Casserole

This casserole is based on a French recipe which cooks the vegetables to perfection by adding them one by one, according to their required cooking time. The result is a tasty mélange of tastes and textures. Use fresh herbs in this recipe, such as a mixture of tarragon, parsley and thyme.

SERVES 4
PREPARATION TIME : *45 minutes*
COOKING TIME : *50 minutes*

INGREDIENTS
1oz (25g) dried mushrooms (optional)
1 medium onion
2-3 cloves garlic
15 small pickling onions
3 large carrots or 12 baby carrots
3-4 parsnips
6oz (175g) fresh mushrooms
½ cauliflower or 4 baby cauliflowers
8 brussels sprouts
1 celeriac root
8oz (225g) green beans
3oz (75g) fresh or frozen peas
1½ oz (40g) butter
1½ tablespoons virgin olive oil
1 bay leaf
Salt and freshly ground black pepper
2 tablespoons chopped fresh herbs
1 small glass dry white wine

Calories per serving : 235 · High in vitamin C from beans · High in carotene from carrots and parsnips

All the different shapes and colours of the vegetables make this a beautiful dish. It can be served as a vegetarian main course, or as a delicious side dish.

If using the optional dried mushrooms, cover them with boiling water and allow them to soak for 30 minutes before using. Reserving the soaking water, strain and set aside.

To prepare the vegetables, peel and thinly slice the medium onion and garlic. Peel the small pickling onions and trim the ends. Peel the baby carrots. Peel, quarter and core the parsnips and cut them into 1in (25mm) lengths. Wipe the mushrooms clean and slice them in half. Break the cauliflower into small florets, and trim the brussels sprouts and cut them in half. Peel and slice the celeriac root into 2in (50mm) pieces that are about ½in (15mm) thick. Top and tail the beans, and shell or thaw the peas.

Melt 1oz (25g) of the butter in a large casserole dish with 1 tablespoon of the olive oil. Add the sliced medium onion, cover and cook for 2-3 minutes. Add the small onions and carrots and cook for 5 minutes. Add the garlic, bay leaf, a pinch of salt and a pinch of the fresh herbs, and cook for 3 minutes. Add the celeriac, parsnips, another pinch of salt and of herbs, and cook for 5 minutes. Add the cauliflower florets, brussels sprouts, another pinch of salt and of herbs, and cook for 6-10 minutes, until slightly tender but crisp.

Meanwhile, heat the remaining butter and olive oil in a saucepan then add the fresh mushrooms. Sauté the mushrooms over a medium-high heat for 3 minutes until the juices are released, then add the optional dried mushrooms and reserved juices, and the wine. Cover the pan and simmer the mixture for 3 minutes before adding to the casserole.

Add the green beans and peas to the casserole and cook for a final 3 minutes. Remove the bay leaf, season with salt and black pepper to taste and add the remaining herbs. Serve immediately.

Spinach, Goat's Cheese and Hazelnut Pancakes

Italians are very fond of stuffed pancakes – spinach and cheese is a favourite filling. This Tuscan recipe uses goat's cheese, toasted hazelnuts and a pinch of nutmeg. Serve with a side salad.

SERVES 4-6
PREPARATION TIME : *15 minutes*
COOKING TIME : *30-40 minutes*
OVEN : *Preheat to 200°C (400°F, gas mark 6)*

INGREDIENTS

PANCAKES
4oz (115g) plain flour
Pinch of salt
1 medium egg
½ pint (285ml) semi-skimmed milk
2 tablespoons sunflower oil

FILLING
1lb (450g) fresh or frozen spinach
¼ oz (7g) butter
3oz (75g) hazelnuts
1 tablespoon sunflower oil
8oz (225g) goat's cheese
6 small spring onions
Pinch of ground nutmeg
Salt and freshly ground black pepper

SAUCE
½ oz (15g) butter
1 tablespoon plain flour
Pinch of mustard powder
½ pint (285ml) semi-skimmed milk
½ teaspoon ground nutmeg
Salt and freshly ground black pepper
3 tablespoons freshly grated Parmesan cheese

Calories per serving : 595 · High in iron from spinach · High in protein from cheese, milk and eggs

To make the pancake mixture, sift the flour into a bowl with a pinch of salt. Whisk the egg and then add sufficient milk to make a smooth, thick batter, beating well. Mix in the remaining milk and oil. Lightly brush a nonstick frying pan with oil and

A nutmeg and Parmesan sauce over light pancakes.

make 12 medium-sized pancakes in the usual way.

To make the filling with fresh spinach, remove any tough stalks and wash thoroughly, then cook the spinach for 1-2 minutes in a pan with only the water that clings to the leaves. Then drain the spinach thoroughly in a colander and chop it roughly. If using frozen spinach, thaw it and heat it gently in a pan with a small nub of butter.

Roughly chop the hazelnuts and cook them in a frying pan over a medium heat in 1 tablespoon of oil for 3 minutes, until they give off an aroma and just start to brown. Crumble the goat's cheese and trim and finely chop the spring onions. Add the cheese and onions to the spinach, along with the hazelnuts, nutmeg, salt and pepper. Mix well together. Spoon a little filling onto each pancake, then roll them up and place in a large, buttered gratin dish.

To make the sauce, melt the butter in a saucepan and gradually stir in the flour and mustard powder. Cook for 1 minute, stirring constantly. Add the milk slowly, stirring until smooth. Add the nutmeg, season to taste, and simmer for 2-3 minutes until it has thickened. Pour the sauce over the pancakes. Sprinkle with the grated Parmesan cheese and bake in the oven for 20-30 minutes, until bubbling and golden. Serve immediately.

Potato and Leek Gratin

This recipe for *gratin dauphinois* uses leeks instead of onions and milk instead of cream. It is a useful dinner-party dish since it can be left unattended in the oven and can be kept warm for quite a long time.

SERVES 4-6
PREPARATION TIME : *25 minutes*
COOKING TIME : *1 hour 40 minutes*
OVEN : *Preheat to 160°C (325°F, gas mark 3)*

INGREDIENTS

1½ lb (700g) King Edward or Desirée potatoes
¼ pint (150ml) milk
Small bunch thyme
2 large leeks
1 clove garlic
4oz (115g) Cheddar cheese, low-fat if desired
½ oz (15g) butter
1 teaspoon ground nutmeg
Salt and freshly ground black pepper

Calories per serving : 235 · Low in cholesterol · High in calcium from cheese and milk

In a small pan, warm the milk over a very low heat with 2 sprigs of the thyme. Do this while preparing the rest of the dish, but do not allow it to boil.

Peel and very thinly slice the potatoes with a mandolin (frame with adjustable cutting blades) or a sharp knife. Put the potato slices into a colander and swill round under cold running water to wash away some of the starch. Drain the potatoes thoroughly. Trim and carefully wash the leeks, then slice them thinly like the potatoes. Crush the garlic clove and grate the Cheddar cheese.

Grease a shallow gratin dish with the butter, and then arrange layers of potato and leek with a little of the garlic, nutmeg and seasoning. After removing the thyme, pour the milk over the vegetables and sprinkle with the grated cheese. Cook near the top of the preheated oven. Be careful not to over brown the potatoes on the top of the dish. Garnish with the remaining sprigs of thyme and serve immediately with meat, poultry or game and green beans.

This impressive and surprisingly light potato dish cooked with milk and leeks has a subtle aroma of thyme.

Carrot and Parsnip Purée

The sweetness of parsnips can bring out the flavour of many foods when it is combined with them, but this mixture of parsnips and carrots is particularly successful – making a delicious creamy purée.

SERVES 4
PREPARATION TIME : *10 minutes*
COOKING TIME : *10-12 minutes*

INGREDIENTS
10oz (275g) carrots
10oz (275g) parsnips
4 tablespoons semi-skimmed milk
¾ teaspoon grated nutmeg
2 teaspoons caster sugar
Salt and freshly ground black pepper
Sprigs of rosemary, thyme or parsley to garnish

Calories per serving : 70 · Low in fat and cholesterol
High in fibre from carrots and parsnips

Bring a saucepan of water to the boil. Peel and trim the carrots and parsnips. Cut them up into similar-sized chunks and cook them in the boiling water for

This sweet purée makes a tasty vegetable side dish.

10-12 minutes, or if you prefer you can steam them in a covered pan for 12-14 minutes, until tender.

Reserving a little of the cooking water, drain the vegetables and put them in a liquidiser (or use a potato-masher). Add the milk, nutmeg and sugar and purée the mixture. If the mixture is still very thick add a couple of tablespoons of the reserved vegetable water. Then season to taste with salt and pepper. Garnish with fresh herbs and serve.

Spinach and Ricotta Roulade

'Roulade' literally means 'a rolling' in French. The spinach soufflé base in this recipe is rolled around a delicious Ricotta cheese and onion filling. You will need a large baking sheet for this recipe.

SERVES 6
PREPARATION TIME : *40 minutes*
COOKING TIME : *40 minutes*
OVEN : *Preheat to 200°C (400°F, gas mark 6)*

INGREDIENTS
2lb (900g) fresh spinach or 1lb (450g) frozen
ROULADE BASE
5 eggs
2oz (50g) freshly grated Parmesan
14fl oz (400ml) milk
2oz (50g) butter
5 tablespoons flour
Salt
Pinch of cayenne pepper
FILLING
½ small yellow onion
2oz (50g) butter
8oz (225g) Ricotta
4 tablespoons milk
1½ teaspoons nutmeg
Salt and freshly ground black pepper
½ teaspoon paprika
2 tablespoons single cream

Calories per serving : 420 · High in protein and calcium · High in vitamin C and iron from spinach

Served with a salad and crisp white wine, this delicate spinach roulade makes an elegant main course.

Cut the stems off the spinach and wash the leaves thoroughly. Cook for 2-3 minutes in a large pan with only the water that clings to the leaves and a pinch of salt. Remove and leave to drain in a colander. If using frozen spinach, follow the instructions given on the packet, then drain and chop finely.

To make the roulade base, line a 10 × 15in (250 × 380mm) baking sheet with greaseproof paper, and lightly butter and flour the surface. Separate the yolks and whites of the eggs. Lightly beat the yolks and grate the cheese and put them both to one side.

Squeeze any remaining water from the spinach, chop it finely and reserve it. Heat the milk and melt the butter in separate pans. Add the flour to the butter and cook over a medium heat for 2 minutes, stirring constantly. Pour in the hot milk and cook for another 3 minutes, while stirring. Season with salt and the cayenne. Remove from the heat.

Whisk a quarter of the mixture into the yolks, return to the pan and add the rest of the mixture. Stir 4oz (115g) of the spinach into the mixture.

In a large bowl, beat the egg whites with a pinch of salt until they form smooth peaks. Stir a quarter of the whites and half the grated cheese into the milk and egg mixture. Gently fold in the rest of the whites.

Pour this mixture onto the baking sheet, spreading it out to fill the corners. Sprinkle the remaining cheese over it. Bake for 15 minutes, or until the top has browned and puffed up. Leaving the oven on, remove the base and carefully turn it out onto a wire rack and remove the paper. Put to one side – the base will cool and collapse into a flat sheet.

To make the filling, finely dice the onion. Melt the butter in a large pan and then cook the onion over a moderate heat for 6-8 minutes until soft. Add the remaining chopped spinach and cook for another 2 minutes, until the butter is absorbed.

Lightly butter a baking sheet. Thin the Ricotta with milk to make it soft, then season to taste with a little nutmeg, salt, freshly ground black pepper and the paprika. Spread the Ricotta over the soufflé, then cover it with the spinach and onion. Roll up the soufflé like a Swiss roll, brush the surface with the cream and place on the baking sheet. Lightly cover with foil and bake for 25 minutes. Cut the roulade into 1in (25mm) slices and serve.

Beetroot with Rosemary

In Britain, beetroot are usually pickled or boiled for salads. In Poland and Russia, however, they are used with more imagination because they are a staple food. Serve this dish with roast or grilled meats.

SERVES 4
PREPARATION TIME : *15 minutes*
COOKING TIME : *1¼ hours*

INGREDIENTS
3 medium beetroot
6 medium red onions
2 tablespoons vegetable oil
4 large sprigs rosemary
½ pint (285ml) red wine
½ pint (285ml) vegetable or chicken stock
1 tablespoon raspberry vinegar
Salt and freshly ground black pepper
Crème fraîche or natural yoghurt
for garnish (optional)
Rosemary sprigs for garnish

Calories per serving : 130 · High in potassium from beetroot · Low in cholesterol

Beetroot and red onions with rosemary in red wine.

Peel and quarter the beetroot and the onions. Heat the oil in a large saucepan and gently sauté the onion quarters. Add the fresh rosemary and cook for 1 minute to release the flavour of the herb. Add the beetroot, wine, stock and vinegar and bring to the boil, then reduce the heat, cover and simmer for 1 hour until the beetroot is tender. Remove the lid and simmer for a further 15 minutes until the liquid reduces to a glaze. Season, and discard the rosemary.

Spoon a little crème fraîche or yoghurt over the dish if desired, and garnish with rosemary sprigs.

Oriental Vegetables

This colourful stir-fry has a tangy orange flavour enhanced by shoyu – naturally fermented soy sauce. Japanese daikon is a long white vegetable also called 'mooli'. This makes a nutritious main course dish.

SERVES 4
PREPARATION TIME : *10-15 minutes*
COOKING TIME : *10 minutes*

INGREDIENTS
4oz (115g) daikon or mooli
4oz (115g) carrots
2 sticks celery
½ green pepper
1in (25mm) fresh root ginger
2 cloves garlic
8oz (225g) packet thread egg noodles
2 tablespoons groundnut oil
3-4 spring onions
4oz (115g) bean sprouts
Salt and freshly ground black pepper
SAUCE
4 tablespoons orange juice
2 tablespoons shoyu
2 tablespoons clear honey
1 tablespoon cider vinegar
1 tablespoon dry sherry
1 tablespoon cornflour
1 teaspoon tomato pureé

Calories per serving : 395 · High in carotene from carrots and pepper · High in protein from noodles

Cut all the vegetables, except the bean sprouts, into strips, keeping them in separate piles. Crush the ginger and peel and crush the garlic. Mix the sauce ingredients in a jug and set aside. Add the noodles to a pan of salted, boiling water and cook according to the packet instructions.

Heat a wok or heavy nonstick frying pan. Add the oil and heat until hot, then add the spring onions and ginger and stir-fry for 2-3 minutes until softened.

Add the daikon, carrots and garlic, and stir-fry for a further 2-3 minutes, leaving them still crunchy.

Add the celery and green pepper and stir-fry for 2-3 minutes. Add the bean sprouts and continue cooking for another 1-2 minutes. Stir the sauce mixture, pour it over the vegetables, add the drained noodles and toss again until evenly combined and heated through. Season with salt and freshly ground black pepper and serve immediately.

Bright and crunchy vegetables in a sweet tomato and orange sauce served with tender vermicelli. The oriental ingredients in this dish can be found in large supermarkets, health food shops, or oriental markets.

Spinach Flan

Spinach was once called 'the herb of Persia', and has long had a reputation for being a source of great strength. Choose young spinach with small, tender leaves. Garnish the flan with rings of pepper.

SERVES 4
PREPARATION TIME : *30 minutes*
COOKING TIME : *1 hour*
OVEN : *Preheat to 190°C (375°F, gas mark 5)*

INGREDIENTS
PASTRY
6oz (175g) wholemeal self-raising flour
Salt
3oz (75g) butter
FILLING
1lb (450g) spinach
1 red or yellow pepper
3 eggs
½ pint(285ml) whole or semi-skimmed milk
5 spring onions
Salt and freshly ground black pepper
½ teaspoon grated nutmeg

Calories per serving : 410 · High in protein from eggs, milk and flour · High in iron from spinach

Tip the flour into a bowl and add a pinch of salt. Rub in all the butter until the mixture resembles fine breadcrumbs, and sprinkle in about 2 tablespoons of cold water to form a firm dough.

Knead the dough on a lightly floured surface until smooth, then roll out and use to line an 8in (200mm) flan or tin. Fill with greaseproof paper and baking beans. Bake for 15 minutes. Remove the beans and paper, bake for 5 minutes more to dry out.

Wash the spinach and cook with just the water that clings to it in a saucepan for 8 minutes, drain well, and chop roughly. Reserving a few rings for garnish, de-seed and dice the rest of the pepper and cook in boiling water for 5 minutes.

Beat the eggs and milk together in a bowl, then add the chopped onions, spinach, pepper, nutmeg and seasoning. Spoon the filling into the flan and cook in the oven for 40 minutes, until set.

Tasty spinach flan is delicious eaten hot or cold.

Sicilian Ratatouille

Aubergines are one of the most popular vegetables in Mediterranean countries. Their peak season is spring, when they are cheaper and you can choose firm vegetables with shiny, unblemished skins.

SERVES 4-6
PREPARATION TIME : *30 minutes*
COOKING TIME : *25 minutes*

INGREDIENTS
2 aubergines
Salt and freshly ground black pepper
1 medium red or yellow onion
½ green pepper
2 sticks celery
4oz (115g) mushrooms
1-2 cloves garlic
4 tablespoons virgin olive oil
14oz (400g) tin plum tomatoes
2 tablespoons capers
1 tablespoon chopped fresh oregano
or 1 teaspoon dried
2oz (50g) green olives
2 tablespoons wine vinegar
2 teaspoons caster sugar
2oz (50g) pine nuts

Calories per serving : 180 · High in fibre from vegetables · Low in cholesterol

In Italy this dish is called 'caponata' and is often served cold as a starter – spread over freshly baked bread.

Peel and dice the aubergines into 1in (25mm) cubes. To extract any bitter juices, place the cubes in a colander, sprinkle with 1 teaspoon of salt and allow to drain for 20 minutes. Slice the onion, pepper, celery and mushrooms and finely chop the garlic. Rinse the drained aubergines and pat dry.

Heat 4 tablespoons of oil in a casserole or frying pan. Sauté the aubergines over medium heat. Stir constantly until softened and slightly coloured. Remove the aubergines and put to one side, then add the onions, garlic, pepper and celery. Cook for 6-8 minutes, stirring occasionally, until quite soft.

Chop and peel the tomatoes and add to the pan along with the mushrooms and capers. Turn down the heat and simmer for 5 minutes, until the tomato sauce has reduced and thickened. Stir in all the aubergines, oregano, olives, vinegar and sugar.

Simmer for another 15 minutes, adding a little water if it is too thick. Season with salt and black pepper, sprinkle with pine nuts and serve.

Easy Bread and Cheese Soufflé

A preheated oven and carefully whipped egg whites will ensure the success of this soufflé. Make bread-crumbs with one-day-old bread either in a liquidiser or by hand. Serve the soufflé straight from the oven.

SERVES 4
PREPARATION TIME : *20 minutes*
COOKING TIME : *40 minutes*
OVEN : *Preheat to 190°C (375°F, gas mark 5)*

INGREDIENTS
4oz (115g) Gruyère or Cheddar cheese
4 eggs
1 clove garlic
6oz (175g) breadcrumbs
1oz (25g) butter
¾ pint (450ml) milk
½ teaspoon cayenne pepper
Salt and freshly ground black pepper

Calories per serving : 370 · High in protein and calcium from milk, cheese and eggs

This cheesy soufflé is virtually foolproof to make.

Grate the cheese, separate the eggs and then crush the garlic. Put the breadcrumbs into a heat-resistant bowl. Use a little of the butter to grease a 1½ pint (850ml) soufflé dish, then sprinkle the sides of the dish with 1 tablespoon of the breadcrumbs.

Gently bring the milk and remaining butter to the boil. Add the cayenne pepper and seasoning, and pour the milk over the breadcrumbs. Add the garlic and cheese and mix. Beat in the egg yolks. Whisk the egg whites until they hold their shape and soft peaks are left behind when the whisk is removed.

Gently fold the egg whites into the mixture. Pour into the soufflé dish, bake for 40 minutes and serve.

Pumpkin Ravioli

Pumpkins make a tasty, alternative filling for ravioli, with their sweet and fragrant flesh. Choose clean, well-matured pumpkins with a firm rind and rich colour, avoiding broken or cracked vegetables. Peak season is from summer to late autumn. Use fresh pasta squares from Italian delicatessens, or wonton skins available from most oriental food stores. Serve with Parmesan and tomato sauce or olive oil and basil.

SERVES 4
PREPARATION TIME : *25 minutes*
DRYING TIME : *10-30 minutes*
COOKING TIME : *1 hour*
OVEN : *Preheat to 190°C (375°F, gas mark 5)*

INGREDIENTS
40 pasta squares or wonton skins
1 small pumpkin
1 shallot
1 clove garlic
½ teaspoon butter
½ teaspoon virgin olive oil
4 basil leaves or ½ teaspoon parsley
1 tablespoon cream
1 teaspoon freshly grated Parmesan cheese
1 tablespoon sweet white wine
Salt and freshly ground black pepper

Calories per serving : 330 · High in carotene from pumpkin · High in protein from cheese

For the filling, cut the pumpkin in two and place both halves on an oven shelf. Roast for 40 minutes until the inside is soft.

Meanwhile, peel and finely chop the shallot and garlic and sauté them in the butter and olive oil until tender. Finely chop the basil leaves or parsley.

Remove the roasted pumpkin halves, then spoon out the flesh and discard the seeds and the tough fibre in the centre. Place 8oz (225g) of the pulp in a mixing bowl – reserving the remainder for another recipe or batch of ravioli if desired.

Stir in the shallot and garlic mixture, the cream, grated Parmesan cheese, white wine and basil or parsley. Season to taste with salt and black pepper.

Lightly flour a flat surface and lay the 40 pasta squares or the wonton skins on it. Place 1 heaped teaspoon of the pumpkin filling in the centre of 20 of the squares or skins. Using a pastry brush dipped in water, brush around the sides of every square. Cover each pumpkin-filled square with an empty square, pressing all four sides down to seal the ravioli, and allow to dry for at least 10 minutes.

Bring a large pan of salted water to the boil. Using a flat spatula, ease the ravioli into the water and cook very gently for 12 minutes. Do not allow it to boil vigorously or the ravioli will break open. Remove them and drain. Garnish with the chopped fresh herbs and serve immediately.

Tender ravioli wrapped around slightly sweet roasted pumpkin makes a delightful starter or main course.

Buckwheat Vegetable Pancakes

Buckwheat pancakes have the attractive dark and speckled appearance of roasted buckwheat flour. They are a speciality of Breton, in north-west France, where pancakes with sweet fillings are called crêpes and savoury ones are called galettes. If you have a blender, pancakes are very easy to make. Pancakes freeze well and can be served with a huge variety of fillings. The leek, aubergine and sour cream filling in this recipe goes particularly well with buckwheat pancakes, making a delicious main course. A salad and a glass of wine turn it into a complete meal.

SERVES 4 (8 pancakes)
PREPARATION TIME : *35 minutes*
COOKING TIME : *50 minutes*
OVEN : *Preheat to 180°C (350°F, gas mark 4)*

INGREDIENTS
1 large aubergine weighing 1½ lb (700g)
2 cloves garlic
1 large or 2 small leeks
1 medium onion
2 tablespoons olive oil
2 teaspoons white wine vinegar
1 level teaspoon cayenne pepper
1 teaspoon caster sugar
½ glass of white wine or vegetable stock
1 tablespoon chopped parsley
Salt and freshly ground black pepper
2 tablespoons natural yoghurt
¼ pint (150ml) sour cream
1 tablespoon chopped chives
PANCAKE
½ pint (285ml) milk or semi-skimmed milk
1 large egg
¼ teaspoon salt
2 tablespoons olive oil
2oz (50g) wholewheat flour
2oz (50g) buckwheat flour

Calories per serving : 315 · High in fibre from flour
High in calcium from milk and yoghurt

Make about 15 small cuts in the aubergine and insert a sliver of garlic into each one. Bake the aubergine for 40 minutes in the preheated oven, turning once. When it has been cooked and is quite soft, leave it in a colander to drain while preparing the pancake batter. Leave the oven on a low setting, ready to keep the pancakes and individual plates warm.

To make the batter put the milk, egg, salt and 1 teaspoon of the oil into a blender and process for 30 seconds. Sift the flour into the mixture and process again for another 30 seconds. Let the pancake batter stand for a few minutes while you make the rest of the filling.

To make the filling, wash and chop the leeks into ½in (15mm) discs. Peel and finely chop the onion. Heat the oil in a large frying pan, add the onion, leeks, vinegar and cayenne pepper and cook over a high heat for 5 minutes, stirring frequently. Add the sugar, white wine, or vegetable stock, and turn the heat down low, stirring occasionally.

Scoop out the aubergine flesh with the garlic, discarding the skin, and add to the simmering pan along with the parsley and season to taste. Mix the yoghurt and sour cream in a bowl.

To cook the pancakes, heat about 1 teaspoon of the remaining oil in a clean nonstick frying pan over

Buckwheat pancakes bursting with fresh vegetables make a well-balanced main course. A dry white wine such as a Muscadet goes well with this dish.

a medium-high heat and add 2 tablespoons of the batter to the pan, quickly tipping the pan so the batter spreads evenly into a circle. Cook for only 2-3 minutes, flip the pancake over with a spatula and cook for another 1-2 minutes. Turn the cooked pancakes onto a warm plate, one on top of the other, and keep warm in a low oven until they have all been cooked. Keep the pan lightly oiled for each pancake.

Divide the filling evenly amongst the pancakes and roll or fold them up on the warm plates. Pour over the yoghurt and cream mixture and sprinkle with the chives. Serve immediately.

French Onion Tart

This succulent tart is called pissaladière in Nice, where the dish originates. The name is derived from pissala, or anchovies, which are used to garnish the tart. Serve hot or cold as a starter or main course.

SERVES 6
PREPARATION TIME : *30 minutes*
COOKING TIME : *1¼ hours*
OVEN : *Preheat to 190°C (375°F, gas mark 5)*

INGREDIENTS
DOUGH BASE
8oz (225g) wholemeal flour
2 teaspoons baking powder
¼ teaspoon salt
1oz (25g) butter or sunflower margarine
1 egg
4fl oz (115ml) skimmed milk
FILLING
3lb (1.4kg) onions
3 tablespoons virgin olive oil
1 tablespoon white wine vinegar
2 teaspoons caster sugar
2 teaspoons freshly chopped herbs
such as basil, thyme and rosemary
Salt and freshly ground black pepper
12 anchovy fillets
12 black olives

Calories per serving : 300 · Low in cholesterol · High in protein from milk, egg and anchovies

Anchovies and olives decorate a French onion tart.

To make the dough base, sift all the flour, baking powder and salt into a mixing bowl and tip in the bran remaining in the sieve. Rub in the butter or margarine and make a well in the centre of the flour. In a separate bowl, beat the egg and mix it with the skimmed milk. Pour this mixture into the well and mix to form a soft dough. Then knead it on a lightly floured surface until smooth and roll out to form a rectangle, about 12 × 8in (300 × 200mm). Lightly oil a large baking sheet and lay out the dough in the centre. Put to one side.

Peel and slice the onions. Add them with the oil and vinegar to a large pan with a lid. Cover and cook very gently for 40 minutes, stirring occasionally.

Add the sugar, herbs and seasoning and continue to cook for 2-3 minutes. Cut the anchovy fillets in half lengthways and stone and halve the olives.

Spread the onion mixture over the dough base and make a lattice pattern of anchovy fillets on top. Place half an olive in the centre of each lattice square and bake in the oven for 30-35 minutes, until the dough base is cooked. Divide into 6 pieces and serve, or allow to cool and refrigerate until needed.

Sweet and Sour Vegetable Strudel

Strudel is an extremely light Austrian pastry that is usually filled with apples or other fruits. This recipe uses fresh vegetables and cashew nuts. Strudel is available in delicatessens and supermarkets.

SERVES 4
PREPARATION TIME : *1 hour*
COOKING TIME : *30 minutes*
OVEN : *Preheat to 200°C (400°F, gas mark 6)*

INGREDIENTS
8 sheets filo pastry
2 sticks celery
4oz (115g) courgettes
4 spring onions
2 carrots
4oz (115g) button mushrooms
1 orange or yellow pepper
2oz (50g) mangetout
2oz (50g) frozen sweetcorn
4oz (115g) bean sprouts
3 tablespoons vegetable oil
2oz (50g) cashew nuts
1 teaspoon ground ginger
2 teaspoons arrowroot powder
1 tablespoon light soy sauce
1 tablespoon tomato purée
3 tablespoons cider vinegar
2 tablespoons brown sugar
1 tablespoon sesame seeds

Calories per serving : 465 · Low in cholesterol · High in iron, fibre and vitamin C from vegetables

Trim and thinly slice the celery, the courgettes and the spring onions. Peel and thinly slice the carrots. Thinly slice the mushrooms. Halve and de-seed the pepper, top and tail the mangetout and chop them into thin strips. Place the sweetcorn in a sieve over a small bowl and soak the bean sprouts in cold water for 5 minutes before rinsing thoroughly.

Heat 2 tablespoons of the oil over a high heat in a large frying pan or wok, and add the cashew nuts.

Crisp stir-fried vegetables in sweet and sour sauce wrapped in light pastry, sprinkled with sesame seeds.

Cook them briefly, stirring continually, until golden. Keeping the oil in the pan, remove the cashew nuts and put them to one side.

Add the celery and carrots to the wok and stir-fry for 2 minutes over a high heat. Add the remaining vegetables one batch at a time, stirring well between each addition, and stir-frying for a total of 4 minutes.

Combine the ground ginger, arrowroot powder, soy sauce, tomato purée, vinegar and sugar, and mix well. Add this mixture to the pan and cook for 2 minutes, stirring well, until thickened. Transfer the mixture to a bowl and leave to cool.

Lay 2 sheets of the filo pastry, slightly overlapping, on a clean work surface. Lay the next 2 sheets on top with the pastry seam lying in the opposite direction. Repeat the process with the next 2 sheets in the original direction and the last 2 in the opposite direction. You should have a square of pastry with sides measuring about 18in (460mm) long.

Carefully spread all the vegetable mixture over the pastry, leaving a 1in (25mm) space around the edges. Fold in 2 sides of the pastry, then carefully roll up the strudel. Transfer to a lightly oiled baking tray. Brush the strudel with the remaining oil and sprinkle with the sesame seeds. Bake in the oven for about 30 minutes until golden-brown. Allow to cool for 5 minutes, then cut into thick slices and serve.

Wilted Spinach Omelette with Nutmeg

Just a small amount of freshly grated nutmeg adds subtle flavour and aroma to the spinach – helping to make this simple omelette rather unusual. Nutmeg is the seed of a fragrant tree that is native to the Molucca Islands of Indonesia, but it is now grown in many other tropical places. Try to buy fresh, whole nutmegs and grate them as required, since the taste and aroma of ground nutmeg is lost quite quickly.

Although eggs contain cholesterol, the yolks also contain lecithin, a substance which breaks down and helps to disperse cholesterol and unhealthy fat deposits in the body. There is no need to cut eggs out of a healthy diet, especially since they are such an excellent source of protein. A little grated cheese can be added with the spinach if desired.

SERVES 4
PREPARATION TIME : *12 minutes*
COOKING TIME : *15 minutes*

INGREDIENTS
1lb (450g) fresh spinach
1oz (25g) butter
1 small onion
1 clove garlic
1 tablespoon olive oil
8 eggs
2 teaspoons grated nutmeg
¼ teaspoon salt and ground black pepper
2 tablespoons chopped parsley

Calories per serving : 245 · High in protein from eggs
High in vitamin D from egg yolks · High in
iron and vitamin C from spinach

Wash the spinach and put it into a large pan with 4 tablespoons of water and the butter. Cook over a medium-high heat for 2-3 minutes, stirring continually, until the spinach has just wilted. Then leave it to drain in a colander.

Chop the onion and crush the garlic clove. Heat the oil in a large pan over a moderate heat and add the onion and garlic. Cook for 7 minutes until the onion is transparent and has just started to go brown.

In the meantime, roughly chop the spinach, and squeeze out any excess water. Break the eggs into a bowl and add 5 tablespoons of water, the nutmeg and the seasoning and beat well with a fork until all the eggs are broken up.

When the onions are cooked add the spinach to the pan, and spread it evenly round the pan. Pour the egg mixture over the vegetables and cook for 2-3 minutes. Carefully lift up the edges of the omelette with a spatula to allow any uncooked egg to run underneath. As soon as the omelette is firm and its underside is golden, fold the omelette in half with the spatula and turn onto a plate. Divide the omelette into four, garnish with the parsley.

Tender spinach that has been lightly cooked in a little butter and seasoned with grated nutmeg and plenty of freshly ground black pepper makes a delicious but simple filling for an omelette.

Baked Courgettes and Aubergines

In most Mediterranean dishes made with aubergines, the vegetable is usually sprinkled with salt before cooking, to draw out some of its water and bitter juices. This process also helps to prevent aubergines from absorbing large quantities of oil when they are fried. In this recipe the vegetables are steamed, so there is no need to cook them in oil at all – creating a much healthier dish.

This dish makes a tasty vegetable accompaniment to almost any type of pork, lamb or chicken dish. It also makes an excellent vegetarian main course if it is served in larger quantities. It can also be topped with a generous helping of grilled cheese.

SERVES 4-6
PREPARATION TIME : *15 minutes*
COOKING TIME : *1½ hours*
OVEN : *Preheat to 190°C (375°F, gas mark 5)*

INGREDIENTS
1lb (450g) courgettes
1lb (450g) aubergines
3 medium onions
2 cloves garlic
3 tablespoons virgin olive oil
1 teaspoon dried herbes de Provence
Salt and freshly ground black pepper

Calories per serving : 110 · High in carotene from vegetables · No cholesterol at all

280

Tender courgettes and aubergines baked with herbes de Provence, onions and just a hint of garlic.

Slice the courgettes and aubergines. Then lay the courgettes in a steamer or covered saucepan with ½in (15mm) of water, steam for 5 minutes and put to one side. Do the same with the aubergines.

Meanwhile, peel and roughly chop the onions and crush the garlic. Heat 2 tablespoons of the virgin olive oil in a pan, add the onions, garlic and herbs, and cook gently for 20 minutes.

Mix the aubergines, courgettes and the onion mixture together and spoon into an ovenproof dish. Season lightly and then sprinkle the top with the remaining tablespoon of olive oil.

Cover the dish and bake it for 30 minutes in the oven. Remove the cover and bake for about another 30 minutes, until lightly browned. Serve hot.

Turkish Stuffed Aubergines

In Turkey this dish is called 'Imam Bayildi', or 'The Imam Fainted', because the religious leader (the Imam) allegedly fainted with delight when he first tasted it. Turks usually eat it cold with rice and salad, but it is also delicious served hot.

Baked aubergines with a tangy tomato filling.

SERVES 4
PREPARATION TIME : *15 minutes*
SOAKING TIME : *30 minutes*
COOKING TIME : *1 hour*
OVEN : *Preheat to 200°C (400°F, gas mark 6)*

INGREDIENTS
*4 small or 2 medium, long, slim aubergines
weighing about 1lb (450g)
Salt
⅓ pint (190ml) tomato juice
½ lettuce or 4oz (115g) rocket for garnish*
STUFFING
*12oz (350g) onions
2 cloves garlic
1 red pepper
6oz (175g) tomatoes
3 tablespoons virgin olive oil
1 tablespoon white wine vinegar
1 teaspoon caster sugar
Salt and freshly ground black pepper
Large bunch of fresh parsley, finely chopped*

Calories per serving : 140 · Low in cholesterol · High in fibre from aubergines and onions

Peel the aubergines if desired but leave a thin ring of skin around each end to hold them together. Cut them in half lengthways, sprinkle with salt and leave to sit for 30 minutes to draw out the juices. Rinse them thoroughly and pat dry.

To make the stuffing, peel and thinly slice the onions, finely chop the garlic and slice the red pepper. Plunge the tomatoes into boiling water for 30 seconds and cold water for 1 minute, then peel away the skins and chop the flesh.

Heat the oil in a frying pan and cook the onions, garlic and vinegar gently for 5 minutes. Add the pepper, sugar, tomatoes and seasoning. Cook gently for about 15 minutes. Stir in the parsley and set aside. Quickly fry the aubergines in hot oil to brown them all over. Drain them on kitchen paper.

Cut a deep slit along the length of the aubergines and spoon in as much stuffing as possible. Lay the aubergines close together, open-side up, in a baking dish with enough tomato juice to almost cover them. Bake for 45 minutes and serve with the salad greens.

Apple, Coriander and Vegetable Curry

The sweetness of the apples in this recipe mingles with the spiciness of a traditional Indian vegetable curry. Serve with rice and a simple green salad.

SERVES 4
PREPARATION TIME : *10 minutes*
COOKING TIME : *50 minutes*

INGREDIENTS
1 large onion
6oz (175g) swede
6oz (175g) carrot
6oz (175g) parsnip
2 tablespoons vegetable oil
½ teaspoon chilli powder
½ teaspoon coriander powder
½ teaspoon turmeric
½ teaspoon cumin seeds
6oz (175g) cauliflower
2 Granny Smith apples
½ oz (15g) butter
½ teaspoon sugar
Fresh coriander for garnish

Calories per serving : 155 · Low in cholesterol · High in fibre and vitamin C from vegetables and apples

Turmeric gives this curry its slightly golden colour.

Peel and finely chop the onion. Peel and roughly dice the swede, carrot and parsnip. Cook the vegetables in the oil in a large pan over a medium heat for 6 minutes, stirring frequently. Add the spices and ½ pint (285ml) water and simmer for 15 minutes. Cut the cauliflower into florets and stir into the pan. Cover and simmer for a further 20 minutes.

Peel, core and roughly chop the apples. Cook over a medium heat for 4 minutes, add the sugar and stir into the curry. Garnish with coriander and serve.

Artichoke and Mushroom Pizza

Wholewheat pizza dough is simple to make, but ready-made pizza dough is sold in supermarkets. You will need a shallow round 8in (200mm) cake tin.

SERVES 2-4
PREPARATION TIME : *25 minutes*
STANDING TIME : *25 minutes*
COOKING TIME : *20 minutes*
OVEN : *Preheat to 220°C (425°F, gas mark 7)*

INGREDIENTS
PIZZA BASE
8oz (225g) wholewheat flour
Salt and freshly ground black pepper
1 tablespoon fresh mixed herbs or 1 teaspoon dried
1 teaspoon sugar
1 teaspoon yeast
TOPPING
8oz (225g) fresh mushrooms
6 spring onions
2 cloves garlic
1oz (25g) butter
2 tablespoons white wine
3 tablespoons virgin olive oil
1 tablespoon fresh mixed herbs or 1 teaspoon dried
Salt and freshly ground black pepper
14oz (400g) tin of artichoke hearts in brine
3oz (75g) Mozzarella or Fontina cheese
1oz (25g) fresh Parmesan

Calories per serving : 420 · Low in cholesterol

Mushrooms and artichoke hearts mingle with herbs and soft Italian cheese on a healthy wholewheat pizza base.

Grease the cake tin using a little butter or olive oil. To make the base, combine the flour, ½ a teaspoon of salt, a few twists of pepper and half the herbs in a bowl. Measure 6fl oz (175ml) of hand-hot water into a jug, then whisk in the sugar and yeast. Leave for 10 minutes until frothy, then stir into the dry ingredients. Mix to a smooth dough with your fingers, kneading if necessary. Press the dough into the cake tin, right up the sides. Cover with a damp cloth and leave for 25 minutes, until risen.

Slice the mushrooms thinly. Finely chop the spring onions and garlic. Sauté the onions in ½oz (15g) butter for 1 minute. Reduce the heat, add the wine and cook for 5 minutes. Remove from the pan.

Heat 1 tablespoon of the oil with the rest of the butter and sauté the fresh mushrooms over a fairly high heat for 3 minutes, until they are soft. Add the garlic to the mushrooms. When the mushrooms begin to release their juices, add the herbs and some seasoning. Add the onion juices and simmer until almost all the liquid has evaporated.

Drain the artichokes. Push the dough lightly back up the side of the tin if it has slipped, then spread the onions on the pizza. Grate the soft cheese and sprinkle over the onions. Spread the mushrooms over the cheese and lay the artichoke pieces in a pattern among the mushrooms. Sprinkle with the Parmesan. Dribble the remaining olive oil over the pizza and sprinkle on the remaining fresh herbs. Bake in the oven for 20 minutes and serve.

Tomato sauce and vegetables liven up this terrine.

Cheese and Nut Terrine

This richly flavoured vegetarian terrine is served in a pool of tomato sauce. You can make your own sauce or, if time is short, there are several good brands of ready-prepared tomato sauce available in the shops.

SERVES 6
PREPARATION TIME : *15 minutes*
COOKING TIME : *1½ hours*
OVEN : *Preheat to 190°C (375°F, gas mark 5)*

INGREDIENTS
4oz (115g) brown rice
8oz (225g) walnuts
8oz (225g) cashew nuts
2 cloves garlic
1 medium onion
3oz (75g) mushrooms
1oz (25g) butter
2 tablespoons chopped parsley
2 teaspoons freshly chopped thyme
or ½ teaspoon dried
1 teaspoon freshly chopped marjoram
or ½ teaspoon dried
Salt and freshly ground black pepper
4 eggs
8oz (225g) Cheddar, Gruyère or Fontina
4oz (115g) cottage cheese
1 small jar tomato pasta sauce

Calories per serving : 560 · High in fibre from rice and nuts · High in protein from eggs and cheese

Cook the brown rice in a pan of boiling salted water according to the packet instructions, drain and leave to cool. Roast the walnuts and cashews on a baking tray in the oven for 5-7 minutes. Allow them to cool then finely chop them. Peel and finely chop the garlic and onion. Clean and chop the mushrooms. Cook the onion with almost all the butter in a large pan over a medium heat for 5 minutes. Stir in the garlic, mushrooms and herbs and season with salt. Cook for 5 minutes, stirring frequently.

Beat the eggs and grate the cheese. Combine the mixture in the pan with the rice, nuts, eggs, cottage cheese and grated cheese. Season to taste.

Grease a loaf tin with the remaining butter, line it with greaseproof paper, then pour in the mixture. Bake in the oven for 1 hour. Leave for 10 minutes. Meanwhile, heat the tomato sauce. Turn the terrine onto a serving plate and remove the paper. Serve with the tomato sauce spooned around the terrine.

Carrots with Broad Beans and Dill

The broad bean is closely related to the field bean, which was probably the first vegetable to be grown by man. Fresh broad beans are available throughout the spring and much of the summer, and if they are picked when young and tender they taste much better than their frozen counterparts.

A side dish of glazed vegetables with fresh dill.

SERVES 4
PREPARATION TIME : *15 minutes*
COOKING TIME : *10 minutes*

INGREDIENTS

1lb (450g) unshelled broad beans or
4oz (115g) frozen broad beans
12oz (350g) carrots
½ pint (285ml) vegetable stock
2 teaspoons freshly chopped dill
½ oz (15g) unsalted butter
½ teaspoon arrowroot powder
Salt and freshly ground black pepper

Calories per serving : 70 · Low in fat · High in fibre
from broad beans and carrots

If using fresh broad beans, remove them from their pods. Peel and trim the carrots and cut them into thin sticks approximately ¼in (5mm) wide and 2in (50mm) long.

Place the carrots in a saucepan, add the stock, bring to the boil and cook for 2 minutes. Add the broad beans and cook for 3 minutes. Reserving the stock, drain the vegetables and set aside.

Return the stock to the saucepan with half the dill and the butter. Mix the arrowroot with 1 tablespoon of water and stir into the liquid. Bring to the boil, stirring until the mixture has thickened, and then cook for about 5 minutes, stirring occasionally, until it is reduced to a syrupy glaze.

Return the vegetables to the pan with the rest of the dill. Season to taste with salt and freshly ground pepper and reheat gently before serving.

Spicy Spanish Potatoes

'Tapas' are snacks that are served as appetisers in Spanish bars, and this dish is a typical savoury tapas. Passata is a sauce made from sieved and strained tomatoes, and it is available from large supermarkets in jars and cartons. Alternatively, you can substitute 1 pint (570ml) of tomato juice. This dish is delicious warm or cold, and can be served on its own as a snack with wine or sherry. It also goes well with salads or grilled meats, to make a tasty main course.

A rich and spicy tomato sauce coats new potatoes.

SERVES 4
PREPARATION TIME : *10 minutes*
COOKING TIME : *30 minutes*

INGREDIENTS

1lb (450g) small new potatoes
½ medium onion
1 tablespoon virgin olive oil
1 teaspoon paprika
1 teaspoon cumin seeds
¼ teaspoon cayenne pepper
½ pint (285ml) passata
Salt
Freshly chopped parsley for garnish

Calories per serving : 140 · Low in fat and
cholesterol · High in vitamin C from passata

Wash the potatoes thoroughly and remove the skins if desired. Finely chop the onion. Heat the oil over a medium heat in a shallow saucepan and add the onion, paprika, cumin seeds and cayenne pepper. Sauté for 5 minutes, until the onion is transparent.

Add the potatoes to the saucepan and stir well, then add the passata with ½ pint (285ml) of water, or 1 pint (570ml) of tomato juice, and bring to the boil. Reduce the heat, add a little salt and simmer gently for about 20 minutes until the potatoes are tender and the sauce has reduced. Spoon into a dish, season with salt, sprinkle with parsley and serve.

Vegetarian Shepherd's Pie

Shepherd's Pie is an old English favourite made with minced beef or lamb. This vegetarian version uses a hearty winter vegetable stew and stock.

SERVES 6
PREPARATION TIME: *1 hour*
COOKING TIME: *2¼ hours*
OVEN: *Preheat to 190°C (375°F, gas mark 5)*

INGREDIENTS
SAUCE
2 medium onions
3 cloves garlic
1oz (25g) butter
1 tablespoon virgin olive oil
1 bay leaf
1 pint (570ml) vegetable stock
1 glass red wine
3 tablespoons flour
4 tablespoons chopped parsley
Salt and freshly ground black pepper
STEW
4 medium carrots
1 celeriac
2 teaspoons lemon juice
10oz (275g) parsnips
10oz (275g) mushrooms
1 small cauliflower
2 cloves garlic
5oz (150g) brussels sprouts
1½ oz (40g) butter
2 tablespoons olive oil
1 tablespoon chopped fresh thyme
¼ pint (150ml) vegetable stock
TOPPING
4 medium potatoes
1oz (25g) butter
4 tablespoons whole or semi-skimmed milk
Salt and freshly ground black pepper

Calories per serving: 350 · High in carotene from carrots · High in vitamin C from sprouts

A casserole of fresh vegetables cooked with herbs and wine, under a crispy golden potato topping.

To make the sauce, dice the onions into ½in (15mm) squares, and finely chop the garlic. Heat the butter and oil gently in a casserole, then add the diced onions, bay leaf and a pinch of salt. Cook over a medium heat for 10 minutes, stirring frequently, until the onion has turned golden. Heat the stock.

Add the garlic and wine to the onions and simmer for 5 minutes. Slowly stir in the flour and simmer for another 2 minutes. Whisk in the hot stock and bring to the boil. Half cover the casserole and simmer for 25 minutes. Add the parsley, season to taste, and remove from the heat.

For the stew, peel the carrots and cut them into pieces 1½in (40mm) long. Peel the celeriac, cut into

large cubes and place in a bowl of water with the lemon juice. Peel, quarter, core and roughly chop the parsnips. Clean the mushrooms and leave them whole if small, or roughly chop them. Break the cauliflower into large florets. Finely chop the garlic.

Boil a pan of water and add the cauliflower. Blanch for 30 seconds, then remove and rinse under cold water and put to one side. Add the brussels sprouts to the boiling water for 1 minute, rinse and reserve.

Melt half the butter and 1 tablespoon of the olive oil in a large pan or casserole, and add the sticks of carrot. Cook over a medium heat for 3-4 minutes, then add the chopped thyme and all but 2 or 3 tablespoons of the vegetable stock. Lower the heat, cover the pan, and cook for 4-5 minutes.

In a second pan, heat the remaining butter and oil and add the mushrooms. Sauté them over a high heat until brown, then add the rest of the stock and the garlic. Cook for 2 more minutes, then add to the carrot sticks in the pan or casserole along with the mushrooms and garlic, the drained celeriac and the parsnips. Cover tightly and cook over a low heat for 3 minutes, then stir in the sauce, cauliflower, sprouts and fresh herbs. Season to taste. Transfer to a casserole, cover and bake for 40 minutes.

To make the topping, boil or steam the potatoes in chunks and lightly mash with a fork. Mix in the butter and milk and season to taste. Raise the oven temperature to 200°C (400°F, gas mark 6). Put the stew in a baking dish and spread the potato over the top. Bake for 40 minutes until the potato browns and the sauce bubbles to the surface. Serve immediately.

Leek and Potato Omelette

This thick vegetable omelette is an adaptation of a tasty dish known as 'kookoo' in the Middle East. There are three types of omelette – folded, flat and soufflé. This dish is similar in style and texture to the Spanish flat omelette. The leeks add colour and a lovely oniony flavour, while the walnuts make an unusual and crunchy topping.

If you want to prepare the potato in advance, it should be soaked in water and thoroughly drained. This helps to avoid any unwanted moisture in the omelette. The leeks should be prepared just before cooking. In the Middle East this dish is eaten cold as well as hot. Cut into thick wedges and serve with a tomato salad and fresh crusty bread.

SERVES 4
PREPARATION TIME : *15 minutes*
COOKING TIME : *20 minutes*

INGREDIENTS
2 medium leeks
1 large potato
2 tablespoons olive oil
4 eggs
3 tablespoons freshly chopped parsley
Salt and freshly ground black pepper
1oz (25g) chopped walnuts
3oz (75g) cottage cheese
1oz (25g) grated Red Leicester cheese

Calories per serving : 300 · High in protein from eggs and nuts · High in fibre from potatoes and leeks

Leek and potato omelette topped with walnuts and cheese is easy to cook and makes a really tasty snack.

Trim the leeks of rootlets and remove any tough outer leaves. Thinly slice the leeks, wash them in a bowl of cold water to remove any dirt, and drain. Peel and cut the potato into ½in (15mm) cubes.

Heat the olive oil in a nonstick frying pan over a medium heat and sauté the potato cubes for 5-7 minutes, until lightly browned and almost tender. Remove from the pan and keep to one side. Add the leeks to the pan and cook for 5-7 minutes, stirring continually, until just tender.

Beat the eggs with 2 tablespoons of the chopped parsley and season generously. Add the potato to the leeks in the pan and stir in the egg mixture until lightly set. Cook for a further 3-5 minutes, pressing down gently on the omelette until it is just firm. Meanwhile, preheat the grill on a high setting.

Remove the omelette from the heat and sprinkle the top with the walnuts, cottage cheese and grated Red Leicester cheese. Cook under the grill until the cheese begins to melt, then remove and sprinkle over the remaining parsley. Serve immediately.

Sorrel and Onion Tart

Sorrel's fresh lemony flavour goes perfectly with the sweetness of cooked onions, making this tart quite unlike a traditional onion quiche. Use spinach and a tablespoon of lemon juice if sorrel is unavailable.

SERVES 6-8
PREPARATION TIME : *15 minutes*
COOKING TIME : *50 minutes*
OVEN : *Preheat to 190°C (375°F, gas mark 5)*

INGREDIENTS
10oz (275g) frozen pastry
1 large or 2 small red onions
2oz (50g) butter
Salt and freshly ground black pepper
8oz (225g) fresh sorrel
2oz (50g) Gruyère or Emmenthal cheese
2 medium eggs
4fl oz (115ml) single or low-fat cream

Calories per serving : 295 · High in protein from vegetables, cheese and eggs · Low in cholesterol

The refreshing taste of sorrel creates an unusual savoury tart that can be eaten hot or cold with salad.

Thaw the pastry and roll it out into a circle that measures 10in (250mm) in diameter and ¼in (5mm) thick. Place it in a greased 8in (200mm) flan tin and prick the bottom with a fork. Cover the pastry with baking beans and bake for 10 minutes in the oven. Remove from the oven, leave the pastry in the tin and allow it to cool for at least 10 minutes.

Peel and thinly slice the onions. Melt 1½oz (40g) of the butter in a frying pan and add the onion and a good pinch of salt. Cover the pan and let the onion sweat over a low heat until tender, but not brown, stirring occasionally to prevent sticking.

Trim and roughly chop the sorrel and grate the cheese. Melt the remaining butter in a pan and add the sorrel, stirring well to coat the leaves. Cook over a low heat for about 4 minutes, then remove from the heat and add to the onion.

Beat the eggs lightly, then add all the cream to the eggs and whisk for 1 minute. Stir in the sorrel mixture, and add 1oz (25g) of the grated cheese and freshly ground black pepper to taste.

Sprinkle the remaining cheese over the bottom of the pastry shell. Cover with the sorrel mixture and bake for 40 minutes, until golden-brown and lightly set. Remove from the oven and allow to stand for a few minutes, then slice and serve immediately.

Sautéed artichoke hearts in a tomato, herb and sherry sauce make a delicious vegetable dish for a dinner party.

Italian Artichoke Hearts with Tomatoes and Sherry

Artichoke hearts come from the young flower buds of the globe artichoke, which belongs to the thistle family. Globe artichokes were cultivated in some Mediterranean countries several thousand years ago. The hearts are covered by tiny spiny filaments and surrounded by tough outer leaves, so it is much easier to buy them ready prepared. Many people still insist that they have medicinal properties, claiming they give ailing livers a boost.

The flavour of Italy is evident in this impressive-looking dish that is surprisingly easy to make. The dish can be served alone, or used as a pasta sauce if the artichokes are cut into smaller pieces. It also goes particularly well with grilled meat.

SERVES 4
PREPARATION TIME : *10 minutes*
COOKING TIME : *15 minutes*

INGREDIENTS
14oz (400g) tin artichoke hearts
1 clove garlic
1 medium onion
½ oz (15g) butter
1 tablespoon virgin olive oil
3 tablespoons sherry
8oz (225g) tin chopped tomatoes
1 teaspoon sugar
1½ teaspoons chopped fresh thyme
Salt and freshly ground black pepper
1 tablespoon shredded fresh basil for garnish

Calories per serving : 80 · Low in cholesterol · Low in fat · High in vitamin C from tomatoes

Drain the artichokes, rinse them under cold running water and drain. Peel and crush the garlic and chop the onion. Gently melt the butter and oil in a frying pan and cook the onion for 2-3 minutes until soft. Stir in the garlic and cook for a further minute.

Halve the artichokes, add them to the pan with the sherry and sauté for 1-2 minutes. Add the tomatoes, sugar, thyme and seasoning. Simmer for 10 minutes and serve garnished with the basil.

Aubergine and Tomato Gratin

The word 'gratin' usually describes a baked crust made from eggs and flour. In this recipe, aubergines and tomatoes are covered with an attractive light soufflé topping and baked in the oven.

SERVES 4
PREPARATION TIME : *30 minutes*
COOKING TIME : *1 hour 50 minutes*
OVEN : *190°C (375°F, gas mark 5)*

INGREDIENTS
1lb (450g) medium aubergines
1lb (450g) large ripe tomatoes
1 large onion
1 clove garlic
1½ tablespoons virgin olive oil
2 tablespoons fresh shredded oregano
2 tablespoons fresh shredded basil leaves
Salt and freshly ground black pepper
SAUCE
½ pint (285ml) skimmed milk
1 small onion
6 black peppercorns
1 clove
2 sprigs fresh thyme or parsley
1oz (25g) butter
1oz (25g) plain flour
1 egg yolk and 2 egg whites
½ oz (15g) freshly grated Parmesan cheese

Calories per serving : 210 · High in fibre from vegetables · High in vitamin C from tomatoes

Thinly slice the aubergines and tomatoes, peel and thinly slice both onions and peel and crush the garlic. Spread ½ tablespoon of the oil and the garlic around the inside of a gratin or baking dish.

Arrange two layers of alternating aubergine and tomato slices over the bottom of the dish. Sprinkle with half the oregano and basil and top with a layer of large onion slices. Season with salt and black pepper, then sprinkle with ½ tablespoon of the oil. Repeat with the remaining vegetables, herbs and oil. The dish may seem rather full, but the vegetables shrink during cooking. Cover the dish tightly with foil and cook for 1½ hours.

Meanwhile, to prepare the sauce, pour the milk into a saucepan with the small onion, peppercorns, clove, thyme or parsley. Bring to the boil, remove from the heat, then cover and leave to stand.

At the end of the cooking time, take the dish out of the oven and remove the foil. Increase the oven temperature to 220°C (425°F, gas mark 7).

Melt the butter for the sauce in a clean saucepan and slowly stir in the flour. Strain the infused milk into the pan a little at a time, stirring continuously, and bring to the boil until thickened. Remove from the heat, beat in the egg yolk and season lightly with salt. Whisk the egg whites separately until stiff, then fold them slowly into the sauce.

Pour the sauce over the top of the vegetables, sprinkle with Parmesan cheese and bake for 15-20 minutes, until the crust is golden-brown.

Succulent aubergines and tomatoes with fresh herbs.

Crunchy vegetables cooked in a slightly sweet oriental sauce make a colourful side dish or light main course.

Stir-fried Vegetables with Oyster Sauce

This delicious vegetable dish is eaten all over the Far East. The oyster sauce gives it a special richness and can be found in almost any large supermarket. The vegetables should still be crisp when served.

SERVES 4
PREPARATION TIME: *25 minutes*
COOKING TIME: *10 minutes*

INGREDIENTS
2 carrots
8oz (225g) broccoli
1 red pepper
8oz (225g) green beans
2oz (50g) spring onions
2 cloves garlic
2 tablespoons vegetable oil
4 tablespoons sesame seed oil
1 small green chilli (optional)
3 tablespoons oyster sauce
6oz (175g) bean sprouts
1 tablespoon light soy sauce
1 tablespoon caster sugar
Juice of 1 lime
Salt and freshly ground white pepper

Calories per serving: 230 · High in fibre and vitamin C from vegetables

Peel and slice the carrots into thin rounds. Divide the broccoli into florets and coarsely chop the stems. De-seed and core the red pepper and cut it into matchsticks. Top and tail the green beans and cut them into thirds. Trim and slice the spring onions and peel and chop the garlic.

Heat the vegetable oil and 2 tablespoons of the sesame seed oil in a wok or large frying pan. Add the garlic and stir for about 1 minute. Then stir in all the remaining vegetables except the bean sprouts and add the oyster sauce. Stir-fry for 3-4 minutes.

Add the remaining ingredients and stir-fry for another 2 minutes. Sprinkle the lime juice over the vegetables, season and serve immediately.

Peppers with a deliciously sweet and moist stuffing.

Peppers Stuffed with Apricots and Pine Nuts

Sweet peppers play an important part in Mediterranean cuisine – stuffed peppers are a particularly popular dish. In the Middle East they are usually served cold as a starter, but they are also delicious eaten hot as a main course. For variety, use a mixture of green, red and yellow peppers. Try to choose thick-fleshed peppers with brightly coloured skins.

SERVES 4
PREPARATION TIME : *30 minutes*
COOKING TIME : *1 hour 20 minutes*
OVEN : *Preheat to 190°C (375°F, gas mark 5)*

INGREDIENTS
4 medium peppers
6oz (175g) short-grain rice
1 large onion
1 clove garlic
3 tablespoons virgin olive oil
2 tablespoons pine nuts
1 tablespoon currants
3oz (75g) dried apricots
½ teaspoon ground cinnamon
Salt and freshly ground black pepper
2 teaspoons sugar
2 tablespoons chopped parsley
2 tablespoons chopped mint
2 medium tomatoes
1 tablespoon tomato purée
5 spring onions

Calories per serving : 350 · Cholesterol free · High in fibre from nuts, apricots and currants

Cut a small slice off the stem end of each pepper and put to one side. Remove the cores and seeds. Wash the rice and drain it thoroughly. Finely chop the onion and crush the garlic.

Bring a pan containing ¾ pint (450ml) of water to the boil. Pour the oil into a separate, large saucepan and fry the onion over a medium heat for 5 minutes, until it turns golden. Add the pine nuts and fry for another 3 minutes, until all the pine nuts begin to colour, then stir in the rice. Add the currants, dried apricots and ground cinnamon, and season to taste.

Stir in the boiling water and add the sugar, parsley, mint, tomatoes, tomato purée, crushed garlic and spring onions. Then mix well and cover. Cook for 10 minutes, leaving the moist rice slightly underdone.

Remove from the heat and spoon the mixture into the peppers, then cover with the reserved tops. Place the peppers upright in an ovenproof dish and pour ¼ pint (150ml) of water around them. Cover with a lid or foil and bake for 40 minutes, then uncover and bake for another 20 minutes. Serve hot or cold.

DESSERTS

Fresh-fruit desserts or old favourites provide the perfect end to any meal. Some can be whipped up in seconds, others look elegant and will leave your guests refreshed and satisfied.

Peaches with Raspberry Sauce

Buy very ripe peaches with a sweet aroma for this dessert. Frozen raspberries make an excellent sauce, or you can use a mixture of other soft red fruits. Serve with light almond biscuits if desired.

SERVES 4
PREPARATION TIME : *15 minutes*
CHILLING TIME : *1 hour*
COOKING TIME : *5 minutes*

INGREDIENTS
4 ripe peaches
8oz (225g) frozen raspberries
1 tablespoon granulated sugar
1 tablespoon Kirsch or Cointreau (optional)
1 tablespoon lemon juice
Sprigs of fresh mint for garnish

Calories per serving : 75 · Low in fat and cholesterol
High in fibre from peaches and raspberries

Refreshing peaches in raspberry sauce with mint.

To make the sauce, put all the frozen raspberries in a covered pan, along with the sugar. Warm over a low heat for 5 minutes until the raspberries have thawed, and the sugar has dissolved in their juice. Press the raspberry mixture through a sieve into a bowl and stir in the optional liqueur. Leave the sauce in the refrigerator to chill.

Put the peaches in a large pan, pour over boiling water and leave them to stand for 1 minute, then drain and allow them to cool. Peel off their skins, and sprinkle with lemon juice to stop them discolouring.

Arrange the peaches on serving plates, whole or sliced without the stone, and pour the sauce around them. Garnish with the fresh mint sprigs and serve.

Apricot Flan

Instead of using the rich shortcrust pastry that is traditionally used for flans, this recipe uses light and crispy filo pastry. Filo pastry is now available from larger supermarkets. A delicious hazelnut mixture is spread into the pastry case before the apricots are added. Apricots retain considerably more flavour than most other fruits when cooked and they make a sweet fresh filling for this flan. Serve either warm or cold, with a little crème fraîche, if desired.

SERVES 8
PREPARATION TIME : *30 minutes*
COOKING TIME : *30-35 minutes*
OVEN : *Preheat to 220°C (425°F, gas mark 7)*

INGREDIENTS
4½ oz (130g) unsalted butter
4oz (115g) filo pastry
4oz (115g) golden caster sugar
2 medium eggs
4oz (115g) finely ground hazelnuts
2oz (50g) plain flour
1 tablespoon Kirsch (optional)
14oz (400g) freshly skinned or tinned apricot halves
1 tablespoon sieved apricot jam
Pistachio nuts for garnish

Calories per serving : 355 · High in protein from nuts
High in fibre from fruit and nuts

Crispy filo pastry topped with hazelnuts and apricots, glazed with apricot jam and sprinkled with pistachios.

Melt ½oz (15g) of the butter. Cut the filo pastry into 8in (200mm) squares and lightly brush each one with melted butter. Brush a 10in (250mm) loose-bottom flan tin with a little melted butter. Line the base and sides of the tin with the filo squares, making sure that each one overlaps the next. Fold in any uneven edges.

Cream the remaining 4oz (115g) butter with the sugar until light and fluffy. Beat the eggs and mix them in gradually, beating well after each addition. Fold in the hazelnuts, flour and Kirsch. Spread the mixture evenly into the pastry case.

Arrange the apricot halves, with their round sides up, on top of the hazelnut mixture. Place the tin on a baking sheet and bake in the centre of the oven for 10 minutes. Reduce the heat to 190°C (375°F, gas mark 5) and continue cooking for 20-25 minutes, until the filling is golden-brown and firm to the touch.

Meanwhile, heat the apricot jam in a saucepan. Remove the flan from the oven, brush the jam over the top and sprinkle with pistachio nuts.

Allow the flan to cool in the tin for 15 minutes, then carefully remove the outer ring and place the flan on a wire rack to cool. Serve warm or cold.

Fresh orange slices served with crunchy golden caramel make a perfect ending to a rich or filling dinner party.

Fresh Oranges with Caramel

If you need a light dessert after a filling meal, try serving this colourful dish in which the freshness of the oranges complements the sweetness of the caramel perfectly. Watch closely when cooking the caramel, as it will turn a dark colour and taste bitter if you overcook it. Timing can vary according to the thickness of the pan, so turn up the heat if the sugar seems to take too long to caramelise.

SERVES 4
PREPARATION TIME : *20 minutes*
COOKING TIME : *5 minutes*

INGREDIENTS
8 large oranges
3oz (75g) granulated sugar
4 small sprigs fresh mint for garnish

Calories per serving : 220 · High in fibre and vitamin C from oranges · Cholesterol free

Cut away the rind, pith and skin from the oranges. Holding each peeled orange over a bowl to catch any juice, divide into segments by sliding a knife down one side of a segment and cutting it from the skin, then cutting down the other side and pulling out the section. Repeat with the remaining segments and then divide the segments and juice into individual serving bowls.

Put the sugar in a heavy-based pan with 2fl oz (50ml) of cold water and bring to the boil over a medium-high heat, stirring occasionally. Boil the syrup for a few minutes, watching very closely to prevent it from burning. Cook until it turns a rich golden-brown, then remove the pan from the heat immediately and trickle over the bowls of oranges.

Garnish with mint and serve quickly, before the caramel starts to dissolve.

Summer Pudding

Wholemeal bread and soft light brown sugar give this healthy pudding a rich mellow flavour. This dessert is quick to make, although it should be prepared a day before serving, to allow the fruit flavours to mature and seep into the bread. The bread should be quite hard and dry for a slightly chewy texture. Almost any mixture of soft or frozen fruits can be used in this recipe.

SERVES 6
PREPARATION TIME : *20 minutes*
CHILLING TIME : *Overnight*
COOKING TIME : *10 minutes*

INGREDIENTS
8oz (225g) fresh blackcurrants
8oz (225g) fresh blackberries
8oz (225g) fresh raspberries
1 lemon
1 large orange
6oz (175g) soft light brown sugar
8 slices wholemeal bread
3 tablespoons Greek yoghurt or cream

Calories per serving : 260 · High in vitamin C from fruits · Low in fat and cholesterol

Remove the stalks from the blackcurrants, wash the fruits and place them in a large stainless-steel saucepan. Hull the blackberries and raspberries, finely grate the lemon and orange rinds and strain their juice. Add the rinds, juice and sugar to the saucepan. Cover and cook gently for 7 minutes until the blackcurrants soften and the juice flows. Add the fruit and continue cooking for another 3 minutes. Reserve 3 tablespoons of the juice.

Remove the crusts from the bread slices. Line the bottom and sides of a 2½ pint (1.4 litre) pudding basin with overlapping slices of bread.

Pour the fruit and remaining juice into the lined basin and then cover with the rest of the bread. To compress the pudding, place a saucer on top with a heavy weight. Refrigerate overnight.

Turn the pudding onto a flat serving dish. Use the reserved fruit juice to cover any areas where the bread has not been coloured by the fruit, and serve with Greek yoghurt or a little cream.

Summer pudding packed with English soft fruits.

Ripe, juicy nectarines filled with curd cheese and yoghurt in a redcurrant sauce, refresh the palate after a meal.

Stuffed Nectarines with Redcurrant Sauce

Succulent nectarines provide a pretty dish for a summer supper party, especially if the edges of the serving plate are decorated with fresh leaves or flowers. At the end of a filling meal, the light taste and scent of nectarines leaves people refreshed rather than sated. If nectarines are unavailable, fresh peaches are just as delicious. When milk has been artificially or naturally soured, the milk separates into a thick creamy curd, used to make curd cheese, and a thin liquid called whey. If you cannot find curd cheese, low-fat cream cheese makes a good alternative. If you prefer to skin the nectarines, plunge them into boiling water for 30 seconds then into cold water. Remove the skins with your fingers.

SERVES 4
PREPARATION TIME : *20 minutes*
COOKING TIME : *3 minutes*

INGREDIENTS
2 tablespoons redcurrant jelly
4 tablespoons tropical fruit juice
2 tablespoons chopped mixed nuts
4 nectarines
A few drops of lemon juice
3 tablespoons strained Greek yoghurt
3 tablespoons low-fat curd or cream cheese
1 tablespoon chopped candied peel
2 teaspoons clear honey

Calories per serving : 185 · High in fibre from nuts and peel · High in protein from yoghurt and cheese

To make the sauce, put the redcurrant jelly and fruit juice into a pan. Heat gently until all the jelly has dissolved, then leave to cool.

Lightly toast the chopped nuts. Cut the nectarines in half and separate them from their stone with a sharp twist. Brush the cut surfaces with lemon juice to prevent discolouring.

Beat the yoghurt into the curd cheese, stir in the peel, nuts and honey, and mix well.

Pile spoonfuls of the mixture onto the nectarines, then arrange them in the serving dish on top of the sauce. Chill until ready to serve.

Salad of Three Fruits with Ginger

Only the ripest fruits should be chosen for this elegant summer dessert. The rich, soft flesh of the dessert Comice pear and the aromatic flesh of the Ogen melon are mixed with tangy pineapple and lifted by a delicious liqueur dressing. Cut the fruit into small pieces of equal size.

SERVES 6-8
PREPARATION TIME : *30 minutes*
CHILLING TIME : *2 hours (optional)*

INGREDIENTS
2oz (50g) caster sugar
1 tablespoon Kirsch, Pear William or Cointreau
1 small pineapple
1 Ogen melon
2 ripe Comice pears
Juice of ½ lemon
2oz (50g) stem ginger

Calories per serving : 120 · High in fibre from pineapple, pears and melon · Low in fat and cholesterol · High in vitamin C from pineapple

Place the sugar in a saucepan, add 1 tablespoon of water and bring to the boil. Simmer until the syrup is clear, then allow to cool. Stir in the Kirsch or other liqueur and put to one side.

Using a sharp, serrated knife, cut off the top and bottom of the pineapple. Using a sawing motion, cut around the fruit in a downward spiral, removing the skin. Push the cylinder of pineapple flesh away from the skin and cut it in half lengthways and in half again. Cut away the pineapple core and cut each quarter in half again and then into small pieces.

Using a sharp knife, cut round and down to remove the melon skin. Cut the peeled melon in half and scoop out the seeds with a spoon. Cut the flesh in the same way as the pineapple.

Peel, core and cut the pears into uniform pieces. Mix them with the lemon juice to retain their colour. Finely slice the ginger. Mix all the fruits and the ginger together in the cooled syrup. Cover with plastic film and, if possible, chill for 2 hours.

Chilled fresh fruit in a ginger and liqueur dressing.

Hot Raspberry Soufflé

Hot fruit soufflés are impressive but are really simple to prepare. The secret to making a light soufflé is to keep as much air as possible in the beaten egg whites. If good fresh raspberries are not available, frozen ones are the best alternative – as they are almost always in perfect condition.

SERVES 6
PREPARATION TIME : *20 minutes*
COOKING TIME : *20-25 minutes*
OVEN : *Preheat to 180°C (350°F, gas mark 4)*

INGREDIENTS
1¼ lb (575g) fresh raspberries
or thawed frozen raspberries
6oz (175g) caster sugar
1 tablespoon Kirsch (optional)
5 egg whites (size 2 eggs)
1 teaspoon icing sugar

Calories per serving : 150 · Low in fat and cholesterol · High in fibre from fruit

---

A light fruity soufflé served with hot raspberry sauce.

Hull the raspberries and press them through a sieve to make a purée. Reserving ½ pint (285ml) of purée for the soufflé, stir 1 tablespoon of caster sugar and the Kirsch, if desired, into the remaining purée to make the sauce. Butter a 6½ × 3in (165 × 80mm) deep soufflé dish and coat evenly with 1 tablespoon of caster sugar.

Whisk the egg whites until they hold their shape, then gradually whisk in the remaining caster sugar, whisking well between each addition until stiff and shiny. In a large bowl, fold a quarter of the egg whites into the reserved raspberry pureé until well mixed, then gently fold in the rest of the egg whites, taking care not to beat any air out of them.

Spoon the soufflé mixture into the prepared dish and mark a deep swirl in the top. Cook in the centre of the oven for 25-30 minutes, until well risen, but do not open the oven during cooking.

Meanwhile, warm the sauce in a small pan, ready to serve in a small jug. Remove the soufflé from the oven and sift icing sugar over the top. Serve immediately with the hot raspberry sauce.

Syrian Fruit Salad

Dried fruit makes a refreshing dessert when served lightly chilled. The fruit is not cooked, but simply left to soak in water and orange juice for up to 48 hours. It can be spiced with a few tablespoons of brandy if wished, and it is delicious served with strained Greek yoghurt. For special occasions, you might like to add an authentic Middle-Eastern touch by garnishing the dish with rose petals.

SERVES 4
PREPARATION TIME : *5 minutes*
SOAKING TIME : *24-48 hours*

INGREDIENTS
8oz (225g) mixed dried fruit
2 large oranges
1oz (25g) blanched almonds and pistachio nuts
Rose petals for decoration (optional)

Calories per serving : 180 · Low in fat and cholesterol · High in fibre from dried fruit and nuts

---

A chilled, dried fruit salad sprinkled with almonds and pistachio nuts, then garnished with scented rose petals.

Roughly chop some of the large pieces of dried fruit, such as apple slices and pear halves, and place them with the rest of the dried fruit in a bowl.

Squeeze the juice from the oranges and pour it over the dried fruit, then pour over ½ pint (285ml) of water. Stir well, cover and leave to soak for at least 24 hours, until the fruit becomes very tender.

Stir in the almonds or pistachio nuts. Turn into a serving bowl and chill in the refrigerator. Remove and decorate with rose petals if wished, and serve.

Scented Pears Poached in Red Wine

Pears turn a deep burgundy colour when they are poached gently in spiced red wine. American Bosc and British Conference are good dessert pears for cooking. Serve with crème fraîche if desired.

SERVES 4
PREPARATION TIME : *20 minutes*
COOKING TIME : *1 hour*
CHILLING TIME : *Overnight*

INGREDIENTS
4 firm dessert pears
½ pint (285ml) red wine
½ glass Cassis (optional)
1½ tablespoons lemon juice
1 cinnamon stick or 2 teaspoons ground cinnamon
4oz (115g) caster sugar
1 teaspoon ground ginger
1 tablespoon honey
6 cloves
4 bay leaves
A twist of freshly ground black pepper
Mint sprigs for garnish
2 tablespoons crème fraîche (optional)

Calories per serving : 235 · Low in fat
Low in cholesterol

Dessert pears poached in wine, liqueur and spices.

Peel the pears and leave them whole with their stalks on. Pour the red wine and optional Cassis into a large pan and add the lemon juice, cinnamon, sugar, ginger, honey, cloves, bay leaves and black pepper. Heat gently, stirring until the sugar has dissolved.

Add the pears, spoon the mixture over them, and cover the pan. Reduce to a low heat and, keeping the liquid just below boiling point, poach gently for 1 hour – turning occasionally – until the pears are translucent and soft, but not mushy.

Remove the pears from the liquid and arrange on a serving dish. Cover and place in the refrigerator. Strain the liquid through a sieve and discard the cloves, bay leaves and cinnamon stick. Pour over the pears and chill overnight.

Garnish with mint sprigs and serve chilled with a little crème fraîche if desired.

Honey, Almond and Orange Flan

Pastry is very high in calories, but this pudding's unusual flan case is made out of almonds and dried dates bound together with honey – the most ancient of all sweeteners. It is based on a traditional Arabic recipe and is very easy to make, provided you have a blender or food processor.

SERVES 6-8
PREPARATION TIME : *15 minutes*

INGREDIENTS
8oz (225g) unblanched almonds
6oz (175g) dried dates
3 tablespoons honey
FILLING
4 large oranges
1lb (450g) fromage frais

Calories per serving : 350 · Low in cholesterol
High in protein and calcium from fromage frais

Put the almonds in a food processor or blender and process them until almost smooth. Add the dates and blend again until they are finely chopped. Pour in the honey and process thoroughly once again.

Fresh orange slices and tangy fromage frais fill a tasty flan case made of crushed almonds, dates and honey.

Press the mixture into an 8in (200mm) flan dish and put in the refrigerator while making the filling.

Finely grate the rind of 2 oranges and add to the fromage frais. Peel all the oranges, removing the white pith, and cut across the core into slices.

Spread half the fromage frais over the base of the flan. Cover with most of the orange slices and top with the remaining fromage frais, spreading it evenly. Finally, arrange the reserved orange slices on top and chill until ready to serve.

Forest Fruits with Blackberry Liqueur

This dessert is healthy and quick to make, and you can use almost any combination of berries and currants that appeals to you. When choosing berries, pick small containers to ensure the fruits are not crushed. All berries should be plump and have a deep colour. Firm berries should also be shiny. Blackberry liqueur, usually called by its French name, Crème de Mûr, is available from some large supermarkets and good off-licences. If you cannot find it, use the blackcurrant liqueur called Crème de Cassis, which is more widely available.

SERVES 4
PREPARATION TIME : *5 minutes*

INGREDIENTS
4oz (115g) strawberries
4oz (115g) raspberries
4oz (115g) cherries
4oz (225g) blueberries
4 heaped tablespoons strained Greek yoghurt
2 tablespoons Crème de Mûr, or Cassis
4 small sprigs of mint for garnish

*Calories per serving : 70 · Low in fat and cholesterol
High in fibre from berries*

An attractive display of berries ready for dipping into creamy yoghurt flavoured with blackberry liqueur.

Hull the strawberries and raspberries, washing them if necessary. Leave the cherry stalks on, but remove any stalks from the blueberries. Then pile a heaped tablespoon of Greek yoghurt on each dessert plate and arrange the fruits around the yoghurt in small clusters. Sprinkle the liqueur over the yoghurt or fruit and garnish with a sprig of mint.

Pineapple and Strawberry Baskets

These elegant tuile baskets can be used with any combination of fruits. The baskets, sauce and filling can be prepared 3 to 4 hours in advance, but the final assembly must be completed just before serving.

SERVES 6
PREPARATION TIME : *1½ hours*
COOKING TIME : *35 minutes*
OVEN : *Preheat to 230°C (450°F, gas mark 8)*

INGREDIENTS
TUILE BASKETS
2 size two egg whites
4oz (115g) caster sugar
1oz (25g) plain flour
2oz (50g) unsalted butter
FILLING
12oz (350g) pineapple pieces
12oz (350g) fresh strawberries
2 tablespoons Kirsch
SAUCE
12oz (350g) fresh or thawed frozen raspberries
1 tablespoon caster sugar
1 tablespoon Kirsch
2 tablespoons thick Greek yoghurt

Calories per serving : 245 · High in fibre from fruit
High in vitamin C from fruit

To make the baskets, put the egg whites into a bowl and beat lightly with a fork until slightly frothy. Blend in the caster sugar, then slowly add the flour and mix until smooth. Melt the butter, allow it to cool, then gradually blend it into the mixture.

Butter a nonstick baking sheet, and put 1 table-

A delicate tuile basket filled with refreshing fruits.

spoon of the tuile mixture in the centre. Using a teaspoon, spread the mixture out thinly, forming a round approximately 8in (200mm) in diameter. Bake for about 5 minutes until golden-brown around the edges. Meanwhile, have an upturned glass tumbler ready for making the tuile baskets.

Remove the tuile from the oven and immediately lift it from the baking sheet and place it over the glass, forming a basket shape. The mixture will cool and harden within seconds. After about 2 minutes, carefully remove the basket by giving the glass a gentle twist, then place the basket on a wire rack to cool. Continue to make the baskets, one at a time, until you have 7 – this includes one extra just in case you have a breakage.

Cut the pineapple into small pieces, hull and quarter the strawberries, and mix together in a bowl with the Kirsch. Leave to stand for 1 hour.

To make the sauce, press the raspberries through a sieve to make a purée. Stir in the caster sugar and Kirsch. Just before serving, pour the sauce onto the serving plates. Using a paper piping bag with a small hole cut in the bottom, pipe a circle of yoghurt on top of the sauce on each plate, and skim a small knife across the yoghurt to create a feathered pattern. Place a basket on each plate, fill with fruit and serve.

Apple Trifle

This is a light and fruity version of the traditional trifle. Choose apples like Granny Smith's or Cox's Orange Pippins for their excellent taste. You can try using different fruits and jams with this recipe.

SERVES 8
PREPARATION TIME : *30 minutes*
CHILLING TIME : *3-4 hours*
COOKING TIME : *15 minutes*

INGREDIENTS
2lb (900g) apples
1 lemon
4oz (115g) granulated sugar
3 tablespoons Grand Marnier
6oz (175g) stale fatless sponge cake
or trifle sponge cakes
2 tablespoons orange marmalade
12oz (350g) thick Greek yoghurt
1 red apple
1 tablespoon lemon juice

Calories per serving : 215 · High in fibre from apples
Low in fat and cholesterol

Peel, quarter, core and slice the apples. Finely grate the lemon rind and squeeze the juice. Put the apples into a saucepan with the sugar, lemon rind and juice. Cover and cook gently for 15-20 minutes until the apples are soft. Place a large sieve over a bowl, and drain the apples in the sieve. Allow to cool.

Mix 8 tablespoons of the apple juice with the Grand Marnier. Cut the sponge cake into slices, and lay out half of them in a glass serving dish. Spoon half of the Grand Marnier flavoured juice over the sponge, and then spread with half of the apples. Repeat with the remaining sponge cake, juice and apples, spreading the apples smoothly. Spread the marmalade evenly over the apple slices. Cover and refrigerate for 3-4 hours, or overnight.

Put 2-3 tablespoons of yoghurt into a piping bag and spread the remainder over the top of the trifle. Pipe the reserved yoghurt around the edge. Decorate with red apple slices tossed in the lemon juice to prevent browning. Refrigerate until ready to serve.

A sumptuous mixture of fruits, sponge and liqueur.

Lemon Soufflé

The secret of making a light and airy soufflé lies in the careful whisking of the egg whites. Use a large metal spoon or a spatula for folding them cleanly into the mixture and be very careful to keep as much air in them as possible.

SERVES 6
PREPARATION TIME : *35 minutes*
SETTING TIME : *2-3 hours*

INGREDIENTS
2 large lemons
5 large eggs
4oz (115g) caster sugar
4 teaspoons gelatine or agar agar
DECORATION
2 tablespoons chilled Greek yoghurt
or whipped double cream
Pistachio nuts

Calories per serving : 155 · High in protein from eggs

Prepare a 6 × 2½in (150 × 65mm) deep soufflé dish. Cut a 5in (130mm) wide, double band of greaseproof paper to wrap around the dish snugly, but not too tightly, with an overlap. Secure with sticky tape. Stand the dish on a flat plate.

Finely grate the rind of the lemons and strain the juice. Separate the eggs, reserving 5 egg whites and 3 of the egg yolks. In a large bowl, whisk the 3 egg yolks with the caster sugar and lemon rind until very thick and pale. Gradually whisk in the lemon juice.

Put 3 tablespoons of cold water in a small saucepan, sprinkle the gelling agent evenly over the surface, and leave to stand until it swells and turns opaque. Heat gently until the gelatine or agar agar dissolves completely and becomes quite hot, then remove from the heat and allow to cool a little.

Whisk the 5 egg whites until stiff, but not dry. Whisk the gelling agent into the lemon mixture, then carefully fold in the egg whites. Pour into the prepared soufflé dish and level the top. Refrigerate for at least 2 hours, until firmly set.

Before serving, remove the sticky tape from the paper, then carefully peel the paper from the side of the soufflé, pulling it back on itself against the back of a palette knife. If you wish, decorate the top with the Greek yoghurt or cream and pistachio nuts.

Egg whites are beaten until they stand up in soft peaks to make a featherlight soufflé garnished with pistachios.

Fruit Fantail in a Scented Honey Dressing

The Ugli fruit is a cross between a tangerine and a grapefruit. When combined with the pink flesh of the ruby grapefruit, and the red flesh of the blood orange, the Ugli fruit makes a colourful dessert.

SERVES 4
PREPARATION TIME : *30 minutes*

INGREDIENTS
1 Ugli fruit
1 ruby grapefruit
2-3 blood oranges (Maltese oranges)
1 lime
DRESSING
6 tablespoons clear honey
2 level tablespoons crystalised orange peel, chopped
6 green cardamom pods, seeds crushed to powder
2 tablespoons rose water

Calories per serving : 180 · Low in fat and cholesterol free · High in vitamin C from fruits

---

Citrus fruits in a honey and rose-water dressing.

Place all the ingredients for the dressing in a small saucepan and stir together over a moderate heat for 2 minutes. Draw from the heat and pour into a china dish. Leave to cool.

Peel all the fruit and neatly trim away the pith using a sharp knife. Cut each fruit lengthways into 4 pieces and slice each piece thinly into segments.

Arrange over 4 dessert plates in fan shapes, using the largest of the fruits at the top of the fan and the smallest towards the centre. Add 1 piece of lime at the base. Pour the honey dressing over the fruit and leave to chill in the refrigerator for 30 minutes.

Strawberry Flan

Strawberries are members of the rose family. Pick-your-own fruit farms are the best places to find flavoursome strawberries that have been ripened fully on the plant. If you are pushed for time – buy a ready-made flan case to use in this recipe.

SERVES 8-12
PREPARATION TIME : *1 hour*
COOKING TIME : *25-30 minutes*
OVEN : *Preheat to 190°C (375°F, gas mark 5)*

INGREDIENTS
FLAN CASE
1oz (25g) unsalted butter
4 large eggs
3oz (75g) vanilla-flavoured caster sugar
4oz (115g) plain flour
SYRUP
4oz (115g) granulated sugar
2 tablespoons Cointreau
or Grand Marnier (optional)
FILLING
1¼ lb (575g) fresh strawberries
2oz (50g) caster sugar
3 teaspoons powdered gelatine or agar agar
8oz (225g) fromage frais
1 egg
1 teaspoon icing sugar

Calories per serving : 225 · High in protein from eggs and fromage frais

---

A simple homemade flan case with a light filling, decorated with a stunning arrangement of fresh strawberries.

To make your own flan case, melt the butter and allow it to cool. Grease and flour a 12in (300mm) flan tin. Separate one of the eggs, reserving the egg white, then whisk it with 3 whole eggs and the caster sugar until the mixture runs off a spoon in a thin trail. Sift the flour into the mixture and fold in carefully. Gradually fold in the melted butter.

Pour the mixture into the flan tin and bake in the centre of the oven for 25-30 minutes until well risen and the sponge shrinks slightly away from the side of the tin. Turn onto a wire rack to cool.

To make the syrup, put the sugar into a saucepan with ¼ pint (150ml) of cold water. Heat gently until the sugar dissolves, then boil for 1 minute and stir the optional liqueur into the syrup. Place the flan on a serving dish and carefully spoon over the syrup.

To make the filling, roughly slice 8oz (225g) of the strawberries, put them into a bowl with the caster sugar and mix well. Cover and leave to stand for 20 minutes, then press through a sieve to make a purée.

Put 2 tablespoons of cold water into a small saucepan and sprinkle over the gelatine. Leave to stand until the gelatine swells and becomes opaque, then heat gently until it becomes hot and dissolves completely. Whisk into the purée, then whisk in the fromage frais. Leave in a cool place until thickened.

Meanwhile, separate the egg, reserving the white, then whisk it until it forms soft peaks. Fold into the strawberry mixture and pour into the flan case. Refrigerate until set. Just before serving, use the remaining strawberries to garnish the flan and a fine sieve to sift the icing sugar over the top.

A fancy jelly mould turns this healthy orange dessert into a spectacular centrepiece for a children's party.

Fresh Orange Jelly

The use of freshly squeezed orange juice makes this jelly taste far better than the commercially produced cubes and, as it contains no artificial colourings or flavourings, it is also much healthier. Set the jelly in a fancy mould if you have one, which adds to the presentation, otherwise a pudding basin can be used instead. Adults as well as children will love this recipe and, if desired, Jamaican rum can be stirred into the strained jelly liquid. Make sure you use gelatine or agar agar which is not too old, otherwise the jelly may not set properly. Serve with crème fraîche or a little whipped cream.

SERVES 4
PREPARATION TIME : *10 minutes*
COOKING TIME : *15 minutes*
SETTING TIME : *1½ hours*

INGREDIENTS
6 large oranges
4oz (115g) sugar
5 × ¼ oz (7g) sachets powdered gelatine
or agar agar
2 tablespoons rum (optional)

Calories per serving : 235 · Low in fat and cholesterol · High in vitamin C from oranges

Pour 4 tablespoons of cold water into a small bowl, sprinkle the surface of the water with the gelatine or agar agar and leave to soak. Squeeze and strain the juice from five oranges and thinly pare the rind of one of them. Put the juice, rind, sugar and 12fl oz (340ml) of water together in a large saucepan.

Place the bowl of gelatine over a pan of hot water and stir until it is completely dissolved. Bring the contents of the saucepan slowly to the boil, stirring until the sugar is dissolved. Reduce the heat, stir in the gelatine and simmer for 10 minutes.

Strain the jelly liquid into a wetted mould and stir in the rum if required. Leave in the refrigerator to set for about 1½ hours. Dip the outside of the mould in warm water. Cover with a plate and turn upside-down and shake until the jelly slips out. Decorate with segments or peel from the remaining orange.

Strawberry Yoghurt Ice Cream

This ice cream's high fruit content gives it a slight texture. It is best eaten when half-frozen. Any soft fruit can be used in this recipe, but you may wish to vary the amount of sugar. You will need a liquidiser.

SERVES 4-6
PREPARATION TIME : *20 minutes*
FREEZING TIME : *8-9 hours*
COOKING TIME : *5 minutes*

INGREDIENTS
6oz (175g) golden granulated sugar
Peeled rind of 1 lemon
¼ pint (150ml) water
1lb (450g) strawberries
½ pint (285ml) low-fat natural yoghurt
4-6 strawberries for decoration

Calories per serving : 195 · Low in fat and cholesterol · High in vitamin C from strawberries

Yoghurt makes a healthy base for delicious ice cream.

Put the sugar, lemon rind and water into a small heavy-based pan over a low heat and stir until the sugar has dissolved. Increase the heat and bring to the boil. Boil rapidly for 2 minutes, then remove from the heat and allow to cool.

Hull the strawberries, then purée them in a liquidiser. Strain in the sugar syrup and purée the mixture again. Pour into a bowl, add the yoghurt and mix well. Turn the mixture into a plastic container and freeze for about 2 hours.

Spoon the mixture into the blender and purée. Return to the freezer for another 2-3 hours, then remove and purée again. Return to the freezer and freeze for about 4 hours, or until firm.

Remove the ice cream from the freezer and leave to soften for 1 hour in the refrigerator. Spoon into small bowls and decorate with fresh strawberries.

Blackberry Fool

A true fool is made with equal quantities of fruit purée and whipped double cream, making it high in cholesterol and calories. A healthy and equally delicious version can be made with a thick custard blended with Greek yoghurt. If fresh blackberries are unavailable use thawed, frozen fruit.

SERVES 4
PREPARATION TIME : *40 minutes*
COOKING TIME : *10 minutes*
CHILLING TIME : *2 hours*

INGREDIENTS
1lb (450g) fresh or frozen blackberries
1oz (25g) custard powder
1½ oz (40g) caster sugar
½ pint (285ml) skimmed milk
4oz (115g) thick Greek yoghurt
1 teaspoon icing sugar (optional)

Calories per serving : 140 · High in fibre from blackberries · High in protein from milk

Put the custard powder into a bowl. Add ½oz (15g) of the caster sugar and blend to a smooth paste with about 4 tablespoons of the milk. Pour the rest of the milk into a small saucepan and bring to the boil, and

Fruit fools, made with yoghurt and custard, instead of cream, taste just as rich and creamy as traditional fools.

then stir the boiling milk into the custard powder.

Return this mixture to the pan and bring back to the boil, stirring constantly until the custard has thickened and no trace of custard powder remains.

Pour the mixture into a bowl and allow to cool a little. Cover with plastic film before refrigerating for at least 1 hour to allow the fool to set.

Reserving 4 blackberries for garnish, put the rest into a pan with the remaining sugar and cook over a low heat for 7 minutes, until the fruit softens. Press the fruit through a sieve to make a purée.

Whisk the chilled custard until very smooth, then whisk in the Greek yoghurt and fold in the purée. Spoon into serving glasses and chill for 1 hour.

Garnish with the reserved blackberries, sprinkle with icing sugar, if desired, and serve immediately.

Honeyed Bread and Butter Pudding

Although it was originally devised as a way to use up stale bread, this traditional family favourite is best made with fresh or day-old bread. To ensure a light and crusty pudding, it is best to let the pudding mixture stand for an hour before baking. This allows the bread to swell and absorb the liquid. Honey is a form of fruit sugar that is less refined than ordinary table sugar. Less honey than sugar is needed to provide the same sweetness, and honey contains some trace elements – minerals which are needed by the body in extremely small amounts. Look for organic honey that is the product of bees fed only on flower nectars, and which often has a scented aroma.

Golden-brown bread and butter pudding has added flavour when it is baked with rum or brandy and a hint of nutmeg. This dish uses less butter than traditional recipes, and sweet honey instead of sugar.

SERVES 4
PREPARATION TIME : *15 minutes*
STANDING TIME : *1 hour*
COOKING TIME : *30-40 minutes*
OVEN : *Preheat to 180°C (350°F, gas mark 4)*

INGREDIENTS
4 thin slices white bread
2oz (50g) butter
4oz (115g) currants
3 medium eggs
½ lemon
½ pint (285ml) whole or semi-skimmed milk
2 tablespoons brandy or rum (optional)
2 tablespoons honey
½ level teaspoon grated or ground nutmeg

Calories per serving : 350 · High in fibre from currants · High in protein from bread, eggs and milk

Butter the slices of bread and cut each slice into 4 triangles. Grease a 1 pint (570ml) pie dish and arrange the bread in layers, sprinkling each with currants. The final layer must be butter-side up.

Separate the yolk from one of the eggs and grate the rind of ½ a lemon. Beat the egg yolk, the 2 whole eggs and the milk together, then stir in the lemon rind. Add the optional brandy or rum. Pour the liquid over the bread and spoon over the honey. Leave to stand for 1 hour.

Sprinkle the top of the pudding with the nutmeg and bake in the oven for 30-40 minutes, until well risen with a golden-brown top. Serve immediately.

Quick Raspberry and Banana Sorbet

Your dinner guests will probably think that this refreshing and healthy dessert takes a long time to prepare, but with a food processor it takes just 5 minutes. The dish is made with only bananas and frozen raspberries but can be quite filling, so keep helpings fairly small. It is best to make this dessert just before serving, but you can make it slightly more solid by keeping it in a freezer for 30 minutes.

Banana and frozen raspberries are whipped up in minutes to create a simple yet impressive sorbet.

SERVES 4
PREPARATION TIME : *5 minutes*

INGREDIENTS
1 large or 2 small bananas
8oz (225g) frozen raspberries
4 sprigs fresh mint for garnish

Calories per serving : 40 · Low in fat and cholesterol High in fibre from banana and raspberries

Put the banana and unthawed frozen raspberries into a food processor and liquidise for 2-3 minutes until the fruit has been puréed. Scrape the sides of the bowl down if this is necessary.

Spoon the fruit mixture into small individual bowls, garnish with the mint sprigs and serve.

Rolled oats combine with yoghurt, honey, raspberries and a dash of whisky to form crunchy, filling desserts.

Scottish Raspberry Flummery

This is a light version of the Scottish Atholl Brose, a rich dessert with an amusing history. It is said that the dessert, originally a mixture of whisky, cream and honey, was used to capture a robber called Big Rory, who stole from passers-by in the woodlands of Lord Atholl. A young man noticed that Rory drank from the same well every day and filled the well with Atholl Brose. Rory became drunk and was captured by the young man who then married Lord Atholl's daughter. This recipe includes raspberries, and it replaces the cream with yoghurt. It is still quite rich, so serve it in small portions. Take care not to over brown the oats as they may become bitter.

INGREDIENTS
4oz (115g) rolled oats
8oz (225g) thick Greek yoghurt
2 tablespoons clear honey
1 tablespoon Drambuie or whisky
6oz (175g) fresh raspberries

Calories per serving : 130 · High in fibre from oats
Low in fat and cholesterol

Spread the oats out evenly on an ungreased baking sheet and roast them in a hot oven for 3-5 minutes until they are pale golden-brown. As soon as their colour has turned, remove them from the oven.

Allow the oats to cool and put them into a large bowl. Add the yoghurt, honey and Drambuie. Mix well together, then cover and chill in the refrigerator for 1 hour.

Spoon the mixture into small glasses or bowls, level the surfaces with a knife or spoon and decorate the tops with fresh raspberries. These desserts will keep in the refrigerator for 24 hours.

Camembert in Filo Flowers with Cranberry Sauce

These light, crispy casings made with filo pastry are served hot from the oven with a centre of soft, melted cheese. Together with a tangy cranberry sauce they can be served as a light snack or as an unusual finish to a dinner party. The uncooked filo flowers can be frozen for future use. You will need 12 round patty-pan moulds for this recipe, which should be about 2in (50mm) across. Serve the filo flowers directly from the oven onto warm plates with the hot sauce. You might like to serve them with some green salad if you are having them as a snack.

Light filo pastry decoratively encases melted cheese.

INGREDIENTS
3-4 sheets filo pastry 13 × 11in (330 × 280mm)
8oz (225g) ripe Camembert
1oz (25g) butter
3 tablespoons cranberry sauce
2 tablespoons orange juice

Calories per serving : 285 · High in protein and
calcium from pastry and cheese

The Camembert should be at room temperature. Grease the tin moulds with half the butter. Using sharp scissors, cut the sheets of pastry into 36 pieces, about 3½in (90mm) square. Cover them with a damp tea cloth to prevent drying out and set aside.

Discarding the rind, mould the Camembert into 10 balls the size of large walnuts. Press 2 squares of the pastry into each mould so that the 8 corners of the pastry are evenly spaced to form the shape of a flower. Wrap the remaining pieces of pastry around each ball of Camembert and seal the edges at the base. Gently press each ball into the centre of a flower. Brush the pastry with a little melted butter and bake in the oven for 5 minutes.

Gently heat the cranberry sauce and orange juice in a pan, pour it around the filo flowers and serve.

The most royal of puddings – breadcrumbs, hot milk and eggs are baked in a pie dish and then covered with jam and meringue. Fresh strawberries add an extra touch of luxury to this low-calorie dessert.

Queen of Puddings

This rich, old-fashioned dessert is a layered pudding of fresh breadcrumbs, strawberry jam and golden meringue. Queen Charlotte, wife of George III, was responsible for the rise in popularity of this pudding. The Queen thought that the sweet was a particularly nutritious and economical dish to serve to all the patients in her hospital – Queen Charlotte's Maternity Hospital, in London. This recipe is a healthier version which uses much less fat and sugar, making a low-calorie dessert. You might like to try serving this pudding with sliced strawberries, as they make a tasty accompaniment and are also very decorative.

SERVES 6
PREPARATION TIME : *20 minutes*
STANDING TIME : *1 hour*
COOKING TIME : *1 hour*
OVEN : *Preheat to 190°C (375°F, gas mark 5)*

INGREDIENTS
1 large lemon
3oz (75g) fresh white breadcrumbs
½ oz (15g) butter
2½ oz (65g) caster sugar
¾ pint (450ml) skimmed milk
3 large eggs
1 tablespoon sugar-free strawberry jam
Sliced strawberries for decoration (optional)

Calories per serving : 170 · Low in fat · High in protein from eggs and milk

Finely grate the rind of the lemon and place it in a bowl with the breadcrumbs, butter and ½oz (15g) of the sugar. Heat the milk until hot, but not boiling, and pour it onto the breadcrumbs. Mix well, cover, and leave to stand for 1 hour.

Separate the eggs, reserving 3 yolks and 2 whites. Whisk the 3 egg yolks into the breadcrumb mixture, then pour into a buttered 1½ pint (850ml) pie dish and cook in the centre of the oven for 45 minutes, until the pudding is lightly firm to the touch.

Leaving the oven on, remove the pie dish and then carefully spread the strawberry jam over the top of the pudding, so that it is even.

Whisk the 2 egg whites in a bowl together, until stiff but not dry, then gradually whisk in the rest of the sugar a little at a time to make a stiff and shiny meringue. Spoon or pipe the meringue on top of the pudding. Return to the oven for about 10-15 minutes, until the top is lightly browned.

Decorate with strawberry slices if desired, or you can serve them separately on the side. Serve the pudding straight from the oven.

SNACKS, DRINKS & SANDWICHES

Quick meals can be healthy and fun to make. Sandwiches with delicious fillings are perfect for picnics. Refreshing homemade drinks are packed with goodness, and for a special treat there are luxurious cakes.

Raspberry or Strawberry Jam with Reduced Sugar

These jams are made with half the amount of sugar normally used for jam making. With less sugar and a short boiling time, all the flavour of fresh fruit is retained. The jams will lose their slight stiffness on removal from the refrigerator. You will need a heavy, stainless-steel saucepan and 3 jam jars.

MAKES : *2½ -3lb (1.1-1.4kg)*
PREPARATION TIME : *20 minutes*
STANDING TIME : *1 hour for strawberry jam*
COOKING TIME : *15-20 minutes*

INGREDIENTS
2lb (900g) fresh raspberries or strawberries
Juice of 1 large lemon
1lb (450g) preserving sugar crystals
5-6 teaspoons gelatine

Calories per serving : 20 · Low in calories
Fat and cholesterol free

If necessary, wash the raspberries or strawberries thoroughly, and remove the stalks.

To make raspberry jam, put the fruit into a heavy, stainless-steel saucepan. Strain the lemon juice, add it to the pan and cover with a tightly fitting lid. Heat gently for 5-10 minutes, until the fruit softens and the juices appear. Add the sugar to the pan and stir over a gentle heat until every granule has dissolved.

Bring to the boil and boil rapidly for 5 minutes and no longer. Meanwhile, put 2 tablespoons of cold water into a small bowl and sprinkle 5 teaspoons of gelatine over the surface. Leave to stand until the gelatine swells.

Remove the jam from the heat. Add the gelatine and stir gently until it has completely dissolved. Pour the jam into 3 clean, warm jam jars and place a waxed paper disc on top of each jar, wax side down. Allow the jam to cool, then cover with lids or with clear, Cellophane covers. If you prefer, strain the jam through a nylon sieve to remove the pips. The jam will last much longer if it is stored in a refrigerator.

To make the strawberry jam, put the strawberries into a heavy-based, stainless-steel saucepan, add the strained lemon juice and crush with a stainless-steel vegetable masher. Add the sugar, stir well, cover and leave to stand for 1 hour. Then proceed as for the raspberry jam, using 6 teaspoons of gelatine. Allow the jam to stand for 10 minutes before potting.

Wholemeal Bread

Wholemeal flour contains the whole of the wheat and is a balanced source of nutrition; supplying vitamins, minerals, protein and fibre. Instructions for 12 rolls, a cob loaf, or a flowerpot loaf are given in this recipe, but you can make any shape you wish. Bread freezes well, so it saves time to make a batch.

MAKES 12 rolls or 2 loaves
PREPARATION TIME : *2½ hours*
COOKING TIME : *35-40 minutes*
OVEN : *Preheat to 230°C (450°F, gas mark 8)*

INGREDIENTS
3lb (1.4kg) wholemeal flour
1 tablespoon salt
2 tablespoons caster sugar
2oz (50g) butter
3 sachets easy-blend dried yeast
or 2oz (50g) fresh yeast
½ pint (285ml) skimmed milk
1 tablespoon sunflower seeds

Calories per serving : 245 · High in fibre, protein and iron from flour, and zinc from sunflower seeds

Sift the flour, salt and sugar into a large bowl. Add the bran remaining in the sieve to the bowl. Rub the butter into the flour. Add easy-blend yeast to the flour and mix well, or dissolve fresh yeast in ½ pint (285ml) of tepid, skimmed milk.

Make a well in the flour and pour in the milk and 1 pint (570ml) of tepid water. Mix to form a dough. Turn onto a lightly floured surface and knead well for 10 minutes, until the dough is elastic.

Place the dough in a clean bowl, cover with plastic film, and leave in a warm place for about 1½ hours

Wholemeal dough can be moulded in a flowerpot, or into rolls, and spread with homemade fresh-fruit jam.

until the dough has doubled in size. Meanwhile, grease two large baking sheets and, if you wish to make a flowerpot loaf, thoroughly clean and grease a 6½in (165mm) clay flowerpot.

Turn the risen dough onto a lightly floured surface and with clenched fists, flatten out the air bubbles. Re-knead for 2-3 minutes.

For a flowerpot loaf, cut off a quarter of the dough and shape it into a smooth ball, then place in the flowerpot. To make the rolls, cut off 12 × 2oz (50g) pieces of dough and shape each one into a smooth ball. Space well apart on a baking sheet. To make two

cob loaves, divide the dough equally, and shape them into neat rounds, about 7in (180mm) in diameter. Place them on a large baking sheet.

Loosely cover the bread with plastic film, and leave somewhere warm for 2 hours to double in size.

Brush the flowerpot loaf with cold water and sprinkle with sunflower seeds. Sprinkle wholemeal flour over the cob loaf. Leave the rolls plain.

Bake the rolls for 15-20 minutes and bake the loaves for 35-40 minutes until golden-brown, and there is a hollow sound when they are tapped on the base. Cool on wire racks.

Delicate coffee éclairs with a creamy filling and a rich but healthy banana cake make tea-time luxuries.

Banana Loaf

If you pack this delicious banana loaf in kitchen foil, it will keep moist for up to a week. You will need a 2lb (900g) loaf tin for this recipe.

SERVES 8
PREPARATION TIME : *25 minutes*
COOKING TIME : *1¼ hours*
OVEN : *Preheat to 180°C (350°F, gas mark 4)*

INGREDIENTS
12oz (350g) ripe bananas
7oz (200g) self-raising flour
¼ teaspoon bicarbonate of soda
½ teaspoon salt
2oz (50g) butter or sunflower margarine
6oz (175g) light soft brown sugar
2 eggs
3oz (75g) marzipan

Calories per serving : 310 · High in fibre from marzipan and bananas · Low in cholesterol

Grease a 2lb (900g) loaf tin and line with greaseproof paper. Peel and mash the bananas. Sieve the flour with the bicarbonate of soda and salt.

Beat the butter with the sugar until they form a light and fluffy cream. Lightly beat the eggs, then gradually whisk them in with the butter and sugar mixture. Beat in the bananas and fold in the flour mixture. Roughly chop and stir in the marzipan. Turn the mixture into the prepared tin and level.

Bake for 1¼ hours until risen and golden. Turn out to cool on a rack and serve plain or with butter.

Coffee Éclairs

These éclairs contain all the taste and creaminess of normal éclairs but with far fewer calories. The light, creamy filling is made with skimmed milk, Greek yoghurt and only a small amount of cream. You will need a piping bag for this recipe.

MAKES 20 éclairs
PREPARATION TIME : *1 hour*
CHILLING TIME : *2-3 hours*
COOKING TIME : *30 minutes*
OVEN : *Preheat to 220°C (425°F, gas mark 7)*

INGREDIENTS
1½ oz (40g) custard powder
1oz (25g) caster sugar
¾ pint (450ml) skimmed milk
1 teaspoon vanilla essence
2oz (50g) thick Greek yoghurt
2½ fl oz (75ml) double cream
PASTRY
3oz (75g) sunflower margarine or butter
3¾ oz (100g) plain flour
3 eggs
ICING
8oz (225g) icing sugar
1 teaspoon instant coffee granules
1oz (25g) plain chocolate (optional)

Calories per serving : 120 · Low in fat and cholesterol

To make the filling, put the custard powder into a bowl, add the sugar and 2-3 tablespoons of milk and blend to a smooth paste. Heat the remaining milk in a saucepan until almost boiling, then pour it into the custard paste and stir it in.

Return the custard to the saucepan and gently

bring to the boil. Stir well until the custard thickens. Cook for 1-2 minutes, until no trace of the custard powder remains, then beat in the vanilla essence. Pour into a clean bowl and cover with plastic film. Allow to cool, then refrigerate for 2-3 hours.

Meanwhile, to make the pastry, put the margarine or butter into a saucepan with 7½fl oz (215ml) of cold water. Heat gently until the margarine melts, then bring to the boil. Tip the flour into the saucepan and beat quickly, until the mixture forms a stiff paste. Remove from the heat. Whisk 2 eggs and 1 egg white together, then gradually whisk into the paste.

Spoon the paste into a piping bag fitted with a plain ½in (15mm) nozzle. Line 2 baking sheets with nonstick baking paper and pipe 3in (80mm) lengths of paste, spaced well apart, onto the paper.

Bake in the oven for 20-25 minutes, until well risen, golden-brown and quite firm. Remove from the oven and make a small hole in the end of each éclair with a sharp knife, to allow steam to escape. Return to the oven for 5 minutes to dry. Remove from the oven and leave to cool on a wire rack.

Whisk the chilled custard mixture until very smooth, then whisk in the yoghurt. Whisk the cream until stiff, then fold it into the custard. Place this mixture into a clean piping bag and pipe the pastry cream into the hole in each éclair. Shake to ensure the cream is evenly distributed.

Place the icing sugar in a large bowl and dissolve the coffee granules in 1 teaspoon of boiling water. Add the coffee to the icing sugar and add just enough boiling water to make a thick, smooth icing. Dip the top of each éclair in the icing, lift out and drain off any excess. Place on a rack until the icing sets.

If using the chocolate, melt it in a small pan and pour into a small paper piping bag. Cut a small hole in the end of the bag and use to pipe chocolate decoratively. Keep refrigerated until ready to serve.

Country Chicken Burgers

Tasty chicken burgers are a lighter and healthier alternative to eating hamburgers. The burgers can be cooked either under a grill or on an open barbecue, and turkey can be used instead of chicken.

SERVES 4
PREPARATION TIME : *20 minutes*
COOKING TIME : *15 minutes*
OVEN : *Preheat grill on medium setting*

INGREDIENTS
8oz (225g) skinless and boneless chicken thigh meat
1 onion
4oz (100g) sausage meat
2oz (50g) fresh brown or white breadcrumbs
1 tablespoon chopped parsley
1 tablespoon fresh thyme leaves or 1 teaspoon dried thyme

Calories per serving : 195 · High in protein from chicken and sausage meat · Low in calories

Mince the chicken by hand or in a food processor until fairly coarse. Then finely chop the onion and sausage meat. Combine all of the ingredients and work together until evenly mixed, then shape the mixture into 4 burgers.

Cook the burgers under a preheated grill set at a medium setting for about 15 minutes, turning once, until golden on both sides.

Healthy chicken burgers with rolls and a green salad.

Overflowing with tasty chicken and avocado, jacket potatoes are served with a cocktail of fruit juices.

Tropical Fruit Drink

Exotic Brazilian passion fruit are one of the most fragrant and distinctive-tasting tropical fruits available. This subtle blend of tropical fruits provides an excellent alternative to alcoholic drinks at parties. You will need a liquidiser for this recipe.

SERVES 8
PREPARATION TIME : *30 minutes*

INGREDIENTS
1 large, ripe pineapple
8 large, juicy oranges
8 passion fruit
Orange slices and pineapple leaves for decoration

Calories per serving : 90 · High in fibre from fruit

Remove the top and bottom of the pineapple and cut away the skin. Cut the fruit into quarters lengthways, and remove the woody core. Cut the flesh into pieces, place in a liquidiser and blend until smooth. Pass through a sieve to remove fibres.

Cut the oranges in half and squeeze and strain the juice – you will need about 1½ pints (850ml).

Cut the passion fruit into halves, then scoop out the seeds into a sieve placed over a bowl. Mash the seeds into the sieve to extract all the juice, using the back of a stainless-steel spoon. There should be about ¼ pint (150ml) of juice.

Mix the juices in a jug. Half fill serving glasses with crushed ice. Pour the juice over the ice and decorate with orange slices and pineapple leaves.

Jacket Potatoes with Chicken and Avocado

Much of a potato's nutrients are contained in, or just under, its skin. Make the filling for this dish with freshly cooked, boned chicken breasts or with any leftover roast chicken. Serve with a green salad.

SERVES 4
PREPARATION TIME : *20 minutes*
COOKING TIME : *1½ hours*
OVEN : *Preheat to 200°C (400°F, gas mark 6)*

INGREDIENTS
4 large baking potatoes
1 teaspoon olive oil
¼ pint (150ml) sour cream
3 tablespoons snipped chives
1 tablespoon lemon juice
10oz (275g) cooked chicken
1 ripe avocado
Salt and freshly ground black pepper

Calories per serving : 530 · High in fibre from potato
High in protein from yoghurt, potato and chicken

Scrub and prick the potatoes, then rub each one with oil. Cook on a baking sheet for 1½ hours.

Meanwhile, blend the sour cream, chives and lemon juice together in a bowl. Cut the chicken into small cubes and add to the mixture.

Cut the avocado in half and remove the skin and stone. Dice the flesh into ½in (15mm) cubes. Add to the chicken, season to taste and mix well.

Make a diagonal cut in the potatoes and pull them apart. Fill each one with the chicken mixture.

Orange and Apricot Tea Bread

Unlike most shop-bought tea breads, which are served with butter and jam, this high-fibre tea bread is quite delicious on its own. The tea bread will keep moist in an airtight container for 1-2 weeks.

MAKES 20 slices
PREPARATION TIME : *30 minutes*
STANDING TIME : *2½ hours*
COOKING TIME : *1¼ hours*
OVEN : *Preheat to 180°C (350°F, gas mark 4)*

INGREDIENTS
2 large oranges
12oz (350g) dried apricots
5oz (150g) bran
6oz (175g) dark soft brown sugar
½ pint (285ml) warm tea
2 medium eggs
¼ pint (150ml) skimmed milk
12oz (350g) self-raising wholemeal flour
TOPPING
3oz (75g) dried apricots
1½ tablespoons clear honey

Calories per serving : 150 · High in fibre from apricots and flour · Low in fat and cholesterol

Finely grate the rind of the 2 oranges and strain the juice of both fruits into a large bowl. Chop the dried apricots. Add the rind and apricots to the bowl, with

Minted iced tea complements a slightly tangy tea bread that is unusually low in fat and calories.

the bran, sugar and tea. Mix well, cover and leave to stand for 2½ hours.

Line a loaf tin measuring about 12 × 4½ × 3in (300 × 115 × 80mm) with baking paper. Beat the 2 eggs, mix them with the milk and pour into the apricot mixture. Stir well, then fold in the flour. Spoon the mixture into the loaf tin, level the top and bake for 1¼ hours. The tea bread is ready when a skewer comes out clean from its centre.

Remove the bread from the tin and leave to cool on a wire rack. Put the apricots and honey for the topping together in a small saucepan and heat gently for 2 minutes. Spoon evenly over the tea bread.

When the bread is cool, remove the baking paper, cut into thin slices and serve.

Iced Tea

This extremely refreshing drink is very fashionable in the warmer parts of America, where it is usually drunk outside on a 'deck', or verandah. With this method of making iced tea, the tea bags are infused in cold water, which creates a more delicate flavour. You can use other teas apart from Assam – Lapsang souchong and Darjeeling make good alternatives.

SERVES 6-8
PREPARATION TIME : *5 minutes*
STANDING TIME : *2-3 hours*

INGREDIENTS
9 pure Assam tea bags
*3 pints (1.7 litres) still natural spring water
or filtered tap water*
2 large oranges
1 large block ice or ice cubes
1 sprig fresh rosemary
Fresh sprigs of mint

Calories per serving : 25 · Cholesterol free

Place the tea bags in a large jug and pour in the spring water. Cover and leave to infuse for 2-3 hours.

Stir well and remove the tea bags. Slice both the oranges. Put the ice into the jug, add the orange slices, rosemary and mint and allow to stand in a cool place for 10 minutes before serving in glasses.

This nutritious yoghurt drink makes a refreshing partner for curried dishes, like tasty chicken baps.

Indian Yoghurt Drink

This slightly scented drink is known as Lhassi in India, where the recipe originated. It is smooth and mild and particularly refreshing when very cold. You might like to serve it with hot or spicy foods, such as Indian curries. You will need a liquidiser.

SERVES 4

PREPARATION TIME : *5 minutes*

INGREDIENTS

¾ pint (450ml) low-fat plain yoghurt
¾ pint (450ml) semi-skimmed milk
8 drops rosewater
¾ teaspoon ground cardamom
¾ teaspoon cinnamon
4½ teaspoons caster sugar
8 ice cubes
Grated or ground pistachio nuts for garnish
Rose petals for garnish (optional)

Calories per serving : 130 · High in protein from yoghurt and milk · Low in fat and cholesterol

Place all the ingredients, except the pistachio nuts and rose petals, in a liquidiser, add ¼ pint (150ml) of cold water and blend until smooth.

Pour the drink into tall glasses. Keep chilled until needed, then sprinkle with the pistachio nuts and petals, if required, and serve.

Curried Chicken Baps

Garam masala is an elaborate and aromatic mixture of ground spices often used in Indian cooking. It usually includes coriander and cumin seeds, cloves, cinnamon and black pepper. It is normally bought ready-made and, together with the curry powder, adds a slightly aromatic, Indian taste to these simple baps. The word bap is used to describe any soft, round, flat bread roll. It is a traditional name, often used more frequently in the north of England, which dates back to the 16th century. This recipe uses wholemeal baps, which should not be too large.

SERVES 4

PREPARATION TIME : *5 minutes*

INGREDIENTS

10oz (275g) cooked chicken
4 wholemeal baps
¼ Iceberg lettuce
DRESSING
1½ teaspoons garam masala
½ teaspoon curry powder
2 teaspoons lemon juice
1 tablespoon strained Greek yoghurt
1 tablespoon low-calorie mayonnaise

Calories per serving : 445 · High in fibre from baps High in protein from chicken and yoghurt · High in iron from baps and curry powder

Wash and thoroughly dry the lettuce and cut it into shreds using a sharp knife. Dice the chicken into ½in (15mm) cubes and stir it in with all the ingredients for the dressing in a mixing bowl.

Without cutting right through, cut the baps in half and open them out. Sandwich the curried chicken mixture in between 2 layers of lettuce and close the baps. Serve, or wrap well to keep fresh.

Asparagus and Orange Tartlets with Orange Mayonnaise

These tartlets, made with light filo pastry and low-fat orange mayonnaise, make delicious canapés without too many calories. When buying asparagus make sure it is fresh, as stale varieties taste bitter. It is important not to overcook asparagus.

SERVES 4
PREPARATION TIME : *15 minutes*
COOKING TIME : *15 minutes*
OVEN : *Preheat to 190°C (375°F, gas mark 5)*

INGREDIENTS
3 sheets filo pastry 14 × 7½ in (355 × 190mm) plus
3 half-sheets 7 × 3in (180 × 80mm)
1oz (25g) butter
1½ lb (700g) asparagus
1 orange
8 leaves of lollo rosso or other lettuce for garnish
MAYONNAISE DRESSING
2 tablespoons fresh orange juice
3 tablespoons sunflower oil
1 tablespoon white wine vinegar
¼ teaspoon tomato purée
½ teaspoon caster sugar
2 tablespoons crème fraîche
Salt and pepper

Calories per serving : 235 · Low in cholesterol
High in vitamin C from asparagus and citrus juice

Lightly brush melted butter over one of the large sheets of pastry. Lay a second large sheet over the first, lightly butter, then lay over the third. Repeat this procedure with the three smaller sheets and use the large sheets to line 5 small tartlet tins and the small sheets to line 3 more.

Prick the pastry with the end of a sharp knife and bake in the oven for 8 minutes, until it is golden. Then whisk all the ingredients for the mayonnaise dressing together and put to one side.

Tie the asparagus into small bundles and stand upright in an asparagus kettle or in a tall, covered saucepan. The asparagus should stand shoulder high in the water so that the heads steam while the stems cook. Boil for about 4-7 minutes, depending on the thickness of the asparagus.

Cut off the tips of the asparagus, leaving 2½in (65mm) of stalk attached. The rest can be saved and eaten separately or used for soup. Fill the cases with the asparagus spears and add a skinned orange segment for decoration to each one.

Arrange the tartlets on 4 serving plates and pour a little orange mayonnaise over each. Garnish with lettuce and trickle a little orange juice over the leaves. If you are not serving these savoury snacks immediately, store in the refrigerator.

Delicate asparagus and orange tartlets will decorate a buffet table or make beautiful canapés.

Cherry and Vanilla Gâteau

This luxurious cake is made with black cherries and a clear fruit brandy called Kirsch. Ideally you will need a 10in (250mm) expanding cake tin, and a deep 9in (230mm) loose-bottom, round cake tin for this recipe. If possible, use fresh cherries for decoration.

MAKES 8-10 slices
PREPARATION TIME : *40 minutes*
CHILLING TIME : *3 hours*
COOKING TIME : *25 minutes*
OVEN : *Preheat to 180°C (350°F, gas mark 4)*

INGREDIENTS
SPONGE CAKE
3 medium eggs
3oz (75g) caster sugar
3oz (75g) plain flour
FILLING
2 × 14oz (400g) tins pitted black cherries
2 tablespoons Kirsch
6 teaspoons gelatine
10oz (275g) thick Greek yoghurt
4oz (115g) low-fat natural yoghurt
2 teaspoons natural vanilla essence
4 medium eggs
3oz (75g) caster sugar
2oz (50g) plain chocolate for garnish
2oz (50g) thick Greek yoghurt for topping
1 teaspoon icing sugar

Calories per serving : 255 · High in protein from eggs and yoghurt · Low in fat

Grease and flour a 10in (250mm) expanding cake tin, and line the base with greaseproof paper. To make the sponge, whisk the eggs and sugar together until pale and thick. Sift the flour over the mixture and fold it in carefully with a spoon or spatula.

Pour the mixture into the tin and bake for 25 minutes. Turn onto a rack to cool. Cut the sponge into two layers. Line the base of a round 9in (230mm), loose-bottom cake tin with two layers of greaseproof paper. Fit one sponge layer into the tin.

Chocolate cherries garnish a light, creamy gâteau.

Drain the tinned cherries and cut them in half. Reserve 10 tinned or fresh cherries for decoration, put the rest into a bowl with the Kirsch.

Put 5 tablespoons of cold water into a saucepan and sprinkle the gelatine evenly over the surface. Leave to stand until it swells and turns opaque.

In a large bowl, mix the yoghurts and vanilla essence. Separate the eggs and whisk the whites until stiff, then gradually whisk in the caster sugar.

Gently heat the gelatine until it has completely dissolved and becomes hot. Whisk it into the yoghurt mixture and gently fold in the egg whites. Fold in the cherries and pour the mixture onto the sponge in the cake tin. Level the surface and place the other sponge on top. Refrigerate for 2-3 hours, until set.

Slowly melt the chocolate in a double-boiler or bowl resting above a pan of simmering water. Then dip each cherry in the chocolate, place them on greaseproof paper and refrigerate for 1 hour.

Run a palette knife around the side of the gâteau, remove it from the base and place on a serving plate.

Spread the remaining yoghurt over the cake, add the cherries and sprinkle them with the icing sugar.

Homemade Hazelnut and Sultana Rolls

The chopped nuts in these unusual rolls give them a crunchy texture. They taste delicious served warm for breakfast with honey, or as a high-fibre accompaniment to savoury dishes and salads.

MAKES 12 rolls
PREPARATION TIME : *2 hours*
COOKING TIME : *15-20 minutes*
OVEN : *Preheat to 220°C (425°F, gas mark 7)*

INGREDIENTS
1lb (450g) wholemeal flour
1 teaspoon salt
2 teaspoons caster sugar
1oz (25g) butter
1 sachet easy-blend dried yeast
or ½ oz (15g) fresh yeast
2½ oz (65g) hazelnuts
2oz (50g) sultanas

Calories per serving : 170 · High in fibre from flour
High in protein from flour and nuts

Sift the flour, salt and sugar into a large bowl, then tip any bran remaining in the sieve into the bowl. Rub the butter into the flour. Add easy-blend yeast to the flour and mix well, or dissolve the fresh yeast in ½ pint (285ml) of tepid water. Make a well in the centre of the flour and either pour in the water and yeast or ½ pint (285ml) of plain tepid water. Mix to

Elegant vegetable soup makes a refreshing snack or starter with warm hazelnut and sultana rolls.

form a dough. On a lightly floured surface, knead for 10 minutes, until the dough feels smooth.

Place the dough in a clean bowl, cover with plastic film and leave in a warm place for about 1 hour until the dough has doubled in size. Chop the hazelnuts.

Turn the risen dough onto a lightly floured surface and flatten the air bubbles out of it. Re-knead for 2-3 minutes, then flatten again. Place the sultanas and 2oz (50g) of the hazelnuts in the centre and bring the edges of the dough over to enclose them. Knead until the fruit and nuts are evenly distributed.

Grease a baking sheet and divide the dough into 12 balls. Arrange the balls on the sheet and loosely cover with plastic film. Leave in a warm place for about 2 hours, until the rolls have doubled in size.

Brush the rolls with a little cold water or milk and sprinkle with the remaining nuts. Sift a little flour over the tops and bake for 15-20 minutes, until the rolls are golden-brown. Cool on wire racks.

Chilled Vegetable Soup

This cold soup can be made in five minutes, but it looks sophisticated and tastes delicious. Cartons of vegetable juice are sold in supermarkets and grocers, but tomato juice can be used as an alternative.

SERVES 4-6
PREPARATION TIME : *5 minutes*
CHILLING TIME : *2 hours or overnight*

INGREDIENTS
1 pint (570ml) low-fat natural yoghurt
1 pint (570ml) carton vegetable or tomato juice
2 cloves garlic
¼ pint (150ml) semi-skimmed milk
¼ cucumber for garnish
Small sprigs of fresh thyme for garnish

Calories per serving : 90 · Low in fat and
cholesterol · High in fibre from vegetables

Peel and crush the garlic. Thoroughly whisk all the ingredients together in a bowl until smooth. Chill in the refrigerator for at least 2 hours or overnight.

Whisk the soup quickly before serving. Garnish with thin slices of cucumber and thyme sprigs.

Fresh mushrooms with spinach and smoked haddock with potatoes make really tasty fillings for sandwiches.

Mushroom and Fresh Spinach Sandwiches

Fresh, raw spinach is nutritious and extremely tasty in both salads and sandwiches. It complements raw mushrooms very well. Add a mashed anchovy to these sandwiches for extra taste, if you like.

··

SERVES 4

PREPARATION TIME : *15 minutes*

··

INGREDIENTS
6oz (175g) mushrooms
4 spring onions
4oz (115g) young spinach
2 sticks celery
8 slices brown bread
DRESSING
1 tablespoon virgin olive oil
1 teaspoon white wine vinegar
¼ teaspoon smooth French mustard

··

Calories per serving : 180 · High in fibre from bread and vegetables · High in iron from spinach

··

Wash and slice the mushrooms and place them in a bowl. Mix the ingredients for the dressing together, pour the mixture over the mushrooms and stir well.

Trim the spring onions, and finely chop the bulb and about 3in (80mm) of the green stalk. Wash the spinach carefully and remove any damaged leaves and tough stalks or veins. Chop the celery and mash the anchovy, if desired.

Place a layer of spinach and celery on 4 slices of bread and top with a generous helping of mushrooms and spring onions. Sprinkle any remaining dressing over the sandwiches and close them with the remaining slices of bread.

Smoked Haddock and New Potato Sandwiches

Choose a firm brown bread, such as granary or oatmeal, for this filling snack. Fish, potatoes and salad greens provide a complete meal in a sandwich for lunchtime or picnics. The dressing is low in calories and very simple to make. Buy ready-smoked haddock fillets from a supermarket or from your local fishmonger. Try serving the sandwiches with apple or grape juice mixed with sparkling water.

SERVES 4
PREPARATION TIME : *10 minutes*
COOKING TIME : *15-20 minutes*

INGREDIENTS
8oz (225g) smoked haddock
6oz (175g) new potatoes
¼ pint (150ml) milk
4 spring onions
½ Webb's lettuce
or 1 Little Gem lettuce
8 slices firm wholemeal bread
1 tablespoon fresh chopped parsley
DRESSING
2 tablespoons low-calorie mayonnaise
1½ teaspoons smooth French mustard

Calories per serving : 280 · High in fibre from bread
High in protein from haddock, milk and potatoes

Scrub the new potatoes clean. Bring a saucepan of salted water to the boil, add the potatoes and cook for 15-20 minutes, until tender. Drain and cool.

Put the haddock in a pan large enough for it to lie flat. Add the milk and just enough water to cover the fish and gently bring to the boil, then turn the heat down and simmer gently for 5 minutes, until the fish is moist but flakes easily. Lift the fish from the pan, pour away the liquid, or keep it for a soup.

Trim the spring onions, and finely chop the bulb and about 3in (80mm) of the green stalk. Wash and dry the lettuce and chop it into shreds.

Mix the mayonnaise and mustard. Spread the mixture on each slice of bread. Slice the potatoes.

Cover 4 slices of bread with the lettuce, haddock and potatoes and sprinkle with spring onions and parsley. Close the sandwiches and cut diagonally.

Mangetout with Cottage Cheese

The flavour of these tender, edible pea pods (known as snow peas) is preserved by keeping the steaming time down to a minimum. Prepare the mangetout by trimming the tips and removing the strings.

These crispy mangetout canapés can also be served as an elegant starter at a dinner party.

SERVES 4
PREPARATION TIME : *40 minutes*
COOKING TIME : *1 minute*

INGREDIENTS
8oz (225g) large-sized mangetout
7-8 anchovy fillets
12oz (350g) cottage cheese
Salt and freshly ground black pepper

Calories per serving : 135 · Low in calories, fat and cholesterol · High in protein from anchovy

Cut the anchovy fillets into halves and leave to soak for 20 minutes to remove excess salt. Prepare the mangetout and place them in a large steaming basket set over boiling water. Steam for 1 minute, then rinse immediately under cold running water. Chop the anchovies into small pieces. Drain any liquid from the cottage cheese and then mix the anchovies into it, seasoning to taste.

Using a sharp knife, take each mangetout and cut away a sliver along the whole length of the pod on one side, and then ease open. Fill the mangetout carefully with the anchovy-flavoured cottage cheese by pressing it in with a pointed knife or using a piping bag. Dust with pepper and serve.

Jacket potatoes filled with crunchy lemon coleslaw and served with refreshing traditional lemonade.

Jacket Potatoes with Lemon Coleslaw

Cabbage, the main ingredient of coleslaw, was eaten with vinegar before and after a feast by the Greeks and Romans to aid digestion. Choose a cabbage with a firm head for this recipe.

SERVES 4
PREPARATION TIME : *20 minutes*
COOKING TIME : *1½ hours*
OVEN : *Preheat to 200°C (400°F, gas mark 6)*

INGREDIENTS
4 large baking potatoes
½ tablespoon virgin olive oil
COLESLAW
8oz (225g) white cabbage
4oz (115g) carrots
1 small onion
1 lemon
2oz (50g) salted peanuts
2 tablespoons chopped parsley
1 tablespoon virgin olive oil
Freshly ground black pepper

Calories per serving : 440 · High in fibre and vitamin C from vegetables and protein from potato and nuts

Wash the cabbage head and trim any wilted leaves and tough stem end. Cut into wedges and remove the core, then cut the leaves into fine shreds with a large, wide knife. Peel and grate the carrots. Finely chop the onion. Peel and finely grate the lemon rind and squeeze 2 tablespoons of juice. Put all the coleslaw ingredients into a bowl and season with pepper.

Scrub the potatoes and prick them in several places with a fork. Rub each one with a little oil and cook on a baking sheet in the centre of the oven, turning once, until done.

Cut the cooked potatoes almost in half, diagonally. Gently pull apart and fill with the coleslaw.

Old-fashioned Homemade Lemonade

This simple drink is easy to make, refreshing and full of vitamin C. It is not as sweet and heavy as most shop-bought lemonades and is free from artificial colours and flavours. You may need a few extra lemons to make up the amount as they vary in size.

SERVES 8
PREPARATION TIME : *20 minutes*
STANDING AND CHILLING TIME : *2½ hours*

INGREDIENTS
10 large lemons
4oz (115g) caster sugar
1 lime
Sprigs of mint for decoration

Calories per serving : 65 · Cholesterol free

Pare the rind from 9 of the lemons using a vegetable peeler. Take care to avoid the white pith. Squeeze out and strain the juice to make up ¾ pint (450ml).

Put the lemon rind into a large, heatproof bowl, add the sugar and pour in 2½ pints (1.4 litres) of boiling water. Stir until the sugar dissolves, then cover and leave to stand for 30 minutes.

Strain the lemon liquid into a large jug and stir in the lemon juice. Cover and refrigerate for about 2 hours, until it is really well chilled.

Place a big block of ice or ice cubes into a large

serving jug. Cut the remaining lemon and the lime into slices and add to the jug. Pour the lemonade into the jug and decorate with mint leaves.

This lemonade will keep in the refrigerator for a week, but avoid adding any ice before storing as this will dilute the flavour.

Wholemeal Pizza Baps

Wholemeal baps or large rolls provide the perfect, ready-made base for these healthy mini pizzas. They are quick and easy to make – as a filling snack with a tossed green salad, or for a party.

SERVES 4
PREPARATION TIME : *20 minutes*
COOKING TIME : *5 minutes*

INGREDIENTS
4 wholemeal baps
1 clove garlic
1oz (25g) butter or sunflower margarine
1 tablespoon chopped parsley
Salt and freshly ground black pepper
2 large beef tomatoes
2 teaspoons mixed dried herbs
4oz (115g) grated Mozzarella cheese
8 black olives
2oz (50g) can anchovy fillets
2 tablespoons chopped chives

Calories per serving : 510 · High in protein and calcium from baps, cheese and anchovies

Cut each bap in half and place on a large grill rack with the cut sides uppermost. Crush the garlic and blend the butter or margarine and parsley together with the garlic, then season with salt and pepper. Spread the mixture over each bap.

Cut 8 large, round slices from the tomatoes and place a slice on each bap. Season lightly and sprinkle with the herbs, then the cheese.

Cook the pizzas under a hot grill, until the cheese melts and browns slightly. Halve and stone the olives and use them to top the pizzas along with thin strips of anchovy fillets. Sprinkle with chives and serve immediately.

Healthy Strawberry Milkshakes

Raspberry, banana, blackberry and pineapple are some of the other flavours that you can make by substituting fresh fruits for the strawberries in this recipe. You will need a blender or food processor.

SERVES 4
PREPARATION TIME : *10 minutes*

INGREDIENTS
12oz (350g) fresh strawberries
1½ tablespoons caster sugar
1 pint (570ml) chilled skimmed or semi-skimmed milk
½ pint (285ml) natural low-fat yoghurt

Calories per serving : 130 · Low in fat · High in protein and calcium from milk and yoghurt

Chill 4 glasses. Reserve 4 strawberries for decoration and put the rest into a food processor or blender and sprinkle with the sugar. If possible, leave to stand for 20 minutes before puréeing the mixture. Pass the purée through a nylon sieve to remove seeds.

Return mixture to the food processor and add the milk and yoghurt. Blend on a high speed for 1 minute. Pour into the chilled glasses, decorate with the remaining strawberries and serve immediately.

Low-fat strawberry milkshakes and simple but tasty wholemeal pizza baps give children a healthy treat.

Provençal Sandwich

French bread sticks make excellent snacks when they are filled with garlic, herbs, ripe tomatoes, olives, olive oil and all the other flavours of Provence in the South of France. They are especially good for picnics, as they are best made several hours in advance to allow the flavours to mingle. Buy fresh, crusty bread for this recipe and, if the weather is good, eat them outside with a bottle of French wine.

The Mediterranean tastes of olives, garlic, anchovies, peppers and herbs served in crusty French bread with fresh fruit and wine to make the perfect picnic.

SERVES 4-6
PREPARATION TIME : *25 minutes*
COOKING TIME : *15-20 minutes*

INGREDIENTS
1 long French stick
1 red pepper
1 clove garlic
1lb (450g) ripe tomatoes
4oz (115g) stoned black olives
4fl oz (115ml) virgin olive oil
1¾ oz (45g) tin anchovy fillets
3 tablespoons capers (optional)
1 tablespoon fresh shredded basil

Calories per serving : 435 · High in vitamin C from tomatoes · High in protein from bread and anchovies · Low in cholesterol

Place the whole pepper on a baking tray and cook under a hot grill for 15-20 minutes, turning once, until the skin becomes blackened and charred. Remove from the grill, allow to cool, then halve and de-seed the pepper, peel away the skin and cut the flesh into thin strips.

Peel and halve the garlic clove, slice the tomatoes and halve the olives. Cut the French stick in half lengthways, using a sharp bread knife. Rub inside the bread with the cut sides of the garlic clove. Sprinkle each half of bread with the olive oil.

Drain the anchovy fillets and arrange them over the bread. Lay the tomato slices and the pepper strips over the anchovies and scatter over the olives, capers, if used, and finally the fresh shredded basil. Sandwich the bread back together and wrap it tightly in foil until required. Serve in thick slices.

Blue Brie and Radicchio Sandwiches

Tangy blue Brie, crunchy celery and the slightly bitter taste of radicchio make a filling, tasty and healthy snack. Watercress can also be added, or used as a substiute for the radicchio. No butter is really needed on the bread because the Brie is so rich.

INGREDIENTS
2 sticks celery
4 large leaves radicchio
1 small bunch watercress (optional)
1oz (25g) butter (optional)
8 slices wholemeal, rye or poppy seed bread
6oz (175g) ripe blue Brie

Calories per serving : 260 · High in fibre from bread
High in protein from Brie and bread

Wash and dry the celery, radicchio and optional watercress. Butter the bread sparingly, if desired. Add the radicchio to 4 of the slices. Slice the cheese in long thin pieces and arrange over the radicchio. Cut the celery stalks into matchsticks and arrange them over the cheese and finally add the watercress, if desired. Top with the remaining slices of bread and press down firmly. Using a sharp knife, carefully cut each sandwich into triangles.

Blackberry Champagne

This simple fruit syrup uses less than one-third of the sugar normally found in shop-bought syrups, while retaining a full fruit flavour. For special occasions, dilute the syrup with sparkling white wine or champagne. The syrup is also delicious with water or sparkling mineral water. You can also use raspberries and blackcurrants in this recipe.

SERVES 30 glasses
PREPARATION TIME : *10 minutes*
COOKING TIME : *20 minutes*

INGREDIENTS
1lb (450g) fresh or frozen blackberries
3-4oz (75-115g) caster sugar
Chilled sparkling white wine or champagne

Calories per serving : 95 · High in vitamin C from
blackberries

In the summer, low-sugar blackberry champagne is perfect for parties and special occasions, and tangy Brie and basil sandwiches make a tasty light snack.

Wash the berries and remove the hulls. Place them in a bowl over a saucepan of simmering water. Heat gently for about 20 minutes, until the juices flow freely from the fruit. From time to time, crush the berries with a vegetable masher.

Pour the fruit and juice into a sieve over a clean bowl. Leave for 5-10 minutes to allow the juice to drain. Gently press down on the fruit to extract any remaining juice, but do not push the fruit through.

Add the sugar to the juice and return to the saucepan of hot water. Stir thoroughly until every granule of sugar has dissolved. Allow to cool, then pour the juice into a clean jar or bottle and cover with a tightly fitting lid.

This syrup must be kept in the refrigerator and will store for up to a month. When ready, dilute to taste with chilled sparkling wine, mineral water or champagne and serve immediately.

Mixed Nut Cake

Amaretto, a sweet Italian almond-flavoured liqueur, gives this sustaining cake extra flavour. Muscovado is a dark, unrefined sugar which brings the sweet rich taste of molasses to the cake. You will need an 8in (200mm) cake tin for this recipe.

MAKES 16-24 slices
PREPARATION TIME : *30 minutes*
COOKING TIME : *1 hour 40 minutes*
OVEN : *Preheat to 180°C (350°F, gas mark 4)*

INGREDIENTS
8oz (225g) butter or margarine
4oz (115g) pistachio nuts
4oz (115g) muscovado sugar
4oz (115g) caster sugar
4 medium eggs
2 tablespoons Amaretto (optional)
6oz (175g) plain flour
6oz (175g) plain wholemeal flour
1 teaspoon baking powder
3oz (75g) chopped brazil nuts
3oz (75g) chopped hazelnuts
4oz (115g) chopped walnuts
TOPPING
4oz (115g) pecan nuts
2oz (50g) blanched almonds
1 tablespoon apricot jam

*Calories per serving : 360 · High in protein
from nuts, flour and eggs*

Line the cake tin with baking paper greased with butter or margarine. Shell the pistachio nuts. Mix the rest of the butter or margarine with the sugars in a bowl, until light and fluffy. Mix in the eggs, one at a time, beating well after each addition. Beat in the Amaretto and sift in the flours along with the baking powder, adding the bran left in the sieve. Add the nuts and mix thoroughly.

Spoon the cake mixture into the baking tin and smooth the surface with a spatula. Arrange the pecans and almonds in rings on the top.

Bake in the centre of the oven for 40 minutes, then reduce the oven temperature to 160°C (325°F, gas mark 3) and continue cooking for 1 hour, until the cake has risen and is lightly browned. A skewer should come out clean from the centre of the cake.

Heat the apricot jam in a saucepan until boiling hot, then pass it through a sieve. Brush the jam over the top of the cake on removal from the oven.

Leave the cake in the tin for 15 minutes, then transfer to a wire rack to finish cooling.

Chocolate Almond Cake

This rich cake is lower in calories than many shop-bought cakes and makes a treat for chocolate lovers. It is better to undercook than overcook it, as moist, sticky chocolate cake is quite delicious. You will need a liquidiser for this recipe.

SERVES 8
PREPARATION TIME : *40 minutes*
COOLING TIME : *2 hours*
COOKING TIME : *30 minutes*
OVEN : *Preheat to 180°C (350°F, gas mark 4)*

INGREDIENTS
1 tablespoon instant coffee
4oz (115g) plain chocolate
4oz (115g) butter
4oz (115g) caster sugar
3 eggs
2 tablespoons marmalade
3oz (75g) blanched almonds
¼ teaspoon almond essence
Salt
2oz (50g) plain flour
ICING
½ tablespoon instant coffee
2oz (50g) plain chocolate
2oz (50g) unsalted butter

Calories per serving : 390 · High in protein from nuts

Fill the bottom of a double-boiler or pan with water and bring to a simmer. Butter an 8in (200mm) cake tin and dust it with flour. Mix the tablespoon of coffee with 1 tablespoon of boiling water. Place the coffee with the chocolate in the boiler or in a bowl which fits inside the rim of a saucepan without touching the water and slowly melt the chocolate until it is completely smooth, then set it aside.

Soften the butter with a fork and mix it with all but 1 teaspoon of the sugar until creamy. Separate the eggs and beat the yolks and the marmalade into the butter mixture and leave to one side.

Toast the almonds in the oven for 5 minutes, until they begin to colour. Remove from the oven, allow to cool and grind in a liquidiser to a fine consistency.

Stir the melted chocolate into the butter mixture and mix in the almond essence with all but 2 tablespoons of the ground almonds.

Beat the egg whites with a pinch of salt, until soft peaks begin to form. Sprinkle on the remaining sugar. Beat again until stiff and set aside.

With a rubber spatula, fold ⅓ of the egg whites into the butter mixture. Sift ⅓ of the flour over the mixture and fold in. Repeat this process twice.

Scrape the mixture into the cake tin and bake for 25-30 minutes in the oven. The centre of the cake should still be soft when cooked. Remove from the oven and allow to cool for 10 minutes. Turn onto a wire rack and cool for 2 hours before icing.

To make the icing, mix ½ tablespoon of coffee with ½ tablespoon of boiling water. Then melt the chocolate with the coffee as before, stirring until creamy. Remove from the heat and gradually beat in the butter. Allow the icing to cool until it is thick enough to spread over the cake. Dust with the remaining ground almonds.

These nut cakes taste wonderful but are lower in fat and richer in protein than their shop-bought counterparts.

Tasty sandwiches for picnics and special occasions.

Celeriac, Apple and Walnut Sandwiches

These crunchy vegetarian sandwiches are delicious served on their own, or with added cooked chicken or turkey as a filling snack. The lemon mayonnaise brings out the freshness of the celeriac.

SERVES 4-6
PREPARATION TIME : *10 minutes*

INGREDIENTS
½ celeriac
4oz (115g) fresh spinach
2 Cox's or 1 large red apple
1 teaspoon lemon juice
12 slices firm brown bread
3oz (75g) chopped walnuts
4oz (115g) cooked chicken or turkey
DRESSING
2 tablespoons low-calorie mayonnaise
2 teaspoons lemon juice

Calories per serving : 290 · High in fibre from apples, bread and nuts · High in iron from spinach

Peel and grate the celeriac to make about 5oz (150g) of filling. Wash the spinach and throw away any damaged leaves or tough stalks. Core and thinly slice the apples, then sprinkle them with lemon juice.

For the dressing, mix the mayonnaise with the lemon juice and spread onto each slice of bread. Scatter a few leaves of spinach on 6 of the slices, followed by the celeriac, walnuts and apple slices. Cut the chicken or turkey into strips and add it to the sandwiches, if required, then close the sandwiches and cut them into triangles.

Salmon and Caviar Sandwiches

The dark colour of rye bread creates a striking visual contrast in these impressive open sandwiches. Its slightly sour taste blends especially well with the fish and the dill mayonnaise. Lumpfish roe looks just as pretty and tastes almost as good as real caviar.

SERVES 4
PREPARATION TIME : *20 minutes*

INGREDIENTS
4 slices of rye bread
6oz (175g) sliced smoked salmon
2 tablespoons crème fraîche
2 teaspoons caviar or lumpfish roe
Fresh dill sprigs for garnish
DILL MAYONNAISE
1½ tablespoons low-calorie mayonnaise
1 teaspoon smooth French mustard
1 tablespoon lemon juice
3 tablespoons chopped fresh dill
Salt and freshly ground black pepper
½ teaspoon caster sugar

Calories per serving : 160 · High in protein from salmon · Low in fat and cholesterol

Mix the ingredients for the dill mayonnaise together and spread the dressing over the bread. Layer the salmon on each slice, add ½ tablespoon of crème fraîche in the centre, and top with caviar or lumpfish roe and a sprig of fresh dill.

Food and Your Body

The body needs many different nutrients from a wide variety of foods, and to be healthy it needs them in fairly precise amounts. Inevitably, people eat too much of some nutrients and too little of others – in other words they do not have a balanced diet. In order to plan a balanced diet it helps to understand what our food is made of.

The Nutrients in Our Food

Food's nutritional components can be split up into those that we need to eat a lot of (macronutrients), and those we only need in very small quantities (micronutrients). There are three sorts of macro-nutrients: proteins, fats and carbohydrates. These provide us with our day-to-day energy, and enable the body to grow, repair and maintain itself. There are only two kinds of micronutrients – vitamins and minerals – and these enable the body to carry out specific functions such as digesting food, helping the nervous system work, and maintaining the right levels of important chemicals in the blood.

Dietary fibre (also called roughage) from plants has no nutritional value, but helps to maintain good health by adding bulk to the diet and pushing waste products through the system.

Finally, water is of course also essential to our diet – over 60 per cent of the body is composed of this vital fluid, which it uses for all its functions.

Nutritionists have identified about 40 different essential nutrients that the diet has to provide regularly (though not necessarily daily) in the right amounts and proportions for good health, and life itself. We need proteins, fats, carbohydrates, vitamins and minerals in order to sustain a healthy and active body. An understanding of what our food is made of, and which foods belong to which category, will help us to work out our optimum needs and get the balance right. Healthy eating follows naturally.

Proteins

Proteins are involved in thousands of the body's vital functions, including the growth, maintenance and repair of cells. It is used to form about 17 per cent of the body (muscle and bone, skin, hair and nails) and to produce many enzymes and hormones that keep the body working efficiently.

If the body is not getting enough carbohydrates or fats to meet all its energy needs, proteins can be broken down and used as a source of energy – but they are really far too valuable for tissue building and repair to be used in this way.

Proteins are the most complex of all the food compounds; built up of a mixture of more than 20 amino acids – molecules containing carbon, hydrogen, oxygen, nitrogen, and other constituents.

Eight of these amino acids can only be obtained through food and so must be present in the diet. The body uses the amino acids to make its own proteins and any excess is then returned to the liver for energy use, storage or elimination.

Eating a variety of different protein foods will ensure that you get enough of each amino acid, especially of the eight essential ones. Combining different foods (such as beans or pulses with grains) usually makes the proteins easier for the body to use.

The main dietary sources of protein are meat, poultry, fish, shellfish, eggs, cheese, yoghurt, milk, pulses (beans, peas and lentils), nuts, potatoes, bread and cereals (pasta), rice, oats and rye. Variety is important for people who eat no animal foods. Pulses and cereals are complementary proteins that are often combined in vegetarian and vegan diets to ensure a proper balance of amino acids. Vegans must take special care to get their protein from dried pulses, bread, potatoes, porridge, rice and vegetables. Protein deficiency is rare in the average Western diet. Exceptions include slimmers on some peculiar diets, old people who have lost interest in food, and individuals who are careless of themselves and who do not bother to eat properly. Too little protein, a problem in developing countries, can lead to a breakdown of muscle tissue. Too much can put a strain on the liver and the kidneys, as well as reducing the mineral balance in the body.

The average British intake of protein is well above the RDA (Recommended Daily Amount), and so most people need have no concern about getting enough. Do not be beguiled by processed foods advertised as being 'protein-rich'.

Fats

The relationship of fats to health is often misunderstood; many people believe that fats are something to be avoided at all costs. Although it is true that a very fatty diet leads to obesity – with its many attendant health risks – fats are still an essential part of our diet. They are a principal source of energy and play a vital role in bodily functions.

All fats contain a mixture of different fatty acids: saturated fatty acids which come mainly from animal fats, and are solid at room temperature (such as butter and lard), and unsaturated fatty acids which come from vegetable (such as olive oil) and fish oils, and are generally liquid at room temperature. There are two vegetable oils that are rich in saturated fats – coconut and palm oil.

An excess of saturated fats can lead to a harmful increase in the amount of cholesterol circulating in the blood. Cholesterol is needed for a healthy brain and nervous system, and for the production of hormones, but too much can create a risk of heart disease if your diet and health are already poor.

Eating oily fish regularly is now thought to help to prevent heart disease by keeping arteries clear.

There are two 'essential' fatty acids important to health that need to be supplied by the food we eat. All unsaturated vegetable oils such as sunflower, safflower and soya bean are good sources of these.

If an oil is labelled 'cold pressed' or 'virgin' it has come from the first pressing which is carried out at a low temperature, and is of a better quality. This distinction is important with olive oil which is graded according to acidity. Extra virgin olive oil is considered the best as it has the lowest acidity.

'Britain is starting to eat less fat. Since 1983 our consumption of whole milk has actually dropped by over 20%, and has been replaced by a healthier preference for skimmed and semi-skimmed milk.'

A moderate amount of fat is needed in everyone's diet. According to the British Medical Association, 30-35 per cent of all our calories should come from fats – but the current figure is 40 per cent. We have the highest incidence of heart disease in the world, and this is due largely to too much saturated fat, and probably too much sodium.

We get most of our fats from margarine, butter, cooking fats and oils, meat, milk, cheese, eggs, and from 'hidden' fats in cakes, biscuits and crisps.

How to Reduce Fats Fats are a very concentrated form of energy, and it is easy to get too much of them. Aim for a moderate intake and cut down on saturated animal fats.

■ Cut down on high-fat meats (such as sausages, bacon, lamb chops and minced beef), dairy products (especially cream and hard cheeses), eggs, peanuts and peanut butter.

■ Buy lean cuts of meat and trim visible fat. Poultry has little fat with the flesh, but the skin is fatty and should be removed before sautéing, grilling or casseroling, and after roasting. Game is lean meat.

■ Eat more fish. White fish is low in fat, and oily fish such as herring, mackerel, trout and salmon are rich in an unsaturated oil, not widely available in other foods, which helps to prevent heart attacks.

■ Choose cottage cheese, Camembert, Brie and reduced-fat cheeses in place of fattier varieties such as Cheddar and Stilton. Substitute skimmed and semi-skimmed milk in recipes and for drinking. Use yoghurt or single cream instead of double cream.

Use butter, margarines and even low-fat spreads sparingly. Only use soft margarines made from sunflower or soya oils which are labelled as being 'high in polyunsaturates'. Other margarines may have started out being high in polyunsaturates, but they have been through heat or chemical processes which harden and saturate the oils.

Use less cooking fat, oil, salad oil, mayonnaise, or other high-fat salad dressings and sauces.

Avoid fried food. Use low-fat cooking methods such as grilling, roasting, stewing and baking. Steam or boil where possible.

If you do fry chips or other foods occasionally, cut them into large pieces. Drain off as much fat as possible after cooking, and pat off excess oil with kitchen paper before serving. Never reuse oil, as reheating it makes it saturated.

Always skim any fat off the top of casseroles, curries, soups and stews before serving them.

Try to have chocolate, cakes, pastries, biscuits and crisps only occasionally, and to include more fruits and vegetables in your diet.

Carbohydrates

Carbohydrates provide energy for both physical and mental exertion. They are present in large amounts in cereals, bread, rice, pasta and potatoes, and are also found in fruits, vegetables and some dairy products. The sugars, starches and cellulose (main component of fibre) in foods are all different forms of carbohydrates. Starchy carbohydrate foods are excellent sources of energy and essential nutrients, while sugar sweeteners have no nutritional value, apart from providing calories.

Sugar

The body breaks both sugar and starch down into glucose sugar for energy, but whereas starch is a nutritional requirement of the body, sugar is not. Table sugar (called sucrose) is a popular part of our

everyday lives simply because we like the taste of sweet food, but it contains only calories, and no nutrients. Although it is obtained from sugar cane and sugar beets, it is produced by a complex refining process which robs the beets and cane of their nutrients. Even brown sugar, which many people think of as being healthy, is chemically almost identical to white table sugar.

Natural sugars such as the fructose and glucose found in fruits, lactose found in milk, and maltose found in grain, are packaged with vitamins and minerals, and so are more acceptable forms of sugar. But all sugars are more or less equal in calorie content, and their only benefit is to provide us with a source of 'quick energy'.

Excess sugar consumption leads to obesity and tooth decay, but it has not been proven to cause

'The average person in Britain consumes about 77lb (35kg) of added sugar in their diet each year.'

diabetes or coronary heart disease, as some have claimed. Being easily digestible, sweet foods and sugar, especially glucose, are useful for people who have difficulty eating (the sick, the convalescent, the elderly) and people who need sudden 'top ups' of energy, such as endurance athletes. But any sugar that is not used as a source of energy is stored as fat.

How to Reduce Sugar In large quantities sugar is fattening, causes tooth decay, and can even become addictive. Here are some ways to cut down.

The palate adjusts quickly to less sweet food. Persevere for a few days and things will soon get easier. Try not to use artificial sweeteners; they will simply reinforce your craving for sweetness.

Use less packet sugar in drinks, with breakfast cereals, and when cooking. If you can, persist to the point where you can do without it altogether. When cooking, you might try other flavourings, such as cinnamon, ginger or lemon.

Watch out for 'hidden sugars' in foods like tinned soup and vegetables, cakes, pastries, biscuits, 'frosted' breakfast cereals, chocolates and sweets. Look on the label for the calorie content and any mention of added sugars such as dextrose, fructose, glucose, lactose, maltose and sucrose.

■ Many drinks – fizzy drinks, colas, squashes and even juices – contain large amounts of added sugar. Drink mineral water, unsweetened herb teas, milk, or low-calorie drinks instead.

■ Cut down on jam, marmalade, lemon curd, honey and tinned pie fillings. Instead of tinned fruit in syrup, use fresh fruit or fruit tinned in juice.

Starch

Starches are a major component of cereals, flour, pulses and vegetables. They once acquired an unfair reputation for not being good for you, but bread, pasta, rice and porridge are now regaining popularity as energy foods. Starchy foods should make up at least 55 per cent of our total energy intake.

Obviously you should choose unsweetened and unrefined foods. Grains, pulses, vegetables and fruits provide a steady stream of energy when eaten

----

'Pasta is a popular endurance food with athletes in stamina-based sports as it offers a slow and steady release of energy to the body. It is well-balanced nutritionally and not very fattening.'

----

in as natural a state as possible, and they contain vitamins, minerals and protein, as well as plenty of fibre. Potatoes, sweetcorn, turnips, beans, peas and lentils are an excellent source of starch.

How to Eat More Starch Starchy energy foods are not fattening when eaten in moderation, and should make up most of your daily carbohydrate intake.

■ Eat more bread but less spread. Cut thicker slices.

■ Eat more boiled and baked potatoes, but try to use any margarine and butter toppings very sparingly. Experiment with yoghurt, cottage cheese, low-fat toppings, and gherkins. Cut down on roast, sauté and thinly chipped potatoes. If you must eat chips, they have less fat when they are thickly cut, crisp outside, and fluffy inside. Use sunflower or corn oil for the occasional times you need to do deep-frying.

■ Eat more beans, peas and lentils. They are good sources of healthy starch, as well as providing useful amounts of protein and other essential nutrients.

Salt

Salt (sodium chloride) is a micronutrient containing the minerals sodium and chlorine. It is a vital dietary ingredient and a popular additive. We need to replace what we lose in urine, faeces and sweat, but too much can be as harmful as too little. Although it is an essential nutrient, if taken in excess the sodium in salt can cause health problems. People who are especially sensitive to sodium can respond with rises in blood pressure which can lead to stroke, heart disease and kidney failure.

The recommended daily amount of sodium is no more than 6g (about ¼oz) per person a day. Present intake is high – on average about 9g (⅓oz). Many foods contain salt or other forms of sodium naturally, and substantial amounts of sodium are added to processed foods, mainly as a preservative or flavouring. Fortunately, an increasing demand for low-sodium products has led to many manufacturers reducing the amount of salt in many processed foods.

How to Reduce Salt Consumption Your salt intake builds up over the day to a surprising extent – be aware that many common prepared foods add little by little to the total.

■ Cut down on the use of salt in cooking or at the table, as this accounts for about a third of our intake.

■ Season food with garlic, herbs, spices, freshly ground black pepper or lemon juice. The palate usually adjusts quickly to a reduction in salt in food.

■ Check food labels for the following ingredients: sodium nitrite (a curing agent and a preservative), sodium benzoate (a preservative), monosodium glutamate (a flavour enhancer), sodium bicarbonate (baking soda, a leavening agent).

■ If you want to avoid salt or cut it down, check labels to see how high salt or sodium is on the list.

The following products have added salt or sodium: salted meat and fish; processed and tinned meats; vegetables, olives and fish canned in brine; canned and dried soups; tomato juice; salad dressings; some breakfast cereals; ice cream and cakes.

Fibre – Nature's Broom

Dietary fibre from plant foods (cereals, leafy and root vegetables, fruits, salads, beans, peas and other pulses) helps to get rid of waste products left after digestion, by sweeping them through the body. Fibre has no nutritional value, and cannot be digested or absorbed, but it adds bulk to foods passing through the digestive system.

Bulk stimulates the muscular wall of the large intestine, helping to keep it in good order. The waste products then move along quickly and are eliminated regularly, reducing any strain on blood vessels and the lower bowel. The fibre itself passes virtually unchanged through our intestines, to be excreted as waste matter, making it entirely non-fattening.

Passing waste matter through our bodies quickly helps to remove any harmful substances from the body before they can cause disease; decreasing the risk of bowel disorders, as well as piles. Fibre is also important for regulating sugar absorption and the amount of cholesterol in our blood.

It is not necessary to add bran to foods in order to get enough fibre. Daily helpings of white or brown bread, oats, fresh vegetables, raw and dried fruits, and pulses will carry you to the daily fibre target of 1oz (25g). Any increase in high-fibre foods should be gradual – especially in older people – or you may experience wind and abdominal bloating while the bowels accustom themselves.

Vitamins and Minerals

Vitamins and minerals are called micronutrients because they are only needed in tiny amounts for thousands of daily bodily reactions. They work together in groups – for example, vitamin D regulates the absorption of calcium, and so both are equally important for healthy teeth and bones. All vitamins occur exclusively in living tissues and fall into two groups: water and fat-soluble. Any water-soluble vitamins are easily eliminated from the body in sweat or urine, and must therefore be replaced regularly by a balanced diet.

Our bodies cannot store the water-soluble vitamins B and C, and any excess not taken up and used by the body is passed out in the urine. For this reason we need a daily supply of these vitamins.

The fat-soluble vitamins (A, D, E and K) are less widely distributed in nature. Found in such foods as liver, fish liver oils, egg yolk, margarine and greens, they are neither soluble in water nor easily excreted. They can be stored in the liver for several days but still need to be replaced regularly.

Minerals are essential for health and growth and perform many important functions in the body, such as the formation of bones and teeth. We obtain our minerals through food, but unlike vitamins, which plants are able to manufacture, minerals have to be extracted from the earth by plants.

Once their work is done, minerals are excreted in the urine and sweat, and so they have to be replaced regularly. If you are already in good health and eat a balanced diet, vitamin and mineral supplements are not normally needed.

Micronutrients and Your Diet

Although micronutrients are essential for health, they are not elixirs of life, and have no energy value. Good health and vitality come from a balanced combination of foods – micronutrients do not usually work in isolation but as functional groups. Too much of one can interfere with the function of another, and some nutrients in excess can kill – vitamins A and D, for example. Others are harmful, though not lethal, in excess.

Many people take vitamin and mineral supplements, but these are not necessary if you are in good health and eat a balanced diet. The times when supplements may be necessary are when there are extra demands or stresses on the body, such as during pregnancy. Women taking contraceptive pills may need some extra micronutrients, as may post-menopausal women, elderly people, and anybody who smokes heavily or drinks a lot of alcohol.

What Vitamins and Minerals Do and Where They Come From

Vitamins help the body to process nutrients and combat infection and disease. The body makes some vitamins and gets others from food. Most minerals perform similar functions, while others form part of the body's structure. This chart shows which foods provide which vitamins and minerals.

Some vitamins are soluble in water, while some are soluble in fat. Water-soluble vitamins, such as B and C, cannot be stored in the body and need to be replaced daily. Fat-soluble vitamins, A, D, E and K, can be stored in the liver for approximately one week. Some minerals, such as calcium, are present

Vitamins	Major Sources	Major Functions
Fat-soluble Vitamins		
A (retinol and carotene)	Liver, fatty fish, fish liver oil, egg yolk, carrot, whole milk, margarine, butter, greens, full-fat cheese.	Bone growth; skin repair; maintenance of mucous membranes; colour and night vision; immune system.
D (calciferol)	Produced by action of sunlight on human skin; found in fish liver oil, oily fish, yeast, egg yolk, margarine.	Regulation of calcium and phosphorus for growth and maintenance of bones and teeth.
E (tocopherol)	Vegetable oil, egg yolk, nuts, seeds, peanuts, polyunsaturated margarine, wholegrains, greens.	Protection of cell membranes from damage, so may retard effects of ageing; needed for tissue handling of fatty substances; protection of vitamins A and C; skin repair.
K (phylloquinone)	Synthesised by bacteria in the large intestine; found in liver and greens.	Prevents haemorrhaging; stimulates production of substances involved in the normal blood-clotting process; processing of energy in the liver.
Water-soluble Vitamins		
B1 (thiamin)	Wheatgerm and wholegrain cereal, fortified white flour, soya flour, bread, brewer's yeast/yeast extract, meat, nuts.	Breaks down carbohydrates to provide energy, maintains healthy nervous system.
B2 (riboflavin)	Brewer's yeast/yeast extract, cheese, milk, yoghurt, meat, egg, fortified cereal, greens.	Processing of energy; forming enzymes (proteins that break down food and carry out other bodily functions); production and repair of body tissue; maintains healthy mucous membranes.
B3 Nicotinic acid (niacin)	Liver, lean meat, oily fish and tuna, brewer's yeast/yeast extract, potato, bread, fortified cereal, wheatgerm, peanuts.	Works with thiamin and riboflavin in energy-producing reactions in cells; efficient blood circulation; control of blood cholesterol; healthy skin and nervous system.
B5 (pantothenic acid)	Liver, kidney, bean, egg yolk, wholegrain cereals, wheatgerm, peanuts.	Needed by cells for energy; breaks down carbohydrates, proteins and fats; healthy skin and hair; healthy nervous and immune systems.
B6 (pyridoxine)	Liver, brewer's yeast/yeast extract, wholegrain, fatty fish, nuts, egg yolk, banana, potato, lean meat, avocado, spinach, green bean.	Processing of proteins, maintenance of nervous system; production of haemoglobin (a protein for the transportation of oxygen in red blood cells); control of body water; healthy skin.

in the body in quite large quantities – there is almost 3lb (1.4kg) of calcium in the average healthy adult. Other minerals, which can be just as important, are only needed in tiny amounts, and these are called 'trace element minerals'.

Requirements for vitamins and minerals vary from one individual to another and may change as a person gets older. Vitamins and minerals are needed in complex combinations by the body – many of them depending on the presence of other vitamins and minerals to carry out their functions. But a well-balanced diet should contain all the nutrients needed for a healthy life. The best sources are fresh or unprocessed fruit, vegetables, dairy products, cereal foods, meat and fish. Some of these nutrients can be destroyed in the processing of refined foods, and careless storage or cooking can destroy water-soluble vitamins unnecessarily. It is important to pay attention to the way food is cooked and include plenty of raw fruit and vegetables in your diet.

Vitamins	Major Sources	Major Functions
Water-soluble Vitamins *continued*		
B12 (cobalamin)	Lean meat, liver, kidney, milk, fish, shellfish, egg.	Red blood cell formation; breaks down fats, proteins and carbohydrates; protein production; maintenance of nervous system; formation of DNA (main constituent of chromosomes) and RNA (essential for the function of proteins).
Folic acid	Liver, kidney, raw or lightly cooked greens, brewer's yeast/yeast extract, nuts, citrus fruit, banana.	Production of red blood cells; maintenance of nervous system; formation of DNA and RNA.
Biotin	Liver, kidney, egg yolk, yeast.	Processing of fats and proteins.
C (ascorbic acid)	Citrus fruit and juice, blackcurrant, tomato, sweet pepper, berries, potato, greens.	Maintenance of connective tissues, including tendons, ligaments and cartilage; production of hormones in adrenalin glands; general chemical and physical processes; protects vitamin E.
Minerals		
Calcium	Milk, cheese, yoghurt, bread, greens, almond, sesame seed, shellfish.	Growth and maintenance of healthy bones and teeth; essential for blood clotting; hormone release; muscle and nerve functions; cell regulation.
Chloride	Salt in foods.	Works with sodium to maintain body water; protein digestion in stomach; muscle tone; enzyme activation.
Magnesium	Milk, bread, leafy green vegetables, pulses, nuts, shellfish.	Muscle tone; function of enzymes.
Phosphorus	Foods rich in protein.	Energy storage; maintenance and strength of bones; function of membranes (thin layers of separating or connecting tissues); growth.
Potassium	Wholegrain, vegetables, meat, milk, fruit and fruit juice, nuts, pulses, coffee.	Part of the structure of bones and teeth; major mineral found in cell fluids; membrane function and control of muscle functions; regulating blood pressure; energy production.

continued on next page

continued from previous page

Vitamins	Major Sources	Major Functions
Minerals *continued*		
Sodium	Table salt, bread, meat, milk, tinned and salted meat and fish.	Major mineral in fluids surrounding cells; nerve and muscle functions; membrane movement; blood pressure control.
Sulphur	Foods rich in protein, egg, fish and shellfish, pulses, meat, poultry, milk, nuts.	Water balance in body; present in blood; maintains bones; part of some amino acids (essential components of proteins); nerve and muscle functions.
Trace Element Minerals		
Chromium	Wholegrain, fresh fruit, nuts, liver, kidney, beef, molasses, cheese.	Constituent of proteins; enables cells to use glucose efficiently.
Cobalt	Greens, scallops, liver, kidney.	Important part of vitamin B12; glucose control.
Copper	Liver, crustacea, shellfish, brazil nut.	Enzyme function; blood formation; bone growth and function; immune system; nerve function and breakdown of energy.
Fluorine	Fish, sea salt, cereal, meat.	Resistance to dental decay; strong bones.
Iodine	Seafood, shellfish, fish.	Production in the thyroid gland of hormones which determine the rate of body metabolism, and therefore healthy growth and development.
Iron	Meat, bread, greens, dried fruit, pulses, nuts.	Production of haemoglobin in red blood cells; activation of enzymes.
Manganese	Wholegrain, avocado, nuts.	Activation of enzymes; cell structure.
Molybdenum	Buckwheat, barley, oats, liver, pulses.	Enzyme functions.
Selenium	Wholegrain flour, cereal and products, liver, kidney, meat, fish and shellfish.	Protecting cell membranes and fats from damage.
Zinc	Meat, milk, cheese, bread, nuts, oily fish, shellfish, egg yolk, wholegrain cereals.	Growth and sexual development; bone metabolism; activation of enzymes; release of vitamin A from the liver; healthy maintenance of the immune system; sense of taste; insulin storage (a hormone to control blood glucose levels).

How to Improve Your Micronutrient Balance The natural place to get micronutrients is in a varied and balanced diet. Balance is the important thing – we need enough – but not too much.

- Eat plenty of different fruits and/or vegetables.

- Adjust your diet rather than take tablets if you know you are deficient in some vitamin or mineral. If you lack iron, look to your meat, eggs and greens. If calcium, look to dairy produce and greens. If vitamin B12, eat more lean meat, liver, kidney, milk, fish, shellfish and eggs. Vegans may need to take vitamin B12 pills and increase their yeast intake.

- Follow the cooking and storage instructions given in this book to minimise vitamin wastage. As a general rule, don't overcook vegetables.

How Our Bodies use Food

When sitting down to a meal most of us are normally concerned only with the appearance, the taste, the smell and the texture of our food, not about the energy and nutrients it is providing us. Our food provides our fuel; it keeps us warm and supplies the energy we need to stay alive and move around. It also supplies the necessary materials for growth and repair of worn tissues, and the vitamins and minerals and other substances that are necessary for the chemical processes that take place inside our bodies. The digestion of food, and the distribution of energy and nutrients, is an incredible journey.

Digestion

It may help us to picture the digestive tract as a processing plant that consists of a series of conduits and food-processing chambers, each with its own functions. It breaks down the components of our food for absorption from the intestines into the bloodstream, and expels the waste products.

From the first bite we take, our digestive juices begin to work. As we chew our food, its pleasant taste creates a stimulus for continued eating, and for the secretion of saliva. Saliva contributes fluid and enzymes for the first stage of digestion.

From the mouth the food passes with little or no change into the stomach. As it enters, it is acted upon by acid and more enzymes from the stomach lining, and is turned into a semifluid mass known as chyme. This semidigested food then passes into the first part of the small intestine where more enzymes from the pancreas, and bile from the liver, set to work on breaking down the food further.

By now the protein, carbohydrate and fat in the food have been digested into units that are tiny enough to be able to pass through the intestinal wall into the bloodstream, together with the vitamins, minerals and trace elements.

Amino acids (the sub-units of proteins), together with glucose (the result of starch and sugar digestion), go straight into the blood circulation system. Most of the fatty acids are transported to the blood via the lymphatic system – a major route for the absorption of nutrients into the tissues – so that all the nutrients are distributed throughout the body.

Fuel for the Body

When food is burned up by the body cells, it liberates the energy we need to sustain life. About 70 per cent of this energy is used to keep the essential processes going within the body; to maintain our normal body temperature, the normal tone of our muscles, and to keep our heart and other organs functioning healthily. If we did nothing but rest in bed all day we would still need about two-thirds of our normal food intake to provide this basic energy. The rest is used for daily activities: dressing, eating, walking, working and playing.

Foods vary in their energy content, depending on how much water, alcohol, sugar, starch, fat and protein they contain. The energy values of foods are commonly thought of in terms of 'calories'. (In fact, what we commonly call a calorie is actually called a kilocalorie or 1000 calories, in nutritional terms.)

When your diet supplies just the amount of fuel or calories the body needs, all the food energy will be used. But when the diet supplies more calories than are needed, the excess fuel is stored in the body as fat. When the diet supplies fewer calories than are needed, the body converts its fat stores to energy to make up the difference, and weight is lost.

The number of calories an individual needs daily depends on their age, sex, size and level of physical activity. For example, a sedentary male between the ages of 35-64 will need about 2400 calories, but a man in the same age group with a physically active job will need about 3350.

Metabolism

Our need for energy is constant; the cells send out a steady stream of energy and are ready to respond to demands for 'instant energy' – such as having to react quickly in an emergency. This daily balancing act of energy intake and output is the job of your 'metabolism' – a term that describes the sum total of all the chemical activities of the body in taking in food, using what it can, and getting rid of the rest.

Your 'metabolic rate' is the rate at which your body converts fats, carbohydrates and proteins into energy. Burning more energy than you eat will make you lose weight, and eating more than you burn leads to a gain in weight because the excess is then stored in the body as fat.

Scientists are discovering more about the metabolism every year. There are all sorts of sophisticated controls that regulate how fast our fuel is used. You can rely on your body to do the job for you as long as you have a balanced diet, with all the essential nutrients and ample starch for energy.

Glucose for Energy

Foods that contain a lot of starch are best for the human body when it comes to energy, as they provide us with most of our glucose. Bread and potatoes were once the staples of the British diet, and should be restored to pride of place. Glucose (blood sugar) is the fuel that your cells prefer to use as a basic source of energy. It is the fuel that the muscles first turn to for the body's activities, and the only fuel that the brain uses in normal situations.

All carbohydrates are converted to glucose in the small intestine. The hormone insulin is essential for 'glycosis' – a process that turns glucose into energy for the body. Diabetics produce insufficient insulin to convert enough glucose into energy, causing their blood-sugar levels to rise beyond normal limits.

Glucose can be used as an immediate source of energy, or stored for a short time in the muscles and liver. Excess amounts of glucose are stored as fat.

Glycogen Glucose is stored in the body as 'glycogen' (animal starch) which consists of many glucose molecules joined together, and which can easily be broken down into glucose when needed. As the muscles and liver can only store limited amounts of glycogen (enough for one day at the most) we need regular starch in our diet to keep our metabolism and brain working properly.

The liver reserve is for the use of the brain, which needs a constant supply of glucose. The brain has no access to the glycogen stored in the muscles. Once inside the muscles, this glucose cannot get out

again – it acts exclusively to keep the muscle-energy metabolism working properly. It also meets any sudden demands for extra muscle energy.

The importance of muscle glycogen is vividly illustrated in feats of endurance. For example, when a marathon runner runs out of glycogen, his legs will wobble and give way.

Sugars All sugars are either used as a source of energy or stored as fat. Because sugars are relatively simple structures they are broken down into glucose much more quickly than starch, which is a complex structure. This is why sweets or chocolate can give you that feeling of an immediate 'lift' – they raise the blood-sugar level quickly and temporarily satisfy any feelings of hunger. However, the body responds by producing more insulin to remove excess glucose from the blood. This soon causes blood-sugar levels to fall even lower than they were before, leaving you feeling hungry, tired and irritable. By contrast, high-fibre starch gradually releases a steady stream of energy, because it takes longer to metabolise.

Vitamins and minerals are necessary for the efficient digestion of sugar. The body has to take these from its own stores in order to turn sucrose (table sugar) into a useful form of energy.

Unrefined starchy staple foods which contain vitamins and minerals therefore provide a far better way of building up the body's glycogen reserves.

Storing Food for Energy

Fatty acids, the sub-units of fat, are distributed to special fat storage (adipose) cells around the body. The primary function of fat is as a long-term energy reserve. Stored in the liver and muscles, it takes longer to convert into energy than glycogen, but the reserves are much greater. Fat is ideal for keeping extra reserves of calories (energy) because it stores them in such a concentrated form. An ounce of fat contains well over twice as many calories as an ounce of starch, sugar or protein.

In addition to storing energy, fat insulates the body, protecting us from changes in external temperature and helping to maintain a fairly constant internal temperature. It also prevents the skin from becoming dry, acts as a lubricant for joints and cushions vital organs like the heart, kidneys and those of the reproductive system.

Body fat is quite an active tissue. It replenishes itself in two main ways. First, dietary fat and alcohol go directly to form body fat. And second, after the body's relatively small stores of carbohydrates and protein have been topped up, any surplus glucose is also converted into body fat. So it does not matter what form calories are in when they arrive, all surpluses finish up as fat. When there is an extra demand on the body, fat tissue provides fatty acids to other body tissues to burn as energy.

Once calories have been converted into fat, the fat can be burnt to fuel the muscles (physical work) or used to maintain the chemical processes of the body's metabolism (chemical work). It is only burnt up in significant quantities with regular exercise or if food intake is cut to below daily requirements.

Focus on Everyday Food and Drink

Many people are particularly concerned about everyday foods and drinks because we consume them in such large quantities. This section takes a close look at some of the most popular foods and drinks in this country – helping you to choose a healthy diet for your family.

Water

Although water contains no calories, it is our prime nutritional need. An adequate and regular intake is fundamental for good health. The quality of our drinking water varies from one region to another. Nitrates washed into rivers from fertilisers, and contaminants discharged into rivers from industrial waste, can find their way into local water supplies. The local authorities continually check that these contaminants remain within legal limits. The current concern for environmental issues, combined with stringent European Community standards, should soon lead towards safer and purer tap water.

Although our water is purified and disinfected to remove pollutants and infectious organisms, tap water may still contain traces of potentially harmful substances from old pipework, crumbling water mains and the chemicals used in treating water.

Lead from lead piping in old houses accumulates in the water overnight, so run the water for a few minutes before use. Hot water contains more lead than cold, so boil cold water for cooking rather than using hot water straight from the tap.

Fluoride is a mineral which, in small amounts, is vital to the formation and strength of healthy teeth and bones. In some areas where it is added to the water there have been difficulties in keeping fluoride levels constant. Too much fluoride is harmful to the body – preventing it from absorbing vital calcium. Other added substances that give cause for concern are aluminium and chlorine.

Spring and Mineral Waters In the last few years the sales of bottled spring and mineral waters has boomed. The land around the underground source of water is usually protected so that chemical fertilisers and pesticides cannot leach through the soil and taint the water. The difference between spring and mineral waters is that spring waters do not make any claims for their mineral content, only for their purity. Claims that these waters have therapeutic powers remain unproven. Mineral content varies from brand to brand. Check the labels if you are on a restricted diet – some brands contain six times more sodium than others, for example.

Water Filters An easy way to combat contaminants in tap water is to use a home water filter. The cheapest and simplest type is a jug filter. In tests these have been shown to remove lead, some chemicals, and most of the chlorine. Some can reduce aluminium, but only a few remove nitrates. The filter cartridges need to be changed regularly.

Soft Drinks

Fruit squashes and fizzy drinks are enormously popular but most are made entirely of water, sugar, artificial colourings and flavourings, sodium and carbon dioxide. These soft drinks are high in calories and sugar but low in nutrients. A can of cola contains about seven teaspoons of sugar; a glass of blackcurrant cordial or bitter lemon contains about five teaspoons; a medium-sized bottle of tonic water contains four teaspoons; and a glass of orange squash contains about two teaspoons. Although diet soft drinks are low in calories they usually contain even more additives, such as sodium for flavour.

Healthy alternatives to these soft drinks are now available in the form of a range of 'elixirs' and 'tonics' that are blends of spring water, fruit juice, vitamins and herbs. The drinks make several claims, such as helping to restore the body's alkaline balance, or to act as a natural pick-me-up. These drinks are usually quite low in calories but tend to be more expensive than other soft drinks.

After-sports drinks are fairly new on the market in Britain. They are designed to help the body recover quickly after exercise, by replacing the body fluids and minerals that are lost in sweat. They are therefore only of any real benefit to people who take strenuous exercise. However, sports drinks are healthier thirst quenchers than many soft drinks. Some contain a lot of glucose or dextrose, making them high in calories, so check the labels.

Sports drinks have various concentrations which determine how quickly the body can use the drinks to replace lost fluids and absorb the nutrients they contain. Hypotonic drinks are less concentrated than body fluids and are therefore more easily absorbed by the body – ideal for sportsmen who want to replace lost nutrients and fluids as quickly as possible. Hypertonic drinks are more concentrated and absorbed more slowly by the body, making them suitable for people to drink before or during long periods of exertion. Isotonic drinks have the same concentration as body fluids.

Colas The stimulant caffeine is found in high levels in colas – 20 to 50mg in a drink. While a moderate intake of caffeine is thought to be safe in healthy adults, children may be ingesting as much as an adult coffee drinker from soft drinks and chocolate.

Fruit and Vegetable Drinks Pure fruit and vegetable juices are high in important nutrients. Tomato juice, for example, is rich in vitamins A and C; and citrus juices, especially orange juice, are rich in

vitamin C. Commercial fruit juices may have sugar and other substances added, and they are usually pasteurised to prevent fermentation and spoilage; a process which destroys some of the nutrients.

The labelling of fruit drinks is confusing for consumers. 'Whole orange' means that the drink includes the pith, skin and flesh, to which water and sugar is added, and 'orange flavour' means that it contains artificial flavourings, colour and perhaps a little orange essence. Most types of fruit squash and cordials only contain about 5 per cent fruit juice. High juice squashes contain more, but are also more expensive. Vitamin C levels fall quickly if juice is stored for a long time. Most juices are extracted in their country of origin – where they are made into a concentrate by removing the water. They are then rehydrated and packaged in this country. Freshly squeezed orange has the highest vitamin C content, but is expensive and deteriorates quickly.

Tea and Coffee

Vast amounts of coffee and tea are consumed in the West, both of which contain the stimulant caffeine. Coffee is made from an infusion of the roasted and ground seeds of the coffee plant. Instant coffees are made from infusions that have been spray or freeze-dried, and contain less caffeine than freshly ground coffee. A cup of ground coffee contains about 90 to 150mg per cup, and a cup of tea contains about 50 to 80mg per cup. Caffeine gives us a temporary lift because it stimulates the central nervous system and the heart.

An excessive intake of caffeine (six to eight cups or more per day) can result in a variety of serious disorders. Its stimulation of the heart can bring on anxiety symptoms such as irritability, headaches and insomnia; its stimulation of the pancreas to produce more insulin can lead to low blood sugar and fatigue; and its stimulation of acid in the stomach can lead to ulcers. You do not have to give up coffee altogether, just cut down to a moderate level – about two or three cups a day.

Some decaffeinated coffees use chemical solvents to remove the caffeine – check the labels and choose those that are made with a steam process instead. You can buy coffee substitutes from health food stores that are made from roasted grains with added flavourings such as chicory. You can also buy instant coffees that have been blended with chicory or grains; making their caffeine content much lower.

Tea is the world's most popular beverage. It has a lower caffeine content than coffee, but it contains a drug called tannin (about 60 to 280mg a cup) which can cause digestive problems and lead to constipation if people drink too much.

Herbal teas are healthier and available in many flavours. Rosehip and hibiscus teas contain vitamin C and are said to be stimulating, while peppermint tea is claimed to aid digestion. All herbal teas are normally drunk without milk or sugar.

Alcoholic and Low-alcohol Drinks

If people drink in moderation, alcohol need not be harmful – in fact it can even have positive medicinal qualities. However, it cannot be stressed too strongly that in the long term anything much more than a glass or two a day will damage your mind and body.

Counting the Calories Alcoholic drinks are high in 'empty' calories that contain no useful nutrients. Low-alcohol drinks are usually lower in calories than standard alcoholic drinks. A standard glass of full-strength wine may contain about 125 calories whilst the equivalent amount of low-alcohol wine ranges from 20 to 55 calories. The difference between low-alcohol and standard beers is not so great – low-alcohol beers range from 40 to 80 calories for half a pint compared to around 80 to 120 calories for a full-strength lager. A drink which is labelled 'low-calorie', 'low-carbohydrate' or 'light' may in fact have a normal-strength alcohol content.

Benefits of Alcohol

An occasional glass of wine can help some people to relax. However, if you get into the habit of having a daily glass of wine to help you unwind, for example, you will find your alcohol consumption starts creeping up as your body needs more of it to bring about the same effect. Alcohol, drunk in moderation, is believed to help people who suffer from hardened arteries. This is because it causes the arteries to dilate slightly, allowing the blood to flow more freely around the body, so putting less strain on the heart. A tot of brandy before bedtime is especially good.

Organic Wines

Grown without artificial pesticides or fertilisers, organic wines are gaining popularity in Britain and are widely available. Because fewer chemicals are used in their production, the manufacturers claim that you are less likely to suffer from a hangover.

Low-alcohol drinks

Low-alcohol drinks can make a good alternative to soft or alcoholic drinks, as long as you do not drink them in larger amounts. Most 'low-alcohol' drinks still contain varied amounts of alcohol, so be careful to check labels for strengths.

Low-alcohol wines or beers can still give you a hangover. They contain substances called 'high alcohols' which are thought to contribute to the same morning-after symptoms as too much alcohol. Many low-alcohol drinks also contain more chemical additives than their alcoholic counterparts.

Extra-strength lagers (where all the sugar turns to alcohol) live up to their name. They are almost three times as strong as ordinary beers.

Low-alcohol beers can either be brewed in the usual way and then have their alcohol removed, or there are various methods that make it possible to produce less alcohol from the start. Additives may be added to low-alcohol beers, since the alcohol that has been removed would normally have provided the flavour and colour, and acted as a preservative. Low-alcohol wines always start with a normal level of alcohol, which is then reduced by distillation.

Labelling Standard lagers contain between 3 to 4 per cent alcohol, and most wines have an alcohol content of about 11 per cent. There are regulations covering some of the drinks that contain less alcohol than normal: 'alcohol-free' means that the drink should not contain more than 0.05 per cent of alcohol, and 'de-alcoholised' means it should not contain more than 0.5 per cent. But there are various non-regulated terms that beers can also use. These include: 'low-alcohol', 'reduced alcohol', 'greatly reduced alcohol', 'light', and 'lite' which typically contain up to 1.2 per cent alcohol – about a third of the alcohol in a standard alcoholic beer.

Bread

Bread is one of the most nutritionally balanced foods available and provides us with an easily digested source of energy. We eat an average of just under three slices a day in Britain, and many nutritionists feel our consumption should be increased, especially if it is eaten instead of fatty or sugary foods.

Bread is not particularly high in calories and it is not fattening unless eaten in excessive amounts, as with most other foods. White bread has roughly the same number of calories as brown and wholemeal bread, but the bran in wholemeal bread makes you feel full and you are therefore less likely to overeat. Avoid spreading bread too thickly with butter or margarine and sugary spreads.

Bread provides carbohydrates (mainly as starch), fibre, protein, calcium, iron, and the B vitamins called thiamin, niacin and riboflavin. High intakes of dietary fibre and the carbohydrates (starches) found in bread are associated with a reduced incidence of coronary heart disease, bowel disease and diabetes, particularly if it replaces fat and sugar in the diet.

Types of Bread

Brown About 15-20 per cent of the wheat grain is removed and so it contains more bran-fibre and sometimes more wheatgerm than white bread, as well as more minerals and vitamins. It must have vitamins and minerals replaced by law. It may also have added caramel to give it colour.

Fibre-enriched These breads, made from either white, brown, wheatgerm or wholemeal flour, have extra fibre added to them after milling. High-fibre white is still usually lower in fibre than wholemeal.

Malted or Granary Malted whole grains (grains that have been allowed to partially sprout) are added to white or brown flour. Malted and granary breads contain all the nutritional value of the whole grain.

Wheatgerm Only 10-15 per cent of the wheat grain is extracted. Wheatgerm bread contains more bran and much more wheatgerm than brown bread.

White Roughly 30 per cent of the wheat grain, which consists of bran and wheatgerm, is removed to make white bread. In Britain, any B vitamins or iron and calcium that are lost in the milling process must be re-added to the bread by law.

Wholemeal Wholemeal bread, or 'wholewheat' bread has no wheat grain removed at all. It contains all the nutrients of the whole grain, including traces of chromium which diabetics often lack.

Baking Bread

Before about 4000 BC all bread was flat or 'unleavened' like Indian chappatis and Mexican tortillas, but then it was discovered that adding yeast caused the dough to rise. Yeast is a living organism which is rich in vitamin B. When it is warmed it produces gases which are trapped by gluten in the dough, making the bread rise. Other grains and meals are added to wheat flour to give bread distinctive tastes, textures and colours, such as oats, barley, rye, buckwheat and cornmeal.

Preservatives and Stale Bread

Preservatives are added to slow down the growth of mould – some breads are available without them, but they have a reduced shelf life. Freezing bread prevents staling. Storing it in the refrigerator helps prevent the growth of mould, but speeds up staling.

Butter, Margarine and Low-fat Spreads

The long-running controversy over whether butter, margarine or low-fat spread is best for your health has caused a great deal of confusion. Butter and margarine have about the same number of calories – only low-fat spreads have significantly fewer. The fat contents vary considerably from one spread to another – both in quantity and type. Lards and drippings made from animal fat contain 99 per cent fat and are very high in cholesterol and saturated fat. Some low-fat spreads have only 25 per cent fat and are high in unsaturated fats and cholesterol-free.

Butter Most people prefer the taste of butter compared with other spreads, but have been discouraged from buying it by publicity connecting it with heart disease. Butter is high in cholesterol and saturated fat and low in unsaturated fat, and if it is eaten in excess it can cause a build-up of cholesterol in the blood. However, many nutritionists believe that if eaten in moderation it can be preferable to margarine which is a highly processed food and contains many additives. The only additives allowed in butter by the EC are salt and natural colourings.

Margarine Making margarine involves heating oils, then refining, deodorising and bleaching them. Vegetable oils are used either on their own or combined with animal or fish oils. Margarine also usually contains water, whey, emulsifiers to bind the oil and liquids, salt, colouring and flavouring agents. By law it must contain vitamins A and D.

Hard margarines are high in saturated oils and fats. Some of the soft 'easy-spread' margarines are high in polyunsaturates, but even if a margarine is high in polyunsaturates, some of them are converted to saturated fats during processing. Legally, margarines must contain 80 per cent fat – giving them roughly the same calorific value as butter. To be labelled 'high in polyunsaturates' a margarine must contain no more than 25 per cent saturated fat. Margarines claiming to be 'low in cholesterol' may not necessarily be low in saturated fat.

Soft margarines made from sunflower or soya oils are high in polyunsaturates and they contribute essential fatty acids and vitamin E to the diet. There are some specialist margarines on the market which do not use artificially processed oils, and others are made with no whey for people with a milk allergy.

Spreads Spreads have less than 80 per cent fat and have fewer calories than butter or margarine. They can be divided into the following categories:

1. Blended-fat spreads made from beef fat, cream, butter, milk and oil are about 70-75 per cent fat.
2. Reduced-fat spreads contain approximately 60 per cent fat. These are largely sunflower-oil based and high in polyunsaturates.
3. Low-fat spreads contain about 40 per cent fat, although there are no laws currently governing their content. They may be based on sunflower oil, butter or a mixture of animal and vegetable fats. Because of their high water content, low-fat spreads are not suitable for frying or cooking.
4. Very low-fat spreads contain approximately 25 per cent fat and 75 per cent water. They are also unsuitable for cooking.

Comparing Organic and Conventional Foods

Despite its high price, organic food is becoming increasingly popular. Farmed without the use of the man-made fertilisers, pesticides, growth regulators and additives in animal fodder that are used in conventional farming, organic farmers rely instead on crop rotation, animal and plant manure, and biological pest control.

Scientific tests have shown that organic foods are generally no higher in nutrients than conventional foods. However, organic fruit and vegetables are much lower in levels of pesticides, and organic animal and dairy foods are produced without artificial hormones and antibiotics.

Look for The Soil Association symbol on organic foods, which guarantees high standards. To be able to use the symbol, farmers have to adhere to very rigorous standards and keep to strict guidelines for the rearing of animals.

Food Irradiation

Irradiated food is exposed to a radioactive source in a process that is similar to taking an X-ray. The radiation kills any bacteria and other contaminants, enabling food to look fresh for much longer than normal. This reduces the need for preservatives and other additives, but there is concern that the process may destroy vitamins in the food. Although there is no evidence of a health risk, some scientists are concerned about the long-term effects of irradiation.

Food Directory

This directory gives useful tips and information on a broad range of food and drinks. Each entry contains a breakdown of the nutritional value of a typical serving. Some foods that are not generally regarded as 'healthy' have been included for comparison.

The food directory is broken down into main groups, such as cereals and grains, for example.

Within these groups the foods are listed alphabetically. The nutritional figures are given for a typical serving. So, for each 3½oz (90g) serving of pasta, you will see the calories (Cals) per serving, the grams of protein, fat, sugar and fibre and the milligrams of sodium per serving. Water and carbohydrates will usually make up the rest of the serving weight.

Fruits

A TYPICAL 3½OZ (90G) SERVING

Apples, cooking Bramleys are the most famous cooking apples with their firm flesh and a sharp taste. Granny Smiths are good for cooking and eating.

Cals	Protein	Fat	Sugar	Fibre	Sodium
37	0.3	0	9.2	2.4	2.0

Apples, dessert Homegrown Worcester Pearmain and Cox's Orange Pippin, and imports such as Golden Delicious keep dessert apples available year-round.

Cals	Protein	Fat	Sugar	Fibre	Sodium
46	0.3	0	11.9	2.0	2.0

Avocado An avocado is ripe when the bulbous end yields to pressure. They can be scarce between June and August.

Cals	Protein	Fat	Sugar	Fibre	Sodium
223	4.2	22.2	1.8	2.0	2.0

Bananas Underripe, slightly green bananas are cheaper and will eventually mature in a warm room, but avoid very green ones.

Cals	Protein	Fat	Sugar	Fibre	Sodium
79	1.1	0.3	16.2	3.4	1.0

Blackcurrants Full of vitamins and with a strong, sharp flavour, blackcurrants are ideal for pies and puddings. In season in the summer.

Cals	Protein	Fat	Sugar	Fibre	Sodium
28	0.9	0	6.6	8.7	3.0

Cherries, whole There are black, white and sour types of this fruit, which are plump, well-coloured and shiny when ripe for eating. They are all in season late spring to late summer.

Cals	Protein	Fat	Sugar	Fibre	Sodium
41	0.5	0	10.4	1.5	1.5

Figs, fresh Fresh figs are only really ripe when they are soft to the touch. In season August to September.

Cals	Protein	Fat	Sugar	Fibre	Sodium
41	1.3	0	9.5	2.5	2.0

Grapes It is important to buy grapes at their peak – underripe grapes tend to be acidic and overripe ones mould easily. There are several varieties available all year round.

Cals	Protein	Fat	Sugar	Fibre	Sodium
51	0.5	0	13	0.3	1.0

Grapefruits A firm, heavy grapefruit with a smooth skin indicates juiciness, while a rough, spongy skin means that a grapefruit will be dry. Pink grapefruits are sweeter but more expensive.

Cals	Protein	Fat	Sugar	Fibre	Sodium
22	0.6	0	5.3	0.6	1.0

Kiwi Fruit Because kiwi fruits do not discolour when cut, they can be used in open fruit tarts and salads. They are in season from July to February.

Cals	Protein	Fat	Sugar	Fibre	Sodium
37	0.3	0	9.2	7.3	2.0

Lemons Thin-skinned lemons tend to be much juicier than thick-skinned ones. A sprinkling of lemon juice stops other fruits discolouring. Organic unwaxed lemons are now widely available.

Cals	Protein	Fat	Sugar	Fibre	Sodium
15	0.4	0	3.2	5.2	6.0

Limes Lime juice is an excellent substitute for lemon juice and is frequently used in Asian cooking. In season February to July.

Cals	Protein	Fat	Sugar	Fibre	Sodium
15	0.4	0	9.2	7.3	2.0

Mango Ripe mango is the perfect foil for smoked meats, chicken and turkey. Mangos are ripe when they give slightly to the touch and have a pungent aroma. In season for most of the year.

Cals	Protein	Fat	Sugar	Fibre	Sodium
59	0.5	0	15.3	1.5	7.0

Melon Varieties of melon include the round, yellow honeydew, the large, green-skinned watermelon, the small, sweet-tasting ogen melon and the oval, sweeter-tasting canary melon. Melons are ripe when their ends are soft.

Cals	Protein	Fat	Sugar	Fibre	Sodium
24	1.0	0	5.3	1.0	14

Oranges Look for firm, shiny oranges with smooth skins. Sour oranges such as Seville are suitable for making marmalade whereas sweet oranges are usually used for juices.

Cals	Protein	Fat	Sugar	Fibre	Sodium
35	0.8	0	8.5	2.0	3.0

Peaches Ripe when the stalk end is soft to the touch, and not necessarily when they are tinged red. Peaches are in season from July to October.

Cals	Protein	Fat	Sugar	Fibre	Sodium
37	0.6	0	9.1	1.4	3.0

Pears This fruit can be divided into cooking and dessert varieties. Several varieties of pear cook well including Conference and the American Bosc. Choose both when they are fairly firm but yielding at the stalk end.

Cals	Protein	Fat	Sugar	Fibre	Sodium
41	0.3	0	10.6	2.3	2.0

Plums The British purple damson is sour and often used in pies or preserves. The green varieties are sweet and ideal for eating from August to October.

Cals	Protein	Fat	Sugar	Fibre	Sodium
38	0.6	0	9.6	2.1	1.0

Prunes These dried plums are used in desserts, ices and stuffings. They go especially well with pork and can be bought tinned or dried.

Cals	Protein	Fat	Sugar	Fibre	Sodium
82	1.3	tr	20.4	8.1	7.0

Raspberries Firm raspberries freeze well. Do not buy soft or mildewy ones. In season June to September.

Cals	Protein	Fat	Sugar	Fibre	Sodium
25	0.9	0	5.6	4.4	2.0

Strawberries An intense perfume is the best sign of good quality strawberries that are really ripe. In season from late spring to early summer.

Cals	Protein	Fat	Sugar	Fibre	Sodium
26	0.6	0	6.2	2.2	2.0

Vegetables and Pulses

Vegetables

A TYPICAL 3½OZ (90G) SERVING

Artichoke, globe, boiled Try to find compact green heads with no dark patches or dry streaks. In season spring to autumn.

Cals	Protein	Fat	Sugar	Fibre	Sodium
7.0	0.5	tr	1.1	13	6.0

Aubergine, raw Large aubergines often contain bitter juices. Even smaller ones may need to be cut open and salted to reduce their bitterness and the amount of fat they absorb when fried. In season July to October.

Cals	Protein	Fat	Sugar	Fibre	Sodium
14	0.7	0	2.9	2.5	3.0

Beans, broad Their distinctive flavour makes them good for soups and purées. In season June to late July.

Cals	Protein	Fat	Sugar	Fibre	Sodium
48	4.0	0.5	0.5	4.0	1.0

Beans, butter, boiled One of the fullest flavoured beans which are delicious in soups or served cold as a starter. In this country you can either buy butter beans ready-cooked in tins, or dried. Dried beans are normally covered with cold water, soaked for a couple of hours and cooked for about 45 minutes.

Cals	Protein	Fat	Sugar	Fibre	Sodium
95	7.1	0.3	1.5	5.1	16

Beans, French The slender pods have no strings and only need topping and tailing. Flat, fairly large pods are the best. In season June to August.

Cals	Protein	Fat	Sugar	Fibre	Sodium
7	0.8	0	0.8	3.2	3.0

Beetroot The smaller they are, the more tender and sweet they will be. Baked, steamed or boiled whole, they pair well with dark meats and spicy sausage. In season June to September.

Cals	Protein	Fat	Sugar	Fibre	Sodium
44	1.8	0	10.0	2.6	64

Broccoli Otherwise known as calabrese. Avoid any that have started to turn yellow. Can be bought as whole heads or as small florets. In season September to April.

Cals	Protein	Fat	Sugar	Fibre	Sodium
18	3.0	0	1.5	4.0	1

Brussels Sprouts Look for undamaged, tightly closed heads. Avoid any with yellow leaves. The Germans often serve them with fried, chopped bacon and onion. In season September to March.

Cals	Protein	Fat	Sugar	Fibre	Sodium
18	2.8	0	1.6	2.9	2

Butternut Squash The North American club-shaped squash tastes like a nutty version of the pumpkin. It can be steamed, sautéed or added to soups.

Cals	Protein	Fat	Sugar	Fibre	Sodium
28	0.9	tr	2.3	8.9	3

Cabbage, common green Choose tight-headed cabbages with bright colour. They should not smell strongly. At least one variety is in season all year round.

Cals	Protein	Fat	Sugar	Fibre	Sodium
7	1.1	0	0.8	2.2	12

Carrots New carrots are sweeter than mature ones, and are best eaten whole. Larger carrots are delicious when sliced very thinly and sweated for 2-3 minutes with a pinch of sugar, a little butter and fresh herbs. In season May to August.

Cals	Protein	Fat	Sugar	Fibre	Sodium
19	0.5	0	4.0	3.0	50

Cauliflower A good cauliflower should have green leaves and a firm, compact, white head. Available whole or in small florets. In season all year round.

Cals	Protein	Fat	Sugar	Fibre	Sodium
9	1.5	0	1.0	2.0	4

Celeriac Sometimes also called celery root. It is a large, knobbly root vegetable with a tough skin that must be peeled before cooking. It can also be grated raw to make a delicious salad. In season September to March.

Cals	Protein	Fat	Sugar	Fibre	Sodium
44	1.8	0	10.0	2.6	64

Courgettes They are best when grown less than 6in (150mm) long. In season May to September.

Cals	Protein	Fat	Sugar	Fibre	Sodium
25	1.5	0	0	0	1.0

Cucumber All cucumbers should be firm and crisp; if soft, they are past their best. In season July to September.

Cals	Protein	Fat	Sugar	Fibre	Sodium
10	0.6	0.1	1.8	0.4	13

Fennel Sweet Florence fennel has a distinctive aniseed flavour. It is used a great deal in Italian cooking – raw in salads, or cooked in soups and stews. In season June to November.

Cals	Protein	Fat	Sugar	Fibre	Sodium
27	1.5	0	0	0	331

Leeks Chunky leeks with thick stems are the best. Avoid ones with yellow leaves. Leeks often retain grit within their layers and must be well cleaned. In season September to May.

Cals	Protein	Fat	Sugar	Fibre	Sodium
24	1.8	0	4.6	0	6.0

Lettuce, raw There are an increasing number of lettuces available. Some have decorative leaves which make beautiful salads. It can also be cooked and added to soup or used to wrap fish and other foods.

Frisée

Radicchio

Cals	Protein	Fat	Sugar	Fibre	Sodium
10	1.0	tr	1.0	1.5	10

Mangetout Bright green flattish pea pods which can be eaten raw, stir-fried or steamed until just tender but still quite crisp.

Cals	Protein	Fat	Sugar	Fibre	Sodium
42	3.0	0	1.5	2.0	4.0

Mushrooms, raw Common white are sold as young button mushrooms, as standard size and as mature. Flat or field mushrooms have a slightly more intense flavour.

Cals	Protein	Fat	Sugar	Fibre	Sodium
13	2.0	0.5	0	1.0	9.0

Onions, raw Included in the onion family are red, white, yellow, pickling and spring onions. Shallots are also related to onions. All should be firm not shrivelled or soft.

Cals	Protein	Fat	Sugar	Fibre	Sodium
23	0.9	0	5.2	1.3	2.0

Parsnips Small to medium parsnips are best. Their sweet, nutty taste is good in soups or vegetable purées. In season September to April.

Cals	Protein	Fat	Sugar	Fibre	Sodium
56	1.5	0	2.5	2.5	4.0

Peas Wrinkled pods usually indicate old and hard peas that should be avoided. Fat pods also tend to contain older peas. In season May to October.

Cals	Protein	Fat	Sugar	Fibre	Sodium
52	5.0	0.5	2.0	2.0	0

Potatoes, boiled (see Convenience Foods for chips) New potatoes should be scrubbed and boiled. They can be eaten hot or used cold in salads.

Cals	Protein	Fat	Sugar	Fibre	Sodium
80	1.4	tr	0.4	1.0	3.0

Potatoes, jacket A lot of a potato's fibre and nutrients are contained in its skin or just below it. Pierce large potatoes to help them cook right through.

Cals	Protein	Fat	Sugar	Fibre	Sodium
105	1.4	tr	0.4	4.3	3.0

Potatoes, roast 'Old' potatoes are best roasted around a joint for the last hour of the joint's cooking time. Potatoes may be boiled gently for 8-10 minutes before roasting for a crisper finish.

Cals	Protein	Fat	Sugar	Fibre	Sodium
157	2.8	4.8	0	0	9.0

Potatoes, sweet, boiled These can be boiled, baked or puréed and have a sweet chestnut flavour. In season September to June.

Cals	Protein	Fat	Sugar	Fibre	Sodium
85	1.1	0.6	9.1	2.3	18

Spinach You will need 2¼lb (1kg) of spinach to serve four people as the leaves diminish dramatically during cooking. Cooked spinach flavoured with lemon or nutmeg makes an excellent filling for omelettes, pasta or crêpes.

Cals	Protein	Fat	Sugar	Fibre	Sodium
30	5.1	0.5	1.2	6.3	120

Sweetcorn Cobs should be cooked in boiling water from 3 to 20 minutes, depending on freshness and size. Sweetcorn can be served on the cob with a small knob of butter. In season from July to October.

Cals	Protein	Fat	Sugar	Fibre	Sodium
123	4.0	2.0	1.5	4.5	1.0

Sweet Peppers Mild chillies may be red, orange, purple or yellow and can be stuffed, marinated or used to make colourful salads. They are from the same family as smaller chilli peppers, such as the small, Mexican green Serrano chilli.

Cals	Protein	Fat	Sugar	Fibre	Sodium
15	0.9	0.4	2.2	0.9	2.0

Watercress, raw As a highly perishable vegetable, watercress should be eaten quickly or stored briefly on ice. It is available all year round in bunches.

Cals	Protein	Fat	Sugar	Fibre	Sodium
15	3.0	0	0.5	3.5	60

Pulses

A TYPICAL 3½OZ (90G) SERVING

Chickpeas, tinned These peas range from yellow to black in colour and have a rich, nutty flavour, suited to meat stews or salads. They are puréed to make the Middle-Eastern hummus.

Cals	Protein	Fat	Sugar	Fibre	Sodium
75	4.8	1.3	0	3.9	0

Lentils, dried Lentils range greatly in colour, but in general the smaller the lentil the better the taste. They do not all need pre-soaking, but some varieties are highly toxic if unsoaked.

Cals	Protein	Fat	Sugar	Fibre	Sodium
99	7.6	0.5	0.8	3.7	12

Soya beans, dried These are sold in supermarkets as well as health food shops and are often processed to make vegetable protein or soya 'mince'.

Cals	Protein	Fat	Sugar	Fibre	Sodium
135	13.9	6.6	0	3.0	0

Fish and Shellfish

Fish

A TYPICAL 3½OZ (90G) SERVING

Cod, grilled Cod yields plenty of white, flaky flesh. It can be grilled, sautéed, poached or steamed and served with a wide range of sauces.

Cals	Protein	Fat	Sugar	Fibre	Sodium
88	21.0	1.0	0	0	110

Haddock, steamed Haddock is smaller and less abundant than cod and slightly softer in texture. It is best steamed or gently poached and is often smoked.

Cals	Protein	Fat	Sugar	Fibre	Sodium
98	11.4	0.4	0	0	60

Halibut, steamed The largest flatfish of all, halibut can weigh 500lb (230kg). It is cheapest in December, but best from August to April.

Cals	Protein	Fat	Sugar	Fibre	Sodium
131	23.4	4.0	0	0	110

Mackerel, grilled This nutritious, oily fish can help prevent heart disease. Its firm, strongly flavoured flesh is often smoked. Best from November to March.

Cals	Protein	Fat	Sugar	Fibre	Sodium
188	21.5	11.5	0	0	150

Monkfish, raw Usually only the large tail of this fish is found on sale. Its sweet, slightly chewy flesh is easy to fillet.

Cals	Protein	Fat	Sugar	Fibre	Sodium
76	14	2.0	0	0	18

359

Salmon, poached The middle cut of this delicately flavoured fish is the most popular choice. Salmon is now cheaper than several other types of fish. In season February to August.

Cals	Protein	Fat	Sugar	Fibre	Sodium
197	20	13	0	0	110

Salmon, smoked, 2¼oz (60g) serving An expensive delicacy, smoked salmon ranges in fat content from about 3-20%. Vacuum-packed slices must be chilled or frozen for long-term storage.

Cals	Protein	Fat	Sugar	Fibre	Sodium
80	25.4	4.5	0	0	1050

Sardines, in oil These oily fish are the young of pilchards, available tinned. Fresh ones come largely from France, March to December.

Cals	Protein	Fat	Sugar	Fibre	Sodium
217	23.7	13.5	0	0	650

Sole, poached All types of sole have a low-fat content and white flesh. Do not buy large fish as they may be old and less tender when cooked.

Cals	Protein	Fat	Sugar	Fibre	Sodium
91	20.6	0.9	0	0	120

Tuna, in brine Nutritious tuna fish are cooked in herbed brine and then tinned in water or oil. Tuna in oil has more than twice the number of calories as tuna in brine, unless it is well drained.

Cals	Protein	Fat	Sugar	Fibre	Sodium
120	27	1.1	0	0	350

Shellfish

Crab Edible members of the crab family are either large-bodied or long-legged varieties. Available fresh, tinned and frozen. In season from May to October.

Cals	Protein	Fat	Sugar	Fibre	Sodium
64	10	2.5	0	0	185

Mussels, boiled Look for mussels with tightly closed shells that have a clean, sweet smell. Mussels are available from September to March. They are at their cheapest in March.

Cals	Protein	Fat	Sugar	Fibre	Sodium
44	8.6	1.0	0	0	105

Oysters, raw (6) Oysters are graded according to their size, which is reflected in their price. They can be cooked or eaten raw with a little lemon juice or Worcestershire sauce. In season from September to April.

Cals	Protein	Fat	Sugar	Fibre	Sodium
30	6.6	tr	0	0	1530

Prawns, boiled Prawns are boiled and often shelled before being sold. Though they are low in fat, they are high in cholesterol. In season June to August.

Cals	Protein	Fat	Sugar	Fibre	Sodium
54	11.3	0.9	0	0	795

Scallops, steamed The attractive fan-shaped shells of scallops are often used to display food. Scallops can also be pan fried or grilled. They are in season from September to March.

Cals	Protein	Fat	Sugar	Fibre	Sodium
105	23.2	1.4	0	0	270

Squid, raw Many different varieties of squid are sold in the Mediterranean region, where it is enormously popular. Look for sweet-smelling moist meat.

Cals	Protein	Fat	Sugar	Fibre	Sodium
75	15.3	0.8	0	0	176

Meat

Beef

Beef, roasted topside Topside of beef comes from the rear end of the steer and is the most popular Sunday roast joint. Secure it with string before roasting.

Cals	Protein	Fat	Sugar	Fibre	Sodium
156	29	4.4	0	0	49

Beefburger, 4oz (115g), without bun Coarsely minced beef is shaped into patties and fried or grilled. The mince of commercial burgers may be fatty and 'fillers', such as breadcrumbs, are often added for bulk.

Cals	Protein	Fat	Sugar	Fibre	Sodium
280	21	18	0	0.3	940

Calf's Liver This is the best liver for grilling, frying and sautéing. It is very tender and only needs cooking for a couple of minutes. Buy it when it is deep pink or beige rather than red.

Cals	Protein	Fat	Sugar	Fibre	Sodium
153	20.1	7.3	0	0	93

Corned Beef, 1¼ oz (30g) slice This beef does not contain any corn but is cured with salt, sugar and saltpetre and pressed together with gelatinous material and fat.

Cals	Protein	Fat	Sugar	Fibre	Sodium
65	8.1	3.6	0	0	285

Fillet Steak, grilled The fillet steak is considered to be the finest cut of beef, but it is high in fat. Tender and juicy, it goes well with baby vegetables and small, fried potatoes.

Cals	Protein	Fat	Sugar	Fibre	Sodium
168	28.6	12.5	0	0	56

Minced Beef, raw Quality can vary a great deal with minced beef. Generally, cheaper mince will contain more fat and gristle. Buy it as fresh as possible or, better still, mince your own at home.

Cals	Protein	Fat	Sugar	Fibre	Sodium
221	18.8	16.2	0	0	86

Lamb

A TYPICAL 3½OZ (90G) SERVING

Lamb's Liver This is less tender than calf's liver, but it sautées and braises well and is often used in pâtés.

Cals	Protein	Fat	Sugar	Fibre	Sodium
250	26.9	13.2	0	0	160

Leg of Lamb, roasted The most popular red meat in Britain, lamb is very tender and so almost all cuts can be roasted.

Cals	Protein	Fat	Sugar	Fibre	Sodium
191	25.6	21.1	0	0	67

Pork

A TYPICAL 3½OZ (90G) SERVING

Bacon, grilled, 1oz (25g) Look for very lightly cured bacon which is pale pink with a supple rind.

Unsmoked back

British Streaky   *Suffolk back (sweet cure)*

Cals	Protein	Fat	Sugar	Fibre	Sodium
101	7.6	4.7	0	0	505

Ham, 2oz (50g) Ham is the matured and salted hind leg of the pig, and as such is high in sodium. It may be smoked or enriched with honey or spices. Commercially cured pressed pork shoulder is not strictly a ham.

Parma

Ardennes

Cals	Protein	Fat	Sugar	Fibre	Sodium
60	9.2	2.6	0	0	625

Liver Pâté Pâté is the French word for pie – literally a pie without the crust, usually made of minced meat, fats, a variety of herbs and seasonings, and often natural meat jelly.

Cals	Protein	Fat	Sugar	Fibre	Sodium
138	7.5	11.6	0	0	290

Pig's Liver Dark red and shiny, with a strong flavour, pig's liver blends well in pâtés. It is the cheapest type of liver.

Cals	Protein	Fat	Sugar	Fibre	Sodium
77	10.6	3.4	0	0	43

Pork Sausage, grilled (2) A mixture of minced pork and spices are stuffed into a casing to be fried, grilled or baked.

Cals	Protein	Fat	Sugar	Fibre	Sodium
285	11.8	15.6	0	0	900

Roast Pork Roasts need cooking slowly and basting as pork can easily dry out. Cook pork until its juices run clear. Leaner pork usually has less flavour.

Cals	Protein	Fat	Sugar	Fibre	Sodium
185	30.7	6.9	0	0	79

Salami (2 slices) These dried, smoked sausages are made from finely chopped pork, beef and fat, and often flavoured with garlic and other spices.

Chorizo   *Milano*

Cals	Protein	Fat	Sugar	Fibre	Sodium
83	3.3	7.7	0	0	315

Poultry and Game

Poultry

A TYPICAL 3½OZ (90G) SERVING

Chicken Breast, skinned Chickens are available in many sizes, from 1lb (450g) baby birds to 10lb (4.5kg) capons. The white, boneless meat of the chicken is often breaded and fried.

Cals	Protein	Fat	Sugar	Fibre	Sodium
142	26.5	4.0	0	0	71

Chicken, roasted with skin Roast a chicken in a hot oven and baste it every 10 to 15 minutes to create a juicy bird with a crisp skin. Self-basting roasting chickens are widely available.

Cals	Protein	Fat	Sugar	Fibre	Sodium
216	22.6	14	0	0	72

Duck, skinned A duck that is to be roasted should not be wrapped in foil, the fat must escape or the meat and skin will be greasy. The fat can be allowed to drip off the bird from a roasting rack.

Cals	Protein	Fat	Sugar	Fibre	Sodium
189	25	10.5	0	0	96

Game

A TYPICAL 3½OZ (90G) SERVING

Pheasant A hen bird will normally feed two to three people and a cock three to four. Make sure that the bird is not badly shot when buying and try to remove all lead shot.

Cals	Protein	Fat	Sugar	Fibre	Sodium
213	32.2	9.3	0	0	100

Rabbit, stewed Wild rabbit is lean and gamey, while domestic rabbit is light and delicate and tastes similar to the meat of chicken. Like other lean meats, wild rabbit must be kept moist during cooking. Domestic rabbit is excellent cut into pieces and stewed with herbs.

Cals	Protein	Fat	Sugar	Fibre	Sodium
179	23.2	6.6	0	0	32

Venison The best venison meat is dark red. Venison is usually sold in joints and then roasted or stewed. It can often be tough, in which case it needs to be tenderised and cooked very slowly.

Cals	Protein	Fat	Sugar	Fibre	Sodium
198	35	6.4	0	0	86

Herbs, Sauces and Pickles

A TYPICAL 1 TABLESPOON SERVING

Parsley, fresh Mildly flavoured and rich in iron and vitamins, fresh parsley can be used in soups as well as whole or chopped up finely for garnish. Dried parsley has a concentrated flavour, but it does not contain as many vitamins.

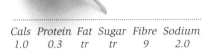

Cals	Protein	Fat	Sugar	Fibre	Sodium
1.0	0.3	tr	tr	9	2.0

Brown Sauce Meat or vegetable stock is flavoured with dripping, spices and herbs to make a brown savoury sauce.

Cals	Protein	Fat	Sugar	Fibre	Sodium
15	0.7	0.5	3.5	tr	147

Chutney Many different combinations of fruits and vegetables are preserved in spiced vinegar to form a wide range of chutneys.

Cals	Protein	Fat	Sugar	Fibre	Sodium
23	0.2	0.5	6.0	0.4	20

Mayonnaise A creamy sauce made from egg yolks and large quantities of oil, making it very high in calories. Different flavours are now available.

Cals	Protein	Fat	Sugar	Fibre	Sodium
103	0.1	11.4	tr	1.0	72

Mayonnaise, low-fat The calories and fat content are greatly reduced but significant quantities are still left.

Cals	Protein	Fat	Sugar	Fibre	Sodium
43	0.1	4.2	0.7	1.0	141

Tomato Ketchup Tomatoes are combined with vinegar and spices to form this sauce. It is quite high in sodium.

Cals	Protein	Fat	Sugar	Fibre	Sodium
13	0.4	0.8	1.2	1.0	168

Worcestershire Sauce Made from soy sauce, matured vinegar and spices.

Cals	Protein	Fat	Sugar	Fibre	Sodium
14	0.4	0.4	6.8	tr	238

Dairy Products

Milk

A TYPICAL ½ PINT (285ML) DAILY INTAKE

Milk, condensed (1tsp) Whole milk has its water content reduced and is sweetened with large amounts of sugar to make a thick and syrupy consistency.

Cals	Protein	Fat	Sugar	Fibre	Sodium
50	1.5	1.5	8.0	0	21

Milk, evaporated (1tsp) The water content of evaporated milk has been reduced so that it contains about double the solids of ordinary milk by volume.

Cals	Protein	Fat	Sugar	Fibre	Sodium
23	1.5	1.5	1.0	0	27

Milk, semi-skimmed About half the fat content of whole milk is removed by separation to form semi-skimmed milk. Other constituents are barely affected.

Cals	Protein	Fat	Sugar	Fibre	Sodium
131	9.4	4.5	14.2	0	105

Milk, skimmed Practically all the fat is removed or skimmed from whole milk. Skimmed milk is useful for people on diets or with cholesterol problems.

Cals	Protein	Fat	Sugar	Fibre	Sodium
94	9.4	0.3	14.2	0	103

Milk, whole (regular or silvertop) Milk has all the nutrients needed by children and adults; it contains good quality protein, digestible fat, sugar, vitamins and minerals, but no fibre.

Cals	Protein	Fat	Sugar	Fibre	Sodium
187	9.1	11.1	13.6	0	105

Cream

A TYPICAL 1OZ (25G) SERVING

Cream, double In Britain, double cream has a fat content of 48%. Avoid boiling or freezing sauces with cream in, otherwise they may curdle or separate.

Cals	Protein	Fat	Sugar	Fibre	Sodium
125	0.5	14.5	0.8	0	11

Cream, single Cream is a concentration of the fatty solids of whole milk. Single cream contains no less than 18% fat and is thinner than other creams.

Cals	Protein	Fat	Sugar	Fibre	Sodium
59	0.7	5.7	1.2	0	15

Cream, whipping The fat content of whipping cream is high – ranging from 30-60%. The high fat content causes the whipping characteristics.

Cals	Protein	Fat	Sugar	Fibre	Sodium
113	0.6	11.8	0.9	0	0.1

Eggs

A TYPICAL SIZE 3 EGG

Egg, boiled Although egg yolks are high in cholesterol, they also contain lecithin which breaks down cholesterol and disperses fatty deposits in the blood.

Cals	Protein	Fat	Sugar	Fibre	Sodium
74	6.2	5.4	0	0	140

Egg, fried The fried egg contains more calories than a boiled egg, because of the cooking fat that clings to it.

Cals	Protein	Fat	Sugar	Fibre	Sodium
90	6.8	7.0	0	0	80

Yoghurts

A TYPICAL 5FL OZ (150ML) CARTON

Yoghurt, fruit low-fat Live cultures are often destroyed during the production of fruit yoghurts because the fruit and milk combine during fermentation.

Cals	Protein	Fat	Sugar	Fibre	Sodium
135	6.1	1.1	26.7	0	96

Yoghurt, Greek The flavour and texture of yoghurt depends on the bacterial culture used to make it. Greek yoghurt is particularly thick and creamy and makes a good substitute for cream.

Cals	Protein	Fat	Sugar	Fibre	Sodium
175	9.6	13.6	3.0	0	107

Yoghurt, natural live Yoghurts that are labelled 'live' are made from pasteurised milk. The milk is heated at a low temperature which kills disease allowing the live bacteria which give the yoghurt its flavour to survive.

Cals	Protein	Fat	Sugar	Fibre	Sodium
119	8.6	4.5	11.7	0	120

Yoghurt, natural low-fat Yoghurt is fermented using skimmed or low-fat milk and can make an excellent base for a low-fat salad dressing.

Cals	Protein	Fat	Sugar	Fibre	Sodium
84	7.7	1.2	9.3	0	125

Ice Cream

A TYPICAL 2¼OZ (60G) SCOOP

Ice Cream, dairy Normally, it is only the more expensive ice creams that are made with a lot of real cream. Lard and synthetic additives and flavourings are often used to give the cheaper varieties a rich and creamy texture.

Cals	Protein	Fat	Sugar	Fibre	Sodium
116	2.2	4.0	13.6	0	48

Ice Cream, low-fat The fat content of ice cream is greatly reduced by using low-fat dairy ingredients. As much as 65% of ice cream can be air, which is pumped into it to make it soft and light.

Cals	Protein	Fat	Sugar	Fibre	Sodium
40	1.0	1.7	4.3	0	25

Sorbet These desserts are made from sugar, syrup and flavourings. Fruits, liqueurs or chopped herbs may be added. Sometimes savoury sorbets, such as tomato and basil, are served in expensive restaurants to clear the palate in between courses.

Cals	Protein	Fat	Sugar	Fibre	Sodium
79	0.5	0	20.5	0	35

Cheese

A TYPICAL 1OZ (25G) SERVING

Camembert types These are delicately flavoured cheeses that soften as they mature. At their peak, they ooze when they are cut open. They should not be refrigerated when ripe.

Cals	Protein	Fat	Sugar	Fibre	Sodium
89	6.3	7.1	0	0	195

Cheddar English Cheddar can be mild or strong in flavour, and can often be substituted for expensive hard cheeses.

Cals	Protein	Fat	Sugar	Fibre	Sodium
124	7.7	10.3	0	0	201

Cottage Cheese This is a fresh curd cheese which is very low in fat compared with cream cheese, which contains five times as many calories.

Cals	Protein	Fat	Sugar	Fibre	Sodium
29	4.0	0.5	0.5	0	114

Edam type A mild, Dutch, hard-pressed cheese that is often thought to be a low-fat cheese. It is medium to high-fat.

Cals	Protein	Fat	Sugar	Fibre	Sodium
100	7.8	7.6	0	0	306

Feta Medium-fat Greek Feta is made from either goat's or sheep's milk. Fresh Feta is moist and crumbly but becomes dry and salty as it ages.

Cals	Protein	Fat	Sugar	Fibre	Sodium
75	4.6	6.1	0.5	0	432

Fromage Frais This light, fresh French cheese has the consistency of thick yoghurt. It has a refreshing, slightly tart taste. Low-fat varieties are available which make healthy low-calorie sauces, salad dressings and dessert toppings.

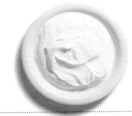

Cals	Protein	Fat	Sugar	Fibre	Sodium
34	2.0	2.0	1.7	0	33

Mozzarella Italian Mozzarella is one of the best soft cheeses for cooking as it melts so easily. It is used frequently in Italian dishes like pasta and pizza.

Cals	Protein	Fat	Sugar	Fibre	Sodium
87	7.5	6.3	0	0	183

Parmesan (1tsp) This hard, strong-tasting cheese is ripened for two years before it is sold, making it rather expensive. Buy it in a block if possible, as a lot of rind is used in ready-grated varieties.

Cals	Protein	Fat	Sugar	Fibre	Sodium
23	2.0	1.5	0	0	55

Ricotta Fresh Ricotta is a soft versatile cheese used in cooking both savoury and sweet dishes. It forms the basis of many Italian pasta fillings. It can also be pressed and served as a table cheese.

Cals	Protein	Fat	Sugar	Fibre	Sodium
43	2.8	3.3	0.6	0	30

Stilton The process by which English Stilton is made; with double cream and marked by blue veins, gives it a piquant flavour. It crumbles easily for whisking into white sauces or dressings.

Cals	Protein	Fat	Sugar	Fibre	Sodium
133	6.8	10.6	0	0	279

Fats, Spreads and Oils

A TYPICAL ½OZ (15G) SERVING

Butter, salted Rich in fat and vitamins A and D, salted butter is cheaper and usually sweeter than unsalted varieties.

Cals	Protein	Fat	Sugar	Fibre	Sodium
111	tr	12.3	0	0	130

Margarine All modern margarines are made from around 85% vegetable oil, with colour, flavourings, salt and preservatives. Many are high in saturated fats to keep them firm.

Cals	Protein	Fat	Sugar	Fibre	Sodium
110	tr	12.2	0	0	120

Low-fat Spreads These contain about half the calories and fat of ordinary margarines but should not be used for cooking because of their water content.

Cals	Protein	Fat	Sugar	Fibre	Sodium
55	tr	6.1	0	0	103

Cooking Oils These include sunflower oil (which is high in the healthier polyunsaturated fats) and olive oil (the finest and dearest oil) containing only polyunsaturated fats. Virgin olive oil is actually cholesterol-free.

Greek virgin olive oil   *Spanish virgin olive oil*

Cals	Protein	Fat	Sugar	Fibre	Sodium
134	0	15.0	0	0	0.3

Lard and Dripping Dripping is mutton and beef fat; lard is the softer fat of pork. Both are fat and cholesterol-rich and can often be made at home.

Cals	Protein	Fat	Sugar	Fibre	Sodium
134	0	15.0	0	0	0.3

Nuts

Shelled Nuts

A TYPICAL 1OZ (25G) SERVING

Almonds, whole There are two types of almond: bitter almonds that are used to make oil, and sweet almonds which are used in cake-making as well as in desserts and even meat dishes.

Cals	Protein	Fat	Sugar	Fibre	Sodium
130	5.1	16.1	1.3	4.1	2.0

Chestnuts A sweet and starchy nut that is low in fat and often used in stuffings. Store chestnuts in a cool place, as they mould quickly at room temperature.

Cals	Protein	Fat	Sugar	Fibre	Sodium
51	0.6	0.8	2.1	2.0	3.0

Hazelnuts Hazelnuts have been collected and eaten by man since the Bronze Age. For most cooking purposes, hazelnuts can be bought ready-shelled, chopped or ground. Shelled hazelnuts, like almonds, keep better than most nuts.

Cals	Protein	Fat	Sugar	Fibre	Sodium
98	4.3	20.5	1.1	2.8	0.6

Peanuts, fresh This highly popular snack food is the seed of a tropical pulse. They can become soft and lose their taste if overcooked.

Cals	Protein	Fat	Sugar	Fibre	Sodium
132	7.3	14.7	0.9	2.4	2.0

Pine Nuts, fresh The seeds of certain pine trees, pine nuts are usually sold blanched, and after toasting to improve their sweet aroma they may be ground for adding to savoury dishes, or sprinkled whole on salads and desserts.

Cals	Protein	Fat	Sugar	Fibre	Sodium
140	6.2	16.5	1.1	2.1	1.9

Pistachios Fresh pistachio nuts have a much stronger flavour than older ones. They are used frequently in patés, stuffings and terrines, as well as in cakes and sweets.

Cals	Protein	Fat	Sugar	Fibre	Sodium
136	6.0	16.2	0.9	2.6	2.2

Walnuts Whole walnuts tend to have more flavour than ready-chopped ones. They can be bought shelled or chopped and used in sauces and salads.

Cals	Protein	Fat	Sugar	Fibre	Sodium
121	5.0	21.3	3.2	5.2	0.6

Breads, Grains and Cereals

Bread

A TYPICAL 1OZ (25G) SLICE

Bread, brown Brown bread is richer in fibre and vitamins than white bread. Some brown breads have extra wheat-germ or bran added to them, giving them an even higher fibre content.

Cals	Protein	Fat	Sugar	Fibre	Sodium
65	2.5	0.6	3.0	1.8	162

Bread, white White bread is often cheaper than unrefined breads but, although it is comparable in terms of fat and protein, it lacks some vitamins. However, it is still a good source of fibre.

Cals	Protein	Fat	Sugar	Fibre	Sodium
71	2.5	0.6	0.8	1.1	156

Bread, wholemeal This bread is made from the whole wheat kernel, making it rich in vitamins and high in fibre. It is one of the healthiest types of bread available and is an easily digestible source of protein.

Cals	Protein	Fat	Sugar	Fibre	Sodium
65	2.8	0.8	0.5	2.2	165

Bread, white pitta A pale, speckled flat bread which forms a pocket for savoury fillings like goat's cheese or Middle-Eastern aubergine mixtures. Pitta bread does not contain as much fibre as other breads because the flour is highly refined.

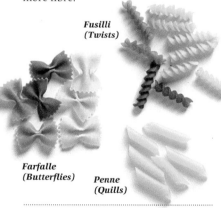

Nan

Pitta

Cals	Protein	Fat	Sugar	Fibre	Sodium
80	3.1	0.4	0.7	1.3	160

Pasta and Grains

A TYPICAL 3½OZ (90G) SERVING

Pasta, white White pastas are made with refined flour. One of the healthiest types of pasta is made with flour from 100% durum wheat which contains more fibre.

Fusilli (Twists)

Farfalle (Butterflies)

Penne (Quills)

Cals	Protein	Fat	Sugar	Fibre	Sodium
104	3.6	0.7	0.5	1.8	1.0

Pasta, wholemeal The whole wheat grain is used to make the flour for wholemeal pasta, which may take a little longer to cook.

Cals	Protein	Fat	Sugar	Fibre	Sodium
113	4.7	1.9	1.3	4.0	4.5

Rice, cooked brown As brown rice is unpolished, the bran layer is left intact. It is more filling and nutritious than white varieties because of the vitamins and fibre contained in the rice husk. It may sometimes take longer to cook.

Cals	Protein	Fat	Sugar	Fibre	Sodium
141	2.6	1.1	0.5	1.5	1.0

Rice, cooked white This is polished to remove the bran and wheatgerm. There are several types, the most popular being easy-cook. Try basmati with curries and short-grain arborio rice for Italian risottos.

Cals	Protein	Fat	Sugar	Fibre	Sodium
123	2.2	0.3	29.6	0.8	2.0

Rice, wild Wild rice is the seed of an aquatic grass. It goes well with poultry and makes delicious rice salads. You can buy it in health food shops.

Cals	Protein	Fat	Sugar	Fibre	Sodium
147	3.6	0.8	tr	5.2	4.0

Cereals

A TYPICAL 1¼ OZ (30G) SERVING

Bran The high-fibre, protective outer coat of grains, called bran, which is often lost during the manufacture of commercial breakfast cereals. It is not necessary to add bran to foods if you are eating a wide variety of wholefoods.

Cals	Protein	Fat	Sugar	Fibre	Sodium
83	4.5	1.7	4.6	8.0	22.4

Cornflakes Grains of corn are rolled flat and baked with additives which give them their taste, colour and texture. Like many modern breakfast cereals, cornflakes are fortified with vitamins and iron, and many have added sugar.

Cals	Protein	Fat	Sugar	Fibre	Sodium
107	2.4	0.2	2.2	1.0	333

Muesli, unsweetened Many mueslis are now available with no extra sugar, making them a healthier breakfast food. A muesli cereal will typically contain wholewheat and oat flakes, dried fruits and mixed nuts.

Cals	Protein	Fat	Sugar	Fibre	Sodium
110	3.2	2.4	5.0	3.3	0.9

Porridge Traditional porridge oats – actually rolled oats which are rich in soluble fibre – are still one of the cheapest and best balanced breakfast cereals available. To eat porridge the healthy way, mix it with hot water and add a little salt instead of sugar.

Cals	Protein	Fat	Sugar	Fibre	Sodium
120	3.7	2.6	0	1.9	10

Biscuits and Baking

Biscuits

ONE BISCUIT

Crispbread, rye These thin rectangular biscuit-like breads are often used as part of a diet. They are usually based on rye flour, but are also sometimes made with wheat flour.

Cals	Protein	Fat	Sugar	Fibre	Sodium
32	0.9	0.2	0.3	1.2	22

Chocolate Digestive Plain digestive biscuits are coated with a thin layer of either plain or milk chocolate.

Cals	Protein	Fat	Sugar	Fibre	Sodium
84	1.6	4.1	4.8	0.5	77

Flapjack Flapjacks are varied by the use of different flours, such as cornmeal and buckwheat. Each country has its own speciality, but they all contain a lot of sugar and are very high in calories.

Cals	Protein	Fat	Sugar	Fibre	Sodium
423	4.8	12.7	13.3	2.4	108

Meringue These light and decorative dessert casings are made with whipped egg whites and sugar. They should be baked in a very low oven.

Cals	Protein	Fat	Sugar	Fibre	Sodium
106	1.5	0	26.7	0	110

Water Biscuit These light biscuits are made largely from flour and water, and are one of the most suitable biscuits to have with cheese.

Cals	Protein	Fat	Sugar	Fibre	Sodium
35	0.9	1.0	0.2	0.5	38

Flour and Sugar

A TYPICAL 2OZ (50G) SERVING

Flour, plain white The wheatgerm and the bran are almost entirely removed during the refining processes that are used to make the flour white. Until recently, white flour has always been seen as a pure and desirable product.

Cals	Protein	Fat	Sugar	Fibre	Sodium
175	4.9	0.6	0.8	1.7	75

Flour, wholemeal This flour is very nutritious because nothing is removed from the wheat grain in milling.

Cals	Protein	Fat	Sugar	Fibre	Sodium
159	6.6	1.0	1.1	4.8	17.5

Sugar, white, 1 teaspoon (5g) Refined from sugar cane or sugar beet, white sugar provides fast-releasing energy but hardly any nutrients. It is known to be the major cause of tooth decay.

Cals	Protein	Fat	Sugar	Fibre	Sodium
20	0	0	5.0	0	0

Pastry

A TYPICAL 1OZ (25G) SERVING

Pastry, filo Consisting of several thin leaves of pliable dough, this delicate pastry goes well with a range of fillings, such as fresh fruit, meat and cheese.

Cals	Protein	Fat	Sugar	Fibre	Sodium
97	2.0	3.7	0.2	0.7	0

Pastry, shortcrust This pastry is the most versatile and easiest to make of all. Butter, flour, water and an optional egg yolk are simply mixed quickly together in a bowl. It is important that the fat is chilled to keep it firm for mixing.

Cals	Protein	Fat	Sugar	Fibre	Sodium
135	1.5	8.3	0.3	0.7	123

Jams and Preserves

A TYPICAL ½OZ (15G) SERVING

Honey Usually the paler the honey, the milder its flavour. Comb honey and chunk honey both come straight from the beehive and contain some bits of honeycomb. Honey can often be used in cooking instead of sugar.

Cals	Protein	Fat	Sugar	Fibre	Sodium
43	tr	tr	11.2	0	1.7

Raspberry Jam A conserve of whole fruit boiled with sugar, British jam differs from jelly which is made from fruit juice boiled with sugar.

Cals	Protein	Fat	Sugar	Fibre	Sodium
39	0	0	10.4	0.1	2.4

Reduced-sugar Jam The sugar content of jam is reduced by substituting water and gelling agents.

Raspberry

Apricot

Cals	Protein	Fat	Sugar	Fibre	Sodium
21	0	0	5.0	0.2	2.4

Marmalade The term marmalade is usually reserved for jams made from citrus fruits. Traditionally, marmalades are made from bitter Seville oranges.

Cals	Protein	Fat	Sugar	Fibre	Sodium
39	0	0	10.4	0.1	2.7

Peanut Butter Smooth peanut butter is essentially mashed peanuts, which seep oil when pounded. The germ of the nut is removed to prolong the shelf life. Organic brands are made without any added sugar.

Cals	Protein	Fat	Sugar	Fibre	Sodium
94	3.4	8.1	1.0	1.1	52.5

Cakes and Pies

A TYPICAL 4OZ (115G) SERVING

Black Forest Gâteau, 3oz (75g) This rich chocolate cake, sandwiched with black cherries and cream, is named after the Black Forest in Germany because of its dark colour – arguments still rage over whether it was first made there.

Cals	Protein	Fat	Sugar	Fibre	Sodium
215	2.6	12.2	24	0	0

Apple Pie, 4oz (115g) Apples such as Cox's Orange Pippins, Granny Smiths and Bramleys are baked with sugar and cinnamon. Check shop labels for additives. Pastry is high in fat and sugar. Cream adds 110 calories per serving.

Cals	Protein	Fat	Sugar	Fibre	Sodium
180	2.0	7.6	14.2	2.2	110

Sweets

ONE SWEET

Boiled Sweets Simple, uncoated boiled sweets usually contain nothing more than sugar, flavourings and colourings.

Cals	Protein	Fat	Sugar	Fibre	Sodium
23	0	0	6.1	0	0

Chocolate, milk, 2oz (50g) Whole milk is flavoured with a chocolate syrup or powder and set to form a variety of different brands.

Cals	Protein	Fat	Sugar	Fibre	Sodium
265	4.2	15.2	28.5	0	120

Chocolate, plain, 2oz (50g) Plain and milk chocolates are sweetened to make them palatable. The amount of cocoa solids varies from brand to brand.

Cals	Protein	Fat	Sugar	Fibre	Sodium
263	2.4	14.6	29.7	0	11

Toffee Toffee is made by adding butter to sugar that is boiled with a little water.

Cals	Protein	Fat	Sugar	Fibre	Sodium
4	0.7	0.8	5.7	0	26

Convenience Foods

Baked Beans in tomato sauce, 4oz (115g) Nutritious, high-fibre haricot beans are baked and served in a tomato sauce which contains a lot of sugar and sodium. Reduced-sugar tins of beans are now available.

Cals	Protein	Fat	Sugar	Fibre	Sodium
64	5.1	0.5	5.2	7.3	480

Chicken Curry, 11oz (300g) portion As with many precooked foods, ready-made curry needs quite a lot of sodium and preservatives in order to reach you in a palatable condition.

Cals	Protein	Fat	Sugar	Fibre	Sodium
627	28.7	54	6.2	0.3	1221

Chips, deep fried Oven-ready varieties contain up to 40% less fat than ordinary fried chips. Do not repeatedly use the same deep-frying oil.

Cals	Protein	Fat	Sugar	Fibre	Sodium
253	3.8	10.9	0	0	12

Crisps, 1¼ oz (30g) packet Although crisps are usually cooked in unsaturated fat, as much as 38% of it is absorbed by the crisp. Most low-fat crisps contain only a little less fat than ordinary ones.

Cals	Protein	Fat	Sugar	Fibre	Sodium
149	1.8	10	tr	3.3	154

Fish Fingers, fried Cod or hake pieces are shaped and deep-fried in breadcrumbs. They can be cooked from the freezer or grilled in a few minutes.

Cals	Protein	Fat	Sugar	Fibre	Sodium
233	13.5	12.7	0	0	350

Hamburger with Bun, 4oz (115g) The hamburger is made of minced meat of varying purity and grilled or fried. It is often topped with various condiments, cheese or onions.

Cals	Protein	Fat	Sugar	Fibre	Sodium
246	13.7	10	1.4	3.1	386

Lasagne, 8oz (225g) portion Squares or wide strips of pasta are layered and baked with minced meat, tomato and a cheesy Béchamel sauce that is made with butter, flour, milk or cream.

Cals	Protein	Fat	Sugar	Fibre	Sodium
403	23.7	19.6	1.8	1.5	638

Pizza, 4oz (115g) tomato and cheese slice It is easy to prepare a homemade pizza with a dough base and toppings of your choice. Ready-made pizza slices are not usually as nutritious as fresh, homemade versions.

Cals	Protein	Fat	Sugar	Fibre	Sodium
235	9.0	11.2	2.2	1.8	570

Ravioli, in tomato sauce, 7oz (200g) Small casings of pasta are filled with chopped meat, cheese and served in a tomato sauce. Quite a lot of sugar and other flavourings are often used.

Cals	Protein	Fat	Sugar	Fibre	Sodium
70	3.0	2.2	2.2	1.8	420

Tomato Soup, tinned, 7oz (200g) serving Tinned tomato soup is second best to fresh soup, but it does provide a convenient and tasty snack. Beware of high sugar and sodium contents.

Cals	Protein	Fat	Sugar	Fibre	Sodium
110	1.6	6.6	5.2	0	920

Non-alcoholic Drinks

Chocolate, Coffee and Tea

A TYPICAL CUP OR GLASS (100ML)

Chocolate, Hot, powder (1tsp) Sweetened cocoa or powdered chocolate is mixed with hot water or milk to make a hot drink that is high in calories.

Cals	Protein	Fat	Sugar	Fibre	Sodium
55	2.0	1.1	11.1	tr	53

Coffee, infused, black no sugar Filtering coffee removes the natural oils from the coffee beans. Freshly roasted and ground coffee is the purest and most flavoursome you can drink.

Cals	Protein	Fat	Sugar	Fibre	Sodium
2.0	0.2	tr	tr	0	tr

Tea, milk no sugar Made from the leaf of various tea bushes, which naturally contain caffeine, the flavour and quality of tea depends on the leaf variety and how it is prepared. Tea tastes much better when made with soft water.

Cals	Protein	Fat	Sugar	Fibre	Sodium
0-1	0.1	tr	0	0	tr

Soft Drinks

A TYPICAL GLASS (100ML)

Apple Juice The juice of apples contains vitamins and energy in the form of natural sugar which is released slowly into the body. However, these sugar levels are surprisingly high.

Cals	Protein	Fat	Sugar	Fibre	Sodium
47	0.8	tr	16.6	0	4.2

Cola, 12fl oz (340ml) The tropical cola nut contains caffeine and other stimulants. Our Western cola drinks contain cola-nut extract, large amounts of sugar, flavourings and colourings. The sugar can seriously damage children's teeth.

Cals	Protein	Fat	Sugar	Fibre	Sodium
129	0	0	34.7	0	26

Cola, diet The sugar content of ordinary cola is replaced with artificial, calorie-free sweeteners to form diet cola. It has no nutritive or calorific value. Caffeine-free diet cola is now available as well.

Cals	Protein	Fat	Sugar	Fibre	Sodium
0	0	0	0	0	36

Lemonade, 12fl oz (340ml) Lemonade can be still or carbonated, clear or cloudy. It is made with either natural lemon juice or lemon flavouring together with a lot of sugar and water.

Cals	Protein	Fat	Sugar	Fibre	Sodium
69	0	0	18.5	0	21

Orange Cordial, diluted All cordials are made from sugar, or sweetening agents, colourings and flavourings. Some brands contain the concentrated juice of real fruit with added vitamins.

Cals	Protein	Fat	Sugar	Fibre	Sodium
21	tr	0	5.7	0	4.2

Orange Juice, freshly squeezed Juice is easy to extract from oranges and has a much higher vitamin C content than processed varieties.

Cals	Protein	Fat	Sugar	Fibre	Sodium
38	0.6	tr	9.4	0	2.0

Strawberry Milkshake Thick brands of milkshake which have cream and ice cream added are very high in calories. Lower-fat, healthy milkshakes can be made at home using skimmed or semi-skimmed milk and fresh fruit.

Cals	Protein	Fat	Sugar	Fibre	Sodium
126	3.5	4.0	10.3	tr	736

Tomato Juice, tinned As with other tinned or cartoned fruit juices, check tomato juice labels to see if sugar has been added. Make your own juice with fresh, vitamin C-rich tomatoes.

Cals	Protein	Fat	Sugar	Fibre	Sodium
16	0.7	tr	3.2	tr	230

Tonic Water This carbonated drink is usually used as a mixer with spirits, especially gin. It contains high levels of quinine, a toxic stimulant which is derived from tree bark.

Cals	Protein	Fat	Sugar	Fibre	Sodium
56	0	0	16.9	0	18

Alcoholic Drinks

Beers

A ½ PINT (285ML) MEASURE

Bitter, best Draught beers include light ale, pale ale and export ale, as well as popular best bitter. The nutritional figures below represent an average.

Cals	Protein	Fat	Sugar	Fibre	Sodium
88	tr	tr	6.5	0	23

Lager, ordinary Fermented at a lower temperature and matured for longer than other beers. Light-coloured lagers are tangy and sharp – they are usually better for cooking than darker brews which are stronger and very smooth.

Cals	Protein	Fat	Sugar	Fibre	Sodium
83	0.6	0	4.3	0	11

Lager or beer, strong The difference between strong and ordinary beer is surprisingly large both in terms of calories and alcohol content.

Cals	Protein	Fat	Sugar	Fibre	Sodium
175	0.6	0	4.3	0.5	11

Stout, dry Dry Irish stout gets its black colour and flavour from black malt and bitter hops. It is sometimes added to beef casseroles or stews to add richness to the gravy.

Cals	Protein	Fat	Sugar	Fibre	Sodium
105	0.9	tr	11.9	0	65

Wines

A ONE GLASS (125ML) MEASURE

Champagne Normally a blend of wines which get their sparkling quality, characterised by very small bubbles, from a second fermentation in the bottle. Always serve chilled.

Cals	Protein	Fat	Sugar	Fibre	Sodium
79	tr	0	1.8	0	5.0

Red Wine Generally speaking, red and rosé wines are made from the black grape and white wine from the white grape. Black grape skins are left with red wine during fermentation for colour.

Cals	Protein	Fat	Sugar	Fibre	Sodium
85	0.3	0	0.4	0	13

White Wine, dry The classic French wines now have to compete with Spanish, Italian, German and New World wines. Sweeter white wines do tend to have more calories.

Cals	Protein	Fat	Sugar	Fibre	Sodium
83	0.1	0	0.6	0	5.0

Fortified Wine

A ONE GLASS (50ML) MEASURE

Port When port is made, the grape fermentation is stopped quite early on by the addition of brandy. With rare exceptions, port is quite sweet.

Cals	Protein	Fat	Sugar	Fibre	Sodium
79	0	0	6.0	0	2.0

Sherry, medium Sherries are fortified by adding pure alcohol before they are blended but after fermentation. Most sherries are sweetened, but very dry styles, such as finos and olorosos, can come straight from the cask.

Cals	Protein	Fat	Sugar	Fibre	Sodium
58	0.1	0	1.4	0	2.0

Cider

A ½ PINT (285ML) MEASURE

Cider, dry The basis for cider is apple juice which is fermented in large vats. It has been made since Roman times.

Cals	Protein	Fat	Sugar	Fibre	Sodium
103	0	0	2.6	0	20

Cider, sweet Dry ciders are light and give a dry finish to dishes, with only a hint of apple. Sweet ciders, by contrast, have a much stronger apple taste. Dry ciders are good in winter stews and for basting hams, while sweet ciders are often used in desserts.

Cals	Protein	Fat	Sugar	Fibre	Sodium
118	tr	0	12	0	19.6

Spirits

A ONE SHOT (25ML) MEASURE

Gin, 70% proof Juniper berries are fermented to make this spirit. Although white gin hardly ever figures in recipes, sloe gin is occasionally used in cooking.

Cals	Protein	Fat	Sugar	Fibre	Sodium
51	0	0	0	0	0

Whisky, 70% proof This spirit is distilled from fermented grain, typically barley and maize in Scotland and Ireland. The figures for whisky apply to all 70% proof spirits.

Cals	Protein	Fat	Sugar	Fibre	Sodium
51	0	0	0	0	0

Brandy Fermented and distilled grapes produce brandy. Spirits distilled from other fruits have their own names.

Cals	Protein	Fat	Sugar	Fibre	Sodium
55	0	0	0	0	0

Eating and Exercise for a Healthy Life

Food and exercise are the key to enjoying a healthy life. A well chosen diet and some gentle exercise will give you more energy to lead your life to the full, and fight off any ailments. Physical health makes people more attractive and promotes mental well-being too. Every individual has different priorities, tastes and needs, but what they choose to eat and how they choose to exercise is determined by their lifestyle and influenced by the society around them.

The Great British Diet

In Britain a new awareness of health and fitness has begun to dawn as studies and surveys by leading nutritionists continue to show that what we eat directly affects our health. We have been advised to cut down on saturated fats and so reduce our cholesterol levels, to cut down on salt and sugar, and to increase our intake of fibre, carbohydrates, fresh fruit and vegetables – especially raw vegetables.

But the new emphasis on health and fitness has still not taken full effect. There is still a high incidence of diet-related diseases which shows that for many of us, old eating habits die hard. As a nation, only 12 per cent of men and 15 per cent of women have daily fat intakes that are as low as the recommended amount. Consequently, Britain has one of the highest rates of heart disease in the world. Heart disease is still the most common single cause of death in this country.

Although we have started to eat far more skimmed milk, low-fat spreads and wholemeal bread in our diet, we are still eating too many sweets, crisps, biscuits, cakes, soft drinks and processed meats. Sugar and salt intakes are still rising – largely due to their use by manufacturers in processed foods. And we still need to eat more dietary fibre.

Surprisingly, a recent survey shows that we are eating less than the recommended daily amounts of calories. But largely because of an inactive lifestyle, about 36 per cent of women and 45 per cent of men still weigh significantly more than they should.

The eating habits of men and women in this country show marked differences. While men are more likely to eat fried fish, sausages, meat pies and chips, women prefer to eat wholemeal bread, low-fat milk, salad, vegetables and fresh fruits – although they also have a weakness for cakes and biscuits. Older people eat more milk puddings, potatoes, butter, jam and marmalades than average while young people crave takeaways and snack foods.

Is the British diet showing any real signs of improvement? The signs are encouraging when you consider our busy lifestyle, and the wide availability of ready-prepared foods. Public demand for natural, unrefined foods and fresh foods has risen dramatically in the last few years – a demand that is being met by many supermarkets. It would seem that at last we have learnt how to eat a healthier diet and are starting to put theory into practice.

Planning for Health

The secret to improved health is to make subtle but permanent changes to your attitude towards food and exercise. There is no point trying to dramatically change your diet and take lots of exercise if you are only going to keep it up for a few days. You will find it much easier to keep to your new resolutions by making small changes that suit your lifestyle and naturally become part of your routine.

The Balanced Diet

Your body is continually trying to supply you with just the right amount of energy and nutrients you need. Under normal circumstances, your body will be able to compensate for days when you eat more, or less, than usual, and be ready to supply extra energy if you start taking vigorous exercise.

Most people only have to make small changes to their eating habits to ensure they have a varied diet which supplies them with the right number of calories and a good balance of carbohydrates, fats, proteins, vitamins and minerals. But people who persist in eating an unbalanced diet for a long time

Daily Menu Planning Guide

A varied and balanced diet containing plenty of fresh fruit and vegetables will ensure that you achieve your required daily vitamin and mineral intake. A diet comprising plenty of carbohydrates (pasta, bread, potatoes, rice) will provide the body with enough energy to function properly, reducing the need for excess fats. This chart breaks common foods down into five food groups and recommends the daily servings needed from each group. Add to your daily menu if you see that your diet is lacking in any group and cut down on fats and other foods if these should exceed the recommended servings.

Food Group	Daily Serving	One Serving	Tips
Bread, cereals and potatoes	6	1 large slice bread 2 small slices bread 1oz (25g) cereal 4oz (115g) potatoes 3½oz (90g) cooked pasta, rice etc	Choose from as many different serving options as possible. Use wholegrain bread and cereal products when you can.
Meat, fish, poultry, eggs, cheese and pulses	2	3½oz (90g) cooked lean meat, fish or poultry 2 eggs 6oz (175g) cooked pulses (beans, peas, lentils) 1oz (25g) hard cheese 1½oz (40g) medium-fat cheese (Edam, Camembert, Brie, Ricotta) 4oz (115g) low-fat cheese (cottage cheese, low-fat soft cheese)	If you are vegetarian or vegan, take care to combine pulses with cereals for a balanced intake of protein.
Milk and yoghurt	2	⅓ pint (190ml) milk 5oz (150g) yoghurt	Calcium-enriched soya milk can be included in this group. It is highly nutritious and ideal for anyone who is allergic to dairy products.
Fruit and vegetables	5	1 piece of fruit 3½oz (90g) cooked vegetables Large salad portion	Include at least one vitamin-C-rich fruit, such as citrus fruit, kiwi fruit or berries.
Fats and oils	½-1oz (15-25g)	Butter, polyunsaturated margarines, low-fat spreads Refined oils such as olive oil, groundnut, sunflower, corn or soya oil	There is a lot of hidden fat in foods without adding any extra, so use fats and oils sparingly on bread and in cooking or salad dressings.

make the body's task of matching supply with demand almost impossible. In the long-term they run a high risk of having poor health in later life.

Exercise

Boosting your energy levels, building up immunity against disease, and losing excess weight, can all be achieved by combining a healthy diet with regular exercise. While good food provides essential nutrients, exercise will build the body's strength and stamina. Exercise should not feel too strenuous or painful, and it need not be boring if you choose the right kind. It is never too late to build some form of enjoyable activity into your daily routine.

The Benefits

Good Health Vitality, improved general health, good posture, suppleness, a sense of well-being and a longer life expectancy are among the major benefits that regular exercise can bring. As your body's flexibility, strength and endurance increase, you become far better equipped to fight any tiredness, stress, stiffness and disease.

Scientific research has shown that exercise can help to prevent and relieve many medical complaints. It reduces your chances of getting heart disease, improves circulation and controls blood pressure. In the case of diabetics, it has been shown to improve tissue sensitivity to insulin, making treatment of this condition more effective.

People who exercise regularly spend fewer days away from work due to illness. They suffer less from stress, and their increased concentration levels enhance their performance at work. A healthy body leads to a healthy mind.

Weight Loss For the overweight, regular exercise is an essential part of long-term successful dieting, making it easier and quicker to lose weight on a calorie-controlled diet. Exercise helps to curb the appetite by preventing a drop in the blood sugar levels that cause hunger. It also speeds up the time that it takes for food to be processed in the digestive

system, and the rate at which the energy in food is burnt up – known as the metabolic rate.

Fat and muscle are two different kinds of tissue. Dieting without exercising weakens the muscles and causes the loss of valuable muscle tissue, whereas aerobic exercise burns away fat and builds firm muscle tissue. Because muscle weighs more than fat, actual weight loss may take longer to register on the scales when you combine diet with exercise, but your body will look leaner, and your weight loss is more likely to be permanent.

It is important to regulate your weight loss on a diet; a loss of no more than 2lb (900g) per week is recommended. If a large amount of weight is lost too quickly, muscle tissue is lost as well, and there is a greater risk of putting the weight back on.

Well-being Many people find that regular exercise relieves stress and tension and helps them cope better with everyday life. This may be because exercise stimulates the release of certain natural hormones in the brain, called endorphins, which mimic the action of morphine and have a pleasurable and pain-suppressing effect. This explains why athletes experience a 'natural high' after vigorous exercise, and why the regular exerciser will feel a general sense of self-satisfaction and well-being. Other benefits include being able to relax and sleep more easily, and having a more enjoyable sex life.

Preparing for Fitness

Exercise is an individual concern, and it is important to find the right type and level of exercise that suits you. Before beginning any regular exercise routine, you should first gauge how fit you are. Seek medical advice if you have ever suffered from high blood pressure, heart disease, chest trouble (such as asthma or bronchitis), joint pain, back pain or arthritis. Older people, or anyone with any doubts about their level of fitness, should either have a fitness test or a general medical.

Exercise before and during pregnancy can make labour and delivery much easier – consult your doctor if you are already pregnant. Antenatal clinics will recommend special exercises that are suitable during and after the pregnancy, to prevent strain on the body and to get you back into shape.

Warming Up and Cooling Down

You should always warm up and cool down before and after exercise to regulate the heart rate and to stretch and relax muscles. It is dangerous to start a vigorous exercise routine while the muscles are still cold, as this can easily lead to stiffness and injury. Warm-up exercises prepare the body properly for the task ahead, by gently stretching the muscles and improving blood circulation.

Of equal importance is the cooling-down phase, as the body can suffer from shock if you stop exercising abruptly. The pulse rate should be slowed gradually. To do this, spend the last five minutes or so of your chosen exercise routine slowing down the pace, and finishing with gentle stretching. After the cool down, relax tired muscles in a warm bath or shower.

Whatever your present level of fitness, it is vital that you warm up and cool down. Try beginning and ending your chosen exercise routine with the following gentle stretches. If you are swimming, running or cycling, start slowly for five minutes, gradually increase the pace, and then make sure you ease down the pace for the last five minutes.

If you have not taken any exercise for a while, you would do well to spend a few weeks just doing the warm-up exercises, a five-minute warm-up walk and a faster ten-minute walk, followed by a five-minute cool down and the stretching exercises again.

Remember these are gentle stretching exercises, not training exercises. The aim is to loosen and stretch muscles, tendons and ligaments and so reduce stiffness. Most of these stretches only need to be done once.

1 *Side Bends* Sit with your legs crossed. Keeping your body straight and shoulders back, raise your left arm above you and gently lean your arm and upper body over to the right. Use your right hand to support you and hold the stretch for 5 seconds on each side.

2 *Lower Back Extension* Lie on your front, lift your upper body away from the floor and support it with your elbows positioned directly underneath you. Your hands should face forwards. Keeping your elbows on the floor at all times, and your head pointing forwards, gently push your upper body an inch (25mm) or two farther away from the floor, breathing out as you push, until you feel the stretch in your lower back. Repeat 8 times, gently lowering your body to the floor between each stretch.

3 *Thigh Stretch* Place your right hand against a wall to help get your balance. Bend your left knee and lift your leg behind you. Gently hold your foot with your left hand and pull it towards your bottom. With your right leg slightly bent, look straight ahead and straighten your back. Point your left kneecap towards the floor. Hold the stretch for 8 seconds. Repeat with the other leg.

4 *Spine Stretch* Crouch on all fours and breathe in as you gently arch your spine upwards. Relax and breathe out as you slowly let your stomach drop. Concentrate on arching the upper spine. This exercise mobilises the spine and is excellent for good posture.

5 *Upper Body* Stand straight and raise your left arm in the air. Bend the arm back at the elbow so that the left hand touches the back of your right shoulder. Grasp your left elbow with your right hand and gently push back and down to stretch out the shoulder. Hold for 5 seconds. Relax and repeat with the other arm, stretching a little farther each time.

7 *Hamstring Stretch* Lie on your back and slowly bring your right knee into your chest. Holding the knee with both hands, gently pull it farther into your chest. Hold the stretch for 8 seconds. Repeat with your left leg.

8 *Overhead Stretch* Stand with your feet shoulder-width apart and extend your arms above your head and slightly backwards. Pull your stomach muscles in, straighten your back and stretch your arms high. Squeeze your palms together firmly for 5 seconds. Relax and lower your arms straight out in front of your chest. Squeeze your palms together, then repeat the exercise 8 times.

6 *Calf Stretch* Lean against a wall using both arms. Bend your left leg in front of your right, keeping your right leg straight. Feel the stretch in your left calf. To increase the stretch, lean closer to the wall, keeping your left heel on the floor. Hold the stretch for 8 seconds on each leg.

9 *Neck Turns* Stand with feet shoulder-width apart. Relax your upper body and gently turn your head around to the right, hold for 5 seconds, then turn it around to the left. Repeat 8 times in each direction, always holding the stretch for 5 seconds before changing direction.

It is important to try and choose a realistic exercise programme – one that will fit easily into your daily routine. Don't make keeping fit harder by joining a health club that is an awkward journey away from home or work, or by placing too many demands on your body too soon and straining your muscles. If exercise becomes a chore, you will find it hard to maintain your motivation. As motivation is the key to successful exercising, choose activities that are both accessible and enjoyable.

If you have not done any regular exercise for a long time, begin with some caution. It is important to build up gradually and gently so that you do not overwork your heart, lungs and muscles. If you feel very short of breath, or experience pain or tightness in the chest, dizziness, nausea, or loss of muscle control during exercise, it means that you must be pushing yourself too hard. You should always stop exercising if you experience any pain.

However fit you are, there are certain times when you should never exercise. Always wait until two hours after eating a meal, and refrain from exercise if you have a fever or viral infection, or if you feel giddy, faint or sick.

The Pulse Test Your 'resting' pulse – the rate at which your heart beats – is a useful indicator of your aerobic fitness level. In adults it normally beats 60-80 times per minute; in children it may be higher. You can measure this by pressing your first two fingers on the thumb side of your wrist (never use your thumb as this has a separate pulse), counting the number of heartbeats for 15 seconds and then multiplying the figure by four.

'In a study of 50,000 people, exercise was related to feelings of general well-being, positive moods and lower levels of anxiety and depression.'

Aerobic exercise will raise the pulse to well over 100 beats per minute. You can check the maximum rate that your pulse reaches during exercise and then note how long it takes to return to normal once you have stopped. After one minute, it should come down by at least ten counts. After ten minutes it should be below 100 and you should be breathing normally. After 20 minutes it should be back to the normal resting pulse – if not, then your exercise has been too vigorous and you need to follow a less-demanding routine. Build up slowly and surely.

As your aerobic fitness level goes up, your resting pulse rate will actually start to come down. This signifies an improvement in the blood circulation and an increase of oxygen supply; giving the heart more time to rest between beats.

It really helps to chart your exercise progress by measuring your chest, waist, hips, legs and arms, and keeping a regular record of your measurements as your body starts to firm and tone up.

Always start by taking things slowly and gradually, especially if you have been inactive. You'll make better progress if you take things easy. Even fit people should rest for at least 24 hours between exercise sessions to allow the body to recover.

Exercise and Age

It's Never too Late to Exercise Nearly everyone, regardless of age or physical condition, will benefit from regular exercise. Inactivity can prove to be highly disabling, especially among the elderly, as it causes muscles to grow weak, joints to stiffen, and the heart and lungs to function less effectively.

Although it is true that the capacity for aerobic fitness declines with age, aerobic exercise will slow the rate of this decline, and after a few weeks of increased activity there will be a considerable improvement in energy, alertness, flexibility and strength. Weight gain, caused by the slowing down of the body's metabolism, will also be under control.

The extra leisure time available to retired people provides the ideal opportunity, not only to build more exercise into their daily routine, such as gardening and extra walks, but also to take up a favourite sport, such as golf or tennis.

Exercise classes for all age groups are widely available, although it is advisable to choose those that are properly supervised. Always check to see that the level of a class is suitable for you.

Exercise must be regular. A month's activity, followed by months of inactivity, will be of little benefit. Exercise that is gradually developed into a permanent routine is of immediate and long-term benefit at any age. Making exercise a part of daily life when you retire, helps you to stay physically fit and mentally alert well into your 80's.

Which Sport is Best for You?

This chart offers a guide to the different benefits gained from popular sports and pastimes. These benefits will largely depend on how much effort goes into an activity; you may swim gently to relax and unwind or swim lengths for serious fitness training.

The calories used during a football match, for example, will depend on whether you are a forward or a goalkeeper. Similarly, you will burn far more calories by digging a garden trench than by pruning roses. The chart gives a range of calories used per minute – reflecting the intensity of each exercise.

Calorie expenditure also varies from one individual to another. The developed muscles of a person who has undergone endurance training will use up fat for energy at a faster and more efficient rate than someone with a greater proportion of body fat. At the same time, a heavier person will use more calories than a lean person to exercise. A person weighing 18 stone (114kg), for example, will use twice the calories needed by a 9 stone (57kg) person to climb stairs. This is because of the extra energy required to carry the excess weight.

Activity	Aerobic Fitness	Muscular Strength	Coordination	Relaxation	Sociability	Calories used per minute
Aerobic dancing	★★★★	★★★★	★★★★★	★★★★★	★★★★	8-12
Badminton	★★★★	★★★	★★★★★	★★★	★★★	9-18
Bowls	★	★★	★★★	★★★	★★★★	3-4
Cricket	★★	★★★	★★★★	★★★	★★★★★	3-6
Cycling (13mph)	★★★★★	★★★★★	★★★★	★★★	★★	5-11
Football	★★★★★	★★★★★	★★★★	★★★	★★★★★	10-20
Gardening	★★★	★★★	★★★	★★★★★	★	4-10
Golf	★★	★★	★★★★	★★★	★★★★★	5
Hill walking	★★★	★★	★★	★★★	★★★	8-15
Horse riding	★	★★★★	★★★★	★★★★	★★★	3-10
Netball	★★★★	★★★	★★★★★	★★	★★★	6-9
Rowing (100m/min)	★★★★	★★★★★	★★★★	★★	★★★	4-11
Rugby	★★★	★★★★★	★★★	★★	★★★★★	6-12
Running (5mph)	★★★★	★★★★	★★	★★★	★★	9-10
Running (10mph)	★★★★★	★★★★★	★★	★★★	★★	9-20
Skiing (downhill)	★★★	★★★★	★★★★★	★★★★	★★★★	10-20
Squash	★★★★★	★★★★	★★★★★	★★	★★★★	10-20
Swimming	★★★★★	★★★★★	★★★★	★★★★★	★★★★	11-14
Tennis	★★★	★★★★	★★★★★	★★★	★★★★	8-10
Walking	★★	★★	★	★★★★	★★	3-5
Weight training	★★	★★★★★	★★★★	★	★	3-5

The Live Better Workout

In addition to increasing your general aerobic fitness, you may wish to stretch and tone specific parts of your body. This simple 20 minute workout will exercise all your major muscle groups. Begin the workout using the minimum number of repetitions for each exercise, and gradually increase the number as your muscle tone improves. If you work this programme into your daily routine three or four times a week, you will soon feel and see the benefits.

As you become stronger, you can repeat a set of exercises after a 20 second rest, but never force your muscles or cause yourself pain.

1 **Bent Knee Leg Lifts** Sit with your bottom against the wall and your arms by your sides. Bend your right knee. Gently press your back into the wall and lift your left leg off the floor, keeping the knee slightly bent and your shoulders against the wall. Repeat 8 times for each leg.

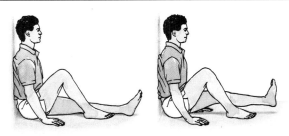

2 **Reverse Lunges** Stand in an upright position with your hands straight out to the sides for balance. Slowly take a large step back. Bend your front leg and lower your back knee until it is an inch off the floor. Keep your back straight and both feet pointing forwards. Gently straighten and repeat 8 times for each leg.

3 **Side Leg Lift** Stand sideways to the wall and extend one arm for support. Keeping your hips still, slightly bend your left leg and then cross it in front of your right leg, sweeping the floor with the outside of your left foot. Lift your left leg out to the side, and sweep it behind the right leg. Repeat the exercise, crossing your right leg over your left. Repeat 8 times for each leg.

4 **Knees to Chest** Lie on your back and tuck your hands under your bottom. Pull your stomach muscles in, push your back into the floor and lift your head off the floor and slowly bring your right knee into your chest, keeping your left leg straight. Gently pull in your left knee while you straighten your right leg. Repeat 20 times as a continuous cycling motion.

5 **Bottom Leg Lifts** Crouch on all fours and support your weight on both forearms and your left knee. Extend your right leg out behind you, keeping it slightly bent and in line with your neck. Hold your stomach muscles in to support the back and gently lift and lower your right leg, using small, controlled movements. Repeat 20 times for each leg.

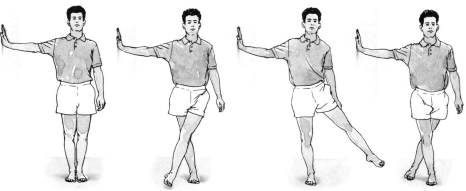

6 *Arm Dips* Sit on the floor with your knees bent. Place your palms flat on the floor either side of you, facing forwards. Gently bend your elbows and tighten the stomach muscles, then move your bottom a little nearer your feet. Lift your body up until your arms are straight. Keep your hips still as you lift. Repeat 8 times.

7 *Back Lifts* Lie on your stomach with your arms stretched out in front. Gently lift the right arm and left leg off the floor, breathing out as you lift, and raising your head. Alternate with the left arm and right leg. Repeat 4 times on each side.

8 *Side Bends* Stand with feet a bit more than hip-width apart and knees slightly bent. Gently lean over to the right, facing forwards, sliding your left arm up towards your armpit and your right arm down the side of your leg. Keep your stomach muscles pulled in, your shoulders back and your body straight. Repeat 8 times on each side.

9 *Elbow to Knee* Lie on your back with your hands either side of your head, elbows out to the side. Pulling in your stomach muscles, bring your right knee to your left elbow, straighten and bring your left knee to your right elbow. Repeat 10 times as a continuous motion.

10 *Wall Press-ups* Stand upright facing a wall with your feet about 15in (380mm) apart. Place your hands flat against the wall at shoulder height and gently lean your body into the wall, bending the elbows as you lean. Keep your elbows high and your back straight. Push away from the wall until your arms are straight and you have returned to the starting position. Repeat 8 times as a continuous motion.

11 *Half Sit-up* Lie on your back with your knees bent and your arms out straight behind your head. Pulling your stomach muscles in, gently swing your arms over your head and lift your upper body so that it is halfway towards a sitting position. Gently curl your lower back down to the floor. If this is easy, put your hands either side of your head. Repeat 8 times.

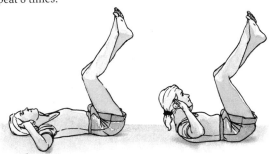

12 *Abdominal Curls* Lie on your back with your legs in the air, slightly bent and crossed. Place your hands on either side of your head and point your chin towards the ceiling. Pulling your stomach muscles in but relaxing the upper body, gently lift your head and shoulders towards your knees. Do not jerk your body forwards. Repeat 8 times.

It is important to find the kind of exercise that suits your age, temperament and preferences. There are many systems to choose from; all excellent ways to get you into shape and build up energy reserves.

Choosing Your Exercise

There are three basic types of exercise – aerobic (which means 'with oxygen'), anaerobic ('without oxygen') and isotonic. Aerobic activities are sustained and rhythmical exercises that increase the body's ability to deliver oxygenated blood to the muscles and organs, such as dancing and jogging.

Anaerobics relies on short, sudden bursts of energy for brief periods, rather than a sustained rhythmic routine. Sports in this category include sprinting and some forms of gymnastics.

Isotonic exercise is designed to develop muscular strength and flexibility, so that the body is supple and graceful. Included in this category are yoga, stretching and weight training. Stretching exercises are particularly good for easing tension out of tired muscles, and for firming up slack muscles if you're on a weight-reducing diet. They also make a good start to a fitness programme for an inactive person.

The Many Benefits of Aerobics Aerobic forms of exercise include jogging, cycling, swimming, skipping, rowing, modern aerobic dancing, and good old-fashioned brisk walking. As well as sport and exercise, any continuous activity which increases your breathing and heart rate is aerobic, such as gardening or chopping wood.

Aerobic exercise improves the functioning of your heart, blood vessels and lungs. As your body uses oxygen more efficiently, the heart becomes stronger and the arteries and veins become more elastic and free from any harmful blockages. As your breathing improves and becomes deeper, you are able to process oxygen more efficiently, and your ability to clear out carbon dioxide and other toxic waste products from the lungs improves. Aerobics also makes cell regeneration more efficient, which may help to slow down the ageing process.

To achieve maximum aerobic benefits, exercise must be sustained for a minimum of 20 minutes, three times a week, adding ten minutes to this time for warming up and cooling down.

Combining the Benefits Ideally, the three basic forms of exercise will be combined in a complete fitness schedule. You might choose to go for a run three times a week to increase your stamina and the fitness of your heart and lungs, while performing some stretching and toning exercises at home to maintain overall muscle tone and greater flexibility. Swimming is a good all-round exercise that builds strength and flexibility. Any risk of injury is lessened as the body is supported in the water.

There are many opportunities to add a little activity to your daily routine. Vigorous housework, gardening and brisk walking, all provide good exercise. Make a point of using your body as much as possible. Walk upstairs rather than using the lift, or walk to the shops instead of taking the car or bus. Get off before your usual stop for work and walk the rest of the way. Do not sit for too long – get up from time to time and move about.

Eating to Look Better

If you have ever longed to change the way you look, you will know what a frustrating and pointless exercise it can be. But it is still possible to improve on nature with a little extra attention to diet, good sleep and regular exercise. After all, a healthy-looking person is an attractive person.

Your diet affects the condition of your hair, skin, nails and the size and tone of your body, at a far more basic level than any face lotions or hair treatments you can buy. Special diets, and certain vitamin and mineral supplements, are often prescribed to help treat problems such as dull skin or split nails, but the fundamental aim in looking better must be to eat a well-balanced diet with plenty of fibre, fresh fruit and vegetables, and water to cleanse the system.

Skin

The skin is the body's largest organ. Although it renews itself, it must be fed properly to look its best. Vitamins, minerals and trace elements are all vital to the skin's health – vitamins A, C and E are especially important. Vitamin A from dairy products, liver, most fish and vegetables helps skin cells to shed smoothly and maintain the oil balance in the skin. Vitamin C from citrus fruit and some vegetables helps to repair the skin and form collagen (a protein which forms new skin). Vitamin E, found in most foods but especially vegetable oils, egg yolks, whole grains and green vegetables, protects cell membranes from damage and strengthens the immune system against infections which can adversely affect your looks. Zinc also promotes skin repair – zinc supplements are prescribed to help reduce stretch marks during pregnancy.

Plenty of fresh foods, especially fruit and deep-coloured vegetables, together with pulses, grains and fibre, form a good basis for a diet that will improve your skin. You should also eat the correct amount of calories per day for your height, build and sex, and drink plenty of water – about eight glasses a day if possible – to keep the fat layers under the skin plump, promoting a smoother complexion. If you maintain a steady weight, this will help to prevent your skin from losing its elasticity with age.

One of the skin's most important functions is to excrete toxins through its pores. The most common toxins that we regularly take into our body are alcohol, coffee, tea, refined starches and sugars. You do not have to cut these things out completely but limit them, and of course any other food that seems to aggravate a skin complaint.

Many people are sensitive or allergic to a particular food without realising it, and a poor complexion is one of the most common results of having a food sensitivity. The presence of excess toxins in the body can cause skin problems, and constipation can cause the skin to be dull because toxins are not being expelled. A reduction in the consumption of toxins will help the skin cleanse itself and aid regular bowel movement.

Protect your skin from the sun's harmful rays which can age it prematurely. When you sunbathe, drink plenty of water to rehydrate your body.

Exercise According to a study published in the *British Journal of Dermatology*, people who exercise regularly tend to have thicker, stronger and more flexible skin. Exercise increases the circulation which stimulates the supply of nutrients to the skin and makes the elimination of toxins and wastes more efficient. It also promotes production of the hormones which are essential for skin softness and resiliency. Sweating is an entirely healthy part of exercise – it eliminates body wastes, regulates temperature and helps to keep you cool.

Hair

Healthy hair reflects a healthy body. Although the basic character of your hair depends on four features that are due to heredity – density, texture, pattern and colour – its actual strength and condition are determined by the food you eat. Many of the things people do to their hair, such as dyeing it or having it permed, can seriously damage it, but illness or emotional stress can also cause hair to be dull and lifeless. Your hair condition can be an early warning of lowered vitality caused by a poor diet.

The very best way of ensuring you have healthy-looking hair is to adopt a wholesome and balanced diet, but if you are particularly worried about the condition of your hair, you should boost your intake of the vitamin B complex which is important for maintaining shining hair. It also helps to guard against premature hair loss. The best sources of this are liver, wholegrain cereals, bread and brewer's yeast. Vitamin C is also very important because it maintains the strength of the capillaries supplying blood to the hair follicles. You can buy multivitamin and mineral tablets from health shops that have been specially prepared to help promote healthy hair. Some nutritionists claim that including oily fish regularly in your diet keeps hair healthy and glossy.

As the years pass, production of sebum decreases (an oily secretion that serves to protect the hair) making hair dry and brittle, and loss of pigment causes it to become increasingly susceptible to damage. These changes, which are primarily age-related, are accelerated if there are vitamin or mineral deficiencies in the body.

Teeth

Cutting down on foods which are high in sugar is the most important step in tooth care. The bacteria which cause plaque feed on the sugar that collects on uncleaned teeth. They convert the sugar to acids which then eat into the tooth. This process is greatly hindered if you clean your teeth regularly – as soon as possible after meals and just before you go to bed.

Calcium and vitamin D are essential for the healthy development and maintenance of teeth and bones, especially in children. The minerals potassium and magnesium are equally important. Good sources of calcium are dairy produce and green vegetables. Vitamin D is found in oily fish (herrings, pilchards and sardines), dairy produce and eggs, potassium is found in avocados, bananas, meat and potatoes, and magnesium in pulses, nuts and cereals and leafy green vegetables.

Fluorine helps to protect teeth from decay, which is why it is commonly injected into local water supplies. If you are not receiving fluorine in your water, fluoride toothpaste will do the same job. Fluorine taken in excessive amounts, however, can upset the balance of other minerals in the body.

Nails

The rate of nail growth varies with the individual, but is most rapid in youth, pregnancy and warm weather. The nail weakens as it grows from the base, so healthy nails should be kept fairly short and curved to help prevent them breaking or splitting. Illness, stress and a poor diet can all affect their texture and condition.

Misshaped or spoon-shaped nails can be caused by anaemia – a shortage of the oxygen-carrying red haemoglobin in the blood. The most common cause of this is iron deficiency, due to dietary deficiences or excessive loss of blood during menstruation or an accident. Foods that are rich in iron include kidneys, liver, beans, nuts and red meat. Combine them with vitamin C which aids iron absorption. White spots or bands on the nail may indicate a zinc deficiency, in which case you should increase your intake of seafood, cereals and red meat. Alternatively, you can take zinc tablets or brewer's yeast.

Eyes

Our eyes reflect our state of well-being and the quality of our diet. Ensuring that you have a good light for reading and that you rest your eyes regularly will help to avoid eyestrain caused by overworked muscles. Your eyes should be checked regularly, as any faults in vision can lead to eyestrain, migraines and tiredness and must be detected at an early stage.

The brightness and clarity of eyes are improved by a good diet and by regular exercise, which increases the supply of blood and oxygen to them.

Muscle Tone

The condition of muscles surrounding a joint depends on the functional demands on the joint and the range of movement required of it. To be fit, joints and their muscles need to be stretched and exercised regularly. To grow in size, muscles need to be used to bear loads or to resist weights. Exercise also stimulates the release of certain hormones from the adrenals and sex glands, without which muscles and bones start to degenerate.

Muscles that are surrounded by fat will appear poorly defined, no matter how well exercised or developed they are. Rapid weight fluctuations tend to diminish the muscle tissue. Magnesium from pulses, nuts, cereals and leafy green vegetables and chloride from the natural salt in food are both beneficial to the maintenance of muscle tone.

Cellulite Lumpy, dimpled flesh that can appear on some women's bodies – usually on the buttocks and upper thighs – is called cellulite. The exact cause of it remains unproven, but it is commonly believed to be the result of a build-up of waste materials in the body tissues, creating pockets of water, fat and impurities. To eliminate an excess of toxins in your diet, stop smoking and cut down on coffee, alcohol, cakes, sweets and refined produce. Eat plenty of fresh fruit and vegetables, and take regular exercise to encourage good circulation.

Looks and Ageing

Experts in ageing have discovered that the ageing process is a combination of many changes in the body: we have internal 'body clocks' that switch off various functions as we grow older and slow down the production of important hormones; the immune system weakens and we become less resistant to illness; and then there is a lifetime's general wear and tear on the body. These factors all contribute to the formation of highly active atoms or molecules, known as free radicals, which will then react with other molecules to damage cells and collagen fibres (elastic tissues in the skin). This in turn leads to a process called 'cross-linking' which causes collagen fibres to become tangled. The skin then loses its suppleness and becomes wrinkled. Advancing age and cross-linking also cause veins and arteries to harden, muscles to soften and limbs to stiffen.

Lack of exercise and obesity are thought to speed up the ageing process. Nutrition is therefore thought to play an important role in longevity. A well-balanced, low-calorie diet that includes plenty of fresh fruit, raw vegetables and wholegrain foods may result in a longer life expectancy, a stronger immune system, and continued mental alertness.

Naturopaths claim that the following vitamins have 'anti-ageing' qualities when taken together in a multivitamin and mineral supplement: vitamin A stimulates the immune system; vitamin C is said to boost the immune system and help fight off infection and diseases; zinc rebuilds skin proteins; vitamin E is believed to slow the ageing of body cells and ward off infection and damage from air pollution; and a mixture of B vitamins prevents a range of deficiencies from loss of appetite to tiredness.

Lack of exercise is responsible for many age-related changes, both inside and outside the body. Regular exercise maintains the circulation and helps to ensure that our body tissues receive maximum amounts of oxygen. This means that you look healthier and more vibrant, and that your body is able to combat the development of many circulatory problems that are characteristic of ageing. Varicose veins, for example, can be prevented or improved with regular exercise. Aerobic exercise protects your cardiovascular system from atherosclerosis (hardening of the arteries in old age). Exercise also slows the spread of excess weight and its related diseases, and in later life it helps prevent osteoporosis – the thinning and weakening of the bones, which leads to hunched shoulders and a curved spine.

Looking Good The following are simple guidelines designed to help you make the most of your looks and your health as you get older:
- Eat a balanced but varied diet, including plenty of raw vegetables, fruit and wholegrain foods for vitamins and minerals.
- Try to exercise for 20 minutes three times a week.
- Limit your consumption of alcohol, coffee and tea.
- Avoid smoking or taking unnecessary drugs.
- Avoid too much sunbathing.
- Take up a new hobby and try using relaxation techniques such as meditation to reduce stress and keep your mind active and agile.
- Monitor your weight regularly and reduce your calorie intake slightly if it starts to rise.

Fitting Health into your Lifestyle

Many people think that organising a healthy diet is time-consuming, but eating good food takes no more effort than eating an unhealthy and badly balanced diet. Once you have made positive changes to your diet you will be much better equipped to cope with life's stresses and strains.

Fast Food There is nothing innately wrong with fast food, but if people rely too much on foods like hamburgers, milkshakes and chips, their diet is likely to contain too much fat, refined sugar and salt and not enough fresh fruit and vegetables.

On the Move If you know you are going to be travelling for most of the day and you are not going to have time to eat a proper meal, have a good breakfast and try to prepare some food at home, or perhaps buy something before you start your journey. Although the odd bar of chocolate or packet of crisps will not do you any harm, do not substitute a lot of these snack foods for a proper meal. If you are feeling a bit flat, eating a lot of sweets will boost your blood-sugar level quickly, but then as your body adapts to cope with the large influx of refined sugar you will soon be left feeling worse than ever. Nuts and fruit, or sandwiches, make a much more sustaining and healthier snack. Muesli bars contain more fibre than a chocolate bar, but most of them still contain a lot of sugar and are high in calories.

Sandwiches One of the most healthy convenience foods is sandwiches. Bread is a well-balanced source of energy, and as long as you do not spread it too thickly with butter or margarine it is not very fattening. If possible, avoid fillings which are made with a lot of mayonnaise, which is very high in fat and calories, and try replacing fillings such as processed meat or hard cheese with chicken, fish, tuna or cottage cheese and some salad. To ensure you have a well-balanced meal, complement sandwiches with a piece of fruit and buy a fruit juice or mineral water occasionally instead of tea or coffee .

Making a packed lunch for work is not only cheaper but lets you choose exactly what you want to eat, and is often a good way of using up leftovers. Making sandwiches for children is also a good way of encouraging healthy eating habits and stopping them from buying so many sweets and fizzy drinks.

Eating Out If your work or social life leads you to eat out a lot you probably need to keep a close eye on your weight and your alcohol intake. However, by choosing carefully from a menu you can ensure that you have an enjoyable meal without feeling bloated or guilty. Chicken Tikka is one of the healthiest choices in an Indian restaurant, and most Chinese vegetable, rice or noodle dishes are good for you. There is very little evidence that the amount of monosodium glutamate used by Chinese restaurants to enhance the flavour of their food poses any sort of serious health risk.

French restaurants will often use a lot of rich ingredients such as butter or cream, but there should also be plenty of soups and salads. Italian menus normally have a lot of healthy dishes, like grilled chicken or fish and most pasta dishes.

If you are concerned about your weight, limit yourself to two courses, or order a side salad or an extra portion of vegetables instead of having a rich dessert. Many people choose not to drink alcohol at lunch time and most restaurants now offer a selection of mineral waters and low-alcohol wines.

Alcohol

As long as people drink in moderation, alcohol will not do them any harm. However, many people are not sure how much they can safely drink, and may be drinking enough to seriously damage their health without even realising it. The chart on the opposite page is a guide to the maximum amount of alcohol a man and a woman can safely drink in a week.

Alcohol is usually measured in units – one unit of alcohol is approximately equal to half a pint (285ml) of ordinary beer or cider, one-third of a pint (190ml) of strong ale or vintage cider, a single pub measure of sherry, port, spirits and liqueurs, or a single pub glass (100ml) of wine. These equivalents only apply in England and Wales – a pub measure is 20 per cent larger in Scotland and 50 per cent larger in Northern Ireland. For men, the maximum weekly allowance with a relatively low health risk is 21 units, and no more than three units should be consumed in any one day. The consumption of these units should be staggered over the week and no more than 1½ pints (850ml) of ordinary beer or three single whiskies should be drunk in any one day. For women, the maximum weekly allowance is 14 units, with no more than two units in a day. Alcohol consumption within these limits can relieve tension, encourage a sense of well-being and is unlikely to be harmful to health. Like any drug, however, alcohol can have drastic effects on mental and physical health if taken in excess. The physical effects might include damage to the brain, liver and kidneys and cancer. Mental effects can include a failing memory and intellect, social problems and depression.

'In 1987, 35 per cent of men and 52 per cent of women in England and Wales did most of their drinking at home. In the same year, 30 per cent of expenditure on alcohol was via off-licences and the rest via pubs, bars and restaurants.'

It is not always easy to keep track of the number of alcohol units you consume over time, especially when drinking alternately between the pub, your home and friends' houses. It is easier to keep track of the number of measures you consume in a pub or bar, but you might try noting how long it takes you to finish bottles and cans that are drunk at home, especially as 'home measures' are often far larger than pub measures. Pay special attention when you are mixing your drinks. At a dinner party, for example, an apéritif, a glass of wine and a liqueur will comprise your daily limit.

A man should take 11 days to consume a standard bottle of spirits and a woman should take 16. A standard bottle of sherry should last a man four

How to Monitor your Drinking

This chart will help you to monitor your alcohol intake. It outlines how many calories are contained within alcohol and the maximum recommended weekly rates of consumption for one person. If your alcohol consumption significantly exceeds these rates, you should take steps to reduce your intake. You could limit your drinking to special occasions and have soft, or low-alcohol drinks at other times.

Item	Units	Maximum Weekly Consumption		Calories per item	Calories per 100ml
		Men	Women		
Spirits					
Standard bottle (750ml)	32			1650	220
Single pub measure	1	⅔ (21)	½ (14)	50	220
Sherry					
Standard bottle (750ml)	12			885	118
Single pub measure	1	1¾ (21)	1 (14)	75	118
Wine					
Standard bottle (750ml)	7			600	80
Standard pub glass	1	3 (21)	2 (14)	85	80
Ordinary Beer or Lager					
1 pint	2	10½	7	175	40
Large can (440ml)	1½	14	9	140	40
Small can (275ml)	1	21	14	85	40
Strong Beer or Lager					
1 pint	3	7	4½	350	80
Large can (440ml)	2	10½	7	280	80
Small can (275ml)	1½	14	9	170	80

383

days and a woman six, a bottle of wine should last two and a half days for a man and three and a half for a woman. A four-pack of 440ml cans of ordinary beer should be drunk in no less than two days by a man and three days by a woman; with strong lager, the limits are four days for a man and six for a woman. Pregnant women should try to avoid alcohol completely. However, if they do drink they must never drink more than four units in one week and no more than two units in a day.

Coping with Stress

There is no such thing as a stress-free existence and a little stress can actually be good for you. Challenges and goals at work, for example, keep you motivated and content. However, continual exposure to high levels of stress can seriously damage your health and make it difficult for your body to fight off illness.

The first step in alleviating stress is to identify the cause of it. It may come from within, such as an emotional or financial worry, or from outside – a noisy environment at work perhaps. A major change in life, such as retirement or having your first child, can also be stressful. Even if you cannot avoid the cause of stress, you can change your response to it.

There are many measures that you can take to avoid or relieve stress. If you find yourself constantly busy and rushing around, try establishing a set of priorities and foregoing some of the activities that are not so important. Keep some time free to be on your own and deal with the most important things in your life first. One of the most enjoyable aspects of relieving stress is learning how to relax.

Being able to relax is as important to your health as exercise. Ten minutes a day is enough to feel refreshed. Make yourself comfortable, either sitting or lying down, stretch and then concentrate on relaxing each part of the body in turn, working from the toes upwards. Then close your eyes and breathe slowly and deeply, listening to your breathing for ten minutes, or longer if you wish. Yoga, taking up a new sport, or simply talking about the causes of your stress may also help you to relax.

When under stress our bodies use up more of some nutrients than others – a lot of the B vitamins and vitamin C, sometimes known as the 'anti-stress

vitamins', are used. We need a daily supply of these as our bodies cannot store them, and they can easily be destroyed by food processing and overcooking, for example. Furthermore, B vitamins are destroyed by alcohol, and vitamin C by smoking and aspirins (each cigarette destroys 25mg of vitamin C in your body). A balanced diet, including fresh, unprocessed food, will provide these vital vitamins. Limit your intake of caffeine drinks like coffee, tea and cola, and do not miss meals.

The mineral calcium is important in combatting depression, anxiety, panic attacks, insomnia and hyperactivity, which are all signs of stress. Milk, cheese and yoghurt are rich sources of calcium, and it is also found in smaller quantities in wholegrains, nuts, dark green leafy vegetables and pulses.

Sleep

Sleep provides a chance to rest the mind and repair the body. Individuals need different amounts of sleep, our needs change throughout our lives and as we age it becomes normal to sleep less, to take longer to get to sleep and wake more often during the night. Too much as well as too little sleep can cause irritability and lack of concentration. The quality of sleep is also known to be important. There are two kinds of sleep: slow-wave orthodox sleep which is essential for our physical health, and rapid-eye movement (REM), also called dreaming sleep, which is essential for mental health. During the night, we alternate between periods of each. As many as 10 million people in Britain suffer from sleeplessness.

Do's and Don'ts for poor sleepers Do not rely on sleeping pills or other drugs for more than a few days without seeing a doctor. Use the tips below instead.

■ Do keep your sleep schedule as regular as possible.

■ Do try a milk drink, it contains an amino acid that causes the brain to release a mildly tranquillising substance that encourages drowsiness. But do not have a drink before going to bed if you are prone to waking up to go to the lavatory.

■ Do try to relieve stress (see Coping with Stress).

■ Do exercise during the day, the sense of mental well-being that accompanies regular exercise helps to promote good sleep, especially when combined with a healthy diet.

■ Don't eat indigestible or high-fat foods in the evening as they will keep your digestive system active. The later in the evening you eat, the lighter your meal should be.

■ Don't drink strong coffee or tea just before going to bed as caffeine is a powerful stimulant.

■ Don't eat foods you know you have a sensitivity to just before going to bed. For example, fruit and raw vegetables give some people gas, and cheese can give some people nightmares.

Food Poisoning and other Food Scares

Food poisoning is caused by the growth of bacteria in food and it can easily go undetected because infected food does not necessarily look or taste 'off'. Buying fresh food, storing it properly and cooking and preparing it hygienically will dramatically reduce the risk of food poisoning.

Salmonella By far the most common form of food poisoning is salmonellosis – caused by salmonella bacteria. It is caught from food that has not been sufficiently heated to kill the bacteria. There are hundreds of different strains of salmonella but only a few of them can cause food poisoning. Symptoms of salmonella poisoning include diarrhoea and vomiting between 12 and 48 hours after eating infected food. This is often accompanied by a temperature and headache. Cases involving the very young and elderly should be treated immediately by a doctor – very occasionally salmonella can be fatal.

Salmonella is commonly found in unpasteurised milk and milk products, eggs and raw-egg dishes like mayonnaise, and poultry products – particularly in improperly thawed and undercooked chicken. Be especially careful with these foods at parties or other functions where it is possible that food has been prepared a long time in advance or has been left standing in a warm room – both these factors can increase the risk of food poisoning substantially.

Botulism The most serious of all forms of food poisoning is botulism. Unless it is treated quickly it can quite frequently be fatal, but fortunately it is extremely rare. Botulism is usually found in tinned food, where the tin has been damaged or has blown out at the ends, like the back of a spoon.

Listeria Although listeria is not as common as salmonella, there are still thousands of cases a year. Occasionally, listeria can prove fatal for unborn children, the very young and the elderly, but unlike salmonella it has little effect on most healthy adults.

Listeria bacteria are destroyed by cooking, and they are most commonly found in milk and dairy products, particularly unpasteurised milk and soft cheeses like Brie and Camembert. Uncooked meat, prepacked salads, pâtés, poultry and seafood, and vegetables fed with animal manure are also prone to listeria. Pregnant women should be particularly careful to avoid all these foods. Precooked meals which are then rapidly cooled, known as cook-chill products, have also been linked to listeriosis.

Liver and Vitamin A

Pregnant women should be particularly careful to avoid eating a lot of liver, due to its high vitamin A content. A number of disabled babies were born to women with very high intakes of retinol – the form of vitamin A found in animal products. Animals were being fed high levels of the vitamin in their fodder and so were storing high levels in their livers. Animal feed suppliers have since been asked to reduce the amount of vitamin A in their feed.

Mad Cow Disease

Although media coverage on BSE or Bovine Spongiform Encephalopathy has decreased, cows in Britain are still being slaughtered because of it. Scientists believe it was caused by farmers who fed reprocessed, contaminated sheep carcasses to their cows. Sheep have long been known to carry the disease called 'scrapie' (a degenerative disease of the central nervous system). BSE affects more dairy cattle than beef cattle and can take up to ten years to show itself. So far there is no evidence that BSE can spread to humans or affect them in any way, but it will probably be some years before we fully understand all the effects of the 1980s outbreak.

Aluminium

The metal aluminium is used in the making of many forms of kitchenware. It is found in kitchen pots and pans, household utensils, packaging materials and aluminium foil. It is also added to table salt to prevent it from attracting water and to medicines that neutralise acid in the stomach.

Aluminium in a soluble form readily dissolves in water and can therefore be absorbed into the human body. If acidic foods, such as fruit or vinegar, are cooked in aluminium pans the food will corrode the aluminium and it will then leach into the cooking water. Food that is wrapped in foil for long periods of time may also become tainted.

An excess of aluminium in the body damages the central nervous system, and is now believed to be associated with Alzheimer's disease – a form of premature senility. It can also accumulate in the liver and kidneys, making them less efficient.

Plastic Film

Fine plastic wrapping used to cover food for storage or microwave cooking is now usually labelled 'Non-PVC' – meaning it is made without any poly-vinyl chloride – the chemical thought to be responsible for tainting food wrapped in film. But many scientists now advise people to avoid using even Non-PVC plastic film in direct contact with food, particularly with high-fat foods, such as cheese, pastry and meat.

Common Food Myths

Many of the miracle cures we hear about are merely old wives' tales passed down by relatives, or new fads that are championed by the media. Or are they? Here are some of the most popular myths about foods and the realities behind them.

Brown sugar is better for you than white False. Refined white sugar is 99.9 per cent pure sucrose. Brown sugar is less refined but is still 98 per cent pure sucrose and 1 per cent water. Although it does retain tiny amounts of minerals and vitamins, these amounts are far too small to do you any good.

An apple a day keeps the doctor away False. While it is true that eating plenty of fruit can help you obtain adequate fibre, vitamins and minerals, just one apple a day cannot. An apple will provide about 40 calories of energy, 3 grams of dietary fibre, 2 milligrams of vitamin C and very small amounts of iron, thiamine and niacin.

Meat is essential for strength False. There are large numbers of strong and healthy vegetarians and vegans, who eat no animal foods at all.

Margarine is less fattening than butter False. By law margarine must contain at least 80 per cent fat – the same as butter. Only low-fat spreads have fewer calories than butter and margarine.

Spinach makes you strong False. There is no medical basis for this idea. Spinach is a good source of vitamins A and C and contains the minerals iron and copper, but it is no more or less nutritious than other leafy green vegetables.

Garlic is a herbal cure-all Partly true. There is a firm scientific basis for the old belief that a few raw garlic cloves (or garlic oil capsules) a day are beneficial to health. Various studies show that garlic can lower blood pressure and cholesterol levels, so helping to prevent heart disorders, and there is some evidence that it can help prevent colds, chills, flu, sinus problems and bronchial complaints.

Bran is best to regulate the bowels False. It is better to eat more food that is naturally high in fibre than to sprinkle bran on top of a refined carbo-hydrate diet. Include lots of fibrous vegetables like celery, cabbage, carrots, fresh fruit and whole-grain cereals. Too much bran can irritate the bowels and cause uncomfortable bloating and wind. It should only be taken in small amounts in conjunc-tion with a fibre-rich diet, and plenty of fluids.

Special Diets for Special Needs

Almost any condition can be helped by eating the right diet. If you have high cholesterol levels, suffer from food allergies or digestive problems, want to lose weight, or have some other special need, it is still possible to enjoy your food and alleviate your condition – and you may overcome it altogether.

Food and Growth

Even before you are born you need food, and the body's need for nutrients changes as you grow and develop. Armed with a general knowledge of these important changes, you will easily be able to adapt your diet accordingly throughout your life.

Nutrition and Conception

It is now believed that the diet before conception contributes almost as much to a healthy pregnancy as what the mother eats while she is pregnant. Both partners are advised to establish good dietary habits for three months before a planned conception, and to only drink alcohol in moderation.

Pregnancy Pregnant women need a varied and well-balanced diet which contains all the essential nutrients, and the Recommended Daily Amount of calories is 2400. It is not true that a pregnant woman has to 'eat for two' – eating a normal amount, plus the odd extra serving of bread, potatoes or cereals, should cover all her needs. A pint of milk or its equivalent as yoghurt or cheese is also necessary to cover the increased requirements for protein and calcium. The average weight gain is 8lb (3.6kg) by the end of the first 20 weeks of pregnancy, then about 1lb (450g) a week until the birth. A total gain of about 28lb (12kg) is average and desirable.

Pregnant mothers need extra amounts of calcium, iron, folic acid and zinc. Iron and folic acid help to treat and prevent anaemia, a lack of folic acid can also lead to deformities in a child. Too little zinc can cause slow growth and sexual development.

To help prevent constipation (a frequent problem during pregnancy because the body's muscles are slacker) eat wholegrain cereals, fruit, vegetables and pulses to provide fibre, and drink plenty of water and healthy drinks throughout the day.

Babies

A baby grows more during its first two years than it does in the rest of its life. Milk, whether it is breast milk or manufactured infant milk, supplies all the necessary nutrients during the first six months. Breast milk is the first choice as it provides energy and nutrients in the right amounts, and is less likely to cause digestive problems or allergic reactions.

The first fluids which a mother's breast excretes, called colostrum, are a rich source of the mother's antibodies which protect the baby against many diseases. Even if a mother does not go on to fully breast feed, provided she gives her baby colostrum in the first few days after birth, she has lined her baby's gut with this infection-fighting fluid.

Weaning, or getting a baby accustomed to solid foods, is best done between four to six months, during which the baby will get used to new tastes and textures. This should help to prevent picky eating habits as the child grows. Avoid adding salt or sugar to food from the start – salt can overload the baby's kidneys, and sugar can encourage a taste for sweet things which may lead to tooth decay.

Milk will continue to feature as a major food, but by the first birthday other foods should be part of the daily intake too, and breast or manufactured infant milk can be replaced with ordinary cow's milk. Semi-skimmed milk is not recommended before the age of two years, or skimmed before a child is five.

Young Children

Because of their rapid rate of growth, children need proportionately more of all nutrients than adults. Good eating habits need to be established as early in life as possible, so avoid giving sweets and cakes as rewards. Children can be picky or faddy eaters. Offer a variety of foods without commenting too strongly, but if the child's health seems to be suffering as a result of fussy eating, seek professional advice.

Puberty

As children approach their teen years and puberty, there will be another growth spurt and a greater need for all nutrients. An addiction to fast foods or the desire to turn vegetarian are common at this time. It is important to try and find foods that teenagers enjoy, and which are also good for them.

Girls in particular will develop an awareness of their body and may become obsessed with their weight. Missing breakfast or school lunches in an attempt to lose weight will result in an unbalanced diet. If a child is overweight, missing meals is not advisable as this can affect their metabolism and concentration. A balanced and sensible diet should be followed (see Slimming Advice, page 393).

Adulthood

An adult's dietary needs vary according to sex, age and level of activity. Men require more calories than women, partly because women store more of their body weight as fat, and fat uses fewer calories than muscle. Average requirements for men and women are outlined in How Many Calories do you Need? on page 389. However, some individuals may require more than suggested, others less.

Middle Age As we reach middle age our nutrition remains just as important. Our energy and calorie requirements may drop if we become less active – but regular exercise is as beneficial as ever.

The Menopause When women stop ovulating and experience the 'change of life' (between the ages of 45 and 55) they must be careful to maintain a good calcium intake to help protect against osteoporosis (brittle bones). Excess caffeine, salt, smoking and alcohol all increase the risk of osteoporosis. For those suffering with symptoms of fatigue and depression, a balanced and wholesome diet will help improve vitality and general well-being.

Old Age In old age we need nourishing foods more than ever, because the body is less able to absorb certain nutrients. If an elderly person is living alone or suffering from illness, they may take less interest in their food. Stocking up an emergency food store (see pages 18-19) can overcome difficulties in getting to the shops. Try to cook fresh homemade soups, stews and casseroles if possible, and make sure you are getting plenty of fibre and vitamin C, which is easily destroyed by storage and cooking.

Slimming for the Overweight

There is nothing mysterious about what causes people to be overweight, and if we understand why we put weight on, we stand a better chance of taking it off – and keeping it off. People become overweight for three main reasons: they eat more food than they need – perhaps out of habit or due to stress; they lead an inactive life and do not use up enough calories; or they have inherited a slow metabolism (which means that they do not use up calories as quickly as most people).

With so many convenience foods about, there is a great temptation to eat far too much, and yet our need for calories has decreased with our modern lifestyle. Nowadays we rely more on electricity and petrol to run our lives than the energy we get from our food, and unused food energy is stored as fat. Excess weight is the result of long-term, consistent consumption of excess calories. It takes months, even years, to build up, so no one can expect to lose the surplus in just a few days of crash dieting.

Getting your calorie balance right is a long-term task. You need a method of weight control that fits easily into your lifestyle.

Who is Overweight?

More than a third of people in Britain are overweight. Half of those are just 'plump', while the other half are sufficiently overweight for dieting to be recommended on health grounds. We tend to accept obesity as a normal condition, but it can actually present a serious risk to life. Diseases which are more frequent in overweight people include arthritis, kidney disease, some types of cancer, piles, coronary heart disease, respiratory infection, diabetes, strokes, gallstones, high blood pressure, and varicose veins. It is also difficult and more dangerous to carry out surgery on overweight people.

Overweight Families Fat parents are more likely to have fat children. When both parents are overweight, there is an 80 per cent chance of their children being overweight at some stage in their lives. This can be a genetic tendency, but bad dietary habits acquired early in life are far more likely to cause weight problems in adulthood. It is therefore essential to teach sound eating habits to children.

Fat children do not necessarily become fat adults, though about 60 per cent of overweight adults have telltale signs by the age of 11. When obesity in early childhood is severe there is a high probability of the problem persisting into adulthood. Obese children have a tendency to respiratory illness, raised blood pressure, and high blood cholesterol levels.

Weight correction is easier in growing children than adults. Calorie restriction can be quite gentle, allowing height to gradually catch up with weight.

Crash Dieting

The body does not like any sudden or drastic changes in diet or lifestyle. Slimming should be gradual, and while calories are reduced, attention to nutrients is particularly important. The success of any crash diet is short-lived because water, glycogen and protein are lost from the body – rather than excess body fat. Once normal eating is resumed, body fluids are quickly replaced and there is an immediate gain in weight. Each time you lose and regain weight in this way, your body becomes a little 'flabbier' and your metabolic rate falls – and with it your calorie requirement. Weight gains therefore become more rapid, while slimming becomes even more difficult. So what is the solution?

The secret is to make as few changes as possible to your eating habits. Instead, make adjustments that you know you can follow for life. Even if you have to halve your intake of calories during the weight-reduction stage you will still be able to eat most of the foods you like and follow a meal pattern that suits your lifestyle. Once you have reached your target weight you can start increasing your calorie intake again, and your body will not have been faced with a major change in eating habits.

How Many Calories do you Need? People require different daily calorie intakes according to their age, sex and level of activity. A one-year-old baby, for example, requires approximately 1150 calories per day. A 12-14-year-old boy will need 2650, and a girl of the same age will need 2150. A 15-17-year-old boy will need about 2900 calories, whereas a girl of the same age will still only need 2150. In adult life, calorie requirement is no longer needed for growing. An inactive man with a desk job who doesn't take any exercise will only require 2500 calories a day, but a man who takes moderate regular exercise will need at least 3000. An inactive female will need 1900 calories but an active female can use up to 2500. Energy requirements gradually slow with age – a woman's requirements generally slow earlier.

Before planning a diet, assess how much weight you really need to lose; how balanced your normal diet is; and whether your lifestyle as a whole is working for or against your health. Try to identify the habits which caused your weight problem in the first place. Make a note of the situations in which you are most likely to consume extra calories, so that you can try to avoid them in the future.

If a low energy expenditure or requirement is at the root of the problem – because your metabolism is efficient at conserving energy or because your lifestyle is sedentary – your health stands to gain

Monitoring Your Weight

This chart is a guide to a desirable range of weights according to height and build for men and women. The range for a healthy person can be quite broad. Because muscle weighs more than fat, it is possible for a muscular athlete who has very little body fat to be above his maximum desired weight.

There is no hard and fast rule about age and weight – it depends on the individual, but it is quite

Women

Height		Slight Build				Medium Build				Large Build			
		minimum		maximum		minimum		maximum		minimum		maximum	
ft in	m	st lb	kg	st lb	kg	st lb	kg	st lb	kg	st lb	kg	st lb	kg
4 9	1.45	7 1	44.9	7 10	49.0	7 8	48.1	8 6	53.5	8 3	52.2	9 2	58.1
4 10	1.47	7 2	45.4	7 12	50.0	7 10	49.0	8 8	54.4	8 5	53.1	9 5	59.4
4 11	1.50	7 3	45.8	8 0	50.8	7 12	50.0	8 11	55.8	8 7	54.0	9 8	60.8
5 0	1.52	7 5	46.7	8 3	52.2	8 0	50.8	9 0	57.1	8 10	55.3	9 11	62.1
5 1	1.55	7 7	47.6	8 6	53.5	8 3	52.2	9 3	58.5	8 13	56.7	10 0	63.5
5 2	1.57	7 10	49.0	8 9	54.9	8 6	53.5	9 6	60.0	9 2	58.1	10 4	65.3
5 3	1.60	7 13	50.3	8 12	56.2	8 9	54.9	9 9	61.2	9 5	59.4	10 8	67.1
5 4	1.63	8 2	51.7	9 1	57.6	8 12	56.2	9 12	62.6	9 8	60.8	10 12	68.9
5 5	1.65	8 5	53.1	9 4	59.0	9 1	57.6	10 1	64.0	9 11	62.1	11 2	70.8
5 6	1.68	8 8	54.4	9 7	60.3	9 4	59.0	10 4	65.3	10 0	63.5	11 6	72.6
5 7	1.70	8 11	55.8	9 10	61.7	9 7	60.3	10 7	66.7	10 3	64.9	11 10	74.4
5 8	1.73	9 0	57.1	9 13	63.0	9 10	61.7	10 10	68.0	10 6	66.2	11 13	75.7
5 9	1.75	9 3	58.5	10 2	64.4	9 13	63.0	10 13	69.4	10 9	67.6	12 2	77.1
5 10	1.78	9 6	60.0	10 5	65.8	10 2	64.4	11 2	70.8	10 12	69.0	12 5	78.5
5 11	1.80	9 9	61.2	10 8	67.1	10 5	65.8	11 5	72.1	11 1	70.3	12 8	79.8
6 0	1.83	9 12	62.6	10 11	68.5	10 8	67.2	11 8	73.5	11 4	71.7	12 11	81.2
6 1	1.85	10 1	64.0	11 00	69.9	10 11	68.5	11 11	74.8	11 7	73.0	13 00	82.5

The figures in these charts are approved by the British Medical Association.

most by increasing your rate of calorie burn-off. This can be achieved with a half-hour brisk walk or swimming three or four times a week. A simple course of exercises is given on pages 376-377.

Why Activity is Helpful to Slimmers When your calorie intake decreases, your body responds by trying to save calories. It shuts off access to the fat stores that you are keen to use up, so that you do not burn up unnecessary calories. But if you start to take up regular exercise, the body will respond in the opposite way – you burn more calories, and use up more of the body's stores of fat to help provide the necessary fuel. This makes the process of slimming much quicker and easier. Replacing fat with extra muscle also aids slimming because muscle uses more energy than fat, helping you to stay slim once you have lost weight. Many people also find that exercise helps to take their mind off eating.

Seeing an Improvement

Everyone likes to feel that they are making real progress, and it's a good idea to keep a record of your weight and measurements, as well as details of your diet. You can then ensure that you prevent your weight from creeping up, and your diet from becoming disrupted. Measuring your progress every week instead of every day allows you to monitor overall progress rather than a series of fluctuations which may be discouraging. If you have one lapse you will have the rest of the week to make up for it.

normal for some people to put on a little weight as they get older due to internal or external changes.

The desirable range for each build is between the minimums and maximums shown. Only if you weigh significantly more or less than your desired range should you become concerned. A small degree of excess weight does not present a serious health risk, especially compared with the risks of smoking and heavy drinking. There are, however, advantages in losing weight if you are above the desirable range. It is easier to become fit if you are slim, and less weight means less strain on your joints, heart and other vital organs. The improvement in physical appearance will often increase your confidence.

Men

| Height | | Slight Build | | | | Medium Build | | | | Large Build | | | |
| | | minimum | | maximum | | minimum | | maximum | | minimum | | maximum | |
ft in	m	st lb	kg	st lb	kg	st lb	kg	st lb	kg	st lb	kg	st lb	kg
5 1	1.55	8 11	55.8	9 3	58.6	9 00	57.1	9 10	61.7	9 7	60.3	10 5	65.8
5 2	1.57	8 13	56.7	9 5	59.4	9 2	58.1	9 12	62.6	9 9	61.2	10 8	67.1
5 3	1.60	9 1	57.6	9 7	60.3	9 4	59.0	10 0	63.5	9 11	62.1	10 11	68.5
5 4	1.63	9 3	58.5	9 9	61.2	9 6	60.0	10 3	64.9	9 13	63.0	11 1	70.3
5 5	1.65	9 5	59.4	9 11	62.1	9 8	60.8	10 6	66.2	10 1	64.0	11 5	72.1
5 6	1.68	9 7	60.3	10 0	63.5	9 11	62.1	10 9	67.6	10 4	65.3	11 9	73.9
5 7	1.70	9 9	61.2	10 3	64.9	10 0	63.5	10 12	68.9	10 7	66.7	11 13	75.7
5 8	1.73	9 11	62.1	10 6	66.2	10 3	64.9	11 1	70.3	10 10	68.0	12 3	77.6
5 9	1.75	9 13	63.0	10 9	67.6	10 6	66.2	11 4	71.7	10 13	69.4	12 7	79.4
5 10	1.78	10 1	64.0	10 12	68.9	10 9	67.6	11 7	73.0	11 2	70.8	12 11	81.2
5 11	1.80	10 4	65.3	11 1	70.3	10 12	68.9	11 11	74.8	11 5	72.1	13 1	83.0
6 0	1.83	10 7	66.7	11 5	72.1	11 1	70.3	12 1	76.7	11 9	73.9	13 5	84.8
6 1	1.85	10 10	68.0	11 9	73.9	11 5	72.1	12 5	78.5	11 13	75.7	13 10	87.1
6 2	1.88	10 13	69.4	11 13	75.7	11 8	73.5	12 9	80.3	12 3	77.6	14 1	89.4
6 3	1.91	11 3	71.2	12 3	77.6	11 12	75.3	13 0	82.5	12 8	79.8	14 6	91.6
6 4	1.93	11 7	73.0	12 7	79.4	12 2	77.0	13 5	84.7	13 0	82.5	14 12	94.3
6 5	1.96	11 11	74.8	12 11	81.2	12 6	78.9	13 9	86.6	13 4	84.4	15 2	96.2

Doctors recommend a safe maximum weight loss of no more than 2lb (900g) a week. During the first fortnight, however, you may lose considerably more because of water loss. Once you are at your target weight, keep monitoring yourself to check that your weight remains stable. If your weight continues to drop it may be a sign that there is something wrong, and you should seek the advice of your doctor.

Which Diets Work?

Every year a 'revolutionary' new diet captures our attention, claiming to be able to help us shed pounds and feel healthier. There is no magic way to lose weight and the healthiest, safest and ultimately the easiest way of slimming and staying slim is to eat a balanced diet including fibre, while cutting down on sugary and fatty foods. Many people, however, turn to one of the diets listed below. While some are based on sound nutritional principles, others are deficient in certain nutrients and are not balanced.

Slimming Diets

Dr Atkins Revolutionary Diet A low-carbohydrate and high-protein diet that is high in total fat, saturated fat and cholesterol. You can expect to lose up to 8lb (3.6kg) in the first week, but this is mainly water. Once you start eating normally again the weight will go back on. This diet could be dangerous for people who are suffering from kidney disease.

BBC Diet A sensible diet that advocates less fat and sugar and more fibre and exercise. The guidelines include how to make the healthiest choices on the three-meals-a-day plan.

Beverly Hills Diet A low-calorie diet which relies heavily on exotic fruits such as pineapple, papaya and mangoes, eaten in a certain order on specific days. Deficient in many nutrients including protein.

F-plan Diet The first book to come out extolling the virtues of high-fibre foods when dieting. Based on 1000-1500 calories per day, the F-plan diet is low-fat and nutritionally balanced. But anyone not used to a high-fibre diet may experience excess flatulence.

Hip and Thigh Diet This low-fat diet provides between 1000-1500 calories per day. Forbidden foods and menu options are listed. Dieters are advised to include foods from certain groups, and take a multivitamin supplement whilst on the diet.

Mayo (Grapefruit) Diet Half a grapefruit or some grapefruit juice accompanies every meal; consisting of unlimited amounts of meat, fish and eggs. The diet claims that the grapefruit 'burns' fat – which is untrue. The diet is potentially unbalanced and it is high in saturated fat and cholesterol.

Metabolic Diet This diet is based on low-fat, low-sugar and high-fibre foods yielding 1500 calories per day. The diet also contains a daily programme of vitamin and mineral supplements which it claims maximises the metabolic rate.

Scarsdale Diet Based on a 14 day crash diet. It is very low in starch and is therefore deficient in certain nutrients. The amount of fluid allowed is restricted, which could lead to serious dehydration.

Rotation Diet A three-week cycle with different energy levels, followed by a diet-free week designed to increase motivation – 600, 900 and 1200 calorie days are mixed, averaging out at 900 calories over the three-week cycle for women. Men are given higher calorie allowances. Exercise forms part of the programme and a multivitamin and mineral supplement is advised if the diet is not followed carefully.

Weight Watchers Nutritionally sound, the diet has three programmes: reducing, levelling and maintenance. Exercise is also incorporated into the diet.

Very Low-calorie Diets

These diets are usually based on fluid preparations which are the dieter's sole source of calories and nutrients, although some have added solid foods such as muesli bars. These diets can cause the body's metabolism to drop lower than normal. This means that when the dieter starts to eat normally again, the weight not only returns but is also more difficult than ever to lose.

These diets do not encourage healthy eating habits which lead to a more gradual but permanent weight loss. Very low-calorie diets should only be used by the seriously overweight, and they should not be used by anyone for longer than three weeks.

Health Diets

Bircher Benner Diet A diet based mainly on raw fruit, vegetables, cereals and milk products. Dr Bircher Benner was the first to promote the breakfast cereal muesli at his clinic in Switzerland at the turn of the century. Only unrefined organic foods are allowed, and no stimulants like alcohol or coffee.

Food Combining – The Hay Diet Devised by an American doctor, William Howard Hay, to combat digestive problems such as ulcers. Many people have claimed dramatic improvements in their health after adopting the Hay Diet, but medical proof of its effectiveness is still limited.

Hay recommended that carbohydrates (sugars and starches) should not be eaten with high-protein foods or acid fruits (such as apples, pears and oranges) at the same meal. He pointed out that protein stimulates the production of acid in the stomach, and that the acid interferes with carbohydrate digestion, which needs an alkaline medium.

The major part of the diet comprises vegetables, salads and fruits. Only small quantities of fats, proteins and starches are eaten. All starches must be obtained from wholegrain products. Apart from digestive disorders, the diet also claims to help people suffering from arthritis and food allergies.

Raw Energy Diet Like Dr Bircher Benner before her, health and beauty writer Leslie Kenton promotes a diet high in raw foods and very low in fats which is claimed to be healing and health-promoting. A very small amount of meat, fish and poultry is included in the diet, but no processed foods, and no stimulants.

Slimming Advice

If you grill or steam instead of frying food, eat low-fat varieties of dairy products, and cut down on alcohol and sugar, natural weight loss can be dramatic. Choose fish, skinless chicken and lean meat, and eat plenty of fruit and vegetables. Unwanted weight can then be shed effortlessly while you continue to eat normal quantities of bread and cereals.

The recommendations for Menu Planning on page 370 will provide roughly 1400 calories per day. These quotas provide the minimum daily intake of protein, carbohydrates, fat, vitamins and minerals required by a typical adult on a balanced diet.

If you require more calories, especially if you are very active, choose extra portions from the bread, cereal and potato section (which contain about 70 calories each). It is also important to try and have something from this section at each main meal. Reduce your intake of butter, margarine and oil to just ¼ -½ oz (7-15g) per day. Remember, ordinary margarine has the same calories as butter.

> Don't Miss Meals in Order to Lose Weight. If you skip a meal, your blood sugar level drops and this leads to cravings for high-energy foods such as chocolate and sweets. Missing meals can also lead to bad long-term eating habits.

Suggested Meal Pattern Based on 1400 Calories

Breakfast 1 piece of fruit (½ grapefruit, small orange, banana etc) or 4oz (115g) of fruit juice.
1oz (25g) of low-sugar wholegrain breakfast cereal with ⅓ pint (190ml) skimmed milk.
1 slice of wholemeal bread, to be thinly spread with butter, margarine or one of the low-fat spreads.
Tea or coffee with semi-skimmed milk but no sugar.

Mid-morning Low-calorie drink of your choice, such as coffee or tea with skimmed milk, no sugar.

Midday Low-calorie soup, any flavour.
2 portions from bread section of Menu Planning.
Lean meat, chicken, fish, cheese, eggs or pulses.
Large portion of salad (with low-calorie dressing, no mayonnaise) or lightly cooked vegetables.
Fresh fruit or low-calorie fruit yoghurt.
Tea or coffee with semi-skimmed milk but no sugar.

Mid-afternoon Low-calorie drink of your choice, such as black coffee, and a piece of fruit.

Evening Low-calorie soup, any flavour.
2 portions from bread section of Menu Planning.
Lean meat, chicken, fish, cheese, eggs or pulses.
Large portion of salad (with low-calorie dressing, no mayonnaise) or lightly cooked vegetables.
Fresh fruit or low-calorie fruit yoghurt.
Tea or coffee with semi-skimmed milk but no sugar.

Bedtime Low-calorie drink made with skimmed or semi-skimmed milk but no sugar.

Vegetarianism

Vegetarianism is becoming increasingly popular in the West and, providing the diet is properly planned and varied, vegetarians and vegans are as healthy as meat eaters. True vegetarians do not eat red meat, poultry or fish, but many will eat eggs, milk and cheese. Some partial vegetarians eat fish. A vegan diet consists entirely of foods of plant origin.

Are Vegetarians Healthier?

Vegetarians eat a greater variety of plant foods than people on a meat-based diet, and there is little doubt that their diet is usually very healthy. They avoid ingesting the synthetic hormones and other chemical residues found in animal carcasses, and their diet is generally lower in saturated fats (unless they rely too much on eggs and cheese) and higher in fibre.

Research shows that vegetarians usually weigh less, suffer less from constipation, and also have lower cholesterol levels. Statistically, they are less likely to suffer from heart disease, high blood pressure, and digestive diseases. Whether this is linked to their diet, or general lifestyle, is as yet unclear.

Is Protein a Problem? If eggs, dairy products or fish are included in the diet, vegetarians will meet their protein needs. The value of any source of protein is measured in terms of both how much it contains (the quantity), and how efficiently it can actually be used by the body (the quality).

The term NPU (net protein utilisation) is used to indicate the proportion of protein in foods which is used by the body. The NPU value of eggs at 94 per cent, and cow's milk at 82 per cent, is higher than that of meat at 67 per cent. Other examples include fish at 80 per cent, cheese at 70 per cent, and tofu (soya-bean curd) at 65 per cent.

Animal proteins (including milk and dairy products) are 'complete' because they contain all the amino acids we need to build human proteins. Vegetables are 'incomplete' proteins and have to be eaten in larger quantities, as well as in combinations that have a proper balance of amino acids. As the four 'essential' amino acids are in short supply in vegetables – vegans must take special care. Complementary proteins can be combined as follows:
□ Vegetarians should combine eggs or dairy products with any vegetable protein (cereals and milk, cheese sandwich, pasta and cheese, vegetables or potatoes served with a cheese sauce).
□ Vegetarians and vegans should combine beans, dried peas and pulses with grains (rice and lentils, beans on toast). Nuts and seeds should be combined with pulses to obtain a balanced protein.

Vitamin and Mineral Deficiencies

Because vegetables are low in certain vitamins and minerals, the following list will help you to plan your meals carefully so you meet all your requirements.

Iron Eggs are a good source of iron for vegetarians. Both vegetarians and vegans need to eat a large variety of iron-rich plant foods such as broccoli,

dried apricots and figs, pulses and nuts – especially almonds. Because iron from animal sources is more easily absorbed by the body, it is important to eat foods that are rich in vitamin C (such as broccoli and tomatoes) at the same meal, as this will aid the absorption of iron. Vegetarian women who experience heavy blood loss at menstruation should pay particular attention to boosting their iron intake.

Calcium Milk, cheese, yoghurt, greens, nuts and beans are the primary sources of calcium in a vegetarian diet. Vegans need to get this mineral from grains, pulses, nuts, seeds and dried fruits. As fibre-rich foods make calcium more difficult for the body to absorb, vegans need to eat a good supply of dark green leafy vegetables and beans. Some soya milks are calcium-enriched.

Vitamin D Calcium absorption relies upon the presence of vitamin D. In summer the body is able to manufacture its own vitamin D from the action of sunlight on the skin. In winter we have to rely on food sources such as butter, margarine and some breakfast cereals. During the winter months, vitamin D supplements are recommended for vegans.

Vitamin B12 This very important vitamin is found almost entirely in animal and dairy products. Supplementation is essential for vegans, as a lack of B12 can lead to anaemia and damage to the central nervous system. Vegans can spread B12-enriched yeast extract on their bread, and drink B12-fortified soya milk. Breast-fed infants of vegan mothers must receive supplementation after consulting a doctor.

Zinc Found more in animal than in vegetable foods; vegetarians get their zinc from wholegrain cereals. As dietary fibre makes zinc more difficult for the body to absorb, a plentiful supply of zinc must be included in the diet. Good sources are whole grains, (particularly if sprouted), nuts, beans and seeds.

First Steps to Vegetarianism

The human body likes to adapt to a new diet gradually, so start with a few vegetarian dishes a week – increasing to two or three entirely vegetarian days a week – before cutting out meat altogether.

Avoid the temptation to consume large amounts of eggs, milk and dairy produce instead of meat. Some of these foods, such as cream and hard cheeses like Cheddar, contain large amounts of fat and calories. The same is true of many nuts.

The best method is to use more pulses and lentils, which are low in fat and high in fibre. Introduce them slowly if you are not used to them, or you may experience wind and abdominal bloating.

Vegetarian Recipes You will find a list of recipes that are suitable for vegetarians in the Index.

Digestive Problems

Digestive problems can arise from the type of food we eat, the way we eat it or from infection and disease. A healthy digestive system and regular bowel movements generally reflect good overall health and a balanced diet.

Wind (Flatulence) Passing wind is quite normal, and no cause for worry unless it becomes excessive or is accompanied by abdominal discomfort or other digestive changes. If this is the case, your diet and eating habits may be the cause. If you eat in a hurry, you may swallow air with your food, which is then passed along your digestive system. You should slow down and chew for a little longer. If you have only recently started eating high-fibre foods, especially beans, peas and lentils, this may also cause flatulence. High-fibre foods should be introduced to the diet very slowly indeed. Excessive flatulence may indicate a bowel problem or food allergy.

Constipation Constipation can be relieved if you eat high-fibre foods such as fruit and vegetables, wholegrain products (wholemeal bread, brown rice, oats) and pulses (beans, peas and lentils). It is very important to drink plenty of fluid (six to eight glasses) each day. As the fibre absorbs water, dietary waste is passed easily through the bowel.

Diarrhoea Causes of diarrhoea include anxiety or fear, food poisoning, viral fever, antibiotics, food intolerance, highly sugared or salted drinks, too much sun or an overindulgence of summer fruit.

Consult your doctor if symptoms persist for more than 24 hours or are accompanied by dizziness and fever. Doctors must also be consulted if babies have diarrhoea and/or vomiting for more than one hour. They can become dehydrated very quickly and need speedy replacement of body fluids. You can buy sachets of rehydration powders from a chemist, or make your own rehydration drink (for babies and adults) using 2 pints (1.1 litres) of boiled water, 6 teaspoons of sugar and 1 teaspoon of salt. Sip throughout the day when cool.

Adults with diarrhoea should avoid drinking any alcohol. Stomach upsets often occur abroad because the tap water contains different strains of bacteria which your body is not used to.

When you feel like eating again after an attack of diarrhoea, high-fibre foods (boiled rice, wholemeal bread, apples, cherries, bananas and citrus fruit) are good to eat first because they absorb some of the excess fluid from the lower bowel. They also provide plenty of potassium which is lost during an attack.

Irritable Bowel Syndrome Both constipation and diarrhoea can be caused by this condition, sometimes one followed by the other. Both are usually accompanied by flatulence. The abdomen can also become distended and rather painful. Irritable bowel syndrome is often experienced by people who are feeling very anxious or under a lot of stress. Women between the ages of 25 and 40 years are especially prone. Treatment of irritable bowel often includes slowing down and learning to relax, eating more slowly, chewing well and taking time to enjoy food. Coffee can speed up the process of digestion and may aggravate the problem, so it often helps to cut down. A high fibre, low-fat diet and plenty of fluids (six to eight glasses daily) is usually recommended. If a particular food, such as milk, or a wheat product seems to make the problem worse then you should ask your doctor to refer you to a dietitian. Keeping a diary of everything you eat and drink and noting bowel habits will help to identify problem sources.

Diverticular Disease (Diverticulosis) In Western countries one in ten people over the age of 40 and one in three over the age of 60 suffer from this disease. Evidence suggests that it is caused by diets of refined foods which block the bowels and cause infection and straining over bowel motions. Eating high-fibre foods and drinking plenty of fluid will make bowel motions easier and more regular.

Haemorrhoids Also known as 'piles'. These are enlarged veins in the wall of the anus which can be very painful and sometimes bleed. Like diverticular disease, haemorrhoids can be relieved by eating a high-fibre diet and drinking plenty of liquid to soften stools and ease their passage through the gut.

Coeliac Disease This disorder of the small intestine affects mainly young children, and is caused by an inability to absorb gluten – a protein found in some grains. Wheat products must be eliminated from the diet, as well as oats, rye, barley and processed foods that contain flour as a thickener. Sufferers can eat other cereal products such as rice, tapioca, cornmeal and cornflour. Gluten-free bread, pasta and other cereal products are now quite widely available from large supermarkets and health food shops.

Ulcers

These are small sores on the wall of the stomach or small intestine. They are either caused by an excessive production of acid in the stomach (the stomach naturally produces acid to break down food for digestion but sometimes produces too much) or a progressive breakdown of the stomach lining. Stress, smoking, excess coffee and alcohol, and possibly diets which are high in refined foods, can all upset the stomach's acid balance and harm its lining.

Many ulcers heal themselves, but some can lead to internal bleeding and in extreme cases they can be fatal. Traditionally, ulcers were treated with milk and a bland diet, but studies have shown that milk causes the release of acid in the stomach and further aggravates ulcers.

Coping with Ulcers The following tips will help to alleviate stomach ulcers, but any severe abdominal pain should be treated by a doctor immediately.

■ Learn to manage your stress (see Coping with Stress, page 384).

■ Eat a balanced diet including wholegrain cereals, breads and fresh vegetables. Avoid refined and spicy-hot foods. Eat little and often. Never rush your meals and always try to chew your food thoroughly.

■ Drink sparingly at meals (this will ensure that your food is more thoroughly chewed) but drink plenty of fluid during the rest of the day.

■ Avoid aspirin because it can harm a sensitive stomach lining or small intestine.

■ Drinking very hot drinks may cause or aggravate ulcers, so let them cool a little first.

■ Reduce alcohol and coffee consumption, and the number of cigarettes you smoke if you cannot give up. Drinking alcohol or coffee on an empty stomach is particularly bad as the lining is vulnerable.

The Heart

The heart is the strongest muscle in the body. It beats about 75 times per minute, pumping the 9 pints (5 litres) of blood in your body around the circulatory system. It contracts and relaxes like any other muscle, forcing blood away from the heart through arteries and into tiny capillaries which feed the body's tissues, then back to the heart through veins.

Blood Pressure

When your blood pressure is measured, two readings are recorded; one is taken when the heart beats and the blood is at peak pressure, and the other when the heart relaxes and exerts least pressure. These two readings are combined as a fraction to give your pressure measurement – normally around 120/80, although there will be individual variation.

High Blood Pressure (Hypertension) Arteries and veins that are healthy can expand and contract easily with each heartbeat, but as you grow older, or disease intervenes, elasticity decreases. This creates a stronger resistance to blood flow. The blood pressure in the arteries rises causing high blood pressure, known medically as hypertension. When someone gets upset, frightened or excited, their heart beats faster and pushes more blood through the blood vessels. If their arteries are inelastic, they will then develop hypertension. High blood pressure can cause strokes (a blood clot or burst blood vessel prevents blood getting to the brain), heart attacks and kidney disease. The causes of high blood pressure are not completely understood but studies have shown that too much salt in the diet may harden the arteries. Our bodies need only a little salt to function – no more than we get from a balanced diet – but in the West we eat an extra 10-12 grams per day on average (ten times more than we need). Remember that there is a lot of 'hidden' salt in processed food as well as the salt you may add at the table. You may be surprised how salty processed foods taste once you start to reduce your intake. (See section on Salt, pages 344-345.)

Heart Disease

There are many different types of heart disease including angina pectoris, thrombosis and heart failure. Heart disease is the most common cause of death in the Western World. Although the rate of deaths from heart disease has been dropping in the USA over the past few years, figures have not changed significantly in Britain, where one person dies every three minutes from coronary heart disease – equivalent to 175,000 people each year.

> *'There is less heart disease in areas of the UK that have "hard" water – which contains higher levels of calcium and magnesium. It is thought that these minerals help to guard against heart disease.'*

A combination of stress, smoking, high alcohol intake, lack of exercise, obesity, and a diet that is high in saturated animal fats, have all been linked to high levels of cholesterol in the blood. Research indicates that people and populations with high blood cholesterol levels have a higher incidence of heart disease and heart attacks.

What is a Coronary? For your body to function efficiently your heart must pump blood, which carries oxygen, through arteries. Any blockage in these arteries strains the heart and reduces the amount of oxygen being delivered around the body. The most common cause of a blockage is athero-sclerosis, a condition in which arteries narrow and become more susceptible to being blocked by fatty deposits which are partly made up of cholesterol. Heart attacks can also be the result of a blood clot forming in the coronary artery (which serves the heart directly). This is termed coronary thrombosis. Angina, a severe pain in the chest which can spread to the neck, jaw and arms, is also caused by the narrowing of the arteries. The lack of oxygen to the heart causes the heart muscles to 'cramp'.

Mediterranean Diet There is plenty that you can do to reduce your chances of heart disease. The traditional Mediterranean diet provides an excellent example of healthy eating for the heart. It incorporates plenty of fresh fruit and vegetables, pulses and cereals, olive oil, fish and moderate amounts of chicken and red meat. The incidence of heart disease in the Mediterranean tends to be low. This low-fat, low-cholesterol, high-fibre diet can also play an important role in recovery after a heart attack.

What is Cholesterol? Cholesterol is a fatty substance contained in some foods and made mainly by our livers. People usually think of it as a harmful substance that clogs arteries and leads to heart attacks, but cholesterol actually has a number of important uses. The body uses it to make vitamin D and hormones, to produce bile, to insulate nerves and form cell membranes.

The reason that cholesterol has been considered so harmful is that the typical Western diet contains far more than we need – about 500mg per day. Our bodies can regulate the amount of cholesterol they produce according to the amount contained in our food. Most people are able to manufacture enough cholesterol on a very low or cholesterol-free diet. The type of fat we eat also affects the amount of cholesterol in our blood. Unsaturated fats are much less likely to raise cholesterol levels than saturated fats. (See Fats, pages 342-343.)

Prevention and Treatment

Self-help Check list Switch to a diet that is lower in saturated fat by cutting down on meat. Buy only lean cuts of meat and trim off any visible fat. Avoid fried food (see How to Reduce Fats, page 343).
■ Include oily fish (mackerel, kippers, pilchards, sardines, salmon and trout) in your diet and eat

them regularly. The fats in these fish contain 'omega 3' fatty acids, a type of unsaturated fat which helps to eliminate cholesterol. You can also buy omega 3 tablets in health shops. Studies indicate that a 4oz (115g) portion of any oily fish twice a week can significantly reduce the chance of a heart attack.

■ When buying oils for cooking, choose specifically named oils such as virgin olive, corn, soya bean or sunflower oil. Avoid 'blended' oils because they are often high in saturated fats.

■ Try to avoid pastries, cakes, crisps, chocolate and puddings which contain hidden fats.

■ High-fibre foods have been found to reduce blood cholesterol, especially foods which contain fibre in the form of pectins and gums found in fruit, vegetables, oats and pulses.

'The vitamin C that is present in fresh (or quickly frozen) fruit and vegetables is believed to help balance our blood cholesterol levels.'

■ Limit the amount of sugar you eat or, better still, avoid all additional sugar. It is preferable that any sugar included in the diet should be eaten with high-fibre foods because this controls the sugar entering the bloodstream. Check the labels of breakfast cereals as they are often high in sugar and salt.

■ Smoking: If you are seriously concerned about the condition of your heart, you must try to give up smoking altogether. At the very least, try to cut right down on the number of cigarettes you smoke.

■ Alcohol: Refer to the maximum recommended amounts per week for men and women on pages 382-383, and restrict your drinking accordingly.

■ Exercise: If you do not lead an active life, then you should start to introduce some gentle exercise into your routine. A 30 minute brisk walk three or four times a week can greatly improve your circulation.

■ Stress and relaxation: Allow yourself plenty of time to get things done to avoid unnecessary stress. Free radicals (see page 381) can damage the blood circulatory system if the body is under severe stress. Carotene and vitamins C and E can help prevent this damage – the vitamin and mineral chart on pages 346-348 tells you which foods they are found in.

■ Weight: Find out what your weight should be by referring to the weight chart on pages 390-391 and try to achieve and then maintain your target weight.

Recipes for the Heart You will find a list of recipes that are suitable for people who are suffering with a heart condition in the Index.

Diabetes

Diabetes is caused either because the pancreas fails to produce enough insulin or because the body is unable to use insulin efficiently. Insulin is a very important hormone that is needed by the human body to turn the glucose in food into energy.

During digestion, glucose is produced from the carbohydrates present in food and drink (see Carbohydrates on page 343). Glucose from refined, sugary foods, such as cakes and biscuits, enters the blood far more quickly than glucose from unrefined starchy foods that have natural fibre (see How to Manage Diabetes, facing page).

Diabetics are unable to control sudden bursts of glucose into the blood and so must reduce their intake of sugary foods. Diabetes must be treated, otherwise glucose imbalance will cause other chemical imbalances in the body, which will affect the nervous and circulatory systems. Long-term complications may arise, such as heart disease, strokes, gangrene, kidney disease and blindness.

'Research shows that in the West, the incidence of common diabetes is doubling every ten years.'

Doctors think that this increase may be linked to the number of people eating larger amounts of refined, sugary foods. Diabetes affects men and women of all ages and is always treated with a diet that is low in sugar and fat, and high in unrefined starchy carbohydrates such as wholemeal bread, porridge oats and potatoes.

The main symptoms of diabetes are excessive thirst, frequent passing of water, weakness, leg cramps, tingling in the hands and feet, weight loss, and reduced resistance to infection. Sometimes diabetics become very irritable because of their high blood-sugar levels, and they can even lapse into a coma if these levels rise too high.

Diabetics should also be careful not to include too many fatty foods in their diet which can make you put on weight. Being overweight further upsets blood-sugar control. In addition, diabetics already run a higher than average risk of heart disease, which is linked to eating too much fat.

How to Manage Diabetes

▪ Eat regular meals and always include high-fibre starchy foods at each meal such as wholemeal bread, wholegrain cereal, rice, pasta, or potatoes in their skins. If you have a weight problem, include smaller portions of these foods. The fibre in pulses helps to control the speed at which glucose enters the blood. Ordinary tinned baked beans serve this function, but they are best with no added sugar.

▪ Avoid eating very sugary and fatty foods. Glucose, dextrose, maltose, syrup and honey are all sugars. Up to 1oz (25g) of sugar per day as part of a diet that is high in fibre will not cause any harm, as long as your weight is normal. No sugar at all is even better.

▪ Choose fresh fruit or fruit tinned in natural juice rather than syrup. Jams and preserves with no added sugar can be used in moderation. Use artificial sweeteners if necessary, but always add them to food after cooking otherwise they lose their sweet taste. Unless you are overweight, high-fibre cakes and biscuits made with ordinary sugar and whole-meal flour can also be eaten occasionally.

▪ Consider the amount of fat you include in your diet. Even if your weight is normal, you should choose low-fat foods, and try to prepare and cook food so that the fat content is kept to a minimum.

▪ Sweet alcoholic drinks, like some sherries, wine, cider, liqueurs and stout, should be avoided. For special occasions, dry wine, sherry and cider, lager, beer, spirits and low-alcohol drinks can be drunk instead, but keep well within the limits detailed on pages 382-383. Alcohol should only be taken with food. Some low-alcohol drinks are low in sugar and are particularly suitable for diabetics.

▪ Keep your weight within healthy limits (see the weight chart on pages 390-391). There are special diabetic cakes, biscuits, sweets and chocolates, but these are not necessary and can be fattening. They are often sweetened with sorbitol, which contains as many calories as ordinary sugar and if taken in excess can cause diarrhoea. Artificially sweetened low-calorie squashes and fizzy drinks are valuable because they do not contain sugar in any form.

Recipes for Diabetics A list of recipes suitable for diabetics appears in the Index. No diabetics should change their diet without consulting their doctor first, especially those taking insulin.

Food Allergies and Sensitivities

Many people suffer unpleasant reactions, such as nausea, skin problems or migraines, when they eat an everyday food that most of us enjoy with no ill effect. Almost any food can trigger an attack – anything from chocolate to wheat.

Adverse food reactions can be caused in different ways. A true food 'allergy' will cause an abnormal reaction by the body's immune system, which is sensitive to a particular food.

Food 'intolerance' is a general term used to cover reaction to food, some of which may not stimulate an immune response. It can be caused by common foods and fertilisers or pest sprays used on farm produce, or artificial colourings, preservatives and flavourings added to processed foods. Food intolerance can also be caused by enzyme deficiency, which prevents the digestion of certain foods. For example, babies have the enzyme lactase in their intestines which is essential for the digestion of milk sugar called lactose. It is quite common for people to lose the ability to digest large amounts of milk as they reach adulthood.

A food 'aversion' is when someone has developed a reaction to a certain food because of a psychological problem connected to it. For example, if a child is continually forced to eat his greens against his will, a psychosomatic reaction can then build up.

Who is Susceptible? Various medical authorities have estimated that one person in six suffers from some form of food allergy and half of those are allergic to more than one food. Many allergies are hereditary. For instance, eczema and asthma often develop in children whose parents also suffer. It is also known that we are more susceptible to allergies when we are tired or under stress, and there is a lot of evidence to show that children are more likely to have allergies than adults. But in many cases doctors

Food Allergies and Their Symptoms

Almost any food can cause a wide range of reactions, but allergies to most foods are quite rare. This chart lists the foods that most commonly cause allergies, and gives an approximate indication of how many people are affected by them. The chart also lists the most common allergic reactions to each food.

Product	Numbers Affected	Symptoms
Milk	1 person in 25	Constipation, diarrhoea, flatulence. Babies allergic to milk protein may also suffer from wind, colic, catarrh and swollen sinuses, and they may go on to develop asthma and eczema.
Eggs	1 person in 40	Rashes, swelling, stomach upsets. Egg protein can cause asthma and eczema.
Shellfish	1 person in 60	Migraine, nausea, prolonged stomach upsets.
Nuts	1 person in 66	Rashes, swelling, asthma and eczema.
Cheese	1 person in 66	Some people may be able to eat some dairy products but not cheese. Migraine, asthma and eczema.
Wheat and Flour	1 person in 70	Migraine, coeliac disease (diarrhoea and weight loss) can be caused in adults and young children by the protein called gluten, which is present in wheat, oats, rye and barley.
Chocolate	1 person in 100	Migraine, rashes, swelling, asthma and eczema.
Fish	1 person in 150	Migraine, nausea, rashes, swelling, stomach upsets.
Food Additives and Colourings	1 person in 150	Hyperactivity and other behavioural changes can be caused in some children by food additives and colourings. The colouring agent tartrazine, the food preservative benzoic acid, and antioxidants BHA and BHT are the most likely additives to cause a reaction.

still do not understand exactly what causes allergies or intolerances. Children will often grow out of allergies, but it is also quite possible for people to suddenly develop them – this is more likely to happen relatively early in life.

What Can You Do? Food allergies are difficult to trace. If a simple skin-testing technique does not produce a clear result, your doctor may recommend an elimination diet as a means of identifying an allergy. Culprit foods are eliminated for about two weeks, then reintroduced one at a time, and the effect assessed. Self-diagnosis and treatment of allergies is both extremely difficult and unwise. Even if you know you are allergic to a certain food, you will still need to seek professional guidance. A dietitian can tell you how to cut out any culprit foods, yet still maintain a well-balanced diet.

Recipes for Various Allergies See Index for recipes that contain no dairy products, gluten or eggs.

Diet and Cancer

Cancer can develop in any part of the body when normal cell maintenance and growth becomes uncontrolled. Usually, the body's immune system stops abnormal cell growth, but if the immune system is inefficient, then a cancer can develop.

There is mounting evidence to suggest that a healthy diet and lifestyle, which includes regular exercise, periods of relaxation and a positive approach to life, helps to prevent this disease.

Many scientists believe that it is the difference in diet that explains why specific cancers are common in some countries and so rare in others. Much medical research has shown that bowel, breast and stomach cancers occur less in societies where the diet is low in fat and meat, and high in fibre. Fibre may be of benefit because of its ability to speed up the movement of the body's waste products through the digestive tract, so that any cancer-causing substances do not have a chance to linger.

There are several vitamins that are believed to be important in cancer prevention because of their ability to slow down the destruction of body cells and strengthen the immune system: beta carotene (a form of vitamin A), vitamin C, vitamin E and the mineral selenium. It is best to get these from a well-balanced diet rather than taking supplements. Various cleansing diets have been developed by alternative therapists to help rid the body of toxins. These focus on raw, unprocessed and unrefined foods such as fresh vegetables, fruit, nuts and seeds.

Factors Linked with Cancer In scientific research, the following factors have been linked with cancer: diet; smoking; heavy alcohol consumption; environmental factors, such as overexposure to sunlight in susceptible individuals, and radiation from nuclear waste; and psychological factors, such as mental stress, an inability to express anger, depression and grief – all of which depress the immune system.

Eating to Reduce the Risk

■ Avoid eating too many refined and processed foods as the chemicals used in them may be harmful.
■ Eat wholegrain cereals, rather than refined cereals, which contain vitamin E – present in wheatgerm.
■ Eat plenty of fresh fruit and vegetables and include at least one raw salad in your diet every day. Beta carotene is found mainly in carrots, apricots and dark green leafy vegetables such as broccoli and cabbage. Vitamin C is abundant in citrus fruits, berries, kiwi fruit, red and green peppers. Vitamin E is found in avocados, blackberries and most nuts.

■ Include fatty fish in your diet at least once a week – it contains valuable fatty acids and vitamins.
■ Avoid eating too much fat to maintain healthy circulation and digestion.
■ Give up smoking or cut right down, and try not to exceed the recommended weekly alcohol allowances (see Alcohol Chart, page 383).
■ Moderate your salt intake.

Arthritis

There are about 100 different types of arthritis, all involving some disorder or inflammation of the joints. Individuals respond to treatment differently. Some people who suffer from rheumatoid arthritis have been known to respond to a low-fat diet; others to supplements of zinc, vitamin C and vitamin E, which should not really be taken without a doctor's supervision. If people are overweight, they are often advised to diet – by losing weight they will help to relieve the strain on their joints.

Naturopathic treatment, which helps the body to heal itself with natural therapies – including diet – is said to have had success in treating arthritis. A wholefood, largely vegetarian diet is followed which avoids red meat, salt, sugar, white flour products, cow's milk, artificial additives, tea, coffee, alcohol and acidic foods like lemons and vinegar. Plenty of raw vegetables and vegetable juices such as celery, carrot, cucumber and beetroot are recommended.

Convalescing

If someone in the family is recovering from an illness and only feels like eating a bland diet, try giving nutritious foods like natural yoghurt, porridge, clear soup, and boiled brown rice or steamed white fish with lightly cooked vegetables. Add an attractive garnish to make meals more appealing, and don't put too much on the plate. Unless a special diet is necessary, the patient can return to his normal diet when he feels ready, but rich foods should be reintroduced gradually to avoid any upsets. If meals are being served in the bedroom, ensure that the food is easy to eat, and that your patient is able to sit up straight, well supported by pillows.

Index

Page numbers in **bold** type indicate a reference to a photograph, illustration or chart.

A

Activity
  chart showing benefits of various sports **375**
  see also Exercise
Additives on food labels 10-11
Ageing
  diet and 388
  looks and 380-1
Alcohol/Alcoholic drinks
  benefits of 353
  calories in 353, 383
  diabetes and 399
  health and 382
  heart disease and 398
  labelling 353-4
  low-alcohol drinks 353
  monitoring your intake 382-4
  nutritional values 368
  organic wines 353
Alfalfa and beansprout salad 111, **111**
Allergies and sensitivities
  food 'aversion' and food symptoms **400**
Almond(s)
  and orange flan 304, **305**
  and sherry vinegar, beef strips with 206, **206**
  broccoli and nutmeg soup 62, **62**
  chocolate cake 338, 339
Aluminium
  dangers of 386
  foil 21, 386
Alzheimer's disease 386
Amino acids 341, 349
Anchovy and mayonnaise dressing 105
Antioxidant, explained 10
Antipasto, tomato, avocado and Mozzarella 48, **48**
Apple(s)
  and celeriac salad 82, **82**
  and parsnip soup 46, **47**
  and raisins, quail with 224, **224**
  and rhubarb sauce 150
  and vegetable curry 282, **282**
  'apple a day . . .' myth 386
  celeriac and walnut sandwiches 340, **340**
  juice, nutritional values 367
  lamb chops with 184, **185**
  nutritional values 356
  Parmesan and rocket salad 88, **88**
  pie, nutritional values 366
  potato and pork cakes 196, **197**
  trifle 308, **308**
  walnut and celeriac salad 92, **92**
Apricot(s)
  and mint, roast leg of lamb with 178, **179**
  and orange teabread 326, **327**
  and pigeon stir-fry 220, **220-1**
  and pine nuts, peppers stuffed with 294, **294**
  and rice salad 89, **89**
  baked ham and candied sweet potatoes with 186, **187**
  flan 296, **297**
Arrabbiata pasta 256, **256**
Arthritis 401
Artichoke(s)
  and mushroom pizza 282, **283**
  and mushroom salad 94, **95**
  chicken and tarragon pasta 121, **121**
  cups with cottage cheese 70, **70**
  fennel and lamb hotch-potch 192, **192**
  hearts with sherry 290, **290**
  nutritional values 357
Ascorbic acid 347
Ash Wednesday fish pie 159, **159**
Asparagus
  and orange tartlets with orange mayonnaise 329
  with orange dressing 44, **44**
Atholl Brose, light version of Scottish raspberry flummery 318, **318**
Atkins (Dr) Revolutionary Diet 391
Aubergine(s)
  and chickpeas, curried lamb with 206, **207**
  and courgettes, baked 280, **280**
  and tomato gratin 291, **291**
  nutritional values 357
  Sicilian ratatouille 272, **273**
  stuffed 281, **281**
Avocado(s)
  and orange salad 66, **66**
  crab and orange salad 77, **77**
  dip 156
  jacket potatoes with chicken and 326, **326**
  nutritional values 356
  sauce 182
  spinach, smoked chicken, mushroom and avocado salad 106, **106**
  tomato and Mozzarella antipasto 48, **48**

B

Bacon
  and mangetout salad 86, **86**
  and mushrooms, roast fillet of beef with 190, **190**
  nutritional values 361
Baked
  beans in tomato sauce, tinned, nutritional values 367
  cod with devilled topping 148, **148**
  courgettes and aubergines 280, **280**
  ham with apricots and candied sweet potatoes 186, **187**
  polenta with tomato and cheese 123, **123**
  scallops with garlic and herbs 53, **53**
  spare-rib chops with sweet potato 199, **199**
  squash with turkey 246, **246**
Bakery items, purchasing 9
Baking
  storing items in freezer, tables for **26**
  tins for 21
  vegetables 13
  white fish 15
Balsamic vinegar 160, 183
Banana(s)
  and raspberry sorbet 317, **317**
  loaf 324, **324**
  nutritional values 356
Baps
  curried chicken 328, **328**
  wholemeal pizza 335, **335**
Barbecuing
  meat 17-18
  white fish 15
Barley, roast leg of lamb with 178, **179**
Basil
  and sweet pepper salad with Feta 109, **109**
  and tomato sauce 34, **35**
  and tomato soup 60, **61**
BBC Diet 392
Bean curd *see* Tofu
Bean(s)
  and alfalfa sprout salad 111, **111**
  and tuna salad 106, **106**
  broad, nutritional values 357
  butter, nutritional values 357
  butternut squash and white bean soup 40, **40**
  carrots with broad beans and dill 284, **285**
  dried, destroying toxins in 13
  french, nutritional values 357
  haricot, with smoked pork 241, **241**
  mixed chilli con carne 176, **177**
  stew of duck, vegetables and dried beans 228, **228-9**
  three-bean pâté 40, **41**; salad 84, **84**
Beef
  bourguignonne 202, **202**
  braised in Burgundy wine 202, **202**
  braised, with field mushrooms 242, **243**
  braised, with Guinness 204, **205**
  bresaola with pears 43, **43**
  calf's liver with lime and sage leaves 174, **175**
  chilli con carne 176, **177**
  Chinese rolled, with vegetables 200, **201**
  Italian meatball casserole 244, **245**
  nutritional values 360
  raisin and walnut burgers 210, **210**
  roast fillet with bacon and mushrooms 190, **190**

spaghetti bolognaise
134, **135**
steak, *see that title*
stock 28
strips, with almonds and
sherry vinegar 206, **206**
tacos 182, **182**
traditional pot roast
252, **252**
veal, *see that title*
Yorkshire puddings filled
with minced 178, **178**
Beer
labelling 353-4
low alcohol 353
nutritional values 368
Beetroot
and orange salad 76, **76**
nutritional values 357
with rosemary 270, **270**
Beverages *see* Drinks
Beverly Hills Diet 392
Bircher Bonner Diet 392
Biscuits, nutritional values
365-6
Blackberry(ies)
champagne 337, **337**
fool 314, **315**
liqueur, forest fruits with
306, **306**
Blackcurrants, nutritional
values 356
Black Forest gateau,
nutritional values 366
Blood pressure 396-7
Blue Brie and radicchio
sandwiches 336, **337**
Body fat 350-1
Boiled sweets, nutritional
values 366
Botulism 385
Bouillabaisse 32, **32**
Bowls and jugs 20
Braised
beef with field mushrooms
242, **243**; with Guinness
204, **205**
pork with leeks 184, **184**
vegetable casserole
264, **265**
Braising meat 18
Bran
myth concerning 386
nutritional values 365
Brandy
and game soup 68, **69**
nutritional values 368
Bread
baking of 354
benefits of eating 354
brown 354
fibre-enriched 354

malted or granary 354
nutritional values 364-5
orange and apricot tea
bread 326, **327**
preservatives in 354
storage in refrigerator 354
types of 354
wheatgerm 354
white 354
wholemeal 354; recipe
for 322, **323**
Bread and butter pudding
with honey 316, **316**
Bread and cheese soufflé,
easy recipe 274, **274**
Bresaola with pears 43, **43**
Broccoli, almond and nutmeg
soup 62, **62**
Brussels sprouts, nutritional
values 357
BSE (Mad Cow Disease)
385-6
Buckwheat vegetable
pancakes 276, **276**
Bulgur salad with lime 81, **81**
Burgers
beef, raisin and walnut
210, **210**
country chicken 325, **325**
Butter
beans, nutritional
values 357
beans, potato and chicken
stew 254, **254**
in the diet 355
nutritional values 364
Butternut squash
and white bean soup 40, **40**
nutritional values 358
Buying food
cleanliness 10
convenience foods 10
store cupboard, stocking
the 18-19
supermarkets 9

Cabbage
nutritional values 358
pork chops with 204, **204**
potato and chilli soup
68, **68**
red cabbage ragout with
chestnuts 262, **263**
red cabbage with guinea
fowl 254, **255**
with walnuts and sesame
seeds 262, **262**

Caesar salad 100, **100**
Caffeine
in colas 352
in tea and coffee 352-3
Cajun-Creole cod 164, **164**
Cakes
banana loaf 324, **324**
cherry and vanilla gateau
330, **330**
chocolate almond 338, **339**
coffee éclairs 324, **324**
mixed nut 338, **339**
nutritional values 366
Calabrese *see* Broccoli
nutritional values 357
Calcium, source of 347, 394
Calf's liver with lime and
sage leaves 174, **175**
Californian strawberry and
spinach salad 78, **78**
Calories
expenditure of, sports
chart guide **375**
explained 11
individual daily needs
349, 389
Camembert in filo flowers
with cranberry sauce
319, **319**
Cancer
diet and 400
eating to reduce the risk
of 401
factors linked with 401
Canned food 10
Cannelloni
stuffed with spinach and
cheese 142, **142**
with crab and tomato
sauce 126, **127**
Caramel, fresh oranges with
298, **298**
Carbohydrates 11, 343-4
Cardamom, carrot and
tomato soup 37, **37**
Carrot(s)
and parsnip purée 268, **268**
courgettes and, with pasta
137, **137**
nutritional values 358
tomato and cardamom
soup 37, **37**
with broad beans and dill
284, **285**
Carotene 346
Casseroles
beef with Guinness
204, **205**
duck with peaches 222, **223**
farmhouse chicken
236, **236**
Italian meatball 244, **245**

pheasant with chestnuts
and orange 234, **234**
pork chops with savoy
cabbage 204, **204**
vegetable 264, **265**
Catalana, paella 238, **239**
Cauliflower
nutritional values 358
prawn and pasta salad
105, **105**
Caviar (or lumpfish roe),
smoked salmon and rye
bread sandwiches
340, **340**
Celeriac
and apple salad 82, **82**
nutritional values 358
sandwiches 340, **340**
split pea soup with ham
and 60, **60**
walnut and apple
sandwiches 340, **340**
Celery, walnut and apple
salad 92, **92**
Cellulite 380
Champagne
blackberry flavoured
337, **337**
nutritional values 368
Charts, *see* Tables and Charts
Cheddar, nutritional
values 363
Cheese
and bread soufflé, easy
recipe 274, **274**
and nut terrine 284, **284**
artichoke cups with cottage
cheese 70, **70**
blue Brie and radicchio
sandwiches 336
Camembert in filo with
cranberry sauce 319, **319**
cannelloni stuffed with
spinach and 142, **142**
Cheddar, nutritional
values 363
chicken with cheese and
courgette stuffing 216, **216**
Cottage cheese, nutritional
values 363
Edam, nutritional
values 363
eggs with blue cheese and
Ricotta 42, **42**
Feta, nutritional values 363
Feta, sweet pepper and
basil salad 109, **109**
figs with ham and goat
cheese 54, **54**
freezer, tables for **25**
Fromage frais, nutritional
values, 363

Cheese *continued*
  goat cheese, hazelnut and spinach pancakes 266, **266**
  goat cheese toasts 61, **61**
  goat cheese with winter salad 92, **93**
  light cheese mousse: with smoked salmon 74, **74**
  mangetout with anchovy flavoured cottage cheese 333, **333**
  Mozzarella antipasto 48, **48**
  Mozzarella, nutritional values 363
  Parmesan, nutritional values 363
  polenta baked with tomato and 123, **123**
  Ricotta, nutritional values 363
  Roquefort pears 64, **65**
  spinach and Ricotta roulade 268, **269**
  Stilton, nutritional values 364
  tomato, avocado and vegetable terrine in a light cheese mousse 58, **59**
Cherry(ies)
  and vanilla gateau 330, **330**
  nutritional values 356
Chestnuts
  and orange, casserole of pheasant with 234, **234**
  nutritional values 364
  red cabbage ragout with 262, **263**
Chicken
  and mushroom risotto 136, **136**
  and vegetable salad 98, **99**
  artichoke and tarragon pasta 121, **121**
  baps, curried 328, **328**
  breasts with raspberry vinegar 230, **230**
  burgers 325, **325**
  casserole 236, **236**
  chop suey 256, **257**
  curry, ready-made, nutritional values 367
  goulash 226, **226**
  grilled baby chickens with chilli 222, **222**
  in mustard sauce with leeks 225, **225**
  jacket potatoes with avocado and 326, **326**
  livers, bacon, mushrooms and sage with polenta 125, **125**

Mediterranean drumsticks 218, **218**
Moroccan couscous 240, **240**
nutritional values 361
orange chicken 216, **217**
potato and butterbean stew 254, **254**
pot roasted, with cranberries 250, **251**
prawns and garlic sausage with rice 120, **120**
salmonella bacteria 385
satay 64, **64**
simmered with spicy dried fruit 247, **247**
spinach, smoked chicken, avocado and mushroom salad 106, **106**
stock 27
strips in yellow-bean sauce 212, **212**
Thai chicken and coconut soup 62, **63**
tikka 232, **233**
with cheese and courgette stuffing 216, **216**
with coriander stuffing 248, **248**
yakitori 234, **235**
Chickpeas
  and aubergine, curried lamb with 206, **207**
  salad 78, **79**
  tinned, nutritional values 359
Chicory, pigeons with 215, **215**
Children
  coeliac disease 396
  dietary needs 388
Chilled vegetable soup 331, **331**
Chilli
  con carne 176, **177**
  grilled baby chickens with 222, **222**
  potato and cabbage soup 68, **68**
Chinese
  chicken strips in yellow-bean sauce 212, **212**
  chop suey 256, **257**
  prawn, mangetout and mango stir-fry 144, **144**
  rolled beef with vegetables 200, **201**
  spare ribs with five-spice marinade 195, **195**
  spicy prawns with noodles 146, **146**
  turkey stir-fry 227, **227**

Chips, nutritional values 367
Chloride 347
Chocolate
  almond cake 338, **339**
  hot drink, nutritional values 367
Cholesterol 342, 397
Chopping boards 20
Chop suey 256, **257**
Chowder
  crab 38, **38**
  ham and sweetcorn 242, **242**
Chromium 348
  and diabetes 354
Chutney, nutritional values 362
Cider
  and grapes, sausages with 252, **253**
  chicken casseroled in 236, **236**
  nutritional values 368
  pork braised in 184, **184**
  Wiltshire ham cooked in 200, **200**
Citrus fruits in a scented honey dressing 310, **310**
Cleanliness, consideration when buying food 10
Coconut
  spicy spinach soup with 72, **73**
  Thai chicken and coconut soup 62, **63**
Cod
  baked with devilled topping 148, **148**
  Cajun-Creole 164, **164**
  nutritional values 359
  Spanish marinated 154, **155**
Coeliac disease 396
Coffee
  decaffeinated 352
  nutritional values 367
  substitutes 352-3
Coffee éclairs 324, **324**
Colas
  caffeine in 352
  nutritional values 367
Cold leftovers, eating 18
Coleslaw, lemon flavoured 334
Colouring additives in food 11
  allergic to 400
Constipation 395
Convalescence, eating during 401
Convenience foods 10, 381, **382**

nutritional values 367
Cooking
  loss of nutrients 12, 13
  retention of nutrients 12, 13
Copper pans 21
Coriander stuffing 248
Corner shop, buying food at 9
Cornflakes, nutritional values 365
Coronary, explained 397
Cottage cheese
  artichoke cups, with 70, **70**
  nutritional values 363
  with mangetout 333, **333**
Country baked mushrooms 66, **67**
Country chicken burgers 325, **325**
Courgettes
  and aubergines, baked 280, **280**
  carrots and, with pasta 137, **137**
  chicken, with cheese and courgette stuffing 216, **216**
  nutritional values 358
  soup 57, **57**
Couscous
  Moroccan chicken 240, **240**
  with seven vegetables 128, **128-9**
Crab
  cakes 153, **153**
  cannelloni with tomato sauce 126, **127**
  chowder 38, **38**
  nutritional values 360
  orange and avocado salad 77, **77**
  with marinated sweet peppers in filo pastry 72, **72**
Cracked wheat salad with lime 81, **81**
Cranberries, pot-roasted chicken with 250, **251**
Cream, nutritional values 362
Creamy mushroom and walnut pasta 134, **134**
Crispbreads, nutritional values 365
Crisps, nutritional values 367
Croutons 86, 100
Crudités with tofu mayonnaise 71, **71**
Cucumber
  and dill salad 96, **96**
  Lebanese soup 50, **51**

nutritional values 358
sauce 161, 173
Cumin and parsnip soup
52, **53**
Curry/curried
apple and vegetable
282, **282**
chicken baps 328, **328**
lamb, with aubergine and
chickpeas 206, **207**

D

Dairy foods, freezer tables
24-25
Depression *see* Stress
Dextrose, defined 11
Diabetes
alcohol and 399
diet 399
explained 398
weight and 398-9
wholemeal bread,
beneficial in 354
Diarrhoea 395
Diet(s)
achieving a balanced
370-1
appearance, effects of
healthy diet on 378-81
babies 387-8
cancer and 400-1
children 388
daily menu planning
guide **370**
fats *see* Fats in the diet
1400-calorie diet 393
(The) Great British 369
menopause 388
middle age 388
old age 388
planning for health
369-70
pregnancy 387
puberty 388
salt in the 344-5
specific slimming diets
391-3
starch in the 344
sugar, how to reduce
intake 343-4
very-low-calorie 392
young children 388
Digestion, process of 349
Digestive problems 395-6
Dill
and cucumber salad 96, **96**
carrots, broad beans and
284, **285**

Recipes for Diabetics

This is a selection of recipes that are low in sugar or completely sugar-free, suitable for diabetics.

SOUPS · STARTERS · SALADS

Spiced lentil soup 45, **45**
Mushroom soup 50, **50**
Spinach and salmon
terrine 56, **56**
Cracked wheat salad with
lime 81, **81**
Parmesan, rocket and
apple salad 88, **88**

Apricot and rice salad
89, **89**
Tuna and bean salad
106, **106**
Mangetout stuffed with
cottage cheese and
anchovy 333, **333**

MAIN COURSES · VEGETABLE DISHES

Lamb with yoghurt and
Indian spices 188, **188-9**
Fettucine with two pepper
sauce 132, **132**
Baked cod with devilled
topping 148, **148**
Cajun-creole cod 164, **164**
Calf's liver with lime and
sage leaves 174, **175**
Pan-fried steak with green
peppercorn sauce
176, **176**
Roast leg of lamb with
barley 178, **179**
Pork chops with orange
and ginger 181, **181**
Veal with balsamic
vinegar and sultanas
183, **183**
Paella catalana 238, **239**
Chicken simmered with
spicy dried fruit 247, **247**

Steamed chicken with
coriander stuffing
248, **248**
Mushroom bake 250, **250**
Guinea fowl with red
cabbage 254, **255**
Pork goulash 258, **258**
Spicy Mexican pizza
260, **261**
Wilted spinach omelette
with nutmeg 279, **279**
Artichoke and mushroom
pizza 282, **282**
Aubergine and tomato
gratin 291, **292**
Italian artichoke hearts
with tomato and sherry
290, **290**
Jacket potatoes with
chicken and avocado
326, **326**

DESSERTS · SNACKS · DRINKS

Honeyed bread and butter
pudding 316, **316**
Queen of puddings
320, **320**

Tropical fruit drink
326, **326**
Healthy strawberry
milkshake 335, **335**, 368

dressing 96
mayonnaise 340
with salmon sauce 94, **94**;
160, **160**
Directory of foods **356-68**
Diseases, diet related 369
Diverticular disease
(diverticulosis) 395-6
Dressings
anchovy 105
celery seed 77
crème fraîche 114

curry 328
dill 96
fromage fraise and
mayonnaise 92
fruit vinegar and garlic 105
garlic 112
garlic and yoghurt 107
ginger and liqueur 301
herb 70
honey 92, 264, 310
lemon 106, 109, 112
mustard 92

mustard and orange 66, 77,
78, 88 107
mustard mayonnaise 333
onion 99, 109, 112
onion, garlic and mustard
99
orange 45
orange mayonnaise 329
oregano 49
peanut 87
persimmon 91
sherry vinegar 89
soy 264
spicy 85, 87, 91, 110
tahina 111
tarragon, for fish 163
tofu mayonnaise 71
yoghurt and orange 107
Dried fruit, orange and nut
salad 302, **303**
Drinking *see* Alcohol
Drinks
alcoholic *see* Alcohol/
Alcoholic drinks
blackberry champagne
337, **337**
coffee 352-3
healthy strawberry
milkshakes 335, **335**
iced tea 327, **327**
Indian yoghurt drink
328, **328**
nutritional values 367-8
old-fashioned homemade
lemonade 334, **334**
tea 352-3
tropical fruit drink
326, **326**
see also Soft drinks
Dripping, nutritional
values 364
Drumsticks, Mediterranean
218, **218**
Duck
bean and vegetable stew
228, **228-9**
casserole with peaches
222, **223**
nutritional values 361
roast, with mango sauce
214, **214**
salad, warm 96, **97**

E

Earthenware cooking
dishes 21
Easy bread and cheese
soufflé 274, **274**

Egg-Free Recipes

This is a selection of the egg-free recipes in the book for people with an intolerance to eggs.

SOUPS · STARTERS · SALADS

Courgette soup 57, **57**
Goat's cheese toasts 61, **61**
Broccoli and almond soup 62, **62**
Kipper and mushroom salad 85, **85**

Warm duck salad 96, **97**
Fresh pear salad 104, **104**
Turkish salad 108, **108**
Asparagus and orange tartlets with orange mayonnaise 329, **329**

MAIN COURSES · VEGETABLE DISHES

Marinated fish in lime juice 116, **116**
Italian pea and ham risotto 118, **118**
Pasta quills with salmon, broccoli and tarragon 130, **131**
Salmon kedgeree 150, **151**
Plaice with watercress sauce 154, **154**
Ash Wednesday fish pie 159, **159**
Grilled lamb cutlets with spiced mangoes 174, **174**
Beef tacos 182, **182**
Chinese spare ribs 195, **195**

Pork, potato and apple cakes 196, **197**
Szechuan pepper lamb 198, **198**
Chinese rolled beef with vegetables 200, **201**
Smoked pork with haricot beans 241, **241**
Turkey hotpot 244, **244**
Sweet and sour vegetable strudel 278, **278**
Italian artichoke hearts with tomatoes and sherry 290, **290**
Braised vegetable casserole 264, **265**

DESSERTS · SNACKS · DRINKS

Scented pears poached in red wine 304, **304**
Honey, almond and orange flan 304, **305**
Blackberry fool 314, **315**

Quick raspberry and banana sorbet 317, **317**
Hazelnut and sultana rolls 330, **331**
Wholemeal pizza baps 335, **335**

Eating, appearance related to good eating 378-81
Eating habits of the British 369
Eating out 382
Eclairs, coffee 324, **324**
Edam, nutritional values 363
Eggs
    hard-boiled with pesto 34, **34**
    nutritional values 363
    purchasing 10
    storage in refrigerator 21
    with blue cheese and Ricotta 42, **42**
Emulsifiers, defined 11
Energy, body's fuel for 349

glucose for 350
metabolism and 349-50
'Enriched', explained 11
Equipment for the kitchen 20-21
Exercise
    aerobic 374, 378
    age and 374, 381
    anaerobic 378
    as aid to slimming 371-90
    benefits of 371, 379
    choosing type and level of 375, 378
    good health and 371
    heart disease and 398
    importance of regularity 374

isotonic 378
muscle toning 376-7
pulse test 374
weight, losing weight as result of 371
well-being as result of 371
Exercises, programme of **372-3**, **376-7**
    stretching and loosening up **372-3**
    stretching and toning **376-7**
    thigh stretch **372**
    upper-body **373**
    wall press-ups **377**
    warming up and cooling down **372-3**
    workout **376-7**
Eyes, care of 380

Farmhouse
    chicken casserole 236, **236**
Fast food 381; see also Convenience foods
Fat
    'fat' explained 11
    removing from casseroles 18
    removing from meat-roasting juices 17
Fats in the diet
    'essential' fatty acids 342
    how to reduce 342-3
    relationship to health 342-3
    saturated 342
    storage in the body 350-1
    unsaturated 342-3
    vegetable oils 342
    see also Butter, Margarine and Spreads
Fennel
    artichoke and lamb hotchpotch 192, **192**
    nutritional values 358
    tomato and orange salad 98, **98**
Feta salad with sweet pepper and basil 109, **109**
    nutritional values 363
Fettucine
    primavera 126, **126**
    with two pepper sauce 132, **132**
Fibre in the diet 341, 345
Figs
    fresh, nutritional values 356

with prosciutto ham and goat cheese 54, **54**
Filo pastry
    apricot flan made with 296, **297**
    Camembert in filo flowers with cranberry sauce 319, **319**
    crab with marinated sweet peppers in 72, **72**
    nutritional values 366
    pork tenderloin in 208, **209**
    spinach triangles with tomato and basil sauce 34, **35**
Fish
    see individual references, Cod, Tuna, etc.
    baking in foil or parchment 15
    benefits of eating 15, 342
    cooking of 14-15
    directory of **359-60**
    fingers, nutritional values 367
    freezer tables **22-23**
    grilling or barbecuing 15
    oily types, beneficial to health 15, 342
    poaching 15
    preparation for cooking 14
    raw fish, preparation of 15
    steaming 15
    stock 28
    white fish, cooking of 15
    see also Shellfish
Flan
    apricot 296, **297**
    honey, almond and orange 304, **305**
    spinach 272, **272**
    strawberry 310, **311**
Flapjacks, nutritional values 365
Flatulence 395
'Flavouring' explained 11
Flour, nutritional values 366
Flummery, Scottish raspberry 318, **318**
Fluoride in water 351
Fluorine 348
Food
    allergies and sensitivities, see that title
    as fuel for the body 349
    digestion of 349
    directory of **356-68**
    freezer tables **22-26**
    irradiated 355
    labels, see Labels on food
    myths concerning 386
    organic v. conventional 355

poisoning 18, 385
processing for canning, freezing and ready-made dishes 10
processors and blenders 21
reheating of 18
safety regarding 9-10
shopping for, *see* Buying food
Fool, blackberry 314, **315**
Forest fruits with blackberry liqueur 306, **306**
'Fortified' explained 11
F-Plan Diet 392
Free radicals 381
Freezer
  defrosting and cleaning 21
  food storage tables **22-26**
  freezing foods, process of 10
  'head space' in containers **22-26**
  temperature 21
  thawing food from the **22-26**
French onion
  soup 49, **49**
  tart 277, **277**
Fresh
  orange jelly **312-13,** 313
  oranges with caramel 298, **298**
  pear salad 104, **104**
  vegetable timbale 36, **36**
Fromage fraise, nutritional values 363
Frozen food cabinets, purchasing items from 10
Fructose, defined 11
Fruit(s)
  cooking 14
  directory of **356-7**
  discoloration of peeled flesh 14
  fantail in a scented honey dressing 310, **310**
  forest fruits, with blackberry liqueur 306, **306**
  freezer tables **25-26**
  loss of vitamins and minerals in preparation 14
  nutty fruit risotto 133, **133**
  oriental salad with 90, **91**
  preparation of 14
  purchasing 9
  purée, preparation of 14
  spicy dried, simmered with chicken 247, **247**
  storing 13-14
  summer pudding 299, **299**
  venison stew with 231, **231**
see also Apple(s), Banana(s) etc.
Fruit drinks
  labelling of 352
  milk shakes 335, **335**
  tropical 326, **326**
  see also Drinks
Fruit salad
  Syrian 302, **303**
  three fruits with ginger 301, **301**
Frying meat 18
Fuel for the body, food as 349

G

Game
  and brandy soup 68, **69**
  freezer tables **23**
  nutritional values 361
  see individual references, Pheasant, Venison etc.
Gammon and mushroom bake 250, **250**
Garlic
  as herbal cure-all 386
  baked scallops with herbs and 53, **53**
  prawns, spicy 38, **39**
Gâteau
  Black Forest, nutritional values 366
  cherry and vanilla 330, **330**
Gazpacho 32, **33**
  salad 110, **110**
Gin, nutritional values 368
Ginger, three-fruit salad with 301, **301**
Glucose
  defined 11
  for energy 350
Glycogen, glucose stored in the body as 350
Goat cheese
  figs with prosciutto ham and 54, **54**
  hazelnut and spinach pancakes 266, **266**
  toasts 61, **61**
  winter salad with 92, **93**
Goulash
  chicken 226, **226**
  pork 258, **258**
Grains (*see under* Pasta)
Grapefruit, nutritional values 356
Grapes
  and cider, sausages with 252, **253**

Gluten-Free Recipes

This is a selection of the gluten-free recipes in the book for people who need to avoid wheat, oats, rye, barley and any processed foods that contain flour.

SOUPS · STARTERS · SALADS

Watercress soup 42, **43**
Parsnip and apple soup 46, **47**
Artichoke cups with cottage cheese 70, **70**
Smoked salmon rolls 74, **74**
Oriental salad 90, **90**

Tomato, orange and fennel salad 98, **98**
Warm salad of scallops 100, **101**
Spinach, smoked chicken, avocado and mushroom salad 106, **106**

MAIN COURSES · VEGETABLE DISHES

Italian pea and ham risotto 118, **118**
Spanish rice 120, **120**
Chicken and mushroom risotto 136, **136**
Prawn, mangetout and mango stir-fry 144, **144**
Salmon with dill 160, **160**
Spicy lamb kebabs with yoghurt and cucumber sauce 172, **172**
Roast loin of pork with prunes and sloe gin 180, **180**
Pork chops with orange and ginger 181, **181**
Navarin of lamb 193, **193**

Beef bourguignonne 202, **202**
Braised beef with field mushrooms 242, **243**
Chicken simmered with spicy dried fruit 247, **247**
Potato gratin with leeks 266, **267**
Beetroot with rosemary in red wine sauce 270, **270**
Sicilian ratatouille 272, **273**
Apple and vegetable curry 282, **282**
Carrots with broad beans and dill 284, **285**

DESSERTS · SNACKS · DRINKS

Salad of three fruits with ginger 301, **301**
Forest fruits with blackberry liqueur 306, **306**
Lemon soufflé 308, **309**

Strawberry yoghurt ice cream 314, **314**
Old-fashioned homemade lemonade 334, **334**
Healthy strawberry milkshakes 335, **335**, 368

  and kiwi fruit, pheasant with 224, **225**
Gratin
  aubergine and tomato 291, **291**
  potato and leek 266, **267**
Grilled
  baby chickens with chilli 222, **222**
  lamb cutlets with spiced mangoes 174, **174**
Grilling
  meat 17-18
  white fish 15

Guinea fowl with red cabbage 254, **255**
Guinness, beef with 204, **205**

HI

Haddock
  fillets with coriander and orange 168, **168**
  smoked, and new potato sandwiches 332, **332**

Haddock *continued*
    steamed, nutritional
        values 359
Haemorrhoids (Piles) 396
Hair
    diet and healthy hair 379
    vitamins and minerals,
        beneficial to 379
Halibut, salmon and
    vegetable pasta 148, **149**
Ham
    and pea risotto 118, **118**
    and sweetcorn chowder
        242, **242**
    baked, with apricots and
        candied sweet potatoes
        186, **187**
    chicken (or turkey) and
        vegetable salad 98, **99**
    cooked in cider 200, **200**
    figs and goat cheese with
        54, **54**
    nutritional values 361
    split pea soup with celeriac
        and 60, **60**
Hamburger with bun,
    nutritional values 367
Hard-boiled eggs with
    pesto 34, **34**
Hay Diet 392
Hazelnut
    and sultana rolls 330, **331**
    spinach and goat's cheese
        pancakes 266, **266**
    wild rice and orange salad
        112, **113**
Health diets 392-3
Healthy strawberry
    milkshakes 335, **335**
Heart attack explained 397
Heart disease
    cholesterol and 397
    diet and 369
    Mediterranean diet and 397
    oily fish as aid to
        preventing 15, 342
    self-help checklist 397-8
    see also Exercise
Herbal teas 353
High blood pressure 396-7
Hip and Thigh Diet 392
Homemade
    hazelnut and sultana rolls
        330, **311**
    lemonade 334, **334**
Honey
    almond and orange flan
        304, **305**
    and soy dressing, sweet
        peppers in 264, **264**
    bread and butter pudding
        316, **316**

Recipes for a Healthy Heart

This is a selection of low-fat and low-cholesterol recipes that are suitable for people with heart disease.

SOUPS · STARTERS · SALADS

Bresaola with pears 43, **43**
Parsnip and cumin soup 52, **53**
Game and brandy soup 68, **69**
Thai fish salad 90, **90**
Caesar salad 100, **100**

Gazpacho salad 110, **110**
Potato salad with walnuts and lemon dressing 114, **115**
Savoury mangetout with cottage cheese 333, **333**

MAIN COURSES · VEGETABLE DISHES

Marinated fish in lime juice 116, **116**
Spaghetti with mussels 118, **119**
Spaghetti Bolognaise 134, **135**
Mackerel with rhubarb and apple sauce 150, **150**
Mexican style trout 156, **157**
Haddock fillets with coriander and orange 168, **168**
Mixed bean chilli con carne 176, **177**
Braised beef with Guinness 204, **205**
Curried lamb with aubergine and chickpea 206, **207**

Moroccan chicken couscous 240, **240**
Chicken, potato and butter-bean stew 254, **254**
Guinea fowl with red cabbage 254, **255**
Sweet peppers in honey and soy dressing 264, **264**
Beetroot with rosemary in red wine sauce 270, **270**
Oriental vegetables with vermicelli 270, **271**
Braised vegetable curry 282, **282**
Vegetarian shepherd's pie 286, **286-7**
Aubergine and tomato gratin 291, **291**
Jacket potatoes and lemon coleslaw 334, **334**

DESSERTS · SNACKS · DRINKS

Summer pudding 299, **299**
Stuffed nectarines with redcurrant sauce 300, **300**

Provençal Sandwich 336, **336**
Scottish raspberry flummery 318, **318**

    dressing, citrus fruits in
        310, **310**
    nutritional values 366
Hotpot
    lamb 193, **193**
    turkey 244, **244**
Hot raspberry soufflé
    302, **302**
Hungarian pork goulash
    258, **258**
Hygiene in the kitchen 20
Hypertension 396-7

Ice cream
    nutritional values 363

strawberry yoghurt
    314, **314**
Iced tea 327, **327**
Icing, coffee/chocolate 338
Illness, eating during
    convalescence 401
Indian spices and yoghurt
    with lamb 188, **188-9**
Indian yoghurt drink
    328, **328**
Indonesian pineapple salad
    86, **87**
Iodine 348
Irish stew 196, **196**
Iron, sources of 348, 394

Irradiated food 355
Irritable bowel syndrome 395
Italian
    artichoke hearts with
        tomatoes and sherry
        290, **290**
    meatball casserole
        244, **245**
    pea and ham risotto
        118, **118**

Jacket potatoes
    with chicken and avocado
        326, **326**
    with lemon coleslaw
        334, **334**
Jam
    nutritional values 366
    reduced-sugar raspberry
        and strawberry 322, **323**
Jelly made with fresh oranges
    312-13, 313
Juniper berries, pork chop
    with 203, **203**

Kebabs
    prawn 170, **170**
    spicy lamb 172, **172**
Kedgeree, salmon 150, **151**
Kipper and mushroom salad
    85, **85**
Kitchen
    health in the 20
    utensils 20-21
Kiwi fruit
    and grapes, pheasant with
        224, **225**
    nutritional values 356
Knives 20

Labelling on food
    alcohol content, lagers and
        beers 353-4
    fruit drinks 352
    understanding 10-11
Lactose defined 11
Lager
    alcohol content 353-4
    labelling 353-4
    nutritional values 368
Lamb
    chops with apple 184, **185**

curried, with aubergines and chickpeas 206, **207**
cutlets with spiced mangoes 174, **174**
fennel and artichoke hotchpotch 192, **192**
Irish stew 196, **196**
liver parcels with herbs 173, **173**
marinated in yoghurt and spices 188, **188-9**
navarin of 193, **193**
nutritional values 361
roast leg, with barley, apricot and mint stuffing 178, **179**
spicy kebabs with yoghurt and cucumber sauce 172, **172**
stew with lentils and spinach 248, **249**
Szechuan pepper 198, **198**
Lard, nutritional values 364
Lasagne
    mixed fish 130, **130**
    ready-made, nutritional values 367
Lebanese cucumber soup 50, **51**
Leek(s)
    and potato gratin 266, **267**
    and potato omelette 288, **288**
    chicken breasts in mustard sauce with 225, **225**
    nutritional values 358
    pork braised with 184, **184**
    with monkfish 147, **147**
    with red and yellow peppers 260, **260**
Leftovers, eating cold 18
Lemon(s)
    coleslaw, jacket potatoes with 334, **334**
    dressing 106, 109, 112, 114
    nutritional values 356
    soufflé 308, **309**
Lemonade
    nutritional values 367
    old-fashioned homemade 334, **334**
Lentils
    lamb stew with spinach and 248, **249**
    Lincolnshire sausages with 190, **191**
    nutritional values 359
    soup, spiced 45, **45**
Lettuce, nutritional values 358
Lhassi yoghurt drink 328, **328**

Lime(s)
    calf's liver with sage leaves and 174, **175**
    cracked wheat salad with 81, **81**
    juice, fish marinated in 116, **116**
    nutritional values 356
Lincolnshire sausages with lentils 190, **191**
Linguine with mushroom sauce 122, **122**
Listeria bacteria 385
Liver
    calf's, with lime and sage leaves 174, **175**
    lamb's liver parcels with herbs 173, **173**
    nutritional values 360, 361
    vitamin A in 385

MN

Mackerel
    nutritional values 359
    marinated with tarragon 166, **166**
    with rhubarb and apple sauce 150, **150**
Macronutrients 341-4
Mad Cow Disease (BSE) 385-6
Maltose, defined 11
Mangetout
    and bacon salad 86, **86**
    and prawn and mango stir-fry 144, **144**
    and scallop salad, warm 100, **101**
    nutritional values 358
    with anchovy-flavoured cottage cheese 333, **333**
Mango(es)
    and prawn cocktail 58, **58**
    nutritional values 357
    sauce, duck with 214, **214**
    spiced, with grilled lamb cutlets 174, **174**
    spicy fish with 168, **169**
Margarine
    hard 355
    'less fattening than butter' myth 386
    nutritional values 364
    soft 355
Marinated
    cod 154, **155**
    lamb with spices 188, **188-9**

mackerel with tarragon 166, **166**
mullet with mango 168, **169**
mushroom and artichoke salad 94, **95**
spare ribs 195, **195**
sweet peppers with crab in filo pastry 72, **72**
white fish in lime juice 116, **116**
Marmalade, nutritional values 366
Mayo (Grapefruit) Diet 392
Mayonnaise
    anchovy-flavoured 105
    dill 340
    mustard 333
    nutritional values 362
    orange 329
    tofu 71, 83, 92
Meat
    barbecuing 17, 18
    braising 18
    buying 9, 10
    cooking of 17
    'essential for strength' myth 386
    fat in 16, 342
    freezer tables 22
    frying 18
    grilling 17-18
    keeping fresh 16
    nutritional values **360-1**
    preparation for cooking 16
    removing fat from roasting juices 17
    resting time after cooking 17
    retaining moisture during cooking 16-17
    roasting times 17
    storage in refrigerator 16, 21
    thermometers 17
    see also under individual references e.g. Beef, Lamb, Pork, etc.
Meatball casserole 244, **245**
'Meat products', defined 11
Mediterranean
    diet 397
    drumsticks 218, **218**
Melon, nutritional values 357
Menu planning guide 370
Meringue, nutritional values 365
Metabolic Diet 392
Metabolism explained 349-50
Mexican
    pizza 260, **261**
    -style trout 156, **157**

Micronutrients 344-8
Microwave cooking
    cold spots 20
    plastic film 21
    standing times 20
Milk
    as part of the diet 342
    nutritional values 362
Milkshakes
    healthy strawberry 335, **335**
    nutritional values 368
Minerals
    function 347-8
    sources of 347-8
    supplements 345
    the body and 345
    trace elements 348
    vegetarianism and 394
Mineral water 351
Mixed
    bean chilli con carne 176, **177**
    fish lasagne 130, **130**
    nut cake 338, **339**
    root salad 107, **107**
    sprout salad with tahina dressing 111, **111**
Monkfish
    nutritional values 359
    peppered fillets of 158, **158**
    roast tail 166, **167**
    salad 90, **90**
    with leeks 147, **147**
Moroccan chicken couscous 240, **240**
Mousse
    light cheese with smoked salmon rolls 74, **74**
    vegetables 58, **59**
    watercress, with red pepper sauce 46, **46**
Mozzarella
    avocado and tomato antipasto 48, **48**
    nutritional values 363
Muesli, nutritional values 365
Mullet, spicy with mangoes 168, **169**
Muscle tone 380; *see also* Exercise
Mushroom(s)
    and artichoke pizza 282, **283**
    and bacon, roast fillet of beef with 190, **190**
    and chicken risotto 136, **136**
    and fresh spinach sandwiches 332, **332**
    and kipper salad 85, **85**
    and walnut pasta 134, **134**

Milk-Free Recipes

This is a selection of recipes that do not contain any dairy products for people who need to avoid milk in their diet.

SOUPS · STARTERS · SALADS

Carrot, tomato and cardamom soup 37, **37**
Three bean paté 40, **41**
Split-pea soup with ham and celeriac 60, **60**
Crudités with tofu mayonnaise 71, **71**

Crab, orange and avocado salad 77, **77**
Chickpea salad 78, **79**
Indonesian pineapple salad 86, **87**
Squid and tomato salad 103, **103**

MAIN COURSES · VEGETABLE DISHES

Spaghetti with mussels 118, **119**
Courgette and garlic spaghetti 124, **124**
Couscous with seven vegetables 128, **128-9**
Spanish marinated cod 154, **154**
Trawlerman's stew 156, **156**
Skate with tarragon dressing 162, **162-3**
Roast monkfish tail 166, **167**
Lamb's liver parcels with herbs 173, **173**
Beef tacos 182, **182**

Steak with orange and walnuts 186, **186**
Pork chops with barbecue sauce 194, **194**
Wiltshire ham cooked in cider 200, **200**
Lamb stew with lentils and spinach 248, **248**
Leeks with red and yellow peppers 260, **260**
Sweet peppers in honey and soya dressing 264, **264**
Stir-fried vegetables with oyster sauce **292-3**, 293
Chop suey 256, **257**
Baked courgettes and aubergines 280, **280**

DESSERTS · SNACKS · DRINKS

Fresh oranges with caramel 298, **298**
Quick raspberry and banana sorbet 317, **317**

Tropical fruit drink 326, **326**
Mushroom and fresh spinach sandwiches 332, **332**

Mushrooms *continued*
bake 250, **250**
braised beef with 242, **243**
country baked 66, **67**
marinated mushroom and artichoke salad 94, **95**
nutritional values 358
sauce with linguine pasta 122, **122**
soup 50, **50**
spinach, smoked chicken, avocado and mushroom salad 106, **106**
Mussels
boiled, nutritional values 360

in white wine 52, **52**
with spaghetti 118, **119**
Mustard sauce 54
chicken breasts in, with leeks 225, **225**
with peppercorns 176
Myths concerning food 386

Nails
diet and 380
vitamins and minerals beneficial to 380
Nasturtium flowers 114
Navarin of lamb 193, **193**
Nectarines, stuffed, with redcurrant sauce 300, **300**

Niacin 346
Nicotinic acid 346
'No added sugar' defined 11
Noodles, spicy prawns with 146, **146**
Nut(s)
and cheese terrine 284, **284**
cake 338, **339**
nutritional values 364
nutty fruit risotto 133, **133**
Nutmeg
and spinach omelette 279, **279**
broccoli and almond soup 62, **62**
Nutrients
carbohydrates 343-4
fats 342-3
macronutrients 341-4
micronutrients 345
proteins 341-2
Nutritional values of food 356-68
Nutty fruit risotto 133, **133**

Oils, cooking
nutritional values 364
see also Vegetable oil
Old English vegetable salad 98, **99**
Old-fashioned homemade lemonade 334, **334**
Olive
oil 342
tomato and pepper pasta salad 102, **102**
Omelette
leek and potato 288, **288**
spinach with nutmeg 279, **279**
Onion(s)
and sorrel tart 288, **288**
French onion soup 49, **49**
nutritional values 358
tart, French 277, **277**
Orange(s)
and apricot tea bread 326, **327**
and asparagus tartlets with orange mayonnaise 329, **329**
and avocado salad 66, **66**
and beetroot salad 76, **76**
and chestnuts, casserole of pheasant with 234, **234**
and coriander with haddock fillets 168, **168**

and ginger, pork chops with 181, **181**
and walnut salad 114, **114**
and walnuts, steak with 186, **186**
chicken 216, **217**
cordial, nutritional values 367
crab and avocado salad 77, **77**
dressing, asparagus with 44, **44**
honey and almond flan 304, **305**
jelly made with fresh fruit **312-13**, 313
juice, fresh, nutritional values 368
mayonnaise 329
nutritional values 357
sauce 168, 208; with lemon and redcurrant 200
tomato and fennel salad 98, **98**
wild rice and hazelnut salad 112, **113**
with caramel 298, **298**
Organic
v. conventional foods 355
wines 353
Oriental
chicken and coconut soup 62, **63**
salad with fruit 90, **91**
vegetables 270, **271**
Oyster(s)
nutritional values 360
sauce, stir-fried vegetables with 293, **293**

Packaged foods, sell-by dates 10
Paella Catalana 238, **239**
Pancakes
buckwheat vegetable 276, **276**
spinach, goat's cheese and hazelnut 266, **266**
Pan-fried steak with mustard and green peppercorn sauce 176, **176**
Parmesan
nutritional values 363
rocket and apple salad 88, **88**
Parsley, nutritional values 362

Parsnip
and apple soup 46, **47**
and carrot purée 268, **268**
and cumin soup 52, **53**
nutritional values 358
Pasta
benefits of eating 344
nutritional values 365
Provençale 139, **139**
Pastry
nutritional values 366
see also Filo pastry
Pâté, three-bean 40, **41**
Pea(s)
and ham risotto 118, **118**
nutritional values 358
split with ham and celeriac
soup 60, **60**
see also Mangetout
Peaches
casserole of duck with
222, **223**
nutritional values 357
with raspberry sauce
296, **296**
Peanut
butter, nutritional
values 366
dressing 87
sauce 64
Pear(s)
Bresaola with 43, **43**
nutritional values 357
poached in red wine
304, **304**
rabbit stew with 218, **219**
salad 104, **104**
with Roquefort cheese
64, **65**
Pepper(s)
and tomato sauce 152
basil and Feta salad
109, **109**
crab with marinated sweet
peppers in filo pastry
72, **72**
fettucine with two-pepper
sauce 132, **132**
lamb 198, **198**
nutritional values 359
red and yellow, with leeks
260, **260**
sauce 46, 54
stuffed with apricots and
pine nuts 294, **294**
sweet, in honey and soy
dressing 264, **264**
tomato and olive pasta
salad 102, **102**
Peppered
lamb steak 198, **198**
monkfish fillets 158, **158**

Persian pilaf 138, **138**
Persimmon, orange and
water chestnut oriental
salad 90, **91**
Pesto, hard-boiled eggs
with 34, **34**
Pheasant
casserole with chestnuts
and orange 234, **234**
nutritional values 361
with grapes and kiwi fruit
224, **225**
Pie(s)
apple, nutritional values
366
fish 159, **159**
vegetarian shepherd's
286, **286-7**
Pigeon(s)
and apricot stir-fry 220,
220-1
with chicory 215, **215**
wood pigeon and brandy
soup 68, **69**
Pilaf, Persian 138, **138**
Piles (Haemorrhoids) 396
Pineapple
and strawberry baskets
307, **307**
salad 86, **87**
Pine nuts and apricots,
nutritional value 364
peppers stuffed with
294, **294**
Pizza
artichoke and mushroom
282, **283**
baps, wholemeal 335, **335**
readymade, nutritional
values 367
spicy Mexican 260, **261**
Plaice with
orange and lemon sauce
164, **165**
watercress sauce 154, **154**
Plastic film 21, 386
Plums, nutritional values 357
Poaching white fish 15
Polenta
baked with tomato and
cheese 123, **123**
with chicken livers and
sage 125, **125**
Pork
baked spare-rib chops with
sweet potato 199, **199**
braised, with leeks
184, **184**
Chinese spare ribs with
five-spice marinade
195, **195**
chop suey 256, **257**

chops with: barbecue
sauce 194, **194**; juniper
berries 203, **203**; orange
and ginger 181, **181**; savoy
cabbage 204, **204**
Hungarian goulash
258, **258**
nutritional values 361, 368
potato and apple cakes
196, **197**
roast loin of, with prunes
and sloe gin 180, **180**
smoked pork and haricot
beans 241, **241**
tenderloin in filo pastry,
with orange sauce 208, **209**
Porridge, nutritional
values 365
Port, nutritional values 368
Potassium 347
Potato(es)
and leek gratin 266, **267**
and leek omelette 288, **288**
boiled, nutritional
values 358
butter-bean and chicken
stew 254, **254**
cabbage and chilli soup
68, **68**
jacket, nutritional
values 359
jacket with: chicken and
avocado 326, **326**; lemon
coleslaw 334, **334**
pork and apple cakes
196, **197**
roast, nutritional
values 359
salad with walnut, and
lemon dressing 114, **115**
smoked haddock and new
potato sandwiches
332, **332**
spicy Spanish 285, **285**
sweet potatoes, *see*
that title
Pot roasts
beef, traditional 252, **252**
chicken with cranberries
250, **251**
Poultry
cooking of 16
fat in 16
freezer tables **23**
nutritional values 361
preparing 15-16
roasting times 16
skin of 16
storing of 15
storing of, in refrigerator 21
stuffing 15-16
see also Chicken, Duck, etc.

Poussins grilled with chilli
222, **222**
Prawn(s)
and mango cocktail 58, **58**
boiled, nutritional
values 360
cauliflower and pasta salad
105, **105**
chicken and garlic sausage
with rice 120, **120**
mangetout and mango stir-
fry 144, **144**
skewers with lime and
tamarind 170, **170**
spicy garlic 38, **39**
with Chinese noodles
146, **146**
Pregnancy
diet during 387
liver and vitamin A,
warnings 385
Preservative
defined 11
in bread 354
Pressure cooking
vegetables 13
Protein(s)
deficiency 342
defined 11
recommended daily
amount 342
sources of 341-2
vegetarianism and 394
Provençal sandwich 336, **336**
Prunes
and sloe gin, roast loin of
pork with 180, **180**
nutritional values 357
Puddings
bread and butter 316, **316**
Queen of 320, **320**
summer 299, **299**
Pulses
cooking 13
nutritional values 359
Pulse test 374
Pumpkin
and white bean soup 40, **40**
baked spare-rib chops with
sweet potato and 199, **199**
ravioli 274, **275**
Purée(s)
carrot and parsnip 268, **268**
fruit, preparation 14

Quail with apples and raisins
224, **224**
Queen of puddings 320, **320**
Quick raspberry and banana
sorbet 317, **317**
Quick spaghetti carbonara
140, **141**

411

R

Rabbit
  nutritional values 361
  stew with pears 218, **219**
Radicchio and blue Brie
  sandwiches 336, **337**
Ragout of red cabbage with
  chestnuts 262, **263**
Raisins
  and apples, quail with
  224, **224**
  walnut and beef burgers
  210, **210**
Raspberry
  and banana sorbet
  317, **317**
  flummery 318, **318**
  jam, reduced-sugar recipe
  322, **323**
  nutritional values 357
  sauce 296, 307
  soufflé, hot 302, **302**
  vinegar, chicken breasts
  with 230, **230**
Ratatouille, Sicilian 272, **273**
Ravioli
  in tomato sauce, tinned,
  nutritional values 367
  pumpkin-filled 274, **275**
Raw Energy Diet 393
Ready-to-cook foods 10
Ready-to-eat foods 10
Recommended Daily Amount
  (RDA) defined 11
Red cabbage
  ragout with chestnuts
  262, **263**
  with guinea-fowl 254, **255**
Redcurrant sauce 56, 300
Red pepper sauce, watercress
  mousse with 46, **46**
Reduced-sugar raspberry and
  strawberry jam 322, **323**
Red wine, scented pears
  poached in 304, **304**
Refrigerator
  defrosting and cleaning 21
  fruit in 14
  keeping food separate 21
  meat in 16, 21
  poultry in 15, 21
  store-cupboard role 19
  temperature 21
  vegetables in 12
Reheating of food 18
Restaurant meals 382
Retinol 346, *see* Vitamin A

Rhubarb and apple sauce
  150, **150**
Riboflavin 346, *see* Vitamin B
Rice
  and apricot salad 89, **89**
  chicken and mushroom
  risotto 136, **136**
  Italian pea and ham risotto
  118, **118**
  nutritional values 365
  nutty fruit risotto 133, **133**
  Paella Catalana 238, **239**
  Persian pilaf 138, **138**
  salmon kedgeree 150, **151**
  Spanish rice 120, **120**
  wild rice, orange and
  hazelnut salad 112, **113**
Ricotta
  and spinach roulade
  268, **269**
  nutritional values 363
Risottos *see under* Rice
Roast
  duck with mango sauce
  214, **214**
  fillet of beef with bacon
  and mushrooms 190, **190**
  lamb 178, **179**
  loin of pork 180, **180**
  monkfish tail 166, **167**
  pork 180, **180**
  stuffed venison 212, **213**
Roasting
  meat 17
  poultry 16
  tins for 21
Rocket salads
  and lettuce 108, **108**
  Parmesan and apple 88, **88**
Rolls
  hazelnut and sultana
  330, **331**
  smoked salmon with light
  cheese mousse 74, **74**
Root salad 107, **107**
Roquefort pears 64, **65**
Rosemary, beetroot with
  270, **270**
Rotation diet 392

S

Safety, food and 9-10
Salad
  dressings, *see* Dressings
  of three fruits with ginger
  301, **301**
Salami, nutritional values 361
Salmagundi 98, **99**

Salmon
  and caviar (or lumpfish
  roe) sandwiches 340, **340**
  and sole roulades 145, **145**
  and spinach terrine 56, **56**
  broccoli and tarragon with
  pasta quills 130, **131**
  halibut and vegetable pasta
  148, **149**
  kedgeree 150, **151**
  poached, nutritional
  values 360
  tartare 94, **94**
  with dill 160, **160**
  see also Smoked salmon
Salmonella poisoning 385
Salt in the diet
  how to reduce 344-5
  recommended daily
  amount of sodium 344
Sandwiches
  as convenience food 381-2
  blue Brie and radicchio
  336, **337**
  celeriac, apple and walnut
  340, **340**
  mushroom and fresh
  spinach 332, **332**
  Provençal 336, **336**
  salmon and caviar (or
  lumpfish roe) 340, **340**
  smoked haddock and new
  potato 332, **332**
San Francisco salad 114, **114**
Sardines in oil, nutritional
  values 360
Satay sauce, chicken in
  64, **64**
Saucepans, types of 20-21
Sauces
  arrabbiata (spicy tomato)
  256
  avocado 182
  barbecue 194
  bolognaise 135
  brown, nutritional
  values 362
  cucumber 161
  dill 94
  freezer tables **23-26**
  mango 214
  mushroom 122
  mustard 54, 225
  mustard and green
  peppercorn 176
  nutmeg and Parmesan 266
  orange 208
  orange and dill 149
  orange and lemon 164
  orange, lemon and
  redcurrant 200
  oregano 245

oriental 264
  oyster 293
  peanut 64
  pepper 54
  peppercorn 176
  pesto 34
  raspberry 296, 302, 307
  redcurrant 56, 300
  red pepper 46, 54
  rhubarb and apple 150
  satay 64
  sweet and sour 257, 278
  tomato 58, 127
  tomato and basil 34
  tomato and pepper 152
  tomato ketchup,
  nutritional values 363
  watercress 154
  Worcestershire, nutritional
  values 362
  yellow bean, for chicken
  212, **212**
  yoghurt and cucumber 173
Sausages
  nutritional values 361
  with grapes and cider
  252, **253**
  with lentils 190, **191**
Scallops
  baked with garlic and
  herbs 53, **53**
  steamed, nutritional
  values 360
  warm salad of 100, **101**
Scarsdale Diet 392
Scented pears poached in red
  wine 304, **304**
Scottish raspberry flummery
  318, **318**
Selenium 348
Sell-by date
  in supermarkets 9
  packaged foods 10
Sesame seeds and walnuts,
  cabbage with 262, **262**
Shelf life of food produce 9
Shellfish
  *see under individual
  references*, e.g. Crab,
  Prawns, etc.
  cooking of 15
  crab, nutritional values 360
  directory of **360**
  nutritional values 360
Shepherd's pie, vegetarian
  286, **286-7**
Sherry
  nutritional values 368
  vinegar 206
Shopping, *see* Buying food
Sicilian ratatouille 272, **273**
Sieves and colanders 20

Skate with tarragon dressing 162, **162-3**
Skin
  diet and the 378-9
  effect of food allergies and sensitivities on the 379
  toxins excreted through the 379
  vitamins and minerals beneficial to 378-9
Sleep
  importance of 384-5
Slimming
  advice 393
  crash dieting 389-90
  daily calorie intake 389-90
  exercise helpful to 390
  1400 calorie diet 393
  fruits beneficial to 14
  missing meals, caution 393
  monitoring weight 390-1
  specific diets for 391-3
Sloe gin, 180
Smoked haddock and new potato sandwiches 332, **332**
Smoked pork and haricot beans 241, **241**
Smoked salmon
  nutritional values 360
  rolls with light cheese mousse 74, **74**
Smoking 381, 398
Sodium
  recommended daily amounts 344
  sources and functions 348
Soft drinks
  after-sports drinks 352
  colas 352
  diet types 352
  'elixirs' and 'tonics' 352
  fruit juices 352
  hypertonic 352
  hypotonic 352
  isotonic 352
  nutritional values 367-8
  sugar in 352
  see also Drinks
Soil Association, symbol on organic foods 355
Sole
  and salmon roulades 145, **145**
  poached, nutritional values 360
Sorbet
  nutritional values 363
  quick raspberry and banana 317, **317**
Sorrel and onion tart 289, **289**

Soufflés
  bread and cheese 274, **274**
  hot raspberry 302, **302**
  lemon 308, **309**
Soups
  bouillabaisse 32, **32**
  broccoli, almond and nutmeg 62, **62**
  butternut squash and white bean 40, **40**
  carrot, tomato and cardamom 37, **37**
  chilled vegetable 331, **331**
  cold 32, 50, 57, 331
  courgette 57, **57**
  Crab chowder 38, **38**
  freezer tables **23**
  French onion 49, **49**
  game and brandy 68, **69**
  gazpacho 32, **33**
  ham and sweetcorn chowder 242, **242**
  Lebanese cucumber 50, **51**
  mushroom 50, **50**
  parsnip and apple 46, **47**
  parsnip and cumin 52, **53**
  potato, cabbage and chilli 68, **68**
  spiced lentil 45, **45**
  spicy 68, **68**, 72, **73**
  spinach with coconut, spicy 72, **73**
  split pea, with ham and celeriac 60, **60**
  Thai chicken and coconut 62, **63**
  tomato and basil 60, **61**
  watercress 42, **43**
  wood pigeon and brandy 68, **69**
Soya beans, dried, nutritional values 359
Spaghettata 124, **124**
Spaghetti
  bolognaise 134, **135**
  carbonara 140, **140**
  with mussels 118, **119**
Spanish
  marinated cod 154, **155**
  potatoes, spicy 285, **285**
  rice 120, **120**
Spare-rib chops with sweet potato 199, **199**
Spiced lentil soup 45, **45**
Spicy
  arrabbiata pasta 256, **256**
  fish with mangoes 168, **169**
  garlic prawns 38, **39**
  lamb kebabs with yoghurt and cucumber sauce 172, **172**

Mexican pizza 260, **261**
  prawns with Chinese noodles 146, **146**
  Spanish potatoes 285, **285**
  spinach soup with coconut 72, **73**
Spinach
  and Ricotta roulade 268, **269**
  and salmon terrine 56, **56**
  and strawberry salad 78, **78**
  and turkey rolls 232, **232**
  cannelloni stuffed with cheese and 142, **142**
  flan 272, **272**
  goat cheese and hazelnut pancakes 266, **266**
  lamb stew with lentils and 248, **249**
  'makes you strong' myth 386
  mushroom and fresh spinach sandwiches 332, **332**
  nutritional values 359
  omelette with nutmeg 279, **279**
  paste 240
  smoked chicken, avocado and mushroom salad 106, **106**
  soup (spicy) with coconut 72, **73**
  spaghetti and, with olive oil and garlic 124, **124**
  triangles with tomato and basil sauce 34, **35**
  vegetable terrine 58, **59**
Split-pea soup with ham and celeriac 60, **60**
Spoons 20
Sport
  after-sports drinks 352
  chart showing benefits from various sports **375**
Spreads, low-fat 355
  nutritional values 364
Spring water 351
Sprout salad with tahina dressing 111, **111**
Squash
  butternut, and white bean soup 40, **40**
  butternut, nutritional values 358
  stuffed with turkey, baked 246, **246**
Squid
  and tomato salad 103, **103**
  grilled, with tomato and pepper sauce 152, **152**
  nutritional values 360

paella Catalana 238, **239**
Stabiliser defined 11
Starch
  how to eat more of 344
  sources of 344
Steak
  fillet, nutritional value 360
  pan-fried with mustard and green peppercorn sauce 176, **176**
  preparation for cooking 17
  with oranges and walnuts 186, **186**
Steamed chicken with coriander stuffing 248, **248**
Steamers 21
Steaming
  vegetables 13
  white fish 15
Stews
  chicken, potato and butter-bean 254, **254**
  duck, bean and vegetable 228, **228-9**
  fish 156, **156**
  Irish 196, **196**
  lamb with lentils and spinach 248, **249**
  meat 18
  rabbit with pears 218, **219**
  vegetable, for shepherd's pie 286, **286-7**
  venison with fruit 231, **231**
Stilton, nutritional values 364
Stir-fry 13
  chicken strips in yellow-bean sauce 212, **212**
  oriental vegetables 270, **271**
  pigeon and apricot 220, **220-1**
  prawn, mangetout and mango 144, **144**
  sweet peppers in honey and soy dressing 264, **264**
  turkey 226, **227**
  vegetables with oyster sauce **292-3**, 293
Stocks
  beef 28
  chicken 27
  cubes 27
  fish 28
  freezing of 27
  veal 27
  vegetable 27
Storage of food
  fruit 13-14
  poultry 15
  vegetables 12
  see also Freezer and Refrigerator

Store cupboard, the
  basic ingredients of 19
  buying for the 18
  dried foods 19
  stocking the 18-19
  storage times for dried and
    tinned foods **19**
  tinned foods 18, 19
Stout, nutritional values 368
Strawberry
  and pineapple baskets
    307, **307**
  and spinach salad 78, **78**
  flan 310, **311**
  jam, reduced-sugar recipe
    322, **323**
  milkshakes 335, **335**
  nutritional values 357, 368
  yoghurt ice cream 314, **314**
Stress
  coping with 384
  measures to relieve 384
  relaxation and 384, 398
  vitamins and minerals for
    relief of 384, 346-8
Strudel, sweet and sour
  vegetable 278, **278**
Stuffed
  aubergines 281, **281**
  mushrooms 66, **67**
  nectarines with redcurrant
    sauce 300, **300**
  peppers 294, **294**
Stuffing
  cheese and courgette 216
  coriander 248
  turkey, for squash 246
Sucrose defined 11
Sugar
  body's use of 350
  brown *v.* white myth 386
  how to reduce intake 343-4
  nutritional values 366
'Sugar-free' defined 11
Sultana and hazelnut rolls
  330, **331**
Summer pudding 299, **299**
Sunbathing 379
Supermarket chain stores,
  buying food at 9
Sussex lamb chops 184, **185**
Swedish dill and cucumber
  salad 96, **96**
Sweet and sour
  sauce 257
  vegetable strudel 278, **278**
Sweetcorn chowder with
  crab 38, **38**
  ham 242, **242**
Sweetcorn, nutritional
  values 359
Sweeteners defined 11

Sweet pepper(s)
  and basil salad with Feta
    109, **109**
  in honey and soy dressing
    264, **264**
  marinated with crab in filo
    pastry 72, **72**
  nutritional values 359
Sweet potato(es)
  baked spare-rib chops with
    pumpkin and 199, **199**
  candied, with baked ham
    and apricots 186, **187**
  nutritional values 359
Syrian fruit salad 302, **303**
Szechuan pepper lamb
  198, **198**

T

Tacos with beef 182, **182**
Tagine 247, **247**
Tagliatelle
  salmon, halibut and
    vegetable pasta 148, **149**
  with chicken, artichoke
    and tarragon 121, **121**
  with courgette and carrot
    ribbons 137, **137**
  with tomatoes and olives
    140, **140**
Tahina dressing 111
Tamarind, prawn skewers
  with lime and 170, **170**
Tarragon dressing 163
Tarts/tartlets
  asparagus and orange, with
    orange mayonnaise
    329, **329**
  crab with marinated sweet
    peppers 72, **72**
  French onion 277, **277**
  sorrel and onion 289, **289**
Tea
  caffeine in 352, 353
  herbal 353
  iced 327, **327**
  nutritional values 367
  tannin in 353
Tea bread, orange and
  apricot 326, **327**
Tea-towels 20
Teeth
  diet and 379-80
  fluoride and 380
  vitamins and minerals
    beneficial to 380
Terrines
  cheese and nut 284, **284**

spinach and salmon 56, **56**
  vegetable 58, **59**
Thai
  chicken and coconut soup
    62, **63**
  fish salad 90, **90**
Thermometers, meat 17
Thiamin 346 (*see* vitamin B)
Three-bean pâté 40, **41**
Three-bean salad 84, **84**
Thyroid gland, 348
Tikka, chicken 232, **233**
Tinned food, *see* Canned food
Tins, roasting and baking 21
Toffee, nutritional values 367
Tofu mayonnaise, crudités
  with 71, **71**
Tomato(es)
  and aubergine gratin
    291, **291**
  and basil sauce 34
  and basil soup 60, **61**
  and olives with tagliatelle
    140, **140**
  and pepper sauce 152
  and sherry, artichoke
    hearts with 290, **290**
  and squid salad 103, **103**
  avocado and Mozzarella
    antipasto 48, **48**
  carrot and cardamom
    soup 37, **37**
  juice, tinned, nutritional
    values 368
  ketchup, nutritional
    values 362
  orange and fennel salad
    98, **98**
  pepper and olive pasta
    salad 102, **102**
  polenta baked with cheese
    and 123, **123**
  sauce 58, 127
  soup, tinned, nutritional
    values 367
Tonic water, nutritional
  values 368
Traditional pot-roast beef
  252, **252**
Travelling, eating during 381
Trawlerman's stew 156, **156**
'Tricolore' (tomato, avocado
  and Mozzarella antipasto)
  48, **48**
Trifle, apple 308, **308**
Tropical fruit drink 326, **326**
Trout
  Mexican-style 156, **157**
  parcels with cucumber and
    lemon 161, **161**
Tuna
  and bean salad 106, **106**

nutritional values 360
  salad 112, **112**
Turkey
  and spinach rolls 232, **232**
  hotpot 244, **244**
  stir-fry 226, **227**
  -stuffed squash, baked
    246, **246**
Turkish
  salad 108, **108**
  -stuffed aubergines
    281, **281**

Ulcers, stomach and small
  intestine 396

Vanilla and cherry gâteau
  330, **330**
Veal
  stock 27
  with balsamic vinegar and
    sultanas 183, **183**
Vegans 394
  calcium 394
  iron 394
  protein 394
  Vitamin B12 394
Vegetable(s)
  and apple curry 282, **282**
  baking 13
  boiling 13
  buckwheat pancakes
    276, **276**
  casserole 264, **265**
  chopping 12
  directory of **357-9**
  drinks 352
  freezer tables 22-26
  loss of nutrients 13
  margarine 355
  oil, source of 'essential'
    fatty acids 342
  olive oil 342
  oriental 270, **271**
  peeling 12
  platter 54, **55**
  preparation for cooking 12
  preparation for freezing 24
  pressure-cooking 13
  preventing deterioration 12
  soup, chilled 331, **331**
  steaming 13
  stir-fried, with oyster
    sauce **292-3**, 293
  stir-fry 13
  stock 27
  storage of 12